EVOLUTIONARY ECOLOGY
AND
HUMAN BEHAVIOR

FOUNDATIONS OF HUMAN BEHAVIOR
An Aldine de Gruyter Series of Texts and Monographs

SERIES EDITOR
Sarah Blaffer Hrdy
University of California, Davis

EVOLUTIONARY ECOLOGY
AND
HUMAN BEHAVIOR

Eric Alden Smith and Bruce Winterhalder

EDITORS

ALDINE DE GRUYTER

New York

About the Editors

Eric Alden Smith is Associate Professor of Anthropology, University of Washington. He has conducted fieldwork on subsistence ecology and economics among Hudson Bay Inuit, and is currently analyzing demographic data collected in the same area.

Bruce Winterhalder is Professor and Chairman, Department of Anthropology, and a member of the Ecology Curriculum, University of North Carolina at Chapel Hill. He has carried out fieldwork on various evolutionary ecology topics among the Cree of northern Ontario and the Quechua of highland Peru.

ALDINE DE GRUYTER
A division of Walter de Gruyter, Inc.
200 Saw Mill River Road
Hawthorne, New York 10532

The paper used in this publication meets the minimum requirements of American National Standard for Information Sciences—Permanence of Paper for Printed Library Materials, ANSI Z39.48-1984.

∞

Library of Congress Cataloging-in-Publication Data

Evolutionary ecology and human behavior / Eric Alden Smith, Bruce
    Winterhalder, editors.
        p.   cm. — (Foundations of human behavior)
    Includes bibliographical references and indexes.
        ISBN 0-202-01183-6 (cloth : alk. paper). — ISBN 0-202-01184-4
    (paper : alk. paper)
        1. Human evolution—Philosophy.   2. Human ecology.   3. Social
    evolution.   4. Behavior evolution.   5. Sociobiology.   I. Smith,
    Eric Alden.   II. Winterhalder, Bruce.   III. Series.
    GN365.9.E97   1992
    304.2—dc20   92-696
                                                                         CIP

Manufactured in the United States of America

10 9 8 7 6 5 4 3 2 1

Contents

Part IV.   Reproduction and Social Relations

List of Tables

List of Boxes

List of Figures

Chapter 11

Chapter 12

Preface

SCOPE AND PURPOSE

Since 1859 evolutionary biologists have used the Darwinian concept of natural selection to explain the origin, diversification, and adaptive design of living things. For perhaps an equally long time, various social and natural scientists have examined human and animal societies in their ecological context. But only in the last 30 years has a systematic framework emerged for analyzing animal behavior within a simultaneously evolutionary (selectionist) and ecological perspective. Analysis of human behavior from this perspective has an even shorter duration. Despite its relative youth, theory from what is now called evolutionary behavioral ecology has begun to make a distinct and productive contribution to the biological and social sciences. The primary goal of this volume is to document these contributions to the study of human social behavior.

The chapters herein summarize current theory and empirical research in human evolutionary ecology. They focus on topics lying at the intersection of evolutionary biology, behavioral ecology and human social behavior. Our goal is to describe the current state of the art in this complex, relatively new and sometimes controversial area straddling the boundary between the biological and social sciences.

Certainly the century after Darwin saw a variety of evolutionary approaches applied to humans, with a mixed record of success, failure, and sometimes notoriety (reviews in Hofstadter 1944; Gould 1981; Kitcher 1985; Ruse 1986). Although they shouldered the Darwinian mantle, these schools assumed premises and pursued analyses rather different from those recently developed under the rubric of evolutionary ecology. The studies summarized in this volume fully embrace Darwin's central tenet that differential reproduction is the primary force shaping biological adaptation and diversity. But in addition they focus on the ecological context of adaptation, and they employ a model-based methodology capable of unleashing the power of Darwinism to analyze complex, flexible phenotypes. As a result, they take up topics of central concern to the social sciences with fresh perspectives and methods.

For sake of coherence and because of space limitations, we have limited ourselves to research that is fundamentally *ecological* in nature. By this, we mean research that makes environmental variation an essential element in the explanation of behavioral variation. The volume does not pretend to cover the full range of studies of human behavior that are guided by evolutionary biology. For example, the field known as "evolutionary psychology" is not represented, nor do we encompass all topics commonly included under the label "sociobiology."

We have endeavored to present human evolutionary ecology in a form accessible to advanced undergraduates, graduate students and professionals in the social and biological sciences. Those familiar with the field should profit from the comprehensive treatment of concepts, methods and subjects. However, the volume is not intended exclusively for those already proficient in this area, nor is it only for those already committed to a neo-Darwinian explanatory framework. To the contrary, we hope that it will make the subject interesting and accessible to scientists without prior experience with such research. To further this aim, the authors of each chapter have drawn on convergent or complementary aspects of conventional social science. Because evolutionary ecology avoids the nature/culture polarization that has often characterized discussions of evolution and human behavior, we expect the volume to appeal to a broad audience interested in the causes of variation in human social behavior.

The approaches and topics that constitute human evolutionary ecology began to coalesce abut 15 years ago. They have now reached the point that a preliminary synthesis is opportune. The questions addressed in this field have concerned anthropologists, archaeologists and other social scientists for many years. They include such topics as the logic of different systems of production, the relation between subsistence and social relations, the causes of variation in gender roles, the problem of collective action in nonstate societies, the forces generating equality and inequality, and the relationship between culture and natural selection. We are confident that evolutionary ecology offers a new and cohesive perspective on these and other topics.

ORGANIZATION AND PROSPECT

The present work is like the typical edited volume only to the extent that it is a collection of chapters written by different authors. Unlike many anthologies it is not an afterthought to a conference symposium or workshop, nor a collection of papers connected by topic but uncoordinated in coverage or approach. When the editors first conceived the project in June of 1987, we drafted the broad outlines of the volume. We then drew up a list of chapter topics and approached the authors we felt would be best qualified to write them. We required each author (ourselves included) to agree to a lengthy protocol of outlines, abstracts, and manuscript revisions, with review at every stage. This procedure was adopted in an attempt to produce a unified, coherent, and comprehensive survey of human behavioral ecology. We have sought the consistency of an advanced textbook, but also the authority and vividness of original research papers. Our goal has been chapters that present central concepts, key models, and exemplary studies, rather than a complete review of what has been accomplished in each field of study.

The volume is divided into four sections. In Part I the theoretical foundations of the field and its implications for analyzing human behavior are described. These are placed within the context of the history and current status of relevant branches of social science (particularly nature/culture debates, ecological anthropology, and decision theory). Part II ("Closest Kin") contains chapters that examine the evolutionary ecology of pre-*sapiens* hominids and nonhuman primates. It thus provides a broader comparative perspective, illustrating both differences and similarities between human evolutionary ecology and that of other species. Part III ("Resources, Work, and Space") treats core areas of human ecology: foraging strategies, production intensification, time allocation, and territoriality and land tenure. Part IV ("Reproduction and Social Relations") contains discussions of cooperation, collective action, competition, sociopolitical inequality, mating and parenting strategies, and population dynamics.

ACKNOWLEDGMENTS

Nearly any scholarly work depends on the assistance of many individuals; the present work is certainly no exception. The editors wish to thank four sets of people to whom we feel particularly indebted: the chapter authors, who suffered patiently our repeated demands for revisions and then exceeded what was asked; our editors at Aldine (Richard Koffler and Trev Leger) and the series editors (Sarah Blaffer Hrdy and Richard Wrangham), who responded with enthusiasm, tolerated delays in the production schedule, and instructed us in the inexact art of counting manuscript pages; the evolutionary biologists who first introduced us to this exciting body of theory, particularly those we have known personally as teachers, mentors or colleagues: Ric Charnov, Steve Emlen, Gordon Orians, and Ron Pulliam; and our families, for the usual and eternal reasons that make simple acknowledgments insufficient.

Eric Alden Smith
Bruce Winterhalder

THEORETICAL FOUNDATIONS

Evolutionary Ecology and the Social Sciences

Bruce Winterhalder and Eric Alden Smith

1

1.1. INTRODUCTION

1.1.1. Problem and Rationale

Put as briefly as possible, evolutionary ecology is the study of evolution and adaptive design in ecological context. The contributors to this volume believe that evolutionary ecology is poised to make significant contributions to our understanding of human behavior. But we realize that acceptance of this approach within the human sciences is hampered by a history of controversy surrounding the use of evolutionary biology to analyze human behavior. Our hope is that careful integration of this approach with more standard social science, and a presentation of contemporary evolutionary ecology that makes clear its complexity and sophistication, will blunt much of the criticism that might otherwise arise.

The first two chapters of this volume are directed principally to social scientists for whom evolutionary terminology or ideas may be relatively unfamiliar. Evolutionary ecology depends on a coherent, well-defined investigative apparatus—premises, concepts, conventions, and terms that define a disciplined framework of study. We set out this framework and locate it with respect to other approaches to analyzing human evolution and behavior. This first chapter provides a broad overview of the questions addressed by evolutionary ecology with respect to human behavior. It relates evolutionary ecology to the approaches and concerns of social science generally. Chapter 2 provides a summary of the basic theoretical principles used throughout the volume, and compares these in some detail to selected social science frameworks.

Perhaps the first question that might occur to a social scientist is, Why *should* an evolutionary approach be applied to human behavior, especially social behavior? After all, the skeptic might argue, this can only confuse levels of analysis and is likely to resurrect thoroughly discredited notions of biological determinism and innate differences between races and sexes. We will deal with the matter of biological determinism below (1.3). The more fundamental question—Why bother with evolution at all?—deserves an immediate response.

Put simply, our answer is that any comprehensive explanation of human behavior *requires* evolutionary forces. At the most basic level, humans, like other species, are products of biological evolution. Human societies are products of cultural evolution (which in turn is conditioned by biologically evolved propensities). Thus, evolutionary forces acting on both genetic and cultural variation are directly involved in making us, and our societies, what they are. A more detailed discussion of the necessary causal role of evolutionary forces in shaping human behavior is provided in section 1.3, as well as in Chapters 2 and 3. The fundamental point made here is that there is simply no alternative to evolutionary analysis with respect to origins and maintenance of certain primary beliefs and preferences shaping human action.

The qualities of behavior impose special demands on its analysis. Individual behavior and social life are complex and diverse, ephemeral in their observable manifestations, and subject to rapid change over time. They are shaped by several different kinds of causes ranging from genes to symbols. The evolutionary analysis of behavior provides an abundance of difficult materials. One can despair of finding regularities or explanations for them. Evolutionary ecologists seek to order investigation through clear theoretical, methodological, and topical commitments, as spelled out below.

1.1.2. Chapter Overview

In section 1.2.1 we describe the origins and basic premises of evolutionary ecology, discuss various ways to include environmental context in evolutionary analyses, and examine the different kinds of explanation that can be classified as evolutionary. From this theoretical beginning we shift to questions of methodology, starting with a brief description of the hypothetico-deductive method and the role of simple models in analyses of biological and social phenomena. We then appraise the difficulties of evaluating behavioral ecology hypotheses (1.2.2).

Section 1.3 examines some of the issues raised by the claim that an evolutionary and ecological framework is a necessary component of any comprehensive view of the causes of human behavior. We discuss problems associated with a biocultural framework (1.3.1) and then posit that a synthesis of biological and cultural views can be justified on both ontological (1.3.2) and methodological (1.3.3) grounds. The chapter concludes with a summary (1.4).

1.2. WHAT IS EVOLUTIONARY ECOLOGY?

1.2.1. Substantive Features

Evolutionary ecology is the application of natural selection theory to the study of adaptation and biological design in an ecological setting. When the features under examination involve behavior, as is the case in this volume, then the subset of evolutionary ecology is often termed *behavioral ecology* (e.g., Krebs and Davies 1991). If the behavior involves social interactions, then the term *socioecology* may be employed (e.g., Crook 1970). In any case, evolutionary ecology is simultaneously concerned with natural selection (or its effects) and ecological context.

Historical Origins.   As a well-defined and integrated body of theory and research, evolutionary ecology is no more than about 30 years old. To be sure, styles of thought that are both evolutionary (in the Darwinian sense of giving explanatory precedence to natural selection) and ecological (i.e., focusing on organism–environment relations) predate the term itself. In fact, we might identify Darwin himself as the first evolutionary ecologist. But for reasons too varied to discuss here, ecological and evolutionary biology developed more or less independently.

Some groundwork for modern evolutionary ecology was laid in the 1930s through 1950s when mathematical biologists such as Lotka, Volterra, Gause, and Hutchinson developed the seminal mathematical models of ecological processes such as population dynamics, competition, and predation. These models were comparable in logical rigor and predictive power to those of population genetics (see Kingsland 1985; Hutchinson 1978). Building on this work, the two most prominent figures to forge an evolutionary ecology approach were David Lack (e.g., 1954, 1968) in England and Robert MacArthur (e.g., 1958, 1960, 1961) in the United States. MacArthur in particular brought all the elements of evolutionary ecology together in a creative synthesis: definition of central topics (e.g., community diversity, population regulation, sex ratios, feeding strategies, competitive equilibria), explicit Darwinian premises, hypothetico-deductive methods, and a reliance on simple mathematical models. When assessed against the highly descriptive tradition of 1950s ecology and the functionalism that then pervaded attempts to understand evolution in ecological terms, MacArthur's approach was radical. He inspired a generation of students and colleagues (Fretwell 1975) to pursue open-minded creation of abstract models and hypotheses, followed by their skeptical, empirical appraisal. Although Lack placed less emphasis on mathematical modeling, he played a similar role in the history of British biology.

MacArthur and Lack were key figures, but they did not define evolutionary ecology by themselves. By the 1960s, important work in this tradition was being done by many researchers. On the theoretical front, prominent contributions include Levins's (1968) monograph on adaptation to changing environments, MacArthur and Wilson's (1967) on island biogeography, along with papers by MacArthur and Pianka (1966) and Emlen (1966) on foraging strategies, and Orians (1969) on the evolution of mating systems. Contributing to these advances were exemplary field studies, including those by Crook on weaverbirds (Crook 1965) and primates (Crook and Gartlan 1966). These showed clearly that variation in social organization between and within species could be analyzed as evolutionary responses to local social and ecological conditions. By the 1970s, the blossoming of evolutionary ecology as a distinct field of study was formalized with the publication of several textbooks and edited volumes (Emlen 1973; Ricklefs 1973; Pianka 1974; Cody and Diamond 1975; May 1976; Krebs and Davies 1978; Roughgarden 1979).

One early paper by Brown (1964) is particularly illustrative of the move from descriptive and functional studies to the kind of analysis developed in evolutionary ecology. Brown noted that the diversity observed in avian territorial systems had so far confounded specific, functional explanations. There seemed to be no consistent pattern, no means of generalizing about the different beneficial consequences that had been offered to explain territorial behavior. Brown sought to shift the reasoning used to examine this question in a manner suggested by his title, *The Evolution of Diversity in Avian Territorial Systems.*

Brown argued that for natural selection to favor territoriality—aggressive behavior with respect to a resource such as space—there must be some relative advantage to it. Since the argument was couched in neo-Darwinian terms, the advantage must be enhanced probability of survival and reproduction. That will depend on the balance of costs and benefits or, more specifically, on the cost of defending the resource and the competitive benefits gained by its exclusive use. Brown argued that resources are more defendable where they are concentrated and predictable in location and that the benefits of defense grow with the degree of competition for the resource (its effective scarcity).

Brown argued that these two factors, defendability and competition, are jointly necessary for aggressive defense of the resource to evolve. For instance, if the resource is not economically or physically defendable, even very intense competition for it could not lead to the evolution of territoriality. Neither would territoriality evolve if the resource were defendable but not the object of competition; for instance, if it were localized but so abundant that nothing was gained to offset the costs of safeguarding its exclusive use.

This model is explored in more detail below (8.4.3). Its general significance for the logic of evolutionary ecology models has several aspects:

1.   As highlighted by his title, Brown's model begins with the evolutionary process, specifically with natural selection. His argument takes the form of a thought experiment: In what environmental circumstances will differential fertility and mortality select for defense of resources?

2.   Brown's objective is to explain the acknowledged *diversity* of territorial systems, from complete defense to lack of it. Further, since the model does not specify a particular type of resource, it can be applied to food, space, mates, or any other factor that contributes to an organism's fitness. A population might express territoriality differently for each of these factors, and might switch its territorial behavior over time, as the relevant independent variables change (e.g., seasonal changes in the dispersion or predictability of resources, or in their scarcity).

3.   Brown's thought experiment is an excellent example of a simple evolutionary ecology model. He has isolated a particular behavior and identified how it should vary as a consequence of a few independent variables. The verbal argument can be represented in the form of simple graphs or equations. Both the behavior and the variables are observable, making any particular application of the model a test of a hypothesis.

4.   Finally, there is a more subtle point. Imagine Brown had given his essay this superficially similar title: *The Function of Territoriality in Avian Species*. Gone would be the explicit reference to an evolutionary approach and to the explanation of diversity. In their place would be a search for the function(s) of territory. These two titles might promise the same kind of analysis, but the differences are fundamental. Territoriality presumably has (or had) one or more functions. But the evolutionary ecologist seeks explanation causally in the process of natural selection in specified environmental conditions. A function or functions (e.g., ensuring adequate food supplies) may be identified by Brown's explanation, but the explanation does not begin or end with this.

Neo-Darwinism.   Brown based his analysis solidly on the principle of natural selection. The observations that Darwin assembled in creating the concept of natural selection (Mayr 1977) are roughly the same that constitute its most parsimonious formulation today: More individuals are born than can live to reproduce, due to the constraints of environment; individuals show heritable differences that affect their relative ability to survive and reproduce; over time (multiple generations) their differential mortality and fertility will accumulate the more fit (or adaptive) of these variants in the population (see 2.2.1 for further discussion). The evolutionary ecologist typically studies the consequences of these principles at the phenotypic level (see 2.2.2). He or she focuses on the social and ecological processes and relationships—many of them behavioral—through which the implications of differential mortality and fertility are worked out.

Evolutionary ecology embraces a wide range of phenomena, from the behavioral strategies of individual organisms to the structure and evolution of ecological communities. Topically, the field embraces foraging strategies, spatial organization, group size and formation, sex allocation, mating systems, life history patterns, interspecific coevolution (of predators and prey, competitors, mutualists, and parasites and hosts), the evolution of niches, and the equilibrium structure and dynamic behaviors of ecological communities (see Krebs and Davies 1991; Roughgarden et al. 1989). Evolutionary ecology unites this diverse set of topics and foci by virtue of its base in neo-Darwinism, its focus on explaining phenotypic design, and its use of relatively simple mathematical models (often drawing on optimization or game theory) to understand complex systems.

Role and Characterization of Environment.   Evolutionary ecology directs our attention to the role and characterization of the environment in which organisms live, reproduce, and die. In the drama of evolutionary ecology the "ecological theater" is as fundamental as the "evolutionary play" (Hutchinson 1965). In fact, we might say about evolution what Simon (1969) has said about human behavior: It is the product of simple rules played out in an exceptionally complex environment. For neo-Darwinism, the rules are given by natural selection, the structure of inheritance (haploid, diploid, cultural, etc.), population structure, and the like. Simon's observation challenges us to determine appropriate means of describing and evaluating the short- and long-term environmental influences on behavior.

In the studies that follow, environment is defined as everything external to an organism that impinges upon its probability of survival and reproduction. The effects can bear on development, physiology, or behavior, and their sources can be physical, biological, or social. Broadly, we distinguish between *strategic* and *parametric* environmental contexts (Elster 1986:7). Strategic contexts (or variables) are those in which the consequences of a behavior depend on the frequency of it and alternative behaviors in the population. There is an "interdependence of decisions," which means among other things that there are no truly independent variables in the analysis. Typically, an organism's social environment is one of strategic variables. For instance, a courting warbler changes behavior in concert with the response of potential mates and competitors. In evolutionary ecology, strategic processes are studied using the concept of evolutionarily stable strategies (ESS), with concepts and models that are based in game theory (2.2.3).

In contrast, decisions made in a parametric context do not yield different outcomes depending on their own frequency. The independent variable may be deterministic or probabilistic and uncertainty may be low or high, but it is nevertheless independent. Typically the physical environment consists of parametric variables. A migrating warbler need not concern itself with the possibility that its decision to go south will provoke a change in the latitudinal distribution of seasonal climates. Decisions made in parametric situations can be analyzed with simple optimization models (2.4).

After deciding whether the environmental variables are strategic or parametric, it becomes important to decide how to reduce their complexity and to characterize them in a manner that best suits analysis of evolutionary questions. This is rarely easy or straightforward. At the simplest level a normative description of a few features of environment might suffice, for instance, to explain bird migration. But most behavior is a result of evolutionary mechanisms and processes operating on several scales of space and time. Behavioral responses, especially those involving learning, are most likely when the relevant environment has qualities of high variance, novelty, and unpredictability (Mayr 1974; Boyd and Richerson 1985). The spatial and temporal *pattern* of the relevant environmental features must be characterized with appropriate variables and in sufficient detail to capture these qualities (see Southwood 1977; Wiens 1984; Winterhalder 1980).

The attention of evolutionary ecology to the great complexity of the organism's environment helps to distinguish it from narrow versions of sociobiology. Key sociobiological models (kin selection, parent–offspring conflict, sexual selection, sex ratio manipulation) are derived from the basic features of Mendelian rules. They base predictions mainly on the properties of genetic inheritance systems, which are rather uniform. Because of this they achieve a high degree of generality. But sociobiological models without ecological variables can be *too* general if one is interested in the exceptional plasticity and diversity of behavior found *within* the human species.

In contrast, evolutionary ecology models give greater attention to the organism's environment. They predict diverse and flexible behavior, contingent on localized and often changing conditions. The great variety of states possible in the organism's immediate environment leads behavioral ecologists to expect a corresponding variety in the expression of behavior. While the chapters to follow sometimes draw upon sociobiological models, they attempt to complement these by being sensitive to the behavioral nuances arising from the socioecological setting.

Evolutionary Questions. Evolutionary biologists rarely dispute what questions are possible or even which kind of question is being asked in a particular instance. Compare programmatic statements by two evolutionary biologists, an ethologist (N. Tinbergen) and a systematist (E. Mayr). Tinbergen's (1968) commentary argues that it is the methods, not the results, of ethology that ought to be emulated by social scientists. Mayr's (1976 [1961]) views are stated in an essay titled, "Cause and Effect in Biology." Each sets

Table 1.1.   A Comparison of Statements by Tinbergen (1968) and Mayr (1976) on the Forms of Explanation in Biology

Tinbergen	Mayr
I. Ultimate analysis in terms of Neo-Darwinian process	
1. In what ways does this phenomenon (behavior) influence the survival, the success of the animal?	1. An ecological cause. The warbler . . . must migrate, because it would starve to death if it should try to winter in New Hampshire.
II. Proximate analysis in terms of mechanism	
2. What makes behavior happen at any given moment? How does its "machinery" work?	3. An intrinsic physiological cause. The warbler flew south because its migration is tied in with photoperiodicity. It responds to decrease in day length.
	4. An extrinsic physiological cause . . . on the 25th . . . the sudden drop in temperature and the associated weather conditions affected the bird . . . so that it actually took off.
III. Proximate analysis in terms of ontogeny	
3. How does the behavior machinery develop as the individual grows up?	
IV. Ultimate analysis in terms of evolutionary history	
4. How have the behavior systems of each species evolved until they became what they are now?	2. A genetic cause. The warbler has acquired a genetic constitution in the course of the evolutionary history of its species which induces it to respond appropriately to the proper stimuli from the environment.

out four components to his scheme. Tinbergen poses his components as questions, whereas Mayr defines four "equally legitimate" types of causation, which he illustrates with answers to the general question: "Why did the warbler on my summer place in New Hampshire start his southward migration on the night of the 25th of August?"

In Table 1.1 the statements of these two authors are listed in parallel columns. We have added headings but have retained the numbering and wording of the authors. There is a high degree of correspondence between these outlines despite their different forms and independent development. Mayr's warblers almost perfectly answer three of Tinbergen's behavioral questions. The modest deviations also are revealing (the following comments are keyed to the headings):

I.   Both Tinbergen and Mayr draw attention to the mechanisms and processes of evolution, chiefly natural selection. Mayr calls this an "ultimate" source of causation; it refers to the evolutionary origins of the trait. It answers a *why* question: Why did the trait come about? We can generalize Mayr's reference to suit our present purposes by adding social causes to his ecological ones.

II.   Mayr distinguishes two types of answers that match one of Tinbergen's inquiries: "What makes behavior happen at a given moment?" There is an intrinsic cause (characterizing the state of the organism) and an extrinsic cause (which characterizes its environment). For Mayr these are "proximate" causes located in the individual and its immediate circumstances. They answer *how* questions: How does the adaptation function?

III.   Mayr's scheme of four parts omits reference to Tinbergen's question about ontogeny: How does the behavioral response develop? With our focus on complex phenotypes, we cannot afford to overlook this question. The study of learning during growth is vital to the analysis of behavior, especially human behavior. In fact, humans are so powerfully receptive to socialization that it constitutes the basis for a parallel system of inheritance (Chapter 3). Adapting Mayr's terminology, we might say that ontogeny falls closer to the proximate realm of functional inquiry. But for humans, or any creature heavily dependent on learning and social transmission of knowledge, ontogeny has engendered its own, partially independent mechanisms of evolutionary change.

IV.   For both Tinbergen and Mayr the fourth realm of inquiry is a phylogenetic or historical one. It also is an ultimate or *why* type of inquiry. But phylogenetic analysis concerns evolutionary origins in the narrow historical sense and not the reasons why selection might continue to stabilize some phenotypic feature within a population.

1.2.2. Research Strategy

Evolutionary ecologists generally follow the research strategy known as the *hypothetico-deductive method*. This method involves a cyclical movement between the creation of abstract models and their testing against the empirical evidence. The logic and structure of this cycle is the concern of the present section.

Hypothetico-deductive Method.   The hypothetico-deductive (HD) method consists of procedures that adhere to specific rules of logic and evidence, but also attempt to reflect the way scientists actually think and work. It is pragmatic science, somewhat wary of the more formal (and occasionally dogmatic or disputatious) philosophies of scientific method, which have contended for the attention of the physical, biological, and social sciences. Although anticipated by Kant and advocated at length by Popper, we prefer

Medawar's (1982:73–135) more accessible summary (see also Fretwell 1972:viii–ix).

The HD method distinguishes between the creative and evaluative components of scientific research; it acknowledges and draws our attention to differences between the processes of discovery and those of verification. HD advocates do not believe that the inventive stage of science can be formalized in a methodology. It depends rather on such scientifically elusive elements as the felicitous guess or inspired insight. These elements clearly are helped by experience with the relevant data and by knowledge of related theory, hypotheses, and concepts, but they cannot be reduced to a protocol of logical procedures.

The generation of theory or hypotheses is followed by processes of evaluation. Hypotheses are tested by experiment and observation and gain our respect by outliving the twin assaults of logic and evidence. In Medawar's (1982) words, "there is . . . reciprocation between an imaginative and a critical process, between imaginative conjecture and critical evaluation" (p. 100). The result is a "running adjustment" (p. 105) of ideas and data. The kind of confidence accruing to a veteran HD hypothesis falls short of notions such as proof, but it is consistent with contemporary views on logic and our normal experience with human intellectual fallibility. The HD method accepts the sharp distinction offered by logical positivism: Hypotheses cannot be strictly proven, only soundly disproved. But it insists that the practice of science is considerably less tidy. Some hypotheses are accepted with a high degree of confidence, while others are occasionally wrongly rejected. Evolutionary science in practice must work the more ambiguous middle ground between surely right and certainly wrong. It is rare, at least in the biological and social sciences, for an hypothesis to be rejected outright; an unequivocal disproof is hard to obtain. Rather, hypotheses are more commonly subject to tinkering, adjustment, and repair. They are assimilated into other ideas or, if unproductive or repeatedly unsubstantiated, they simply fade away.

Medawar describes the HD method as one that "potentiates common sense." It does not rest on claims that logical procedures (deductive or inductive) are infallible guides to truth; it does not grant unquestioned authenticity to facts but, rather, sees them as perceived and selected according to preexisting ideas. It thus allows for the influences of culture, context, and personality, while cautiously insisting that biases of each can be found out and corrected if the practice of science is disciplined.

Simple Models in a Complex World.   Upon hearing Darwin's idea of natural selection, Huxley is supposed to have remarked, "How extremely stupid not to have thought of that" (Huxley 1920:94). Natural selection itself—differential survival and reproduction—is a simple notion (see 2.2.1).

But the consequences of the concept, its operation in the process of evolution, are anything but simple. Between the straightforward logic of the idea and the bewildering complexity and variety of the products of the evolutionary process lies the key to understanding the place of models in evolutionary ecology analyses. From a premise of a few sentences we must generate ideas adequate to explain the detail and complexity, say, of a primate troop or a tropical rain forest. Models are our best means of surmounting this detail while preserving at least some fidelity to its reality.

"We . . . build models to explore the consequences of what we believe to be true" (Starfield and Bleloch 1986:3). Models are especially useful when there is some understanding of the problem, but ideas about how to analyze the data are limited. They help to (1) define the problem, (2) organize thought about it, (3) understand data, (4) test the understanding, and (5) make further predictions. In effect, they are heuristic tools that discipline our attempts to work from general premises to concrete and testable illustrations of them.

Levins (1966) defined three desirable qualities of any model: realism, generality, and precision. Though each has clear virtues, one cannot pursue all three at once with equal vigor. One can get high precision, for example, but only at the cost of reduced generality or realism. Thus, an optimization model may specify a single currency to be maximized, which allows precise predictions about optima but overlooks the diversity of goals that may pertain in the real world. Similarly, maximal realism usually entails reduced generality or precision; a model that exactly fits a particular case will probably not fit other cases nearly so well (sacrifice generality) and may be so complex as to make precise prediction (and hence empirical test under changed conditions) impossible.

Evolutionary biologists typically emphasize particular qualities, depending on the question being asked or the answer sought. If fisheries management or economic policy, for example, is the objective, realism has high priority. If inferences that will contribute to the construction of theory with broad applicability are the objective, then generality will have a high priority. The attempt to establish recurrent relationships between types of food webs and community structure might be an example. If clearly distinguishing between competing hypotheses is desired, precision may be the most important quality. Whatever the balance of these qualities that the analyst seeks, models are devices to make complex problems tractable.

Models, however, may invite criticism because of their simplicity. Superficially there is an intuitive appeal to such critiques. The models of evolutionary ecologists are orders of magnitude short of the complexity and variety of the phenomena they purport to explain. They invite the accusations of simplemindedness and reductionism. But simple is not simpleminded. Simple models are a necessary, not a temporary or primitive stage

of scientific development. This is because "simple models are caricatures
. . . capturing a few essential features of the problem in a recognizable but
stylized manner, and with no attempt to represent features not of immediate
interest" (Richerson and Boyd 1987:35). They often are implicit in our
ability to understand the more complex models that may grow out of or
supersede them. The Hardy–Weinberg formula and the logistic growth
curve are examples of models that survive, enshrined in thought and textbooks, because they do enduring heuristic work.

In evolutionary ecology no single model exists or is used in isolation. Any
subject is analyzed through a collection or family of models. Each model
addresses a particular topic and has its own limitations. Their articulation
into a more comprehensive account is a task that requires that we know
their limitations, applicability, and representativeness. In particularly well-
developed areas (e.g., optimal foraging theory—see Chapter 6), a set of
complementary models can develop into a comprehensive analytical tool—
a *theory*.

Reductionism. The use of simple models in the social sciences also invites
charges of reductionism, especially if the models have a biological origin.
To address this issue, we first define and distinguish among several different
meanings of reductionism, following Mayr (1988:10–11). Mayr specifically
examines the reduction of biology to physics, but his analysis is applicable
one step up the scientific hierarchy, where the social sciences look back
uneasily to their relationship with biology.

Constitutive reductionism applies to the "dissection of phenomena,
events, and processes into the constituents of which they are composed"
(Mayr 1988:10). It claims that higher-level phenomena are constituted of
lower-level events and processes, which preserve their integrity whatever
their context. A behaving human is constituted of organs, organs of cells,
cells of molecules. Comprehending higher levels does not fundamentally
change understanding of the lower ones, which have properties and processes that remain valid and applicable from whatever level they are studied. Thus, a molecule is not different by virtue of being in an organism;
chemical reactions follow the same rules whether located in a puddle or the
stomach of a tuna.

To the extent that higher levels are unique, their novel properties and
processes emerge from differences linked to increased organizational complexity. Life is constituted of nonliving materials but has emergent properties
all its own; the living brain is an organic structure, but mind is a different
matter.

Novel emergent properties raise the issue of *explanatory reduction*, which
"claims that all the phenomena and processes at higher hierarchical levels
can be explained in terms of the actions and interactions of the components
at the lowest hierarchical level" (Mayr 1988:11). In the extreme (signified by

reduction across several levels, or to the lowest level) explanatory reductionism is a failure. It is impossible to explain socialism in terms of molecular bonds. But a more modest claim to partial explanation at a lower level can be defended in many circumstances. Within this more limited scope, explanatory reductionism is a standard procedure of scientific analysis. The understanding to be gained from explaining a conditioned reflex in terms of neural circuitry illustrates its merits. However, in many circumstances it is difficult to evaluate the power and limitations or establish the appropriate degree of explanatory reductionism. This leaves room for controversy.

Finally, *theory reduction* implies that theories at one level are only special cases of theories formulated for lower levels and ultimately can be reduced to them. Theory reduction enjoys a limited success in physics but is almost universally rejected elsewhere (Mayr 1988:11). It confuses processes (for example, biochemical), which are common across levels (as recognized by general acceptance of constitutive reductionism), with concepts, which are not. The brain operates according to standard biochemical processes, but the workings of the mind cannot be explained in purely biochemical terms. The same can be said of natural selection and Mendelian inheritance relative to chemistry.

Evolutionary ecology presumes constitutive reductionism. It practices a limited degree of explanatory reductionism, as do most biological or social sciences. For example, a commitment to self-interest explanations permeates most of the models discussed in this book; many social science analyses also attempt to analyze social phenomena as the product of self-interested behavior (albeit for different theoretical reasons), although such reductionism sometimes is controversial in the social sciences (see 2.3.1). Finally, there is little if any theory reduction invoked in the studies summarized in this volume. Rather, evolutionary behavioral ecology involves a blending of complementary theoretical approaches: neo-Darwinism, cultural transmission models, decision theory, population ecology, and even models of bargaining and political dynamics. Thus, evolutionary ecology as exemplified by the studies summarized herein does not require or advocate greater amounts of reductionism than can be found in many realms of social science, nor does it invoke the most problematic form, theory reduction.

There is another property of human behavior that elicits the charge of simplicity and sometimes that of reductionism: It is multicausal. Multicausality arises because any and all behavior results from the interacting effects of genes, environment, and learning. The classical example in biology is bird song (Lehrman 1970), but the issues are the same for human musicians. The primary question to be asked (but what a question!) is how and to what degree each of these causes leads to the behavioral variation seen in musicianship (or any other trait), avian or human. Whatever their relative importance, separate study of each of these factors is necessary to

understand their consequences taken all together. Once their separate effects can be predicted, it is an empirical matter to determine if any factor
predominates.

This point bears emphasis. To study the causes of phenotypically complex
traits like behavior one must analyze the causes of behavioral variance
(Lewontin 1974). For individuals of a species formed through complicated
and prolonged processes of growth and development, this entails analyses
in which genotype, experience, and learning are the minimum set of independent variables. One can wrongly assess the relative importance of those
variables, but there is no logical basis for claiming that analysis of one or
another of them is in itself reductionism.

When charges of biological reductionism are evaluated by the distinctions
Mayr outlines:

1.   Many collapse, usually because they confuse or fail to distinguish
among the various types of reductionism, or because they treat as reductionism legitimate analytical choices (see 1.2.1).

2.   Some raise important and thought-provoking issues, although often
they must be shorn of rhetorical baggage and exaggerated claims of critical
impact.

3.   Those which constitute valid critiques thereby assume an important
role in the self-correcting processes of the HD method.

The analysis of human behavior from an evolutionary ecology perspective
will benefit from more careful and tolerant understanding of the role of
simplifying models. Specialized analyses that take up a limited set of problems or causal factors do not for that reason alone represent inappropriate
instances of reductionism.

Evaluation.   Evolutionary theory is multifaceted and the determinants of
behavior are diverse. The questions we might ask are various, and they must
be asked by means of families of models that represent a sometimes uneasy
compromise between the complexity of the situation being investigated and
analytical feasibility. As argued above, the HD method alerts one to the
potential for errors in the process of theory evaluation. What sense then can
we make of the claim that an idea has survived empirical test?

First, hypothesis testing allows us to correct our view of the world as it is
expressed in choices about the variables, constraints, currencies, and other
concrete elements that we use to construct an evolutionary ecology model.
It helps to articulate theory. For instance, in the prey choice model (6.2.3)
we make certain assumptions about the environment (random distribution of
prey), about the organism (that it can sense and assess the costs and benefits
associated with different prey species), about selection (that it has acted to
enhance the prey capture abilities of the predator), about the value of the

prey to the predator (calories are more important than nutrients), and so on. Based on these assumptions, the model provides explicit predictions. If empirical observations do not conform to those hypotheses, at least they may provide clues concerning which of the model assumptions were wrong. The formal structure of the model becomes the template upon which we use data to track down and correct errors in our initial understanding.

Second, most evolutionary ecology models produce hypotheses concerning the form, direction, and degree of the relationship between variables. Precision often has a low priority to the kind of knowledge being sought. Hypotheses like the following are common: As resource density and predictability increase, territoriality is more likely. If prey density increases, the diet breadth of the organism (the number of prey types it pursues) will diminish. Females in better than average health and resource circumstances should, if they can expect their offspring to experience the same, produce more of the sex that most benefits from the maternal condition. Note that these hypotheses are stated in the form of inequalities, correlations, and functions without constants. They distinguish among qualitative possibilities and often are tested through comparative research designs. When evolutionary ecology models *do* seek quantitative precision, it is usually in order to maximize the power of the empirical test, rather than to obtain precision for its own sake or for the reasons that policymakers might wish to have precise predictive accuracy.

Third, evolutionary ecology models are quite explicit about the kinds of information required to evaluate them. Unfortunately, their data requirements often are extensive and difficult to meet. They also may be novel relative to information already collected on the topic. For instance, before optimal foraging theory was applied to hunter–gatherers, most anthropologists studying hunter–gatherers assumed that prey selection was a function mainly of prey abundance. In contrast, the prey choice model suggested that other variables, such as the food value of prey types and their pursuit and handling costs, likely were equally or more important. Making such measurements became a new task for fieldwork. Because they make broad and sometimes unexpected demands on our empirical resources, evolutionary ecology models can appear to be far ahead of their empirical validation. This also is a strength, as they direct us to new data and novel ways of the seeing the old.

Fourth, neither these observations on data nor the HD method itself suggest that we should expect definitive results from single tests. Evolutionary ecologists have learned to be patient with somewhat fuzzy data, suggestive results, and tests of hypotheses that result in partial acceptance or modification of the prediction rather than its outright rejection. A sound empirical investigation can weigh for or against a hypothesis but also may be inconclusive. The analyst must tolerate some ambiguity and partial resolution.

1.3. EVOLUTIONARY ECOLOGY AND THE SOCIAL SCIENCES

Social scientists often ignore or actively discourage linkages between their studies and evolutionary theory. In contrast, the authors of this volume believe that the relationships are direct and compelling. Underlying this claim are the biological origins and continuing biocultural character of human capacities and behavior. These alone are sufficient to motivate a comprehensive search for an integrated, evolutionary science of human behavior. However, any synthesis must come to terms with the troubled history of biocultural analyses of human behavior. And it must identify clear ontological and methodological grounds for such synthesis.

1.3.1. Skirmishes Along the Biocultural Frontier

The long history of battles over the causation of human behavior has left many biological and social scientists wary of the whole enterprise. Unpleasant scientific and ideological skirmishes have tended to alternate with periods of uneasy standoff. The more prominent battles—over Darwinism, social Darwinism, and sociobiology, in turn—have been episodic and inconclusive. The reasons for this procession of relatively unproductive disputes are various. Here we briefly consider three of the more important ones.

First, analysts of all persuasions frequently conflate scientific issues with ideological ones. By historical precedent, Western academics associate biology with politically conservative views and culture with liberal ones. Once established, these associations are reinforced by academic traditions and polarization. Conservatives frequently advance the cause of biology, and radicals that of culture.

But there are good reasons to reject these associations, on both logical and empirical grounds. Empirically, there are many historical and contemporary examples where biology is the basis for radical views and culture the redoubt of conservative ones. The later work of A. R. Wallace (e.g., 1913) is an excellent example of the former. Contrary to the conservative, laissez-faire social Darwinism of the day, Wallace argued that Darwinism substantiates the case for political socialism. Similarly, the radical environmentalism of B. F. Skinner (e.g., 1972), although not linked by Skinner himself to conservative views, certainly was attacked by progressives as robbing humans of dignity and self-determination. In the contemporary scene, we have to look no farther than the debate over evolutionism and creationism to see that the denial of biology in human affairs is not necessarily a progressive view. The feminist sociobiology of Hrdy (1981) is another striking disconfirmation of the conventional wisdom. More generally, there is no necessary or logically invariant relationship between biology or culture as a causal influence on behavior and the ethical or political content or implications of that behavior. In sum, although biological determinism *can* be used to bolster conservative views, to think it *must* be so used is a prejudice, albeit a widespread and sometimes self-fulfilling one.

Second, among the many unnecessary and unfortunate associations that inhere to the nature–nurture dichotomy of Western thought is the belief that nature constrains and culture facilitates the expression of variety in human behavior. When someone refers to "human nature" versus culture, it is predictable that nature and not culture is seen as setting the boundaries (cf. Young 1974). While it is true that species-specific behaviors exist, much vertebrate social behavior varies dramatically depending on ecological circumstances, stage of life cycle, and other factors, which we can attempt to understand by means of evolutionary ecology models. The models are deterministic in that they attempt to analyze diverse manifestations of behavior using a common causality; but they do not predict a uniform outcome.

Conversely, anthropologists repeatedly emphasize (even while avoiding the word) the determining character of cultural life. When Geertz says that "man is an animal suspended in [cultural] webs of significance" (1973:5) the captive, constraining (and naturalistic) imagery evokes no cries of reductionism, determinism, or conservatism. Conversely, if a biologist says that humans are "entangled in the message of DNA" an uproar is likely to follow. A priori there is no justification for the automatic association between biological causation and determinism or limitations, nor between cultural causation and flexibility or variety.

Evolutionary ecology is more heterogeneous as a theory, more probabilistic as a process, and in outcome more productive of diversity and flexibility than is commonly believed by social scientists. The role of culture currently advanced by several approaches in the social sciences may be more causally restrictive or deterministic than is the case for the evolved propensities assumed in human behavioral ecology.

Third, disagreement has been exacerbated by the ambitious tone of some recent biological analyses of human social behavior (Kitcher 1985) and the disputatious replies of some social scientists. The contributors to this volume offer a cautious assessment of what evolutionary ecology has to offer to social science. We are acutely aware of limitations, some due to the youthful state of evolutionary ecology and others to the very nature of evolutionary explanations. The authors of this volume do not claim that natural selection and ecological adaptation *by themselves* explain all of human action, only that they are important causes of its variation. And even when selection and adaptation are the prime causal forces, they do not necessarily produce uniformity; instead, they often produce patterns of (adaptive) phenotypic variation keyed to varying environmental states, historically unique evolutionary trajectories, or indeterminate outcomes with multiple possible equilibria. Each of these possibilities is discussed in models and empirical analyses throughout this volume.

Environmental Determinism. Because evolutionary ecology gives the environment a central explanatory role (see 1.2.1), it may appear vulnerable to the charge of environmental determinism. The debate over environmental determinism has a long history in social science (reviewed in Vayda and Rappaport 1968; Ellen 1981:Chapters 1 and 2); it remains a loaded issue, subject to frequent misapprehensions.

Taken literally, environmental determinism is indefensible: No aspect of the environment *in itself* directly and solely determines features of human behavior or society. There is always an interaction between environmental problems or opportunities, and the beliefs, goals, and capabilities of the human actors who confront them. The environmental determinism that found favor in scholarly circles early in this century erred in overlooking the great differences in beliefs, goals, and capabilities found in different human societies. It thus ignored important intervening variables (technology, social structure, economic organization, etc.).

But simply refuting environmental determinism (as Franz Boas and his associates were so fond of doing) yields the equally problematic environmental possibilism. Possibilism holds that the environment sets *limits* (usually broad ones) on the forms of behavior that can occur but plays no determining role within those limits. Possibilism is not wrong; it is just incomplete—hopelessly so. To say that the environment only limits, and therefore does not play any determining role, is to ignore more subtle forms and degrees of causation. For example, Kroeber is often quoted for his statements that climate cannot explain why agriculture spread where it did, only why it failed to spread to some areas (i.e., those too dry or cold). But more recent analyses suggest that some areas that are not physically too extreme for agriculture nevertheless are marginal enough that other forms of subsistence *are more profitable*, and hence preferred by inhabitants of these regions.

To a large degree, it was this last type of argument that Julian Steward (1955) introduced in his pathbreaking theory of "cultural ecology." Steward wished to go beyond the sterility of the possibilist/determinist debate and "the fruitless assumption that culture comes from culture" (p. 36) offered by Boasian possibilism. In Steward's formulation, heavily influenced by his training in evolutionary biology, environment determined the payoffs to various behavior patterns and thus exercised influence even within the limits of what was possible:

> Over the millennia, cultures in different environments have changed tremen-
> dously, and these changes are basically traceable to new adaptations required
> by changing technology and productive arrangements. . . . Whether or not
> new technologies are valuable is, however, a function of the society's cultural
> level as well as of environmental potential. (pp. 37–38)

Thus, Steward took full account of intervening variables and of degrees of
adaptive advantage.

In sum we might say that cultural ecology replaced the possibilism of the
Boasians with a rather primitive notion of adaptive optimization, fore-
shadowing the approach of contemporary evolutionary ecology. However,
Steward—and cultural ecology in general—never came up with an explanation or mechanism for adaptive optimization. Only two plausible mechanisms have yet been proposed: rational choice and natural selection. The
former is a powerful element of human adaptation (and seems to operate in
other species with complex nervous systems as well); but it implies preexisting preferences for options with high-payoffs and hence ultimately depends
on a history of natural selection (see 2.3.2). Natural selection can shape
preferences and resulting behavioral patterns not only via genetic evolution,
but also via cultural evolution (see Chapter 3). By bringing both these
explanatory mechanisms to bear, and by utilizing a methodology based on
model-building and HD processes, evolutionary ecology promises to put
Steward's seminal insights on a more solid and productive footing.

1.3.2. Ontological Syntheses

One encouraging basis for synthesis between evolutionary biology and
social science is ontological. Humans are evolved creatures that through
their history have been subject to the same evolutionary processes as other
organisms (see Chapters 3 and 5). Our cultural capabilities, to whatever
degree they constitute emergent properties, are a product of that process.
Further, in evolutionary terms, they are a fairly recent phenomenon. They
had their beginnings in creatures that anatomically and physiologically were
quite like us. These observations do not necessarily provide grounds for a
thoroughgoing reductionism, however. We cannot simply replace culture
theory with evolutionary biology. The problem is that while culture may
have begun simply enough as an aspect of phenotype, it has properties that
made it into a parallel, partially independent, and very powerful evolutionary mechanism (see Chapter 3). The result is a creature heavily dependent
on learning and experience. Whatever the relative balance of causation in
human behavior, its analysis requires theory that can deal synthetically with
our biocultural heritage.

It is no surprise that solid understanding of the relationship of culture to biology is yet modest and that consensus remains elusive. Indeed, the contributors to the present volume occasionally do not have complete agreement on these issues. Nevertheless, we all believe that evolutionary ecology can contribute substantially to the resolution of many of these disagreements. We also agree that the conventional terms of debate— biology versus culture, determinism versus intentionality, reductionism versus holism, biological versus social science—are now unproductive and need to be left behind for more sophisticated ways of framing the issues.

1.3.3. Methodological Syntheses

Methodology is another area of potential synthesis. The models employed in evolutionary ecology often transcend the conventional division between the biological and social sciences. They do so in at least two ways.

First, they create a more general arena for the use of concepts that span the biology/culture dichotomy. Those familiar with the history of the social sciences (especially economics) immediately will recognize many of the premises and concepts used in this volume. Optimization, rational choice, game theory, and methodological individualism are tools familiar to many social scientists. Evolutionary ecologists use this terminology with some caution. The precise meaning of terms can shift or become ambiguous in a new context, and simple borrowing of terms rarely is analytically rewarding. But here we believe that the rationales for common usage are sound (see 2.3 and 2.4).

Second, there are methodological issues common to the biological and social sciences. To what degree is microlevel theory sufficient to explain macrolevel phenomena? In the biological sciences, to what extent are macroevolutionary phenomena susceptible to microevolutionary explanation? In the social sciences, to what degree are the broad phenomena of human history (e.g., the origin of the state) explicable through principles of methodological individualism, what Elster (1983) calls "microfoundations"? Within a comprehensive, evolutionary framework these become versions of the same question: To what extent are the properties of complex systems (ecosystems or societies), including their historical development, the product of microlevel processes channeled through the actions of individuals? Similarly, what are the proper form and limits of functionalism or (as it is often termed in evolutionary biology) adaptationism? We defer discussion of these issues to Chapter 2, but their listing here should give ample evidence of the common methodological issues linking evolutionary ecology and conventional social science.

1.4. SUMMARY

The main arguments presented in this chapter can be summarized as follows:

1.   Synthetic studies combining evolutionary and ecological elements in the study of behavior are fairly recent. Evolutionary behavioral ecology is characterized by a reliance on natural selection theory, a hypothetico-deductive methodology based in models, and a focus on the levels of individual phenotypes and social systems.

2.   Simple models are a necessary tool for the analysis of complex systems. The competing characteristics of generality, precision, and realism cannot be simultaneously maximized in any model or analysis. The analyst must make choices about which to emphasize in a given inquiry.

3.   Evolutionary ecology analyses typically take the form of the following question: In what environmental circumstances are the costs and benefits of behavior X such that selection would favor its evolution? Framing the analysis this way encourages the search for general (widely applicable) answers, without ignoring the importance of individual and populational diversity.

4.   Behavioral diversity is largely the result of diversity in the socio-ecological environment of the organism. Strong attention to this environmental setting distinguishes evolutionary ecology from narrow forms of sociobiology.

5.   Most evolutionary ecology analyses take up ultimate or *why* questions, while giving less attention to (though not denying the importance of) questions of proximate mechanisms.

6.   The charges of determinism and reductionism leveled by critics of evolutionary analyses of human behavior often are misdirected complaints about legitimate analytical choices and procedures. Analyses based on natural selection and environmental variables are not inherently more deterministic or reductionistic than those based on cultural or social variables.

7.   The need for synthetic, evolutionary analyses of human behavior rests on both ontological grounds (humans have evolved as biocultural creatures) and methodological ones (the biological and social sciences share important issues and can profitably share certain methods).

ACKNOWLEDGMENTS

Robert Bettinger, Monique Borgerhoff Mulder, Kristen Hawkes, and John Terrell offered useful criticisms of earlier versions of this chapter.

Natural Selection and Decision-Making: Some Fundamental Principles

Eric Alden Smith and Bruce Winterhalder

2

2.1. INTRODUCTION

This chapter provides an introduction to the main theoretical principles employed throughout this volume. It is organized into three sections. In section 2.2 we present an overview of contemporary evolutionary theory, emphasizing the explanatory logic of natural selection. We describe the complexities imposed by the hierarchical organization of living systems and the techniques currently used to analyze the evolution of social interactions. Section 2.3 surveys selected theoretical and methodological issues in the social sciences. We emphasize methodological individualism and rational choice, topics that provide natural avenues for linking social theory and evolutionary ecology. In section 2.4, we summarize the general principles of simple optimization analysis, a framework commonly employed in both evolutionary ecology and the social sciences. We pay special attention to problems that can arise in applying optimization methods in an evolutionary context.

2.2. NATURAL SELECTION AND EVOLUTIONARY ECOLOGY

Any survey of the theory of natural selection limited to a few pages must be highly abbreviated. Our goal is to present those principles that are most relevant to the questions and findings raised in the later chapters of this volume, in a way that is accessible to readers unfamiliar with this body of theory. We begin (2.2.1) with a discussion of natural selection and its key components, as well as other evolutionary forces and constraints. Section 2.2.2 discusses problems surrounding levels of selection and adaptation:

What kinds of traits are favored by natural selection, and at what levels (genes, individuals, groups, etc.)? In section 2.2.3, we introduce the theory of evolutionarily stable strategies, the primary framework used by evolutionary ecologists in analysis of social interactions.

2.2.1. Selectionist Analysis and Its Limitations

What Is Natural Selection? In outline, natural selection is a simple process. Three conditions are required:

1. There must be phenotypic variation (differences between individuals).
2. Some of this variation must be heritable (transmitted to offspring).
3. Variants must differ in their ability to survive and reproduce (there must be fitness differences).

The term *phenotype* refers to characteristics of an organism other than DNA—its morphology, physiology, and behavior.

Some *phenotypic variation* is due to differences in genotype, some is due to environment (which influences phenotypes during ontogeny and also elicits short-term behavioral responses), and in the human case some is due to culturally acquired information (which may either be considered an aspect of environment, or be defined as heritable information analogous to genotype—see Chapter 3). The portion of phenotypic variation that is not attributable to differences between the environments of individuals is said to be *heritable*. Phenotypic characters are heritable if faithfully transmitted to offspring, even by nongenetic means. For selection to act, there must be heritability, but it need not be 100% (although the lower it is, the slower or less effective selection will be). *Fitness differences* must also exist if natural selection is to occur. It is possible to have heritable variation without fitness differences—differences in fingerprint patterns, or equally effective enzyme variants, for example—but the types of variation studied by evolutionary ecology (foraging patterns, mating systems, birth spacing, etc.) are unlikely to be selectively neutral.

Given heritable variation with fitness consequences, variants that reproduce at a higher average rate will tend to become relatively more numerous; in a finite environment, this process will eventually lead to the replacement of less "fit" variants by those with higher rates of replication. Of course, there are many subtleties and complexities hidden behind this simple statement (e.g., Darwin 1859; Williams 1966; and Krebs and Davies 1991). Some of them have to do with the concept of Darwinian fitness, our next subject.

What Is Fitness? In an important paper on life history theory (see Chapter 11), the evolutionary ecologist Stephen Stearns offered a somewhat tongue-in-cheek definition of fitness as "something everyone understands but no one can define precisely" (Stearns 1976:4). This ambiguity has led some critics to judge evolutionary theory as fundamentally confused or even tautological. Such charges are unjustified.

In evolutionary biology, the term *fitness* derives from Herbert Spencer's phrase (later adopted by Darwin) "survival of the fittest." The potential for confusion arises from both terms. Survival colloquially means staying alive; but Darwin's theory is not about survival in this sense, except as such survival increases lifetime reproductive output. The second term also confuses: fittest colloquially means strongest, healthiest, whereas what Darwin and his successors mean is relative reproductive success. But this explication of "survival of the fittest" invites the charge of tautology. What is fit? That which survives (reproductively). What survives (reproductively)? That which is fit.

One sensible solution to this quandary is that proposed by Mills and Beatty (1984). They define the fitness of an organism or a type (a "variant" or "trait" in our terminology) as "its *propensity* to survive and reproduce in a particularly specified environment and population" (p. 42). Fitness then refers to the *expected* number of descendants of a type (relative to other variants in the population), whereas the *actual* number of descendants generated by a given individual is determined by a number of factors, some of which might be unrelated to adaptive design (see also Williams 1966a: 102ff.; Brandon 1990:14–24). For example, we would not want to conclude that water-conserving traits have lower fitness in an arid environment just because one year's data indicate that a disproportionate number of organisms with these traits died from lightning strikes. The propensity measure of fitness cautions us to look beyond limited data such as these, and to ask if *on average* water conservers have higher fitness than nonconservers. In effect, fitness propensity is a probabilistic measure. It focuses attention on adaptive *design* for reproduction rather than actual number of offspring per se.

The propensity interpretation of fitness helps us understand what evolutionary biologists mean by adaptations. For Darwin, adaptations were any characteristics that make an organism better fitted to survive and reproduce in its environment. What saves selection theory from tautology is that there is a highly regular relationship between an organism's way of life, its environment, and the kinds of characteristics that will actually improve its fitness: Desert dwellers improve their adaptedness by traits that conserve water, water dwellers by hydrodynamic efficiency, nocturnal creatures by sensitive sight, hearing, or echolocation, and so on. Hence, fitness is the product of interactions between two sets of characteristics: those of the environment (including other organisms) and those of the organism or type being studied. The more we understand about an organism and its environment, the better we are able to predict what kind of traits—should they arise—will be favored by selection. Fitness itself is tautological (as is any definition), but the explanatory framework of natural selection in which fitness is embedded is not.

What then is the significance of natural selection? Darwin's fundamental insight was this: *If* some process is at work generating new variants (with genetically transmitted variation, we now know these to be mutation and recombination), and *if* the relevant aspects of the interaction between organism and environment ("selection pressures") remain relatively stable, then natural selection will increase the adaptive fit of descendant members of the population relative to their ancestors. In addition, selection (in concert with other factors) will lead to the evolution of organisms with novel characteristics or abilities, and to new, reproductively isolated species. In this way, a blind mechanistic process creates adaptive design in nature, and provides a nonteleological and naturalistic explanation for such design.

Other Evolutionary Forces.   Natural selection is only one of the elements involved in evolution. Mutation, recombination, and diploid reproduction all introduce random genotypic variation into populations. Genetic drift (sampling error due to small effective population size) and founder effects (when a small emigrant group is not representative of its original population) operate primarily to reduce genetic differences within groups, but increase it between them. There are also macroevolutionary processes (such as differential survival of species or higher taxa) that shape the diversity of living things. Most of these are random with respect to adaptive design (e.g., mass extinctions due to catastrophic events) but some may be directional (Gould 1982; Stanley 1975, 1979; Eldredge 1985; cf. Charlesworth et al. 1982).

While all of these factors play important roles in evolutionary theory, only natural selection has broad relevance to the questions addressed in this volume, which mainly concern variation and adaptive design in human behavior.

Constraints on Selection.   Evolutionary ecologists make selection the centerpiece of their analytical efforts, but do so aware of various limitations on its effectiveness. Their models make implicit assumptions about the availability of well-behaved genetic variation, consistency of selection pressures, and predominance of selection over other evolutionary factors (2.4.1). They assume that various types of interactions (among physically or functionally linked portions of the genome; among various competing adaptive demands) do not impede selection for the trait(s) under analysis. They give secondary attention to questions of psychological and physiological mechanism that fall under the rubric of proximate analysis (1.2.1).

These assumptions sometimes will be inaccurate. Less often will they be so wrong as to debilitate the analysis. There are two reasons for this. First, among all the traits available for study, evolutionary ecologists tend to focus on those most likely to meet the conditions just stated—that is, traits with large effects on fitness, which do not rely on specific forms of genetic inheritance. Second, partially as a result of the simplification gained by ignoring some factors, the results of evolutionary ecology models usually can be reliably tested. The risks that arise from simplifying assumptions are more than offset by the likelihood of discovering and correcting the mistake.

2.2.2. Levels of Selection

The Group Selection Controversy. In 1962 the Scottish ethologist Wynne-Edwards provoked a major evolutionary debate with this simple proposition: Many behavioral features of social animals are signal mechanisms by which individuals become aware of population crowding and subsequently act (individually and voluntarily) to reduce their own reproduction. They do this, said Wynne-Edwards, because otherwise depletion of resources and starvation or even group extinction would follow; hence natural selection has favored reproductive self-restraint and the social signals whereby it is maintained.

A flurry of rebuttals (Maynard Smith 1964; Williams 1966a; Wiens 1966; Lewontin 1970) followed on this work. The criticism focused attention on the units upon which natural selection acts. If we arrange the possibilities in a hierarchy of size and inclusiveness—genes, genotypes, isolated aspects of phenotype, whole phenotypes (individuals), kin (groups of related individuals), groups of randomly related individuals, breeding populations, communities, ecosystems, the biosphere—then we can say that the Wynne-Edwards proposal stimulated an extensive and productive debate on the *level of selection*. Wynne-Edwards was claiming that selection acted effectively at the level of groups, to maximize group rather than individual benefit. The critics claimed that selection is ineffective at this level, and any group benefits are simply by-products of individual ones. Newly sensitized by the level of selection debate, evolutionary biologists quickly realized that some of their favorite evolutionary explanations unwittingly relied on group selection and would need to be rethought.

As will become clear shortly, the meaning of the term *group selection* is itself controversial. For present purposes, the following definitions are sufficient. *Individual selection* is the form of natural selection that Darwin described; it "selects" between individuals who differ in heritable characteristics, and favors the characteristics that cause individuals to leave the largest relative number of surviving offspring. *Group selection* acts on heritable variation between groups of individuals; it favors characteristics that result in increased survival of groups (vs. extinction) and in increased reproduction of groups (through immigrants who disperse to found new groups or join other existing ones). "Groups" is general enough to include the various units lying between individuals and the biosphere in the list above, but has usually referred to demes (isolated breeding populations) or subsets of demes. Finally, *kin selection* acts via the effects of characteristics expressed in one individual on the reproductive success of itself and its close relatives; it favors characteristics that have highest "inclusive fitness" (see below).

The problem with Wynne-Edwards's proposition is evident if we consider the effect of natural selection on the frequency of alternative traits (and underlying genetic variants), not on the condition of individuals or groups per se. Imagine that a growing population faces a shortage of some essential common resource. Further population growth would lead to resource depletion, increased mortality, and possibly even extinction of the population. This could be averted if individuals voluntarily and unilaterally limited the number of offspring that they bear and successfully raise to maturity. We might well expect such restraint, and explain it in terms of the benefits to group survival and well-being. But is it feasible that natural selection would produce such an outcome?

In most circumstances, the answer is no. The rationale for restraint is that otherwise the population will grow and cause resource depletion; but this means that it is possible (in the short run, at least) to raise additional offspring. Under these conditions, a strategy of reproductive restraint will always be of lower relative fitness within the group than one that causes the production of slightly greater numbers of offspring that survive to reproduction. The more profligate members gain the immediate fitness advantages of additional offspring. Whenever the undesirable costs of overpopulation are shared equally by all, they gain a long-term reproductive advantage as well: Even if resource depletion brings population stasis or decline, their descendants will be represented in relatively greater numbers. Thus, even though in the long run all individuals would be healthier and the population would be larger if resources were not overexploited, selection within groups will relentlessly favor the more prolific. This is the evolutionary equivalent of the tragedy of the commons (Hardin 1968).

We might save the proposition if the differential extinction of groups was frequent enough, and the opportunities for emigration from crowded groups to less crowded ones scant enough. In other words, group selection for population control (with selection favoring groups with high frequencies of restrained reproducers) would have to be stronger than individual selection for increased reproduction. But considerable analysis has cast doubt on this possibility, at least in the form envisioned by Wynne-Edwards. Individuals generally both reproduce and die at higher rates than the groups of which they are members. Furthermore, genetic variation is generally greater within groups (among its members) than between them (within a single species).

Since selection can only operate on heritable variation associated with differential fertility and mortality, the two facts just stated tell us that while group selection of the Wynne-Edwards sort might occur, it will generally be a weak evolutionary force when measured against the pervasiveness and effectiveness of selection on individuals.

Since the critical reaction to Wynne-Edwards, a second family of group selection models has been produced. These "structured-deme" models make different assumptions and yield different results. First, the structured-deme models include an intermediate level of organization between individuals and the deme or breeding population: a temporary association of interacting individuals, often termed a "trait group" (Wilson 1977, 1980). Members of trait groups interact, and traits that are "altruistic" (costly to individual fitness but beneficial to the fitness of other group members) are expressed at this point. Subsequently, members disperse, and contribute to the next generation in the population at large. Second, rather than differential *extinction* of groups as in the Wynne-Edwards formulation, in the newer models group selection is fueled by differential *propagation* of group-advantageous traits in the dispersal (or population-mixing) phase. This is actually the original approach to group selection developed by Sewall Wright (1945) in his pioneering model; it has only recently been given detailed theoretical treatment (Harpending and Rogers 1987; Rogers 1990b).

The structured-deme or trait group approach to group selection avoids many shortcomings of Wynne-Edwards's version; and it overlaps considerably with the kin selection inclusive-fitness approach pioneered by Hamilton (1964; see below). Thus, there has been renewed debate in the last decade concerning the significance of group selection as an evolutionary force. The analytical nuances of this debate are extensive and important, but cannot be detailed here (see Maynard Smith 1976, 1987; Wade 1978, 1985; Uyenoyama and Feldman 1980; Michod 1982; Wilson 1983; Grafen 1984; Brandon and Burian 1984; Sober 1984; and Nunney 1985). Nevertheless, it seems fair to make some summary statements. Evolutionary biologists are quite skeptical of unsupported claims that, because a given characteristic is or would be beneficial to the survival or well-being of one or more supraindividual units, it has or will be favored by natural selection. On the other hand, the extent to which the newer, more sophisticated models of group selection may account for various biological phenomena is more open to debate and empirical assessment. In addition, some researchers have argued that human societies show much higher levels of cooperation between unrelated individuals than is found in other species or can be derived from individual and kin selection. Prominent explanations for this include a history of particularly potent intergroup competition (Alexander 1974; Hamilton 1975) and particular features of culturally inherited variation (Boyd and Richerson 1982, 1985; see 3.4.4). Resolution of the role of group selection thus awaits further work, although many evolutionary biologists remain convinced it plays a role only in special and relatively rare circumstances.

Kin Selection. With individual selection a trait spreads solely through its fitness-enhancing effects on the actor, measured in terms of direct descendants. This is selection as envisioned by Darwin. By contrast, kin selection (Maynard Smith 1964) expands the assessment of fitness to include the fitness-enhancing effects of an organism on biologically related individuals with which it interacts. Kin selection is often measured in terms of inclusive fitness ("inclusive" of related individuals), referring to the net effect of a particular trait or pattern of behavior on Ego's own fitness, plus its net effect on the fitness of related individuals, each devalued by their degree of relationship to Ego (Hamilton 1964).

Kin selection has been frequently invoked as a neo-Darwinian explanation of the evolution of altruistic behavior between closely related individuals (e.g., the members of a colony of social insects, which is generally a large family group). The altruist actor by definition suffers some loss of individual fitness, but the genotype for altruism can still increase in the population if the behavior results in sufficient fitness benefits to nondescendant kin. Depending on their genealogical closeness to the actor, kin have specific probabilities of sharing the same genotype by common descent. The aggregate fitness consequences of the altruist's phenotype on the survival and reproduction of kin carrying these shared genes may more than offset the loss in individual fitness incurred by the altruist. Specifically, Hamilton's rule says that altruism will be favored by selection when $C < rB$, where C is the fitness cost paid by the altruist, B is the benefit received by the recipient, and r is the coefficient of relationship by immediate descent (e.g., 0.5 for full sibs or parent to offspring, 0.25 for grandchildren, nephews, and nieces).

Although theory in evolutionary ecology has made relatively little use of the logic of kin selection or inclusive fitness, it is worth stressing two points. First, there is a widespread belief that kin selection theory predicts that altruism will characterize most interactions between kin, and in proportion to the genealogical closeness (the coefficient r); but this notion is mistaken (Dawkins 1979; Altmann 1979; Harpending 1981). For example, it is easy to see that Hamilton's rule allows the evolution of competition between kin, even infanticide or fratricide; simply make C the fitness gain to Ego, B the loss suffered by Ego's kinsman of relatedness r, and ask whether the gain to Ego is sufficiently great to offset the fitness loss to the kinsman, devalued by r. There is no reason the answer must be no (and history is replete with cases of siblings fighting to the death over inheritance of the throne or family estate).

Second, much discussion of kin selection, by both proponents and critics (e.g., Sahlins 1976), is phrased as if r were the only factor that really mattered. To the contrary, treatment of kin of a given degree of relatedness (e.g., offspring) varies greatly between and within animal species and human societies, and Hamilton's rule predicts that these differences must be due primarily to variation in costs and benefits (*C* and *B*). In turn, variation in *C* and *B* is determined by social, ecological, and life history circumstances. Hence any deep understanding of variation in kin interactions will require the insights of social and ecological theory; focusing on relatedness alone yields an extremely truncated version of Hamilton's model (Smith 1979b).

The Phenotypic Gambit. Beginning in the 1920s with the work of Fisher, Haldane, and Wright, the mathematical theory of population genetics has given precision to that part of natural selection theory dealing with inheritance and genetic variation in populations. The analysis of organism–environment interactions that is the focus of evolutionary ecology arose later, and has required somewhat different conceptual tools.

The phenotypic traits of greatest ecological interest (including behavioral traits) are not controlled by single genes. Their expression is complex and multicausal, and dependent on environment in ways not easily captured in exact genetic models. Because of this, evolutionary ecologists typically treat the observable phenotypes of organisms (including behavior) as adaptations, avoiding detailed assumptions about heritability. In effect, they postulate that some underlying "strategies" or "decision rules" have been shaped by selection so as to produce adaptive phenotypes. According to this approach, it is neither necessary nor feasible to demonstrate the exact heritable basis of every trait of interest. Instead, one should proceed as if the precise nature or details of the link between heritability and phenotype were unimportant.

Grafen (1984) calls this research strategy the "phenotypic gambit" (see also Maynard Smith 1978). The phenotypic gambit analyzes a trait

> as if the very simplest genetic system controlled it: as if there were a haploid locus at which each distinct strategy was represented by a distinct allele, as if the payoff rule gave the number of offspring for each allele, and as if enough mutation occurred to allow each strategy the chance to invade. (Grafen 1984:63–64)

Since few if any of the traits studied by evolutionary ecologists are controlled by single loci in a haploid system, the phenotypic gambit is really based on the premise that selection will favor traits with high fitness (or evolutionary stability; see 2.2.3) irrespective of the particulars of inheritance. In fact, behavioral ecologists usually assume extreme phenotypic plasticity, a wide array of feasible strategies, and the ability of the actor to assess payoffs and choose or learn the best alternative under any given set of circumstances.

Further, since the fitness consequences of different strategies often are difficult to assess, evolutionary ecologists frequently employ more tractable measures such as energy capture per unit time, or fertility rates (see 2.4.3). The key assumption here is that these "proximate currencies" are highly correlated with fitness—that they are good indices or proxy variables for fitness, to use the language of the social sciences.

In summary, there are two ways in which evolutionary ecology diverges from evolutionary genetics: (1) the phenotype, not the genotype, is taken as the unit of study; (2) some correlated but more readily measurable index of evolutionary success is substituted for fitness. Lacking the mechanistic dynamic inherent in population genetic models of evolution, evolutionary ecology has substituted alternatives suited to its focus on phenotypic strategies and proximate currencies. The most popular approaches have been evolutionary game theory (2.2.3) and simple optimality models (2.4).

2.2.3. Evolutionary Game Theory

Natural selection results from the interaction between a population of organisms and the environment. As long as "environment" is external to the evolving population, selection generally favors those alternatives that confer the highest average fitness on their bearers. But when the relevant aspect of the environment consists of conspecifics (as in the case of social interactions), selection operates in a more complex, reflexive manner: The fittest strategy must do well in competition with (copies of) itself, not just in competition with other strategies. The first situation allows for simple optimization analysis (2.4); the latter requires the strategic analysis of evolutionary game theory.

An analytical framework for strategic contexts was first formalized by mathematical economists under the rubric of "the theory of games" (von Neumann and Morgenstern 1944; Luce and Raiffa 1957) and subsequently given a neo-Darwinian application in the theory of "evolutionarily stable strategies" or ESS (e.g., Maynard Smith 1974a, 1982a; Parker 1984; Parker and Hammerstein 1985). The key insight in ESS theory is this: When the relative payoff of alternative strategies or phenotypic traits depends on what other individuals in the population are doing, the outcome favored by natural selection depends on which alternatives are *unbeatable* rather than on which has the highest average payoff. A strategy that has high payoff when it is rare (and rarely encountered) in the population may have low payoff when common, or vice versa. In strategic contexts the payoff from each strategy must be calculated in light of all the possible strategies that can be played against it, including itself. A standard example of an ESS is the Hawk–Dove game (Box 2.1).

ESS Models and Behavioral Ecology.   ESS theory involves complexities beyond the scope of this chapter, but it has two implications that need to be

Box 2.1. *The Hawk–Dove Game.* Imagine a situation in which there are frequent pairwise contest over possession of some resource. Suppose there are just two tactics (possible ways of behaving) in such a contest, Hawk and Dove. The Hawk tactic is to fight aggressively over the contested resource; the Dove tactic involves peaceful bluffing, and yielding as soon as real aggression seems likely. Hence, Hawk always beats Dove. The problem is to determine the ESS, i.e., the ratio of Hawk:Dove that will be unbeatable in terms of average fitness payoffs per player.

Suppose the resource itself is worth 100 fitness points, and that fighting and losing exacts a larger cost, say -300 points, while simply giving up without a fight (the tactic Doves follow when encountering Hawks) yields 0 points (no change in fitness). Suppose further (for simplicity) that when Hawk plays against Hawk, or Dove against Dove, each player has an equal probability (.5) of winning or losing.

Given these assumptions, the average payoffs to each tactic for the three possible types of contests are as follows:

1. Hawk vs. Hawk $= (100/2) + (-300/2) = -100$
2. Hawk vs. Dove: Hawk $= 100$, Dove $= 0$
3. Dove vs. Dove $= (100/2) = 50$

It is conventional in both classical and evolutionary game theory to present such a payoff structure in matrix form, with the tactics of one player listed at the top of columns, and the tactics of the other listed by row on the left. For simplicity, payoffs in the cells are those gained by the "row" player only.

For the Hawk-Dove game as described, the matrix is:

	Hawk	Dove
Hawk	-100	100
Dove	0	50

The evolutionary equilibrium is reached when the average payoff to Hawk equals the average to Dove, given the frequency of each strategy in the population. In the present hypothetical case, this equilibrium ratio works out to 1:2. That is, the ESS is to play Hawk one third of the time, and to play Dove in the remainder of encounters; alternatively, one could be Hawk or Dove for life, and the 1:2 ratio would express the ratio of each type of individual in the population. In ESS terminology, the first case is termed a "mixed strategy" (e.g., play Hawk with probability .33, play Dove with probability .67); the second is a balanced polymorphism (analogous to that maintained by heterozygote superiority with sickle-cell vs. normal hemoglobin in a malarial environment).

To see why this ratio is the ESS, consider a population consisting initially of all Dove. A single Hawk mutant will win every contest, because Hawk always beats Dove. Since the prize for winning is defined in fitness gains, Hawks will increase in the population (assuming simple inheritance). But as the Hawk tactic proliferates, it begins playing against itself with appreciable frequency; every time it does, the average payoff to Hawk is -100, much worse than Dove gets playing against itself (50) *or* against Hawk (0). At a certain point (which defines the ESS), the frequency of the Hawk tactic will be such that its average payoff will be no higher than the average payoff to Dove. The same kind of argument applies to a population of all Hawk that is invaded by a mutant playing Dove.

To check that the 1:2 ratio is the ESS, we can compute the average payoffs to each tactic given the expected encounter frequencies. At 1 Hawk:2 Doves, each player plays against a Hawk in ⅓ contests, and against Dove in the remaining ⅔. The computations are:

Tactic	Average payoff from		Overall average
	Plays against Hawks	Plays against Doves	
Hawk	$.33(-100) = -33$	$.67(100) = 67$	33
Dove	$.33(0) = 0$	$.67(50) = 33$	33

Using this method, the reader can easily check that any deviation from the 1:2 ratio will result in a player obtaining a lower average payoff. In fact, the general solution to the Hawk–Dove ESS is that the equilibrium Hawk frequency equals V/C, where V is the value (fitness gain) of winning the contest and C the cost of losing a fight (in the present example, $V/C = 100/300 = 0.33$). (If $V \geq C$, the equilibrium frequency of Hawk reaches 1.0, and pure Hawk is the only ESS.)

Sources: The Hawk–Dove game was first described in the seminal paper on ESS theory by Maynard Smith and Price (1973). A detailed review of this and many other evolutionary games is found in Maynard Smith (1982a). Dawkins (1976:Chapter 5) provides a clear and non-technical discussion, from which we have borrowed heavily for this exposition. In classical game theory, a formally identical payoff structure is found in the game of Chicken (Rapoport et al. 1976). Further discussion of Hawk–Dove, and applications to human social behavior, can be found in sections 9.5.3 and 10.3.2.

emphasized. First, to apply ESS theory one asks what strategy or set of strategies will be unbeatable over evolutionary time. A strategy is an ESS if when common in the population it cannot be replaced (via natural selection) by specified alternative strategies. Second, ESS theory shows that conflicts of interest between actors result in evolutionarily stable outcomes that often have lower payoffs than could be achieved if cooperation could be somehow ensured. An ESS is the optimal strategy to follow, but only in the special sense that any actor who deviates from it will be worse off (have lower fitness), even though if *all* deviated in concert they might all be better off. Thus, in the Hawk–Dove game, a "conspiracy of doves" would yield a higher per capita fitness, and indeed higher fitness for every member of the population (Dawkins 1976:77). For the hypothetical payoffs listed in Box 2.1, all-Dove would yield 50 fitness points per individual per interaction, versus the 33 obtained with the ESS; but an all-Dove population can be invaded by Hawks, who will gain higher fitness than Doves when rare, and thus be favored by selection. As this example illustrates, there is no guarantee at all that the ESS will correspond to the strategy that maximizes average fitness in the population.

The implications of this disjunction between the evolutionary equilibrium and the possible individual fitness maximum are quite significant. ESS theory shows that selection may move individual behaviors in directions that produce collective consequences that are suboptimal for everyone. It suggests that the evolution of social phenomena is riddled with pervasive or even insoluble contradictions between the interests of each individual and their collective interests as realized through social interaction. The paradigm illustration of this point is the Prisoner's Dilemma game (Box 2.2).

Although the prisoner's dilemma structure is one that seems to characterize many collective-action problems, it is certainly not the only possible payoff structure (see 9.5.3 and 10.2.2). Some social interactions are characterized by a more mutualistic structure. But the general argument applies: Social interaction always holds at least some likelihood of strategic conflicts of interest. These require that we analyze the consequences of natural selection and rational choice according to the competitive optimum predicted from game theory.

In summary, ESS theory combines the methods of economic game theory with the explanatory logic of natural selection theory. In the place of the economist's assumptions of rationality and self-interest, the evolutionary ecologist substitutes evolutionary stability and fitness (Maynard Smith 1982a :2). While not as rigorous as explicit genetic or cultural-transmission models, it provides a convenient and robust approximation when the details of inheritance are unknown and the "phenotypic gambit" (2.2.2) is adopted. ESS models (or their equivalent) are warranted whenever conflicts of interest or frequency dependence effects apply to the characteristics being investigated. In such cases, the optimum is a competitive (evolutionarily stable) rather than simple (average fitness-maximizing) one.

Box 2.2. *The Prisoner's Dilemma*. In the two-person version of this game, the payoffs have the following pattern:

1.   If both cooperate, each player gets *c*.
2.   If both defect (fail to cooperate), each gets *b*.
3.   If one defects and the other cooperates, the Defector gets *d* and the Cooperator (in this case, altruist) gets *a*.
4.   The payoff values are ordered $a < b < c < d$.

Using the payoff matrix conventions introduced in Box 2.1, we can list Ego's actions by row (on the left), Alter's by column (on top), with the payoffs to Ego given in the cells of the matrix:

		Alter's actions:	
		Cooperate	Defect
Ego's	Cooperate	c	a
actions:	Defect	d	b

Since the payoffs will be the same regardless of which player is desig-
nated Ego, this is termed a symmetrical game.

Clearly, as long as $2c > (a + d)$, the strategy with the highest average
payoff (for Ego and Alter combined) would be to cooperate. But the best
strategy in terms of self-interest is to defect, regardless of whether the
other actor cooperates. In game-theoretical terminology, we say that in
the prisoner's dilemma (PD) game, defection is the "dominant strategy."

As with the Hawk–Dove game (Box 2.1), the ESS can be grasped
more easily if we consider whether one strategy (cooperate or defect)
can invade a population consisting of the other. The defect strategy can
invade a population of Cooperators, because the payoff to defect is
greater than that to cooperate both for Defector–Cooperator interactions
($d > a$) and for interactions between Cooperators ($d > c$). But the
cooperate strategy cannot invade an all-defect population, because its
payoff is lower both against defect ($a < d$) and as compared to the
common defect–defect interaction ($a < b$). This is true even though a
population of pure Cooperators is characterized by a higher average
payoff than a population of all Defectors ($c > b$), and indeed mean
fitness declines with each increase in the number of Defectors.

In sum, if there is no way to enforce cooperation, selection (or
rational self-interest) will drive the noncooperative strategy to fixation,
hardly the best result from anyone's (or everyone's) standpoint. There
are circumstances in which a less dismal result could prevail, both in the
context of rational-choice models (Taylor 1987) and via natural selection (Axelrod and Hamilton 1981); and of course cooperation may have
a non-PD structure. Both points are discussed elsewhere in this volume,
particularly in Chapters 9 and 10.

Sources: The PD has a long history in classical game theory (Rapoport
1974; Sugden 1986; Taylor 1987). The earliest application of PD logic
to an evolutionary context is probably that of Trivers (1971), although he
did not use explicit game theory techniques. Axelrod (1984; Axelrod
and Hamilton 1981; Axelrod and Dion 1989) and Hirshleifer (1982;
Hirshleifer and Martinez Coll 1988) make extensive use of PD structures
for analyzing the evolution of cooperation. Maynard Smith
(1982a:Chapter 13) reviews the theory, and Boyd (1988, n.d.) discusses
the way in which the PD can be generalized to cover a variety of
reciprocal interactions.

2.3. THEORY AND METHOD IN THE SOCIAL SCIENCES

Since theory and method in the social sciences are highly diverse, we
must be selective in discussing their relationship to evolutionary ecology.

Decision theory (particularly rational-choice models) has the clearest relevance to and compatibility with evolutionary ecology; hence it is what we focus on here. We concern ourselves with two main issues: the significance of methodological individualism (2.3.1), and the relationship of intentional explanation (of which rational choice accounts are a subset) to explanation in general and selectionist explanation in particular (2.3.2). Richerson and Boyd (3.5.2) discuss some additional linkages between evolutionary ecology and the social sciences, revolving around the effects of cultural transmission.

2.3.1. Methodological Individualism and Social Analysis

Definition.   Methodological individualism (MI) holds that the properties of groups (social institutions, populations, societies, economies, etc.) are a result of the actions of its individual members. By "properties of groups" we mean rules, practices, and the like. By "actions" we mean both intentional and unintentional behavior (see 2.3.2). MI stands in opposition to various forms of methodological collectivism, which hold that group properties cannot be reduced to those of its members and their interactions.

The main corollary of MI (and what most people have in mind when they invoke it) is that explanation of the properties of groups should in principle be derived "from the bottom up," in terms of the actions and intentions of individuals. Stated so simply, MI may strike many readers as unproblematic, or even uninteresting. Certainly most of us agree that societies or cultures or bureaucracies do not literally have minds that choose or hands that move. Nevertheless, conventional analyses often proceed as if they did. Hence, if followed consistently MI has consequences that challenge many explanatory practices in the social sciences—including ecological anthropology (Vayda 1986)—in a way that is similar to the subversive effect that individual-level selectionism and ESS theory have had on functionalist explanation in evolutionary biology (see 2.2.2).

The Role of MI in Social Analysis.   The primary goal of MI is to provide "microfoundations" or "actor-based accounts" for social phenomena by analyzing the extent to which they are the aggregate outcomes of individual beliefs, preferences, and actions (Homans 1967; Elster 1982; Roemer 1982a). In this sense, MI takes the "black box" of social institutions and processes apart, in order to discover the individual-level mechanisms that provide its workings.

In practice, MI is usually linked to a number of corollary assumptions. One of these is that individual actions result primarily from rational-choice processes. Another is that individuals are basically selfish—guided in their choices by self-interest. Although we will have more to say about these matters below (see 2.3.2), it is worth noting here that these assumptions are not actually entailed by MI: It is logically defensible to adhere to individualism in a methodological sense without adopting the rational-choice and self-interest corollaries, or any kind of substantive (ethical, political, etc.) individualism (Elster 1982:453). It does not violate MI as such to show that individuals make nonrational decisions, take the welfare of others into consideration, adopt beliefs and preferences from their cultural milieu, or let beliefs about supraindividual entities shape their actions. MI simply holds that in each case these processes originate in and are maintained by the actions of individuals.

In the social sciences MI is most firmly established in neoclassical economics, which postulates individual decision-makers as the fundamental units of action and causality, and views social phenomena like markets and prices as the aggregate outcome of individual choice. Even here, however, MI has proven impractical or inappropriate for some questions, hence the development of macroeconomics and the use of supraindividual actors such as firms, households, and interest groups as analytical shortcuts in economic analysis. Economics, of course, also adheres rather closely to the rational-choice and self-interest assumptions. But many schools of psychological analysis are equally based in MI, yet abjure rational choice as a corollary. Nor does MI necessarily entail orthodox political or economic views: There is a very active branch of Marxist political and economic analysis that is explicitly based in MI and rational-choice/game theory (Elster 1982, 1985; Roemer 1982a, 1982b, 1986).

Some schools of social science research implicitly or explicitly reject MI in favor of methodological collectivism. They postulate collective entities or goals—such as classes, development of the productive forces, cultural systems of meaning, social or ecological equilibrium, or population pressure— as the prime movers of history and social structure. In fact, underlying much of the theoretical discord in the social sciences is a contest among differing interpretations of the relative power and appropriate realm of application of individualist and collectivist approaches. Whatever their virtues may be, collectivist approaches are much less compatible with evolutionary ecology than those that rely on MI, for reasons we discuss next.

MI and Evolutionary Ecology. The levels-of-selection controversy (2.2.2) resulted in a general consensus among evolutionary biologists that adaptations will rarely be found that increase group persistence or well-being at the expense of its individual members. For instance, the notion that populations evolve so as to regulate their size or maximize ecosystem stability or efficiency seems implausible once one attempts to specify the individual-level mechanisms that would produce such outcomes and to explain why natural selection would favor them. Setting aside technical details, it is fair to say that something rather close to MI is the working assumption of evolutionary ecology analyses of behavior. Indeed, it has been said that the ultimate goal of evolutionary ecology is to explain the structure and functioning of populations and ecosystems in terms of the properties and evolutionary history of their individual members (e.g., Orians 1973; Pulliam 1976).

The close parallels that often exist between evolutionary ecology and methodological-individualist social science are nicely illustrated by the issue of population regulation. The notion that "population pressure" (imbalance between resources and population size) is something human groups seek to avoid and that many social practices are designed to maintain population–resource balance by either restricting population growth or increasing resource productivity, has been very popular in the history of ecological anthropology and related fields (review in Bates and Lees 1979). Most of these theories assign collectivist notions like "societal homeostasis" the role of agency in sociocultural evolution, and pay little attention to the beliefs and actions of individuals. The MI critique of such views is quite similar to the selectionist one we have sketched above (2.2.2). Both focus on the "free-rider" problem of reproductive restraint, and both caution that group benefits may be only incidental outcomes of individual self-interest. They differ, of course, in the causal mechanisms invoked: Selectionist explanations emphasize population structure and group versus individual mortality and fertility rates, while MI social science points to rational self-interest (i.e., individual incentives to have offspring and disincentives to sacrifice for the collective good).

This example illustrates how, even though starting from rather different premises, both MI and evolutionary ecology make one skeptical of arguments purporting to explain individual characteristics in terms of their group-level benefits, unless it can be shown that special circumstances (centralized coercion, powerful group selection, or highly biased cultural transmission [see 3.4.4 and 3.5.2]) prevail. Similar arguments can be made with respect to conservation of game (Hames 1987b; see 7.5.1), ritual regulation of warfare (Peoples 1982; Vayda 1986; see 10.4.1), or many other group benefit arguments common in the social sciences (a number of which are discussed in other chapters of this volume). The general point, for either MI social scientist or evolutionary ecologist, is that explanation of social phenomena, including group-level benefits, should pay attention to individual-level mechanisms.

2.3.2 Intentional Behavior and Rational Choice

Despite the convergence of evolutionary and rational-choice accounts of collective action, there remain some salient differences. One of the most obvious is that the primary causal force in evolutionary theory is natural selection, while in rational-choice theory it is individual decision-making. One possible way to bridge this gap is to nest one approach within the other. If the mechanisms of individual decision-making are themselves products of evolution, they should be explainable in selectionist terms: Rationality is an evolved adaptation. But the tidiness of this resolution is somewhat deceptive, for it glosses over a number of complex issues. To understand these, we need to place both evolutionary and rational-choice accounts within a more general philosophical framework.

Modes of Explanation.   Following Elster (1983), we distinguish three modes of scientific explanation: causal, functional, and intentional. Causal explanation is the scientific "ideal," and the only accepted mode in the modern physical sciences. While the subtleties of this mode are too involved to discuss here, the basic logic is simple enough: Causal explanations specify the physical mechanisms involved when one event or process determinatively leads to another. Causal explanation is typically reductionist, in the sense that it proceeds by explaining the properties of objects or processes in terms of the interaction of component objects or processes—the properties of a gas by its pressure, temperature, and chemical composition, and the properties of an organism by those of the DNA molecules that it inherited and the environment within which it develops.

Functional explanation is the most controversial of the three modes under consideration. It can be outlined succinctly as follows (simplified from Elster 1983:57):

1.   There exists one or more actors (A) who possess some characteristic (C).
2.   C produces some beneficial consequence (B)—beneficial for A.
3.   B is unintended, and perhaps unrecognized, by A.
4.   B maintains C by a causal feedback loop passing through A.

To summarize, one might say that functionalism explains characteristics by virtue of their *unintended beneficial consequences.* Following Froemming (1986), we can represent the argument graphically thus:

Functional explanation is not employed in the modern physical sciences, where "beneficial consequence" has no acceptable meaning, but it plays distinctive roles in (evolutionary) biology and in the social sciences. In biology, B properly refers to fitness, with other benefits being relevant only to the extent that they are good correlates of fitness. The causal feedback loop is simply natural selection: C increases in frequency if it yields a higher B than some alternative C possessed by other A in the same population. In contrast to causal explanation then, biological functionalism accounts for the properties (C) of organisms (A) by their fitness benefits (B). It explains the characteristics of organisms in terms of selective advantage: Phenotypes and their underlying DNA sequences are the way they are because they have evolutionarily outcompeted the alternatives that have been tried on the field of organic evolution. (The use of function here is distinct from its meaning in proximate analysis [1.2.1]. In the one case we are explaining the ultimate evolutionary origins of a phenotypic design, in the other its proximate operation.)

While functional explanation is distinct from causal explanation, it is not independent from it. Specifically, if a functional explanation in biology states that B *maintains* C, this makes sense only if C *causes* B (i.e., the characteristic yields a fitness benefit), and if in turn the causal mechanisms of heredity ensure that C recurs in at least some descendants of A. More generally, we can say that any functional explanation depends for its validation on an underlying causal explanation, and thus is less fundamental than the latter:

> We can use functional explanation in biology because we have a causal theory—the theory of evolution by natural selection—that licenses us to explain organic phenomena through consequences that are beneficial in terms of reproductive capacity. Even if in a given case we are unable to tell the full causal story, we may be able to advance an explanation in terms of these beneficial consequences. (Elster 1983:21)

This is precisely the tactic of evolutionary ecology.

In the social sciences, functionalism takes various forms, but the structure sketched above is common to them all. In comparison to biological functionalism, however, in social science there is much greater ambiguity concerning the kinds of beneficial consequences involved, the identification of the beneficiaries, and most importantly the causal feedback loop of proposition (4). Elster (1983:56ff.) suggests that sociofunctionalism occurs in at least two varieties: Strong forms (a la Malinowski) propose that *all* social phenomena have beneficial consequences that explain them; weak forms (a la Merton) propose that *whenever* social phenomena produce unintended benefits, they can be explained by these benefits. Topically, sociofunctionalism covers a wide range. In addition to Malinowski and Merton, prominent examples include British structural functionalism (e.g., Radcliffe-Brown 1952), cybernetic human ecology (e.g., Rappaport 1968), cultural materialism (e.g., Harris 1979b), and historical materialism (e.g., Cohen 1978; cf. Elster 1982).

The attraction of functional explanation in the social sciences is that it relieves one of the admittedly implausible assertion that all social institutions or practices were created or persist because of consciously perceived beneficial consequences—that (for example) Yanomamo warfare exists because its practitioners recognized its efficacy in regulating population. But because functional explanation relies on unrecognized and unintended relationships, to be convincing it must provide a specified causal feedback mechanism:

> A functional explanation can succeed only if there are reasons for believing in a feedback loop from the consequence to the phenomenon to be explained. In the case of functional explanation in biology . . . we have general knowledge—the theory of evolution by natural selection—that ensures the existence of some feedback mechanism, even though in a given case we may be unable to exhibit it. But there is no social-science analogue to the theory of evolution, and therefore social scientists are constrained to show, in each particular case, how the feedback operates. (Elster 1983:61)

Unfortunately, that is rarely done. Existing functional explanations in social science almost invariably fail to postulate any explicit feedback mechanisms, let alone to demonstrate their existence or causal efficacy. The absence of a causal foundation for sociofunctionalism has lead to a proliferation of types of beneficial effects, units proposed as beneficiaries (ranging from individuals to ecosystems), and time scales over which the benefits are assessed. This ambiguity gives sociofunctionalism a tremendous degree of license in constructing explanations that are broadly plausible but lack rigorous theoretical foundation or empirical evaluation.

The third mode of explanation is *intentional*. It is virtually limited to the social sciences—we no longer argue that water seeks its own level or light finds the shortest path in any but a metaphorical manner. Some analyses of animal behavior make reference to intentionality (e.g., Griffin 1981, 1982), but ever since Darwin we do not explain most biological characteristics of living things via intentionality: Natural selection, unlike a deity (or an animal breeder), has no intentions.

Intentional explanation accounts for actions in terms of the beliefs and preferences of the actor; both are necessary constituents of intentional explanation (Elster 1983:Chapter 3). We might know that someone prefers intellectual stimulation to high salary, but in order for that to explain why she or he chose a career in anthropology over one in law we must invoke her or his beliefs about a number of things: the intellectual content of each profession, the likelihood of succeeding in either, and so on.

But if beliefs and preferences provide the foundations of intentional explanation, they also define its limits. In order to explain *them*, we must eventually invoke some other explanatory mode—causal (as in the neurophysiology or ontogeny of learning) or functional (as in the biological evolution of our cognitive machinery or the cultural evolution of our values). While it is possible to derive some beliefs and preferences from "higher-order" beliefs and preferences, this procedure (like the joke about what the turtle holding up the world is standing on, "It's turtles all the way down!") cannot go on indefinitely. As with functional explanation, then, intentional explanation is inherently incomplete.

Rational Choice. The paradigm form of intentional explanation is rational-choice theory. As used here, the term *rational* refers not to ends, but only to the relation between ends and means. Rational actors are those who pursue their ends (whatever they might be) as effectively as possible, and who do not commit logical errors in ordering their preferences. To explain the second point briefly, a rational actor has what is called "transitive preference rankings": if she or he prefers A to B, and B to C, then she or he will prefer A to C.

This restricted meaning of *rational* is sometimes referred to as "thin rationality," to emphasize that it does not make any substantive predictions about what it is actors actually value or prefer. In this view, it is not the purview of economics (for example) to explain why some people prefer to maximize pecuniary benefits and others prestige or patriotism or piousness. In principle, then, rational-choice theorists are no more committed to "materialistic" measures of value such as wealth or hedonistic satisfaction than they are to preference rankings that put spiritual enlightenment or service to humanity above all else. But in developing any particular model or hypothesis, one must move beyond thin rationality and posit something substantive about preferences. Preference rankings can be derived inductively (by observing what actors choose, or asking them what they would choose, under specified conditions) or deductively (from some additional assumptions about the cultural or biological determinants of preferences).

Rational choice obviously implies that actors do indeed have a choice. More specifically, rational-choice theory divides the factors determining outcomes into two categories: choices and constraints. Choices refer to the elements over which the actor can exercise intentional control; constraints are everything else (see 2.4.4). Where preferences are known or presumed, rational-choice theory is tested by observing situations where constraints change in a certain manner, then comparing changes in actual choices to those predicted from the theory (given the specified shift in constraints and the original preferences).

In order for choice—rational or otherwise—to operate, an actor must have beliefs as well as preferences; this raises what economists call the problem of information. Rational-choice theory assumes that actors possess (or can gain) "sufficient" information to make an informed choice. The simplest models assume that actors possess "complete information" (in the sense of knowing at least the probability distribution of outcomes—"the odds") if not "perfect information" (knowing the outcomes with certainty). More complicated models relax this assumption, and allow actors to gain information (at some cost) as they make choices or otherwise sample reality. This allows predictions to be made about the optimal degree of ignorance, based on the marginal costs and benefits of information. While the postulate of complete information may often be unrealistic, it is a useful simplification, in that it allows one to build relatively simply, general, and testable models. In the case of creatures that have elaborate means of obtaining, storing, and transferring information (i.e., humans) it is not such an unreasonable assumption if the relevant sector of the environment does not change too rapidly (see 2.4.4 for further discussion).

In addition to assuming that actors know what they want and how to get it, most rational-choice theorists assume that actors are utility maximizers. In essence, utility is economists' way of talking about the *relative* amount of *satisfaction* derived from *consumption* of any *good*. The four italicized terms in this definition need to be explained.

Like preferences, satisfaction is individually defined, and rational actors are assumed to be able to weigh the satisfaction derived from alternative uses of their time and other resources. Although the classical economists (Adam Smith through Ricardo) thought that utility was something that could be measured on an absolute scale ("cardinal utilities"), neoclassical economics abandoned this assumption in favor of relative ("ordinal") utility. The most behavioristic of contemporary economists simply speak of "revealed preference," that is, the relative preferences for alternative goods implied by the actor's actual choices. "Consumption" and "good" are used in a very broad sense: One "consumes" food, but also sleep, theories, and mating opportunities. All of these (and anything that yields satisfaction, including pursuit of ideals) are "goods."

Rational-choice theory has been repeatedly criticized for taking as given that which needs most to be explained: the preferences and beliefs of individuals, and the social milieu, which determines to a considerable extent the rewards to different choices. In defense of the rational-choice framework, two things bear mentioning. First, it *can* explain in a limited but important sense, by holding preferences and beliefs constant and then allowing one or two other factors to vary. For example, if we know the relationship between wealth and consumption, we can use microeconomic models to predict the effect of changes in prices or income on consumption levels. This can even be done on a historical time scale, as in the attempts of economic historians to explain long-term socioeconomic changes on the basis of changes in technology, population, and market opportunities (e.g., McCloskey 1975b; North 1981). Following the principle of methodological individualism, social institutions and milieus are analyzed as products of past (and continuing) individual actions, not of some independent force.

Second, some preferences and beliefs can be derived from other, more fundamental ones. For example, preferences for achieving or maintaining social status might lead us to alter our preferences for particular goods or activities as these become more or less fashionable. And of course it may be in the interests of those with exceptional influence or power to manipulate the beliefs and preferences adopted by the less influential or powerful—both in the domestic (familial) and extradomestic (political) domains.

But even accepting these two points, it remains true that rational-choice theory fails to explain much about variation in preferences and beliefs. It is possible that evolutionary ecology can fill at least part of this gap. Preliminary evaluation of this possibility is one important goal of this volume.

Evolutionary Ecology and Intentionality. If evolutionary ecology is to contribute to social science, it will have to come to terms with the role of intentionality. Although a measured discussion of this issue is complex, and made more difficult by the long and acrimonious history of debate on Darwinian analyses of human behavior (1.3.1), it is useful to consider four distinct viewpoints:

1. Intentionality is autonomous and supersedes organic evolution.
2. Intentionality has no explanatory role to play in science.
3. Intentionality is a set of genetically evolved proximate mechanisms.
4. Intentionality is shaped by both cultural and genetic evolution.

(In all cases, by *intentionality* we mean conscious elements of decision-making—beliefs and preferences—as these are used in intentional explanations.) Let us briefly consider each of these positions.

Position (1) is widespread in the social science literature, but takes various forms. Some see the autonomous status of human intentionality in a historical dimension (e.g., Bock 1980; Slobodkin 1978), an intellectual tradition that can be traced back to Marx. Others emphasize the social matrix in which intentions are formed and enacted, and see this social process as contradicting or eluding Darwinian reductionism (e.g., Sahlins 1976; Ingold 1986). Still others do not appear to deny Darwinism a limited explanatory role, but see the causal distance between genes and human action as a major impediment to evolutionary analysis (e.g., Reynolds 1976; Kitcher 1985).

At the other extreme is position (2), which denies explanatory validity to concepts such as intentionality, decision-making, choice, and rationality (e.g., Dunnell 1980; Rindos 1985). In this view, evolutionary change takes place independently of the vagaries of human intentions; to grant intentions a causal role is to succumb to teleological thinking. Thus, whatever force intentionality might have in a psychological sense, to proponents of (2) it cannot explain the trajectory of social evolution any more than mutation can explain the outcomes of organic evolution. Indeed, Rindos (1989) explicitly compares intentional phenomena to the random-variation-generating mechanisms organic evolution (mutation, recombination, etc.). This view has historical precedent in the superorganicism of Kroeber (1917) and the cultural-evolutionary philosophy of Leslie White (1949), both of whom ardently denied that the direction of cultural evolution could be explained by human choices.

The simplest way in which evolutionary ecology could give explanatory depth to rational choice theory would be to derive fundamental beliefs and preferences from neo-Darwinian principles. This is position (3), the program of human sociobiology (e.g., Alexander 1979; Chagnon and Irons 1979; Harpending et al. 1987). A common way of expressing this position is to refer to intentionality—or more precisely, the cognitive mechanisms underlying intentional phenomena—as proximate mechanisms (1.2.1). Like other proximate factors, these mechanisms are evolved characters; they can be analyzed in and of themselves (like a physiologist studies the digestive system, for example) or they can be analyzed as adaptations that have been shaped by natural selection to serve certain (fitness-enhancing) purposes.

This sociobiological view of human action is particularly instructive with regard to explaining preferences. While economics or psychology can derive second-order preferences from more basic ones (as noted above), there comes a point at which fundamental preferences or goals (conscious or unconscious) must be taken as given in order to anchor the entire analysis. Intentionality, like learning, is a *derived* force (Boyd and Richerson 1985; Campbell 1965; Rosenberg 1980). In principle, evolutionary biology offers a way to identify fundamental preferences that are likely to be favored by natural selection. A completely convincing account would require demonstration of the proximate cognitive mechanisms and their specific genetic bases (Kitcher 1985; Tooby and Cosmides 1989; Symons 1989). But many feel that a plausible initial case can be based on the fit between adaptive predictions and the empirical facts of human action (Alexander 1990; Irons 1990; Smith 1987c; Turke 1990).

The sociobiological view of human decision-making offers a special refinement of the concept of self-interest. As we noted above, the "thin" version of rational-choice theory does not specify the content of self-interest. It proposes simply that actors are goal-seeking, whatever their individual goals may be. In practice, social scientists invoke various kinds of self-interest (well-being, wealth, power, status, etc.). But they rarely agree on the exact list involved or the rank order of its elements, perhaps because the goals are not derived from any underlying theoretical principles. In contrast, sociobiology specifies a single underlying maximand: inclusive fitness. As described earlier (2.2.2), inclusive-fitness interests sometimes are "selfish" in the colloquial sense, but can also be self-sacrificing (to offspring and other close kin, and in the short run even to unrelated reciprocators) in specified evolutionary contexts (9.4, 10.4). Evolutionary theory can even be used to predict when it would be fitness enhancing to violate the canons of rationality and be swayed by benevolent or malevolent emotions (Hirshleifer 1987; Frank 1988). It offers explicit predictions about the exact form and content of "self-interest," and of evolved preferences and inclinations in general, in different environmental circumstances. In this it goes beyond the thin rationality of neoclassical economics or decision theory.

We have already argued that this viewpoint does not necessarily entail the narrow sort of genetic determinism that most social scientists rightly reject (1.3). It does, however, remain problematic, since neither humans nor other animals actually seem to hold fitness maximization as a goal. Rather, they possess various psychological mechanisms that lead them to learn some things easily, other things with difficulty or not at all, and to invest outcomes with specific positive or negative valences. In other words, actors may be utility maximizers, but they are fitness maximizers only to the extent that the utility functions defined by their evolved cognitive and emotional machinery are correlated with fitness. Given the logic of Darwinian evolution, high correlation of fitness and utility is the most reasonable expectation, but even ardent sociobiologists recognize that rapid environmental change and perhaps other factors can reduce or even destroy this correlation in specific cases (e.g., Symons 1990; Tooby and Cosmides 1990).

The final viewpoint on intentionality, listed above as position (4), holds that human preferences are best explained as the *joint* product of genetic and cultural evolution. In contrast to (3), this position holds sociobiological theory to be incomplete, and cultural inheritance to be an independent determinant of human action. In contrast to (1), and to the received view in contemporary social science, it adopts an explicitly Darwinian approach to understanding cultural variation, including the preferences and beliefs that inform intentional action (for further discussion, see Chapter 3).

In summary, both functional and intentional explanation of human behavior either require evolutionary analysis or at minimum are complementary with it. In the case of functional explanation, natural selection is currently the only process capable of providing the causal feedback element necessary for a convincing analysis. In the case of intentional explanation, natural selection is needed to underwrite a theory of preference formation. In neither case is there presently a well-established or compelling alternative to selection theory. However the problems of reconciling evolutionary biology with intentionality and culture are eventually resolved, the evidence summarized in this volume suggests strongly that some significant portion of the preferences and beliefs exhibited by human beings in diverse times and places have been shaped directly or indirectly by natural selection. While it is certainly too early to draw firm conclusions about the explanatory limits or potential of evolutionary ecology in the human sphere, we are confident that it has an important role to play in explaining human social and behavioral patterns.

2.4. OPTIMIZATION ANALYSIS

Optimization theory is one of the most frequently used analytical tools in evolutionary ecology. It is also one of the more controversial. In this section, we offer a brief summary of the explanatory logic behind the optimization approach, its relation to natural selection and to human decision-making, and the general elements common to any optimization model. Although optimization underlies ESS analyses of selection in a strategic context (2.2.3), the term itself is more closely associated with analyses in a parametric context (as defined in 1.2.1).

2.4.1. The Logic of Optimization Analysis

Elements.   While optimization analysis is used in many diverse settings, from decision theory and economics to engineering, all optimality models share certain basic elements: (1) an *actor* that chooses or exhibits alternative strategies or states; (2) a *strategy* set defining the range of options available to the actor; (3) a *currency* in which the costs and benefits of alternatives are measured; and (4) a set of *constraints* that determine the feasible strategies and the payoffs associated with each.

In keeping with methodological individualism (2.3.1) and the presumed prevalence of individual-level selection (2.2.2), in evolutionary ecology actors are usually defined as individual organisms. Each of the other three elements is discussed in some detail in sections 2.4.2–2.4.4, following consideration of some general issues.

Epistemology.   What is the relationship between optimization analysis and the logic of explanation? Optimization is not some general principle of nature, nor are optimality models intended as realistic descriptions of the behavior of individual actors or the process of adaptation by natural selection. Instead, research using optimality models tests particular hypotheses, each of which shares the elements and structure common to optimization analysis.

It is certainly possible to analyze biological diversity without employing optimization analysis. Consider the example of hunter–gatherer prey choice. We could describe each instance of prey choice in terms particular to the specific group being studied. We might note that the prey chosen varied systematically, and perhaps isolate a statistical relationship between prey abundances and the size or caloric value of chosen prey. But these findings would be specific to that case and lack any broader relevance. We would have an observation or correlation in search of an explanation.

In contrast, by using optimization analysis we can apply a general methodological framework to any particular case, and thereby test and refine models that have widespread applicability (cf. 1.2.1). For example, the prey choice model (6.2.3) can be applied whenever some basic assumptions about prey distributions and currency are met. It yields a set of simple yet powerful predictions about prey choice that might apply equally to seed-gathering Paiutes and seal-hunting Inuit. Although the assumptions and predictions of this optimization model might not precisely fit any particular case, it appears to capture the basic elements of diverse cases well enough to have received substantial empirical support in studies of a considerable number of species and situations (see section 6.2.5 for data on humans; Stephens and Krebs 1986 for nonhumans). Furthermore, it can be modified by altering the currency or constraint assumptions to make it more realistic for any particular case under investigation (as discussed in 6.4 and 6.5).

The value of the fine-grained prey choice model is not that it provides realistic descriptions of the cognitive processes or behavioral tactics underlying prey choice in bees, birds, and humans; these doubtless are quite diverse. Rather, it is due to the simplicity and generality of its formulation, its resulting testability, and its potential for analytical manipulation. If empirically successful, this implies that the model has correctly identified the adaptive goals involved in foraging behavior in diverse species.

In sum, optimization is not a theory (in the usual sense of an explanatory framework consisting of substantive propositions about the real world), but a method. Put succinctly, the epistemological role of optimization analysis is to provide a systematic means of generating hypotheses about the structure and function of living things. In other words, "the role of optimization theories in biology is not to demonstrate that organisms optimize [but] . . . to understand the diversity of life" (Maynard Smith 1978:52). Thus, for evolutionary ecology the optimization approach serves as a bridge between the abstract principles of natural selection theory and the diverse empirical facts of any real-life case. But the legitimacy of recasting evolutionary processes and outcomes in terms of optimization analysis is itself subject to debate, an issue we take up next.

Optimization and Evolution.   Simplifying somewhat, three views on the link between optimization analysis and evolutionary theory can be found in the literature: (1) evolution via natural selection is an optimizing process; (2) optimization analysis has little or no valid relation to evolutionary theory; (3)

optimization analysis is a convenient heuristic tool or simplification for analyzing evolutionary outcomes.

The first view holds that optimality models merely formalize the process underlying Darwinian evolution (e.g., Cody 1974). This view was propounded during the early period of ecological optimization research, but has since been qualified in significant ways. First, natural selection is not the only evolutionary force, so even if selection is an optimizing process, other forces (drift, pleiotropy, etc.) and constraints (developmental, genetic, etc.) may produce nonoptimal outcomes. Second, the identification of selection with optimization is inexact. Selection favors existing variants with higher fitness, not necessarily the best possible or imaginable variant; it trades in relative rather than maximum advantage.

The second view holds that the criticisms just outlined identify crippling or even fatal weaknesses in the analytical partnership of evolution and optimization (e.g., Sahlins 1976; Gould and Lewontin 1979; Lewontin 1987). One version of this critique argues that evolutionary optimization analysis proceeds from a "Panglossian" assumption that all is for the best in this best of all possible worlds. This assumption is then easily demolished by showing that selection may instead lead to inefficiency, waste, conflict, and even extinction. Other critics have pointed out that individual organisms face a variety of adaptive problems, which involve trade-offs or compromise. For example, the most efficient foraging strategy might constrain the organism to suboptimal predator avoidance.

The solution offered by natural-selection theory to this latter criticism is in principle quite straightforward. Since other traits possessed by an organism are part of the environment of any one trait, the optimal strategy for any given trait is defined as that member of the feasible set that contributes the greatest fitness to the organism, *given the other traits that the organism possesses and given that each of these is optimal in the same context.* But in practice, this principle brings an intractable complexity to the analysis of any particular adaptive problem, for to understand one problem/trait/ strategy properly, one would have to understand all of them.

Although important work is being done in analyzing optimal trade-offs between two major strategy sets (e.g., predation and foraging), evolutionary ecologists have not shown much interest in tackling whole-organism adaptation with formal optimality models. Indeed, it is not clear that this is even possible within existing theoretical and practical constraints. Instead, analyses have typically focused on a single optimization problem at a time, as if it were isolated from other (potentially interacting) problems. Some critics charge that this amounts to an illegitimate "atomizing" of organisms into component traits, each removed from the integrated matrix of the organism and its historical changes (e.g., Lewontin 1979; Gould and Lewontin 1979).

Whenever these single-trait analyses fail and the analyst cites competing adaptive goals as a possible explanation, the critics see this as a cover-up aimed at obscuring failure of the enterprise by post hoc rationalization.

This is a serious criticism, which has engendered an extended discussion (e.g., Maynard Smith 1978; Dawkins 1982; Oster and Wilson 1984; Krebs and McCleery 1984; Kitcher 1985:Chapter 7; Williams 1985; Dupré 1987; and articles by Gould and Lewontin, cited above). Perhaps the best that we can add here is that it remains a rather hypothetical problem. We rarely know in fact what degree of contradiction and compromise exists among the various traits of an organism; the most direct way to find out is to take the atomistic or "piecemeal" approach and test models of trait optimization. Given the numerous reasons why particular optimality hypotheses might fail, simple models have been empirically successful to a surprising degree.

We believe the third view listed above underlies the great majority of optimization analyses in evolutionary ecology. Optimality models are useful tools for ecological analysis even though they are not "true" in any simple sense (1.2.2). It is especially important not to confuse the process of selection with its results. In the narrowest sense, the process is one of relative advantage only. But selection is persistent and cumulative. Given sufficient genetic variation and consistency of selection pressures, it is plausible that one of its cumulative results will be a trajectory of improvement in designs. The result may be a design that can fairly be characterized as optimal with respect to the fitness currency, the design problem, and the relevant constraints.

A skeptic might still object that environmental change is ubiquitous, hence consistency of selective pressures unlikely. But this is a matter for empirical resolution (Jochim 1983). A more interesting reply is that selection can favor, and demonstrably has favored, the evolution of capacities for phenotypic adjustment to rapidly shifting environmental conditions. Such abilities are central to behavioral aspects of phenotype, including human learning abilities, rationality, and cultural transmission—all arguably products of selection for optimal (fitness-maximizing) phenotypic design (2.3.2, 3.3).

When evolutionary ecologists invoke optimization arguments then, they are not granting omniscient directionality to natural selection. Rather, they are postulating the evolution of phenotypes whose attributes are "optimal" in the specific sense expressed in the hypothesis under test (e.g., a foraging strategy that maximizes energy efficiency, presuming that the latter is a robust correlate of fitness). Viewed this way, optimization models are simply shortcuts to understanding the outcome of evolutionary history, "a tactical tool for making educated guesses about evolutionary trends" (Oster and Wilson 1984:284).

2.4.2. The Strategy Set

A strategy set (sometimes termed "phenotype set" or "feasible set") consists of the options (choices, decisions, alternative states) available to the actor. The content of the strategy set may be limited to a very few alternatives (e.g., Hawk vs. Dove, see Box 2.1), or it may be more complex (e.g., the various combinations of prey types a forager might harvest, which for just 5 possible prey types amounts to 31 alternative combinations). Specification of the strategy set is obviously a critical step in optimization analysis.

In some cases, optimization theory may provide considerable guidance in defining the strategy set. For example, in the prey choice problem, the fine-grained prey choice model (see 6.2.3) tells us to rank the prey types by return rates, reducing the strategy set to just 5 alternatives (take only the highest-ranked type; take the 2 highest ranked; etc.). But there are many cases in which the specification of the strategy set is an empirical or inductive problem, for which theory (including optimization theory) offers little assistance.

Satisficing versus Maximizing. If the analyst faces difficulties in defining and characterizing the strategy set, so might the actor. Does the actor know all of the possible solutions to a given decision problem and their payoffs? Can she or her calculate the optimal one? Mindful of these questions, some propose an alternative to optimization analysis, termed *satisficing.* Rather than expect the actor to be an optimizer (an impossible task, in this view), we might expect him or her to choose any alternative that is "good enough" (Simon 1955; Winter 1964; Elster 1983:74ff.).

Satisficing has two major analytical limitations, however. First, there is no general criterion by which the analyst or the actor can decide what is "good enough." Thus, satisficing remains an ad hoc method; the goal (satisficing) must be determined empirically by observing an actor assumed to have that goal. If satisficing is then used to explain the actor's behavior, the circularity is evident. Second, satisficing has no clear meaning in an evolutionary context (Krebs and McCleery 1984:119ff.; Foley 1985:224). A "satisfaction threshold" is irrelevant to selection, which in parametric contexts favors the best (fitness-maximizing) alternative among those available in a population. And in strategic contexts, satisficing can never be an ESS, because a strategy that is closer to the optimum will invade and outcompete the satisficing strategy. There is no "good enough" in the eyes of selection, only "better than."

Satisficing is sometimes advocated by analysts who wish to acknowledge the actor's incomplete information or cognitive limitations. But in these cases, satisficing is best replaced by an optimizing approach with appropriate information constraints (see below). Proponents of satisficing might reply that without knowing the costs of acquiring information, the optimal amount of information remains unknowable, causing an "infinite regress" problem in determining how much information to gather to determine the value of information (Winter 1964; Elster 1983:139ff.). This is a serious problem for single actors using rational choice in a novel situation. It may be less of a problem for actors who pool their experience (through observation and cultural transmission). And it is certainly less problematic if the optimizing force is natural selection rather than choice, for then selection "does the work" of determining which of the existing heritable strategies in a population actually comes closest to the optimum.

2.4.3. Currency

The currency in an optimization model calibrates the costs and benefits of alternatives in the strategy set, in order to rank preferences and to determine the optimal solution. Once a currency is chosen, the analyst can manipulate the optimization model to produce a set of predictions. For example, the currency in the fine-grained prey choice model (see 6.2.3) is some measure of food value (typically calories) obtained per unit foraging time. The different costs (in foraging time) and benefits (in food value) obtained from various prey choice combinations define the net benefit.

Ideally a currency would be characterized by maximal generality, precision, and realism. But this combination is rarely possible (see 1.2.2). The most general currencies commonly used in optimization models are fitness and utility. But these present problems, particularly in obtaining precise measurements of choice outcomes.

Fitness offers the strongest deductive basis for ranking different outcomes in terms of selective value. But because it is a lifetime measure summing the effects of many different phenotypic characters, it is generally impractical as an empirical currency. In addition, it can be argued that fitness is an inappropriate empirical measure for behavioral choices. As noted above (2.3.2), organisms do not rank alternatives by fitness consequences per se, but rather by various cognitively defined costs and benefits. Furthermore, fitness is a probabilistic measure (2.2.1), and the issue of evolutionary interest is really *design* for fitness rather than current fitness outcomes themselves (Williams 1966a:102). To study the costs and benefits of short-term behavioral choices in an evolutionary framework then, we need a proxy for fitness, a measure that we have reason to believe is correlated with fitness (or has been so in the evolutionary past) but that is more suitable for empirical research.

Utility has proven to be a useful theoretical construct in the development of economics and decision theory. Actors exhibit preferences that reflect psychological valuations of the consequences of alternative choices. Since the psychological mechanisms underlying these evaluations are at least in part genetically evolved, it is a reasonable presumption that utility is a fairly robust correlate of fitness. Of course, this is less likely when conditions are evolutionarily novel (2.3.2), or when the relevant preferences are strongly shaped by certain forms of cultural evolution (3.4). But if utility is a good proxy for fitness on theoretical grounds, it is not much help on methodological ones. Utility (like revealed preferences or satisficing) cannot be established independently of the actual choices made by an actor. It is a descriptive term for inferred preferences. To say that rational actors maximize utility is thus true by definition (Krebs and McCleery 1984:94).

In sum, to advance the goal of understanding organisms as products of evolutionary design we need currencies that are less general and more operationally useful than fitness or utility. Depending on the problem under analysis, the currency of choice might be reproductive success, mating frequency, survival frequency, resource harvest rate, and so on (as detailed in subsequent chapters of this volume). No single currency is best for all analyses, but some have proved useful for large domains of evolutionary ecology.

2.4.4. Constraints

The elements of any optimization model can be divided into two categories: variables that are subject to choice on the part of the actor, and those that are not. The latter are termed constraints. Stephens and Krebs (1986:9) suggest the following classification of constraints:

1. Extrinsic
2. Intrinsic
   a. of abilities
   b. of requirements

Extrinsic constraints are exogenous to the actor, features of the social or natural environment that are beyond the actor's control—at least under the ceteris paribus ("all else being equal") assumptions of a particular optimization model. For example, in the Hawk–Dove model (Box 2.1), the value of the contested resource is an extrinsic constraint.

Intrinsic constraints are those endogenous to the actor's phenotype. They include abilities (behavioral, cognitive, and the like) and requirements (physiological, nutritional, etc.). The simplest and most general models assume few intrinsic constraints. For example, in the Hawk–Dove game, the analysis is considerably simplified if we can assume that all players employing the same tactic have equal ability, so that any Hawk has an equal chance of winning against another Hawk, or any Dove against another Dove. This simplification obviously exacts some price in terms of reduced realism or empirical accuracy.

The specification of constraints involves a balance among the competing goals of realism and generality, a compromise between our desire to be faithful to the facts and the demands of analytical tractability (the ease of mathematically manipulating and comprehending the model). In general, an increase in realism is obtained by adding constraints. For example, in the Hawk–Dove game we might include intrinsic constraints like differences in fighting ability (e.g., Maynard Smith and Parker 1976), or such extrinsic constraints as nondivisibility of the resource so that Doves cannot share (e.g., Maynard Smith 1982a:Chapter 3). But increased realism often comes at the price of diminished generality, testability, and analytical comprehension (see 1.2.2). The most efficacious balance must be judged relative to specific research goals and current theoretical and empirical understanding.

Cognitive Constraints.   One class of intrinsic constraints of particular interest to social scientists is that imposed by limitations in the cognitive mechanisms and information that actors possess. There are two distinct issues here: the relationship between cognition and selection, and the way in which limited information affects decision-making.

Many optimization models assume the actors possess complete information in the relevant domain. If one seeks to understand what information an actor actually possesses, how it is acquired and updated, and its role in decision processes, then the complete-information assumption is clearly inappropriate. Instead, one needs to build and test models that incorporate information constraints. Bayesian decision theory, models of cultural transmission (3.3.1), and sampling models are appropriate avenues for this research. Some of these analyses treat the acquisition of information as an optimization problem in which there is a trade-off between the value of increased knowledge and the cost of acquiring it (Stephens and Krebs 1986:Chapter 4).

To return to the prey choice problem, it might be that prey that superficially resemble each other (e.g., belong to a single species) in fact differ significantly in their expected return rates. In some cases, gathering the information needed to discriminate prey types might have low cost (e.g., stranded vs. free-swimming whales). In others, the cost of obtaining the requisite information might outweigh any possible benefits (e.g., if one needs actually to capture the prey item before assigning it to one or another type).

Actors are also constrained by their cognitive and cultural capabilities for processing information. Formal optimization models define solutions using geometric tangents, partial derivatives, algebraic inequalities, or the like. These mathematical techniques provide convenient and elegant means of arriving at general and precise solutions, but they certainly do not replicate the everyday decision processes of actors. Instead, real actors (including people) are likely to use rules of thumb, less robust but far simpler ways of comparing outcomes and finding the (approximately) best solution. For example, instead of ranking prey types by net caloric return per unit handling time (6.2.3), foragers might use cruder but fairly effective rules involving the size and fat content of available prey (Jochim 1983).

While the relationship between cognitive constraints and evolutionary forces is complex, two general points can be made here. First, widespread rules of thumb are probably products of cultural or genetic evolution that have had robust selective advantages. If so, their primary adaptive value may be that they offer low-cost solutions to problems that are difficult or even insoluble when tackled by rational choice or individual trial-and-error learning. Actors may not replicate the procedures of an optimization model, but simple rules of thumb or cognitive algorithms provided by natural or cultural selection may allow them to approach the solution quite closely under conditions approximating the environments in which these "shortcuts" evolved.

Second, human actors in particular may increase their probability of attaining the optimum in complex decision problems by drawing on the accumulated experiences of others, as transmitted through conversation, lore, and culturally acquired beliefs. Indeed, this may underlie the evolution of the elaborate system of cultural transmission in the hominid lineage (3.3).

Individually Variable Constraints.   We usually think of optimization models as prescribing a single best solution to a given problem. From this perspective, it is reasonable to average together the actions of a set of individuals, and to view individual variation in choices as random "noise" due to errors in measurement, decision-making, or both. But the process of selection and the logic of methodological individualism both suggest otherwise. Since individuals (and classes of individuals) can be expected to differ in their intrinsic constraints (due to their age, experience, etc.) we should not expect them to share the same optimum for a given decision problem, even in the same environmental situation.

There are at least three distinct explanations for individual variation, besides the observational and decision errors mentioned above. First, individuals exhibiting what appear to be suboptimal responses may be making "the best of a bad job" (Dawkins 1980). That is, such individuals may temporarily or permanently lack the abilities or resources to achieve the outcomes with highest fitness payoffs. That would be the case, for example, with a forager who could not efficiently pursue a normally high-ranked prey type because of some physical handicap, and therefore wisely chose to ignore it. To average his or her response in with those of nonhandicapped foragers, or treat it as nonoptimal, would be to ignore the relevant difference in constraints.

Second, individuals (or classes of individuals) may differ in their constraints, and hence in their optima, in ways that cannot be ranked as "better versus worse" or "more versus less constraints." A good example of this is constraint difference between males and females, which can affect optima for such decision categories as foraging (Chapter 6), time allocation (Chapter 7), or use of space (Chapter 8), as well as the more obvious domains of mating and parenting strategies (Chapter 11).

Finally, even individuals who do not differ in their constraints may display different but equally optimal phenotypes. This will be the case whenever the evolutionary equilibrium includes two or more tactics, and tactic differences are either a facultative response of individuals (a mixed strategy) or heritable (a polymorphism; see 2.2.3). In such a situation, it makes no sense to say that one phenotype is superior (optimal) compared to another. Because "superiority" is frequency dependent, at equilibrium the payoffs to each will be equal. Prominent examples include "ideal-free" habitat distributions (8.3.2), evolutionarily stable group sizes (10.2.1), and female choice of polygyny versus monogamy as a function of variable male resources (11.3.2). To characterize one strategy (living in the "richest" habitat, foraging alone, being monogamous, etc.) as the optimal one is to overlook the differences in constraints created by the actions and characteristics of other actors.

2.5. CHAPTER SUMMARY

This chapter has surveyed the central ideas of evolutionary biology and social theory relevant to human behavioral ecology. The main points are as follows:

1. Natural selection requires three conditions: individual variation, heritability, and differential fitness.

2. Natural selection favors variants with highest *fitness* or *evolutionary stability*. Fitness refers to the statistical propensity of a variant to leave descendants, rather than to actual numbers of descendants of any given individual.

3. When fitness is frequency dependent, as is true in many social interactions, natural selection favors an *evolutionarily stable strategy* (ESS). An ESS is the variant (or combination of variants) that, when characteristic of most members of the population, cannot be replaced by another variant through natural selection. There is no reason to expect that an ESS will maximize average population fitness.

4. Evolutionary biologists distinguish between individual selection, group selection, and kin selection. Individual selection favors variants with maximal surviving offspring; kin selection favors variants with maximal surviving genetic relatives (including nondescendant kin); group selection favors variants producing maximal survival or colonizing success of groups

(trait groups, demes, etc.). The balance among these forms of selection is currently debated, but most evolutionary ecology models emphasize individual selection.

5. Because the exact mode of inheritance of behavioral phenotypes is usually unknown, evolutionary ecologists often adopt the "phenotypic gambit." That is, they assume that inheritance is simple, phenotypes are highly flexible, and proxy currencies are robust fitness correlates.

6. Methodological individualism analyzes social phenomena in terms of the actions and interests of individuals; it is adopted in several areas of social science, and is generally compatible with the analytical approach of evolutionary ecology.

7. Explanations can be classed as causal, functional, or intentional. Evolutionary explanations are often functional in form, but full explanation requires that they incorporate the causal process of natural selection. Intentional explanation has a complex relation to evolutionary analysis. Some see intentions as overriding evolutionary analysis, others claim they have no explanatory role in science, and still others incorporate them as a genetically or culturally evolved set of mechanisms with fitness consequences.

8. Optimality models are very commonly used in evolutionary ecology. Their elements include a decision-maker (actor), a set of alternatives (strategy set), a currency (specifying the variable maximized), and a set of constraints (variables outside the actor's control). Optimization models can be powerful tools for analyzing adaptations, even though they are not fully realistic descriptions of the evolutionary process.

ACKNOWLEDGMENTS

We thank the following individuals for providing detailed comments on earlier versions of this chapter: Robert Bettinger, Rob Boyd, Monique Borgerhoff Mulder, Raymond Hames, Kristen Hawkes, Sarah Blaffer Hrdy, and Michael Taylor.

Cultural Inheritance and Evolutionary Ecology

Peter J. Richerson and Robert Boyd

3

3.1. INTRODUCTION

Humans are uniquely reliant on culture as a means of adaptation. To be sure, some human variation results from genetic adaptation. Like most other animals, we adapt using individual learning. Unlike other creatures, however, humans acquire a great deal of adaptive information from other conspecifics by imitation, teaching, and other forms of "cultural transmission."

It is important to distinguish between culture and individual learning. Culture is often lumped with ordinary individual learning and other environmental effects under the heading of "nurture," to be contrasted with genes—"nature." This way of thinking is responsible for much confused thinking about the evolution of human behavior. Culture differs from individual learning because variations are acquired from other individuals. For the most part, humans do not learn their language, occupational skills, or forms of social behavior for themselves, they learn them from parents, teachers, peers, and others. Cultural variants are more like genes than are ordinary learned variants. Like genes, they are inherited and transmitted in a potentially endless chain, while variants acquired by individual learning are lost with the death of the learner.

Because culture is transmitted, it can be studied using the same Darwinian *methods* used to study genetic evolution. Human populations transmit a pool of cultural variation that is cumulatively modified to produce evolutionary change, much as they transmit an evolving gene pool. To understand cultural change we must keep track of all the processes in the lives of individuals that increase the frequency of some cultural variants and decrease the frequency of others. Of course, these processes do differ substantially from the processes of genetic evolution. Most important perhaps,

culture allows inheritance of acquired variation; individually learned variants can be taught or imitated.

Culture can also be studied using the *substantive* conclusions of Darwinism. It is plausible that natural selection has shaped the human psyche so
that people tend to acquire adaptive beliefs and values, however culture
may work in detail. If not, how can we account for the evolution of the
complex, costly organ that manipulates culture, the human brain? To the
extent that this premise is correct, human behavior can be predicted using
theory drawn directly from behavioral ecology, and no special account
need be taken of the processes by which people acquire that behavior. The
gambit of ignoring the details of how genes, learning, and other factors
actually produce adaptive behavior has proven to be very successful in the
study of the behavior of other animals. The substantive use of Darwinism to
understand behavior is defended in greater detail in the first two chapters of
this book, and exemplified by the following chapters.

There is an irony in the history of the application of Darwinian concepts
and methods to cultural evolution. Darwin (e.g., 1871) believed that the
inheritance of acquired variation was a general feature of all systems of
inheritance. He did not make a rigid distinction between organic inheritance and culture because he thought that habits acquired by individuals
could be inherited. Darwin is often accused of biologizing culture (Alland
1985), but the truth is almost the opposite. By modern standards, Darwin
had a shamelessly anthropomorphic view of the animal world. He seems to
have believed that the advantages of the inheritance of acquired variation
were obvious: Parents spend a lot of effort learning the details of how to
behave in a local environment, and it seems a waste to dissipate this effort
by requiring offspring to relearn everything anew each generation. Humans,
Darwin could observe, used imitation and instruction to transmit the results
of learning, and it suited his intellectual agenda to minimize the difference
between humans and other animals in order to bring all organisms into the
compass of his theory (Gruber 1974). It was thus easy for him to imagine that
culture was the model inheritance system. The irony is that, although
Darwin's view that acquired variation and natural selection interact to guide
evolution is seriously wrong for the genetic system of inheritance, it *is* quite
apt for human culture. Although after many twists and turns to correct his
errors, Darwin's theory became the heart of evolutionary biology in the
1930s (Provine 1971), it was ignored by the emerging social sciences in
favor of the very different progressive evolutionary schemes of Herbert
Spencer and his followers.

It is only in the last few decades that biologists and social scientists have
returned to try to complete the project initiated by Darwin in the *Descent*.
One of the earliest and most important figures in this renaissance is Donald
Campbell (1965, 1975), who argued that the general similarities of genes

and culture meant that the same methods that evolutionary biologists use to study genetic evolution would prove successful in the investigation of culture. Beginning in 1973, L. L. Cavalli-Sforza and M. W. Feldman (1981) initiated a series of theoretical and empirical investigations of culture using the techniques of population genetics. About the same time, Richard Alexander (1974) and E. O. Wilson (1975) reinvigorated the evolutionary study of humans by proposing that much of the substance of human behavior could be understood in adaptive terms no matter how it was acquired— genetically, culturally, individually learned, or a complex mixture of all three. Several workers, including ourselves, have attempted to combine the methodological and substantive questions, using models inspired by population genetics to understand how culture works as a system of adaptation (Pulliam and Dunford 1980; Lumsden and Wilson 1981; Boyd and Richerson 1985; Rogers 1989a).

In this chapter our task is to present this last, hybrid body of work. There is little doubt that the organic capacities that underlie human learning and behavior were shaped by natural selection, and thus that the behavior resulting from these capacities must have been adaptive, at least in past environments. Nonetheless, attention to the processes of cultural evolution is important for human evolutionary ecology. First, the rate at which a population adapts to changing circumstances depends on the mechanism of adaptation. Genetic adaptation by natural selection is a relatively slow process, individual learning is fast, and as we shall see, cultural adaptation may range from one extreme to the other. For some disciplines, such as archaeology, the rate of adaptation may be of great interest. Second, the rapidity of adaptation itself is a kind of adaptation to variable environments, and is of interest in its own right. Finally, we will argue at length below that cultural adaptation can yield qualitatively different outcomes than those predicted from conventional fitness optimizing theory, even if one assumes that the *capacity* for culture has been shaped solely by natural selection acting on genetic variation.

3.2. PROCESSES THAT GENERATE ADAPTATIONS

A number of processes act to change the cultural composition of a population through time. We refer to these processes as the "forces" of cultural evolution. Some are analogous to the forces of evolution operating on the genetic system—drift, mutation, natural selection, and so forth. Others have no close analog in genetic evolution. Some of these processes tend to produce adaptation in a reasonably straightforward sense. Others result in evolutionary outcomes that cannot be predicted without taking into account the details of cultural evolution. We begin by considering processes that give rise to ordinary adaptations—that is, forces that tend to produce fitness-maximizing behavior.

3.2.1. Guided Variation

Because culture is acquired by copying the phenotype, culture allows the inheritance of acquired variation. Individuals acquire beliefs and values by social learning. Such culturally acquired information is often affected by individual learning during the individuals' life. People may modify existing beliefs, or even adopt completely new ones, as a result of their experiences. When such people are subsequently imitated, they transmit the modified beliefs. The next generation can engage in more individual learning and change the trait even further. When the beliefs of one generation are linked to the next by cultural transmission, learning can lead to cumulative, often adaptive, change. We say that such change results from the force of *guided variation*.

If individual learning is not to be random, there must be some rules that govern which behaviors are acquired and which are rejected. The strength and direction of guided variation depend on the nature of these learning rules. Operant conditioning provides a good example of how such rules work. An animal's nervous system causes some environmental events to be reinforcing and others aversive. The behavioral variation that individuals exhibit is shaped by such stimuli so that reinforced (generally adaptive) behaviors are retained, while those that result in aversive stimuli (normally maladaptive) disappear. Other forms of individual learning involve more complex, cognitively mediated rules. In every case, however, the kinds of traits acquired by learning depend on rules expressed in the nervous system, which were acquired genetically or during an earlier episode of cultural transmission.

Thus, the kinds of traits increased by guided variation depend on the nature of the evolutionary forces that shaped the learning rules. The case in which learning rules are genetically transmitted and shaped by natural selection is of particular interest. First, this is the primitive case and thus is important for understanding the evolutionary origin of guided variation. Second, evidence suggests that it is common in contemporary humans (Lumsden and Wilson 1981:Chapters 2 and 3; Tooby and Cosmides 1989; Cosmides and Tooby 1989). Finally, if learning rules were shaped by guided variation or some other force of cultural evolution, we then must ask how those prior learning rules were acquired. A chain of cultural rules will often end in genetically acquired traits of some kind.

Guided variation allows populations to adapt relatively quickly and effectively to changing environments. This is easiest to see when the goals of the learning rules are closely correlated with genetic fitness. If human foraging practices are adopted or rejected according to their energy payoff per unit time (as is typically assumed in optimal foraging theory—see Chapter 6), then the foraging practices used in the population will adapt to changing environments much as if natural selection were responsible. If the adoption of foraging practices is strongly affected by consideration of prestige, say that associated with male success in hunting dangerous prey, then the resulting pattern of behavior may be different. However, there will still be a pattern of adaptation to different environments, but now in the sense of increasing prestige rather than calories.

The rate at which a population can adapt by guided variation depends on how hard it is to evaluate alternative behaviors. When individuals can easily learn that some alternative behavior is better than their existing behavior, then guided variation can transform a population very quickly. On the other hand, when it is difficult to evaluate which cultural variant is best, some people will switch from an inferior variant to a superior one, but many others will switch the other way, and the net change will be small. It may often be the case that it will be difficult to determine which variant is best, even if different variants have very different fitnesses. When learning is difficult, culture can also accumulate small learned steps over many generations, leading to larger changes than would be possible when each generation has to learn anew. Box 3.1 shows how simple mathematical models are used to make verbal arguments like this one more precise.

3.2.2. Biased Transmission

People do not just imitate others at random and then modify behavior on the basis of their own experience; they also pick and choose whom and what to imitate in the first place. We call this process *biased transmission*. The simplest form of biased transmission, *direct bias*, can make use of the same guiding motivations as are used in guided variation. With direct bias, there is no need to invent or reinvent the behavior concerned, but only to evaluate alternative behaviors and choose among them. If behavior is at all complex, it is much easier to evaluate available alternatives than it is to invent for oneself. Plagiarism is usually easier than invention, so the distinction between these two forces is not trivial. We will consider other forms of biased transmission below.

Again, if we suppose that selection on genes is responsible for the guiding rules behind the people's choices, direct bias will tend to cause adaptive cultural variants to spread. A seventeenth-century New Guinea population might have been exposed to American sweet potatoes for the first time when some neighbors began cultivating them. Some individuals in the population likely tried cultivating sweet potatoes, evaluating whether they were superi-

Box 3.1. *A Model of Guided Variation.* Mathematical models are often useful for deducing the long-run evolutionary consequences of events in the lives of individuals. Here we illustrate this idea with a simple model of guided variation. Consider some basic subsistence behavior with two cultural variants—say whether to pursue individual or cooperative foraging. To make learning useful, we assume that the environment is variable—cooperative foraging is best in some environments and individual foraging is best in others. Suppose young people acquire their initial beliefs about which mode is best in the local environment by imitation of a single adult (say children imitate their mothers). As they mature they attempt to evaluate which technique is better, say by trying out the two techniques. If such trials convince them that the other technique is superior, they switch; if not, they stick to what they learned from Mom.

Let us suppose that a population has recently moved from an environment in which cooperative foraging was favored to an environment in which individual foraging is favored. Because there are only two cultural variants we can describe the state of the population by the fraction, or "frequency," of individuals who forage individually, labeled q. Then the rate of increase in the frequency of individual foraging as a result of guided variation, Δq, will be

$$\Delta q = \alpha(p - q)$$

where α = the probability that behavior is acquired by individual learning, and p = the probability that the best behavior is chosen given that behavior is acquired by individual learning.

Notice that the frequency of individual foraging converges toward the probability that it is chosen when individuals rely on their own experience. Thus, if it is easy to discern the advantages of individual foraging, we would expect almost everybody to forage individually once the population reaches equilibrium. In contrast if it is hard to discern which is better, then many individuals may err and the equilibrium frequency of individual foraging will be lower. If "learning" is merely random ($p = \frac{1}{2}$), then the equilibrium frequency is $\frac{1}{2}$.

The rate at which the population approaches equilibrium depends on how often individuals are convinced to switch foraging techniques based on their own experience, which is measured by α. If $\alpha = 1$, everyone learns individually, and equilibrium is reached in the first generation, and if $p = 1$, everyone who does learn for him- or herself does get the correct answer. If $\alpha = 1$ and $p = 1$, the whole population gets the new answer without error in the first generation—perfect individual learning. Smaller values of α and p indicate some reliance on social learning and errors in individual learning.

While an analysis limited to so few features of the cultural system is quite unrealistic, it does model one of its distinctive features, the inheritance of acquired variation. The hope is that the lessons of the simplified analysis remain as we add complexity.

or to existing cultivars. If, on average, individuals perceived sweet potatoes as superior, they adopted sweet potato cultivation, exposing more people to the practice and so on until it spread throughout the population.

Like guided variation, biased transmission will cause a trait to spread more rapidly if it is easy to determine that the trait is better than the alternatives. If the new sweet potatoes have substantially higher yields than older cultigens like yams, then it will be easy for horticulturalists already accustomed to evaluating alternative breeds of yams to determine that sweet potatoes are better. However, the benefits of many other very desirable traits may be hard to detect. The practice of boiling drinking water substantially reduces infant mortality due to diarrhea. Nonetheless, the practice may fail to spread because its effects are confounded by many other sources of diarrhea, because it conflicts with folk medical theory, and because the causative agents killed by boiling, bacteria, are invisible. Traits whose net beneficial effects are only apparent when averaged over substantial periods of time may be especially difficult to evaluate.

Unlike guided variation, the strength of biased transmission depends on the amount of cultural variation. Bias is a culling process analogous to natural selection. Individuals select which variants to adopt from among the variants that are available. This means the force of bias has it greatest effect when alternative variants have approximately equal frequencies, and is weak when one variant is rare. This property of direct bias is easily seen in the context of the simple model sketched in Box 3.2.

3.2.3. Example: The Diffusion of Innovations

Studies of the diffusion of technical innovations illustrate how the strength of guided variation and direct bias varies in response to circumstances. It is well-known that humans make extensive use of pragmatic decision-making techniques when considering adopting potentially useful innovations. Rogers (1983) reviews many studies that suggest that the perceived advantage of new technology relative to old is one of the most important variables in explaining why particular innovations spread. In conformance with the theory, people with more education and more resources are more likely to be the early adopters of innovations. The difficulty of evaluating innovations and the impact of costly errors weigh more heavily against less educated and poorer people adopting innovations on the basis of their own evaluations. They, sensibly, wait for those who can better bear the costs of independent decision-making to try them out, and imitate earlier adopters later in the cycle of innovation adoption. The very rapid rate of technical evolution at the present time is probably a result of the fact that high rates of literacy, related phenomena such as the existence of libraries, and prosperity equip

Box 3.2. *A Model of Direct Bias.* Let us illustrate these ideas with a very simple model of direct bias. Again suppose, as in Box 3.1, that individuals must choose between individual and cooperative foraging. As before, individuals acquire their initial beliefs from their parents. But now assume that as adults, if they encounter another person who has different beliefs, they attempt to evaluate the relative merit of their beliefs and those of the person they have encountered. If they decide the other person's beliefs are better, they switch. Then the change in frequency of individual foraging is:

$$\Delta q = 2\alpha(p - \tfrac{1}{2})q(1 - q)$$

The rate of increase of individual foraging is proportional to the probability that individual evaluation is decisive, just like guided variation. If $p < \tfrac{1}{2}$, cooperative foraging is favored; if $p > \tfrac{1}{2}$, individual foraging is. Unlike guided variation, the effect of direct bias is proportional to $q(1 - q)$, the amount of variation in the population. When either one of the traits is rare—(q or $(1 - q) \approx 0$)—direct bias becomes very weak. Thus even very advantageous variants will spread slowly when they are rare, assuming direct bias is the only force causing them to increase. When both variants are equally common—($q = (1 - q) = \tfrac{1}{2}$)—and the rate of change is a maximum for a given α and p. Also, note that in the long run, direct bias completely eliminates the inferior variant from the population, albeit very slowly toward the end, while guided variation reduces its frequency to $1 - p$. In the case of guided variation, everyone who has the right trait by inheritance can make an error in individual learning and convert back to the wrong behavior. In the case of direct bias, as the frequency of people with the favored trait goes up, fewer people observe the unfavored behavior at all, and thus fewer people are tempted to err.

many people with the capacities to make fairly effective individual decisions and to tolerate the cost of mistakes.

However, the technology of preindustrial societies can also be transformed quite rapidly. The most dramatic examples are those in which population growth leads to increased competition for resources. Exponential population growth is a very rapid process, and when it drives cultural change those processes can be rapid as well. Kirch (1984) describes the response in Polynesian societies to population growth. The Polynesian islands were apparently settled by very small groups of voyagers, and it took several hundred years for the population of larger islands to become overcrowded. However, as populations did reach these levels, considerable environmental deterioration occurred. At the same time, dense populations stimulated considerable technical innovation. On Hawaii, for example, irrigation, sophisticated dryland farming systems, and aquaculture on a considerable scale allowed for an intensification of production in response to rising populations and deteriorating resources. Although status competition between chiefs (who supervised the larger-scale economic enterprises) played an important role in the evolution of late Polynesian technology, the basic decision-making forces of direct bias and guided variation must have been major elements of the process of invention and diffusion of the technology of intensification in response to more intense competition for a diminishing stock of traditional resources.

Sometimes the diffusion of improved practices proves exceedingly slow. Bettinger and Baumhoff (1982) describe the case of the several-century-long episode of the expansion of Numic speaking (Shoshone, Ute, Mono) peoples across the Great Basin of North America. The Numic speakers made intensive use of high-processing-time plant resources, such as grass seed, for their subsistence. Because this strategy supported relatively denser populations that also exploited higher-quality game and plant resources, previous populations that restricted themselves to the high-quality resources were displaced (see Chapter 6 for the optimal foraging theory that in part underpins this analysis). What kept the people being displaced from adopting Numic technology to defend themselves against the slow incursion of the Numics? Bettinger and Baumhoff argue that the key cultural trait was not the processing technology itself, which was relatively simple and widely known, but a social-organizational innovation that placed greater value on women and women's labor. In general, the utility of various subsistence techniques is easy to observe and evaluate. Alternative variants can be tested and retained or discarded as experience dictates. The consequences of social organizational variables are often harder to observe. What sort of woman should a man marry? How many should he attempt to marry? How should he treat her? The consequences of such decisions are worked out over an entire lifetime and few people get to make more than one or two experiments. It makes sense that people should rely more on tradition with regard to social organization and less with regard to subsistence techniques, even when, as perhaps with the pre-Numic peoples, clinging to traditional social organization results in displacement.

3.3. CULTURE AS AN ADAPTATION

If the massive use of culture is, like bipedalism and large cheek teeth, a distinctive human trait, what adaptive role does it play and how did a capacity for it evolve? In this section we try to understand the circumstances under which culture is superior to genetic transmission and individual learning as a means of adaptation. Understanding culture as an adaptation is important for two reasons: First, the usual approach to this problem is an anthropocentric rush to judgment. It is assumed that culture is an inherently superior mode of adaptation, and the question reduces to the breakthroughs required to achieve it. It is salutary to reverse this presupposition. Darwin erred; the inheritance of acquired variation is rare in nature. What is so *wrong* with culture that it should be really conspicuous in only one species? Second, below we will argue that some cultural processes may lead to "maladaptive" outcomes, but only if guided variation and direct bias are weak forces. Thus, it is important to know under what conditions selection might favor a strong reliance on social learning.

3.3.1. The Advantage of Cultural Adaptation in Variable Environments

To understand the evolution of social learning we ask: What sorts of selective pressures might have favored the expansion of a capacity for social learning? When will a tendency to depend on an inherited tradition become important relative to genetically inherited patterns of behavior, or a combination of genes plus individual learning?

As we have already noted, social learning is similar to both individual learning and genetic inheritance. Individual learning is a pure system of phenotypic adaptation to environmental contingencies, but the acquired adaptation perishes with the individual learner. A pure system of inheritance (genetic or cultural) does not allow the individual any flexibility, but the fitness consequences of heritable variation cause the population to become adapted. Social learning allows both modes of adaptation. This mixed mode of adapting has two distinct advantages.

First, social learning may be favored because it allows individuals to avoid costs associated with learning. Individual learning may often be costly; it takes time and energy, exposes the organism to risk, and may require a larger brain. Rogers (1989a) analyzes a simple model in which there are two types of individuals—individual learners who evaluate alternative behaviors and choose the best one, and social learners who copy the behavior of a randomly chosen individual from the previous generation. He assumes that occasionally the environment changes from generation to generation. If individual learning is more costly than social learning, then social learners always increase in frequency when they are rare since they are virtually certain to acquire the best behavior without bearing the costs of individual learning. However, as social learners become more common, fewer people are learning for themselves and errors begin to accumulate in the population. Those that merely copy have a greater chance of copying another social learner, and thus acquiring an inferior behavior learned in a different environment. Rogers shows that at equilibrium there is always a mix of social and individual learners—the greater the environmental variability the lower the frequency of social learning. This model also has the property that the average fitness of the equilibrium mix of social and individual learners is the same as a population composed only of individual learners. Culture is favored by selection, but it does not increase average fitness. The equilibrium mix of social and individual learning is an ESS (see 2.2.3).

Second, social learning may be favored because it allows individuals to avoid learning errors. Virtually all learning mechanisms allow the possibility of error. Consider, for example, an individual trying to decide which of two foraging techniques is better. She tries them both out, and chooses the one that yields the highest return. In a noisy world, small samples may often yield erroneous results—the technique with the higher return in the sample may have a lower return over the long run. Costs and errors may be linked, since making learning more sophisticated and costly will tend to reduce errors. Social learning can reduce the importance of such errors by allowing individuals to be more selective in their use of learned information. A social learning forager can use a rule like: Try out the two techniques and if one yields twice as much as the other adopt that technique; otherwise use the technique that Mom used. The use of such a rule will reduce the number of learning errors; however, it will also slow down the rate at which the population adapts. We have analyzed a simple model that incorporates this idea, which is sketched in Box 3.3 (see Boyd and Richerson 1988b, 1989a, for more detailed analysis). This model suggests that at equilibrium (the ESS) individuals always depend on a mix of social and individual learning, and the average dependence on social learning increases as the environment becomes less variable in either time or space. Unlike Rogers's model, the equilibrium population has higher average fitness than a population that depends only on individual learning; the cultural system for the inheritance of acquired variation is adaptive in changing environments.

So far, we have ignored genetic adaptation. We have seen that cultural inheritance is favored as environments become less variable. However, these are exactly the conditions under which selection will allow a population to adapt genetically to changing environments. What if we compare a system of genetic transmission plus individual learning with a cultural transmission system plus learning for the same subsistence trait? We have done such an analysis for a model that is conceptually similar to the one just presented, but using a different detailed structure (Boyd and Richerson 1985: Chapter 4). This model shows that the inheritance of acquired variation is favored relative to genetic inheritance plus individual learning unless the environment is either nearly constant or nearly random. In the context of this model, the range of environments under which culture or a similar system should be favored is rather broad.

This family of models gives as much support as a simplified theoretical model can to our intuitive argument. A cultural system of inheritance

Box 3.3. *The Optimal Dependence on Culture*. Consider the same model of guided variation as presented in Box 3.1. Now, however, we assume that the learning rules that govern acquisition of subsistence technique are genetically variable. The question is: How will natural selection acting on this variation shape the learning rule?

Suppose that the fitness of each behavior in each environment is given by the following matrix:

| | Fitness associated with | |
	Cooperative foraging	Solitary foraging
Dry conditions	$W + \delta$	W
Wet conditions	W	$W + \delta$

where W represents a baseline of fitness having to do with things other than choice of subsistence, and δ is the component of fitness due to subsistence choice. The environment varies from generation to generation. The probability that parent's and offspring's environments differ is m. When $m = 0$, the environment never changes; when $m = \frac{1}{2}$, the environment varies randomly on the time scale of a generation.

To consider the evolution of learning, we need to model learning in a little more detail than we did in Box 3.1. Suppose that the individual evaluates the two alternatives by trying each method and comparing their net yields. Let the observed difference between the net yields of individual foraging and cooperative foraging in a particular trial be x. Thus if $x > 0$, the net yield from solitary foraging is greater. However, due to the finite sample and the noisiness of the world, x will vary from trial to trial, even in the same environment. Thus, sometimes individuals will achieve a higher yield with the technique that is inferior on the average. We assume that individuals deal with this problem as a statistician might—they begin by acquiring an initial technique by imitating another individual; then they switch to the other technique only if the difference in yield is greater than a threshold value d, which we assume is genetically determined and variable. Individuals with larger values of d require more convincing evidence to switch and thus tend to rely on social learning more when compared with individuals characterized by smaller values of d.

As is illustrated in Figure 3.1, increasing d decreases the probability α that the individual learning trial will be decisive, but it increases the probability p of acquiring the best foraging technique given that individual learning is decisive. If d is made small, individuals will act as if they have great confidence in their own experience. However, if S, the noisiness of the environment, is large, they will very frequently adopt the wrong strategy by mistake. A large d avoids the possibility of making a mistake, but it will cause individuals to be more likely to depend on social learning. If the environment has recently changed this may be deleterious.

Elsewhere (Boyd and Richerson 1988b, 1989a) we have determined the evolutionarily stable value of α, which we label α^*. Figure 3.2 illustrates the results of this analysis. The relative importance of social and individual learning depends upon two things: the noisiness of the

(Box 3.3. *Continued*)
environment (more generally, the difficulty of accurate individual learning) and the degree of similarity of the average environmental condition from generation to generation. If there is a reasonable degree of resemblance between parents' and offspring's environments and individual learning is fairly inaccurate, strong dependence on social learning can be favored. This simplified analysis is extended in various ways in the papers cited above, and this essential behavior does not change.

combining individual and social learning ought to provide adaptive advantages in environments with an intermediate degree of environmental similarity from generation to generation. This is the regime where the faster tracking due to the evolutionary force of cumulative, relatively weak, low-cost individual learning pays off most. Most individuals can depend primarily on tradition, yet the modest pressure of individual learning is sufficient to keep culture "honest."

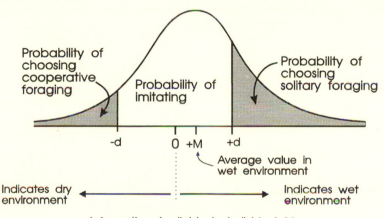

Figure 3.1.   The effect of the learning threshold (d) on the probability of acquiring the best behavior by individual learning or tradition. The curve shows the probability of obtaining a given estimate x of the average difference in yield between the two environments (2M) from the small sample of years a young person experiences before choosing his strategy, assuming that environment is actually wet. If x exceeds +d, the young person ignores tradition and chooses the strategy best for a wet environment, solitary foraging. If x is less than −d, he mistakenly chooses the best strategy for a dry environment, cooperative foraging. If x is between −d and +d, the young person follows tradition (adopts mother's strategy). The width of the bell-shaped curve gives the variability of the individual's estimate. When the variability of the sample is large compared to the average difference between environments, most individuals will find it difficult to determine the best strategy. Note that for the value of S illustrated, the probability of choosing the wrong strategy will be quite high unless the d interval is fairly wide; individuals should have only modest confidence in their own experience in this case.

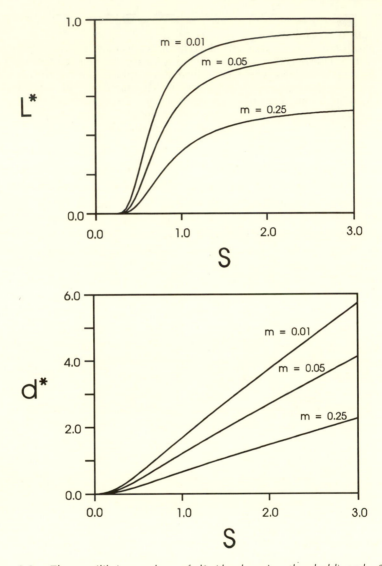

Figure 3.2.   The equilibrium values of d* (the learning threshold) and α* (the fraction of a population acquiring a trait by individual learning) as a function of information quality (S) for three values of environmental variability (m). The upper panel plots the evolutionary equilibrium value of d, d*, as a function of the quality of information available from individual learning (S), for three levels of environmental variability measured by the probability of parents' and offsprings' environments being different (m). The lower panel plots the fraction of the population that acquires the trait by individual learning at evolutionary equilibrium (α*) as a function of S for the same three values of m. Individual learning becomes less important and therefore cultural transmission becomes more important as the quality of information from experience deteriorates (S increases) and the environment becomes more stable (m decreases).

Existing data do not allow a critical empirical test of this adaptive rationale for culture. Two lines of inquiry might be pursued to develop such tests. First, many animals seem to have simple capacities for social learning (Zentall and Galef 1988). Two animals for which social learning is apparently quite important are rats (Galef 1988) and pigeons (Lefebvre and Palametta 1988). These are weedy generalists that certainly have to adapt to variable environments. If a broader comparative study of animal social learning showed a significant correlation between environmental variability and capacities for social learning, the models would be supported. Second, humans are an extreme example of "encephalization" (brain enlargement), but many other animal lineages show more moderate encephalization during the Tertiary Epoch (the last 65 million years, Jerison 1973; Eisenberg 1981). At least the last 2 million years of the Pleistocene Era seem to have much more variable climates than the past (Shackleton and Opdyke 1976). It is perhaps not a coincidence that highly cultural hominids arose during the Pleistocene. The beginnings of the enlargement of the neocortex to the contemporary human scale began about the beginning of the Pleistocene as *Australopithecus* gave way to *Homo*, and fully sapiens-sized brains only evolved during the latter part of the Pleistocene with its high-amplitude glacial cycles (Klein 1989; Foley this volume). Studies of patterns of paleoclimatic variation are not yet sufficiently detailed to know whether the relationship between increasing encephalization and increasing environmental variability is a close one on geological time scales across the broad spectrum of encephalizing lineages. If large brains are used for individual learning and social learning, the models suggest that increasing rates of environmental variation should have driven the Tertiary encephalization trends.

3.4. CULTURAL EVOLUTION NEED NOT YIELD FITNESS MAXIMIZATION

Thus far we have seen how the forces of guided variation and direct bias can cause cultural evolution to mimic the results of genetic evolution. At equilibrium, individuals will act as if they chose the behavior that maximizes fitness. It may be that this behavior actually evolved over many generations as a result of guided variation and direct bias. However, for many purposes this fact will be irrelevant, and it will be possible to predict behavior based on fitness maximization.

Other forms of cultural adaptation are not so simple. In this section we argue that there are processes of cultural adaptation that (1) lead to different outcomes than would be predicted based on fitness maximization, but (2) are nonetheless favored by natural selection because they make social learning more effective.

3.4.1. Natural Selection of Cultural Variation

Natural selection can act on cultural variation to produce evolutionary change in the same way that it acts on genetic variation. For natural selection to occur there must be variation and variants must differ in ways that affect the number of copies of each variant that are present in the next generation (see 2.2.1). Many culturally transmitted traits have substantial effects on fitness. Belonging to a pronatalist religion tends to increase fecundity, and belonging to an abstemious one tends to increase survival. Thus, if religious beliefs are transmitted from parents to offspring, selection on cultural variation can produce adaptations in the metric of genetic fitness.

People often acquire beliefs and values from individuals other than their parents. Such "asymmetric" cultural transmission makes adaptive sense. Direct bias is more effective if naive individuals survey many models before they make up their minds whose trait to adopt. If Dad is a poor hunter, why not observe the strategies of several other men before making up your mind how you will approach the problem? Thus, selection may favor a tendency to imitate nonparental individuals.

When cultural variation is transmitted nonparentally, natural selection may favor genetically maladaptive cultural variants. Whenever individuals are culturally influenced by grandparents, teachers, peers, and so on, natural selection acting on cultural variation can favor the increase of behaviors that increase the chance of attaining such nonparental roles. When the traits that maximize success in becoming a parent are different from those which maximize success as a teacher, priest, or grandparent, natural selection acting on cultural variation can cause genetically maladaptive traits to spread. In most past societies, various risks ensured that few people lived to see their grandchildren. Surviving to grandparental age might require being unusually cautious, more cautious than would be optimal from a genetic fitness point of view. Too-cautious behaviors might easily spread throughout a society if grandparents play any significant role in socialization. This effect is easily seen in a simple model—see Box 3.4. The result is intuitively reasonable and is robust to the relaxation of many of the special assumptions of this simple model (Boyd and Richerson 1985:Chapter 6).

Example: The Demographic Transition. Human demography may provide examples of this effect. Many urban populations, especially elite populations, throughout recorded history seem to have reproduced at rates below replacement despite an economic capacity to out-reproduce nonelites (Knauft 1987). Ancient cites were like tar pits, drawing country folk into their alluring but disease-ridden precincts. The modern demographic transitions that occurred in Europe at various times from the beginning of the

Box 3.4. *Natural Selection on Cultural Variation.* Suppose that, in some given society, people acquire (culturally) beliefs about the existence of an afterlife in which believers are rewarded. For simplicity, further suppose that there are only two variants—believers and unbelievers. Children acquire their beliefs by imitating one parent and one priest. Parents and priests have different weights in socialization processes, such that the importance of parents can be measured as A and of priests as $1 - A$. Beliefs in an afterlife will affect the chance that their bearer will become a priest or a parent. Let the relative superiority of one variant of the trait at helping their bearers become parents or priests be v and w, respectively. Suppose that believers are more likely to become priests than unbelievers, and thus w is a small positive fraction. Further suppose that believing reduces the likelihood of becoming a parent, and v is a small negative fraction.

The change in the frequency of people who value piety, Δq, is approximately

$$\Delta q \approx q(1 - q)(Av + (1 - A)w)$$

Thus, one of the two beliefs will increase at the expense of the other. Which one depends on the relative magnitude of their effects on life chances and the weight of parents versus priests in what children learn. For example, belief in an afterlife will increase whenever $Av + (1 - A)w > 0$. We might suppose that parents are rather more important in socialization than are priests, so that A is larger than $1 - A$ (say 0.75 and 0.25, respectively). However, becoming a priest may be a more selective process than becoming a parent—almost all priests are believers, while there are many parents of each type. If so, w will be a larger positive fraction than v is a negative one (say 0.1 versus -0.01). If so, $Av + (1 - A)w$ may be positive even if the importance of priests in socialization is relatively small. In our example, the value is $+0.0175$. It is only necessary that becoming a priest is sufficiently more selective to compensate. (See Richerson and Boyd (1984) for details of the analysis. Some generalizations are examined in Boyd and Richerson 1985:Chapter 6.)

nineteenth century onward are another striking example. As people have become wealthier in the industrialized countries, they have tended to lower their fertility and completed family sizes to replacement or even below. This reverses the correlation between wealth and reproductive success often found in rural pastoral and agricultural societies (see Chapters 11 and 12). Coale (1986) has collected some examples of strong fertility control and population declines among rural populations in Europe before the main transition, but these are rather isolated cases, because only urban societies could draw enough cultural recruits to sustain a demographic transition given premodern rates of mortality. Other fertility-controlling subcultures seem to have simply gone extinct.

At least for the modern European transition, a good case can be made for the spread of low-fertility norms due to their effects at promoting cultural success. The modernization of Europe greatly increased the social complexity of European societies. Many new professions arose that were allocated on the basis of achievement, rather than upon inherited rank as was common in premodern Europe. Professional educators to serve the need for universal literacy are one example. Professional entrepreneurs are another. Many of these new roles besides the formal teaching ones carried responsibility for education. Entrepreneurs and business managers had an important role in training factory workers, clerks, and so forth for the new occupations of the industrial era.

Relative to the previous agrarian society, European modernization must have resulted in more nonparental transmission from more competitively selected individuals. Modern data (Terhune 1974) suggest that raising children who are likely to be successful in competition for such roles conflicts with having a large family. Children who do well in school and acquire similar skills for professional and entrepreneurial competition require considerable parental investment. Many readers will be familiar with the conflicts between having families, especially large families, and the demands of modern careers. It seems likely that the occupants of the new competitive roles tended to be drawn from a fraction of the population that already valued small families within which greater investments of parental effort per child were possible. As the weight of "teachers" in cultural transmission increased, and as these roles became allocated on the basis of achievement rather than inheritance, low-fertility norms could spread to the whole population.

Similarly, Knauft suggests, preindustrial cities could draw their population from the countryside despite being demographic "black holes" because of the cultural dominance of the city over the rural population. City elites tended to define the norms and values of the whole society because of their dominance of governmental, economic, and spiritual institutions effective in nonparental transmission of culture, and hence to draw replacement personnel from among members of the demographically successful countryside "infected" with these values.

3.4.2. Why Selection May Allow Culture to Deviate

The fact that natural selection may favor genetically maladaptive traits does not mean that cultural evolution will necessarily result in maldaptive outcomes. Many core beliefs and values are usually acquired from parents and other close relatives, and selection on variants so transmitted will tend to favor genetic-fitness-maximizing behavior. Even if selection acts to increase the frequency of maladaptive beliefs, the effect may be unimportant if direct bias and guided variation are sufficiently powerful to keep genetically maladaptive variants at low frequency. Suppose, for example, natural selection acting on cultural variation favors a belief in a god who rewards the pious in heaven, and that this belief causes people to have families that are smaller than the genetic optimum, either because they join religious orders, or because they devote resources to support the church. Family sizes still might be optimal if the effect of selection is counteracted by direct bias. The evolved predispositions that underlie direct bias (e.g., sexual desire and a love for children) might cause people to reject these religious beliefs, or at least to obey them mainly in the breach.

On the other hand, direct bias and guided variation may often fail to counteract the effects of selection on non–parentally transmitted variation because it is too difficult to determine which beliefs best serve the individual's genetic interest. Earlier we showed that the optimal reliance on cultural transmission depends on the cost of learning and the likelihood of learning errors. When it is difficult to determine which of two variants is best, learning is costly and error prone, and therefore natural selection acting on genes favors a heavy reliance on cultural transmission. Does God exist? If He does, and He rewards the pious, some evolved predispositions—fear of death, love of comfort—may overbalance the desire for a large family and lead people preferentially to adopt the practices sanctioned by religion. But determining whether God exists and exactly what He (She, They) expects of us has proven to be very difficult over the millennia.

The idea of a god who rewards the pious is only an especially striking example of a much larger class of cultural variation about which it is difficult and costly to apply evolved predispositions to make adaptive choices in real environments. The natural world is complex, hard to understand, and variable from place to place and time to time. Is witchcraft effective? What causes malaria? What are the best crops to grow in a particular location? Are natural events affected by human pleas to their governing spirits? The relationship between cause and effect in the social world is often equally hard to discern. What sort of person(s) should one marry? What mixture of devotion to work and family will result in the most happiness or the highest fitness? People can make some intelligent guesses about such decisions, but compared to the variation we observe in others' behavior, the number of alternatives we can investigate in any detail is quite limited. Even if individuals are willing to devote substantial effort to particular decisions, each of us faces too many decisions to make costly investigations concerning all of them. The picture that emerges from behavioral decision theory (Nisbett and Ross 1980) is that people commonly rely on simple, often misleading rules of thumb to make complex decisions. Human decision-making skills seem empirically to be a compromise between the rewards of accurate judgments, and the costs imposed by enlarging the cognitive apparatus and increasing the information collected from the environment.

As the effect of direct bias and guided variation weakens, culture becomes more and more like a system of inheritance. Much of an individual's behavior is a product of beliefs, skills, ethical norms, and social attitudes that are acquired from a set of other people by social learning. To predict how an individual will behave, one must have knowledge about his or her cultural milieu. This does not mean that the evolved predispositions that underlie individual learning become unimportant. Without them cultural evolution would be uncoupled from genetic evolution, and would provide none of the fitness-enhancing advantages that must have favored the evolution of capacities for culture. However, it is also likely that cultural variation often responds to selection for behaviors that conflict with genetic fitness. Selection on genes that regulate the cultural system may still favor cultural transmission, because *on average* it does better than genes could do alone.

These ideas are consistent with much behavioral variation both within and among societies being genetically adaptive. In the view proposed here, people strive to satisfy evolved goals, but in the context of culturally acquired beliefs. Thus, *if the cultural context is taken as given, we would expect that much variation in behavior would be explicable in sociobiological terms*. For example, we would expect that a believer's decision to join a monastery will be influenced by what he or she must give up in order to do so. A wealthy woman may well be more likely to enter a convent than a poorer one if it is customary to marry hypergynously, even if the religious beliefs of the rich and the poor are equally fervent. The same argument applies to variation among societies. People are more likely to become a celibate in a society where they can enhance their relatives' reproductive success because celibates are admired, wealthy, or powerful than in one in which such people are recruited by poor, despised religious minorities that restrict opportunities for nepotism.

More generally, we think it is plausible to view genetic and cultural evolution as a tightly coupled coevolutionary process in humans. In some cases, forces like guided variation and direct bias will be based on genetic variation, strong, and expressed in the environments under which selection produced the guiding rules. In such cases, fitness will be increased by the presence of the cultural system, and behavior may be accurately predicted without explicit reference to the dynamics of cultural evolutionary processes. In other cases, the decision-making forces will be weak, or expressed in a cultural environment that distorts their effects. In these cases, even when the cultural system does act to increase fitness, it will be necessary to account for cultural effects in more detail.

3.4.3. Indirect Bias

A similar argument can be made for two other bias forces, *indirect bias* and *frequency-dependent bias*. These forms of biased transmission allow individuals to better their chance of acquiring adaptive behavior, but at the same time give rise to processes that may not always result in fitness-maximizing behavior.

Indirect bias results when individuals use some traits, for example, those connoting prestige, as an indicator of whom to choose as a cultural model. Once chosen, one may imitate many characteristics of an admired other without further bias. If variants of these latter traits are correlated with the variants of the indictor trait, the correlated variants will increase due to this indirect bias. This process may favor ordinary adaptations and these rules are effective at economizing on information costs. Indirect bias may also allow cultural variation to respond to evolutionary forces in ways that can, under some circumstances, yield different outcomes than would be predicted based on fitness maximization models that ignore cultural inheritance.

There are often likely to be easily visible traits that are correlated with fitness, such as wealth, even when the exact behaviors that contribute most to fitness are very hard to evaluate. In such cases, it makes sense to imitate everything that wealthy people do in an effort to acquire the traits that make them wealthy, but without actually trying to determine exactly how wealth is produced. Irons (1979a) presented evidence from a group of Iranian Turkomen pastoralists that showed social status and biological reproductive success to be strongly correlated. High-status men had larger herds and more wealth, and translated these economic advantages into more wives and more and healthier children. As Borgerhoff-Mulder notes in Chapter 11, a number of studies have documented a similar correlation in other subsistence societies. If wealth partly derives from subsistence or social skills that can be acquired by imitation, it makes adaptive sense to imitate the wealthy. The assumption that wealth is correlated with adaptive behavior is perhaps generally correct; if so it would be sensible to imitate wealthy people even if it is not always very clear just what components of wealthy people's behavior are adaptive.

Studies of the diffusion of innovations (Rogers 1983) document that people use prestige systems in a sophisticated way to acquire new traits. Especially in the case of the poor and less educated, whose ability to bear the costs of direct evaluation of innovations is limited, people tend to adopt the practices of "opinion leaders" of higher status. However, it is people of high *local* status who are preferentially imitated, not socially distant elites whose life situation is very different from potential adopters. When information about a novel behavior is difficult or expensive to acquire, the simple rule, Imitate the most successful people whose general situation is roughly comparable to mine, is likely to be an effective mechanism for acquiring adaptive traits so long as the correlation between cultural and biological success is high. A poor Turkomen herdsman is probably well advised to imitate the herd management practices of his wealthier neighbors and ignore the advice of technical experts whose recommendations may derive from principles developed in Colorado, Switzerland, or New Zealand. The wealthy man, who perhaps can read manuals for himself and can afford to make a few mistakes in search of a high-payoff new method, is more likely to make effective use of such technical experts.

The indirect bias force can lead to dynamics that are similar to runaway sexual selection. Darwin (1871) believed that mate-choice sexual selection (see Chapter 11) was responsible for the maladaptive elaboration of secondary sexual characters such as the feather displays of male peacocks. When there is mate choice based on some visible trait, a trait that was originally correlated with fitness might become wildly exaggerated as evolution comes to respond more to the choice process itself than to ordinary natural selection. This subject remains controversial in evolutionary biology, but in theory this mechanism can operate (Lande 1981; Pomiankowski 1988) and seems to account for otherwise mysterious characters such as the elaborate penises of many insects (Eberhard 1985). The indirect bias process works in a similar way except that individuals choose their cultural parents in addition to their mates based on criteria such as indicators of prestige. Models show that the runaway dynamic is also possible in the case of indirect bias (Boyd and Richerson 1985:Chapter 8). We have argued that many phenomena ranging from maladaptive fads and fashions to group-functional religious beliefs to symbolically marked boundaries between groups might result from the properties of indirect bias (Boyd and Richerson 1987, 1990a; Richerson and Boyd 1989).

3.4.4. Frequency Dependent Bias

Guided variation, direct bias, and natural selection on parentally transmitted variation will tend to cause the most adaptive behavior to be more common than alternative behaviors. Thus, when it is difficult or costly to determine which variants are adaptive, it may be best to bias imitation in favor of the commonest type in the population. Recall the aphorism, When in Rome, do as the Romans do. We label this process *frequency-dependent bias*. Humans are widely suspected of conformity in their behavior, and this bias rule is quite plausibly important.

Frequency-dependent bias may cause group selection to be a more important process in cultural evolution than it seems to be in genetic evolution (see 2.2.2). Consider a large population subdivided into many smaller, partially isolated groups. Frequency-dependent bias reduces variation within groups because rarer variants are less likely to be imitated and therefore to become even rarer. At the same time, frequency-dependent bias increases variation between groups because immigrants entering a group will be rare and also subject to discrimination in transmission. For this reason, group selection may be more important in shaping cultural variation than it is in shaping genetic variation. If so, group level adaptations may be more common in the human species than in other species (Boyd and Richerson 1982, 1985:Chapter 7, 1990b).

Example: Cooperation among Nonrelatives. Human societies exhibit much more cooperation than is typical of vertebrate societies. This tendency is most marked in the complex societies of the last few millennia, where the degree of division of labor, amount of altruistic self-sacrifice, and coordination of complex activities rival and exceed that of the advanced social insects (Campbell 1983). Even the simplest hunting and gathering societies are much more complex and cooperative than the societies of any other social mammal. The human sexes cooperate in an extensive division of labor between hunting and gathering. There is much sharing of food and other resources, especially within bands. Relatively peaceful, cooperative relations are generally maintained between several bands that share a common language and culture, numbering a few hundred to a few thousand individuals. By contrast, even among our closest relatives the chimpanzees, the sexual division of labor is absent, food sharing (other than mothers with offspring) is minimal, and political cooperation is restricted to the handful of closely related males that form the core of a troop (Goodall 1986).

In other animal societies, patterns of cooperation are well explained by kin selection and reciprocal altruism. For example, the complex societies of the social insects are based on kin selection. Only a few closely related individuals are reproductively active in the colony, and the cooperating sterile workers are their offspring (Wilson 1975). The best documented cases of reciprocal altruism, involve pairs of individuals, as in the example of the species of "cleaner" fish and shrimps that eat ectoparasites from the mouths and gills of larger fish (Trivers 1971).

It is an open question whether either of these two mechanisms is sufficient to explain the scale of cooperation observed in even the smallest-scale human societies. The problem with explanations based on kin selection is that humans cooperate with nonrelatives in large-scale societies. Van den Berghe (1981) has proposed that kin selection will account for patterns of cooperation observed in small-scale societies, and that cooperation in complex societies is the result of a cognitive mistake. The empirical problem with reciprocal altruism is that there are no known cases of large-scale cooperation attributable to reciprocity (unless humans are such). Alexander

(1987) proposed that human cooperation is supported by complex webs of "indirect reciprocity" that is restricted to humans because only our species has the cognitive sophistication to keep track of the complex webs of interactions that result.

Darwin (1871) was first to advance the notion that human societies might be subject to group selection, although he was not generally attracted to such explanations. Hamilton (1975) has elaborated this hypothesis, especially in connection with warfare as an agent of effective selection between groups. The empirical problem with this hypothesis, it seems to us, is that human groups are genetically open systems. As Chagnon et al.'s (1970) data for the Yanomamo suggest, groups that are successful in warfare often incorporate female and juvenile captives, and marriage across ethnic boundaries is common in any case. In the famous case of the Nuer expansion in the Sudan in the nineteenth century, wholesale capture and ordinary marriage of the defeated and surrounded Dinka was the demographic mainstay of the expansion (Kelly 1985). In small-scale societies, individuals in groups defeated in war typically disperse to other groups where they have relatives or other connections. These sorts of patterns, if they are indeed general, are those that will tend to reduce any genetic differences between groups and increase genetic heterogeneity within groups. As noted in Chapter 2, lack of genetic isolation of groups is the main difficulty with group selection.

Group selection based on cultural variation is a possible explanation for the evolution of human cooperation. Frequency-dependent bias may maintain enough cultural variation between groups for group selection to be important. It has the by-product of discriminating against rare variants in the population. Thus, a fair amount of immigration of less altruistic individuals (say from bands defeated in war) will not convert a more altruistic group to a less altruistic one. As long as the less altruistic variants are a minority, the conformity effect acts as a powerful impediment to this variant's increase despite assuming the usual within-group advantage to less altruistic behavior. This mechanism does not even require the demographic annihilation of groups with too few altruists, merely their disruption and dispersal of their members. So long as it is rare for such dispersal events to tip more altruistic populations over the threshold where the less altruistic variant begins to increase, between-group selection can be a potent force (Boyd and Richerson 1982, 1985:Chapter 7).

None of these hypotheses is completely implausible. Our theoretical studies of reciprocity in large groups, including models incorporating Alexander's idea of indirect reciprocity and models of punishment, suggest that reciprocity should be restricted to quite small groups (Boyd and Richerson 1988a, 1989b, in press b). Even in groups as small as 6–10, reciprocity is much more difficult to get started in a population than it is when only pairs interact. The models also indicate that a synergistic combination of kin selection and reciprocity does not tend to make it easy to get reciprocity started when rare in larger groups, unlike the case for pairs. However, this area is still poorly explored, and it may be that strategies as yet unmodeled will be more effective. It is certainly possible that some combination of kinship and reciprocity can explain cooperation in small-scale, face-to-face societies. Campbell (1983) argues that cultural group selection is only necessary to explain the levels of cooperation and integration in the complex, large-scale societies of the last few thousand years. These societies are so large as to involve extensive cooperation among largely anonymous masses of people. It is harder to see how kin altruism and reciprocity can knit these societies into workable complexes than in the case of hunting and gathering societies where much of the political power may reside in 100 or so adult males, who cooperate for the most part in coresidential groups of only 10 or so. Critical theoretical and empirical work is only beginning on this important problem.

3.5. RELATIONSHIP TO OTHER VIEWS

3.5.1. Human Sociobiology

The publications of Alexander (1974) and Wilson (1975) mark the advent of human sociobiology. Although neither of these works was primarily concerned with human behavior, both insisted that the rapidly developing evolutionary theory of ecology and social behavior was applicable to the human species. Much of the work in this book has been stimulated by this claim, and, as you have read in Chapters 1 and 2, the commonest method of studying human behavior is the use of fitness optimization and ESS models. Oversimplifying somewhat, human sociobiology has mainly added a genetic evolutionary component to classical rational-choice models (Hirshleifer 1977; Boyd and Richerson 1985:157–166).

Human sociobiologists differ about whether cultural variation within and among contemporary human groups is adaptive. Some (Alexander 1979; Betzig 1986; Turke 1984; Durham 1976) believe that a great deal of contemporary variation is adaptive, that is, that one can generally predict variation in behavior by determining what is fitness maximizing. Of course they admit that exceptions exist: Mistakes occur, many behaviors have little impact on fitness, and even important traits may temporarily drift away from the fitness optima. In general, however, these authors believe that cultural differences represent adaptations. Others, including Tooby and Cosmides (1989) and Barkow (1989), argue that behavior represents an adaptation to

the social and ecological conditions that confronted Pleistocene food foragers (see also Konner 1982; van den Berghe 1981). According to this view,
some cultural variation may be adaptive because the relevant aspects of the
environment have not changed very much. However, there will be much
behavior that is not fitness maximizing under current conditions because the
environment imposed by farming and industrial life is so different from food
foraging. We can still understand human behavior in Darwinian terms, but
only as the result of now outmoded evolved predispositions interacting with
contemporary environments. Symons (1989) has labeled proponents of
these two hypotheses *Darwinian anthropologists*, and *Darwinian psychologists*, respectively.

Our view is both something like Darwinian anthropology and something
like Darwinian psychology. From the former perspective, apparent departures from fitness-optimizing behaviors can be viewed as fitness optimizing
under a constraint of information cost. Like most adaptations, a capacity for
culture has costs as well as benefits. Culture is peculiar only in that some of
the costs of having culture are tolerating its evolutionary activity. Ordinary
learning will often lead to maladaptive behavior because unless it is easy to
learn, individuals will often, more or less at random, learn the wrong thing.
In the case of culture, the errors made will tend to be systematic rather than
random, but so long as the systematic errors are less costly than the unsystematic ones, natural selection will favor capacities for culture. Since all
evolutionary optimization arguments involve constraints (see 2.2.4), the
costly-information argument could be subsumed under Darwinian anthropology.

On the other hand, the key postulate of Darwinian psychology (Barkow
1989; Cosmides and Tooby 1989) is that departures from the expectations of
simple models can be traced to specific evolved psychological mechanisms
acting in specific environments. The costly-information argument similarly
suggests that a tendency to depend upon nonparental transmission, the use
of conformist transmission, and so forth must, averaged over many societies
and long periods of time, be adaptive. These mechanisms, a propensity for
which might well be organic, only go wrong in some times and places. We
suspect that there is nothing magical about the hunting and gathering past.
Even in such societies the evolutionary dynamics of culture likely mattered
because culture helped people to adapt to an environment that was highly
variable in space and time. If so, all the considerations of information cost
constraints we have discussed would have applied. It seems unlikely that a
static "environment of evolutionary adaptedness" would have favored the
evolution of culture capacities in the first place since culture is mainly an
advantage in variable environments. However, it is certainly plausible that
some kinds of departures from basic fitness-optimizing expectations may
have become more dramatic since agriculture so changed the subsistence

and social environment of human populations. It is easy to imagine that the institutions of complex societies are built willy-nilly using a psychology adapted for hunting and gathering.

3.5.2. Darwinism Is Consistent with Many Views of Human Nature

The idea that the human psyche has been shaped by natural selection allows human sociobiologists to make general predictions about human behavior. Darwinian anthropologists think that the beliefs and values that predominate in a particular culture should be the ones that maximize reproductive success in the environment at hand. Darwinian psychologists must understand what past conditions were like, then deduce what kinds of predispositions would maximize fitness under those conditions, and finally predict the effect of the atavistic predispositions in contemporary environments. In either case, making predictions often requires detailed knowledge of the relationship between behavioral variation and variation in reproductive success in particular environments, either past or present. However, there are many behaviors that would seem to be maladaptive in any environment, so both kinds of Darwinians are prepared to agree about a range of general predictions.

Most human sociobiologists agree that the following two principles are necessary consequences of this argument:

> *No group-beneficial explanations*. Human behavior can never be explained in terms of group benefits. Selection should have shaped the human psyche so that individuals' choices increase their reproductive success and that of their relatives, either in contemporary environments or under Pleistocene foraging conditions. In neither case should selection favor behaviors because they benefit a social group. Any observed group benefits must be side effects.

> *No mentalism*. Human behavior is only proximally, not ultimately, the result of cultural rules. Selection should have shaped the human psyche so that individuals constantly modify their behavior in their own interest. Human behavior cannot be explained in terms of cultural history. Rather, it must be explained in terms of the pragmatic consequences for survival and reproduction. This means that behavioral differences between groups are usually the result of environmental or technological differences, not of history.

These two principles are *deductions*, consequences of the belief that natural selection has shaped psychological predispositions that govern human behavior, and given an understanding of what kinds of outcomes are favored by selection. We believe that these deductions do not necessarily follow from Darwinian premises. There is little doubt that the human psyche was shaped by natural selection. However, if our view of culture and its evolutionary origin are correct, this fact does not force us to accept either of these two principles. It is possible that an evolved psychology could cause the evolution and spread of group-beneficial beliefs and values *because* they are group beneficial. It is also possible that an evolved psychology could cause people to adhere to culturally acquired rules, even though those rules are not in their immediate interest, and therefore that sometimes it may be necessary to explain human behavior in terms of cultural history.

We believe that Darwinian theory is a rich source of models of cultural change. It can play a broadly unifying role in the social sciences; its methods of evolutionary analysis should not be viewed as committing one to narrow conclusions about human behavior. The two sociobiological principles mentioned above are in conflict with a great deal of thinking in the social sciences. Thus, human sociobiologists are in the position of saying to whole schools of social science: "If you took the trouble to learn a little about evolution, you would see that your whole view of society and how it works is obviously and egregiously wrong." In contrast, if our view of culture is correct, these are questions for empirical investigation. Human behavior may or may not be purely selfish or bound by cultural rules, depending on the factors discussed above. Thus the debate between human sociobiologists and their critics can be a matter of empirical test rather than dogma. In what follows we illustrate this argument with two examples.

Group-Level Functionalism.   In the social sciences, there is a long tradition of explaining behavior in terms of group-level functions (e.g., Vayda and Rappaport 1968). The insistence of some human sociobiologists that group selection cannot occur (see Chapter 2) has made it seem to some observers as if Darwinian approaches are inherently incapable of offering group functionalist explanations. Rappaport (1987), in a retrospective discussion of his classic (Rappaport 1968) study of ritual and warfare in New Guinea, is unmoved by the arguments of human sociobiologists, arguing that the evidence that humans have group-level functions is virtually inescapable. We believe cultural evolutionary models furnish the tools to investigate such controversies. If humans are unique in the animal world in some behavior, the processes of cultural evolution are a plausible candidate to explain the difference, since we are unique in our reliance on culture. As we noted in section 3.4.4, conformist transmission effects can set up the preconditions for group selection to operate. This or other cultural mechanisms offer testable hypotheses that might account for why humans cooperate on such a large scale without reproductive suppression of the mass of society's members. Studies of the degree to which people really do conform when they acquire cultural traits relevant to cooperation, and of the degree to which between-group cultural variation is actually maintained, should resolve this question.

History and Diffusion. It is interesting to note that the Darwinian project is far from complete in biology. However, disputes are conducted within a broadly Darwinian framework, which does provide a language of communication at the minimum. The recent dispute over the relationship between the long-run fossil record (macroevolution) and the small-scale changes studied by most evolutionary biologists (microevolution) is an example (see also section 5.2). Some paleontologists (e.g., Valentine, 1973) think that the conventional processes of microevolution, when combined with the known evolution of the earth due to plate tectonics, can account well for the fossil record. Others (e.g., Gould 1982) suppose that biological processes that operate over very long time scales are required to account for the fossil record.

The social sciences have long dealt with similar disputes (Vayda and Rappaport 1968; Renfrew 1984; Nelson and Winter 1982 have good discussions of this issue). To what extent can we account for human behavior in terms of responses to immediate environmental contingencies, and to what extent must we consider the effects of history and diffusion? We have already seen that Darwinian psychologists and Darwinian anthropologists give different answers to this question. Are the differences between, say, contemporary Americans and Japanese primarily a result of adaptation to contemporary local circumstances, or to the fact that these societies have developed historically in near isolation and hence have developed very different solutions to the same problems? Both effects are obviously important, and for some traits one or the other explanation clearly predominates. The linguistic differences between Americans and Japanese are almost wholly a product of a long independent history, while the similarities of industrial technology are the result of conscious borrowings and independent inventions of very similar procedures for common purposes.

The most interesting cases are subtler traits, such as social organization. The Japanese have adopted many Western social institutions, such as parliamentary democracy, yet they remain distinctively Japanese in many respects. Some people in Western nations are intensely interested in adopting those features of Japanese social organization that are responsible for their successes in industrial production, but it is not clear just what needs to be copied to replicate this success. In the worst case, we might imagine that the Japanese tendencies to be very good at industrial production but relatively poor at industrial innovation are strongly linked, so that neither society can acquire the strengths of the other without accepting its weaknesses.

Theoretical investigation of this question is still in its infancy, but the general form it will take is easy to see. For historical factors to be important, there must be constraints that prevent evolutionary optima from being reached quickly (on the evolutionary time scale), or there must be processes that multiply equilibria so that different societies can get stuck at different optimal points. Historians (e.g., McNeill 1963) often picture the last 10,000 years of human history as the working out of the potential inherent in the development of agricultural modes of subsistence. The incipient agricultural societies of 10,000 years ago did not advance to the industrial level in a few generations mainly because the innovations required to create such societies occurred sporadically in different locations. Considerable time was required for each innovation, such as iron metallurgy, to diffuse widely and stimulate the next logical step. In our terms, this hypothesis implies that forces like direct bias and guided variation are relatively weak, and that the uncritical transmission of a cultural tradition is a strong effect. On the other hand, it might that social organizational factors are more important than invention of technology per se. Models of the evolution of cooperation in large groups suggest that many different strategies and combinations of strategies can be ESSes, that there are inherently many different stable forms that human social organization might take (Boyd and Richerson 1988a). If, as Marx argued, technical innovations tend to upset existing social arrangements, then the need for social innovation to accompany technical innovation will act as a substantial brake on the latter. Interestingly enough, strong optimum-seeking forces like direct bias and guided variation will *slow* the rate of evolution when there are multiple ESSes because it will be harder for chance effects to help societies slide from a lower local optimum to a higher one. Only some form of group selection between societies or subsocieties (like classes) will be effective in spreading superior innovations, and this may be a slow process (Boyd and Richerson 1990b). Thus, there are several rather different potentially satisfactory explanations for the long-run historical patterns we observe. (For a longer version of this argument, see Boyd and Richerson in press a.)

These examples illustrate one of the important virtues of Darwinian theory: It can be used to capture many different kinds of explanations in a common framework that makes pointed and critical comparison possible. This makes it an unparalleled device for communication between schools and disciplines in the social sciences (as it is in biology). It is a mistake to identify Darwinism too closely with its substantive discoveries in biology, such as the importance of natural selection and the dubiousness of group selection, especially when the application is to a rather peculiar organism like humans with a peculiar system of inheritance like culture. The application of Darwinian methods to culture does not commit one to the adaptationism that results from the simplest models of natural selection. At least to speak for our own experience, conceiving of Darwinian models of (substantively) "un-Darwinian" hypotheses, analyzing simplified versions of them, and considering the implication of the results clarifies complex long-disputed issues such as the possibility of group functions and the role of historical explanations. We believe that such theoretical clarification will make empirical tests more efficient and thus the ultimate resolution of such questions possible.

3.6. SUMMARY

The main aim of this chapter has been to show that cultural evolution is a Darwinian process. Culture is like genes in the sense that information about how to behave is transmitted from individual to individual. Each individual "samples" the culture of the past by observing others or by being taught, and then potentially becomes sampled in turn. But in many other respects, culture is unlike genes. One or many cultural "parents" may be sampled instead of only two, for example. The most fundamental structural difference between genes and culture is that cultural inheritance is a system for the inheritance of acquired variation. Individuals' capacity for learning and decision-making is harnessed directly to the cultural transmission system in ways that apparently do not exist in the case of genes.

The differences between the genetic and cultural systems gives rise to interesting scientific problems. How does the cultural evolutionary process work? How does it interact with the genetic evolutionary process to produce adaptations? What are we to make of apparently maladaptive cultural practices?

The most important difference between the evolutionary processes of the genetic and cultural systems is the existence of decision-making forces in the cultural system. It is not only the survival and fecundity of variant individuals that causes evolutionary change in the cultural system. The decisions that people make as they learn for themselves or decide whom to imitate or what behaviors to adopt also affect cultural evolution.

The decision-making forces—guided variation and the various forms of biased transmission—are what gives the cultural system of inheritance an adaptive advantage in certain kinds of variable environments, according to the theoretical analysis described in section 3.3.1. When individual learning is coupled to the possibility of transmission by imitation, the cultural system can track environmental fluctuations more quickly than can genes, and at a lesser information cost (or with fewer errors) than relying entirely on individual learning. It is optimal to depend mostly on imitation when learning is costly or error prone, and when the environment does not change too rapidly. Even in this case, the small amount of individual learning is important; it causes the population to track the changing environment more effectively than genes, and can give the cultural inheritance system a considerable advantage over the more familiar genes-plus-individual-learning system. Human diet choices, for example, may well be closer to optimal than they otherwise would be due to this effect.

In addition to making ordinary adaptive processes more efficient, the existence of culture may have contributed to qualitatively new human adaptations. Human eusociality is an example. We hypothesize that cultural processes like conformist transmission permit a measure of group selection on cultural variation. The food sharing and division of labor of hunting and gathering bands appears to have been crucial to the extraordinary geographical expansion of the human species during the Pleistocene. The demographic success of complex societies is clearly dependent on cooperation and the division of labor. Culture may be the analog of the peculiar "haplodiploid" system of sex determination in the ants, bees, and wasps that makes sisters more related to each other, and hence prone to the evolution of sterile-worker eusociality. Conformist transmission can raise cultural "relatedness' far above genetic relatedness, even in large groups. Note that in a group in which the cultural environment has evolved to favor altruistic behavior, genetic impulses to altruism might be favored by mate selection. Those with a genetic predisposition to altruism may have had greater mating success.

Finally, there is no guarantee that all cultural traits will be adaptive from the genetic point of view. As the theoretical analysis described in section 3.4.1 shows, the existence of nonparental transmission, among other things, gives culture a measure of evolutionary activity in its own right. When the decision-making that might more closely control cultural evolution is costly, genetic fitness is best served by a system that tolerates some deviance from genetic fitness optimization. Better some systematic cultural deviations from fitness optima than more severe random ones due to individual error.

A quite suggestive case can be made that the theoretically arresting cases of novel human adaptations and unique kinds of maladaptations due to culture are also real and important. But only suggestive! The amount of critical fieldwork and experimentation that has been undertaken to test these ideas is still quite small. We as yet know far less about cultural evolutionary processes and their interactions with the genetic system than we know about ordinary organic evolution. It is an interesting historical paradox that we know least about evolutionary processes in the animal whose evolution interests us most.

CLOSEST KIN

Evolutionary Ecology of Primate Social Structure

Charles H. Janson

4

4.1. INTRODUCTION

4.1.1. The Diversity of Primate Social Systems

Primates have the greatest range of social organization known in any order of vertebrates. The order includes species that are solitary, monogamous, haremlike, multimale promiscuous, polyandrous, live in extended cooperative families, or show a fission-fusion structure in which individuals join and leave temporary subgroups formed by a larger community of known individuals. Significant variation in social behavior is known within each of these categories as well; for instance, monogamous marmosets (Callitrichidae) generally show substantial male parental care, whereas monogamous gibbons (*Hylobates*) show relatively little. There may exist notable social differences even between populations of a single species; humans are perhaps the best but far from unique example.

Primatologists long have recognized that the social variation exhibited within or between species may be related to differences in ecological or sociodemographic variables affecting these populations (Crook and Gartlan 1966). Understanding the ecological bases of social variation in nonhuman primates may help us explain the diversity of human social systems and perhaps even aid us in reconstructing the social systems of our hominid ancestors.

4.1.2. Known Patterns Relating Ecological and Social Variation

The major method used to document possible links between ecology and primate social behavior has been comparisons of diverse species (e.g.,

Crook and Gartlan 1966; Struhsaker 1969; Clutton-Brock and Harvey 1977a,b; Terborgh 1983). This emphasis contrasts with the more hypothetico-deductive (HD), within-species approach long used to study avian social systems (e.g., Lack 1968). This contrast in study methods has several likely causes. First, the intrinsic interest of primates to humans has promoted a wealth of (sometimes superficial) data on the ecological and social habits of most primate species. Second, it may have initially appeared difficult to apply the predictions of simple evolutionary ecology models to organisms already long known to have very complex social relationships. Third, much of the empirical work on wild primates has been performed by social scientists with strong interests in the details of social dynamics and little interest in ecology. The quality of data on primate ecology has generally lagged far behind that on social structure; it is difficult to test even qualitative predictions from most socioecological hypotheses.

The rationale for the comparative approach is that strong correlations between ecological and social variables may imply a causal link, which could then be examined in greater detail by the HD method (see 1.2.2). It is important to treat such correlations with great care, however, as a variety of methodological problems can confound attempts to interpret them. First, two primate species may be similar in ecology and social structure because of recent shared ancestry (phylogenetic heritage) rather than because they have converged on a successful adaptive mode. For instance, Cheverud et al. (1985) used a hierarchical phylogenetic model to investigate a common pattern that primate species with a larger number of females per male in social groups show greater sexual size dimorphism (e.g., Harvey et al. 1978). Under the assumptions of their model, only a tiny fraction of the variation in body size dimorphism was explained by social or ecological differences among living primate species, after phylogenetic heritage was factored out. It is possible that body size dimorphism was adaptive during the initial divergence of higher primate taxa, but that little evolution has occurred within each taxon in body size dimorphism or socioecological variables.

Second, the assumptions underlying common regression statistics often are not met by the data available for comparative studies, biasing tests in systematic ways. For example, several researchers (e.g., Lande 1979) have noted and tried to explain why brain size increases more rapidly with body size when comparing higher taxa (e.g., families within an order) than with lower ones (species in a genus). Pagel and Harvey (1989) showed that this trend emerges largely because body size is not measured without error (as assumed in conventional regression).

Third, many social and ecological traits are interrelated, so that a significant correlation between a particular pair of variables may imply little about their causal connection unless confounding variables are held constant. In this case one can get the right result for the wrong reason. One example is

Waser and Case's (1981) analysis of how competition between primate species affects their relative abundances. After showing that groups of some primate species predictably displace other species from food trees, Waser and Case use this competitive hierarchy along with observed encounter rates between different species to predict their relative population sizes. The match between predicted and observed population sizes is close and seems to confirm the importance of between-species competition in structuring primate communities. However, a species' population density is largely determined by its territory size, which in turn strongly affects the encounter rate among groups. Waser and Cases's use of encounter rates to predict population densities may reverse the order of cause and effect, and it should produce a good match between predicted and observed population sizes whether or not between-group aggression occurs. Therefore, the importance of between-species food competition in determining primate population sizes is still unresolved.

Despite these methodological difficulties, the comparative method has produced several robust generalizations relating ecology to social structure (Crook and Gartlan 1966; Clutton-Brock and Harvey 1977a; 1977b; Terborgh and Janson 1986). Among the more important are:

1. Nocturnal species are nearly all solitary or live in minimal social units (e.g., a breeding pair with offspring). This pattern is variously interpreted as the result of phylogeny (Clutton-Brock and Harvey 1977a), lack of effective group-based tactics to avoid night predation (Terborgh 1983), or constraints imposed by the food sources of nocturnal species, which mainly are scarce, dispersed insects (Charles-Dominique 1977).

2. Terrestrial species often have much larger groups than do arboreal ones. This contrast may be due to greater predation risk on the ground (Crook and Gartlan 1966) or to the more even distribution of terrestrial versus arboreal food sources (Clutton-Brock and Harvey 1977a).

3. Leaf-eating primates often have smaller groups than do related species that eat more fruit. Since most of these contrasting species are from similar habitats and of similar body size, the social differences likely relate to differences in the abundance and distribution of their food resources. In particular, fruit trees tend to be less common and more productive than are sources of palatable leaves, which are more evenly distributed but of relatively low energy yield (Hladik 1975).

4. Social groups with larger biomass have larger home ranges and travel farther per day than do smaller groups, at least in fruit-eating species (Clutton-Brock and Harvey 1977b). The greater collective energy demands of larger social groups may contribute to such trends (Waser 1977).

These generalizations focus on group size, because the number of animals in a group necessarily constrains most other aspects of social structure (e.g., mating system: Terborgh 1983; Andelman 1986), in addition to which it is one of the easiest aspects of social structure to observe and measure.

In sections 4.2–4.4, I will discuss in detail three major hypotheses suggested to explain the foregoing and other patterns relating to group size. Section 4.5 will examine attempts to integrate several of the preceding hypotheses into a more general theory of social structure. Sections 4.6 and 4.7 will then treat a few hypotheses relating to other aspects of social structure (e.g., territoriality, mating system, aggressive hierarchies, birth sex ratios). Section 4.8 will discuss the shortcomings of existing data and study methods, and will suggest some possible solutions. Finally, section 4.9 will focus on the possible use of these studies in our understanding of human social behavior.

4.2. EFFECTS OF GROUP SIZE ON REDUCING INDIVIDUAL FOOD ACQUISITION

The most intensively studied ecological factor in primates is acquisition of food, at least in part because most primate species spend half or more of their time searching for, traveling between, and consuming food sources (e.g., Clutton-Brock and Harvey 1977a). Early observations suggested that primates were not necessarily food limited, because they often appear very wasteful feeders in fruit trees (e.g., Howe 1980) or spend large portions of every day resting (e.g., Crockett and Eisenberg 1987). Nevertheless, early socioecological models emphasized the likely importance of social group size in either hindering or facilitating individual food intake.

4.2.1. Theory

In separate models, Eisenberg et al. (1972) and Altmann (1974) both postulated that primates in a group would overlap individual search fields and thus reduce each other's rate of encounter with food. They predicted that large social groups could exist only when food occurred in large productive patches, so that competition for the food in a patch would be low (for a more quantitative treatment, see Clark and Mangel 1984). In unproductive patches, members of large groups would suffer reduced food intake and as a result (for females) lowered production of offspring. Natural selection would then favor tendencies of individuals to form smaller groups because such individuals produce more offspring than those that tolerate larger aggregations.

This theory assumes that primates discover new food sources while they forage. How can we deal with the common case in which primate groups exploit a set of previously known food sources (e.g., Milton 1981; Garber 1988a)? In this case, an individual's knowledge of food sources is analogous to its search field. If group members largely overlap in their knowledge of food sources, then each one must share access to food patches it knows without much benefit from using food items known only by other individuals. For members of groups of different sizes to have the same per capita encounter rate with food sources, indvdiuals must not overlap either in their search for new food sources or in their knowledge of previously used food sources (Janson 1988a).

It is sometimes difficult to define a food source. When it is clear that food is discontinuously distributed in space (as is often true for fruiting trees), specifying a distinct source is easy. However, when food is evenly and commonly distributed within a habitat (e.g., leaves), the question arises whether each food item encountered or the entire habitat is a food source. This distinction is important, because individual food items are usually too small to be shared profitably, whereas the habitat may be very large and contain many food items, thus allowing many animals to feed together without competition. This quandary leads to the paradox that sparse, evenly distributed food sources (insects, grass corms) have been used to explain both the solitary life-style of prosimians (Charles-Dominique 1977) and large social groups of baboons (*Papio*; Dunbar 1988).

To help resolve this paradox, it is important to realize that species may differ in how easily group members can stay in contact. If individuals can maintain a cohesive group while far enough apart to exploit separate food sources, then food competition will be low and group sizes large. Conversely, if group members must stay close enough that they usually overlap at a given food source, then food competition will be high and group size small (unless each food source is very productive). Prosimians may be solitary not because insects are evenly distributed in space, but because at night they could not maintain contact over the distances required to avoid competition between neighbors. In contrast, baboons can comprise large groups, despite the small size and even distribution of the grass corms they eat, because the open savanna habitat during daytime allows them to maintain contact while spaced far enough apart to avoid significant food competition (Post et al. 1980).

These examples demonstrate that defining a food patch requires data in addition to the dimensions or productivity of the food source itself. In particular, it is important to know the abundance of food patches relative to the distance required for social contact, which depends on both the physical habitat and the proximate mechanisms (sights, sounds) used to maintain spacing between individuals. A particular distribution or abundance of food sources may produce very different levels of food competition depending on other aspects of a group's social structure.

*4.2.2. Testing Predictions from the Hypothesis
of Within-Group Competition*

The theory discussed above predicts that, within a species and study site, individuals in larger groups should suffer foraging disadvantages relative to members of small groups. Only where compensating advantages exist (see below) is formation of stable groups favored in the face of such foraging costs. These costs are smallest when food occurs in local productive patches, so that there is lots of food to share within a patch, and little food to be found outside it. Thus, a species using highly productive patches can live in larger groups than can another species that feeds on less productive resources (all else being equal).

Several studies compare food distributions and group sizes of two closely related species living in the same habitat. Clutton-Brock (1974) showed that group sizes of two African colobus species fit the theory neatly, with the large-grouped species, red colobus (*Colobus badius*), depending on relatively few, productive patches of new-leaf growth, whereas the small-grouped species, black-and-white colobus (*C. guereza*), fed mostly on common but unproductive sources of mature leaves. Hladik (1975) found similar results in two species of another genus of leaf-eating primates, the langurs (*Presbytis*), and Janson (1986) noted an analogous contrast in the New World fruit-eating capuchin monkeys (*Cebus*). Comparisons across a broader taxonomic range of primates living in a single habitat generally demonstrate the same trends (Klein and Klein 1975; Terborgh 1983).

A few studies try to pinpoint which characteristic of food sources best correlates with foraging group size. Leighton and Leighton (1982) measured both the physical dimensions and number of fruits (using fallen fruit husks) of 18 individual *Trichilia cipo* trees and then recorded the foraging subgroup size of mantled howler monkeys (*Alouatta palliata*) using trees of different physical dimensions. They found that a tree's physical dimension was a good correlate of foraging subgroup size, and concluded that this relationship was due to the larger number of fruits available in larger trees. Terborgh (1983) also showed that food tree crown diameter (and presumed food abundance) was the best correlate of social group size across five fruit-eating primates in Peru. Both outcomes are somewhat tentative because neither study controlled for the spacing between food trees relative to group cohesion (see 4.2.1.).

Comparisons of groups of one species within a single study have examined the interaction between food availability and group size. In black spider monkeys (*Ateles paniscus*), Symington (1988) found that foraging group size increases in parallel with seasonal food availability. Waser (1977) showed that members of large social groups of white-cheeked mangabey (*Cercocebus albigena*) forage farther per day than those in small groups, a pattern he attributed to greater food competition in the larger groups. Larger groups are found to travel farther in several other primate species as well (e.g., Janson 1988b; van Schaik and van Noordwijk 1988; Symington 1988).

4.2.3. Testing Assumptions of the Hypothesis of Within-Group Competition

Many studies on different primate species support the *predictions* of Eisenberg et al.'s and Altmann's models (see 4.2.2), but only recently have detailed feeding studies directly analyzed the central *assumption* of those models: that individual food intake is reduced when the number of individuals foraging together exceeds the local availability of food. Several researchers (Janson 1988b; Chapman 1988; White and Wrangham 1988) have now found that individual food intake is severely reduced (by 50–90%) in larger groups when feeding in small-crowned food trees, but not when using large-crowned ones.

In Janson's study, the average feeding time per group member during a visit to a given species of food tree was examined as a function of group size (number of individuals) in several brown capuchin (*Cebus apella*) groups. In small trees (crown diameter less than 10 m), average food intake was nearly exactly inversely proportional to group size, as though a small constant amount of food was divided among all group members. Conversely, in large food trees (crown diameter of 20 m or more) with abundant ripe fruit, average food intake was the same in small and large groups. The apparent lack of competition in such large trees suggests that each individual eats its fill during a feeding bout. If so, the larger the amount of food in a tree, the more individuals can feed together without reducing each other's food intake and lowering per capita fitness (cf. Whitten 1983). These studies document the mechanism used to explain previously observed correlations between group size and tree size both within and across species.

An additional assumption of Altmann's model is that feeding competition depends on the spacing between individuals. Two studies on spatial structure in capuchin monkeys showed that some group members suffer reduced food intake when they have other group members close to them compared to when they have no near neighbors (Robinson 1981; Janson 1990). Similar work on other species is needed to see if this pattern is general.

Even if individuals in large groups usually have reduced food intake within a food patch, they may not end up with lower daily net energy intake than individuals in small groups. In three recent studies that estimated the effect of group size on an individual's total or net energy intake per day, two (Stacey 1986; Janson 1988b) found no effect of group size, while another (van Schaik and van Noordwijk 1988) found a nonsignificant decrease in net energy intake in larger groups. The most detailed is Stacey's study on yellow baboons (*Papio cynocephalus*). He focused only on the dominant adult male in three groups of different sizes, thus controlling for the effects of age, sex, and dominance status on food intake. By combining intensive measurements of time spent ingesting different food types with their energetic values (from nutritional analysis), he provided an accurate estimate of the total energy consumption of the different males. These values did not correlate with group size, and they were so close to each other that the differences were almost certainly not important. Janson (1988b) found much the same pattern for the average individual in different group sizes of brown capuchins, despite clear evidence that individuals in larger groups had reduced food intake per food patch visited. It appears that individuals in large groups may compensate for reduced foraging efficiency within patches by increasing their daily foraging time or by other means. As Waser (1977) originally suggested, individual members of larger groups do not always suffer nutritionally.

If individuals in large and small groups have equal net energy intake, what limits group size in such a population? To achieve this energetic equality, individuals in large groups often must compensate for lower food intake per patch with increased foraging effort. In this case, the maximum group size may be set by limits on increasing foraging effort. Such limits may occur because of trade-offs between foraging and other fitness-enhancing activities. Individuals that forage longer per day must have less time to spend in other activities such as social interaction or hiding from predators (Janson, 1988b, see also Chapter 7). Such trade-offs are poorly documented (review in Dunbar 1988: 93), and their fitness effects are virtually unknown.

Increased foraging effort may also be limited by absolute constraints such as day length. For instance, in brown capuchins, individuals in the largest observed groups foraged essentially every daylight minute, while individuals in small groups could rest and socialize up to 2 hours per day (Janson 1988b). Because members of the largest social groups cannot increase their foraging time, adding one individual to the current maximum group size should reduce the mean energy intake of other members by about 6%, a magnitude of difference associated with increased death rates and reduced birth rates in other primate species (Dittus 1977). As group size increases, individuals cannot constantly increase foraging effort to make up for reduced intake per food source, so individual food intake must eventually decline.

4.3. EFFECTS OF GROUP SIZE ON INCREASING INDIVIDUAL FOOD ACQUISITION

4.3.1. Theory

Various models postulate foraging benefits for members of larger groups. One possible benefit is a greater discovery rate of food sources when members spread themselves apart and search more area per unit time (Eisenberg et al. 1972; Altmann 1974). This benefit requires that individuals allow other group members to feed in food sources that they discover. Thus, the benefit of an increased group encounter rate with food is offset by the sharing of each food source among group members. In fact, if each food source found could be consumed entirely by the discoverer, then the cost of sharing outweighs the benefit of increased discovery—per capita average food intake rate is independent of or decreases with larger group size (Clark and Mangel 1984; Janson 1988a). Some resources may provide more food than a single individual can consume, either because they produce more food than the animal needs or because the animal's feeding time is limited by some nonsocial circumstance (e.g., limited day length or the arrival of a predator). In this case, individuals in a larger group would benefit from the discovery of such large patches by other group members without incurring the costs of sharing food, at least until group size exceeds the productivity of the food source.

Although this benefit of group foraging has the potential for wide application, its practical significance is probably small. Plant food sources with enough production to satiate more than one animal are generally those most likely to be remembered rather than discovered (e.g., Garber 1988a). Even though such productive trees are often rare and ripen asynchronously, monkeys regularly monitor such trees and seem to have a detailed knowledge of both their locations and approximate ripening status (Milton 1981). As explained above (4.2.1.), if group members overlap in their memory of such sharable food sources, then the total number of food sources available to the group will not increase as rapidly as does group size. There are, however, some food types both productive and ephemeral (thus not worthwhile or possible to remember), such as outbreaks of insects, new leaf growth, and certain synchronously ripening fruit trees.

A second benefit of social foraging might be to reduce the *variation* in food encounter rates (Rubenstein 1982) or to allow the entire group to survive rare crises by sharing in the knowledge that a few individuals retain of unusual or distant food or water sources (Altmann 1974). Reducing variation in resource encounter rates reduces an individual's chance of a critical nutrient shortfall (cf. McNamara and Houston 1986). When resource location or abundance is variable, it may increase an individual's fitness to avoid long periods without food even at the cost of a reduced average food intake due to competition from other group members.

A third benefit of group foraging might be that larger groups of primates are dominant to smaller groups and thus might displace them, gaining preferred access to desirable feeding patches (Wrangham 1980). Wrangham envisions that a small group of cooperating individuals or a large group of noncooperating ones can be displaced from a patch by a large group of cooperating animals. The advantages of cooperation and large group size

Table 4.1.   *Proposed Foraging Costs and Benefits to Individuals as a Function of Increasing Group Size*

Costs	Benefits
1. Reduced food intake within a patch 2. Increased foraging effort and consequent lost opportunities for other activities	1. Sharing access to new-found patches 2. Reduced variation in intake rate 3. Ability to displace smaller groups from preferred feeding patches

are counterbalanced by the costs of within-group food competition. An individual's net benefit of being in a group of a given size will depend on the productivity of food patches and the frequency of between-group contests (Wrangham 1980), although the precise form of this relationship has not been modeled. The effects of increasing group size on average per capita food intake are summarized in Table 4.1.

4.3.2. Data on Group Foraging Benefits

Field data to test whether or not group foraging produces net energetic benefits are scarce. The hypothesis that larger groups may benefit from sharing newly found food patches was tested by Janson (1988b) for brown capuchins. It was often not possible to know whether any given patch visited was newly found by the animals feeding there, but Janson reasoned that if larger groups search for food over a broader swath than do smaller groups, the former should encounter and use more fruit trees per unit distance traveled.

During 18 months, Janson followed four capuchin groups, which had average sizes of 2 to 12 individuals (excluding infants). Each day, all fruit trees fed in for at least 5 minutes by one or more monkeys were identified and labeled. Despite the sixfold variation in group size, larger groups did not predictably use more fruit trees per unit distance traveled. If anything, it seemed that the largest group used slightly fewer (16%) trees per distance traveled than did the smallest group. Similarly, Garber (1988b) found that the rate of fruit trees used per distance actually increased when group size decreased among moustached tamarins (*Saguinus mystax*), although this may have been due to the smaller group's willingness to use less productive fruit trees. Thus, existing data do not support the idea that larger groups encounter food sources more often than do small groups in the same area. The second possibility, that individuals in larger groups may have less variable rates of food intake than those in smaller groups, remains unexamined.

That larger groups compete with smaller ones to gain preferential access to rich food sources is supported by much anecdotal data. Aggressive contests between groups at or near fruit trees are common in many primate species (e.g., Cheney 1981, Garber 1988b). One published study has measured the importance of such between-group competition to the energy budget of a monkey group (Janson 1985). In this study on brown capuchins, larger groups ate at most only 4% more food than did smaller groups because of between-group displacements at food trees. By comparison, the foraging efficiency (food ingested per unit distance traveled) of small groups was up to four times greater than that of large groups (Janson 1988b).

The most convincing evidence for the benefits of sociality in between-group competition comes from aggressive defense of *territories* (not fruit trees as first postulated by Wrangham 1980). Several reports show that larger groups displace smaller groups, restricting the movement of the latter in space (e.g., Garber 1988b), and that home ranges occupied by larger groups may be richer than those of smaller groups (e.g., Cheney and Seyfarth 1987). Such evidence is suggestive but not conclusive, because even without between-group competition, groups that happen to live in richer areas should have higher birth rates and thus grow to larger sizes (Janson and van Schaik 1988).

4.4. EFFECTS OF GROUP SIZE ON AN INDIVIDUAL'S RISK OF PREDATION

A frequently cited benefit of large group size in primates is the reduction of individual risk of predation (e.g., Alexander 1974; Terborgh 1983). There is no question that many primate species are subject to predation (Cheney and Wrangham 1987). However, because of low death rates, it is difficult to estimate even the average rate of predation on a species, let alone predation rates in different sizes of groups. Support for predation avoidance as an important benefit of primate sociality has come largely from theory and indirect tests. Moreover, the costs of group size in attracting predators have been largely ignored.

4.4.1. Benefits of Sociality in Reducing
Individual Predation Risk

There exists a substantial body of mathematical theory demonstrating the potential benefits of social groups in reducing predation rates on individuals (Hamilton 1971; Vine 1971; Taylor 1979; Pulliam 1973). These models focus mostly on two major benefits of group size: the dilution effect and the vigilance effect. The former states that the chance that a particular prey individual is killed per successful predator attack on a group decreases as group size increases (Hamilton 1971). The extent of this benefit depends on how many prey a predator or group of predators can kill per attack on a given prey group. If predators are solitary and can kill only one prey per attack, the probability that a given individual in a group of N animals dies per predator attack is 1/N (Bertram 1978). An individual can reduce this risk by placing other group members between it and the approaching predator (Hamilton 1972). This benefit necessarily comes at a cost to other group members.

The vigilance effect proposes that a predator attack will be detected by some group member earlier if more individuals are vigilant (Pulliam 1973). If the detecting animal alerts other group members, then earlier detection is more likely to cause the attack to fail. This benefit comes at a cost to each vigilant individual—vigilance often requires visual behaviors and careful attention that are incompatible with other routine activities like feeding or grooming. Greater predator detection requires only that *total* group vigilance increases, so individuals in larger groups can each spend less time vigilant and still be safer from predators than members of smaller groups. The "extra" time gained can be devoted to activities that enhance fitness, such as feeding or social interactions (Caraco 1979). A final possibility, that large groups can more successfully deter or counterattack predators, may occur in some primate species (e.g., Altmann and Altmann 1970). However, it is not likely to be important for the majority of primate species that live in closed forests, where counterattack is not usually feasible (Terborgh 1990).

4.4.2. Evidence That Predation Favors Increased Sociality

Attacks on primate groups generally are infrequent and observed deaths from predation even scarcer (Cheney and Wrangham 1987). Without an adequate measure of predation risk, it is not possible to test in detail whether higher rates of predation favor larger group sizes or other aspects of sociality. However, simply comparing a primate species in predator-rich and predator-poor areas could qualitatively test the effects of predation on sociality. Van Schaik and van Noordwijk (1985) found that long-tailed macaques (*Macaca fascicularis*) on mainland Sumatra (with tigers) lived in larger social groups than those living on the island of Siberut (no tigers). This result is consistent with predator theory, but food availability for the two populations was not measured, so food-related explanations for the difference in group size cannot be ruled out. Dunbar (1988) tried to correct this problem in his comparison of gelada baboon (*Theropithecus gelada*) group sizes in different study sites. Dunbar ranked the study sites in terms of (1) risk of predation as measured by the availability of escape routes to the baboons, (2) food abundance as measured by grass cover, and (3) mean foraging party size of the geladas. He found that predation risk was positively related to party sizes across study sites, but that food abundance did not help explain variation in party size either by itself or in conjunction with predation risk.

4.4.3. Testing the Premises of Antipredator Benefits of Large Group Size

It is difficult to test between-population or -species consequences of different levels of predation risk, so most work seeks to verify that the assumptions in models of social predation avoidance are reasonable and to test predictions about *within*-population behavioral responses.

If avoiding predation is a major benefit of sociality, then it should be true that (1) predation is indeed an important source of mortality, and (2) larger groups can either detect or drive away predators more effectively than can smaller groups. With respect to (1), predation has been observed or strongly suspected in nearly all primate species studied for extensive periods (Cheney and Wrangham 1987). Actual deaths due to predation rarely are witnessed, but could be a significant source of selection on animals that are as long-lived as most primate species.

Data on predator detection or deterrence by groups of different sizes are scarce. In a study comparing groups of several species, van Schaik et al. (1983) found that alarm calls were elicited by the approach of humans at greater distances from large primate groups than from small groups. Despite several accounts of primate groups driving away terrestrial predators (review in Cheney and Wrangham 1987), it is not clear if such deterrence is a habitual response or is related to group size. Mobbing of aerial predators by forest primates does occur, but it probably does not drive away the predator by intimidation (Terborgh 1990).

If individuals in larger groups are safer from predation, they may adjust their antipredator behaviors (Caraco 1979). Several studies have shown that individuals do adjust vigilance effort to reflect their predation risk at any given time. For instance, de Ruiter (1986) showed that members of a large weeper capuchin (*C. olivaceus*) group spent significantly less time in vigilance behavior than did individuals in a small group. Likewise, animals on the periphery of a group are more exposed to predators and should spend more time being vigilant than should central ones; such a pattern has been found several times in primates (Robinson 1981; van Schaik and van Noordwijk 1989; Janson 1990). Finally, Boinski (1987) showed that seasonal changes in vigilance by adult squirrel monkeys (*Saimiri oerstedi*) were strongly associated with changing predation risk to the offspring.

Although all members of a group may share reduced predation risk as group size increases, individuals do not necessarily share equally the costs of predator deterrence. In particular, adult males, which are usually larger and stronger than adult females, seem to play a special role in vigilance and defense of group mates from predators, especially in savanna-dwelling primate species (DeVore and Washburn 1963; Rhine 1975). A novel experimental study by van Schaik and van Noordwijk (1989) on forest-dwelling brown capuchin monkeys clearly shows the role of adult males in detecting predators. An artificial model of a Harpy eagle was placed in a tree to monitor the behavior of capuchins as the group approached. After many such experiments, it was clear that subordinate adult males were several times as likely as other group members to be the first to detect the models. This difference was due both to their peripheral location in the group and to vigilance rates sometimes twice as high as other individuals.

4.4.4. When Are Small Groups Safer from Predators?

Individuals in large social groups may also suffer costs with respect to predation. Predators may detect large groups more easily than lone animals, because the former make more noise and have a larger spatial spread (Vine 1973). If so, the rate of predator attacks on groups (and the individuals contained therein) will increase with group size. Even if predators detect large and small groups with equal ease, predators may attack large prey aggregations repeatedly after they detect them. Such multiple attacks might occur for several reasons: (1) The predator may be capable of ingesting more than a single prey (Taylor 1976); (2) even a low chance of capturing prey in an alerted social group might be more rewarding than finding a new group of prey (Stephens and Krebs 1986:42–44); (3) the predator hunts in groups and thus can process multiple kills (as do many human hunters). Multiple attacks and easy detection may increase the rate over time of predator attacks on individuals in larger groups. If this increase in attack rate offsets the benefits to group-dwelling individuals of dilution and vigilance, then a given prey individual's risk of death from predation will increase with group size (Vine 1971, 1973; Taylor 1979).

To date, no published study of predation in primates has had sufficient scope to compare predator attack rates on groups of different sizes. However, evidence from extensive primate censuses performed during the 1970s showed that primates living in large social groups were generally easier for human observers to detect than were species that lived in small groups, and that such a trend could occur even within a species (National Research Council 1981). Studies of greater detail are needed to determine how detectability varies with group size.

The possibility that high predation pressure favors minimal sociality has been suggested for several primate species, all of which employ concealment to avoid predators (Gautier-Hion and Gautier 1978; Terborgh 1983).

These authors argue that hiding effectively from predators can only be achieved by small groups. However, group size in these species may be limited by other factors, so their use of concealment to avoid detection is an adaptive response to small group size, rather than vice versa. For instance, solitary individuals (often males) in otherwise social species are more quiet and cautious than their counterparts in social groups (Tsingalia and Rowell 1984). In one case, social variation within a single monkey species (the simakobu, *Simias concolor*) clearly points to a reduction in sociality where human predation increases (Watanabe 1981). This monkey species lives in both monogamous and small polygynous groups. Comparisons of several populations show that monogamous groups are most common where human hunting is intense, especially near roads. Either small groups evade detection by hunters or hunted populations have been reduced well below densities typical for species in unhunted areas.

4.5. PUTTING DIFFERENT HYPOTHESES TOGETHER

The two major ecological benefits of large social groups are avoidance of predation and access to better resources via between-group food competition (Figure 4.1). Because predation rates are difficult to measure, evidence for predation as a factor favoring large groups rests on a few intraspecific comparisons across several sites with different predation risks and on group size–related trends in vigilance and other antipredator tactics. Such evidence should be collected for many more primate species to evaluate the generality of predation as a selective force on sociality. It is much easier to obtain data on feeding rates, yet quantitative data to show the effect of

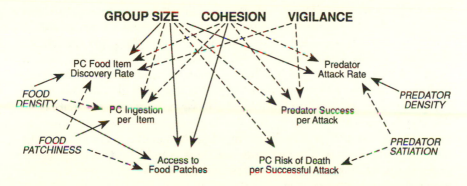

Figure 4.1.   Effects of selected social variables (in bold capitals) and external ecological variables (in italic capitals) on primate foraging success and predation risk. PC signifies per capita. Solid arrows denote positive effects, dashed arrows show negative effects. For details, see text.

between-group competition for food on individual food intake are mostly lacking. Nevertheless, anecdotal data suggest that such competition is widespread among primate species.

Several ecological costs to sociality in primates have been suggested and partly documented (e.g., increased parasitism—Freeland 1976; Hausfater and Meade 1982). Existing models all assume that the most significant of these costs is within-group competition for food, which has been measured in detail for a variety of primate species. Studies suggest that an individual's foraging efficiency is markedly reduced by larger group size, although higher foraging effort or changes in food choice may partly offset this cost. If observed group sizes result from a balance of ecological costs and benefits, the two major trade-offs we can examine are the cost of within-group food competition versus the benefit of between-group food competition (Wrangham 1980) and the cost of within-group food competition versus the benefit of predation avoidance (van Schaik 1983; Terborgh 1983).

4.5.1. Within-Group versus Between-Group Food Competition

Predictions about the effects of within- versus between-group competition for food have focused on either food intake (Wrangham 1980) or reproductive consequences of food intake (van Schaik 1983; Dunbar 1988). In Wrangham's discussion, the benefits to larger groups of increased access to rich food patches would initially outweigh the costs of dividing the food within a patch among more group members; per capita food intake should increase with group size. This increase would continue up to an optimal group size, above which food competition within the group outweighs the benefit of large group size in between-group competition, and per capita food intake would decline. It has proven difficult to verify this prediction since few studies on primates have estimated per capita food intake in groups of different sizes (Janson and van Schaik 1988). However, per capita fecundity should roughly parallel food intake (e.g., Mori 1979), so van Schaik (1983) reasoned that if between-group competition provided a net feeding advantage to larger groups, birth rates should also increase with group size, at least initially (Figure 4.2a). However, in regression analyses of the average numbers of infants per female versus group size in 27 primate populations, van Schaik found only five positive relations and only one of these was significantly different from zero. He concluded that few, if any, populations of primates obtain a net foraging benefit (as measured by fecundity) with increasing group size. Later analyses (see Dunbar 1988) have criticized and revised some of van Schaik's analysis, but do not change the major conclusion that only a few primate species appear to show foraging advantages for larger groups.

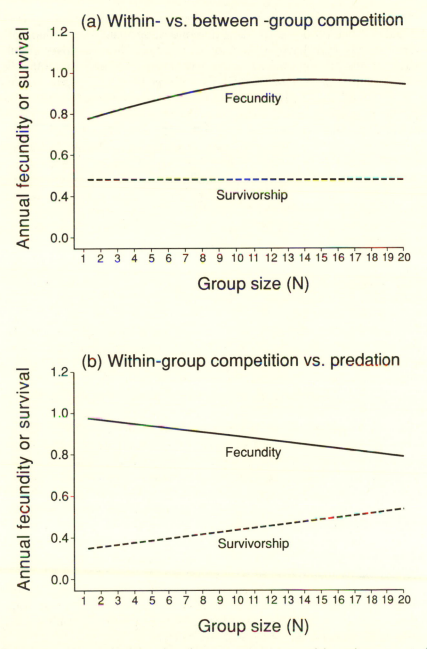

Figure 4.2. *Expected relationships between group size and fecundity or survival when the cost of increasing group size is greater within-group competition for food, and the benefit is either increased access to food patches (a) or reduced risk of predation (b). Redrawn after van Schaik (1983).*

Since van Schaik's paper appeared, several field studies have provided refined and more conclusive data demonstrating that larger groups of a given species may have substantial fecundity advantages over smaller groups (Dittus 1986; Cheney and Seyfarth 1987; Robinson 1988). For instance, Robinson's long-term analysis of birth rates in 10 weeper capuchin groups showed that groups below a critical size (15 individuals) actually had negative population growth rates, while larger groups had reliably positive growth rates. These differences in growth rates were caused nearly entirely by changes in birth rates rather than in death rates. These studies lack detailed data to show that the higher birth rates of females in larger groups are attributable directly to increased food availability. Such ecological data are crucial, because even without preferred access to food, females in larger groups could have higher birth rates because they spend less time being vigilant for predators and thus have more available time for foraging (cf. Caraco 1979).

4.5.2. Within-Group Food Competition versus Predation Avoidance

As noted earlier, evidence for the importance of sociality in avoiding predators is difficult to obtain. In addition, food intake (affected by within-group food competition) and risk of death (from predation) are measured in different units and are therefore hard to compare. These difficulties make existing tests of this trade-off indirect. One approach is to examine the effects of group size on demographic correlates of these ecological factors (Figure 4.2b; van Schaik 1983). Of 27 primate populations analyzed by van Schaik, 22 showed a declining fecundity with increasing group size, consistent with the prediction that within-group competition restricts food intake for individuals in larger groups. Although only 2 of the 22 regression analyses had a significantly negative slope, the chance of finding 22 of 27 regressions to be negative is very small. In most of the same populations, juveniles appeared to survive better in larger groups. This trend is consistent with the notion that predation rates decrease in larger groups, because other likely causes of juvenile mortality (social harassment, starvation) should increase rather than decrease with group size.

An alternative way to examine the interplay of within-group food competition and predation avoidance is to predict group sizes as a function of known ecological conditions. Terborgh (1983) proposed a graphical model of the trade-off between predation avoidance and within-group food competition, later modified by Dunbar (1988) (Figure 4.3). Based on a strong positive correlation between social group size and fruit tree size across five New World primate species, Terborgh reasoned that competition for food within crowns of individual trees would increase rapidly when the number

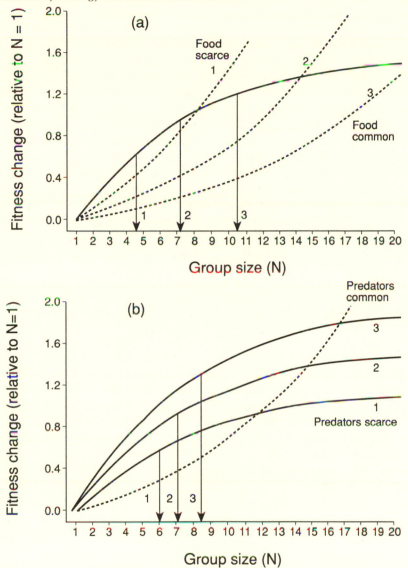

Figure 4.3.   *Predicted effects of variation in food availability or predator density on optimal group size. Fitness benefits are shown as solid lines and costs as dashed lines. (a) Predator density is constant but food availability increases from curves 1 to 3, resulting in lower costs of increasing group size. The predicted optimal group sizes (1–3) increase as food availability increases. Redrawn from Terborgh (1983). (b) Food availability is constant, but predator density increases from curves 1 to 3, resulting in increased benefits to larger group sizes. The predicted optimal group sizes (1–3) increase regularly as predator density increases. Modified from Dunbar (1988). Similar predictions hold for the evolutionarily stable group size (at the crossing of the cost and benefit curves).*

of individuals exceeded the number that could comfortably feed in the average tree crown visited by that primate species. Benefits from predation avoidance were assumed to increase with group size, most rapidly at small group sizes and more slowly for very large groups (Terborgh and Janson 1986; Dunbar 1988) (Figure 4.3a). For example, in the dilution effect discussed above (4.4.1), the increase in per capital survival caused by adding one animal to a group of N is $1/(N^2 + N)$, which becomes minuscule as N grows large. Where predators are more numerous, the predation rate is higher and the potential benefits to be gained from avoiding predators should also be greater. From these assumptions, Terborgh (1983) argued that group sizes should increase linearly with increased food patch size, while Dunbar (1988) added the prediction that group size should increase directly with increased predator density (Figure 4.3b). Broad comparisons across primate species qualitatively support these models (Terborgh and Janson 1986, Dunbar 1988), but additional detailed quantitative comparisons are needed.

4.6. DIRECT EFFECTS OF ECOLOGY ON OTHER ASPECTS OF SOCIAL STRUCTURE

Researchers have documented ecological correlates of many aspects of primate social structure, including territoriality, mating preferences, birth and survival patterns, sex ratio, and competitive and affiliative relationships. These studies can be divided into two general groups: (1) those that deal with the direct influence of ecological variables on social structure; (2) those that deal with the effects of demographic changes on social structure, leaving open the question of what ecological factors (if any) cause the demographic changes. In the next section, I examine examples of studies that show direct ecological effects on social organization: territoriality, aggressive behavior, mating systems, and spatial relationships among group members.

4.6.1. Territoriality

Comparative analyses of territoriality in primates suggested it was associated with small home ranges and evenly dispersed food sources (Crook and Gartlan 1966). However, many species were exceptions to this pattern. Mitani and Rodman (1979) examined the occurrence of territoriality in primates from a more quantitative point of view. They reasoned that territorial defense would occur only if the benefits of exclusive access to the home range exceeded the costs of defense (Brown 1964; see Chapter 8, this volume). Although they could not measure the benefits of territoriality directly, they were able to estimate the costs of territorial defense simply as the ratio (D) of distance a group needs to travel per day to forage (taken as the group's observed daily travel distance) to the distance the group has to travel to defend its area (taken as the mean diameter of its home range). They found that species for which D was below 1.0 were usually (13 of 19 cases) nonterritorial, whereas those with D above 1.0 were all (14 cases) territorial.

They realized that their results could be spurious. Daily travel distance of territorial species may include additional travel related to defense of the territory, thus producing high D values. However, they were able to show that territorial and nonterritorial species of similar body size and diet do not differ in daily travel distance. This analysis leaves unanswered the question of why some species have small enough home ranges to be defensible, while other species of similar body size and diet do not. The possibility that territorial species possess more abundant or predictable resources (Brown 1964) has yet to be tested with primate data.

4.6.2. Within-Group Aggressive Behavior

In most primate species, the outcome of an aggressive contest between two individuals is a foregone conclusion. Usually an individual will not even attempt to behave aggressively toward another that has chased it in previous encounters (e.g., Bernstein 1981). If this behavior is consistent over time, the habitual loser is called the subordinate and the winner the dominant. Because individuals apparently acknowledge their fighting ability against known opponents (see Cheney and Seyfarth 1985), aggressive interactions are usually infrequent and brief. The subordinate animal retreats, the dominant one advances or claims the contested resource.

The ecological benefits of being a dominant can vary widely. For instance, Janson (1985) measured the total amount of food ingested (as the product of the feeding time and ingestion rate) by individuals of different dominance status in a group of brown capuchin monkeys for each of 10 important food sources. At 6 of these food types, dominant individuals ate significantly more than did subordinates, but exactly how much more varied widely. At one extreme food type (the unopened flowering stalk of *Astrocaryum murumuru* palms), the top dominant male ate five times as much as the average group member; at the opposite extreme (while foraging for insects), the top dominant ate no more than the lowest subordinate. These differences were very strongly related to the rate of aggressive interactions performed per unit time per feeding individual. When the rate was high, the dominant did much better than the average, with the advantage decreasing steadily as the rate of aggression declined (Figure 4.4).

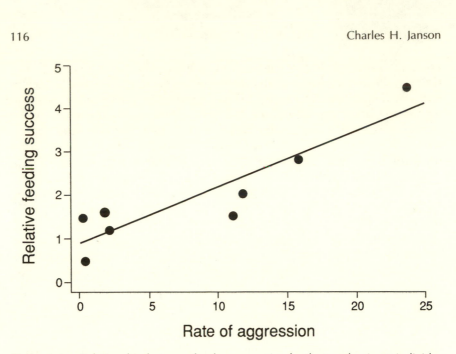

Figure 4.4.   Relationship between food consumption by the top dominant individual in a group of brown capuchin monkeys and the rate of aggression at the food source (Janson 1985b). Relative feeding success is the individual's rate of food intake divided by the mean rate for the entire group. Rate of aggression is the number of aggressive interactions observed among all group members per 100 group feeding minutes. The regression is y = 0.90 + 0.13x (p = .002 that the slope = 0, but the intercept is not significantly different from 1.0).

Similarly, Whitten (1983) found that dominant females ate more and had higher birth rates in one group of vervet monkeys (*Cercopithecus aethiops*) but not in another. The major ecological difference between the groups was in the spatial distribution of one of their most important food plants, acacia flowers. For the group with a clear relationship between dominance status, feeding, and birth rates, flowering acacia trees were clumped in space, whereas in the other group, the trees were randomly distributed. Whitten (1983) suggested that a clumped distribution of trees would be easier to defend by dominants. Harcourt (1989) and van Schaik (1989) have expanded this idea to suggest that primate species with easily defended food sources should show marked dominance hierarchies and a strong effect of dominance on fitness, whereas in species with resources that are hard to defend, aggression should be less common, less clearly structured, and dominance should relate weakly to fitness. This pattern is confirmed in a comparison of two species of squirrel monkeys (*Saimiri*; Mitchell et al. 1991). The species in Central America (*S. oerstedi*) subsists on small fruit trees and dispersed insects, shows a loose female social structure with little evidence of aggressive hierarchy or coalition formation, and females routinely emigrate from their natal group. The South American species (*S.*

sciureus) feeds mostly in scattered but highly productive fig trees, within which fighting is common. This species has a marked female dominance hierarchy, shows frequent coalitions among females, and females remain in their natal group after maturity.

4.6.3. Mating Systems

The correlation between mating system and primate ecology was among the first to be noted (Crook and Gartlan 1966). Many of the results for primates parallel those from other vertebrates (see recent review in Wrangham and Rubenstein 1986). Most primates have a polygynous mating system, as do most mammals. In the earliest classifications of mating systems, much weight was given to whether each primate group had but a single breeding male ("harem" polygyny) or several ("multimale" polygyny). This distinction rapidly blurred, however, as it was recognized that some adult males in an apparently multimale group may not be functional reproductives ("age-graded" male system; Eisenberg et al. 1972). In addition, it was found that both harem and multimale types could be found in populations of the same species, or in the same population over time (e.g., mantled howler monkeys; Crockett and Eisenberg 1987).

To resolve such variation, it became important to understand the costs and benefits of particular mating systems to each sex. Several authors have proposed that a female's fitness is limited primarily by direct ecological constraints on her ability to produce and rear offspring, rather than by the number of mates she has (Trivers 1972; Wrangham 1980). If so, natural selection will favor females that choose socioecological situations that maximize the rate of production of young without regard to the presence of males. In contrast, a male's fitness may often be limited by the number of females he can mate (Trivers 1972). If so, natural selection will favor males that maximize their number of matings with fecund females, constrained by only their personal abilities and the actions of other males in the population. In reality, females may try to influence the number of males in a group (to reduce competition or gain allies; Wrangham 1980), and male fitness may be maximized by helping a single female raise her offspring rather than searching for additional mates (Maynard Smith 1977). In general, however, the reproductive decision for female primates is one of an optimal group size of females, which then constrains the mating options of males.

The influence of female sociality on male mating patterns is clearly seen in the transition between one-male and multimale primate groups. In general, harem polygyny occurs in situations with fewer than about 4 reproductive females per group, while multimale polygyny is prevalent when 5 or more reproductive females occur per group (Terborgh 1983; Andelman 1986). It seems that a single male can defend no more than 4 females from competing males excluded by breeding groups. Primate populations in which a single male accompanies groups of 10 or more females are characterized either by frequent turnover of the resident male (e.g., *Presbytis entellus*; Hrdy 1974) or invasions of nonresident males into a group during the breeding season, when many of them copulate with females and presumably sire offspring (several *Cercopithecus* species; Cords et al. 1986; Rowell 1988).

Once the number of females in the social unit becomes too great, a single male may obtain greater fitness by allowing other males into the group than by attempting to exclude them. By tolerating additional males, a dominant male saves the time, energy, and injury risks involved in fighting off frequent attempts by these males to enter the group or take over the dominant's breeding position (e.g., Hrdy 1974). Thus, these benefits may allow a dominant male to increase his reproductive lifespan. The cost to him is the loss of his potential reproductive monopoly, but this monopoly may never be realized in many haremic species because of seasonal incursions and clandestine copulations by nonresident males (Rowell 1988). Furthermore, the dominant male in a stable multimale social unit may have nearly exclusive access to estrous females, thus achieving reproductive success very similar to that of a harem male (Janson 1984).

Despite the strong constraint of female grouping patterns, male mating options may also be influenced directly by ecological variables. For instance, harem polygyny is more frequent in arboreal than terrestrial primates (Clutton-Brock and Harvey 1977a). One explanation for this trend is that terrestrial primates are more at risk of predation, favoring the presence of several males cooperating in group defense (Crook and Gartlan 1966). In this case, a dominant male may benefit by reducing his own risk of death from confronting a predator by allowing other males into his group. Alternatively, where predators are common, females would gain more antipredator benefit from having extra adult males in their group; thus, females of terrestrial species should tolerate (or even invite) extra males in the group more than those of arboreal species should (cf. van Schaik and van Noordwijk 1989).

Another possible direct influence of ecology on male mating options is the seasonality of breeding (Dunbar 1988). For a group of a given size, the number of females in estrus at any one time increases as the breeding season becomes shorter. Because males are far more likely to compete over estrous than nonestrous females, the total number of females in a group may be less important to male mating strategies than the number of females simultaneously in estrus. Thus, for social groups with equal numbers of females, males should be more likely to tolerate other males when breeding is highly seasonal than when it is very extended. However, if female group size is small and interbirth intervals are long, males may encounter more estrous females by wandering among a large number of females than by defending exclusive access to a particular group or territory containing few females.

Although females in small social groups may have little choice but to mate with the single resident male in their group, there is considerable room for female choice of male partners in species with large social groups. Most researchers are of the opinion that female primates choose males on the basis of possible genetic quality (e.g., dominance status, health; review by Robinson 1982), or on the basis of friendships and potential coalition partners (Smuts 1985; Dunbar 1988). The possibility that ecological benefits may directly motivate a female's choice of mate has been documented rarely in the wild. In one study (Janson 1984), estrous female brown capuchins actively initiate sexual solicitations only toward the dominant male in their group. This male controls access to the small, scattered fruit trees on which females and their offspring depend during the period of food scarcity. The dominant male is tolerant in food trees of all juveniles that he could have sired, but is not tolerant of juveniles that he could not have sired. Thus, females that consistently choose the dominant male as a mating partner may have greater fitness because their offspring have preferred access to food and survive in greater numbers. Brown capuchins thus seem to have a form of resource defense polygyny (see Chapter 11), but here the resource is not a fixed territory as it usually is in birds (Emlen and Oring 1977).

Primates are unusual among mammals in having a relatively high proportion of monogamous species, especially considering that no primate is primarily a carnivore as are most other examples of monogamous mammals (foxes, jackals, etc.). It appears that monogamy in primates has evolved at least twice, probably for different reasons (Rutberg 1983; van Schaik and van Hooff 1983). First, in gibbons, males defend territories that contain a single female, but the males are not active in parental care. Monogamy may have evolved as part of a resource defense strategy because territorial males could not easily defend an area big enough to contain two or more territorial females (Rutberg 1983). Dunbar (1988) disagrees, arguing on energetic grounds that male gibbons should be able to defend much larger territories, suggesting that males are constrained to accompany their mates constantly to watch for either predators (Dunbar 1988) or intruding infanticidal males (van Schaik and Dunbar 1990). Second, in New World primates (callitrichids, *Callicebus, Aotus*), monogamous pairs also defend territories, but male parental care is extensive (Wright, 1984). In this case, monogamy may be advantageous as a form of mate defense by females to increase success in rearing offspring that are either twins or born very large (van Schaik and van Hooff 1983; Wright 1984). In support of this explanation is the fact that groups of some species of callitrichids can peacefully contain two or more adult females, of which only one breeds and suppresses the others (Epple and Katz 1980). Thus, even when in a socially polygynous group, a marmoset female can ensure that she receives all the male's parental care.

In some callitrichids, the benefits of paternal care to offspring survival may be so great that two males even cooperate to rear the offspring of a single female, providing the only documented case of polyandry in nonhuman primates (Garber et al. 1984; Terborgh and Goldizen 1985). Although the advantage of this mating system to a female is clear, males should be selected not to expend energy raising offspring that are not their own. In the saddle-backed tamarin (*Saguinus fuscicollis*), a reproductive female will mate repeatedly with both males in her social group, thus making it difficult for a male to know if a given offspring is his. The sharing is not perfect, however; on occasion, one male may try to monopolize access to a female, and typically one of the males helps to carry the offspring much less than the other (Goldizen and Terborgh 1986). Why doesn't one of the males leave and form a monogamous pair bond with a lone female? Evidence suggests that *only* pairs with helpers (either adult or juvenile) breed successfully (Goldizen and Terborgh 1986). By accepting the help (and tolerating the sexual competition) from a second male, a male can produce the first set of offspring that could act as helpers in future years. Even if the second male does not have equal access to the reproductive female, he might stay in the group because he may inherit the breeding female (with existing helpers) when the first male dies (see Emlen 1984 for nonprimate examples). The subordinate male might also stay in the group if he is thereby helping to raise offspring of close kin, but the relatedness of males in polyandrous groups is not presently known.

4.6.4. Spatial Relationships

Spatial relationships between group members may be important in the context of food acquisition: The closer together individuals forage, the more they will overlap in foraging effort and compete for food (Altmann 1974). Interindividual spacing also affects predation risk, as a predator's chance of discovering a group should increase with group spread, depending on how far apart individuals scatter when they forage (Vine 1973). Group cohesion should reflect a balance between selection pressures to move apart reducing food competition and to bunch together reducing predation risk (van Schaik and van Hooff 1983; Terborgh and Janson 1986; van Schaik 1989). These trade-offs were nicely demonstrated by Robinson's (1981) study of weeper capuchin monkeys. He found that as individuals crowded closer together, their foraging success declined, but the percentage of time spent in vigilance also decreased—animals were hungrier but felt safer. Because most food sources are encountered near the front of the group, this was the best place to forage, but only dominant individuals and their offspring occupied this position. Individuals not tolerated by the group's dominant female were forced to use peripheral areas of low foraging success and high vigilance costs. Similar general patterns were found in a study of spatial relations among individuals in brown capuchin groups (Janson 1990). Janson's study showed by direct measurement of foraging success that dominant individuals foraged where they maximized their foraging success, and juveniles foraged where vigilance behavior reflecting predation risk was least. Subordinate adults foraged where they were least likely to encounter the group's dominant male. Thus, spatial structure in foraging primate groups results from a complex interplay of several ecological and social constraints, each weighted differently for every group member according to its age, sex, and social status.

4.7. INDIRECT EFFECTS OF ECOLOGY ON SOCIAL STRUCTURE VIA DEMOGRAPHY

Many aspects of primate social life depend on the precise balance of different age and sex classes in a group (Dunbar 1979). This balance can change quickly from year to year due to stochastic fluctuations (Altmann and Altmann 1970). For instance, in average-sized primate groups, it is rare for the same number of males and females to be born each year. Likewise, many other demographic parameters vary unpredictably, such as the number of group members lost to predation in a given year or the number of infants born. Extreme values of demographic variables can affect social structure far beyond the year in which they occur, as demographically "unusual" individuals mature (Dunbar 1988). The ecological causes can be many: climatic fluctuations, long-term cycles in forest succession, short-term cycles in predator or prey abundance, and so forth. Demographic influences on primate infanticide have been recently reviewed in Hausfater (1984). In the next sections, I shall discuss two other aspects of social structure thought to depend proximally on demographic parameters, thus eventually on ecological variation: neonatal sex ratio and coalition formation.

4.7.1. Neonatal Sex Ratio

A theorem by Fisher (1930) predicts that a female should invest equal parental effort in sons and daughters. If offspring of one sex require less effort to raise to maturity than the other, then the female should bias the neonatal sex ratio toward the "cheaper" sex. A demographic pattern common to most mammals, including primates, is sex-biased dispersal of young adults, usually males. Given this pattern, a female offspring can grow up to compete for resources with her mother, but a male offspring often leaves before he is likely to compete much with her. If local resource competition from daughters reduces a female's reproductive output, she can raise more male than female offspring per unit time at a given level of reproductive effort. Thus, females competing with their daughters should have a bias toward producing sons. In species with social groups composed of many females, the effects of resource competition are expected to fall most on subordinate females (Silk 1983). It is these subordinate females that should overproduce sons, while dominant females may favor daughters.

An alternative and contrasting explanation for biased sex ratios is non-linear changes in sex-specific fitness as a function of parental investment (Trivers and Willard 1973; see also Chapter 11). If males compete strongly for access to reproductive females, then a small increment in the competitive ability of a son may yield his mother far more grand-offspring than the same increment would in her daughter. A mother's ability to influence her offspring's competitive status should be proportional to the resources that the mother controls, which is usually related to her social status in the group. In primate species where males compete strongly for access to females, dominant females should overproduce sons, while subordinate females should produce relatively more daughters. Local resource competition should produce the same pattern only when sons are philopatric and daughters disperse.

Some of the few documented examples in primates of significant sex ratio bias at birth agree well with the predictions above. Among species with male-biased dispersal, several examples of male-biased sex ratios are known. In galagos (Clark 1978), territoriality between females suggests that resource competition is important, and sex ratios at birth are highly biased toward males. Of species with multifemale groups, one of the best documented cases in nature comes from long-term research on yellow baboons in Kenya (Altmann 1980). Subordinate female baboons favor sons more than do dominant females, and their interbirth intervals are longer after female than male offspring (suggesting greater parental investment in daughters than in sons). Similar results have been documented in some captive macaque (Macaca) populations, although others show no bias or even the reverse pattern (review in van Schaik and Hrdy 1990). Of the few primate species known to have female-biased dispersal, subordinate females overproduce daughters and dominant females favor sons in one species (black spider monkeys; Symington 1987), but no bias is apparent in another (common chimpanzees, Pan troglodytes; Goodall 1986).

Despite these successes, documenting sex ratio biases has been extremely difficult (Clutton-Brock 1982). Primate birth sex ratios often are skewed, but only rarely are statistically different from a 1:1 ratio. The lack of well-documented cases of sex ratio bias is in part due to the large sample sizes needed to demonstrate significant bias, but may also be caused by the mechanistic constraint of the XY system of sex determination, which tends to produce a 1:1 conception sex ratio (Williams 1979).

Equal birth sex ratios may also occur when a primate population is subject to both local resource competition and the Trivers-Willard effect, producing countervailing biases (van Schaik and Hrdy 1990). For instance, the degree of competition between a female and philopatric offspring will depend on the overall abundance of food. When food is plentiful, resource competition will be low and subordinate females should favor daughters, which are virtually certain to reproduce, instead of sons which will face strong competition from the sons of dominant females. When food is scarce, resource competition will be strong, and subordinate females should produce more sons, which will face little harassment, instead of daughters, which are likely to lose in competition with the daughters of dominant females. Existing data from macaques strongly confirm this pattern: Subordinate females overproduce daughters when a population is growing rapidly, whereas they prefer sons when a population is stable or growing only slowly (van Schaik and Hrdy 1990). Thus, how strong and what kind of sex ratio bias occurs in a primate population may depend to a great degree on the degree of resource competition.

4.7.2. Coalition Formation

The common occurrence of male-biased dispersal should also affect the possibility of coalition formation. Although it may be possible for males to recognize and associate with their kin in other groups to which they disperse, the likelihood of two or more closely related males migrating by chance to the same group is low. In contrast, females remain in groups with many close kin. Because coalitions should form more easily among kin than nonkin (see Chapter 10), evolutionary theory would predict that males will form fewer and more temporary coalitions than will females in species with male-biased dispersal. In many Old World primates, dominance hierarchies among females are tightly organized by kinship, largely because mothers are supportive of their daughters (Dunbar 1988). In these same species, coalitions of adult males can occur with little kinship (Packer 1977). Coalitions among unrelated males may be long-lasting when the goal is to maintain exclusive access to a group of females, as in gelada baboons (Dunbar 1984).

Similar demographic constraints may affect the availability and selection of coalition partners for female primates (Dunbar 1988; Datta 1989). In many Old World primates, social groups consist of several *matrilines*, that is social subgroups of related females. All females in a matriline occupy adjacent dominance ranks and thus can defeat any female from a subordinate matriline. Within each matriline, the highest ranking individual is a founder female, and below her rank her daughters in *inverse* order of age (i.e., the youngest daughter is most dominant). Because older daughters are often larger and more experienced fighters, the puzzle is how and why younger daughters come to outrank them. Chapais and Schulman (1980) suggest that mothers usually offer most support in aggressive contests to the youngest of her mature daughters because these have the highest reproductive value. Reproductive value is a measure of an individual's expected genetic contribution to future generations and thus is a good measure of individual (but perhaps not inclusive) fitness (see Chapter 11). Thus, a mother increases her own lifetime fitness. In addition, mothers may favor their youngest daughters because these will have a longer life expectancy and thus can be longer-lasting coalition partners than are older daughters (Dunbar 1988).

The reproductive-value model helps to explain the general inverse relationship between age and dominance among daughters, but not why this pattern often does not occur. This variation is the subject of Datta's (1989) model. Datta demonstrates that quite different dominance structures among related females can arise from a single set of coalition decisions under different schedules of birth and death.

Datta uses rules for the formation of aggressive coalitions derived from intensive studies of rank acquisition by young female rhesus macaques (*M. mulatta*: Datta 1988). First, relatives will intervene in disputes between siblings, usually on the side of the more vulnerable (younger) individual. This rule makes evolutionary sense, because the more vulnerable individual has a greater chance of being injured in a fight, and thus will benefit more from the aid of siblings. Second, a young female will be successful in challenging an older female sibling only if the younger is both relatively similar in size to the older and has the support of kin (mother or other siblings), at least one of which is dominant to the challenged sibling. After several successful challenges, the younger daughter will become dominant to the older.

Datta takes these two assumptions and uses them to form predicted matriline dominance structures for various birth and death rates. She finds that the inverse age dominance pattern of daughters should occur only when birth rates are relatively high or death rates very low. Under these conditions, a younger daughter will be relatively similar in age (and usually size) to her next older sister, and likely to have her mother or other older siblings alive when she is ready to challenge her next older sister. Thus, the youngest daughter can count on much support and will usually win her challenges against the next older sister. Repetition of this process generates the inverse age dominance pattern.

When birth rates are low or death rates are high, the age difference between successive mature sisters will be larger, thus placing the younger at a competitive disadvantage. It is also more likely that the mother or older siblings will have died by the time the youngest daughter reaches maturity, depriving her of coalition partners. In this case, younger sisters cannot successfully challenge older ones, and never come to outrank them. Thus, an inverse age dominance pattern is expected when birth rates are high relative to death rates and matrilines are large. In support of this prediction, the inverse pattern is best documented for provisioned or captive macaque populations, and is much less noticeable or is absent in wild populations and in species with small numbers of females per social group (Datta 1989).

4.8. PROBLEMS OF EXISTING SOCIOECOLOGICAL STUDIES AND SOME POSSIBLE SOLUTIONS

Despite general agreement on the major costs and benefits of sociality for primates and other vertebrates (Wrangham and Rubenstein 1986), the relative importance of different ecological factors in shaping social systems across species is still to a large degree unknown. The scarcity of focused quantitative socioecological studies on primates makes it difficult to compare the intensity of even a single factor (e.g., food competition) across many species or the relative contribution of multiple factors (e.g., predation versus food competition) to social structure within a species. Some ecological factors of potential importance remain nearly unstudied (e.g., parasitism).

To compare the importance of different ecological factors to primate social structure within or across species, it is necessary to express importance on the common scale of individual or inclusive fitness (Vehrencamp and Bradbury 1984). This currency is a natural unit for evolutionary studies as fitness differences are the raw material of natural selection. The next generation of socioecological studies faces the challenge of using natural selection concepts to understand how particular ecological and social traits of individuals interact to affect fitness.

Several problems arise in applying natural selection study methods in primate socioecology: Measuring lifetime fitness for long-lived primates requires improbably long continuous field studies, and showing that natural selection exists on a social trait does not reveal the ecological cause of such selection. I suggest instead a focus on intermediary correlates of fitness, such as individual food intake, energy expenditure, and exposure to predators and parasites (Figure 4.5). The use of these intervening variables is easier than estimating total fitness and reduces the chance that a particular relation between a social trait and fitness will be explained by an incorrect mechanism. Initially, studies may focus on a single interaction between one aspect of ecology and one social trait (e.g., how food production/patch and group size together affect individual energy intake). Eventually, separate studies

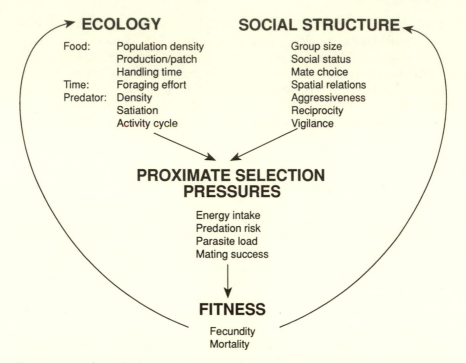

Figure 4.5. This scheme emphasizes the use of within-population variation in ecological and social variables to examine their interaction on fitness. For each social structural trait examined, one can study how variation in a particular ecological variable affects the levels of several correlates of fitness ("proximate selection pressures"). The arrows drawn from fitness back to ecological and social traits emphasize that ecological and social traits evolve at the same time in response to natural selection.

can be combined to give a more detailed picture of how various social traits interact to affect fitness in a given ecological setting, and how changes in ecology affect these relationships (Vehrencamp and Bradbury 1984).

With respect to this research plan, the best data (albeit far from complete) exist for the interaction of ecological and social variables on individual food intake. For instance, one recent analysis (Janson 1985, 1988b) expresses on a single scale (energy intake per day) the importance of three distinct forms of food competition. Other studies have begun to establish the fitness consequences of food competition in wild primate groups (Dittus 1977; Whitten 1983; van Schaik and van Noordwijk 1988; Robinson 1988). No study to date combines detailed and complete ecological and demographic information, so the integration of social and ecological effects on individual fitness remains a goal for the future.

However, it is not clear that even the best quantitative measurements of basic ecological variables (e.g., food and predator abundance) will by themselves clarify their causal effect on social structure. Future studies need to recognize that one ecological factor may affect the importance of another. For instance, primates subject to strong predation pressure may have highly cohesive groups that make it impossible for individuals to avoid food competition by foraging alone (Janson 1988a; van Schaik 1989). Thus, measuring the abundance of food does not by itself indicate the likely importance of food competition.

Understanding the interaction of various ecological and social factors requires explicit mathematical modeling, as verbal models are ill-suited to assess the quantitative trade-offs involved in predicting the kinds of social structure that might be produced by natural selection. Most of the examples cited above relied on explicit, if simple, mathematical formulations. Oddly, such modeling has been virtually absent from the most basic question of primate socioecology: ecological determinants of group size.

As a first step in this direction, I have developed a mathematical model to predict social structure when the benefit of sociality is avoiding predation and the cost of sociality is within-group competition for food. The model starts from three basic ecological parameters: the abundance of food items, the nutritional value of each food item, and the density of predators. Social structure in this case refers to four parameters: number of individuals (group size), between-individual spacing, proportion of individual foraging time spent vigilant, and proportion of daily time budget spent foraging.

For each possible combination of the four social parameters, the model calculates individual (female) fitness for a given set of ecological variables, using explicit assumptions about the interaction of each social parameter with each ecological variable. For instance, to calculate the effect of food abundance on female fitness, the model starts by examining how females in a group find food. For the simple case that all food items are discovered (rather than remembered), the total food discovery rate by the group is proportional to the total search width (W) of the group, which depends on the number of individuals in the group (n), the size of each individual search field (w), and the spacing between individuals (i). If w is greater than i, then individual search fields overlap each other and $W = nw - (n - 1)i$; if w is less than i, then $W = nw$, the sum of all individual search fields. Once a food item is discovered, the amount of food each female actually ingests (I) will depend on both how much food is available in the item (f) and the number of females feeding on it. If the item (or patch) is so large that each female can eat her fill (as might occur in a large fruit tree) then each female eats s, the satiation amount. Otherwise, the model assumes for simplicity that all females share the food equally, so that per capita food intake equals f/n.

The product of the group's total search field (W), per capita food intake per item discovered (*I*), travel rate, and the density of food items gives the per capita rate of food intake per hour of foraging. Total per capita food intake per day is the product of this intake rate and the total time spent foraging (*t*), discounted by the proportion of time spent watching out for predators (*v*). Per capita food intake is transformed into fecundity by a function in which no reproduction occurs if intake is below maintenance costs, and intakes above that level result at first in rapid gains in fecundity, but at large intakes fecundity approaches a maximum. Thus, one component of fitness, fecundity, is given as an explicit function of four parameters of social structure: group size, between-individual spacing, total foraging time, and proportion of time spent vigilant. Similarly, the other component of fitness, mortality, is written as an explicit (but rather more complex) function of these social parameters that reflects their effects in avoiding predation. The model uses the fecundity and mortality rates to calculate total fitness (as reproductive value) using a simplified primate life history.

The results from this model significantly revise some expectations of earlier verbal treatments. In particular, birth rates may not simply decrease with increased group size as predicted under the assumption of increasing within-group competition for food (as drawn in Figure 4.2b). In fact, birth rates can initially increase with increasing group sizes before declining in very large groups (Figure 4.6). This pattern mimics that predicted for the trade-off between benefits of between-group competition and costs of within-group competition (Figure 4.2a) even though my model contains no between-group competition. It appears that the fitness of individuals in small groups may be so dominated by the threat of predation that it is better to sacrifice foraging efficiency to gain protection from predators. As predator density increases, this pattern becomes more marked without appreciably affecting the optimum group size. Thus, the populations in which it is easiest to demonstrate increases in fecundity with group size may be those populations most subject to predation pressure, not those most prone to between-group competition! Although the predictions of earlier verbal models may yet turn out to be correct, the results of the present model suggest that without explicit modeling, biological intuition may be insufficient to capture the complexity of socioecological interactions. Additional mathematical modeling will prove essential to indicate critical parameters to be measured and to sharpen our interpretation of across-species comparative data (see 1.2.2).

The inheritance of social structure remains a difficult problem. Is social structure an "emergent property" of a few fundamental individual behavioral decisions (cf. Datta 1989)? If so, how are those decisions affected by genetic and social factors? The resolution of these questions is likely to require the integration of traditional population genetics, cultural evolution (e.g., Boyd and Richerson 1985; see Chapter 3), and maternal inheritance (e.g., Kirkpatrick and Lande 1989). A related question is to what extent

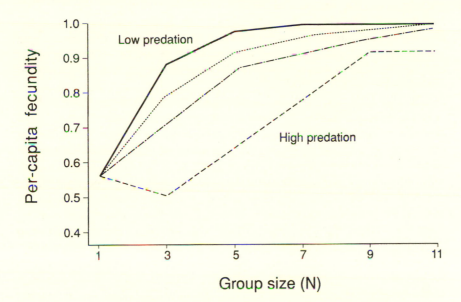

Figure 4.6.   Predicted relationships between per capital fecundity and group size for different densities of predators (from Low to High), based on the mathematical model in text (which excludes between-group competition for food). Compare with Figure 4.2.

social structure represents a "game against the environment" or a "game against conspecifics." In the former case, the optimal social structure can be predicted as a (possibly complex) trade-off between various ecological costs and benefits of sociality. The latter case, however, is likely to produce frequency-dependent fitnesses, which may lead to complex ESS solutions (see 2.2.3). For instance, if individuals independently leave or join groups, even the case of simple ecological trade-offs affecting group size (Figure 4.2) can produce an evolutionarily stable *distribution* of group sizes rather than a single optimal group size (Clark and Mangel 1984).

4.9. APPLYING PRIMATE SOCIOECOLOGY
TO AN UNDERSTANDING OF HUMANS

Ultimately, it may be possible to take the lessons of detailed socioecological studies from within species and apply them to understand the evolution of sociality across primates, including humans. However, common ancestry may confound our ability to predict or interpret differences between species. Two closely related species may have failed to diverge appreciably despite differing selective pressures because of their common origin (cf. Cheverud et al. 1985). Although many modern analyses of traits across primate species try to account for such common origins (e.g., Clutton-Brock and Harvey

1977b), other studies do not (e.g., Mitani and Rodman 1979). In any case there is no guarantee that current methods to account for common ancestry are correct (Felsenstein 1985). The importance of such genetic constraints can be considered small if the behaviors under study are known to be influenced strongly by the local social or ecological context.

It is difficult to interpret the evolution of observed differences in a trait between species unless the mechanism of inheritance is known. Most analyses of natural selection assume that at least some of the variation in a trait has a genetic basis (Endler 1984). However, in species with extensive learning, cultural inheritance of traits may be equally important (see Nishida 1987 for primate examples) and can produce rates of behavioral change much greater than those typical of genetic evolution (Boyd and Richerson 1985). The development of most behaviors depends extensively on environmental feedback (e.g., Tinbergen 1963), with the result that the adult form of a behavior may differ according to the conditions of each individual's ontogeny, including any average differences between populations in ecological or social factors. It may be hard to know if observed social differences between species or populations represent genetic, cultural, or ontogenetically plastic changes.

Regardless of the mode of inheritance, behavioral differences can be considered adaptive if they increase the fitness of their actors relative to other behavioral variants. To assess the ease with which such differences might have arisen among species requires knowing how such differences are acquired. One could propose that the entire diversity of social systems among primate species is due to a single, highly flexible developmental program, which produces distinctive species differences in social behavior in response to differences in ecological circumstances. If so, then studies of nonhuman primate social behavior could offer direct clues to the possible responses of hominids to ecological variation. However, studies of different primate species under standard laboratory conditions suggest that species variation in social behavior is limited and therefore has at least some genetic component (e.g., Rosenblum and Kaufman 1967; de Waal 1989a). To the extent that species differ genetically in social behavior, it becomes more difficult to estimate how social structure will respond to short-term environmental change.

With respect to using results of primate socioecology to understand primitive hominid social structure, it is clear that within-species variation in social structure is extensive in many primate species. Much of this variation may depend on very subtle changes in ecological conditions or variables that are not preserved in the fossil record (e.g., food patch productivity or size). Thus, while studies of primate socioecology may reveal important trends that might be present even in extant human populations, applying these trends to decipher the social structure of fossil man may require more detailed paleoecological data than we currently possess.

Evolutionary Ecology of Fossil Hominids

R. A. Foley

5

5.1. INTRODUCTION

Behavioral ecology has developed in the context of microevolution. Its focus is the pattern of variation within and between living populations. Behavioral ecologists attempt to map the selective processes and adaptive outcomes of events that occur over relatively short time scales. This reflects two elements of modern Darwinian theory. First, evolutionary mechanisms are reductionist, relating to the actual events during an individual's lifetime. Longer-term evolutionary patterns are assumed to be the product of these mechanisms operating over more extensive periods of time. And second, Darwinian theory is mechanistic, and it is easier to study mechanisms operating today than it is to infer them from relics of the past.

However, any synthesis of human behavioral ecology would be incomplete if it did not address the longer-term pattern observable in the fossil record. Macroevolutionary ideas must be compatible with the mechanisms and processes thought to be operating on living or recent populations. The last 5.0 million years have seen the evolution of several primates with highly specialized patterns of locomotion, remarkably eclectic foraging patterns, dispersed spatial organization, pronounced encephalization, distinctive growth and life history strategies, and complex patterns of social organization. This long-term pattern of human evolution is here placed into a context that is consistent with the principles of behavioral and evolutionary ecology.

First, the extent to which a paleobiological perspective offers new insights into human behavioral ecology is considered (5.2). Next, the particular problems of studying human evolution from a behavioral ecological perspective are discussed (5.3). The primary difficulty here is to place hominid characteristics into a cost/benefit framework where the conditions for the appearance of hominid traits can be specified. The solution is to apply a modeling approach that links the characteristics of the hominid fossil record to selective conditions (5.4). A series of models are outlined that build a general model of hominid behavioral ecology. The energetics of bipedalism, the fundamental characteristic of the Hominidae is the point of departure for this (5.5). The conditions under which bipedalism is advantageous serve as a framework for considering foraging behavior (5.6), which in turn is closely linked to dispersal strategies of males and females and the resulting socioecological structures (5.7). These individual strategies themselves relate to the energetic parameters of growth, particularly in the context of enlarged brains (5.8). The model that is developed is then evaluated in terms of its implications for studies of modern human behavioral ecology (5.9).

5.2. PALEOBIOLOGY AND EVOLUTIONARY ECOLOGY

Paleobiology is both the study of evolutionary events in the past and the analysis of evolutionary patterns over longer time scales. Paleobiological approaches offer important new insights into the nature of evolution, but also impose, principally through the nature of the data, certain limitations.

5.2.1. The Role of Paleobiology
in Evolutionary Ecology

Evolutionary and behavioral ecology are characterized by two distinctive traits. The first is an emphasis on the role of the individual. The second is its strongly functional orientation. Its methods, models, and hypotheses derive from these characteristic elements (see Chapters 1 and 2). The central question here is how can a paleobiological perspective be integrated with these approaches and what further insights can be provided by a longer-term perspective.

The first issue is that of scale. Most ecological studies of contemporary populations encompass relatively short periods of times. For example, among chimpanzees and baboons, primates that have been subject to intense study, a "long-term study" covers a maximum of 25 years (Altmann 1974; Goodall 1986; McGrew in press). The evolutionary significance of periods of time depends upon the generational turnover of the species concerned. Twenty-five years for a bushbaby (*Galago* spp.) covers 10 generations; for a baboon (*Papio* spp.) 3.45 generations, and for chimpanzees (*Pan troglodytes*) 1.67 generations (Harvey et al. 1987). During such a period, considerable demographic flux can be observed [see, for example, the population decline among the Amboseli *Papio cynocephalus* population (Altmann and Altmann 1970), or the community changes among the Gombe chimpanzees (Goodall 1986), as well as the flux in social relationships and feeding behavior found in many groups over comparable lengths of time

(Lee 1991)]. Behavioral ecology assigns considerable significance to these changes, and uses such dynamics to provide the lubricants of evolutionary change or stability.

From a paleobiological perspective, however, such periods are diminutive in the extreme, and perhaps more important, seldom observable. For most Pliocene and Pleistocene paleontological situations, a time span of hundreds of thousands of years is involved and, with the exception of the later Pleistocene, temporal resolution does not reach 10,000 years. For a chimpanzee, 10,000 years is 667 generations, and 100,000 years is over 6,000 generations. In other words, a long-term behavioral ecology study represents only 0.025% of a realistic paleontological time unit. During that time a community of Gombe chimpanzees could have consumed several hundred other communities (given an extraordinary run of luck) were the rates for intercommunity violence to be extrapolated from the Gombe data (Goodall 1986).

The problem raised by these simple observations has taken some paleontologists in the direction of various theories of macroevolution (Gould 1980; Stanley 1979). These theories decouple short-term (micro-) evolutionary processes from long-term (macro-) evolution, and erect a hierarchy of evolutionary mechanisms. The net effect of such a strategy is to reduce the patterns observed by neoecologists to a role of stabilizing selection within existing adaptive frameworks. Speciation and the origins of higher taxa must be explained by other mechanisms for which various possibilities have been proposed. However, none of these have proved to be either not reducible to the outcome of microevolutionary mechanisms, and hence consistent with neo-Darwinism (Charlesworth et al. 1982), or lacking in any concrete biological mechanism. Such a mechanism, it might be argued, must reside in the individuals who reproduce or the populations that undergo genetic and evolutionary change. Longer time perspectives do not change this fact, although they may change the conditions (often drastically) under which various biological processes may occur. From an evolutionary perspective the events and patterns observable through paleobiology should be nothing more than neo-ontological ones reiterated over thousands of generations. This chapter attempts to apply this proposal to hominid behavioral evolution.

If paleobiology offers few new theoretical or mechanistic insights into evolution, can it make any significant contribution to evolutionary and behavioral ecology? Two suggestions may be made.

One is that only paleobiology can provide direct evidence of past evolutionary states. An understanding of the antecedent states of living populations is essential for mapping evolutionary trajectories. While identifying ancestor–descendant relationships in the fossil record is by no means an easy matter (and it may indeed be claimed that while all living species have ancestors it is far from clear that any fossil taxa have true descendants; Sarich 1983), nonetheless extinct or fossil species still have an important role to play, for they contribute, regardless of their phylogenetic status, to the sum of biological variability, indeed add to it dramatically. For instance, Martin (1985) has calculated that during the course of their evolution there may have been as many as 6000 species of primate. This compares to approximately 180 living species. Even just taking known fossil taxa, extinct species outnumber extant ones by a considerable margin. The living world represents only a partial set of biological possibilities, and comparative methods that draw theoretical inferences from living variability alone do so on only a small sample of what may have been possible or have existed at some earlier time.

A second important contribution that paleobiology can offer lies in the field of phylogenetic constraints and the importance of historical factors in evolutionary patterns. Natural selection can only operate on what exists. The evolutionary mechanism is one of tinkering, not designing new organisms and traits from scratch. All existing traits are modifications of ones that existed before. While the pattern of evolution may be the playing out of the rules that govern natural selection, change will occur only in specific historical situations, variation that may have extremely significant consequences for the evolutionary direction taken by any lineage. In any complete evolutionary explanation, phylogenetic heritage will play as significant a role as natural selection—indeed it is the interaction of the two that constitutes evolution—and the mapping of evolutionary pathways and the rules that govern such pathways are absolutely critical to the development of evolutionary biology (Foley and Lee 1989; see 5.7).

5.2.2. Limitations of Paleobiology

Having outlined the significance of a paleobiological perspective to evolutionary ecology, it is worth noting the limitations imposed. These have been reiterated many times and principally concern the nature of fossil data (for a discussion see Behrensmeyer and Hill 1981). Fossil evidence is severely limited, both in terms of the numbers of specimens available to represent an immeasurably large number of organisms that have lived in the past, and in terms of the nature of those fossils themselves. Only hard tissues will survive, and these only seldom and partially. Specimens must be fixed in time as well as space, a process that is fraught with potential errors. Paleobiological data must be treated as a sample, and all inferences from that sample should be placed within relatively broad confidence limits.

A further constraint, particularly significant in applying the principles of behavioral ecology to fossil contexts, is that behavior can only be studied indirectly. It is possible to infer behavior from fossils, but only where that behavior can be linked to some morphological trait or environmental condition. It is important to explore the links between behavior and morphological characteristics. This demand forms the basis for the topics developed here—locomotion and foraging behavior, body size and social organization, encephalization, reproduction, and growth.

5.3. FOSSIL HOMINIDS: THE MISSING LINKS IN EVOLUTIONARY ECOLOGY

While paleobiology is central to the development of evolutionary ecology, particularly pressing reasons exist where hominids are concerned. Humans are in many ways a special case in evolutionary biology.

5.3.1. Humans as a Special Case

While the development of behavioral ecology and its sister discipline sociobiology has been remarkably successful, applications to humans have met with considerable opposition (Kitcher 1985; see also Chapters 1 and 2). Objections have ranged from concern about the lack of empirical fit with theoretical expectations, to dissatisfaction with the underlying assumptions, to political distrust. Humans, it may be argued, do not fulfill the basic assumptions of behavioral evolution. Such a view, though, is not possible when a diachronic approach is adopted. If modern humans are compared even with chimpanzees, there is a vast gap in both abilities and achievements. However, this "gap" is unique to a particular period of time—the present—and the further back in time one travels the smaller the gap. The adaptive and behavioral distance between humans and other hominoids is in fact filled with other species (fossil hominids and other extinct apes) and has been created by historical events, in particular extinction. Given this, it is especially important for the successful development of human behavioral ecology that paleoanthropology provides the evidence to reconstruct states intermediate between humans and other animals.

5.3.2. Hominids as a Diverse Group of Species

The discussion above may give the impression that hominid evolution is best viewed as a ladder leading to modern humans, with the hominids on each rung of the ladder approaching more closely the characteristics of modern humans. However, this is far from the case. Perhaps the main insight gained in recent years in paleoanthropology is that hominid evolution is best seen as a series of adaptive radiations, not a ladder of progression

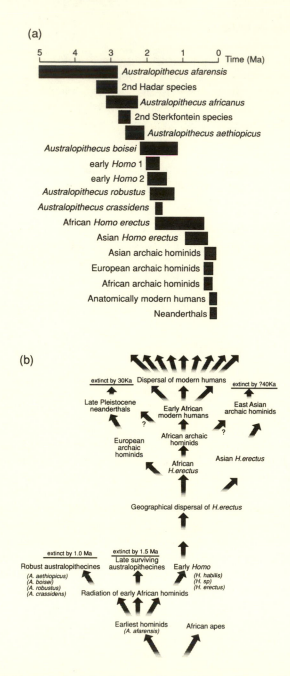

Figure 5.1. (a) *Chronological distribution of hominid taxa discussed in text.* (b) *The overall pattern of hominid evolution. Divergence of African apes and hominids occurs at about 7.0 Ma; the African early hominid radiation between 3 and 1.5 Ma; dispersal into Asia and Europe at about 1.0 Ma; and modern humans appear in Africa between 0.15 and 0.1 Ma.*

(Foley 1987a). The fossil record shows that in the past there was a range of hominid species, many of which were not simply parts of a single evolving lineage. It is these collateral species that provide us with evidence for the range of behaviors and morphologies that have occurred in the past, of which modern humans are a small part, and hence also provide us with a more complete comparative framework for investigating modern human behavioral ecology.

Figure 5.1 shows the broad outline of hominid evolution as it is currently viewed (by this author at any rate), together with the principal taxonomic units that will be discussed here.

5.4. MODELING HOMINID BEHAVIORAL ECOLOGY

The approach adopted here is to use the principles of evolutionary ecology to model the costs and benefits of various hominid characteristics. The parameters for the models are set principally by data drawn from modern humans and living primates, specifically the chimpanzee (*P. troglodytes*, and to a lesser extent *P. paniscus*). The principal purpose of the model is to specify the conditions under which certain features could be expected to be advantageous. Paleobiological evidence may then be used to test whether those conditions occurred at particular points in the past, corresponding to the evolution of these features among hominids.

5.4.1. Costs and Benefits
in Evolutionary Ecology

It is virtually axiomatic to behavioral and evolutionary ecology that adaptive features of organisms are accounted for in terms of fitness costs and benefits. Features should be selected for (and therefore appear and be maintained in lineages) when the benefits of these features exceed the costs, and more precisely, when the cost/benefit ratio of those features is more optimal in the context of reproductive success than alternative features. Humans possess features that are unique in the biological world (as do all species), and therefore an ecological approach to human evolution should identify the costs and benefits of these characteristics and specify the conditions under which benefits exceed costs such that these features would have been selected for. Clearly such a program raises enormous methodological difficulties. The possible phenotypes for early hominids can never be established; neither can the actual costs and benefits of past states be truly measured. To a very large extent, paleoanthropologists have assumed that all human features are self-evidently beneficial. Human features, though, have costs as well as benefits (after all, if they did not, then presumably all species would have developed culture, language, and large brains), and identifying these costs will enable us to posit the conditions under which events in hominid evolution took place.

5.4.2. Modeling Strategies

In attempting to identify the principal selective components in hominid evolution it has been necessary to isolate particular adaptive features and examine their contextual costs and benefits—locomotor behavior, foraging behavior, social strategy, and life history strategy. Such an approach suffers from the limitation that in reality all these features are closely linked to each other. There is, however, an observable chronological pattern to the development of hominid traits, with bipedalism evolving at the outset of the hominid lineage (ca. 4.0 Ma), prior to major craniodental changes (ca. 2.5 Ma onwards), which in turn precede major encephalization and changes in growth patterns (after 1.5 Ma). The sequence of model building here, therefore, may also reflect the sequence of cause and effect in hominid evolutionary change.

5.5. LOCOMOTOR BEHAVIOR AND THE ENERGETICS OF BIPEDALISM

Bipedalism in some form or another appears to be a characteristic of all known hominids, and may lie at the root of all other hominid traits as well as being the principal defining characteristic of the hominid lineage (Howell 1978). The anatomical changes necessary for full bipedalism not only separate hominids very clearly from other hominoids but are also spread widely throughout the skeleton. Bipedalism is of great functional, morphological, and phylogenetic significance in hominid evolution.

5.5.1. Evolutionary History of Hominid Bipedalism

The earliest known hominids date from approximately 5.0 million years (Hill 1985). The earliest tentative evidence for some level of bipedal adaptation comes from femoral fragments dated to between 4.0 and 3.5 Ma from the Middle Awash in Ethiopia (White 1984). More substantial is the evidence of the Laetoli footprints dated to 3.7 Ma (Leakey and Hay 1979), and the partial skeleton known as Lucy (AL-288) from Hadar at 2.9 Ma (Johanson et al. 1982).

It is widely accepted that these early hominids (*Australopithecus afarensis*) were more bipedal than any living anthropoid (Foley 1987a), but there is considerable debate concerning the precise nature of this bipedalism and the extent to which there remained a significant degree of arboreal activity. Lovejoy (1988) has argued that there are few major locomotor differences between *A. afarensis* and modern humans, whereas others (Jungers 1982; Susman et al. 1984; Aiello and Dean 1990) have pointed to the relatively long forearms, long, curved phalanges, and detailed hip morphology as evidence for both biomechanically different bipedalism and retained arboreality.

All later hominids are clearly bipedal, although again both later *Australopithecus* and early *Homo* differ in postcranial anatomy from modern humans. Following the discovery of a relatively complete skeleton from West Turkana (WT-15000) (Walker and Leakey 1986) it is clear that *Homo erectus* possessed body proportions broadly similar to those of modern humans.

Overall bipedalism may be the principal distinguishing characteristic of hominids. The actual extent and form of hominid bipedalism would have varied between taxa and it is only with the later genus *Homo* that fully modern forms of bipedalism appear. Aiello and Dean (1990) have shown that in terms of weight to stature relationships all earlier hominids (up to *H. erectus*) are closer to the apes than to modern humans. There may be significant differences in the form of bipedalism of different hominid taxa. Even within *Homo* considerable variation in morphology can be observed, for example, the different limb proportions and degree of robusticity found in neanderthals (Trinkaus 1983).

5.5.2. Energetics of Bipedalism

Given the pivotal position of bipedalism in both the chronology and anatomical pattern of hominid evolution, the critical question is why should bipedalism have evolved? What benefits accrued to those individuals capable of upright walking, and at what cost?

Energetics should provide an approach to answering these questions, as the principal cost of any locomotor system is energy. A simple hypothesis would predict that bipedalism should, under certain conditions, bestow an energetic advantage relative to other forms of locomotion. Although Taylor and Rowntree (1973) argued that bipedalism was more costly than quadrupedalism, Rodman and McHenry (1980) pointed out that the validity of any comparison depended upon the nature of the quadrupedalism used as a control and the assumed speed of movement. Their recalculation indicated that bipedalism is more efficient than chimpanzee quadrupedalism and bipedalism, the appropriate comparison given hominid ancestry.

Placing average speeds into the context of ranging behavior demonstrates the energetic benefits of bipedalism. Rodman (1984) shows that the maximum day range for a male chimpanzee is 10 km, for a female only 2 km; the mode for males lies between 3 and 4 km. The energetic costs of these day ranges would be about 1000 kJ (Figure 5.2). Modeling with an average of the two speeds used by Rodman and McHenry (1980), a bipedal hominid would make an energetic saving of 405 kJ (assuming a body size of 40 kg, comparable with that of a male chimpanzee) for the same pattern of day ranging. However, the really marked advantages of bipedalism become apparent when increased ranging behavior is modeled. For example, at the same body weight a bipedal hominid could travel up to 11 km for the same level of energy expenditure as a chimpanzee over 4 km (Figure 5.2). In other words, bipedalism can dramatically alter the costs of exploiting large ranges.

Another way of looking at this is in terms of body size constraints. A 40-kg male chimpanzee would expend 3560 kJ traveling the maximum 10-km day range reported by Rodman (1984). In contrast, a 60-kg hominid (about the size estimated for a large *Homo erectus* male) could travel nearly 18 km for the same amount of energy expended (Figure 5.3). In terms of kilojoules expended per kilogram of body weight, hominids have a 36% advantage over the pattern of locomotion seen in the African apes. The adaptive consequences of this can be thought of as a series of constraints that are thereby released—increasing range area, increasing body size, or a combination of these. For females there are also implications for reducing the costs of reproduction.

5.5.3. Costs and Benefits of Bipedalism

Clearly there are energetic benefits in a bipedal mode of locomotion. Other benefits that occur as a result of upright locomotion have been extensively discussed. Of particular note are those of freeing the hands for other activities such as feeding, using tools, and carrying, a proposition made originally by Darwin (1871). Carrying may be important when linked to ranging behavior. Larger day and home ranges must mean greater time spent traveling between food patches, and hence less time spent at food patches and in other activities (Dunbar 1988). The ability to carry food or tools for extracting food may represent a necessary concomitant of more extensive ranging. Among modern humans, carrying a 10-kg load imposes an increased energetic cost of 11.2% (Passmore and Durnin 1955). Assuming the same or greater for quadrupedal or partially bipedal apes, then the energetic savings provided by bipedalism may have been a significant factor in enabling hominids to increase foraging distance without increasing energy expenditure.

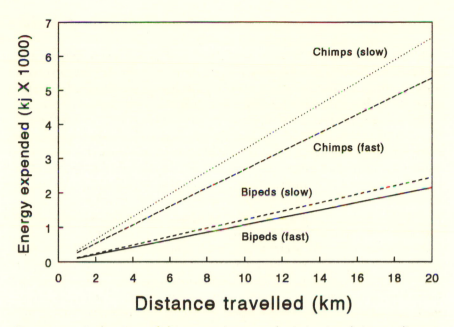

Figure 5.2. *Comparison of the energetic costs of ranging in relation to distance traveled of modern human bipedalism and chimpanzee quadrupedalism at fast and slow speeds (data from Rodman and McHenry 1980).*

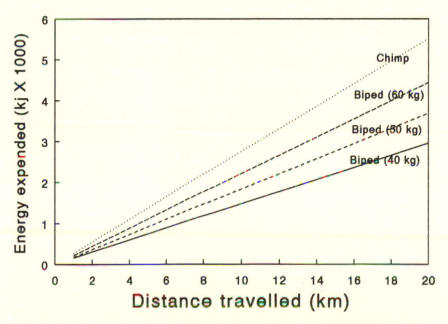

Figure 5.3. *Comparison of the energetic costs of ranging of bipedal hominids at various body weights in relation to chimpanzees. Hominid bipedalism allows much larger animals to forage at energetic costs below those of quadrupedal chimpanzees.*

Wheeler (1985) has also pointed out that bipedalism may provide thermo-regulatory advantages. A bipedal animal exposes a smaller body surface area to solar radiation, and so has a smaller heat load, thus reducing the energetic costs of thermoregulation by a substantial amount.

Once established, bipedalism may provide other benefits. Carrier (1984) has proposed that hominid bipedalism can provide the basis not just for long-distance foraging but also for endurance running and hence the potential for running down prey. As with Wheeler's model, this would be a consequence of the thermoregulatory advantages of bipedalism. Although no specific context for this is proposed, bipedalism allows a different pattern of resource utilization within a home range, both extending the range of potential prey species and increasing the probability of capture.

Bipedalism seems to provide energetic benefits that would be marked under conditions of increasing body size, more extended ranging, greater activity, or solar-induced heat stress. Given the apparent energetic advantages it is perhaps more of a problem explaining why other primates are not bipedal. Some of the costs are clearly related to phylogenetic history. For arboreal quadrupeds it may be argued that the costs of the intermediate stages leading to bipedalism are too high (Aiello 1981; Andrews and Aiello 1984; Foley 1987a). Arboreal primates that are quadrupedal, such as most cercopithecines, have a shorter evolutionary pathway to terrestrial adaptation by maintaining their quadrupedalism. Furthermore, as Taylor and Rowntree have shown, the energetic costs of full quadrupedalism, especially at high speeds, are much lower than for chimpanzees, which are characterized by a greater degree of suspensory behavior. Furthermore, in the case of chimpanzees and other hominoids, the benefits of bipedalism only occur under the specific conditions of foraging over longer distances, a circumstance that does not apply, for example, to the gorilla. More significant, perhaps, is the fact that the principal costs of bipedalism are opportunity costs: the loss of any ability to move efficiently in an arboreal habitat. A species such as the chimpanzee, which obtains a large proportion of its food in the trees, would find this cost to be overwhelming. Energetic and other benefits of bipedalism could only occur under specific ecological conditions.

5.5.4. Ecological Context of Bipedalism

Given the costs and benefits of bipedalism, it is possible to specify the conditions under which it would have been advantageous and therefore positively selected. In brief these are hot, open terrestrial environments where arboreal food resources are limited and where terrestrial resources are distributed in highly dispersed patches over large areas. These ecological conditions would be supplemented by certain socioecological parameters. If females are forced to disperse more widely than is the case with chimpanzees (whose average day range is less than 2 km), then their energetic costs will be greatly increased unless the advantages of bipedalism obtain. For example, a female chimpanzee foraging over 5 km (comparable to some hunter–gatherer females; Blurton Jones et al. 1989; see also Chapters 6, 7, and 8) would be expending an additional 800 kJ per day above the current chimpanzee average, or 9% above estimated total daily expenditure. Following the Wrangham (1980) model, which proposes that males must distribute themselves to maximize access to females, and assuming that early hominids had a pattern of social organization where kin-related males defended areas in which females foraged (Foley and Lee 1989), then males could well have been patrolling some very large areas indeed. Under these circumstances the costs of not being bipedal may have been high. For example, among male chimpanzees modal day range is four times larger than females (Rodman 1984). If female day range increases to 5 km, then male range may increase to 20 km.

The conditions under which bipedalism evolved would be predicted as those in which trees are more dispersed and resources more widely distributed. Hill (1987) proposes this case with the Chemeron environments in which the earliest hominids are found, and Foley (1987a) presents data showing that all early African hominid fossils have been recovered from environments in which tree cover is less than that of most modern chimpanzee populations.

5.6. FORAGING BEHAVIOR

Models of the energetics of bipedalism and ranging patterns clearly show that the conditions under which bipedalism would have been advantageous are intimately linked to the distribution of resources and hence to the foraging behavior of the early hominids.

5.6.1. The Hominoid Diet

There is now substantial data available on the foraging behavior of the living hominoids. However, gibbons, orangutans, and gorillas are probably either too phylogenetically distant or ecologically specialized to provide a suitable model for early hominids. Chimpanzees, apart from being phylogenetically closest (Sibley and Ahlquist 1984), are semiterrestrial, often live in relatively dry African environments, and are of similar body size to some early hominids.

Chimpanzee foraging behavior can best be characterized as eclectic, opportunistic, and dietarily diverse (Wrangham 1977; Kortlandt 1984;

Ghiglieri 1984; see also Chapter 4). Several points may be noted. Diet varies considerably from individual to individual, by sex, through seasons, and from one population to another. Males hunt considerably more than females (Goodall 1986) and, as noted above, forage over larger areas (Wrangham and Smuts 1980; Rodman 1984). The Tai Forest chimpanzees hunt more than those at Gombe (Boesch and Boesch 1989). Among the Mahali chimpanzees diet breadth expands markedly in the dry season (see Collins and McGrew 1988), whereas at Gombe, which is wetter, diet breadth is greater in the wet season (Wrangham 1977). Overall, there is no such thing as a typical chimpanzee diet. Chimpanzees derive most of their nutrition from plant foods, with a very marked preference for fruits and other high-quality items when available. Fruits contribute up to 89% of the diet for the chimpanzees in the Kibale Forest (Wrangham 1986). When these foods are not available, chimpanzees will exploit leaves and other plant materials of lower nutritional value (Hladik 1977). Animal food is nearly always a part of the chimpanzee diet, but this varies considerably with sex, individual, and time of year. In particular, hunting of mammals can fluctuate widely (Goodall 1986). Finally, tools are a variable component of chimpanzee foraging behavior (McGrew 1989, in press). In some populations tool use is confined to termite fishing, while in others stone hammers are used for cracking open palm oil nuts (Boesch and Boesch 1983).

5.6.2. Expansion of the Hominid Diet Breadth

One need not assume that the earliest hominids had a diet similar to that of the chimpanzee, but it is useful to consider the ways in which hominids, during the course of their evolution, have differed in foraging behavior, and diet breadth in particular, from that of living chimpanzees.

There is relatively little evidence for the foraging behavior of the earliest known hominids, *Australopithecus afarensis*. The absence of stone tools rules out the possibility of inferring foraging behavior from archeological deposits. Their tooth morphology, with relatively large incisors and slightly expanded molars, does not differ in a significantly functional manner (with the exception of the reduced canine) from that of the chimpanzee, and studies of dental wear also indicate a largely frugivorous diet (Walker 1981).

By shortly after 2 million years a variety of hominid taxa can be identified. The robust australopithecines (*A. aethiopicus*, *A. robustus*, *A. crassidens*, and *A. boisei*) are all characterized by massive enlargement of masticatory musculature, enlargement of the molars and premolars with flat highly worn occlusal surfaces, and reduced anterior dentition. Dental wear is interpreted as the product of grinding large quantities of hard, coarse plant material (Walker 1981; Grine 1981, 1989; Kay 1985). In contrast, early *Homo* retain generalized dental proportions, with less marked wear. *Homo erectus*, it has been argued, shows a pattern of dental wear indicative of a greater proportion of meat in the diet (Walker, 1981). There is, furthermore, evidence of cut marks on mammalian bones, suggesting that some hominids from about 2.0 Ma were processing meat on a scale unknown among chimpanzees (Potts 1989; Bunn and Kroll 1986). However, the precise interpretation of these animal bone assemblages is a matter of considerable controversy. It is impossible at this point to specify either the extent of hominid meat eating or the means of procurement.

Virtually nothing is known of the foraging behavior of the early Asian hominids (see Pope 1988). By the middle Pleistocene, both African and Eurasian hominids and their artifacts are found with large quantities of animal bones, but generally in cave contexts where there are problems of distinguishing hominid bone accumulations from those of carnivore species (Binford 1984), while open sites are thinly distributed and much carcass deposition may be natural. The nature of plant foraging is unknown.

With archaic *H. sapiens* (especially neanderthals) animal bone accumulations are more marked and have been consistently interpreted by most workers as the product of hunting. Extensive hunting behavior seems to be a general characteristic of anatomically modern humans, although its actual pattern is highly variable (Hayden 1981).

In summary, early hominid diet may overlap considerably with that of the chimpanzee. The principal evidence for any difference lies in the greater use of tools for resource extraction, a greater use of animal products, and an expanded home range. A further difference may be that hominids seem to have focused more food consumption activities at central locations, as shown by stone tool/bone accumulations, than is the case with chimpanzees. However, it should be remembered that the hominids may consist of up to 10 distinct species, and therefore diet is almost certainly highly variable both within and between species.

5.6.3. A Patch Theory Analysis of Hominid Foraging Behavior

Behavioral ecologists have focused on the concept of the resource patch as a useful tool in the analysis of foraging behavior (Wiens 1977). A patch may be defined as a location in either time or space at which resources are available. Usually this refers to an area of the landscape that is relatively rich in resources. Patches have certain qualities: They may be relatively rich or poor (patch quality), large or small, evenly dispersed or clustered, predictable or unpredictable, abundant or rare (see also Chapter 4). Theorists have suggested ways in which changes in any independent patch quality can affect the foraging behavior of a given species. For example, increased patch size is thought to have the effect of increasing group size, while decreasing patch quality will increase foraging time (MacDonald 1981; MacDonald and Carr 1989; Powell 1989).

Although the precursors of the earliest hominids need not necessarily have been similar or identical to chimpanzees in their foraging behavior, it may be useful to employ the patch structure and foraging responses of these apes as a starting point and consider how changes in resource structure altered the foraging activities of the hominids under different ecological conditions. An advantage of this approach is that as the core of any such analysis is based on *relative* values it is not necessary to specify exact quantities, because our knowledge of many elements of early hominid environments and activities is not precise.

Data presented by Dunbar on socioecological variation among the savanna baboons suggest that changes in the predictability, patchiness, and quality of food available and exploited have distinctive effects. This has been used by Lee (1989) and Foley (1989a) to model evolutionary changes in primates and hominids. The essential predictions of this model are:

1. Increasing predictability of resources will result in larger group sizes and more substructuring within these groups.
2. Increasing patchiness of resources will result in larger home and day ranges, more time spent in traveling, and more tightly bonded groups.
3. Increasing food quality will result in greater dietary selectivity.

Figure 5.4A shows the predicted changes relative to a standard value of environmental patchiness and the predictability of resources. It is now necessary to examine the ecological conditions of various situations in hominid evolution in the context of this model and to establish the probable effects on foraging behavior.

5.6.4. The Earliest Hominids

As discussed above (see 5.6.2) the earliest hominids occupied more open, less wooded habitats than living chimpanzees. Relative to the foraging context of chimpanzees this represents increased resource patchiness (Collins and McGrew 1988). Greater environmental uncertainty and seasonality of these environments occurs. There is little evidence to suggest either tool use or increased encephalization, which might indicate an enhanced ability to find patches or ensure a higher rate of return from them (either plant or animal). The expectation is that there should be little change in overall group size or structure at this stage, but considerable increase in day and home range. This is consistent with the energetic basis of bipedalism dis-

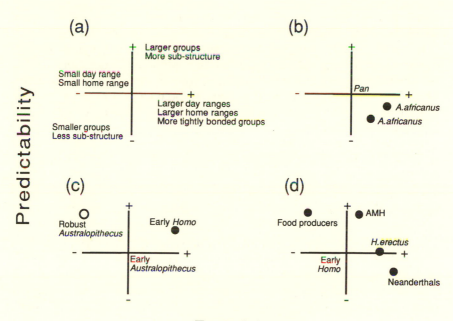

Patchiness

Figure 5.4.   Predicted socioecological effects of changes in resource patchiness and predictability. (a) General model of the effect of increase or decrease of patchiness and predictability of resources. (b) Changes of resource structure for early austra-lopithecines in relation to Pan. (c) Changes of resource structure for robust austra-lopithecines and early Homo relative to early australopithecines. (d) Changes of resource structure for later members of the genus Homo relative to early Homo.

cussed above. Using the predictions outlined above (see 5.6.3 and Figure 5.4A), the earliest australopithecines should have been characterized princi-pally by larger day and home ranges relative to *Pan* (Figure 5.4B).

5.6.5. The Pliocene–Pleistocene Hominid Radiation

From at least 2.0 Ma there is strong evidence for multiple species of hominids (see Figure 5.1) and divergent evolutionary trends. This suggests variable ecological conditions promoting alternative foraging strategies in the highly seasonal environments where the early hominids lived (Foley 1987a). The dental specializations of the robust australopithecines suggests that they were exploiting low-quality plant foods. Unlike the food resources of earlier hominids, these were more likely to occur in large and highly patches. Compared to earlier hominids a reduction in home and day range should have occurred, together with an increase in group size (Figure 5.4C).

In contrast, early members of the genus *Homo* are associated with increased tool use and utilization of animal resources (Isaac 1984). These resources were more patchily distributed, promoting larger day and home ranges. Greater use of tools may have increased their probability of success, thus allowing for larger foraging groups exploiting these rich, high-quality patches (Figure 5.4C).

5.6.6. *Foraging Behavior in Later Hominid Evolution*

It is extremely difficult to plot the changes in socioecology for later hominids in any detail, due to the paucity of evidence and the high degree of environmental variability. By 1.0 Ma hominids were distributed well beyond the dry regions of sub-Saharan Africa, and by 0.1 Ma archaic hominids were dispersed throughout the Old World (Foley 1987a). *Homo erectus* colonized more temperate and seasonal climates, which were characterized by a more patchy resource base compared to early African *Homo*. There is little evidence to indicate much change in their ability to increase the probability of food acquisition. The apparent robustness of middle and late Pleistocene hominids has been linked to long foraging distances (Trinkaus 1983, 1989a), which is consistent with the socioecological prediction of more dispersed foraging patterns (Figure 5.4D). The most extreme response may have been that of the Neanderthals, where reduction in group size would be expected (Binford 1989).

It has been argued (Foley 1989b) that the ecological and morphological characteristics of anatomically modern humans—greater use of high-quality resources, larger home ranges, larger group sizes, and much greater group substructure—may be linked to their ability to ensure foraging, especially hunting, success (see Chapter 6). Through greater planning depth and more effective technology, they turned an unpredictable resource into a predictable one, from which socioecological changes derived (Figure 5.4D). Modern humans were able to sustain much larger group sizes, probably involving considerable substructure. Whether this ability is due to changes in social behavior, mental abilities, or technology remains uncertain. Finally, the development of techniques of food production that occurred at the end of the Pleistocene is also consistent with this model. Modification of the resource base through domestication results in a much less patchy environment, with the reduction in territorial or ranging area that is associated with agriculturalists.

5.7. EVOLUTION OF HUMAN SOCIAL BEHAVIOR

Patterns of social behavior are integrally linked to the structure of resource availability. The foraging behavior discussed in section 5.6 should provide the parameters for modeling the evolution of hominid social behavior. Linkage between resource structure and social behavior is best sought not through broad habitat/social structure correlations, but through the distributional strategies employed by males and females in response to resource availability. Wrangham's (1980) model expresses this as follows: Female reproductive success is principally constrained by access to resources, that of males by access to females. Females will therefore distribute themselves in response to resource distribution, males in response to female distribution. Social structure is the end product of these distributional strategies and the conspecific behavioral interactions that arise from them (see Chapter 4). Where resources occur in large patches, female–female associations should occur. Related females will not disperse from natal groups. Under different ecological conditions, females can be expected to be solitary, in kin-bonded female groups, or in groups of unrelated individuals.

Male distribution responds to female distribution. Where a single male can potentially monopolize one or a group of related females, monogamous or polygynous harem systems will occur. Where no single male is able to gain such reproductive control relative to other males, then (unrelated) multimale systems (including polyandry) develop. If patch structure is such that females do not gain any advantage out of kin-based associations but a male can monopolize a group of females, then groups composed of a single male attached to a group of unrelated females can occur. Where female distribution is dispersed in this manner, males may associate with kin to form coalitions to defend access to females or their resources.

The key element of this model is how males and females distribute themselves. It yields a classification of social groups according to whether there is female dispersal, male dispersal, or dispersal of both sexes from natal groups. Further predictive details involve whether associations between sexes are stable or transient, and whether males will defend females directly from other males or defend the resources on which they depend. The particular power of the model lies in the fact that variation in social behavior is constrained to a series of finite possibilities the conditions for which can be specified (Lee 1989; Foley and Lee 1989).

5.7.1. Principles of Social Evolution

Wrangham's model was developed to account for the variation in social behavior observed in living primates (and other animals). It was extended to explain longer-term patterns of social evolution, and in particular the evolution of hominid social behavior (Ghiglieri 1987; Wrangham 1987; Foley 1987a, 1989a; Foley and Lee 1989). Foley and Lee (1989) proposed a formal basis for such an extension by arguing that each social system may be characterized in terms of three variables (female distributional strategy, male distributional strategy, and male–female relationship) and that the sum of these variables allows the evolutionary distance between social states to be measured. According to this model, some social states are more evolutionarily distant from each other, and possible and probable pathways between them can be specified. Social evolution is seen to consist of alterations in one or more of the key determining variables, the ecological conditions for which could be specified. An expectation of this model is that phylogenetically associated groups should be characterized by adjacent social states. Empirical support for this exists among the hominoids, whose social systems are all adjacent to one another and distinct from the cercopithecines, which are themselves internally coherent (Foley and Lee 1989). The primary advantage of this approach is that social evolution can be assessed in terms of ecological conditions, given that an initial starting point can be established.

5.7.2. Hominoid Social Systems

If changes in social organization follow those in foraging behavior, then it should be possible to map the evolution of hominid social behavior using the hominoids as a baseline for such an analysis. Hominoid social structure shows a strong evolutionary coherence based on female dispersal, with variation in male response to this condition (Foley and Lee 1989). Given the strong phylogenetic links between hominids and African apes, this provides a justification for using ape social strategies as part of the phylogenetic heritage of early hominids (Wrangham 1987; Ghiglieri 1987; Foley 1989a).

Hominoid social organization is markedly diverse. Nonetheless certain patterns can be distinguished. Ghiglieri (1987) and Wrangham (1987) have both argued that the key development in social organization among the hominids is that of female dispersal and the development of kin-based coalitions among males, and Foley (1989a) argues that this is consistent with phylogeny of the hominids. These characteristics become more strongly developed among the African apes. In terms of the model proposed by Foley and Lee (1989) the key variable changes are those relating to the formation of kin associations among males. The pattern of behavior found among chimpanzees is the most evolutionarily derived in this context, and adjacent to the harem-forming gorilla. It may be argued that the hominoids that lie at the base of the hominid clade, at the time of the divergence from *Pan*, lived in social groups where males did not leave their natal group but formed some form of coalition; that females did disperse; and that while females associated with a particular coalition of males as part of a community they did not establish exclusive bonds with particular males. It is also probable that these males did not defend females directly, but rather the territories within which females foraged.

Assuming initial conditions based on the close phylogenetic relationship between hominids and chimpanzees and therefore similar social organization, this model provides a framework for exploring the social structure of the various hominid group sizes discussed in the section on foraging behavior (5.6.3).

5.7.3. Early Hominid Social Behavior

An increased spread of open environments was the key change for the earliest hominids. Resource distribution was more dispersed and patchy, particularly for the relatively large bodied apes. Resource patches would also have been very unevenly distributed and patch size variable. Under these conditions it would be expected that females would have continued to disperse from natal groups and maintained the flexible fission–fusion pattern seen in chimpanzee female foraging groups (see also White and Wrangham 1988). In some cases these would be small dispersed groups exploiting seasonally scarce resources; in others there may have been a tendency toward larger aggregations in response either to larger food patches or to the threat of predation. In either case, day ranges would have been larger. The trend seen in *Pan* towards male territorial rather than female defense would have been enhanced. Larger kin-based male coalitions would be expected, incurring antagonism between groups. This is consistent with the tendency towards larger group size discussed in section 5.6.3.

Such a pattern, rather than monogamous families, single-male harems, or female-bonded groups, is the most parsimonious expectation for the social organization among the early hominids given their phylogenetic context and ecological conditions. There is little reason to expect close and exclusive relationships between individual males and females at this stage.

From these basal hominids (on current evidence, *Australopithecus afarensis*) diverse evolutionary trajectories may be derived, for there is no single trend in hominid evolution. As has been found among both other hominoids and baboons (Dunbar 1988), there would be significant variations in precise structure in response to local conditions. Group size, for example, would have varied markedly, but only within the framework of the general hominoid pattern.

One such variant was the robust australopithecines. Their masticatory specializations, inferred diet, and absence of significant further encephalization indicate ways in which their social organization may have been further modified. They ate principally low-quality plants (either nutritionally poor or requiring considerable processing time), occurring in larger patches. Overall group size probably increased as more females foraged together; male numbers would also increase, weakening the kinship links between them. A rise in the frequency of female defense would be expected under these conditions. A harem structure embedded in larger communities would be the expected outcome. However, unlike the pattern seen in gelada baboons (*Theropithecus gelada*; Dunbar 1988), the longer male tenure associated with the greater longevity of hominoids would inhibit the development of female-bonded harems and the females would be expected to continue to disperse to reduce inbreeding costs and increase mating opportunities. Related males would still be available for group defense against conspecific coalitions on account of the close proximity between harems that would have been maintained (Foley 1989a; Foley and Lee 1989).

Another variation would be associated with the increased encephalization and greater diet breadth of the genus *Homo*. As discussed above (5.6.5), early *Homo*, and especially *H. erectus*, exploited hunted or scavenged mammalian meat on a larger scale than any other living anthropoid. The effect on social organization and behavior may have been marked. Male cooperation among existing kin coalitions may have been enhanced either through territorial defense or collective hunting (as seen, for example, among chimpanzees; Boesch and Boesch 1989). Strongly bonded male kinship groups, possibly extending over more than one generation, would have been likely. What may have been equally significant is the greater reproductive costs for females of larger-brained hominid infants (see 5.8.3). Strengthening of these bonds into long-term stable relationships, most probably polygynously, would indicate and be necessary for greater levels of parental investment in offspring.

The path of social evolution within the genus *Homo* is likely to be diverse and complex. *Homo erectus* (*sensu lato*) occurs in Asia as well as in Africa, and developed *H. erectus* or its descendants is known widely throughout the Old World. Distinctive regional populations of archaic hominids can be identified from at least 200,000 years ago, and these may be associated with specific technologies (Foley 1987b). Given that social behavior is expected to respond to these diverse conditions over a vast area, variability and flexibility may be expected. Smaller group size and less territorially fixed behavior in highly seasonal and colder environments, or smaller but more flexible patterns in tropical forest regions might be predictable trends. What may be argued more strongly is that these variations would be based upon developing patrilineal kinship systems and the further development of male parental investment in the offspring of females to which they are more strongly attached.

5.7.4. The Path to Modern Human Behavior

Against this long-term background it is appropriate to examine the nature of modern human social behavior and problems associated with its emergence. There are several reasons for treating this as more than just a minor modification from that of the more archaic hominids.

Although this is still debated (see Mellars and Stringer 1989; Trinkaus 1989b), there is a case to be made that modern humans had a single point of origin, probably in Africa about 150,000 years ago, and that they dispersed throughout the world, relatively rapidly replacing existing archaic populations (Cann et al. 1987; Stringer and Andrews 1988). Were such an interpretation to be correct, it is reasonable to infer that some major adaptive advantage, and for a hominid—or indeed any hominoid—it is likely that aspects of behavior, especially social behavior, lies at the root of this development. The archaeological record itself displays a marked contrast between archaic and modern forms. The technology of archaic hominids is relatively simple, highly stable spatially and temporally, and generally lacking the range of typological variation seen in modern forms (Foley 1987b). In contrast, after the appearance of modern humans technology is temporally variable, regionally specific, and rapidly characterized by a use of diverse raw materials and the appearance of artistic forms. Again, this is suggestive of marked behavioral differences between archaic and modern hominids. Subsequent to the appearance of anatomically modern humans in many parts of the world, a major change occurs in human subsistence activities with the development of food production at the end of the Pleistocene. Social, spatial, and demographic structure is rapidly and radically transformed in a matter of several thousand years, a pattern that is in stark contrast to the changes seen in the preceding million years.

As discussed in section 5.6.6, there are reasons for relating the appearance of modern humans to increased foraging efficiency, and to the utilization of animal resources. Of particular interest here are the consequences of such a change for social organization. As high-quality food resources become more predictable, there would be the potential for an increase in group size. There may have been greater opportunities for female bonds to occur; for males the implication is larger coalitions, perhaps more intragroup substructuring, and also the potential at least for increased intergroup hostility. Such a pattern would be consistent with the archaeological evidence in some parts of the world for increased population density, greater indications of regional and local patterning, and the relatively high degree of sexual dimorphism in late Pleistocene modern humans (Frayer 1984; Foley 1988). In general terms it might be argued that with the appearance of modern humans the increasingly complex social organization that occurred would itself act as a major pressure for further social evolution and diversification. This may form the basis for both the diversity observable in the recent past and present, and the behavioral flexibility on which it is built (see Chapter 3).

In summary, hominid social evolution appears to display three marked trends: increasing group size, the formation and maintenance of male kin alliances, and strong bonds between individual males and females. Increasing group size is largely associated with the earlier hominids, and group size may be expected to have fluctuated markedly subsequently. Male kin associations probably enabled hominids to occupy and exploit the drier regions of Africa during the late Pliocene and early Pleistocene, and subsequently other parts of the globe. Male–female bonds and more exclusive mating patterns are likely to have been the latest development, possibly associated with the emergence of *H. sapiens* (see Chapter 11). The adaptive basis for this late development may lie in the increased parental investment associated with highly encephalized offspring.

5.8. ENCEPHALIZATION AND LIFE HISTORY STRATEGY

Social organization, deriving from male and female dispersal strategies and consequent mating strategies, reflects resource structure and is the basis for the models presented in section 5.7. Another element that contributes to social organization is parenting strategy, and in particular the costs of raising offspring. All primates have high levels of parental investment, and this is reflected in their life history variables: long gestation, slow postnatal growth, high age of first reproduction, and extended longevity (Harvey et al. 1987). Among humans these are particularly marked, and it may be argued that this is correlated with the high costs of rearing highly encephalized infants (Martin 1983). It is appropriate, therefore, to model the costs, conditions, and consequences of parental investment among hominids.

5.8.1. Pattern of Hominid Encephalization

All assessments of brain enlargement depend upon scaling factors. Among mammals, brain size scales allometrically to body size, and the intercepts of the regressions vary from one lineage to another. Comparisons of hominid absolute brain size can be misleading if body size changes are ignored. Many attempts to estimate body size of fossil hominids have been made (see Foley 1987a for a review). Currently the most acceptable are those of McHenry (1988), which if plotted against time (Figure 5.5) show considerable variation. A general increase would be observable were it not

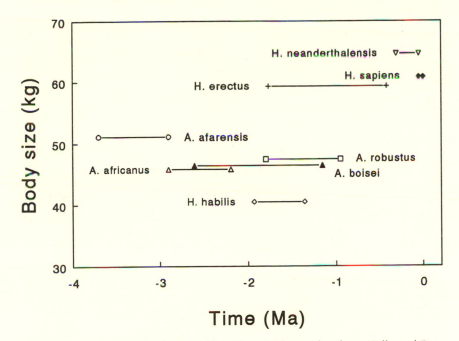

Figure 5.5. Changes in body size of fossil hominid taxa (data from Aiello and Dean 1990).

for the large body size of *A. afarensis*. However, the range for this taxon is from less than 30 kg to about 80 kg, and there are grounds for suggesting that these comprise separate species, in which case there would be both large and small hominids at this early stage. The genus *Homo* displays a gradual increase in body weight, with a slight decrease following the appearance of modern humans. With this in mind, Figure 5.6 plots hominid relative brain size (encephalization quotient or EQ, which is calculated as the observed brain size divided by expected brain size for a particular body size; see Martin 1989 for details) against time. Martin's (1983) EQ based on a 0.75 rather than 0.67 exponent is used. Two inferences to be drawn from these data are that only the genus *Homo* shows a significant increase above that of the great apes, and that modern humans show a major increase.

5.8.2. Theories of Brain Enlargement

Brain enlargement has been explained by both ecological and social factors. Clutton-Brock and Harvey (1980) and Milton (1981) argue that large brains in primates are related to ecological patterns, with frugivores possessing relatively larger brains than folivores. Such an argument can be sus-

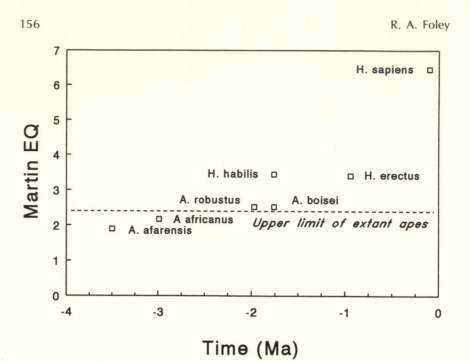

*Figure 5.6. Hominid encephalization quotient (EQ) relative to time. EQ is calcu-
lated by the equation E (observed)/(E (expected) = 0.248W$^{0.76}$ (Martin 1983). Data
from Aiello and Dean 1990.*

tained on the grounds that foraging for patchy and less predictable food
resources, like fruit or animal prey, requires greater levels of information
processing (Parker and Gibson 1979).

Humphrey (1976), in contrast, has proposed a social theory for intelligence, and by implication large brains. The key assertion here is that social
problems require particularly rapid and complex information processing on
account of the flexibility and unpredictability of an individual's behavior,
and hence that large brains will evolve under conditions of social complexity. This hypothesis has been expanded and enlarged by a number of authors
who elaborate on the precise nature of social strategies in primates in
particular (Byrne and Whiten 1986).

Empirical support can be found for each of these hypotheses. Encephalization has been shown to correlate with a large number of life history,
ecological, and social parameters, and many of these parameters change
significantly during hominid evolution (Foley 1990); (see Table 5.1).

Some progress can be made if a distinction is made between the selective
factors that favor brain enlargement and the conditions under which those
factors can successfully operate. For example, possessing a large brain may
be favored in situations where animals must forage widely, exploit patchy

Table 5.1. *Parameters That Have Been Shown to Be Significantly Correlated with Relative Brain Size in Primates and Other Mammals*[a]

Parameters	Significance in hominid evolution
1. *Life history parameters*	
Gestation length[1]	Probably relatively unchanged
Lifespan[1]	Greatly extended
Neonate weight[1]	Modern humans have smaller neonate weight and are more altricial
Weaning age[1]	Greatly reduced in food-producing populations[7]
Age of first reproduction[1]	Marginally later than African apes; males more variable[7]
Interbirth interval[1]	Similar to gorilla, shorter than chimp[7]
2. *Ecological parameters*	
Home range size[2]	Greatly enlarged[8]
Dietary quality[2]	Higher quality[9]
Maternal metabolic rate[3]	Unknown
3. *Social parameters*	
Group size[4]	Larger in modern humans, probably larger in most hominids[10]
Social complexity[5]	Enhanced
Communication[6]	Language, symbolism, etc.

[a]Significance in hominid evolution refers to changes relative to African apes and supporting paleobiological or archaeological evidence (after Foley 1990).
[b]References:

1. Harvey et al. (1987)
2. Clutton-Brock and Harvey (1980)
3. Martin (1983)
4. Dunbar (in press)
5. Humphrey (1976)
6. Parker and Gibson (1979)
7. Lee (1989)
8. Foley (1987a)
9. Hayden (1981)
10. Foley and Lee (1989)

foods, or live a long time in large social groups. Virtually all large mammals fulfil at least some of these conditions and therefore would benefit from a larger brain. The fact that most mammals do not show marked encephalization suggests that there are constraints operating and that only when these are released does a pattern such as that seen in hominids occur. The costs involved in brain enlargement are seldom overcome in evolution to the extent found among genus *Homo*.

5.8.3. Costs of Brain Enlargement

Martin (1983) showed that among mammals brain size scales to body size to the power of 0.75. This is the same scaling coefficient as that of body weight and metabolic rate. It is furthermore well established that most brain growth occurs neonatally or during a short period after birth (Martin 1989). During this time growth rates may be very rapid. Martin has argued on this basis that brain size is constrained by the metabolic costs of growth, and that most species are unable to exceed certain limits. In particular, it is the mothers who must bear the actual metabolic load of brain growth as the vast proportion of this occurs prenatally or very rapidly after birth. It is usually estimated that the average daily metabolic requirements (ADMR) for a pregnant or lactating female are two to three times basal metabolic rate (BMR), and thus higher than the ADMR of other females (Martin 1983).

A comparison of chimpanzees and humans can form the basis for modeling the costs of larger brains. Passmore and Durnin (1955) have suggested that the brain has a very high rate of energy consumption. Using oxygen utilization as a measure, the brain utilizes about 3.5 m/100 g/min[1], or about 20% of human oxygen uptake and energy expenditure. The costs during growth are likely to be higher. Using data on modern human and chimpanzee brain size during growth (Blackfan 1933; Schultz 1940; Passingham 1982) it is possible to calculate the costs of having large-brained offspring. Figure 5.7a shows the daily average costs involved in maintaining the growing human and chimpanzee brain. As can be seen, even the human neonate brain exceeds the costs of a chimpanzee's. By the time the human infant is 5 years old the costs of brain maintenance are more than three times as great. The difference is even more marked when the data on costs are treated cumulatively so that the total costs of a large-brained infant are estimated (Figure 5.7b). By the age of 5 years a chimpanzee will have used 722,658 kJ for brain maintenance (at this level it is irrelevant how these costs are partitioned between mother and offspring). This amounts to a daily average of about 350 kJ. In contrast, by the same age a human will have used 2,108,228 kJ, or a daily average about 1000 kJ. This represents approximately a threefold increase in energy costs during the first years of life on account of an increased brain size.

Whatever the benefits of a large brain, it incurs very high costs that must be met through foraging behavior. Furthermore, in humans brain growth continues for a much longer period; chimpanzees will have achieved virtual adult brain size by between 3 and 4 years of age, whereas in humans even at age 10 there is still a small amount of brain growth. Human mothers, the offspring themselves, or other individuals must provide this additional energy through foraging (see Chapter 9).

To put this into the context of daily energetic needs, Ulijaszek and Strickland (in press) present data showing that the average energy requirement of a human infant in the first 18 months of life is 2556.36 kJ per day.

---

1. The exact ratio between oxygen utilization and energy expenditure varies with the tissue, but a general relationship can be expressed as 1 liter of O_2 = 5 kcal = 20.94 kJ.

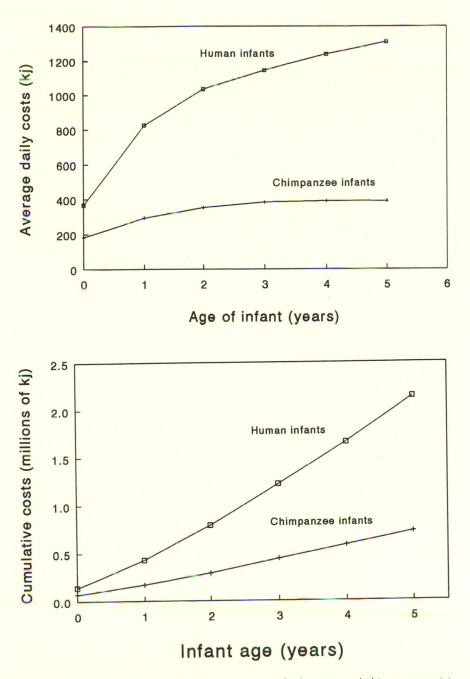

Figure 5.7. *Energetic costs of brain maintenance for humans and chimpanzees. (a) Annual costs in millions of milliliters of oxygen per annum, calculated from the costs of brain maintenance of 3.5 m/g/day (Passmore and Durnin 1955), using human and chimpanzee brain size data for the first 5 years of life. (b) Cumulative costs, using the same data as in (a), but summed through the first 5 years of life.*

Estimating the costs of the human infant's brain during that first year on the basis of the energy costs discussed above, it can be shown that the brain accounts for 494.94 kJ per day of these requirements (i.e., 19.36%). Were those infants to have chimpanzee-size brains, we can calculate the reduced energy requirements; in the first 18 months of life the chimpanzee brain requires an average of 272.88 kJ per day. Average daily energy requirements would therefore be only 2333.48 [total human costs (2556.36 kJ/day) less human brain costs (494.94 kJ/day) plus chimpanzee brain costs (272.88 kJ/day)]. This represents a reduced energy requirement of 222.88 kJ per day. In other words, highly encephalized human infants are approximately 8.7% more costly, assuming other factors are held constant.

Clearly these crude estimates could be improved, but they indicate that high encephalization quotients will only occur among populations that are in some way able to bear the costs (including other opportunity costs) of higher parental effort. Brain enlargement among hominids may be the product of a variety of social and ecological factors, but behaviors underlying them should enhance the energy intake of females and their offspring (see Chapter 9).

5.8.4. Life History Strategy of Encephalized Hominids

The pattern of changes in foraging behavior discussed above (5.6.3) are closely related to this change in the costs of development, and furthermore the development of strategies providing high nutritional returns is necessary for human encephalization. In this sense the causes of large brain size among hominids are ecological. Equally, though, such developments are closely tied in with social factors. As discussed in section 5.7.3, a prominent characteristic of modern human social behavior lies in the strong bonds formed between individual adult males and females. This most probably relates to provisioning of females and offspring or at least enhancement of female access to resources. This more complex social system in which strong relationships form both within kin groups and between the sexes may in turn act as a major selective pressure for increased brain size, and the need for a large brain is reciprocal to the conditions necessary to sustain it.

As can be seen in Figure 5.6, this pattern is characteristic of the genus *Homo*, not the hominids as a whole, and furthermore it is a relatively late development.

Finally, brain size, both adult and neonate, is linked among other species to a whole series of life history parameters: gestation length, weaning age, age of first reproduction, and longevity (Harvey et al. 1987). The pattern of

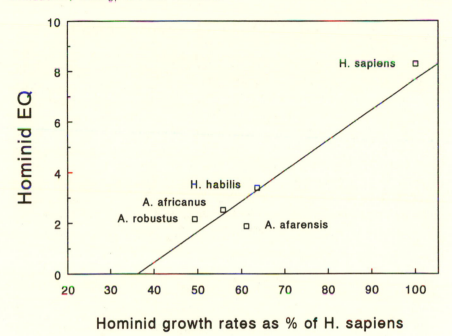

Figure 5.8. *Hominid EQ in relation to hominid growth rates. EQ calculated as in Figure 5.6. Growth rates calculated from data in Bromage and Dean (1985) on calendrical age at death of immature hominids in relation to stage of dental eruption, expressed as a percentage of modern human age/eruption rates. For example, A. afarensis (LH2) has an age estimate from the number of perikymata of 3.6 years; its dental eruption age based on modern human standards is 6 years, which produces a relative value of 60%.*

these changes during the course of hominid evolution is largely unknown, although the recent developments in work on dental tissue formation (Bromage and Dean 1985; Beynon and Wood 1987; Smith 1989) are opening this field up very rapidly. Discoveries of recent years show that hominid development rates during the Pliocene and early Pleistocene are relatively rapid (Bromage and Dean 1985; Beynon and Dean 1988), which provides further support for the suggestion that the major shifts in life history strategy associated with modern humans occur later and are critical to the appearance of modern forms of behavior. Evidence for this is provided by the strong relationship between hominid EQ and growth rates. Figure 5.8 plots estimated hominid EQ against the rate of dental eruption in immature hominids (Bromage and Dean 1985), calculated as a percentage of time of eruption in modern humans. This small set of data suggests that changes in hominid encephalization are strongly related to other life history parameters.

5.9. HUMAN EVOLUTION IN ECOLOGICAL PERSPECTIVE

This chapter has attempted to link the long-term patterns seen in the hominid fossil record to the principles of behavioral and evolutionary ecology, and therefore to explain why hominid evolution took the course it did. Clearly such a venture is fraught with difficulties relating to the particular and relatively impoverished data available. However, it is possible to go beyond phylogenetic and paleoenvironmental reconstructions, and to apply analytical and modeling techniques that relate the observations that are possible to some powerful theories (Foley and Dunbar 1989; Dunbar 1990). The enterprise is very much at an early stage and the patterns suggested here are likely to be modified as new techniques provide additional information about the past. Some preliminary conclusions are possible.

5.9.1. The Ecological Pattern
of Hominid Evolution

Specific models for ranging and foraging behavior and social and life history strategies among early hominids discussed here in isolation can be linked together. A prior condition for hominid evolution appears to be an environmental shift in which there was a reduction of forest cover and expansion of savanna regions in parts of sub-Saharan Africa (Foley 1987a). For the apes living in these conditions, resources became more dispersed and patchy, as well as more terrestrial. Under these conditions there was selection for larger home and day ranges and specialized terrestrial foraging, with concomitant increases in energetic demands. The loss of the ability to forage and sleep in trees was offset by the marked energetic and thermoregulatory advantages of bipedalism. This may have been especially marked among females, whose previous ranges may have been relatively small. With females dispersing further, males would have been even less capable of defending specific females, placing a selective advantage on the formation and maintenance of larger male kin alliances. Overall group size is likely to have increased, with hostility occurring between groups (the early australopithecines).

Continuing environmental change as well as hominid expansion into more variable and drier habitats would have enhanced this situation, leading to considerable adaptive and evolutionary diversity. Among some populations specialization on low-quality plant foods occuring in very large patches would have allowed for a reduction in range size, less dispersed females, and a breakdown in male kin systems, although overall group size permitted by the large food patches may have been high (later australopithecines or paranthropines).

For other populations the ability to exploit diverse resources including seasonally available meat would have been linked to further increases in group size and range size. Both the ecological demands of large ranges and the social complexities of larger groups would have led to pressure for further encephalization, an adaptation that was only possible if high nutritional levels could be obtained, particularly for mothers and their offspring (early *Homo*). The higher costs of offspring with larger brains would in turn have demanded greater levels of parental effort/investment, and females would have benefited from closer associations with males, resulting in increased caretaking or provisioning (evolution through the genus *Homo*). This would in turn produce more complex substructures to the communities, i.e., a hierarchy of social units, mothers and dependent offspring, males and associated females, male kin alliances all within a "community" (anatomically modern humans).

5.9.2. Modern Humans in Paleobiological Perspective

Finally it may be asked to what extent can this analytical survey of hominid evolutionary ecology throw light on the patterns of modern behavior? Several basic points can be established. First, modern human behavior did not emerge as a package at a remote time in the Pleistocene, but has been a process of accretion of new behavioral systems and their biological bases—for example, the early appearance of bipedalism and associated foraging changes, but the late, *Homo*-specific pattern of encephalization. Second, there is no sudden (or punctuated) formation of modern behavior; its antecedents can be mapped through the Pleistocene and back to common roots with the African apes. This is not to say that hominid behavioral evolution is a smooth and continuous process; clearly some changes are more significant and more rapid than others. It might, for example, be argued that the relatively late change in parenting behavior proposed here had major consequences for the whole behavioral and social organization of hominids, resulting in the extraordinarily rapid changes of the last 30,000 years. Third, patterns of hominid evolution and the key elements of modern human behavior appear to be explicable in terms of the general principles of evolutionary ecology extrapolated from studies of living primates. From an ecological perspective there is no evidence for any macroevolutionary mechanisms, although clearly there are events that work themselves out over long periods of time in response to climatic and environmental change (Vrba 1985; Foley 1987a, in press).

Perhaps most important of all, while the patterns of hominid behavioral change are explicable in terms of general principles, the specific pattern is only understandable in the context of the hominid phylogenetic history as an African ape. It is the conjunction of new environmental conditions upon the African pattern of female dispersal and male kin alliances that provides the detailed shape to our evolutionary history. The general run of modern human behavior—the significance of relatively stable male–female relationships, the predominance of patrilineal descent systems, the high levels of parental investment, the slow growth rates and prolonged longevity of modern humans—is the result of the interaction of phylogenetic constraints with novel selective pressures. One of the challenges facing the development of behavioral ecology in anthropology is to show how current variability in behavior has itself arisen from the interaction of the phylogenetic characteristics of the earliest modern humans and the new ecological, social, and demographic environments of the last 30,000 years.

5.10. SUMMARY

1. Human paleobiology, despite the limitations of the fossil record, can significantly contribute to human behavioral ecology through its ability to reconstruct ancestral states and intermediates between humans and other animals.
2. Fossil evidence shows that hominid evolution consists of a series of adaptive radiations, not a single evolving lineage, and so hominid diversity may be expected to reflect diversity of adaptive strategies.
3. Bipedalism, the shared characteristic of all known hominids, confers significant energetic advantages under specific ecological conditions, these being reduced arboreal resources and more extensive ranging patterns.
4. Hominid foraging behavior is best understood in terms of the exploitation of increasingly patchy resources.
5. Hominid socioecology can be seen as the effects of the exploitation of more patchy resources on the ancestral African hominoid social strategies of female dispersal and kin-based male coalitions.
6. Encephalization is a characteristic of the genus *Homo*, imposes major energetic costs that can only be met under specific ecological conditions, and has consequences for life history strategies as a whole.

RESOURCES, WORK, AND SPACE

III

The Evolutionary Ecology of Food Acquisition

Hillard Kaplan and Kim Hill

6

6.1. INTRODUCTION

Evolution is competitive. Variants that can more efficiently harvest resources for reproduction should become more prevalent through time. The nature and distribution of resources are thus primary conditioning factors that determine adaptations. Any comprehensive theory of hominid evolution and contemporary human social behavior will rest heavily upon a theory of resource acquisition.

This chapter will present evolutionary models of food acquisition and discuss examples of the associated empirical research among humans. The principal focus will be upon hunter–gatherers and forager–horticulturalists with little or no market involvement. We will examine subsistence decisions, *given* the technology and resource acquisition abilities of the people in question. We will not address the question of how much time individuals should spend in subsistence activities (see Chapter 7) but instead we consider what people do with the time they devote to food acquisition. We also will assess progress toward the complementary goals of (1) explaining observed variation in diet and food acquisition strategies among and within human groups and (2) developing general models of behavioral decision-making.

Section 6.2 will review the application of optimization theory to dietary decisions and the most general foraging models: prey choice, patch choice, and combined prey and patch choice models. This discussion and the associated mathematical formalisms are drawn mainly from Stephens and Krebs (1986). This will be followed by a selective review of empirical research applying those models to subsistence-level human groups. Section 6.4 will discuss ways in which traditional human economies are likely to violate the assumptions of most existing foraging models, and some areas in which studies of humans are likely to contribute to a general understanding of subsistence behavior in all organisms. We consider central-place foraging, planning and scheduling of activities, incomplete knowledge and information-gathering, the implications of human communication and information exchange, and individual variation in foraging behavior. Section 6.5 treats what we consider to be the two most important unsolved problems in the evolutionary ecology of food acquisition among humans: nutrient complementarity and within-group specialization in subsistence behavior.

6.2. SIMPLE MODELS

6.2.1. The Theory of Optimal Behavior and Its Application to Foraging

Underlying all the models discussed in this chapter is the assumption that organisms will behave as if they are optimizing some fitness-related currency or set of currencies. The logic of cost–benefit analysis is used to justify this assumption. The fitness effects of behavior are multiple and always include some cost. For example, in the act of stalking and firing an arrow at a deer, energy is expended in stalking and shooting, the arrow may be lost or broken and have to be replaced, and if the animal is killed it will have to be butchered and cooked. The hunting attempt also involves *opportunity* costs such as not hunting other animals, clearing gardens, or caring for children.

Natural selection should favor organisms that maximize the *net* (i.e., benefits minus costs) fitness results of their possible behavioral options (e.g., food gains as a function of time and energy spent foraging). This will be true if at least one of the following conditions is met: (1) more food would lead to increased fertility or survivorship; (2) more time spent in one or more nonforaging activities would lead to increased fertility or survivorship; (3) time spent foraging exposes the individual to dangerous predators, pathogens, or environmental conditions that lower fertility or survivorship. Optimization logic does not imply that natural selection will favor the best possible foraging strategy conceivable, but rather that selection will favor the optimal strategy among the *feasible existing* strategies. As long as foragers have valuable ways to spend their time or there are some risks associated with the food quest, efficient foraging will be favored, even when food is not scarce.

6.2.2. The Construction of Foraging Models

Foraging models contain three components: decisions, currencies, and constraints. The decision component is the foraging problem to be analyzed, that is, the phenomenon the model is designed to explain. For example, the prey choice model is designed to explain which of several food resources the forager will eat. The currency component defines the measurement scale for evaluating the effects of alternative decisions. Examples of currencies are energy (e.g., net energy acquired per unit time), protein, survivorship, and fertility. These currencies are intervening variables through which the behavior or morphology under investigation affects fitness. The use of intervening currencies has several advantages. Fitness itself is very difficult to measure and, in long-lived organisms, can require more time than the lifespan of a single investigator. Fitness is also affected by many nonforaging factors. A currency such as energy is directly affected by foraging decisions. Furthermore, determining the pathway through which a decision affects fitness generates a more complete understanding of the phenomenon than would a simple correlation between decisions and fitness.

Constraints are all the other terms in the model. They specify options available to the forager and their effects. Examples of constraints are the density and distribution of potential food resources in the environment, the dangers associated with exploiting different resources, and the forager's technology, ability to exploit those resources, mobility pattern, and knowledge of the environment. The initial selection of currencies and constraints in a model may be incorrect. Failure to confirm the model's predictions often leads to the search for more appropriate constraints. Indeed, most elaborations of the simple foraging models in recent years have involved changes in either currencies or constraints (see Stephens and Krebs 1986).

6.2.3. Modeling Prey Choice

We begin by outlining the simplest and most general model, presented in various forms by MacArthur and Pianka (1966), Charnov and Orians (1973), Schoener (1971), Emlen (1966, 1973), Maynard Smith (1974b), Pulliam (1974), and Stephens and Krebs (1986).

Model Components.　　The model is designed to predict the food items the forager will attempt to exploit ("handle") and those it will ignore in favor of continued search for more preferred foods. Thus, the *decision* component of the model is to *search* or *handle*. Search is time spent looking for prey whether actively moving through the environment or waiting for food items to pass by. Handling prey includes all time devoted to pursuing, capturing, processing (e.g., transporting, butchering, cooking), and eating the prey, once it is encountered.

The *currency* component in the simplest model is *energy*. The model assumes that the forager is designed to maximize the *long-term net rate* at which energy is acquired during foraging.

There are several important constraint components to the model. Searching for and handling prey are *mutually exclusive* activities; they cannot be done simultaneously. Prey are encountered sequentially and randomly, but in proportion to their abundance in the environment. Prey types are *not systematically* clumped into patches or evenly dispersed. The model also assumes that foragers have no impact on resource abundance and distribution. It assumes that encounters without pursuit involve no handling time and do not subtract from search time. Finally, the forager is assumed to know, through past experience, the mean encounter rate, average energy returns, and handling costs associated with each prey type.

Solving for Optimal Prey Choice.   Total foraging time (T_f) may be divided into time spent searching for resources (T_s) and time spent handling resources (T_h). T_h includes time spent in failed pursuits, such as chasing animals that escape, as well as successful ones. The total net energetic returns obtained from resources (E) can be thought of as the food energy acquired (E_a) minus the energy spent searching for (E_s) and handling (E_h) resources. The model then solves for the maximal rate (R_{max}) of net energy acquisition:

$$R_{max} = (E/T_f)_{max} \qquad (6.1)$$

In order to solve for R_{max} one must know three characteristics of every resource i: (1) the average *net* energy acquired from each encounter (e_i); (2) the expected or average handling time per encounter (h_i); and (3) the abundance of the resource, measured by the rate at which it is encountered (λ_i). The return rate on encounter for a resource (e_i/h_i) is termed its *profitability*. In addition, the model includes a term describing the probability that a resource will be pursued if it is encountered (p_i).

Net energy acquired during foraging (E) is equal to net energy acquired from resource pursuits [the sum of all encounters with all prey types ($T_s\lambda_i$), times the probability that they will be pursued (p_i), times the expected net energy returns from encounters with each prey type (e_i)], minus the energy expended in search [the energy costs of search multiplied by time spent searching (sT_s)]. Time spent foraging (T_f) is equal to time spent handling resources [the sum of all encounters with all prey types ($T_s\lambda_i$) times the probability that they will be pursued (p_i), times the mean handling time per encounter (h_i)], plus time spent searching for resources (T_s). Thus, the rate (R) of energy gain for the total set of resources handled by a forager is found in the following expression:

$$R = \frac{\sum_{i=1}^{n} T_s\lambda_i p_i e_i - sT_s}{\sum_{i=1}^{n} T_s\lambda_i p_i h_i + T_s} \qquad (6.2)$$

An algorithm allows one quickly to determine which prey items should be pursued. First, all resources are ranked in descending order of their profitability. The prey type that yields the highest return rate upon encounter [$(e_i/h_i)_{max}$] should always be pursued. Other lower-ranked resources should be included sequentially in the set to be pursued until the next most profitable resource yields a lower rate of return upon encounter than could be obtained by continuing to search for and pursue the more profitable items. None of the resources that are ranked lower in profitability should be pursued when encountered.

The set of resources that result in R_{max} are referred to as the *optimal set* or the *optimal diet*. The total number of resources in the diet, counting from the top of the ranked list, is referred to as *diet breadth*. All resources included in the optimal diet must be characterized by higher return rates on encounter than the average foraging return rate for the forager, including all search time.

To see how this works, consider the following example. There are three resources in the environment. The first resource (r_1) is encountered once in every 5 hours of search ($\lambda_1 = 0.2$ items/hr), yields a net return of 1200 cal, and requires 1 hour to handle ($e_1/h_1 = 1200$ cal/hr). The second resource (r_2) is encountered twice in 5 hours of search ($\lambda_2 = 0.4$ items/hr), yields 450 cal, and requires a half hour to handle ($e_2/h_2 = 900$ cal/hr). The third (r_3) is encountered once an hour ($\lambda_3 = 1$ item/hr), yields 200 cal, and requires 1 hour to handle ($e_3/h_3 = 200$ cal/hr). We begin by considering the most profitable resource (r_1). If the forager only exploits r_1, he or she will on average acquire 1200 cal for every 6 hours spent foraging (5 hours of search plus 1 hour of handling) or a total of 200 cal per hour foraging. Since the second-ranked resource (r_2) will on average result in 900 cal per hour *on encounter*, the forager will increase his or her return rate by pursuing it on encounter. With both items in the optimal set he will make three encounters in 5 hours of search. He or she will spend 1 hour handling r_1 and 1 hour handling r_2 (twice for a half hour each time). Thus, in 7 total hours of foraging (including search), he will acquire 2100 cal (1200 from r_1 and 900 from r_2) or 300 cal/hr, a higher rate than can be obtained by pursuing r_1 alone. Since the foraging return rate of 300 cal/hr is now higher than the expected returns from r_3 after encounter ($e_3/h_3 = 200$ cal/hr), it does not pay to pursue r_3. To prove this, consider what happens if all three resources are taken. In 5 hours of search, the forager will handle r_3 five times for 1 hour each in addition to the 2 hours he will handle r_1 and r_2. Each time he or she handles r_3 he spends on average 1 hour that cannot be used in search. Therefore, in 12 total hours of foraging, he will acquire 3100 cal or 258 cal/hr, less than the 300 cal/hr that could be obtained from exploiting only r_1 and r_2.

Implications. This model has three important implications. First, each individual prey type will always be ignored or always be exploited ($p_i = 0$ or $p_i = 1$), depending upon whether it is in the optimal set. If exploiting a food type will increase the average foraging return rate, there is no reason ever to ignore it. If, on the other hand, exploiting it would decrease the average return rate, it should always be ignored. Second, the food value of a resource type alone is not sufficient to determine whether a forager will pursue it; the costs must be considered as well. Thus, foods are ranked by their profitability (net energy gains divided by handling time) not by their food value. Third, the decision to exploit a food type does not depend on its abundance, but rather on the abundance of the more profitable alternative food types. As the abundance of those more profitable resource types decreases, more time will be spent searching and the overall return rate will decrease. Resources of lower profitability may then be added to the optimal diet.

While the prey choice model is extremely useful, it is unlikely that its predictions will match perfectly the patterns of real foragers, even if they do forage optimally. This is because it is afflicted with a series of restrictive assumptions. For example, the rule that resources should always or never be pursued on encounter will be violated if foragers seek information about resources or if test populations include a mix of individuals with different abilities (Stephens 1985). The ranking of resources may be inappropriate if search and handling time are not mutually exclusive (Hill et al. 1987). Despite these limitations, the optimal-diet model is useful because of its clarity, simplicity, and generality.

6.2.4. Methodological Considerations

In order to perform the strongest test of the prey choice model, it is necessary to measure the values of e, h, and λ for every potential resource encountered by a forager. This often is quite difficult. Even when all variables can be adequately estimated in field studies, the use of observational sampling of naturalistic behavior limits the measurements of profitability to those resources that are actually handled by the forager. This is unfortunate since strong tests of the model require a demonstration that resource types that are ignored yield lower returns upon encounter than the expected foraging returns from exploiting the optimal set.

6.2.5. Anthropological and Archaeological Applications of Prey Choice Models

Prey choice models have been employed in analyzing ethnographic data among the Aché of subtropical Paraguayan forests (Hawkes et al. 1982; Hill and Hawkes 1983; Hill et al. 1987; Kaplan et al. 1990), the Alyawara in the central Australian desert (O'Connell and Hawkes 1981, 1984), the Cree in the boreal forests of central Canada (Winterhalder 1977, 1981), the Machiguenga of tropical eastern Peru (Keegan 1986), the Yanomamo, the Ye'kwana, and the Siona Secoya in Venezuela and Ecuador (Hames and Vickers 1982), Inuit in the Canadian Eastern Arctic (Smith 1991), and the Semaq Beri of Malaysia (Kuchikura 1988).

Most studies have tested the *qualitative* predictions of the prey choice model. Qualitative tests predict *directional* tendencies in prey choice or diet breadth in relation to directional changes in parameters such as return rate or abundance, but do not precisely specify the suite of resources to be exploited. *Quantitative* tests require demonstration that *every* resource exploited increases overall return rate. Ideally, such tests should also demonstrate that *every* resource ignored would decrease overall return rate if it were exploited.

Qualitative Tests. A qualitative prediction of the prey choice model is that low-ranked resources will drop out of the diet when search costs decrease and hence overall return rate increases. Winterhalder (1977, 1981) compared the early historical period when Cree hunters searched for food on foot and paddled canoe with his observational period when they used motorized canoes and snowmobiles. He estimates that snowmobiles for instance cut search time costs by about 75%. Cree hunters pursued more species of animals (especially smaller ones) in the past than in the present, supporting the model's qualitative prediction. A second application of the prey choice model is Hames and Vickers's (1982) analysis of hunting strategies in three Amazonian societies. They test the prediction that diet breadth increases with a decrease in the density of highly profitable prey items by comparing zones of heavy hunting pressure and putatively low animal densities (the areas around older settlements) with zones of lower hunting pressure (areas around new settlements or distant from current settlements). Based on the assumption that large game are more profitable than small, they suggest that: (1) in zones of high hunting pressure, men shoot large animals when they are found but prey on the more abundant smaller game; and (2) in zones of low hunting pressure large game are more abundant and men often ignore small game. In all three cases, the proportion of large game to small game hunted decreased with increased hunting pressure. Among the Yekwana and Yanomamo, significantly fewer kills of small game (pacas and armadillos) occurred in distant zones than would be expected given the probabilities derived from binomial distribution theory.

Quantitative Tests. O'Connell and Hawkes (1981) use the optimal-diet model to predict the resources Alyawara women gather when they are in patches of collectable foods. They estimated the profitabilities of 10 subsistence foods in resource-abundant sandhill patches and found that women only gathered the three most profitable. Many species of ripe seeds, the most abundant food available, were ignored. Collecting experiments indicated that the returns *on encounter* for the ignored seeds were lower than the average foraging return rate, for the three most profitable items. These results are consistent with the prey choice model, but should be interpreted cautiously since the test is based on the assumption that foragers should maximize their return rates *while foraging within a patch*. Combined prey and patch models (see below) suggest that maximizing the rate of net energy acquisition per unit time *within* a patch may *not* maximize overall foraging return rates. In the resource-poor mulga woodland, Alyawara women also ignored ripe seeds. This was true even though their foraging return rate in that patch was so low that they could have increased their energetic return rate by collecting the seeds. Their behavior did not fit the model, perhaps because the handling times for seeds was underestimated or that some other assumption built into the model was faulty. We discuss this result again in a later section.

Research with Aché foragers of Paraguay (Hawkes et al. 1982; Hill and Hawkes 1983; Hill et al. 1987) was conducted to determine if all resources exploited by the Aché increased overall return rates. Experience is that most resources were distributed in ways that were not easily predictable by the foragers and that encounters were approximately random during search. Individuals were followed to determine how much time they spent searching for food items, the rates at which they encountered different resource types, and how much time they spent in pursuit and processing after each resource encounter. The food acquired from these encounters was weighed and converted into caloric equivalents. No attempt was made to measure the caloric costs associated with handling different food items; thus profitabilities were calculated without subtracting energy expended in pursuit and processing. Observed encounter rates by foragers rather than prey census data were used to measure λ_i.

Initial results based upon 4 months of field data (Hawkes et al. 1982; Hill and Hawkes 1983) were consistent with the quantitative predictions of the prey choice model. Aché exploited only those resources whose returns on encounter were greater than the average foraging return rate. No test was carried out to determine whether resources that were ignored when encountered would have increased overall return rates, had they been exploited.

The initial analyses of Aché data aggregated all foragers and activity types. However, since men and women have different skills, abilities, and tools, and exploit different foods, they were considered separately in subsequent studies. Male foraging behavior, when hunting alone is considered, is quite consistent with the quantitative predictions of the prey choice model (Hill and Hawkes 1983, Hill et al. 1987). All 9 meat resources hunted by Aché men increased overall hunting return rate (see Figure 6.1). Sometimes men hunted with shotguns and at other times with bow and arrows. For shotgun hunters, the overall return rate was higher than the return rate on encounter for monkeys and small birds. For bow hunters, however, the on-encounter

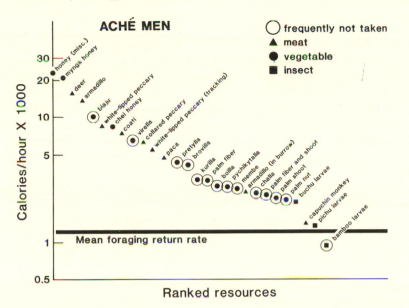

Figure 6.1.   Return rates expected from resources exploited by Aché men in order of descending profitability from left to right. The y axis shows the return rate expected on encounter with each resource type (e_i/h_i). Circled resources are sometimes ignored when encountered (see Hill et al. 1987 for probabilities of pursuit) whereas other resources are always pursued when encountered. Note that 27 of 28 resources handled by Aché men are characterized by higher return rates on encounter than can be expected from overall foraging, as would be expected from Equation (6.2).

profitability for monkeys and small birds was higher than the average hunting return rate, including search. As predicted by the prey choice model, monkeys and small birds almost always were ignored by shotgun hunters but were pursued by bow hunters (Hill and Hawkes 1983). Estimates of return rates for different species of birds led to the calculation that shotgun hunters should take all birds of 1 kg or more and that bow and arrow hunters should take all birds weighing more than 0.4 kg. In fact, the smallest bird shot by shotgun and bow hunters, respectively, was 1.4 kg and 0.4 kg.

Seasonal changes in the pattern of armadillo hunting provide another interesting test of the prey choice model. Aché men always pursued armadillos when they were encountered above ground, but only dug armadillos from their burrows during the late warm–wet and early dry–cold season (Hill et al. 1987). Digging out armadillos greatly increased handling time; however, during the season when armadillos were pursued in their burrows, they were also very fat. They yielded about 3900 cal/hr on encounter. This is much higher than average hunting return rate of 1340 cal/hr. On the other hand, when armadillos were lean in the early wet season, the caloric return rate from digging was about 1220 cal/hr. By ignoring armadillos in burrows when they are lean and pursuing them when they are fat, Aché men appear to have been maximizing their average hunting return rate.

Although these quantitative results are impressive, Aché men's behavior systematically deviated from predictions of the simple prey choice model because men frequently ignored plant foods that would increase their average caloric foraging return rate (Figure 6.1). Although men maximized *meat* calories obtained per hunting time, they did not choose the option that maximized *total caloric* production, which would have consisted mostly of palm fiber. We estimate that Aché foragers encountered an exploitable palm (*Arrecastrum romanzolfianum*) about once every 8 minutes on average. Since each palm can be pounded for fiber for 1–2 hours, Aché men would have spent very little time searching and the vast majority of their foraging day extracting palm fiber, if they always exploited palms upon encounter. The overall energetic return rate from this foraging pattern would be approximately 2600–2700 cal/hr, much higher than the observed male foraging return rate of 1100–1340 cal/hr.

Women's foraging patterns show the opposite trend. They avoided pursuing highly profitable game resources, except under special circumstances (Figure 6.2). Generally, women carried no weapons and directed men to kill the animals they happened to encounter. They sometimes pursued burrowing animals, when no men were present and the kill could be made easily. Women also occasionally participated in group hand-hunts of coatis, pursuing babies and juveniles but leaving the larger, dangerous animals to the men. Thus, the data on women's foraging patterns show that they *could* hunt, but avoided doing so. We believe that this is probably because of the reproductive costs associated with pursuing dangerous, mobile prey (see Hurtado 1985 and Hurtado et al. 1985 for the evidence and a detailed discussion).

The data on both men's and women's foraging behavior suggest that plant foods sometimes are ignored when they would increase overall caloric return rates and foods high in fat and protein are exploited even when they decrease foraging return rates. Within each major food class, however, Aché appear to maximize their overall return rate. We might tentatively draw this conclusion: *Existing optimal foraging models are quite useful for predicting food choice among resources composed of similar macronutrients but may need to be modified to account for sensitivity to the nutrient constituents of foods. The assumption that energy is the sole measure of food value may be inadequate.*

Archaeological Applications of Prey Choice Models. One major goal of archaeological research on diet is to explain long-term shifts in subsistence patterns (for reviews, see Earle and Christensen 1980; Smith 1983; Bettinger 1987). There is an increasing trend toward experimental tests of theories about the archaeological record based on prey choice models. For example,

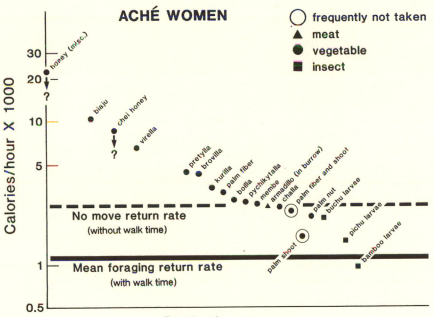

Figure 6.2. *Return rates expected from resources exploited by Aché women (as in Figure 6.1). Note that women do not exploit most game resources taken by Aché men (compare ranked resources to those in Figure 6.1). The two estimates for the profitability of encounters with honey are based on return rates observed for men, since the sample size of honey extraction rates by women is small. The solid line shows the foraging return rate for women if time traveling between campsites is counted as search time. The dotted line shows the return rate for women on days when they do not move camp and all foraging time is spent in search or handling of resources.*

using aboriginal techniques, Simms (1984) experimentally measured return rates from most species of edible seeds in the Great Basin in an attempt to model prehistoric changes in Great Basin foraging patterns. Archaeological data indicated that seeds were ignored by early Holocene foragers but were exploited heavily by later peoples. Simms's data suggested that most species of seeds yield low returns upon encounter because of their high processing time. He used the seed data to predict the threshold at which animal densities would be low enough that prehistoric foragers would have begun to exploit seeds. Such a prediction could be tested using paleoecological and paleontological data. Similarly, O'Connell and Hawkes (1981) used experimentally derived profitabilities from seed exploitation in Australia to postulate that only after the onset of arid conditions in Australia around 17,000 B.P. did Australian foragers begin to use seeds, and eventually populate the central desert regions of the continent.

6.3. PATCH CHOICE

When resource types are clumped together they are said to constitute *patches*. If foragers are able to perceive resource clumping, they are expected to use it to maximize their average foraging return rates. For example, foragers may face the decision of whether to enter a patch or continue searching other portions of the habitat, and if they choose to enter the patch they must decide how long to stay before looking for another patch.

Patch choice models use the same choice principle (mean rate maximization) and many of the same constraints as simple prey choice models, but they differ in their assumptions about prey distributions and net energy gain as a function of handling time. The prey choice model is based upon the assumption that search time is shared among all potential prey because they are encountered at random as a function of their abundance. However, if environments are sufficiently patchy, foragers may alter their return rate by spending more time searching specific portions of a habitat. Most patch models to date are primarily designed to predict how long a forager should remain in a patch once he or she has chosen to exploit it.

6.3.1. Modeling Patch Exploitation Time

Model Components. When a forager enters a patch and begins to exploit it, the rate at which he or she gains energy from the patch may change as a function of time spent there. It is useful to distinguish between three possibilities. First, energy acquired from a patch may increase linearly with patch residence time over a long time span (Figure 6.3a). This would be the case if the forager does not measurably deplete the resources in the patch as he or she forages. For example, spear fishing in the ocean by Australian aborigines may not deplete fish densities significantly. Under these conditions the forager should spend all his or her time in the most profitable patch because any movement entails travel costs and even the next best alternative would be to find another patch of the same type.

Alternatively, energy gain per unit time may remain constant until the patch is completely depleted, and then abruptly fall to zero (Figure 6.3b). For example, if fruits are evenly dispersed on the ground around a fruiting tree and the forager can easily see all of them, he or she may obtain a constant rate of return until the last fruit is collected. Under these conditions, the forager is expected to exploit only those patches whose initial profitability is greater than expected average foraging return rates for the environment as a whole, including travel between patches. He or she should then move to the next patch only after all food items are exploited.

A third relationship between patch residence time and energetic return rate is nonlinear and decelerating (Figure 6.3c). Diminishing return rates

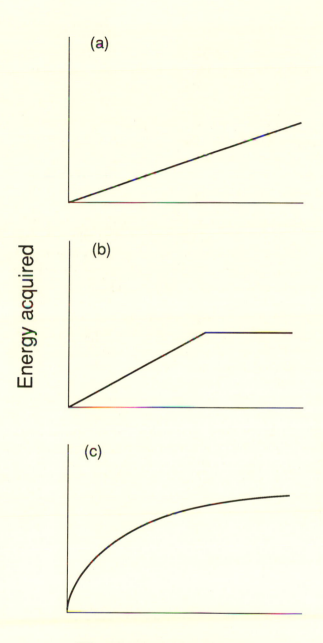

Time spent in patch

Figure 6.3.   Food acquired as a function of time spent foraging in a patch that (a) does not become depleted; (b) provides a constant return rate until the last item is exploited; (c) becomes progressively depleted, or prey items become more difficult to find through time.

will occur if the forager depletes resources while foraging and obtains a lower return rate in a patch after exploiting it for some time, or if prey become increasingly evasive as they are exploited.

Solving for the Optimal Patch Exploitation Time. The marginal-value theorem (Charnov and Orians 1973; Charnov 1976) was developed to determine the point at which the rate-maximizing forager should leave a depleting patch to search for another one. The patch gain function is assumed to be decelerating, and patches are encountered sequentially. The model predicts that a forager should remain in a patch as long as the expected returns from the next unit of foraging time in the patch are higher than expected returns from searching for and exploiting other patches (see Figure 6.4a). Optimal patch residence time will be a function of both how fast in-patch returns diminish and the overall density of patches in environment. As patches become more abundant and the expected search time between patches decreases, the overall foraging return rate will be maximized by shorter residence times (Figure 6.4b). Two important implications of the patch model are: (1) all patches should be exploited until they deplete to the same return rate; and (2) optimal patch residence time will increase as a function of expected search time between patches.

When prey are distributed patchily but in an unsystematic manner within patches, and when some prey are encountered between recognized patches, a combined prey and patch model is appropriate. These models are the most realistic and probably applicable in many human foraging societies, but unfortunately they are mathematically cumbersome and generally require computer simulation rather than algebra to obtain the optimal solution. Stephens and Krebs (1986) have developed a simple combined prey and patch model to predict both patch *choice* and patch *residence time*, to which the reader is referred.

6.3.2. Anthropological Case Studies Using Patch Models

To our knowledge no anthropological studies of patch residence time have been conducted that rigorously meet the assumptions of the marginal-value theorem (or the combined prey and patch model). Most studies attempt to predict which patch types a forager will exploit, given the average return rates associated with each patch in the environment. In these applications, the forager does not sequentially encounter patches but instead chooses which patch to visit each day. For such decisions the patch models described so far are *inappropriate* and may lead to erroneous predictions (Stephens and Krebs 1986:38–45). Choosing the patch with the highest average profitability will not necessarily maximize the overall foraging

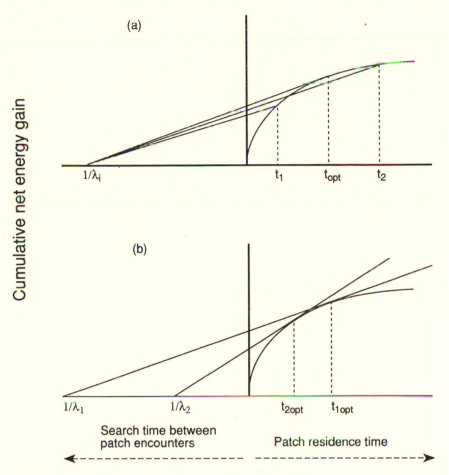

Figure 6.4. *Graphical solutions to the problem of optimal patch residence time: (a) Energy acquired as a function of time spent in the patch (the gain function) is defined by the thin curved line. Overall foraging return rate is defined by the slope of the bold lines [E/T$_{search}$ + T$_{resident}$]. Overall return rate is maximized when the slope of the bold line is maximized. Given the expected search time to encounter another patch (1/λ$_i$) the forager maximizes the average long-term return rate (slope of bold line) at the patch exploitation time (t$_{opt}$), which forms an end point to the line tangent to the gain function. Patch exploitation times t$_1$ and t$_2$ are too short or too long, respectively, thus decreasing E/T. (b) The marginal-value theorem predicts that patch residence time will increase as the search time (1/λ$_i$) for new patches increases. Thus, as it takes more time to find a new patch (1/λ$_1$), it pays to stay longer in a depleting patch (t$_{1\ opt}$).*

return rate. Hill et al.'s (1987) analyses of why Aché hunters choose to exploit lower-ranked peccary patches rather than higher-ranked armadillo patches when both are encountered simultaneously is the only anthropological study that we are aware of that explicitly analyzes this situation. Several examples of patch choice studies among humans are given below.

Smith's (1991) research on Inuit examined time spent hunting in terrestrial and marine habitats as a function of seasonal variability in the return rates obtained from the two habitats. He attempted to determine whether foragers adjusted foraging time spent in each habitat according to their relative profitabilities. Marine habitat profitability peaked in summer (3030 cal/hr) and decreased steadily from fall (2310 cal/hr) to spring (2140 cal/hr). Terrestrial habitats yielded fairly similar returns in spring (1700 cal/hr), summer (1660 cal/hr), and fall (1570 cal/hr), and then peaked in winter (3810 cal/hr). There was no evidence of short-term depletion in either patch; thus return rate is maximized by always selecting the single patch with the highest rate. While it was observed that in each season Inuit hunters spent more time in the more profitable habitat, they did not choose the most profitable patch exclusively. Why might the Inuit sometimes exploit the patches with lower average profitability? Is it possible that patches exploited for several days or weeks in a row yield returns lower than the seasonal average, but recover after some period of nonexploitation? Are there conditions (e.g., weather and recent signs of prey) that reverse rankings of patch profitability on particular days? Investigating these issues should provide a good deal of new information about human subsistence decisions.

Beckerman (1983) examined patch choice among the Bari of Colombia. He measured return rates from fishing and hunting. The findings did not appear to support the prediction that the Bari would choose only the patch that yielded highest average return rate. Specifically, Beckerman showed that for each of 5 time periods sampled, fishing resulted in a higher rate of capture (kilograms of meat/man hour) than hunting, yet in 4 of the 5 time periods men spent more time hunting. Time spent fishing, however, did increase during the months when the ratio of fishing to hunting return rates was higher.

As in the Inuit example, the use of long-term averages limits the test of the patch choice model. First, as Beckerman pointed out, daily changes in environmental conditions may account for the observed pattern. Bari may have chosen to hunt on days when they expected fishing returns to be poor. Second, the gain function of each activity type is unknown. If the number of fishing patches within range was limited, temporary depletion (or changes in prey behavior) might have made hunting the best alternative for several days following fishing expeditions. Third, fishing is associated with a constrained time investment due to preparation and the fact that only one patch can be exploited per day. Conversely, time spent hunting is open-ended for the Bari. It may result in more total food per foraging day than fishing, even though the food is acquired at a less efficient rate. In the Bari case, it may be useful to complement observation naturalistic of foraging behavior with experiments designed to test these alternative hypotheses. For example, it might be possible to ask Bari to fish on some rainy days and just after successful fishing expeditions to determine whether rates are depressed on those days.

O'Connell and Hawkes (1981, 1984) combined prey and patch models in their analysis of Alyawara hunting and gathering. Alyawara men, traveling in O'Connell's vehicle, engaged in two types of hunts, "discretionary" and "embedded." In the former, a decision was made to visit a specific patch in order to hunt there. In the latter, firearms were carried on trips whose primary purpose was other than hunting, such as station work. On those trips, the route taken was determined by the primary purpose and hunts were conducted opportunistically when game was sighted. The embedded hunts allowed the investigator to monitor returns from patches that hunters would not have chosen to visit if the primary purpose of the trip was hunting. Since the returns from embedded and discretionary hunts in the same patches were not significantly different, the data from the two hunt types was comparable. They found that of 11 patches sampled, hunters chose the most profitable patch type most frequently on discretionary hunts. Again, however, the same questions remain unanswered: Why did men spend any time in less productive patches? Were the high-return patches being depleted by hunting? O'Connell and Hawkes attempted to determine if there was temporal variability in patch quality that predicted patch switching. On days when hunting in the grassland was productive (i.e., a kill being made in the first half hour of search), hunters remained in the grassland. On days when it was cool and windy, preventing close approach to kangaroos, kills were not made on the grassland and hunters switched to the hills and ridges. Hunters were apparently acquiring information while hunting.

O'Connell and Hawkes (1981) also examined women's collecting trips. In this case, sandhill patches were characterized by an average return rate 6 times higher than in the mulga woodland. However, on 4 of 9 occasions when women were offered a jeep ride to the patch of their choice, they chose the mulga patches. Exploiting the mulga woodlands results in a much lower energetic return rate but a greater amount of animal flesh in the diet, especially in the hot–wet season. This may be another case of foraging biases on the basis of the macronutrient composition of foods.

Keegan (1986) reanalyzed Johnson and Behrens's (1982) data on Machiguenga forager–horticulturalists combining prey and patch models. He shows that caloric returns per hour of labor investment are about 15 times higher for gardening than they are for fishing or hunting. Yet the Machiguenga were observed to spend only 54% of their food acquisition and production time gardening and the remainder fishing and hunting. Keegan concluded that the simple patch choice model needs to be modified to include the differential nutrient composition of foods. In this case, the vast majority of the calories in Machiguenga gardens were derived from manioc, which is almost pure carbohydrate.

6.3.3. Summary

Simple prey choice models have proven extremely useful in predicting the foods foragers exploit. The tests conducted so far with humans suggest that foragers maximize return rates within classes of foods composed of similar macronutrients but bias resource choice away from calorie maximization in favor of increased protein and lipid consumption. Virtually all applications of patch choice models to human cases have addressed the proportion of time people spend exploiting different food patches when encounters are simultaneous (known locations). Such studies incorrectly assume that foragers should choose the patch characterized by highest returns, but foraging theory clearly specifies that this is *not* the case. Optimal patch choice under conditions of simultaneous encounter is dependent on a number of characteristics (Stephens and Krebs 1986:38–45) that have never been measured in any human study thus far. The gain functions of the patches have not been measured and the reliance on naturalistic observations have limited tests on temporal variation in returns from patches. Foragers sometimes appear to be scheduling short-term patch use in relation to changing return rates, but often there is little information to assess this possibility. At least two applications of the patch model suggest that nutrient differences may be an important criterion affecting optimal patch exploitation time.

6.4. RELAXING AND CHANGING ASSUMPTIONS

6.4.1. Central-Place Foraging

Theory. Humans frequently return to a central place when they forage. Central-place foraging can vary along a continuum from a random search and encounter to targeted search and pursuit. At one end of the continuum, the forager leaves camp, searches the environment for the entire suite of resources that he will exploit upon encounter, and returns to a camp with food (usually but not always, where he began). The Aché and perhaps !Kung hunters exemplify this pattern. At the other end of the continuum, the forager leaves the central place with a specific resource target determined in advance. Binford (1978) suggests that Nunamiut Eskimo men leave camp seeking a specific target, often a specific animal, such as a hibernating bear whose location is known. !Kung women (Lee 1979) visit known mongongo trees and Hiwi foragers visit named resource patches whose characteristics are known in considerable detail (K. Hill, personal observation). Many foraging situations lie somewhere in the middle of this continuum. Machiguenga and Bari men travel to known fishing sites but carry bows and arrows in order to exploit opportunistically encountered game en route (H. Kaplan, personal observation; Beckerman 1983). Cree hunters may leave with moose as their reported prey target, but are prepared to shoot fowl if they are encountered (Winterhalder 1981). These situations present specific problems, each of which require extensions of the simple foraging models.

Central-place foraging imposes special travel costs. Sometimes this is just the cost of returning to a sleeping or activity site. However, if food is brought to another place to be eaten the costs of carrying the food item to the central place must also be considered (Jones and Madsen 1989; Metcalfe and Barlow 1991). In addition, carrying food items can sometimes decrease the forager's ability to capture new food items while he/she searches. Thus, carrying time can be partially or entirely exclusive of search and handling of additional foods. Two questions arise concerning deferment of consumption and transport: (1) Why is consumption deferred? (2) How does central-place foraging affect prey choice and prey handling? We are aware of no explicit models in the human literature that address the first question.

The effects of central-place foraging on prey choice and handling have received formal treatment in Schoener's (1979) encounters-at-a-distance model and Orians and Pearson's (1979) single- and multiple-prey-loader models. Schoener's model imagines a predator that waits at a central place from which it can scan for food items until it observes a prey pass by. The model shows that as distance from the central place to the site of encounter *decreases,* diet breadth increases and includes items of both high and low profitability. Longer distances narrow the diet to include fewer items of high profitability.

The single-prey-loader model (Orians and Pearson 1979) makes a similar prediction but is designed for choices about which prey to handle when resources are *sequentially encountered* in patches at some distance from the central place. Again, as distance increases, the model shows that foragers should return only with higher-ranked resources, passing by low-ranked items. Hames and Vickers's (1982) demonstration that Yanomamo hunters bring back larger prey when hunting in more distant zones is consistent with this prediction.

The multiple-prey-loader model considers a forager who travels to a patch and captures prey items until it returns with those items to a central place. The forager must carry all items it has already captured while it searches for and handles additional items (i.e., until it drops them off at the central place). The efficiency of search and capture within the patch is assumed to decrease as the load increases (e.g., a full beak may inhibit a bird's ability to capture additional prey). Thus the patch shows a negatively accelerated gain function and the forager faces a trade-off between in-patch foraging efficiency and travel time back to the central place. The forager must choose between more trips of smaller loads acquired at a higher return rate, and fewer trips of larger, less efficiently acquired loads. This trade-off can be modeled with the marginal-value theorem and makes a similar prediction: Optimal load size increases with distance to the central place.

Anthropological Applications. Although no field tests of central-place foraging models have been carried out with human populations, some interesting archaeological models have been developed to look at the implications of central-place travel costs. Jones and Madsen (1989) considered the way in which maximum load will affect the ranking of resources located at a distance from a residential site. They conclude that when travel time is high relative to handling time for each resource, and when basket size limits the maximum load that can be carried back, a rate-maximizing forager will exploit resources that provide highest net caloric value per basketload rather than those of highest profitability. Metcalfe and Barlow (1991) have modeled optimal processing times for resources that are acquired at some distance from a residential camp where they will ultimately be consumed. Their model suggests that when transport costs are high, rate-maximizing foragers will often do better to remove low-utility parts in the field rather than transport them to a central place, *even if the parts removed have some utility.* Both of these archaeological models have important implications for the types of refuse likely to be found in archaeological sites distant from resource sources.

6.4.2. Acquiring Information

Theory. The foraging models discussed so far assume that the forager has complete information about resource distributions and yields. This assumption is frequently tenable even though foragers are never fully informed. Often, however, foragers appear to engage in behaviors that *reduce short-term return rates* but provide information that *increases long-term gain.* Information acquisition and the effects of incomplete information are important issues particularly relevant to human foragers, who rely extensively on learning and communication to assess resource distribution, abundance, and profitability.

Foraging models focused on information assume that information acquisition has some cost but provides a benefit. The costs might include time dedicated to sampling and travel to patches in order to determine their productivity. Rate maximization models can be modified to ask: How much effort should a forager expend in information acquisition? Some human foragers such as those in the Great Basin (Steward 1938) and Australia (L. R. Binford, personal communication) apparently travel very long distances to obtain information about food patches. Can we determine if such forays are worth the effort?

To offset its cost, information must increase the foraging return rate. There must be some environmental variability that affects the success of alternative behaviors. Suppose that caribou hunting is more effective in passes and canyons when many animals migrate through and that there is annual variability in the passes and canyons chosen. Knowing the route of the caribou could have a major effect on return rates, but acquiring that information will entail a cost.

These problems can be addressed by models that make interesting qualitative predictions (Stephens and Krebs 1986). If environments change so rapidly that knowing the state at time t provides little information about time $t + 1$, information may be of little value. Knowing that there was a deer in a given location yesterday may not affect return rates today because it will have moved to another unknown location. On the other hand, if the environment does not change at all there is no reason to update knowledge about it. It is in cases of *intermediate rates of change* that information is most useful. A second factor is the range or scale of variability. Aché data suggest that meat returns do not vary greatly from place to place through the seasons. Knowing which animals inhabit a given area may be unimportant if similar returns are found in all areas. On the other hand, the difference in yield between the passes that do or do not contain caribou may be enormous. This suggests that patchy environments that vary temporally at an *intermediate rate* but in *large scale* should be those in which foragers expend the greatest effort in information acquisition.

Information acquisition may pay off in currencies other than calories. Steward (1938) reports that young adult males in the Great Basin frequently traveled great distances to visit and share information about food distributions with their hosts. For their hosts the value of the information may have been increased food yields. The value of the information for the young men might have been to obtain welcome in groups containing marriageable women.

Anthropological Applications.   No anthropological tests of information models have been carried out to date. The Alyawara (O'Connell and Hawkes 1981) and Bari (Beckerman 1983) studies, reviewed above, did invoke information acquisition as an explanation for the exploitation of low-return patches. In neither case, however, were the relevant parameters measured to test those suggestions. Beckerman (1989) presented a model of the value of information to Bari foragers, but concluded based on new data that environmental sampling was an unlikely explanation for the foraging patterns he had described earlier.

6.4.3. *Sensitivity to Variability in Rates*
of Consumption

Theory.   All the models discussed so far have been based upon the premise that *long-term rate maximization* is the goal of human foraging. According to these models, foragers are *insensitive to short-term temporal variation* in the food supply. This assumption, of course, is not necessarily in accordance with the real world. If food intake is highly variable, there may be a chance of starvation. Variation in the amount of food eaten during some time period may also affect fertility and mortality even though the likelihood of starving is low. Under some conditions, foragers will be sensitive to *variability* in foraging returns as well as to *mean rate* of capture. This possibility has been considered for both animals (Stephens and Krebs 1986:Chapter 6) and humans (see Smith 1983; Kaplan et al. 1990; Winterhalder 1986).

When foragers alter their behavior in response to expected variation in rewards, they are said to be *risk-sensitive*. If they adjust their behavior so as to reduce the expected variation in rewards, they are said to be *risk-averse;* and if they act to increase the variation, they are said to be *risk-prone*. Stephens and Krebs (1986) show how the mean and variance in gain rate can be modeled so that risk-aversion and risk-prone behavior can be predicted. Most models of risk-sensitivity among humans have focused on risk-aversion (e.g., Kaplan et al. 1990; Winterhalder 1986), although Hawkes (1990) provides an interesting example of potential payoffs to risk-prone behavior.

Humans can reduce temporal variation in the food supply in at least four ways. First, they can alter diet choice to emphasize less variable resources. Such changes in diet choice may often lower long-term average rate of food acquisition, however. A second method of reducing intake variance is to store foods, which also may involve costs. Processing foods for storage requires time, food value may be lost in processing or later due to spoilage or pests, and storage entails protection and opportunity costs in terms of reduced mobility. A third method of variance reduction is information sharing about food sources. Finally, direct food sharing is another method of reducing expected variation in the food supply. Winterhalder (1986) explored optimal prey choice and risk with a computer simulation. His results suggested that under many conditions, (1) the rate-maximizing and risk-minimizing diets will be the same; (2) food sharing is more effective than changes in diet breadth for reducing risk; and (3) most of the risk reduction obtained from sharing requires only a very small number of participants.

Anthropological Applications.   As far as we know, no direct field tests of risk-sensitive models have been carried out, although Aché research (Kaplan and Hill 1985b) showed that variability in the acquisition of resource types positively correlated with the extent to which they were shared, and that sharing can be an effective method of reducing daily variance in food intake. One simple model showed that food sharing would result in an 80% increase in nutritional status. Given that the Aché never ignore the resources in their environment that are characterized by the highest acquisition vari-

ance (tapirs and peccaries), we speculated that food sharing alone eliminates the need for any other variance reduction strategies (Hill et al. 1987).

6.5. HUMAN SUBSISTENCE PATTERNS: SPECIAL CONSIDERATIONS

6.5.1. Omnivory

Many authors have been skeptical of human foraging models that reduce
the biological value of alternative resource types to energy (e.g., Keene
1981, 1983; Jochim 1983; Sih and Milton 1985). In section 6.2.5.B, we
suggested that Aché foragers bias diets away from energy maximization in
favor of foods containing high proportions of lipids and protein. During the
dry season, Yaminahua foragers of Peru exploited three major food types
(wild bananas, caiman, and several species of fish), but would have maximized energy return rates if they only exploited bananas and caiman (Hill
and Kaplan 1989; Hill 1988). Including fish in their diet decreased overall
return rate. Similarly, among the Hiwi foragers of Venezuela, men pass by
roots that yield 8500 cal/hr on encounter in favor of hunting, which yields
an average of 3070 cal/hr (Hill 1988). Virtually all South American horticulturalists obtain much higher caloric return rates from farming than they
do from hunting or fishing (Beckerman 1989; Hames 1988), yet most spend
considerably more time hunting and fishing than farming (Hames 1988). In
even more extreme cases net energetic return rates from hunting may be
negative, and yet horticulturalists still chose to hunt rather than farm exclusively (e.g., Dwyer 1974; Johnson and Behrens 1982). This bias in favor of
exploiting resources of relatively low energetic profitability but high in
protein–lipid content is found in many other human groups and among
nonhuman primates (e.g., McGrew 1978; Terborgh 1983).

Some nutritional requirements are absolute and inflexible; other nutrient
requirements apparently can be met partially or completely by substituting
sufficient quantities of an alternative nutrient. This introduces complexities
that have yet to receive substantial theoretical or empirical treatment in
foraging research. In fact, with the exception of a few studies (e.g., Belovsky
1988 and Rapport 1981), most foraging research on nonhuman animals has
not been conducted with omnivores. However, several different approaches
have been used to model sensitivity to the nutrient composition of foods.

Linear Programming. Linear programming is a method of solving for
behavioral optima under specified constraints. Belovsky's recent (1987)
application of linear programming to predict !Kung diets illustrates nicely
the advantages and disadvantages of this approach. The model assumes that
hunting and gathering are mutually exclusive activities and attempts to solve

for the optimal allocation of the !Kung foragers' time hunting and gathering. Four constraints (boundary conditions, defining lower or upper bounds of a currency requirement that either must be met or cannot be exceeded) are defined: protein, energy, stomach capacity, and time. Protein and energy are lower-bound constraints (i.e., minimum requirements); stomach capacity and time are upper-bound constraints (i.e., maximum tolerable). Two possible objectives are considered: energy maximization and time minimization. If energy is the goal currency, time is a constraint, and if time is the goal currency, energy is a constraint. When a modified version of this model is developed, taking into account the constraints for an entire family rather than a single adult, the energy-maximizing point predicted by the model matches almost exactly the !Kung diet observed by Lee during July 1964. This success, however, depends heavily on the assumptions underlying the time and stomach upper bounds. For example, the time constraints are based upon a calculation suggesting that longer amounts of time spent foraging would have resulted in net heat loss during the winter months. However, this calculation does not allow !Kung foragers to compensate for heat loss through extra caloric expenditure or through warming themselves by the fire after foraging. As Belovsky notes (1987:41) !Kung foragers frequently violate the time constraint over short time periods. The stomach capacity constraint is also problematic since the maximum food intake that Belosky allows is much lower than observed consumption rates of modern foragers (K. Hill, personal observation). The success of the model is therefore somewhat problematic, since the predicted diet is quite sensitive to the values of both maximum constraints.

In general, linear programming models may be useful for modeling decisions in which constraint and objective functions are linear and all currencies except one may be characterized as constraints. Linear constraint functions are not expected when search costs are shared among resources (the assumption of the prey choice model discussed above) or when costs of acquisition vary nonlinearly as a function of amount produced of each resource (a common gain function in patch models). Modifications and nonlinear programming models are being developed to deal with both problems (Belovsky et al. 1989). Perhaps more problematic is the assumption of linear programming models that the benefits associated with constraint currencies are essentially single step-functions. This means that acquiring more than the minimum of the lower-bound currencies (or utilizing less than the upper bound) is not a better solution for the organism than achieving the constraint boundary. For example, once the protein requirement is satisfied, additional protein is assumed to have no further positive effect. This assumption may not be biologically realistic for many currencies.

Indifference Curves and Nutrient Complementarity Models. One approach to modeling diet choice with multiple goal currencies is the use of indifference curves to model trade-offs in investment among alternative resources. Such models assume that humans make choices that maximize utility gained from investment. Utility generally is defined as the level of satisfaction derived from the consumption of resources and is determined inductively by measuring what people maximize. Biologists who employ the indifference curve approach assume that fitness or some correlate of fitness is the ultimate utility. An additional assumption of indifference curve modeling is that for any two desirable resources, an infinite number of combinations of the two resources would yield equal utility (or fitness). For example, 3 kg of meat and 4 kg of plant food might be equal in utility to 1 kg of meat and 8 kg of plant food. All combinations that yield equal utility define a line (or curve) to which the consumer should presumably be indifferent (hence the name indifference curves). Other combinations yielding higher or lower utilities exist on different indifference curves, and there are an infinite number of indifference lines associated with higher and lower utilities (see Figure 6.5.). Thus, indifference curves are isoclines (analogous to thermoclines or contour lines).

The indifference curve approach assumes that the forager will adopt the strategy that yields the highest utility. Three factors must be specified in order to predict the optimal mix of resources: (1) the total foraging time available, (2) the time cost of each resource or patch (the reciprocal of the return rate for a resource, patch, or foraging strategy), and (3) the shape of the indifference curve set. The first two factors allow for construction of a "budget constraint" function, which defines all the possible combinations of resources that can be acquired given the time available and time costs of resources. For example, if time spent acquiring plant foods is mutually exclusive with time spent obtaining animal foods (i.e., no shared search time), then total time spent foraging is equal to time spent hunting plus time spent collecting: $T = T_h + T_c$. The mix of time spent hunting and time spent collecting is the decision variable in the model (precisely analogous to the linear programing models above). If we know the hunting return rate (R_h) and the collecting return rate (R_c), it is possible to determine all possible combinations of meat and plant foods that can be acquired in time T throughout the range from $T_h = 0$ to $T_h = T$ (or, alternatively, from $T_c = 0$ to $T_c = T$). These values describe the *budget constraint line*. The model predicts that the forager will choose the mix of hunting and collecting times that yields the combination of meat and plant foods with the highest utility. This is the point on the budget constraint line that is tangent to the highest indifference curve (Figure 6.5).

Using data from three South American foragers, the Aché, Yaminahua,

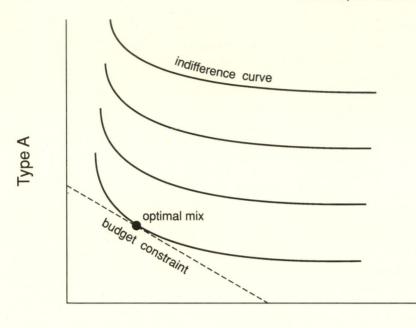

Type B

Figure 6.5.   Indifference curves for two resource types that are partially substitutable and complementary. A budget line can be defined by the amounts of each type of resource that can be acquired given the foraging time available and the time costs of acquiring each. The point at which the budget constraint is tangent to the highest indifference curves is the optimal mix of resources that should be acquired in order to maximize utility gain.

and Cuiva, Hill (1988) derived a composite indifference curve (Figure 6.6) by calculating a series of restriction angles from measured return rates and dietary mixes chosen, and then superimposing each graph on the next. A single indifference curve shape fit all data points. As a test of the generality of this particular model, he then used the derived indifference curve set from the South American data to predict the dietary mix of Pygmy foragers who trade meat for agricultural products with neighboring horticulturists. Since, according to Hart (1978), Mbuti Pygmies receive, on average, 4.6 calories of carbohydrate for every calorie of meat, the slope of the budget constraint line is known. Using this budget constraint and the South American indifference curves, Hill's model predicted a Pygmy diet of 25% meat and 75% carbohydrate, whereas the observed diet is about 30% meat and 70% carbohydrate (Figure 6.6).

The close match between the model derived from the South American data and the observed Mbuti pattern seems encouraging. Nevertheless, the indifference curve approach as applied so far suffers from serious limita-

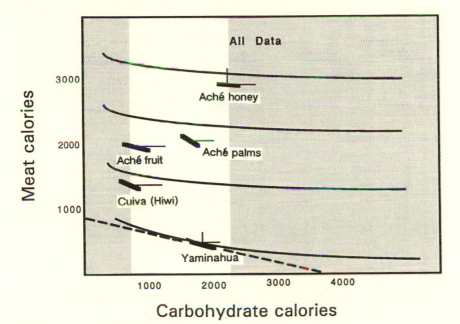

Figure 6.6.   *The measured slope of the budget constraint and the observed choice point define and angle that restricts the possible slope of the indifference curve to the left and right of the choice point. The indifference curve must have a slope between the budget slope and horizontal right of the choice point, and between the budget slope and vertical to the left of the choice point. Restriction angles derived from observed foraging choices of Aché, Cuiva, and Yaminahua foragers can be used to create a composite of the indifference curve shape. Applying the Pygmy budget line (dashed) with a slope of -1/4.6 allows one to predict the Pygmy diet (point tangent to the indifference function) which will maximize dietary utility if Pygmies show the same preferences as South American natives. The predicted diet is about 75% carbohydrate, whereas the observed diet is 70% carbohydrate.*

tions. First, the model Hill developed its two-dimensional and thus can only be used to model trade-offs between two food types. This limits its generality to food types that are either protein/lipid rich or carbohydrate rich. However, many mixes of the three macronutrients are possible. For example, some insect foods that are important in human diets are very lipid rich but not protein rich. Many plant foods contain significant amounts of protein and some fat as well as carbohydrates. Multidimensional models can be developed but they must be solved with differential equations. Second, Hill's application assumes that time costs of hunting and collecting are always exclusive. More likely, however, some time spent looking for hunted resources will also result in encounters with collected resources and vice versa. When search and acquisition costs of different resource types can be partially shared, the budget constraint is not a straight line, but instead bows upward in the middle. Shared search is so common in human foraging that it may turn out that the shape of the budget constraint is more important for determining the diet mix than is the shape of the indifference curves.

Finally, the inductive determination of indifference curves on a case-by-case basis is not satisfying. Using preference curves from one group to predict dietary preferences in another group begs the question of the functional significance of the observed preferences. And it is notoriously easy to generate multiple inductive models a posteriori that are consistent with a set of data. Although these models can later be tested on independent data sets, such models can be empirically adequate for the wrong reasons.

Summary. Each of the models discussed thus far has strengths and weaknesses, and each is designed to explain patterns in a different decision variable. The combined prey and patch model provides the most well developed mathematical tool for measuring the trade-offs in benefits expected from handling or continued search. The model can treat both shared and unshared search and handling costs. It is equipped to deal with both continuous and discontinuous gain functions. The principal problem encountered in applying "handle-or-search" models to human foraging, however, is that the use of calories as a currency in the measurement of gain functions does not generate empirically adequate predictions. Linear programming models are well suited for considering multiple currencies. The major problems with linear programming models are that they assume step-function effects (satisfaction or death) of all constraint currencies and become mathematically complex with multiple resources and shared search or production costs. Indifference curve approaches are well suited to combining distinct objective currencies (e.g., protein and carbohydrate) into a single currency (e.g., utility, nutritional status, or fitness) so that trade-offs between resources can be measured. They are not limited to the step-function assumption, nor do they require linearity of effects. However, they are limited by the fact that the models also become complicated with shared search and many different resource types. Additionally, the shapes of indifference curves are difficult to measure, and the models are inductively derived rather than theoretically based.

6.5.2. Food Sharing and Sex-Dependent Foraging Models

The facts that people share food and that the producers and consumers of food items are frequently different individuals can complicate foraging models. If foragers can expect to exchange food with other individuals, their foraging strategies are likely to be sensitive to those expectations, especially if nutrient complementarity is important. Food sharing is also likely to affect the time individuals allocate to foraging (see Chapter 7). These considerations represent a largely unexplored area of foraging theory (but, see Hawkes 1990; Chapter 9). In addition, the fitness costs and benefits of alternative foraging strategies appear to differ between men and women. Although there are exceptions, women generally avoid activities that involve danger, prolonged high-speed movement, and high mobility (Brown 1970a; Hurtado et al. 1985). Trade-offs between food acquisition, child care, and fertility have been proposed to explain both variation in time allocated to foraging and prey choice by women (e.g., Hurtado 1985; Hurtado and Hill in press).

Factors other than gender may be important as well. For example, Hurtado et al. (1985) found that, among the Aché, nursing women forage less and produce less food than nonnursing women, and that the woman's number of older children is positively correlated with productivity and time allocated to foraging. This pattern was also found among Hiwi foragers, but with additional effects of seasonality (Hurtado and Hill in press). Kaplan and Hill (1985b) showed that there are long-term differences between men in hunting return rates. Children also produce varying amounts of food across societies (Blurton Jones et al. 1989). Their return rate is likely to vary across ecological contexts as a function of the nature and distribution of food resources they can exploit and is probably age and sex specific. Thus, the time that children allocate to foraging and their expected gains is likely to affect parental decisions about what foods to acquire and how much they should provision their children.

It appears that food sharing combined with age–sex differences in goals and constraints leads to a variety of complications when considering the fitness payoff of different foraging patterns. For example, the differences between men and women in prey choice will affect macronutrient-sensitive models of prey and patch choice. In the case of the Aché, the female return rate was approximately 2600 cal/carbohydrate, and almost no protein or lipid per hour spent foraging. For men, the return rate was approximately 600 cal protein, 300 cal lipid, and 400 cal carbohydrate for every hour spent foraging. Since men spend 6.9 hr/day and women about 1.9 hr/day in direct food acquisition, the combined daily diet produced by a man and a woman is 4140 cal protein, 2070 cal fat, and 7770 cal carbohydrate per day. This diet could be easily adjusted if either sex changed their prey selection or time spent foraging. In fact, the observed Aché diet contained even more fat and protein than these numbers suggest because of the high adult sex ratio in observed residential groups.

These types of problems may require the techniques of game theory and frequency-dependent models that solve for equilibria rather than maxima, particularly if the reproductive interests of men and women differ or conflict. Foraging and food production, sharing, and sex differences in behavior are closely related in humans. Eventually these must be incorporated into any comprehensive theory of human food acquisition.

6.5.3. Symbolic Communication

Humans rely heavily upon symbolic communication in the food quest. Symbolic communication can be used to increase the information available to foragers in at least two ways: (1) by increasing their sample size of resource distributions and characteristics; and (2) by providing information on prey or patches that the foragers have never exploited. In fact, effective communication among foragers greatly increases their knowledge of their environment *relative to what is known or measured by researchers attempting to test foraging models.*

The foragers we have observed use both types of information. First, they listen daily to accounts of other foragers. These accounts commonly include details of resource encounter rates (λ_i) and profitability (e_i/h_i) so that the forager is able accurately to assess short-term changes in the environment relevant to prey and patch decisions. The forager's sample of these parameters is a function of how many other individuals in the social group forage independently. Aché men, for example, live in social groups consisting of about 10 hunters, and at the end of day, each man usually reports to the others in considerable detail concerning every game item that he encountered that day, and the outcome of the encounter. At minimal cost, each man gains 10 times as much information about encounter rates as he actually experiences.

Second, foragers learn from older individuals who report on a lifetime of foraging experiences. Most children have detailed knowledge of resource characteristics and capture techniques before ever foraging themselves. In some cases, the knowledge of older individuals has been gained through communication as well, rather than through direct experience. This means that the body of information available covers long time spans and the experiences of hundreds of individuals. Extremely rare events unlikely ever to be experienced by a single forager can be sampled indirectly through information access. Some food taboos may have their origins in long-term information transfer about the low profitability of rarely encountered prey. Whether foragers should pay attention to food taboos and how often they should break them can be addressed in models about the value of information for behavioral decisions (e.g., Stephens and Krebs 1986:Chapter 4) and the conditions that lead to copying others with or without sampling other alternative behaviors (Boyd and Richerson 1985; see Chapter 3, this volume).

The fact that human foragers possess more information than can be gained through personal experience has implications for tests of foraging models on humans. Foragers may adjust their foraging pattern in ways that the researcher is unlikely to understand. The completely informed forager may be sensitive to long-term average conditions, whereas the scientist generally can only measure current conditions. Alternatively, the forager may behave according to knowledge about the specific characteristics of the immediate situation, whereas the researcher must average out the parameter values of his or her model over a much longer period. For example, Inuit foragers may choose terrestrial hunting over marine hunting depending on wind conditions (Smith 1991:Chapter 7), or Bari men may hunt when rainfall patterns suggest that fishing will not be profitable (Beckerman 1989).

A second implication of the information available to human foragers leads to greater optimism. Most foraging models assume complete information on the part of the forager. *This assumption may be more correct for human foragers than for any other species.* Communication systems allow humans rapidly to track changes in their environment, and they actually may be more likely to adhere to the predictions of optimization models than are most other animals, which may instead develop foraging "rules of thumb." Human behavior, in general, is more likely to be adaptive in changing environments than can be expected for other organisms.

6.5.4. Proximate Mechanisms of Change

We have not yet discussed the question of *how* humans come to adapt their food acquisition practices. We know virtually nothing about the specific nature of the cognitive processes governing foraging decisions nor about the developmental processes by which children become adult foragers. Although most observers of human foragers are impressed by the seeming importance of observational learning in the development of foraging skills, the specific nature of these learning processes remains unstudied. We also do not know the extent to which processes of cultural evolution (cf. Boyd and Richerson 1985; Chapter 3) affect human foraging practices and diets. For example, the Aché kill coatis *(Nasua nasua)* and pacas *(Cuniculus paca)* with their hands, using techniques not practiced by other South American foragers. When these techniques are explained to other South American foragers and forager–horticulturalists, they can imagine how they are done but comment on their danger. Were those techniques invented by the cultural ancestors of the Aché and simply not invented by other groups? Could it be that such techniques will only be invented when the costs of injury are outweighed by the benefits of more meat? In general, optimal foraging theories treat capture techniques and the proximate mechanisms that underlie them as givens. Treating them as variables to be explained is an important area for future theory development and research.

6.6. LINKING MODELS OF INDIVIDUAL BEHAVIOR
WITH LARGE-SCALE EXPLANATION

All the models discussed so far have focused on the decision processes of individuals, given a set of assumptions about their abilities and attributes of the environment. How can we account for evolutionary change in foragers' abilities? What factors determine cross-cultural variability in tools, techniques, and the composition of the diet? Perhaps the first and certainly the second set of questions can be productively studied using modifications of current foraging models.

6.6.1. Long-Term Change

Even though prey and patch models treat the abilities, techniques, and technology of the forager as givens, their underlying logic can be used to ask questions about long-term change in those constraints. For example, the domestication of plants and animals is a problem that seems quite tractable using simple modifications of foraging theory.

If we follow the optimal prey and patch choice models we would expect foragers to spend time manipulating the reproductive, growth, or behavioral patterns of protodomestic plants and animals *as soon as such practices would have increased return rate.* The decision variable for a protodomestic would be: How much time should be spent manipulating growth and reproduction of a protodomestic so that it can be harvested at a greater rate? The increase in return rate for the protodomesticate conferred by the manipulation time would be compared to overall return rate for foraging. This is analogous to the decision to add a new prey or patch type to the diet, or to change patch residence time when encounters are simultaneous. Setting the problem up in this manner suggests that investigators search for factors that might have lowered overall foraging return rate in the areas and times of domestication, or that might have raised the rewards associated with manipulation practices. Some possible factors are the terminal Pleistocene extinctions of megafauna and increases in human population density that, in turn, lowered encounter rates with profitable resources.

In order to test these hypotheses, it would be necessary to measure both foraging return rate and the returns from the earliest attempts at domestication. Optimal foraging theory provides the mathematical framework for comparing those return rates, but rigorous tests of hypotheses require data at a degree of precision that archaeologists have not yet been able to obtain. For some kinds of resources (such as fruit collection and seed collection), it may be fairly simple to conduct experiments that will provide robust estimates of return rates (e.g., Simms 1984). For other resources (such as small-game hunting returns for *Homo habilis*), developing adequate estimates of return rates may prove to be a difficult challenge.

6.6.2. Cross-Cultural Variability in Subsistence Patterns

So far, there has been very little work within optimal foraging theory on large-scale ecological trends in the composition of human diets. What kinds of ecological communities are associated with different proportions of meat, plant foods, and insects in the diet, different ratios of male, female, and child labor, and different kinds of foraging practices (ambush hunting, random search, specific-resource-targeting, home base, storage, food sharing, etc.)? What features of the abiotic environment such as rainfall, temperature, and drainage affect human diets? Since humans are part of their own environment, how do demographic processes such as increasing and decreasing population density affect plant and animal communities and human foraging patterns?

Winterhalder et al. (1988) have addressed this last problem in an optimal foraging model that allows the forager to affect the encounter rate of prey types through his or her own prey choice. Surprisingly, the model indicated that population densities were dependent on subsistence work effort, and that both human and prey densities cycled dramatically under a variety of conditions. Both results strongly challenge the utility of the concept of "carrying capacity" that is so common in the anthropological literature. Large-scale subsistence trends in hunter–gatherers have also been modeled by Belovsky (1987) with a linear programming approach. Using an empirically derived relationship between hunting and gathering cropping rates (return rates) and primary productivity, Belovsky develops a model to predict reliance on hunting and gathering as well as the contribution of each sex to the total diet. Binford (1990a) has used a measure (effective temperature) developed by Bailey (1960), which incorporates rainfall, temperature, and drainage to account for both plant and animal productivity in environments and the proportion of meat and plant foods in human diets. Both these models seem to fit well with reported large-scale patterns, although many of the estimates of the relevant dependent and independent variables are very rough.

The development and testing of ecological theories of human dietary variation using the cross-cultural record deserves more emphasis. We are slowly building the quantitative database necessary for conducting those tests. However, more attention needs to be paid to quantitative descriptions of environments, in addition to measuring return rates and foraging decisions.

6.7. CONCLUSIONS

The utility of the optimization approach to subsistence problems must be evaluated in light of what we can learn from it. The models have been better at predicting qualitative patterns in human subsistence than any other current approach. However, many of the predictions drawn from optimal foraging theory have not closely matched the empirical record. To some extent this is inevitable, since the models are explicit simplifications of complex decisions. Why else might the models fail?

One reason is that the empirical data are not suited for testing the foraging model in question. At this stage in the development of human behavioral ecology, it is important to confront squarely the limitations of most tests of foraging models carried out on humans. In many cases, restrictive assumptions of the foraging model under test have been overlooked. Some "tests" have chosen inappropriate models for the decisions being examined. Future research must carefully consider the particulars of each study. What is the decision variable? Are the types to be chosen prey or patches? Has the gain function for different patches been measured? Have encounter rates with types been adequately measured? Are encounters sequential or simultaneous? Is the currency employed adequate for the problem? Careful examination of the character of each foraging model relative to the character of the problem addressed is likely to improve greatly the quality of empirical tests.

Some foraging studies, however, have deliberately violated the assumptions of the model as a means of learning whether those assumptions are important. For example, many early critiques of foraging models (e.g., Keene 1981; Jochim 1983; Sih and Milton 1985) suggested that energy is not the appropriate currency for analyzing human diet choice. Aware of these critiques, we applied the simple prey choice model to Aché foraging to see how it performed in spite of its restrictive assumptions. Our results showed that the Aché *did* bias diet choice away from energy maximization in favor of increased meat and insect consumption. We now know that nutrient-sensitive models are required for many human foraging problems. In this sense, the violations of the predictions of foraging models help us learn about the important constraints on human subsistence decisions.

For those who accept the utility of the approach and wish to apply it to specific problems, the future is indeed exciting. Appropriate modifications of foraging models should allow us to address a broad range of problems in human subsistence practices. The process of discovering the necessary modifications is likely to provide an enormous amount of information about our species. This, then, is the real value of optimization modeling of human behavior. It is a systematic process for learning about ourselves.

6.7.1. Chapter Summary

This chapter has reviewed the basic principles of optimal foraging theory, and their application to human food acquisition. The central points made are these:

1. Behavioral ecologists study food acquisition using an optimization approach. This approach assumes that individuals maximize some currency (usually food energy acquired per unit foraging time), and employs models consisting of decisions, currencies, and constraints (6.2).

2. The classical prey choice model assumes random encounters, a single rank of all prey types, mutually exclusive search and handling costs, and complete information. Tests of the model with human foragers indicate that they generally follow its predictions within choice sets composed of similar macronutrients, but bias resource choice in the direction of protein–lipid maximization in mixed sets (6.2).

3. Optimal patch choice and time allocation depend very much on the shape of the depletion curve, as well as the information available to the forager. The marginal-value theorem (6.3.1) assumes diminishing returns, but existing studies of human patch choice do not adequately demonstrate that this assumption applies to the data analyzed (6.3.2).

4. The classic prey and patch models can be modified in several ways, or incorporated into a combined prey and patch choice model. When food choice involves central-place foraging (6.4.1), acquisition of information (6.4.2), or sensitivity to risk (variance in consumption, 6.4.3), existing theory allows interesting predictions to be made about choice behavior and social interactions (6.4). Little work has yet been done to test such models.

5. The problem of omnivory and multiple components of food value can be addressed in several ways, including linear programming and indifference analysis (6.5). Each approach has strengths and weaknesses, and both suffer from being inductive and succumbing to mathematical intractability when realistic constraints are included.

6. Many possibilities for elaborating simple foraging models to deal with behavioral complexity exist, including food sharing and gender division of labor (6.5.2), symbolic communication (6.5.3), long-term subsistence change (6.6.1), and large-scale cross-cultural variation in subsistence practices (6.6.2).

Time Allocation

Raymond Hames

7

7.1. INTRODUCTION AND PROBLEM

Time allocation studies examine how people expend their effort across a variety of activities. Their analytic aim is to determine whether the duration and scheduling of tasks is consistently patterned and predictable with respect to variables such as sex and age, mode of production, and environment. In order to survive and reproduce, an individual must find food, avoid predators, find a mate, and invest in offspring. Each of these activities uses resources; each detracts from an individual's ability to engage in other adaptive tasks. At the same time, these activities provide benefits that ultimately enhance chances of survival and reproduction. Time allocation studies attempt to assess the factors that determine the costs and benefits of these behavioral trade-offs.

Time allocation presumably is controlled by a number of intrinsic and extrinsic factors that determine the costs and benefits of any activity. Intrinsic factors include an individual's sex, age, physical condition, and social status. Extrinsic factors include environmental variables that are dependent on natural (resource availability, effective temperature, and population density) and social environmental elements (technology and social system). Behavioral ecology provides anthropologists with a rich body of theory, concepts, and models that may prove useful in analyzing variation in human time allocation. It also provides a means of analyzing sociocultural variation.

7.2. THEORY AND CONCEPTS

7.2.1. Theory

Time allocation models are founded on the basic economic assumptions that time and resources are limited and have alternative uses. Through a process of selection (see Chapter 1) optimal use of time will cause certain patterns of behavior to increase in frequency in a population and others to diminish. As a result, time allocation will be consistent depending on local environmental circumstances and the characteristics of individuals. Since fitness payoffs for alternative behaviors are practically impossible to measure, quantifiable measures (e.g., energetic efficiency) that correlate with fitness have been chosen (Schoener 1971; Smith 1979a). However, since fitness is not always a useful concept upon which to base currencies it may be replaced with a situation-specific notion of utility (Winterhalder 1987:326–328). While utility allows greater realism and precision, it is less general. Like most other forms of evolutionary analysis, time allocation theory is founded on a cost–benefit methodology.

7.2.2. Categories of Behavior

Evolutionary analyses of behavior typically identify two types of effort: somatic and reproductive. Somatic efforts promote survival and well-being. Foraging, thermoregulation, and avoidance of predators are good examples. Reproductive effort deals with finding mates and with parental investment. This distinction is somewhat arbitrary in that foraging, for example, can simultaneously serve somatic and reproductive ends—a woman may gather for her own consumption and that of her offspring. Also, given a neo-Darwinian premise, somatic effort ultimately is designed to enhance reproductive effort. For the most part, biological models of time allocation have been devoted to modeling different kinds of somatic effort, especially food-getting activities (Stephens and Krebs 1986). In anthropology the focus has been on the division of labor, labor and social evolution, foraging, cultivation, technology, labor exchange, and child care. Humans also allocate time to social and ritual activities, behaviors that cannot be easily classified from an evolutionary perspective. The problem of time allocated to social activities will be addressed at the end of the chapter. Historically, the recent resurgence of anthropological interest in time allocation coincides with expanded interest in evolutionary biology. Social scientists aware of time allocation problems have reformulated them in evolutionary terms (Rapport and Turner 1977).

In anthropology, time allocation often serves as a method to gain quantitative information on behavior (in biology the corresponding method is known as behavior sampling). While measuring behavior in order to address a problem frequently includes a time component, it could be stressed that the scheduling and duration of an individual's effort in different behaviors is a theoretical problem in its own right.

7.2.3. Costs

Any time an individual engages in an activity two kinds of costs are incurred: opportunity and resource costs. An *opportunity cost* is the amount of benefit forgone by choosing to engage in one behavior instead of another. Costs and benefits always are assessed relative to a feasible set of available options (Figure 7.1). As a result, the optimization approach in time allocation studies is inherently comparative. A *resource cost* is measured by the amount of time, bodily (e.g., calories), or other resources one must expend while performing an activity. In most cases it is difficult to measure resource costs directly. Instead, measures of time expenditure are used as an indirect means of assessing resource costs. While this procedure is satisfactory in many cases, it should not obscure the fact that time expenditure is an index or proximate currency. Therefore, tests of models using time as a cost index are accurate only where there is a good correlation between time and resource expenditure.

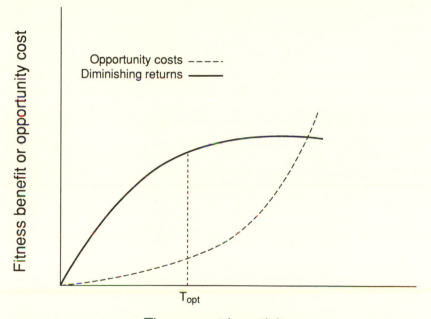

Figure 7.1. Opportunity cost model of time allocation. As an individual persists in an activity, the marginal rate of return decreases (solid curve) and opportunity costs rise (dashed curve). The maximum distance between these lines (at T_{opt}) represents the optimal amount of time that should be allocated to a particular activity.

Humans, unlike many other animals, may incur a social cost or benefit tied to their status in a social group, which affects allocation of time. Much time is expended cooperatively or done on an exchange basis (Hames 1987a, 1989). As a result, choosing to assist another may later lead to a number of outcomes, such as an equivalent return in assistance; a material return (e.g., payment in food for agricultural labor; see Erasmus 1956); or enhanced mating opportunities (Kaplan and Hill 1987). Therefore, the resources an individual has to expend are often not a simple function of body size or physical condition, but a function of his or her status in a local group.

7.2.4. Time Minimization/Resource Maximization

Optimal allocation of time in a particular activity permits an individual either to maximize resource accumulation or to minimize the time devoted to resource accumulation. Furthermore, the principle applies to any activity, not just resource accumulation. For example, efficiency in child care allows more of it to be done in the same period of time or the same amount of care to be accomplished in a shorter period of time. Resource maximizers optimize because it allows them to accumulate resources at the highest rate. Time minimizers optimize because it allows them to complete an activity in the shortest interval possible (Smith 1979a). According to Schoener (1971), an organism is a time minimizer if increased foraging efficiency does not lead to increased foraging. This does not mean increased consumption fails to enhance fitness, but rather, as Winterhalder (1983) points out, that alternative uses of scarce time have a greater positive impact on fitness than does continued foraging. In contrast, an organism is a resource maximizer if increased foraging efficiency increases foraging time or does not change it. For resource maximizers alternative activities (e.g., parental care or rest) are less fitness enhancing than foraging. In either case, for both kinds of organisms, an increase in the net rate of return while foraging would enhance fitness. Time minimization and resource maximization are not mutually exclusive strategies but rather poles on a continuum (Winterhalder 1983).

7.2.5. Modeling Time Allocation

Commonly, evolutionary ecologists graphically develop time allocation models using indifference curves (Winterhalder 1983). In the simplest case, a hypothetical convex rate of return curve is plotted against a hypothetical concave opportunity cost curve along fitness (y axis) and time (x axis) coordinates. The greatest distance between the two curves represents the optimal allocation of time that should be allocated to each activity (T_{opt} in Figure 7.1). It is assumed that this is a diminishings return curve; the value of the next unit of gain (e.g., food) of the activity (foraging) will be less than was the previous unit as need is filled. In contrast, the concave opportunity cost curve is expected to rise and rise more steeply the more time an organism spends in a given activity. Since an organism must engage in a number of mutually exclusive activities in order to survive and reproduce, the longer one refrains from the alternative activity, the more valuable it becomes (or the greater the cost its neglect imposes on fitness). The maximum distance between these two slopes marks the point where an organism should cease its current activity and switch to another.

The location of the origin and exact shape of the opportunity cost and diminishing-return slopes typically are hypothetical. In principle, these curves are measurable but in practice they are virtually never empirically derived. The presumed shape of the curves is informed by a knowledge of the natural history of the population and/or by the assumptions that the analyst wishes to incorporate into the model (Chapter 1). Testing is usually accomplished through statistical comparisons. For example, the graphical model represented in Figure 7.4 (section 7.5.1) predicts that good hunters should hunt more under conditions of groupwide sharing than under conditions of familywide sharing. Demonstration that the model is reasonable is shown by a statistical test indicating that this in fact occurs.

7.3. ANALYTICAL ISSUES AND KEY PROBLEMS

7.3.1. Classifications

Like many other fields of evolutionary biology (e.g., life history and mate choice) time allocation research attempts to make predictions about how individuals will apportion their behavior. This forces one to classify behavior according to what it is designed to accomplish (see section 7.4.4). A fundamental distinction is made between reproductive effort and somatic effort. Ethnographically, there appears to be a close relationship between somatic effort and productive labor (appropriation or transformation of natural resources, as opposed to provisioning of services). Reproductive effort is further divided into mating and parental effort. Most time allocation research in anthropology has been devoted to dealing with differential allocation of time to categories of labor and this will be the central focus of this chapter.

7.3.2. Life History

Nearly all time allocation studies focus on the activities of adults (as locally defined, but this usually means married couples with dependent offspring). Unfortunately, children, subadults, and the elderly are commonly ignored or simply viewed as dependents and thus as causes of a great deal of adult work. However, it is becoming increasingly apparent that children in many societies do productive labor and there are differences in which the rates at which the sexes approach adult labor expenditure patterns. Child labor has clear implications for sex ratio theory since the cost of children is a major factor in that area of research (see Chapter 11). Further, few studies have attempted to look at work effort across the lifespan, an issue explored below (section 7.5.4).

7.3.3. RM versus TM

It is sometimes asserted that tribal people, especially hunter–gatherers, have "limited needs" (Sahlins 1968a; cf. Winterhalder 1990). That is, resource requirements are modest, easily met, and culturally determined. An evolutionary approach to this problem would restate it along a resource maximization/time minimization continuum identifying factors that determine the utilization of one strategy or the other (Winterhalder 1983; and below). To say that resource "needs" are culturally determined, as does Sahlins (1972), is both vague and analytically unfruitful. It prevents the development of models that can both predict why one society has a tradition of low needs (and others do not) and fails to specify how time allocation is adjusted to meet culturally determined needs. An evolutionary ecological approach to this problem begins with theories, concepts, and models that attempt to specify how the local environment and the history of the population affect time allocation patterns. The costs and benefits of various behaviors are measured and then models of time allocation are evaluated. This cost–benefit approach provides a general framework for the explanation of patterns of time allocation and it may shed light on why certain time allocation patterns are highly valued by members of a society.

Recently, a debate among behavioral ecologist over time minimization/energy maximization emerged between Hawkes et al. (1985; Hawkes 1987) and Smith (1987b). It concerns how best to model forager time allocation. Smith (1987b) calls into question two assumptions made by Hawkes et al., specifically: (1) that returns from foraging diminish slowly, and (2) that the value of alternative activities (those forgone while foraging) remains constant through time. To some extent, these assumptions (especially the former) may be reasonable for the Aché, but they may have limited validity for many other foragers. Other issues are addressed such as whether or not a limited-needs view of foragers is congruent with evolutionary ecological models and whether foragers are mainly time or resource limited. These last two issues are not critical theoretical problems. I think it fair to say that Hawkes and Smith both agree that the shape of the diminishing-return curve for foraging and the value of alternative activities forgone while foraging (opportunity costs) cannot be known a priori. The value of any activity is always locally determined and relative to alternative activities.

Local environmental circumstances and technological capabilities determine where an individual may be located on the time minimization/energy maximization continuum for any particular activity. Using standard economic theory (e.g., Hirschleifer 1980) Smith (1987b) notes that it is difficult to predict in advance whether increased efficiency will lead to an increase or decrease in time allocation. This is because increased rates of return have two opposing consequences known as "substitution" and "income" effects. First, the substitution effect raises time allocated to foraging and occurs when increased foraging productivity makes alternative activities more costly since their utility or degree of fitness enhancement is less. Second, the income effect decreases foraging time and occurs when productivity is so high that the producer must take time out to consume that which was produced. Since production and consumption are mutually exclusive, foraging time decreases.

The difficulty in modeling the relationship between optimal time allocation to a particular task and alternative tasks is graphically represented in Figure 7.2 (figure modified after Smith 1987b:76). Concave curves from the origin (A–E) represent different diminishing rates of return for a particular economic activity such as hunting. These rates of caloric return can differ because, for example, A hunts with a blowgun, B hunts with a spear, and C hunts with a shotgun (see section 7.5.3). The convex isoclines represent a series of indifference curves charting increasing fitness from lower right to upper left. In such a graph, "Optimal time allocations to foraging shift as a function of changing rates, and occur at the point vertically below the highest tangency between a [diminishing] return rate [curve] and a fitness isocline (marked by open circles)" (Smith 1987b:76). Fitness isoclines represent opportunity costs of activities forgone while foraging. The shape of the isoclines depends on local factors such as how continued resource accumulation can be used to enhance fitness and the value of activities forgone. Figure 7.2 makes it clear that increases in foraging efficiency (A< B< C< D< E) can lead to increases or decreases in foraging time, or different foraging efficiencies can lead to equivalent time allocated to foraging (B and C) depending on how the isoclines are determined by environmental circumstances.

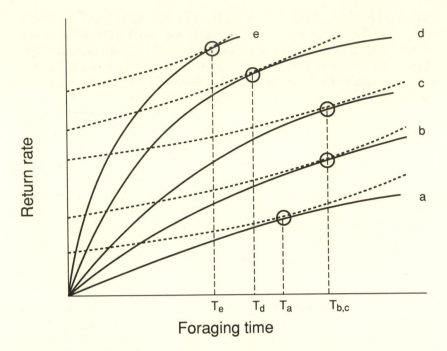

Figure 7.2. Variable rate of return and opportunity costs time allocation model (after Smith 1987b, Figure 1). Dashed lines originating along the y axis represent opportunity costs, while solid lines starting at the origin represent different rates of return that diminish through time. Optimal time allocated to foraging occurs at the point vertically below the highest tangency between a concave return rate line and a convex opportunity cost isocline (marked by an open circle).

7.4. METHODS

7.4.1. Data Collection

The method chosen to generate quantitative measures of behavior depends on the questions asked about time allocation, sample size requirements, and the nature of the ethnographic context. The best single source of wisdom on sampling techniques is still Altmann's (1974) classic article. In addition, Borgerhoff Mulder and Caro (1985) deal with problems inherent in human behavior sampling (particularly Johnson's "spot checks"; Johnson 1975) and review a number of important issues not addressed here. These articles should be read by anyone contemplating the collection of time allocation data (see also Betzig and Turke 1986; Hawkes et al. 1987; and especially the text by Martin and Bateson 1988).

The methods described by Altmann were developed by behavioral biologists whose study subjects cannot speak (i.e. nonhumans). As a result, the methods she describes are strictly observational. Informant self-observation (see section 7.4.3) and recall methods (interviewing an informant at the end of the day) are options for social scientists. Some of the advantages and shortcomings in using informant data will be discussed after a consideration of observational methods.

7.4.2. Behavior Observations

According to Altmann, in sampling behavior one can either record a state or an event. In *state sampling* one records the behavior of a subject the instant the subject is encountered (Johnson's spot checks) or as the subject is observed at regular predetermined time intervals (e.g., recording the behavior of a subject every 5 minutes). The resulting data are akin to a series of photographs, since the duration of the behavior is not recorded. However, with a sufficiently large sample, the frequency of a particular behavior is directly proportional to the length of time the subject engages in it. In *event sampling* (or *continuous sampling*, see Figure 7.3), the researcher continuously records all behavior during a fixed period of observation. The resulting data are like a video of behavior that contains information on duration, sequences, and complexes of behavior.

Crosscutting this distinction is whether one will focus on an individual (focal person) or a group (scan) (Figure 7.3). In *scan sampling* one records the behavior of members of a group. In *focal sampling* one records the behavior of an individual. Normally, scans are done instantaneously and the

	GROUP	INDIVIDUAL
STATE	Instantaneous scan	Instantaneous focal
CONTINUOUS	Continuous scan	Focal follow

Figure 7.3. Sampling methods for observing behavior. In sampling behavior one can record behavioral states or continuous behavior for groups or individuals.

resulting procedure is known as *instantaneous scan sampling.* One may usefully visualize it as taking a group photograph. If the group were limited to about two individuals, a single researcher could, in principle, perform *durational scans* and the result would be like a video. Given limitations in human cognitive and recording abilities, durational scans are difficult unless the categories of behavior are quite broad. If the group were large or transitions from one behavior to another were rapid, the resulting data from a continuous scan would be like a video recorded with the frame speed set too slow. The chief virtue of instantaneous sampling is that a large number of individuals may be included in a sample and it is not very intrusive (observer presence is less likely to affect a subject's behavior). Its chief disadvantage is that duration of behavior and transitions and linkages between behaviors are not recorded. *Event observations,* in contrast, are well designed to sample behavior duration, transition, and linkages. Yet due to the intensive nature of this method, sample size is likely to be small and observer intrusiveness may alter the behaviors observed.

7.4.3. Informants

Informant recall is an alternative to direct observation of behavior. Informants (subjects) may be asked to record their behavior in a variety of ways, such as noting it in a diary at the end of the day, or noting the state of their behavior on a form at fixed time intervals (a kind of self-recorded instantaneous sampling). For nonliterate populations, a researcher may interview subjects and have them recall their behavior. A variant of this recall method may be combined with direct observation and is frequently done in cultural ecological research. In studies of hunting, for example, the researcher notes the time of a subject's departure and return, and then interviews the subject to learn the route taken, locations searched, game spotted and/or pursued, and game taken (Vickers 1988; Winterhalder 1981). In still other situations, instantaneous sampling may be combined with informant statements. In my own studies (e.g., Hames 1979b), when a subject was absent from the village (e.g., hunting) during a scan, I asked a close relative or neighbor where he was and what he was doing and recorded that information as if I actually had made the observation. In most cases the missing subject was interviewed upon return to assess the informant's accuracy.

Aside from intrusiveness and subject bias, the main problem with informant methods is that of recall error. Studies by Engle (1988) demonstrate that recall methods at best are only 70% accurate in estimating the duration of activities. Accuracy may be increased by decreasing the specificity of behavior to be recalled (e.g., asking how much time was spent in food preparation instead of time allocated to the various tasks that compose food preparation) or by combining informant methods with observational methods.

7.4.4. Data Coding and Classification

After a method is chosen one must devise a classification of behavior. Borgerhoff Mulder and Caro (1985) distinguish between two broad types of classification: physical descriptions and description by consequence (see also Betzig and Turke 1986). Elsewhere (Hames in press) I refer to these modes as structural and functional descriptions, respectively. Structural descriptions focus on the body stances and movements inherent in a behavior (e.g., walking at a moderate pace on level ground while carrying a spear; see Denham 1978 for details) while functional descriptions deal with the objective, purpose, or goal of the behavior. Borgerhoff Mulder and Caro (1985) suggest that structural and functional descriptions should be collected simultaneously to heighten the likelihood of accurate cross-cultural comparisons. Structural classifications, in addition, are probably more useful in the calculation of energy expenditure.

Finally, Allen Johnson has developed a standardized and functional classification of behavior in his capacity as editor of Cross-Cultural Studies in Time Allocation (HRAF: New Haven), a comparative time allocation database series published on computer diskette (e.g., Johnson and Johnson 1989). About a half dozen volumes of the series have been published and several either published or in press are authored by contributors to this volume.

Behavior code description can quickly become extremely complex depending on how closely one wants to resolve behavior as it relates to three general issues. Specificity depends with how finely one wants to differentiate the flow of behavior. For example, hunting behavior consists of traveling (normal walking), searching (walking with pauses), pursuing (running), and retrieval (carrying a load). Intensity deals with variation in energetic expenditure of an activity (i.e., the same behavior may vary because of periods of inattention, rest, and the rate at which it is done; Erasmus 1980). Simultaneity deals with a subject doing more than one thing at a time (e.g., a mother nursing a child while conversing as she prepares food). Again, decisions made in coding resolution depend on the problem to be answered and the local environment.

7.5. STUDIES

7.5.1. Foraging

As mentioned previously, organisms may be placed along a continuum from energy maximizers to time minimizers, depending on internal and external variables. Most anthropological studies have not been sensitive to this range of possibilities or to their dependence on very specific ecological conditions. Thus, Sahlins (1972) incorrectly generalizes that all forager time allocation is low (see Hill 1988; Winterhalder 1987; Hames 1989; Sackett 1988; and below for theoretical and empirical refutations). It is low, according to Sahlins, because needs are few and easily met. Needs are few because the culture of foragers, in contrast to settled agriculturalists, places no value on accumulation. Although Sahlins does not use the term *time minimization* he seems to assume that time minimization is a universal condition of hunter–gatherers.

Harris (1979a:81) accepts Sahlins's incorrect generalization about low work levels of foragers and suggests that it is a strategy of conservation: Foragers work little so that they will not degrade the carrying capacity of the environment. Aside from conceptual problems (i.e. failure to specify the conditions under which conservation can be maintained and explicit group selection, see section 2.2.2), it is based on a false empirical generalization about forager work levels (see Figure 7.8). Hill (1982) has shown that foragers such as the !Kung take game and gather foods at rates several orders of magnitude less than would be required to degrade their environment.

In contrast to these views, the selected research reviewed below is generally from investigators who employ formal optimization models and collect detailed behavioral data.

Aché Foraging.   In a number of papers Hill and his coworkers (Hill and Hawkes 1983; Hill et al. 1985, 1987; Hill and Kaplan 1988) have attempted to model Aché male time allocation. Aché foragers are characterized by relatively high levels of hunting effort (Hames 1989:Table 4) and bandwide sharing patterns (Kaplan and Hill 1985a). Approximately 80% of their diet comes from foraging efforts of male hunters. A successful hunter distributes his catch equitably throughout the band (about 30 people) such that his family does not consume a proportionally greater amount of game than others in the camp. In addition, a hunter may not eat of his own kill. Given Aché food-sharing patterns, Kaplan and Hill (1985b) and Hill and Kaplan (1988) argue that foraging is related both to mating effort (hunters exchange game for sexual access to women) and paternal investment (the children of productive hunters are treated better by band members; Hill and Kaplan 1988:284). Given this context, Hill and Kaplan make two predictions regarding male time allocation to foraging and child care: (1) Good hunters should hunt more than poor hunters because "the slope of the fitness/time spent hunting curve for good hunters is steeper initially and probably drops off more slowly than would be the case for poor hunters" (Hill and Kaplan 1988:285); and (2) Males with many dependent offspring should allocate more time to child care than males with few or no offspring (controlling for hunting ability) because the slope of the fitness/time spent hunting curve remains relatively constant for all hunters, while the opportunity costs

increase as a function of number of offspring. Both hypotheses were sub-
stantiated by their observations of individual differences in hunting and
child care time allocation.

It is important to understand the Aché analysis in detail because it is an
excellent demonstration of initially simple optimization models that have
been modified to capture more realistically local constraints identified in
fieldwork. Hill and Kaplan (1988) begin with a standard diminishing-return
model of hunting effort in which the fitness return to hunting is a negatively
decelerated curve. They then modify it by arguing that the rate of decelera-
tion is less for good hunters than poor hunters because food may be
exchanged for sexual favors and better treatment of offspring (Hill and
Kaplan 1988:286). This modification seems to be based on the fact that
although good and poor hunters may initially hunt for equal lengths of time,
a good hunter will return with more game for distribution. Since the good
hunter contributes a greater fraction of the band's total food intake, he is
more likely to outcompete a poor hunter in gaining the benefits of sexual
access and better treatment of offspring. This presumably causes the poor
hunter to decrease time allocated to hunting because he cannot compete
effectively for sex and better treatment of offspring. And since he cannot
compete, the utility of child care and mate guarding may be greater than
continued hunting (A. Hurtado, personal communication). See Hawkes's
(1991) alternative explanation of male time allocation to hunting: the lime-
light theory.

In situations where game is not as widely shared and a hunter contributes
primarily to his family's larder, we expect him to spend less time hunting.
This is because the slope of the fitness return curve declines more rapidly
(Figure 7.4). In other words, returns on hunting time diminish more rapidly
in groups with little game sharing (e.g., Yanomamö–see Hames 1989) than
in groups in which widespread sharing occurs (e.g., Aché).

Hill and Kaplan (1988:285–286) admit that these "result[s] cannot be
considered a test of the model, since the model was partially derived from
the available data." For example, one might just as easily have predicted a
positive correlation between number of dependents and hunting time, controlling for hunting ability. This is based on the assumption that the more
mouths one has to feed the more one must hunt. If game were not widely
shared and unmarried hunters without offspring captured no more game
than necessary to satisfy their own needs, this expectation would be reasonable. For the Aché, however, the opposite of these conditions exists. Thus
men with many dependent offspring should allocate more time to child care
than men with few offspring. Since dependent children require paternal
investment (e.g., grooming, feeding, and monitoring) Hill and Kaplan
(1988) hypothesized that the opportunity cost of child care rises more
rapidly with additional offspring, where increasing time is allocated to

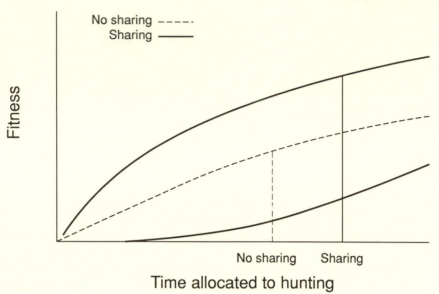

Figure 7.4. *Sharing and its effect on optimal time allocation to hunting. Concave-downward curves indicate fitness return rates from hunting, while the dotted convex curve indicates opportunity costs from time not allocated to other fitness-enhancing activities (see Figure 7.1). Under widespread sharing (solid lines), fitness returns diminish more slowly than when sharing is absent (dashed lines), resulting in greater time allocated to hunting.*

hunting. As a result, hunters with many dependents cease hunting earlier because of the greater fitness-enhancing value of paternal investment.

7.5.2. The Chayanov Slope in Agriculture

Since Sahlins (1972) introduced the research of the Russian rural economist A. V. Chayanov (1966) to the anthropological community, a number of ethnographers have attempted to explore the relationship between time allocation and dependency ratio. Briefly, Chayanov demonstrated that the higher the consumer–producer ratio (or dependency ratio) in a family, the greater the work effort (time) allocated to labor by the producers. The total amount of time worked was determined by the intersection of a decreasing marginal utility curve of production and an increasing marginal disutility curve of labor (Figure 7.5).

The decreasing marginal utility curve is similar to what is assumed in evolutionary models: As more food is produced, succeeding units of food become less valuable. However, the increasing marginal disutility curve of labor cannot be directly derived from evolutionary analogs. According to Chayanov, the more one works the more loathsome or noxious work becomes (this is also known as the "marginal disutility of drudgery"; Durren-

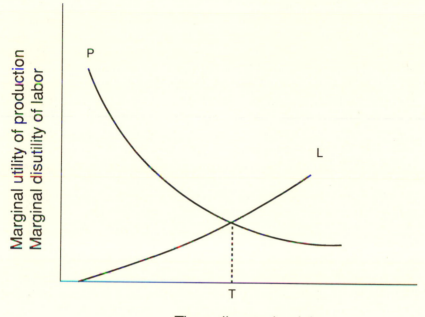

Figure 7.5. *Chayanov's model of time allocation. The optimal time allocated to labor (I) under Chayanovian assumption is determined by the marginal utility of production (P) and the marginal disutility of labor (L) or increases in drudgery.*

berger 1984a:41); or the more one works, the less one wants to work. Marginal disutility appears in the model as a universal psychological assumption about how individuals feel toward labor expenditure. By contrast, in behavioral ecological approaches, such as Hill's above, rising opportunity costs along with decreasing marginal rates of return determine time allocated to labor. Thus assumptions about the pleasures of work or their opposites are avoided.

A Chayanovian approach also differs from behavioral ecology: it presumes (e.g., Durrenberger 1984a:43) that if the productivity of labor (rate of return) increases, the marginal disutility of labor increases at a lower rate and that producers will work longer (see Figure 3.3 in Durrenberger 1984a:45); hence peasant farmers must be energy maximizers because increases in efficiency (e.g., technological innovation) lead to increases in labor time. However, this can only occur if the marginal utility of production (and opportunity costs) remains constant. The unstated assumption is questionable because increased efficiency leads to increased production, which may cause the marginal rate of production to decrease at a faster rate.

Chayanov's ideas were originally derived from the circumstances of Russian peasant communities. His model assumes that nuclear families are self-sufficient and that exchange of labor, economic specialization, markets, and wealth differences are absent. Given these assumptions, anthropologists find tribal and peasant communities ideal for evaluation of what has become known as "Chayanov's slope": the correlation between mean adult labor time and consumer–producer ratio. Although this model is commonly applied to food producers, it may be applied to any group that meets the conditions described above (lack of market economy, etc.). Anthropological evaluations of Chayanov's slope meet with fair to good results (see chapters in Durrenberger 1984b). Some of the problems that may lead to equivocal results stem from poor measures taken of consumers and producers. Normally, individuals older than 14 years are impressionistically scaled as producers and consumers with a value of 1 (see section 7.5.4 on the accuracy of such an assumption). Few studies rely on actual measures of consumption or labor time of community members (for example, see Sahlins 1972). In some cases the amount of land under cultivation is used to index labor time allocation.

A more critical problem is that many of the assumptions made by Chayanov do not fit the reality of tribal or peasant economies. Variations in wealth, family structure, economic specialization, and exchange exist and create analytical problems of their own. For example, a recent study by Fratkin (1989) on East African Ariaal pastoralists found that there was no relationship between labor time and dependency ratio, although there was a negative relationship between labor time and wealth (measured in livestock holdings).

For some anthropologists (e.g., Sahlins 1972) household deviation from the Chayanov slope (households working more or less than they should) is used as a method to determine the degree to which social status determines labor time. In highly competitive egalitarian economic systems (ethnographically known as "big man systems"; Sahlins 1972), big men work more than they should (given their dependency ratio) since they are attempting to acquire capital to maintain their social position. In chiefdom systems (simple stratified societies with hereditary inequality; Sahlins 1972), chiefs work less than they should because their inherited status allows them to appropriate the production of others.

7.5.3. Technological Change and Time Allocation

The introduction of new technology provides important insights into the factors that affect time allocation and energy expenditure. Most studies have focused on the introduction of steel tools and their resulting effect on subsistence activities. Steel tools can either reduce time allocation activities and/or increase total production, because of their greater efficiency (return per unit time) over traditional nonsteel technologies. Theoretically, if new and more efficient technology leads to a reduction in time allocation without a corresponding increase in production, one would conclude that the group is time limited. If the new technology has no effect on time allocation or increases it, thereby increasing total production, then one would conclude that the group is resource limited.

Hunting Technology. A number of recent studies have assessed the impact of firearm introduction (i.e., shotguns) on hunting time allocation. Such studies allow one to determine where a group falls along the time–energy limited continuum. Hames (1979b), in a comparison between shotgun using Ye'kwana hunters and bow using Yanomamö hunters, found that bow hunters hunted for more minutes per day than shotgun hunters (see also Rambo 1978). In an intracultural comparison among the Waorani, Yost and Kelley (1983) showed that acquisition of the shotgun raised hunting efficiency by 33% over the spear and blowgun but that hunting time allocation diminished only by 3%. They concluded that the shotgun had "not significantly changed the amount of time [the Waorani] spent hunting" (Yost and Kelley 1983:221). However, in the same paper (Yost and Kelley 1983:212), data on a larger sample of five villages suggest that increased hunting efficiency does decrease hunting time significantly. Spear hunters were most efficient, at 3.95 kg/hr, and their hunts of shortest duration, at 7.9 hr; shotgun hunters were the second most efficient, at 2.54 kg/hr, and had the second longest hunts, at 9.3 hr; and blowgun hunters were the least efficient, at 1.62 kg/hr, while their hunts were of the longest duration, at 9.6 hr.

Agricultural Technology. While numerous studies have noted in changes in efficiency from stone to steel tools in agriculture (see references in Hames 1979b, 1989) there is only one that attempts to assess the impact of steel tools on efficiency, production, and time allocation. For the Siane, Salisbury (1962) showed that the replacement of stone axes with steel axes reduced labor time but did not affect the size or raw yields of gardens. This suggests that the Siane are time minimizers relative to their agricultural tasks. Hurtado and Hill's (1990) study of the effect of the machete in food processing and harvesting among the Peruvian Machiguenga demonstrates that although the machete is more efficient than traditional scrapers, the tasks to which it is applied are such a small part of gardening costs that total time allocation is not significantly altered. However, it may reduce time allocation significantly in a foraging population.

A number of studies (for references see Ember 1983) have shown that women do less primary food production with the advent of intensive or plow agriculture. With cross-cultural data, Ember (1983) shows that while overall female labor time remains high with the switch from horticulture to agriculture, more time is allocated to the processing of food than to its production (field labor). Therefore, when female time allocation is shifted to agriculture there is no actual decline. Rather it is specialized toward processing the yield. The claim that women's participation in food production declines with the advent of plow agriculture (Boserup 1970) is true but misleading because an unnecessarily restrictive definition of agricultural or horticultural labor mirrors the methodological problems inherent in the comparison of technological efficiency. Subsistence-based societies grow crops to have something to consume. Before consumption can occur land must be prepared, and crops planted, tended, harvested, and processed (winnowing, cleaning, grating, and cooking). The later stages of the production process cannot be ignored if one is to pose useful questions about the division of labor, labor efficiency, and labor organization.

Measurement Problems. Lack of measurement of all relevant costs of production is the most significant problem that plagues the study of technological change. For example, research on the introduction of shotguns to hunting (Hames 1979b; Yost and Kelley 1983) simply compares rates of return in hunting using different technologies. It fails to factor in acquisition, maintenance, and supply (e.g., shells, powder, primers, and shot) costs of the traditional or new technology (Hames 1989). This problem is also seen in studies of "carrying capacity," agricultural change, and the relative efficiencies of hunting versus gathering. In agriculture the efficiency of new crops over old is simply measured as the ratio of clearing, planting, and harvesting costs over yield (Carneiro 1979; Johnson and Behrens (1982). Such comparison are misleading because other necessary costs of production such as food processing and associated processing technology, maintenance, and manufacture are ignored. For example, among the Amazonian Yanomamö and Ye'kwana food processing costs of crops is 50 to 60% of the labor allocated to simple production (clearing, weeding, etc.; Hames 1989; see also Ember 1983).

The importance of measuring all costs sheds light on fundamental issues of hunter–gatherer ecological relations. Lee's (1968) widely cited claim that gathering is more efficient than hunting was shown to be suspect when Hawkes and O'Connell (1983) demonstrated that processing costs of *mongongo* nuts, a staple for some !Kung groups, is greater than acquisition costs. When all factors of production are considered, !Kung hunting and gathering have about the same efficiency. Finally, other tasks such as water and fuel gathering for food processing are necessary costs that have also been ignored (Hames 1988b). While most studies show a decrease in time allocation for specific activities with the introduction of new technology, future studies should pay attention to total costs of production and possible reorganization of labor.

7.5.4. Life History and Time Allocation

While a number of studies have focused on status (marital and number of dependents) as a determinant of time allocation (Hurtado et al. 1985; Hewlett 1988), few have paid sufficient attention to age or to time allocation across the lifespan. How does time allocation to labor vary in respect to life-historic events (e.g., muscular maturation, marriage, or menopause)? Is the division of labor sensitive to age as well as sex? What are the rates and ages at which males and females achieve maximum economic productivity?

Taking into account what we know about human development and senescence, time allocation to labor across the lifespan should exhibit an inverted U-shaped curve, with low points at either end of the lifespan and a high point between. Figure 7.6 shows an empirical curve for Nepalese adults of time allocated to labor (food production and processing, maintenance, and manufacturing) derived from Nag et al. (1978:295–296, Tables 3 and 4). A similar distribution is found by Sackett (1988) in his 104-group cross-cultural sample. Such a curve leads one to ask a series of questions: (1)

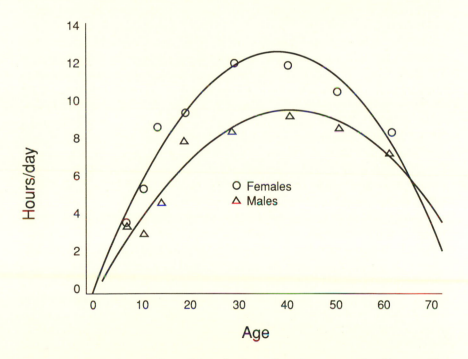

Figure 7.6. *Nepalese male and female time allocation across the lifespan. The inverted U-shaped curves for male and female undoubtedly represent a general but unsurprising pattern of time allocation (Data from Nag et al. 1978.)*

What determines rate of ascent to the peak? (2) What determines the width of the peak? (3) What determines the rate of decline from the peak? Why do male and female curves differ along the same dimension? And, even more importantly, what of the role of life-historic events that are only partially correlated with age (e.g., marriage)?

The article by Nag et al. does not deal with any of these questions directly. However, cross-cultural time allocation research based on a sample of children aged 3 to 9 years in four peasant societies (Munroe et al. 1983, 1984) attempts to deal with several of these questions. Following a simple Chayanovian model (see 7.5.2), Munroe et al. (1984) found that time allocated to labor by young children (largely light household chores) was positively correlated with the consumer–producer ratio (as predicted by a Chaynovian model) but interestingly it was inversely correlated with the amount of time either parent worked. These findings were complicated by the fact that parental work levels were independent of the household consumer–producer ratio, opposite of what the Chaynovian model would predict. Two explanations were offered: (1) The assumption of nonsurplus production is incorrect; and (2) children's work subsidizes adult work (see 7.5.2). Further analysis by Munroe et al. (1984) suggested that the second explanation is most likely.

Whether children begin working at an early age also depends on their possessing the skill and strength to perform economically valuable activities as well as upon the value of economic activities compared to alternative activities (rest, play, socialization). Consistent with other studies, Nag et al. (1978) found that children engage in activities such as child care (Hames 1988), simple household tasks (Munroe et al. 1984), and herding (Thomas 1973) that are well within their skill level and strength. Although child care is a skilled activity, when performed by children an adult is generally nearby to render special assistance (Borgerhoff Mulder and Milton 1985).

In a comparative study of Hadza and !Kung children, Blurton Jones et al. (1989) show that Hadza children begin foraging and making important contributions to their own sustenance at a much earlier age than do !Kung children. These differences appear to be attributable to a lower probability of heat stress and a variety of other environmental factors that permit children to forage safely and effectively.

In extreme cases, for example, Javanese girls (Nag et al. 1970:296) from ages 10 to 16 years may work from 4.9 to 8.4 hr per day. But it appears that in most tribal and some peasant societies children spend more time in noneconomic activities (Munroe et al. 1988) because, as noted, the skill and strength levels for most tasks may be beyond that of a child. Then what fitness-enhancing value do noneconomic activities have for children? More directly, what is the value of play? Much of what passes as child play can be ethnographically interpreted as practice or the development of motor and cognitive skills. For example, Ye'kwana and Yanomamö boys spend about an hour per day play hunting or target shooting. In addition, Ye'kwana and Yanomamö boys and girls play house by building scale models of their parents' houses and emulating appropriate sex roles in the division of labor (Hames 1978; and field data).

Time allocation across the lifespan in many cases has an effect on the division of labor. For example, among the Ye'kwana (Hames 1979b) and Yanomamö most males cease hunting at about age 55 and begin to devote more time to gardening, wood collecting, and other activities that otherwise are dominated by females. This switch in time allocation patterns appears to reflect declining hunting abilities relative to gardening.

Hardworking Grandmothers. In many societies time allocated to labor, arduous labor in particular, declines with age (Amoss and Harrell 1981). In a time allocation study of Hadza women, Hawkes et al. (1989) found that postmenopausal women worked significantly more than childbearing women (22–55% more per day). To account for this difference three hypotheses were posed: (1) postmenopausal women have lower opportunity costs (i.e., do not have to care for children); (2) postmenopausal women exchange vegetable food for meat hunted by men, whereas childbearing women exchange sexual favors for meat; and (3) postmenopausal women use extra resources gained through gathering to invest in daughters who are rearing their grandchildren. Although analytic results were not conclusive, the data best supported the investment in daughter hypothesis. Elevated work loads of postmenopausal women may be designed to subsidize the food production activities of their childbearing daughters. To show that this explanation is correct, Hawkes et al. state that they must demonstrate that food foraged by postmenopausal women is flowing to their childbearing daughters. Such an analysis is currently underway.

7.5.5. Parental Investment

Humans are distinguished by the tremendous amount of time allocated to parental investment (Lancaster and Lancaster 1983). Parental investment is a fundamental theoretical issue in behavioral ecology (Chapter 11). For my purposes it may be defined as time allocated to care, feeding, and nurturing of offspring—a focus on sexual variation in care, the effect of care on other activities, and models that deal with variation in time allocated to child care. To some extent, the parental division of child care is an aspect of the more general division of labor, a full discussion of which is presented below (section 7.5.6).

An interesting theoretical aspect of parental investment, and of the division of labor as well, is the potential for conflicts of interest to develop among married couples (Hill and Kaplan 1988:297–300). Successful reproduction in most environments requires the cooperative allocation of effort between spouses. Conflicts of reproductive interest stem from the fact that males are under greater selective pressure to seek mates of high fertility while females seek mates who are capable investors in offspring (Trivers 1972). As a result, females may expect higher levels of time allocated to parenting than are in a male's reproductive interest and vice versa. This perspective has important implications for behavioral variation as it relates to variation in fertility, social status, and wealth.

According to Katz and Konner's cross-cultural survey (1981), 90% of child care is allocated by the mother of the child or the mother and related females (Babchuck et al. 1985). In most studies, analyses have focused on direct child care: feeding, holding, comforting, and other forms of direct physical interaction between caretaker and child. There are two other forms of parental investment that often are overlooked. Proximity maintenance or monitoring (Hewlett 1988) is a form of care whereby a caretaker remains near an infant or child in order to respond quickly to problems a child may encounter. Indirect investment (Hames 1988, 1992) is a rather broad category of behavior that is frequently reflected in subsistence activities, that is, a parent increasing his or her work load in order to provide food and shelter for a dependent child. At a broader level it may include such things as effort allocated to provide a son with bridewealth or a daughter with a dowry.

According to Hewlett (1988) time allocated to child care varies more among males than females. To account for male variation Hewlett (1988:272) hypothesizes that

> where resources essential to survival can be accumulated or where males are the primary contributors to subsistence, sexual selection theory would predict that fathers in these societies would invest more time competing for these resources and consequently would spend less time with their children. In contrast, where resources are not accumulable or men are not the primary contributors to subsistence, men overall would spend more time in direct care of their children.

He suggests that this model is consistent with the findings of Katz and Konner (1981) and research on the Aché (Hill et al. 1985; Hurtado et al. 1985). However, further quantitative research is necessary to evaluate this hypothesis. Note that this model focuses on variation in time allocated to direct child care and not variation in overall parental investment. In competing for resources (not just material resources but status) males may be providing intangible benefits to offspring such as better treatment by other band members (Hill and Kaplan 1988) or they may be increasing the probability of a male offspring marrying early or polygynously (Chagnon 1979, 1988). Testing hypotheses involving status completion would be demanding and would require methodological innovations.

Variation in Paternal Investment among the Aka. Hewlett's research (1986, 1988) on the Aka Pygmies is the most detailed time allocation database on paternal investment that exists for a tribal population. Predictions made from his general hypothesis (see above) are well-supported. He found that male status is inversely correlated with time allocated to child care. Males who are polygynous, have many brothers, a large hunting net, and who are headmen or are sons of headmen invest less in child care than males who have the opposite characteristics. This implies that such males gain greater fitness returns by engaging in status maintaining or resource accumulation activities than from child care activities, although Hewlett presents no data that would illuminate this hypothesis.

Variation in Maternal Investment among the Aché. The time that females allocate to child care seems to be dependent on four variables: (1) number of dependent children; (2) degree of child dependency (nursing and ambulatory status); (3) degree to which the mother is responsible for providing food for the family; and (4) availability of alternative caretakers. Research by Hurtado et al. (1985) on Aché foragers shows that mothers allocate child care and labor time according to degree of infant dependency (nursing status) and number of dependent nonnursing offspring. Women with nursing infants spend more time in child care and less time working than women without nursing offspring and, controlling for nursing status, women with many dependent offspring spend less time in child care and more time in food getting than women with fewer offspring. This patterning, presumably, reflects trade-offs between two different forms of maternal investment: the value of providing food versus direct physical care of offspring (Hill and Kaplan 1988).

The most interesting finding of the Aché research is that controlling for the number of offspring, nursing women spend less time producing food than nonnursing women, a finding reflected in my own research on Ye'kwana maternal care (Hames 1988). This suggests that nursing women are providing less food to the household than average given the number of dependent offspring in their family. However, one must consider that lactating women are producing food (i.e., milk) 100% of the time that they are breast-feeding. Therefore, it follows that the value of milk production (about 600–800 kcal/day) must be added to the value of food produced through common economic activities. This may erase the differential between nursing and nonnursing women in total food production even though labor time allocation differences would persist. It also suggests that lower levels of labor may be adaptive for nursing women since more energy could be devoted to milk production.

If nursing women work less, then the nutritional status of dependent nonnursing children may suffer, unless older offspring or non–family member compensate. Data on the Ye'kwana indicate that husbands of nursing women do not increase their work loads to compensate for a nursing wife's reduced time allocated to food production. However, it appears that nursing women are given assistance in garden tasks by closely related women in other households (Hames 1987a). For the Aché, extensive bandwide sharing of food appears to be the way in which nursing women may compensate for lower productivity.

7.5.6. *Division of Labor*

In most societies the allocation of many different work activities, or the division of labor, is associated with sex. Tasks may be allocated exclusively, predominantly, or without distinction to males or females. For example, in most groups hunting is done only by males, with the bulk of the hunting done by adult males. For other activities a division of labor by sex is marked in that one sex does significantly more labor than another (e.g., female dominance of food preparation) but the division is not exclusive (Hames 1989). Age also is a significant correlate of labor although it has not been the subject of frequent systematic quantification (see above).

Most theoretical approaches to the division of labor have focused on its sexual dimensions. They suggest that physical and parenting skill differences in males and females are primary determinants of the division of labor. Some of this literature overlaps with studies of parental investment in offspring and its consequent affect on labor time (Chapter 11).

The traditional explanation of the division of labor has focused on physiological differences (aerobic capacity, muscle mass, etc.) between the sexes. Murdock and Provost's (1973) cross-cultural analysis concludes that differences in physical strength determine the division of labor. A major flaw in this work is lack of a clear definition of strength (is it endurance, power, or some other quality of performance?) and absence of a quantitative scale to measure these variables cross-culturally. An interesting attempt to apply the strength model ethnographically comes from Brooke Thomas's thesis (1973) on Andean peasants. He found that women did no arduous foot plowing because they lacked the aerobic capacity for sustained work at this activity. While such findings support the strength model, this model is limited by the fact that many activities that men do are in fact within the aerobic capacity of women.

Judith Brown (1970a) generalized that the division of labor for women will be determined by the degree to which the task done is compatible with simultaneous child care. This generalization assumes that women are the primary caretakers of children. While qualitative research supports this generalization of female-dominated child care, quantitative demonstration (Chapter 11) in support has appeared only recently. Starting with Brown's model, research by Hurtado et al. (1985) on Aché women focuses on three important issues: (1) the degree to which the division of labor is determined by child care differences between the sexes; (2) the possible depressant effect of child care responsibilities on female labor time and efficiency; and (3) the effect that number of weaned dependents has on female labor time. They found that Aché women did restrict themselves to activities compatible with simultaneous child care activities, that nursing women worked less and less efficiently than nonnursing women, and that labor time increased independently of nursing status with the number of weaned dependents a woman had. In addition, husbands of nursing wives allocated more time to child care than males whose wives were not nursing (Hill and Kaplan 1988).

While Brown's generalization has received quantitative support it cannot serve as a general model of the division of labor. It simply states that women will engage in tasks that are compatible with simultaneous child care. However, we know that other family members and kin care for children (Borgerhoff Mulder and Milton 1985; Hames 1987a), that women to some extent engage in activities that are not compatible with simultaneous child care (e.g., female hunting among the Agta; Goodman et al. 1985), and finally that women who do not have young children (e.g., pre- or postmenopausal women) are not burdened by child care obligations.

To deal with these issues, Hurtado et al. (1985) move beyond Brown's model of constraints by developing a simple diminishing-returns model of time allocation to child care and subsistence. They assume that child care beyond a certain point will reach diminishing returns such that it is more adaptive to switch from child care to subsistence (or from subsistence to child care). They hypothesize that for women living in an environment high in sources of trauma, the presence of an unweaned infant will cause the return curve for child care to diminish less rapidly for women so situated compared to women with opposite characteristics (e.g., horticulturalists who clear their settlements of dangerous plants and animals). On the other hand, the diminishing curve for the value of subsistence will remain high for women with weaned dependent children. In both cases the presence of a husband, especially a highly productive husband, will cause the return from a woman's own subsistence effort to decrease more rapidly, leading to higher investment of time in child care.

Hurtado et al. admit that they cannot satisfactorily answer the question of why childless women do not hunt. They speculate, following Frisch (1984) and Bentley (1985), that active hunting may decrease fertility and that postmenopausal women may gain greater fitness benefits by assisting in the care of grandchildren. Another factor to consider is whether women could hunt as efficiently or as effectively as men or whether hunting would produce as high a rate of fitness return as gathering. Hunting is a highly skilled activity that takes years to master. For example, in the case of the Ye'kwana, boys between the ages of 4 and 14 spend, on average, 46 minutes per day playing with bows and blowguns and play hunting (Hames 1978:158). This figure is 70 minutes per day for Yanomamö boys aged 7 to 16. Girls do not engage in any of these activities. Some ethologists note that play is really a kind of practice for activities that have important fitness consequences later in life (Symons 1978). As a result of reproductive activity constraints, young women do not gain the experience to be effective hunters later in life. However, this observation begs the question: Why do girls not play hunt in order to develop skills that in postmenopausal life could be as useful to them as they are to adult males? Cross-culturally it may be the case that skills required to hunt efficiently (e.g., perceptual acuity, aerobic capacity, and strength) decline sufficiently for both sexes in the middle of the fourth decade of life that other activities such as gathering or horticulture are superior alternatives. This perspective would also explain why male hunting effort among the Yanomamö and Ye'kwana declines during this time (Hames 1979b).

7.5.7. Diachronic Time Allocation Patterns

In order to survive and reproduce, humans must engage in a variety of tasks throughout the course of a day, season, or year. As a result, activities must be scheduled through time. Whether and for how long an activity will be done is dependent on its efficiency at a particular time, its diminishing returns, and the opportunity costs of continuing to do that activity compared to alternatives. These factors are the same as those that must be considered when modeling time allocation synchronically. In modeling time allocation diachronically, however, the analyst takes special note of how costs and benefits change as a function of variables that are time dependent. For example, during the course of the day, temperature and humidity rise and fall, thereby affecting the cost of an activity (Durnin and Passmore 1967). For high- and midlatitude foragers, game density or even game quality (see Speth and Spielman 1983 on fat content) is sharply seasonal, requiring high bursts of foraging effort in which nearly all time is allocated to hunting followed by a near cessation of hunting and a switch to food processing, maintenance, or even periods of inactivity (Binford 1980).

Time scheduling is expected to be an adaptive problem when a variety of activities must be done within a particular period of time and when the return to effort of activities varies considerably through time or when it is subject to diminishing returns. What follows are recent examples of attempts to model time allocation over the course of a day and over the course of a year.

Seasonality in Hiwi Work Allocation.   The recent research by Hurtado and Hill (1989, in press) on Hiwi men and women (tropical foragers of the mid-Orinoco River basin of Venezuela) is one of the most comprehensive attempts to deal with seasonal variation in time allocation among foragers. Their research reveals significant variation in time allocated to foraging during the four different seasons that comprise the year for males, post-reproductive and nonlactating women, but not for pregnant or lactating women. Their goal is to account for inter- and intrasexual variation in time allocation on a seasonal basis.

Foraging patterns among the Hiwi are paradoxical: rates of return are relatively high, foraging time never exceeds 3 hr/day in any season (about 1.8 hr/day for males and females over all seasons), yet Hurtado and Hill provide considerable evidence that hunger is a problem (significant seasonal weight loss, anemia, etc.) and appears to have a measurable impact on female fertility and child survivorship. They hypothesize that low work effort and seasonal variation in work effort is largely governed by high labor and opportunity costs. For both males and females, increased labor time leads to weight loss on a seasonal basis. For males, weight loss occurs despite the fact that foraging return rates exceed foraging expenditure by 300 to 400 cal/hr. However, men are required to share what they forage such that increasing foraging leads to a caloric loss (and unlike the Aché but like the Yanomamö in Figure 7.4 they apparently accrue no substantial benefits for sharing; Hurtado and Hill in press). For women, increased labor time during the late wet and early dry seasons coupled with decreased consumption during the early dry season lowers fertility and weight.

Diurnal Patterns in Yanomamö Time Allocation. It is clear in modern society that time allocation in work, leisure, and eating has a diurnal pattern. Ethnographic observation suggests that this is the case too in clock-less tribal and peasant societies, yet it rarely is the topic of systematic investigation or model building (Hanna and Baker 1983). An exception is the study of heat stress in desert and tropical societies by physical anthropologists (Landell 1964). In the tropics, radiant heat, air temperature, and humidity affect the energetic cost of activities: the higher the value of any of these variables, the greater the cost of the activity. This cost is paid by higher energetic expenditure or by the increased probability of stress (heat stroke or prostration). If the energetic cost of an activity is strongly affected by heat stress then one would expect a diurnal scheduling of activities to minimize these costs. At the same time, this does not rule out the innovation of technology such as shelters or clothing to deal with heat stress. However, such innovations must be regarded as costs in themselves because time must be devoted for their manufacture.

The Yanomamö are an Amazonian people living in dense tropical rain-forest 2° north of the equator. In the tropics, overall heat stress approximates an inverted U-curve: Minimum stress occurs in the morning when the temperature is low, humidity moderate, and radiant heat (determined by solar angle) is low; increases throughout the day, peaking at about 1500 hours (Landell 1964); and then declines thereafter to evening. If heat stress is an adaptive constraint, then labor activities should be done at times of the day corresponding to minimum heat stress. Furthermore, activities such as gardening (which lead to high solar exposure and are relatively effort intensive) should be more constrained by heat stress factors than gathering (which is slightly less costly but is done in deep forest shade at a more leisurely pace). Finally, food processing should be least constrained since it is done in the shade and requires little effort. Figure 7.7 displays percentage of time allocated to all labor and gardening, gathering, and food processing by hour of day (an index for heat stress). Total work (which includes all labor activities, is marked by a solid line with open circles and the right y axis) is measured as the percentage of activities that are labor activities at each hour of the day. Gardening, gathering, and food processing (left y axis) are measured as the percentage of the total activity done at each hour of the day. For example, 24% of all gardening is done between 1000 and 1100 hours. An inspection of the figure indicates that, to some degree, the Yanomamö are adjusting their labor activities to minimize heat stress. Labor peaks between 1100 and 1300 hours and declines thereafter. Seventy-five percent of all gardening is done by noon while the 75% level for gathering and food processing is not reached until 1400 and 1500 hours, respectively.

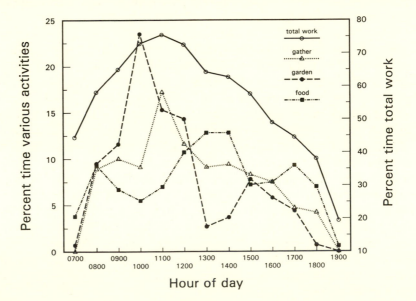

Figure 7.7. Yanomamö diurnal time allocation patterns. The right y axis and solid line measures percentage of all labor at each hour of the day, while the left y axis measures percentage of time allocated to various labor activities (hunting, gathering, gardening, and food preparation) at each hour of the day.

The absence of a perfect correlation between heat stress and labor activities among the Yanomamö may be the result of a variety of factors. Certain activities such as fishing may have greater overall efficiencies (even when heat stress costs are greater) when done at particular hours of the day. Some activities, such as food processing, require the completion of other activities that they necessarily follow (e.g., food can only be processed after it is acquired through hunting or gardening).

7.6. ECONOMIC FORMATION AND LABOR

Stimulated in part by Sahlins's widely read article "Notes on the Original Affluent Society" (1968a) anthropologists in recent years have intensified interest in the relationship between time allocation and economic formation as well as variation in age, sex, and status within economic formations. As Sahlins has noted (1972), some cultural evolutionists generalized that foraging and simple horticulture are inefficient adaptations that require high labor expenditures and correspondingly less leisure time for cultural development. The first systematic attempt quantitatively to deal with the relationship between a group's mode of production (hunting and gathering, horticulture, agriculture, etc.) and labor time allocation was Minge-Kalman's cross-cultural comparison (1980). For her the issue was empirical and encapsulated in the title of her article, "Does Labor Time Increase with Industrialization?" Larger and more recent comparative studies (Hames 1989; and, in particular, Sackett 1988) have addressed the same issue and, in general, have found that labor time allocation does grow with industrialization. However, as seen in Figure 7.8, the relationship is complex, perhaps best described as an S that has fallen on its face, with labor time decreasing from foragers to simple horticulturalists, increasing through peasant societies, and then decreasing, finally, to industrial societies. Sackett's (1988) larger (n = 104) sample shows essentially the same trend.

At this point, it seems unlikely that interesting theoretical issues can be addressed by correlating time allocation with economic formation at this degree of generality. For instance, it is unclear what one can conclude by noting that peasant farmers work more hours per day than simple horticulturalists, or that women in most economic formations work more than men (even when child care is ignored, as in Figure 7.8) (Hames 1989; Sackett 1988). The concepts of foraging, horticulture, and herding are much too indirect and do not adequately directly tap factors responsible for variation in time allocation. For example, foragers, on average, may work more than simple horticulturalists not because wild resources are less plentiful per capita but rather because resources are located at some distance from their residential base. While long distances between a residential base and

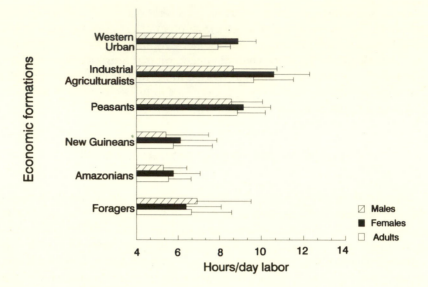

Figure 7.8. Male, female, and adult (average of male and female) labor time, by economic formation. The formations are: foragers (hunter-gatherers); Amazonians (simple horticulturalists with high dependence on foraging); New Guineans (advanced horticulturalists with domesticated animals); peasants (small landholding rural poor); industrial agriculturalists (modern mechanized farmers); and Western urban. Symmetrical I-bars indicate standard deviations. (Data from Hames 1989; n = 27.)

resource locations may be more common for foragers than horticulturalists this may not be true for all foragers (e.g., some Northwest Coast Indians). In some peasant groups, critical resources such as firewood are 2 to 4 hours distant from residences (Panter-Brick 1989).

Furthermore, there is considerable overlap in labor time for different economic formations, a high degree of variability within formations, as well as high variability by sex within and between formations. This variability exceeds the average difference between formations and requires explanation. For example, Hames (1989) and Sackett (1988) both found that women in all economic formations, on average, work about 0.8 hr more per day (child care not included) than men. A productive way to deal with this sort of problem is outlined in the previously described works of Hill et al. (1985) and Hurtado and Hill (1989, in press). For example, in foraging societies it may be the case that men work more than women—a notable deviation from other economic formations—because women are heavily constrained by child care activities (Lee 1968; Blurton Jones and Sibley 1978; Konner and Worthman 1980). Given that gathering frequently requires walking long distances and gathering while caring for an infant reduces foraging efficiency (Hurtado et al. 1985), women may increase fitness better by allocating more time to child care and less to foraging. Although these constraints may be more common in foraging populations than others, they are not exclusively characteristic of foraging populations (e.g., Amazonian horticulturalists spend two to three times more hours per day foraging than they do gardening; Hames 1989). Such time allocation models point to the factors that determine labor and child care expenditure more precisely than broad characterizations that index obscure multiple factors.

7.7. OTHER ISSUES: RITUAL AND MATING EFFORT

With the exception of time allocated to child care, all models and studies reviewed here deal with time allocated to economic activities. This is largely because most of the models employed derive from optimization approaches in microeconomics and foraging theory. Nevertheless, there is no reason to believe that time allocation studies cannot at least be used accurately to describe time allocated to ritual, political, social, and other noneconomic activities. Whether evolutionary theory and time allocation methodology prove useful for modeling these activities depends on how successfully they deal with the following conceptual issues.

As mentioned in the beginning, evolutionary ecology critically deals with how and why individuals allocate time to somatic effort and reproductive effort. If we take the example of ritual curing, an extremely common activity cross-culturally, it is not clear whether the curer is engaging in a kind of reproductive or somatic effort. In some cases the curer receives pay; therefore, we might want to classify it as a kind of somatic effort. But in other cases (e.g., the Yanomamö), a shaman conducting a cure receives nothing, even though he may chant to the spirits all day and night until exhausted and he may have consumed a considerable quantity of hallucinogenic drugs that took additional hours to gather from the forest and to process. Such individuals may gain prestige, but it is unclear how that prestige may be converted to reproductive success.

A closely related issue is choosing a currency. In foraging models the rate of energetic return is used as a proxy or currency for fitness. That is, it is assumed, for good empirical reasons, that rates of return are positively correlated with fitness. Returning to the example of ritual curing, it is entirely unclear what sort of measure analysts would use. Model building and hypothesis testing depend on theoretical variables that clearly specify fundamental relationships. As long variables are well-defined they can be quantified, and the kinds of models reviewed here depend on measurable variables. At this point, time allocation models have virtually ignored noneconomic activities or activities that cannot be easily translated to an economic model. An exception to this generalization is Flinn's work (1988a) on time allocated to mate guarding, reviewed below.

Mate Guarding in Trinidad.   Human reproductive strategies require not only that time be allocated to securing a mate (i.e., marriage) but in some cases that time must be allocated to ensure that the offspring from such a union are genetically one's own and that they receive sufficient care or parental investment. The first problem is exclusively a male concern; Paternity may be uncertain. The second problem is a concern of both sexes; it is more of an adaptive constraint for females than for males (Chapter 11). Flinn (1988a) refers to such problems as "mate guarding," that is, attempts to monitor and/or influence the behavior of a mate to ensure sexual fidelity and investment in offspring. After formulating a series of hypotheses from sexual selection theory, Flinn found the following predictions statistically validated:

1.   Males interact more frequently with female mates when they are fecund (capable of becoming pregnant) than when they are infecund.

2.   Males interact agonistically with their mates more frequently when their mates are fecund.

3.   Males interact agonistically more frequently with other nonrelated males when their mates are fecund.

4.   Females do not interact more agonistically to other females if they are fecund or infecund.

Although Flinn's research was not designed specifically to deal with time allocation issues, it is important to time allocation research in two basic ways. First, it shows the value of time allocation sampling methods for researchers in other areas of evolutionary ecology. And second, it deals with a noneconomic dimension of time allocation that has economic implications. Husbands with fecund wives systematically increased the amount of time they allocated to interaction with their wives, which means they had correspondingly less time to allocate to labor or other activities.

7.8. SUMMARY

Most time allocation research has been devoted to modeling time allocated to economic production such as hunting, gathering, and agriculture: activities, in many cases, representing more than half of all nonsleeping behaviors. Some significant research has been accomplished on child care activities but modeling of time allocated to social activities is still rare. Methodologically, time allocation sampling techniques are potentially useful to most other areas of behavioral ecology because it allows researchers to collect behavioral data necessary to understand variation in diet choice (Chapter 6), parental investment (Chapter 11), exchange (Chapter 9), settlement pattern (Chapter 8), and patch choice (Chapters 6 and 8).

Standard microeconomic theory informs most attempts to model time allocation. Analysts assume that time and resources are limited, are subject to diminishing returns, and have alternative and sometimes mutually exclusive uses. One of the central issues that has emerged is how people respond to changes in resource accrual and production efficiency because of differences in skill (e.g., hunting ability), technology (shotgun and bow hunting), child care constraints (simultaneous child care while foraging), diurnal variation in heat stress, seasonality, and age-related changes in physical ability and conditioning. In some cases, increased efficiency leads to increased time allocation. In other cases it does not. An understanding of the role of opportunity costs (e.g., child care responsibilities) and diminishing returns greatly improves our ability to predict where an individual will fit along this time minimization/resource maximization continuum. At this point, it is unclear whether it is either useful or legitimate to attempt to apply this formal economic approach to noneconomic behaviors. Nevertheless, these concepts are powerful and general enough to serve as a basis for the investigation of social behavior.

ACKNOWLEDGEMENTS

I thank Eric Smith and Bruce Winterhalder for their careful attention to detail in editing several versions of this chapter, Kim Hill and Eric Smith for clarifications on several of the graphs, and Magdi Hurtado for her cogent observations on several of the general issues addressed here. Be that as it may, final responsibility for the chapter rests with me. Research and writing was supported by NSF grant BNS 84-11669.

Spatial Organization and Habitat Use

Elizabeth Cashdan

8

This chapter considers the human use of space from the perspective of behavioral ecology. How do we understand the decisions people make about where to live, how much space to use, and when it pays to defend it? How is human behavior affected by the spatial distribution of resources?

The models discussed below share with the rest of the field the underlying assumption that natural selection favors individuals who behave optimally, in this case optimally with respect to their use of space. Unlike some of the other topics taken up in this book, however, the models discussed in this chapter rarely consider fitness explicitly. Like the models of optimal foraging (see Chapter 6), these are chiefly economic models that use energetic return rates as a proximate currency.

The chapter is organized around three large questions: (1) How can one obtain a reliable supply of food and other resources, when resources vary in time and space? (2) Where should one settle? And (3) how large an area should one use, and when does it pay to defend it against intruders? While one individual's use of space affects the options and payoffs for others, we will ignore this at first, and simply consider the environment as something external to and unaffected by the humans we are studying. The complexities of the social environment—how decisions by one individual affect the optimal strategy of another—will be taken up later in each section.

8.1. DESCRIBING AND MEASURING RESOURCE VARIATION

Resources vary in their distribution through time and across space. How do individuals obtain a consistent supply in the face of this variation? We can think of the solution to this problem as a process of *averaging* over time and space; individuals even out (average over) spatial variation in resources through mobility and trade, and they average over temporal variation through storage. When does it pay to do one rather than the other? And over what scale (time or distance) should one average?

The answers to these questions will depend, in part, on how resources are distributed in time and space; we begin, therefore, with a discussion of how resource variation can be described and measured. Aspects of this that we will consider include the following: Are resources clumped in time or space, or are they evenly distributed? How clumped (i.e, what is the magnitude of variation)? Is the variation predictable or unpredictable? If resources are clumped in time or space, how far apart are the clumps (i.e, what is the frequency, or scale, of variation)? And are patches of different resources found together or not (i.e., do needed resources vary in phase with one another)?

8.1.1. Variation over Time

Figure 8.1 shows two series of data points, which might be yearly rainfall (or some other resource), measured at regular intervals through time. One thing that we might want to know about each time series is the magnitude of the variation: Does yearly rainfall stay close to the average for the series, or does it deviate substantially? One measure of this would be the variance of the data points. A second thing we might want to know is whether the variation is predictable: Is the patterning regular, so that existing data points can be used to predict future ones? This is more problematic, and can be difficult to ascertain by visual examination (compare the upper and lower figures, which show an unpredictable and a predictable time series, respectively). While variance and predictability are different concepts, anthropologists have sometimes confused them, calculating variance when they intend to measure predictability.

One simple yet enlightening way of measuring predictability was proposed by Colwell (1974), who decomposed predictability into two measures, "constancy" and "contingency." If monthly rainfall does not vary at all throughout the year, it is said to be predictable because of high constancy. If it varies, but does so contingent on some other phenomenon (such as season), it is predictable because of high contingency. Both of these are biologically important; if rainfall is highly contingent on season, an animal needing a certain amount of rainfall might do well to use day length as a cue guiding its behavior, whereas day length might profitably be ignored if seasonal contingency is low. Low (1990) has examined the constancy, contingency, and variance of monthly rainfall experienced by a large number of societies, and shows that these variables have significant, but very different effects on behavior.

A limitation of this approach is that rainfall may be predictable at some temporal scales but not at others. Predictability at different scales is best

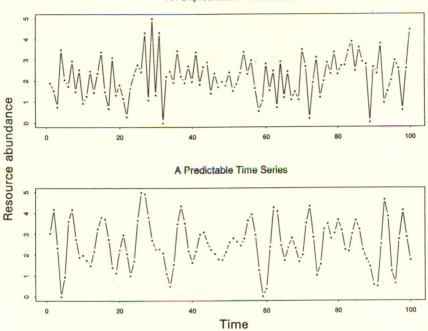

Figure 8.1.   *Predictable and unpredictable time series.*

described by seeing to what extent, and at what time lag, consecutive data points are associated. If there is a significant degree of association between consecutive data points, then past data points can be used to predict future ones. This is done using the techniques of autocorrelation and spectral analysis. We can define a function $\rho(h)$, which is the correlation coefficient between data points, separated by h time units. Therefore, $\rho(1)$ measures the association between data points one time unit apart, $\rho(2)$ measures the association between data points separated by two time intervals (a "lag" of 2), and so on. In the lower time series of Figure 8.1, adjacent points are positively correlated ($\rho(1) = 0.5$), while the association between data points three time units apart is equally strong but negative ($\rho(3) = -0.5$). The correlation at all lags for the unpredictable series is close to zero. The autocorrelation function, then, provides a measure of predictability at different frequencies.

Figure 8.2 illustrates this further by showing variation over time in two hypothetical resources, A and B, with the sum ($A + B$) indicating the total resource abundance. In this figure, B has a frequency of 1 cycle per 5.5 years (1/5.5, or 0.18, cycle per year) and A has a frequency of about 1 cycle per 16 years (1/16, or 0.06). The periodicity of total resource abundance,

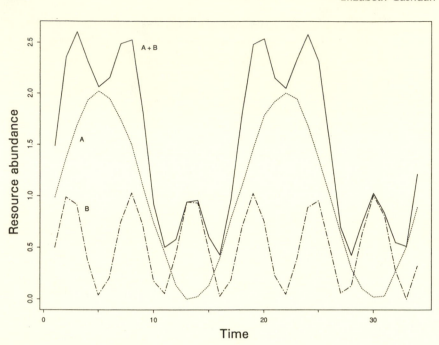

Figure 8.2.   Two time series and their sum.

A + B, can be seen in Figure 8.3, which shows the associated power spectrum for this series. The power spectrum is a way of representing how much of the variance in the time series is accounted for by different frequency bands. The two peaks in the power spectrum of Figure 8.3 indicate that the time series *A + B* has regular cycles at frequencies of 0.18 and 0.06.

Although the lower time series in Figure 8.1 is not obviously periodic, it too can be expressed as the sum of cycles of different frequency in precisely the same way (the power spectrum for the upper, unpredictable series would be nearly flat, since there is approximately equal power at all frequencies). Spectral analysis, then, allows us to measure the *pattern* in any time series by seeing which frequencies are most important in explaining the total variation.

How do people respond to such variation? We will look at a few provocative examples. Jorde (1977), using estimates of yearly rainfall from tree rings, used spectral analysis to compare rainfall patterns before and after 1050 A.D. in the American Southwest. He found that in the later period there was a shift toward more power at lower frequencies (i.e., a tendency to cycle at lower frequencies), implying a greater likelihood of people experiencing several consecutive dry years. Archaeologists have documented some major cultural shifts at this time, including a marked increase in food storage

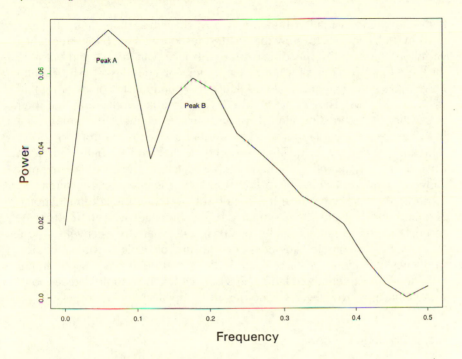

Figure 8.3. Power spectrum of series A + B. *The power spectrum measures the power, or variance, at different frequencies.*

facilities, irrigation, and population aggregation along permanent drainages. Jorde suggests that these cultural responses allowed residents to buffer the longer rainfall cycles.

A related method known as cross-spectral analysis makes it possible to correlate one time series with another. How, for example, do human birthrates track (or buffer) variation in economic or ecological conditions? Because we would not expect the response to be instantaneous, simple correlation of these variables at the same point in time might show no relationship even when one exists. As we will see below, these same methods can also be used to explain variation in space. Cross-spectral analysis can be used to correlate the distribution in space of two different species, or of one species with soil type or topography. The method allows us to explore serial relationships that are out of phase (for example, birth-rates that respond to rainfall levels a year or more later, or plant species that interfere with each other). It also allows us to explore the strength of the relationship at different frequencies.

Jorde and Harpending (1976) have proposed the intriguing and intuitively reasonable notion that, as societies become technologically more complex, they are able to buffer increasingly long-term resource cycles. With the

higher-frequency variation buffered, we might expect population fluctuations in such societies to show the greatest responsiveness to low-frequency
variation. Jorde and Harpending explore this idea with rainfall and birthrate
data for four societies of varying technological complexity. The Ramah
Navajo, a semimobile pastoral population, respond most strongly to rainfall
cycles of 2 years. They do so with a 1 year time lag, indicating that their
population is responding almost immediately to changes in rainfall. The
high *coherence* (correlation between rainfall and birth rate) of .95 shows
that this population is tracking resource fluctuations strongly. San Juan
Pueblo, an agricultural community exposed to the same rainfall regime,
shows much lower coherence; this population is not tracking rainfall as
closely, presumably because it is better able to buffer rainfall fluctuations.
Scotland and England show similarly low coherence, with their strongest
response being to rainfall cycles of 20 and 40 years, respectively. These
technologically complex societies are presumably able to buffer higher-
frequency variation. Lee (1977) and Richards (1983) have used similar
techniques to explore the relationships between demographic and economic relationships over several centuries in European populations.

8.1.2. Variation over Space

Although time series may be more familiar than "space series," variation
in time and space can be conceived of in similar ways and analyzed with
similar methods. We will begin with some traditional measures of patchiness, and then return to the spectral analysis of space series.

Patchiness: Point and Quadrat Methods.   Many ecological models predict that the patchiness of resource distributions will have an important
effect on foraging behavior and settlement patterns. In spite of its importance, however, patchiness can be an elusive variable to measure. Consider
Figure 8.1 again, this time making the x-axis a linear transect in space and
the y-axis the abundance of a resource at different locations along the
transect. Clearly, the peaks correspond to patches (resource clumps). But
what statistic would enable us to compare two distributions and say that one
is patchier than the other? Do we measure total variance? Or perhaps the
distance between peaks?
Plant ecologists have developed many ways of measuring departures from
randomness in plant distributions; these include (a) measures based on the
distance between individual plants and/or between a random point and the
nearest plant, and (b) measures based on the relative abundance of the plant
in different quadrats (see reviews by Grieg-Smith 1983; Kershaw 1973;
Pielou 1977). The most widely known of the former within anthropology is
the nearest-neighbor statistic, the ratio of the observed average distance

between nearest neighbors to the distance expected if the items were distributed randomly (Clark and Evans 1954). Archaeologists interested in spatial patterning of artifacts and sites discovered nearest-neighbor analysis with enthusiasm in the 1970s, but seem to have become disillusioned with it (Pinder et al. 1979; McNutt 1981). In addition to some technical problems, this measure has the conceptual drawback of confounding distance within and between patches; the numerator of this statistic measures the distance between plants *within* a patch, which is usually determined by the reproductive behavior of the species, and is not usually what we are interested in when we speak of patchiness. The technique also requires the precise coordinates of each resource item, which is costly information to collect. If one has only counts per quadrat, other measures are available (see Grieg-Smith 1983; Kershaw 1973, and references therein).

A major difficulty with these measures is that patchiness will normally be ecologically relevant to an organism at only certain scales of distance. Scale is not handled well by either point measures of patchiness (such as nearest-neighbor analysis) or by most quadrat measures; however, some indication of the relative importance of variance at different scales can be obtained by using quadrats that vary systematically in size (see Grieg-Smith 1983; Kershaw 1973; and Whallon 1974).

Autocorrelation and Spectral Analysis. A more sensitive approach to the problem of scale in spatial patterning is through autocorrelation (Cliff and Ord 1973; Voorips and O'Shea 1987) and spectral analysis (Platt and Denman 1975; Roughgarden 1979; Harpending and Davis 1977; Cliff et al. 1975; Rogers and Chasko 1979). Although these methods are usually associated with time series, as discussed above, the problem of scale is analogous and can be dealt with in similar ways.

To make the application more concrete, consider Figure 8.4 (taken from Harpending and Davis 1977), which shows the distribution of apple and orange trees along a hypothetical transect. Apple trees show a cyclical pattern of variation with a frequency of 1 cycle per 50 km, whereas oranges show no clear periodicity. If we graphed the power at different frequencies (as we did earlier with respect to variation over time), we would find that apple trees show a peak in the power spectrum at 1/50, while the graph for orange trees would be more nearly flat (indicating approximately equal power at all frequencies). The power spectrum, therefore, tells us about the magnitude and scale of resource patchiness, even when the patterning may not be apparent in the raw data series.

Of equal importance to a human forager is the relationship between resources. Are clumps of needed resources likely to be found near one another? Cross-spectral analysis, which measures the relationship between two series, can tell us the strength of association between different resources at different frequencies and at different lags. Two resources that respond

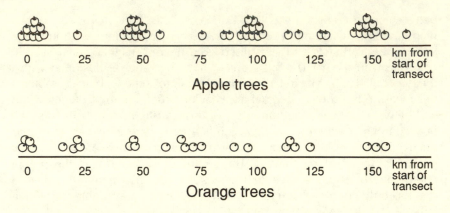

Figure 8.4.   Apple and orange trees along a hypothetical transect (from Harpending and Davis 1977).

similarly to soil and moisture conditions, for example, should be highly correlated and in phase at relatively low frequencies. Resources that interfere with each other should be highly correlated and out of phase at high frequencies.

Spectral analysis is a powerful method for describing variation in spatial patterning, but its potential has not been widely exploited by anthropologists. Yet the attributes of spatial patterning discussed above do seem to have an important effect on human settlement and mobility decisions, as we will see. The discussion of these issues has been hampered not only by a lack of data on the spatial patterning of resources, but by the absence of a clear and appropriate vocabulary for describing and conceptualizing that patterning. The attention given above to spectral analysis was motivated by the belief that an intuitive understanding of the subject can clarify one's thinking about variation in space and time. We will use its vocabulary in the discussion to follow.

8.2. AVERAGING OVER TIME AND SPACE

The problem initially posed in the previous section was how to obtain a consistent supply of resources, given temporal and spatial variation in their abundance or availability. It was suggested that one could think of human responses to this problem as a process of averaging over variation in time and space. The role of storage and other cultural buffers in smoothing out (averaging over) temporal variation in rainfall was discussed briefly above. Here we consider the way mobility allows people to average over spatial and spatiotemporal variation.

8.2.1. Spatial Averaging

One obvious factor affecting range size in human populations is resource abundance. It is reasonable to suppose that a forager in a sparse environment will require a larger range than one in a richer environment, and it will be shown later that this expectation is borne out in both humans and other animals. But is the spatial patterning of those resources also significant?

Obviously, some diversity in resources is necessary (water, shelter, foods with different nutrients), and it is difficult to separate human "needs" from human "wants" in this regard. Harpending and Davis (1977) argue, on the basis of their ethnographic experience, that mobility among the !Kung San is motivated more by a desire for dietary diversity than a desire to obtain some requisite number of calories. While increasing range size will normally increase diversity, the degree to which it does so depends on how the resources are distributed. Harpending and Davis (1977) hypothesize that ranges will be smaller where resources are in phase, since people can remain near the sites of resource concentration; they also predict that ranges will be smaller where there is little spatial variation (patchiness) at relevant frequencies, since increasing range size under these conditions will have little effect on diversity. Larger ranges are expected if resources are patchy but the patches are out of phase.

There is some empirical support for these predictions. Kelley (1983) has shown that hunter–gatherers in colder climates move a greater distance with each residential move, an association he attributes to the greater spatial "segregation" of resources in northern areas (i.e., resource patches that are out of phase at low frequencies).

Foraging range may be affected similarly. The Hadza and the !Kung San make an intriguing comparison in this regard, because their arid savanna environments are superficially similar, yet the !Kung live in an area where important resources (both water and plants) are patchy and out of phase, while resources in the Hadza environment are more evenly distributed (see Blurton Jones et al. 1989 for comparative environmental data; also Yellen and Harpending 1972; and Harpending and Davis 1977:280 for verbal characterization of the !Kung environment). If Harpending and Davis are correct, we would expect to find larger foraging ranges in the !Kung area than the Hadza area, other things equal, and there is some evidence that this is the case. Blurton Jones et al. (1989) and Hawkes et al. (1989) point out that Hadza women do not travel as far as !Kung women do when gathering, due to differences in the way resources are distributed in the two areas. !Kung camps are typically located at sources of permanent water, which are often in fossil river drainages, whereas important food resources are often located miles away on the dune crests between the drainages. The more even distribution of resources in the Hadza area, by contrast, makes it possible to gather successfully near the residential camp; an increase in range size provides little additional diversity.

Where resources are patchy on a scale larger than that of a daily foraging trip (very low frequency variation), and the patches of different resources are uncorrelated or out of phase, moving closer to one resource would simply move the camp farther from other resources. If the different resources are needed simultaneously, therefore, moving the entire camp would not be sufficient to solve the problem of resource acquisition. Binford (1980) argues that this type of resource distribution is particularly characteristic of high-latitude (boreal forest and arctic) regions. The typical response of human hunter–gatherers in such environments is what he terms a "collector" strategy: locate the residential camp at one resource and send out small, specialized task groups to procure the other resources. These task groups will often travel long distances and remain at the other resource locale for several days or weeks, collecting large amounts of the resource for storage. In environments where resources are more evenly distributed, a variety of resources will be within foraging distance of the camp and foragers can simply move the entire residential group as needed. These moves are typically shorter, but more frequent than the residential moves made by collectors (Kelley 1983; Binford 1980, 1990a). The Guayaki (Aché), who live in the tropical forests of Paraguay, are an extreme example of this type of mobility strategy, moving the entire camp an average of only 3.7 miles about 50 times per year (Clastres 1972, cited in Binford 1980).

While the discussion thus far has focused on hunter–gatherers, agriculturalists and pastoralists also use mobility as a way of averaging over spatial variation. This has been documented most extensively for inhabitants of mountain regions, where the altitudinal gradient produces an obvious vertical zonation of resources. Inhabitants of such regions may exploit several different production zones through a pattern of transhumance, or they may remain sedentary and specialized in their procurement activities, but average over the spatial variation through redistribution or trade (Webster 1973; Barth 1956; Orlove 1976; Brush 1976; Rhoades and Thompson 1975).

There is some evidence (Cashdan 1987) that trade replaces mobility as a way of averaging over spatial variation when increased competition, perhaps from increased population density, requires greater productivity and consequently increased specialization of land use. There is a lot of theory in ecology concerning the trade-offs between being a specialist and a generalist, yet trade allows humans to get around this trade-off by combining the efficiency of specialized producers with the diet breadth of generalized consumers. Trade is fundamental to human patterns of space use, but will not be considered further here because it remains theoretically undeveloped within behavioral ecology.

8.2.2. Spatiotemporal Averaging

What do we mean by predictability? One way of describing this, discussed above, is the degree to which a time series is autocorrelated at different time lags. A completely unpredictable time series (white noise) would be uncorrelated at all frequencies, and there would be no more power (variance) at one frequency than at another. The spatial analog of such a measure would be a complete absence of patchiness at all frequencies; resources would be distributed randomly over space. Spatial unpredictability differs from temporal unpredictability by being two-dimensional. If we consider both time and space together ("spatiotemporal" unpredictability), we are looking at variation in the resource distribution in three dimensions. In the following discussion, we will simplify this complex topic by focusing on the degree to which time series at different locations are correlated. If several time series are correlated and in phase, scarcity will be felt regionally. If they are not, it may be possible to buffer scarcity at one location by obtaining resources at another. In this section we will discuss the role of insurance in averaging over unpredictable spatiotemporal variation.

Insurance is a way of coping with unpredictable variation by averaging losses over a large number of independent exposure units. By the law of large numbers, the actual loss approaches the expected loss as the number of independent exposure units is increased. When losses are averaged, therefore, they become more predictable and less variable. Insurance that averages spatiotemporal variation has been described for both hunter–gatherers and food producers. For example, cattle herders in Botswana who have large herds typically keep several cattle posts in different areas, and loan stock to other individuals. Both practices serve as a form of insurance, since drought and disease are unlikely to hit all the cattle posts at the same time.

Agriculturalists, similarly, can buffer spatiotemporal variation in environmental conditions by having fields in different areas, as McCloskey (1975a, 1976) has shown for the preindustrial English peasantry (see also Winterhalder 1990). In England prior to 1700, families held land in large communally owned fields. Rather than having one large plot in each field, families typically had an average of eight small plots scattered widely in each field. While the inefficiency of this system has struck many observers as irrational, McCloskey has calculated that the added cost in average production was outweighed by reduced variance in production. To the extent that climatic conditions and environmental hazards (pests, flooding, etc.) affect the plots differentially, averaging over several dispersed fields will reduce variance and enhance security. McCloskey's analysis of the costs and benefits show not only that scattered fields were advantageous, but that the optimum number of such fields, 8.3, is very close to the number observed. Galt (1979:100), speaking of the farmers of Pantelleria Island, Italy, argues similarly that "land fragmentation . . . acts as a kind of insurance policy which prevents 'all-or-nothing-at-all' years."

Hunter–gatherer visiting patterns have been explained in a similar fashion. Like many hunter–gatherers, the !Kung San maintain a wide network of kin ties across the region. When resources are scarce, people typically respond by visiting kinsmen located in a temporarily more well-favored area. Most anthropologists have interpreted this behavior as an example of "reciprocal altruism" (see Chapter 9); sharing one's resources pays off in the long run because the favor will be reciprocated when circumstances change. It is this assumed reciprocity that makes sharing function as a type of insurance. The problem with this strategy is the difficulty of ensuring that the visitors will, in fact, reciprocate the favor.

Ethnographically, it appears that hunter–gatherers use a variety of mechanisms to reinforce reciprocity. The !Kung San, for example, have an institution called *hxaro,* involving the delayed exchange of gifts between particular exchange partners. *Hxaro* partners are close kinsmen who can be counted on to reciprocate favors when they are needed, and it is these relatives who are visited during times of local scarcity. Wiessner (1982) has shown that the !Kung deliberately choose *hxaro* partners with an eye toward the individual's geographic location and personal abilities, so that they will be protected against risks arising from a variety of sources.

Although anthropologists have been quick to assume that sharing (including sharing access to one's territory) involves reciprocity, they rarely stay in the field long enough to demonstrate this. Since the optimal strategy with interterritorial visiting (allow or exclude visitors) depends on what others do, game theory can be a useful analytical tool in exploring the circumstances that favor it (Smith and Boyd 1990). Hawkes (this volume) uses game theory to analyze the analogous problem of food sharing, and concludes that much of the sharing described in the anthropological literature may, in fact, not be reciprocal at all. The same may be true for reciprocal territorial access. This topic will be taken up further in section 8.5.4.

8.2.3. Spatial versus Temporal Averaging

Foragers can obtain a consistent supply of food either by storing it (averaging over temporal variation) or by increasing their foraging range (averaging over spatial variation). Under what circumstances should they do one or the other? The answer to this question will no doubt depend on both the characteristics of the variation (magnitude, scale, and predictability) in both dimensions, and the relative costs of reducing this variation.

A formal analysis of these trade-offs has yet to be made, but there is some evidence that a greater reliance on storage is associated with a decrease in mobility. Storage among hunter-gatherers is used primarily to buffer predict-able seasonal variation, and is most common in highly seasonal environ-ments (Binford 1980). With increased storage, a decrease in number of residential moves is commonly seen (Kelley 1983). For example, Kelley (1983) notes that the Nunamiut, who store caribou, remain at the winter residential site longer than do the Netsilik, who do not store, and that the Northwest Coast groups, who store salmon, are similarly more sedentary than interior groups of the same latitude who lack access to this resource and do not store. In these cases, the differential dependence on storage reflects the presence or absence of a large, aggregated resource (large caribou herds in the Nunamiut case, large salmon runs in the Northwest Coast). Similarly, the G//ana, who store both food and water, have fewer residential moves per year than do the G/wi, who live in the same environ-ment but do not store (Cashdan 1984a). These examples document a reduc-tion in number of moves, rather than a reduction in range size per se. However, unless the distance covered in each residential move increases with storage, then individual ranges would also be reduced.

The G//ana have been moving from a dependence on mobility to a dependence on storage in recent years, and this shift has been paralleled by a trend toward marrying people from the same area (Cashdan 1984a,b). One interpretation of this reduction in marital mobility is that the greater dependence on storage has reduced the necessity for visiting other territories when resources in one's own area are scarce, and consequently has reduced the necessity for the interband marriages that make such mobility possible.

8.3. HABITAT SELECTION AND SETTLEMENT PATTERN

In this section, we consider the question of where to live. How do the abundance and distribution of resources affect settlement patterns (residen-tial location and group size)? The resource abundance of an area is obvi-ously affected by the number of individuals already exploiting it, and we will consider the effects of density and prior settlement in section 8.4.2. At first, however, let us ignore this and consider only the characteristics of the resources themselves.

8.3.1. Resource Distributions and Efficient Foraging

Unlike most nonhuman foragers, hunter—gatherers usually do not con-sume food when and where they acquire it; most resources are brought back to a residential camp (central place), where they are used by other members of the group. The question of settlement patterns among human foragers, therefore, has at least two aspects: (1) size and location of foraging groups, and (2) size and location of residential groups. Many ecological models exist for the study of foraging groups, and anthropologists have done some excellent work in this area (see Chapter 6).

There are fewer appropriate models for studying the determinants of residential group size and location, although there are some nonhuman parallels. Many species bring food back to a central place, where it may be cached or fed to offspring. One reasonable assumption is that the central place should be located at the place that minimizes travel time to foraging locations. Whether animals in fact locate central places in such a fashion is questionable; Orians and Pearson (1979) point out that finding a safe place to build a nest or a cache may be more important than simply minimizing travel time. Similar nonenergetic considerations may also be important for humans. However, determining the point that minimizes distance to foraging locations is a useful place to begin, if only because deviations from it can be an indication of the importance of these other factors in determining settlement.

Colonial nesting birds are an example of central-place foragers; such birds nest together in large colonies, and bring food back to their young at the nests. Horn (1968) has considered the question of when coloniality pays off, and where the nests should be located. The relevance of Horn's model to human foragers has made it appealing to anthropologists, who have evaluated its predictions for several human populations (Wilmsen 1973; Heffley 1981; Dwyer and Minnegal 1985).

Assuming that we know the minimum area required to support each nest, and the probability of finding food at each location, how do we find out which central-place location minimizes foraging travel time? Horn argues that the average distance traveled bringing food to the central place in a large amount of time, T, is

$$2kT \sum_i \sum_j t(x_i,y_j) \sqrt{(x_i - x_0)^2 + (y_j - y_0)^2} \qquad (8.1)$$

where k is the number of foraging trips per unit time, $t(x_i,y_j)$ is the proportion of time during which foraging is better at (x_i,y_j) than at any other point in the area, and (x_0,y_0) are the coordinates of the central place. In other words, the distance from the central place to a foraging location (the square root quantity) is weighted by the probability that food will be most abundant at that location (the function of t), and these are summed over all foraging locations to give the expected distance. By including the $t(x,y)$ function, Eq. (8.1) considers that food abundance may not be the same from time to time at a given location (either because of mobile prey or simply changes in abundance), and incorporates this spatiotemporal variation into the distance measure.

Horn is wrong in claiming that Eq. (8.1) is minimized at the center of gravity (he would be right but for the square root in the equation). However, the distance can be calculated for specific points, and Horn provides one such example. Horn compares two possible distributions of the same amount of food, one where it is evenly distributed across 16 locations in the foraging area, and the other where it moves around so that only one of the 16 areas contains food at any given time. If the areas can support four nests, where should they be located? In the former case, birds can minimize competition by foraging in separate places, and travel is thus minimized by dispersing the nests. In the latter case, they must all feed together, and distance is minimized by locating all nests at a single location in the middle of the foraging region. It is not clear how general this result is, because it compares two extreme, symmetrical examples of resource distributions. However, Horn also gives a reasonable verbal argument predicting that aggregation should be favored (irrespective of any information sharing or other interaction) if (a) the food is "highly clumped, so that at certain critical times foraging is best at only a single point" (p. 694), and (b) there is enough food at such times to support several foragers.

The predictions concerning aggregation have been applied to a number of ethnographic cases. Heffley (1981) has considered three Athabaskan groups and finds that, in most cases, these foragers live in large aggregated residential settlements when they are exploiting an aggregated, mobile resource such as caribou, whereas they disperse into smaller groups when exploiting more solitary prey with smaller ranges (moose, sheep, and small game). It is not clear whether the aggregated settlements are in the middle of several possible caribou locations or whether the foragers are simply settling where the caribou are predictably most abundant; Horn's model is concerned with the former, but the latter might be optimal if the caribou location could be predicted. In developing an extension of Horn's model, Dwyer and Minnegal (1985) suggest that "clumping" of a resource is not just a matter of its location but also of its size, the technology used to procure it, and the potential to store it and thus extend its abundance through time. When these factors are taken into consideration, they argue, the model also applies to the Mbuti, the Andaman Islanders, and to the exceptions noted by Heffley.

The major finding of these ethnographic studies—that human foragers are clumped when the resources are, and vice versa—is also consistent with predictions obtained by Harpending and Davis (1977). They argue that if the variance in total calories between ranges is large, people should be clumped in large groups at the rich locations; if the variance is small, people should be more uniformly distributed, and in small groups. More interestingly, they then ask: How is this variance in total caloric supply affected by the distribution of *several* resources? Harpending and Davis make the following predictions: (1) Where resources are distributed independently of each other (i.e., low coherence), the variance in total calories between ranges should be small; hence occupations should be uniform. (2) Where resources are correlated and in phase, the variation from place to place is high, and settlement should be aggregated. (3) Where resources are out of phase, the variation in total calories between ranges should be small, and uniform occupation with large ranges would be expected. The latter situation, they argue, typifies the !Kung region. In order to apply these predictions to specific cases, of course, the scale (frequency) of resource variation must be considered in relation to the size of the foraging range.

8.3.2. Effects of Density: Ideal Free Distributions

The models discussed above make predictions about settlement given different resource distributions, but they do not consider the actions of conspecifics in making habitats more or less desirable. An area may be very rich in resources, but if it is crowded with competitors a poorer but empty area may be more desirable. Because the optimal habitat depends on the settlement strategies of other individuals, evolutionary game theory (see Chapters 2 and 9) has recently been the technique of choice for exploring this topic.

Fretwell and Lucas (1970) and Fretwell (1972) modeled habitat selection by assuming a population where all individuals are equal in competitive ability, and where each individual chooses the habitat most suitable (i.e., conferring the highest fitness) at the time of arrival. The first settlers would settle in the best habitats, but as these locations fill up the suitability of these areas would decline. At some point, an individual would do better by locating in another area. If future immigrants continue to choose the best habitat at the time of their arrival, all settled habitats should be of about equal quality. Fretwell (1972) shows that when individuals choose habitats in this way and under these hypothetical circumstances, all individuals will have similar success rates. They call such a settlement pattern an "ideal free distribution"; ideal because the foragers are assumed to be ideal in their ability to select the most suitable habitat, and free because they are free to enter any habitat on an equal basis with residents. Pulliam and Caraco (1984) develop this idea, showing that the behavior that gives rise to the ideal free distribution is an evolutionarily stable strategy, or ESS (see Chapters 2 and 9).

In some species, animals cannot move around freely because some individuals are dominant or defend territories and exclude others. Fretwell (1972) develops a second model in which he assumes that the first settlers will choose the best locations and defend them. The resulting settlement pattern, which he calls an "ideal despotic distribution," differs from the ideal free distribution in that success rates may be much higher at the best locations.

Biologists have shown that a number of different species do choose to settle as the ideal free model would predict (Milinski 1984; Harper 1982; Godin and Keenleyside (1984) although others do not (Sutherland and Parker 1985). A remaining problem, however, is that in at least two of the supporting cases (stickleback fish and mallards) it is known that individuals differ in competitive ability, thus violating one of the assumptions of the ideal free model. Sutherland and Parker (1985) have shown that where individuals differ in competitive ability, there are many different distributions where no individual could do better by moving. Since differences in competitive ability should be the norm, the relevance of the ideal free model is problematical.

There have been no attempts to test these models in human populations, although the polygyny threshold, an analogous model that shows how competing females "distribute" themselves across mates rather than across habitats, has received empirical attention in the human literature (see Chapter 11). In order to test the ideal free distribution on human patterns of settlement, we would like to know the number of individuals in each habitat, how the habitats differ in quality (as measured by such things as feeding rates, fertility, and offspring survival), and the fitnesses of residents. The last of these is rarely available, and differences in habitat quality are rarely measured quantitatively.

A special case of ideal free theory, known as habitat matching (Pulliam and Caraco 1984; Fagen 1987), may be more readily applicable to the environmental data at hand. If we add to Fretwell's assumptions the assumption that an individual's fitness depends solely on the fraction of total resources he or she controls, it can be shown that the relative productivity of two habitats equals (at equilibrium) the relative numbers of individuals that occupy them (Fagen 1987). In other words,

$$n_i/n_j = K_i/K_j \qquad (8.2)$$

where K_i is the total resource in patch i and n_i is the number of individuals in that patch. The question to be answered, then, is: Do human population densities match resource availability in this fashion?

There is abundant evidence in support of a relationship between density and resource availability in human populations, although how closely the ratios conform to Eq. (8.2) is less clear. The classic study is Birdsell's (1953) analysis of population distributions among aboriginal Australian hunter–gatherers. Central Australia is largely desert, and in desert areas rainfall is a good proxy for plant productivity (Pianka 1978:13–14). It would be reasonable, therefore, to expect population density to be positively correlated with rainfall. Although Birdsell had no information on population density, he did know the tribal area of 409 groups. He argued that average group size, which he put at 500 people, varied little from tribe to tribe. If so, then the larger the tribal area, the less dense the population. Birdsell found a strong negative hyperbolic relationship between the size of tribal areas and rainfall, a relationship that became stronger when coastal and riverine groups, and groups that were unusually large or small, were excluded. The y-axis on his original figure is a measure of area per person; transforming it into person/area (population density) would make the relationship between rainfall and population density approximately linear, as we would expect from the habitat matching rule.

A strong relationship between density and rainfall also exists for the Marshall Islands in Micronesia (Williamson and Sabath 1982). Williamson and Sabath had the advantage of census data to determine population density, and were able to show that it was strongly related to rainfall in these islands (r^2 of 0.42 and 0.72, depending on census year).

Both Birdsell and Williamson and Sabath interpret their results to mean that populations are regulated by resource abundance. Their data, however, bear on population distributions and settlement, and do not necessarily imply that demographic processes are regulating population numbers; if the population of Australia were twice as large, for example, the same *relative* densities might still be expected from habitat matching.

Since the habitat matching rule assumes that fitness is determined solely by food intake, we should not be surprised to find counterexamples. These should be expected both where fitness is heavily influenced by factors other than food intake (see Chapters 9 and 11 for some examples), and where food intake is not directly related to habitat productivity. The latter should be increasingly important as economies move toward industrialization and toward greater involvement in interregional trade.

A common empirical finding in the animal literature, one that contradicts the expectations of the ideal free model, is that intake tends to be higher at the best sites (see Sutherland and Parker 1985 for a review of the evidence). It is likely that this is also the case for humans. For example, a comparison of !Kung and G/wi Bushmen shows that the G/wi work about twice as hard as the !Kung to get about the same number of calories (Lee 1979; Tanaka 1980). The two groups have similar technologies and are in adjacent areas of the Kalahari Desert, but rainfall (hence productivity, see above) is considerably lower in the G/wi region (Cashdan 1983). If distribution were really ideal free, we would expect that densities in the !Kung region would rise to the point where return rates in the two regions were equal. But they have not. Sutherland and Parker (1985) suggest that where individuals differ in competitive ability, even without territoriality, higher intake rates at the best sites are to be expected. A strong competitor would do more poorly if it moved to inferior sites, while a weak competitor might do more poorly if it moved to a better site, because of interference. While this may not explain the !Kung advantage, it does seem applicable to southern Africa as a whole, where the politically and militarily strongest groups inhabit the most productive regions.

8.3.3. Other Reasons for Aggregation

In the discussion thus far, it has been argued that foragers aggregate where resources are most abundant or where such aggregation minimizes travel time. Conspecifics have thus far been regarded solely as competitors whose presence depresses return rates. Ecologists, however, have suggested a large number of factors that might make group living desirable. To the extent that coresidents *enhance* fitness, the assumptions of these models are not met, and settlement patterns can be expected to differ accordingly. We will return to the question of where to settle, therefore, after briefly discussing some of the reasons that have been given for group living. Smith (1981) provides an excellent review of these, with references both to the theory and to examples from the human and nonhuman literature. In addition to the factors discussed previously, Smith considers benefits to group living arising from enhanced reproductive opportunities, better predator avoidance, enhanced ability to defend resources, and increased foraging efficiency. The latter takes many forms, and can include increased encounter rate, increased capture rate from group hunting, increased prey size taken, reduction in foraging area overlap, information sharing about the location of resources, and risk reduction due to resource sharing. We will review a few of these briefly, focusing on increased foraging efficiency and enhanced defense.

Information sharing and efficient foraging.   Some social carnivores can kill more or larger animals in a group than they can by hunting separately (Schaller 1972:445; Nudds 1978), and an advantage in return rates is no doubt an important motivation for the frequent practice of group hunting described for human foragers. The size of human residential groups, the focus of discussion here, may also be affected by foraging considerations if group size affects the costs of gathering information about resources.

In a number of species, especially birds, individuals learn about resource locations by watching other successful foragers (Krebs et al. 1972; Horn 1968; Ward and Zahavi 1973; Pitcher et al. 1982). If patch size is large relative to individual food requirements, the advantages of foraging in groups could outweigh the costs of competition. Information sharing of a more active sort is, of course, ubiquitous among humans, and may sometimes affect residential group size and settlement. When hunter–gatherers visit groups in other areas, visitors can benefit by learning about resource locations from the residents, and both can benefit from considering the others' foraging plans (Smith 1981 and references therein; Hames 1983:404 and references therein; Smith and Boyd 1990; Cashdan 1983). One of my //Gana informants told me that while permission to enter is never refused, the owners may tell the newcomers "which side to use and which side not to use." In both human and nonhuman foragers, resource locations that are unpredictable and highly variable should enhance the foraging benefits of information sharing (Smith 1981). Kurland and Beckerman (1985) have suggested that the advantages of information sharing in a savanna habitat may have facilitated the development of collective foraging among early hominids, and that sociality arising for this reason may have set the stage for the ubiquitous food sharing characteristic of extant human foragers.

Defense against Predators and Conspecifics.   An individual may be better protected against the risk of predation when in a large group. A bird, for example, must interrupt its feeding periodically to scan for predators, but if individuals in a flock share this task and alert others to danger, the birds can spend more time feeding (Elgar and Catterall 1981; Bertram 1980; Pulliam et al. 1982). Grouping may also enhance ability to defend against a predator. Grouping is not necessarily an unmitigated advantage, even with regard to predators, since it may make prey more conspicuous and more desirable to a predator. While predators are not normally a major risk factor for humans, enhanced defense may have been important in hominid evolution, and might possibly affect the interhousehold spacing of extant human foragers (Gould and Yellen 1987; cf. O'Connell 1987; and Binford 1991).

Groups may also enhance defense against conspecifics. For example, solitary chickadees receive more aggression from other solitaries than do chickadees in flocks (Barash 1974). Hyenas, which form patrols to monitor their territories and engage in considerable intergroup aggression, may also benefit from large group size (Kruuk 1972; Pulliam and Caraco 1984). Similar advantages accrue to large groups among the horticultural Yanomamo, whose groups are larger and more widely separated where intervillage warfare is intense (Hames 1983). While success at warfare may motivate aggregation among the Yanomamo, declining efficiency at food procurement and increased fighting within the village are countervailing forces that lead to group fission (Hames 1983; Chagnon 1968).

8.3.4. Ideal Free Theory Revisited

The ideal free model assumes that patch quality and fitness decline as the number of individuals increases, due to competition with other group members for resources. But if living in groups confers fitness benefits for other reasons, such as those discussed above, then this assumption will not hold. Pulliam and Caraco extend the ideal free model to consider optimal habitat selection when fitness first increases with additional group members (due to benefits of group living), and then decreases after an optimal group size is reached. In Figure 8.5, the top graph corresponds to the assumptions of the ideal free model, while the lower two graphs show what can happen where

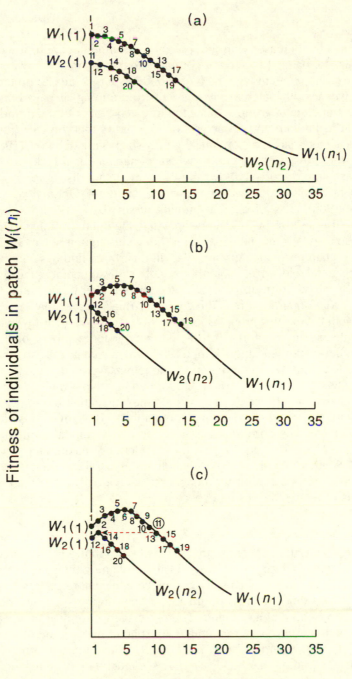

Figure 8.5. Effects of conspecifics on habitat selection (from Pulliam and Caraco 1984).

fitness initially increases with group size. In the middle graph, the optimal group size for patch 1 is 6, but it continues to pay the next 5 newcomers to join that group, even though the fitness of the group decreases. In the lower graph, where both patches have benefits to grouping, it pays one of the existing members of group 1 to switch to patch 2 after the 12th individual settles in it. Pulliam and Caraco's example shows that the ESS group size may be larger than the "optimal" group size; Slobodchikoff (1984) has shown the same thing for groups where dominance is a factor.

The example discussed above shows clearly that a discussion of optimal settlement requires that we consider the question, Optimal for whom? Smith's (1985) study of optimal hunting group sizes among the Inuit addresses this question by modeling separately the optimal strategies of existing group members and newcomers. Although his argument concerns foraging rather than residential groups, we will review the findings here because of their general relevance. In Smith's model, a newcomer faces the choice of joining an existing group of $n - 1$ members (thereby becoming the nth member) or foraging alone. The "joiner's rule" shows that newcomers should join the existing group as long as $\bar{R}_n > R_1$ (where $\bar{R}_n$ is the per capita return rate for a group of size n). The decision rule for members, on the other hand, is different; their fitness is increased by newcomers only so long as $\bar{R}_n > R_n - 1$. Optimal sizes for members and joiners were the same for most of the hunt types analyzed by Smith, but for two hunt types (beluga whale and breathing hole seal hunting) joiners could maximize their returns by joining groups larger than would be optimal for members. The group sizes predicted by the joiner's rule correspond more closely to empirical group sizes for these hunt types than does a rule based solely on maximizing per capita returns. Smith's model, like that of Pulliam and Caraco, underscores the importance of focusing on the benefits to individuals rather than groups. Conflicts of interest are to be expected.

Where to Settle: A Brief Summary.   We have seen in this section that settlement patterns are strongly affected by the distribution of resources, and simple models can go a long way toward explaining them. However, the presence of conspecifics can make a place either more or less desirable. Where conspecifics depress return rates, one might expect an ideal free distribution, or one of its variants. There is evidence for distributions of this type in both humans and nonhumans, in spite of the fact that the assumptions underlying the model may not be met. Where fitness is *enhanced* by coresidents, on the other hand, we may see much larger aggregations than would otherwise be expected. Understanding the social relationships among coresidents, therefore, is a necessary prerequisite for a complete understanding of settlement patterns.

8.4. TERRITORIALITY

In the preceding section, we discussed the problem of where to live. Having made this decision, the individual faces another strategic choice: Should he defend his territory against outsiders, or should he let them come in and share the booty? And how large a territory should he defend?

These two questions, which we address in this section, are closely related. Territorial defense has the benefit of reducing competition for resources and enables the individual to monitor their availability more easily. Monitoring and defending a territory exact a cost in time and energy, however, and expose the individual to some risk of injury. When do the benefits exceed the costs? One important consideration is territory size. As the area to be patrolled increases, so do the costs of territorial monitoring and defense. Very large territories may not be economical to defend. Figure 8.6 illustrates this graphically: In this figure, it is assumed that costs and benefits both increase with territory size, but costs continue to rise proportionately while benefits increase at a decreasing rate as territories have more resources than the animal can efficiently use to enhance fitness. Terri-

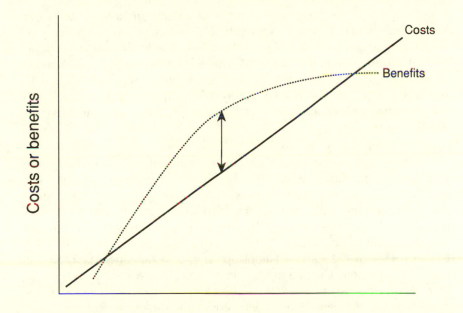

Figure 8.6. Costs and benefits as a function of territory size.

toriality would pay off wherever benefits exceed costs; assuming that animals are trying to maximize immediate benefits, the optimal territory size would be the point where the difference is greatest. (The shape of the benefit curve may differ markedly among species, as will be discussed below.)

In considering the pros and cons of territoriality, therefore, we will first consider the determinants of range and territory size. In the following discussion, we will follow conventional usage and define a *range* as the area exploited by an individual, whether defended or not, and a *territory* as a range (or resources within it) that is defended against outsiders.

8.4.1. Some Determinants of Range Size

How much space does an animal use? In section 8.3.1, we showed that the distribution of resources could be expected to influence range size. Larger ranges are to be expected where resources are patchy and out of phase, and this prediction was shown to receive some empirical support among human foragers. Many other factors have been shown to influence range size, and we consider some of them below.

Body Size.   Among a variety of types of animals (mammals, birds, lizards), home range increases approximately linearly with increasing body size (Harestad and Bunnell 1979; Calder 1984). The relationship is no doubt due, at least in part, to the increased energy requirements of larger animals (McNab 1963), but large animals have larger ranges than their metabolic needs would suggest (Harestad and Bunnell 1979). One reason for this may be that large animals also live in larger groups, with ranges that overlap (Calder 1984).

Trophic Level.   Trophic level also affects range size. Mammalian carnivores have larger home ranges than herbivores or omnivores of the same size (McNab 1963; Harestad and Bunnell 1979), as one would expect given the greater energy available in primary production (green plants) than secondary production (herbivores). The range size of carnivores also increases faster (hyperallometrically) with body size (Harestad and Bunnell 1979; Calder 1984). If the same relationships apply to humans, Harestad and Bunnell's equations indicate that a human carnivore weighing some 65 kg should require a range size of about 3863 km^2, whereas an omnivore of the same size would need about 16 km^2 and an herbivore only 2 km^2.

In general, trophic level affects human range size as we might expect; human foragers in the topics, who depend largely on plant foods, have smaller ranges than do those in northern environments, where animal foods make up a larger fraction of the diet (Binford 1980, 1990a; Kelley 1983). The actual range sizes of terrestrial human hunters appears to be even larger than we would predict from Harestad and Bunnell's equations, due to the reliance of these hunters on domesticated animals for transport (Binford 1990).

Sex. Since females of most mammalian species are smaller than males, the allometric relationships discussed above would lead us to expect smaller ranges for females. Females typically do have smaller ranges than males, although the difference is less than one would expect given the differences in weight (Harestad and Bunnell 1979).

In polygynous species, however, the sex difference in range size may be considerable. In most species, a female's fitness is determined chiefly by her ability to provision her offspring, and her territory size reflects her needs for material resources (food, water, nest sites, etc.) within the territory. For polygynous males, where paternal investment is typically low, fitness is affected chiefly by success in mating with a large number of females. A polygynous male's territory, therefore, should reflect not only his need for material resources, but his desire to gain access to a large number of females. In many polygynous species, where a male's fitness is enhanced by maximizing his number of mates, a male's territory may encompass those of several females. Gaulin and Sailer (1985) have shown that the ranges of males and females do not differ significantly in size among monogamous primates, whereas those of polygynous primates do. In these species, females have range sizes that would be predicted on energetic grounds, while the males have ranges that are considerably larger. Gaulin and FitzGerald (1986) have shown similar patterning among monogamous and polygynous species of voles.

Humans have been described as a mildly polygynous species; does a sex difference in range size characterize humans as well? There is considerable support for such a sex difference, both from the child development literature and from cross-cultural ecological studies (see review in Gaulin and Hoffman 1988). There is also some evidence that greater male ranging in humans may be determined by the need to find a mate, as Gaulin and Hoffman suggest. Hewlett (1988) found that male Aka Pygmies had larger "exploration ranges" than did females, and that, among the males, there was a correlation between exploration range and "mating range" (the distance between birthplace of spouses). Such a correlation did not exist for Aka females.

8.4.2. Resource Abundance and Optimal Territory Size

Range size is also strongly correlated with the abundance of resources. An inverse relationship between territory size and resource density has been shown for a number of species, including wrens (Cody and Cody 1972), iguanas (Simon 1975), sunbirds (Gill and Wolf 1975), and hummingbirds (Kodric-Brown and Brown 1978). The same pattern appears to hold for at least some human foragers, such as the Cree-Ojibwa Indians of eastern subarctic Canada (Rogers 1969:45), the Kalahari San (Cashdan 1983:54), and Australian foragers (Peterson 1972:24; Birdsell 1953).

Why should this relationship exist? One possible reason is that ranges are larger where resources are sparser because a larger area is required to satisfy an animal's resource needs. This idea has intuitive appeal, but it may not be correct. The animal studies cited above refer to defended territories, and Myers et al. (1979) and Ewald et al. (1980) have suggested that the relationship may be a consequence of the greater intrusion rate that comes with increased abundance. Rich territories may be smaller, in other words, because with more intruders an animal cannot defend as large an area. The argument also assumes that an animal will occupy (and defend) an area no larger than it "needs." But what determines these "needs"? For energy maximizers, who can use food in excess of maintenance to increase fitness, there is no reason to expect animals to defend only the minimal area required for basic maintenance (Ebersole 1980; Kruuk and MacDonald 1985).

An animal trying to extend its territory faces competition from neighbors and intruders. The outcome of that competition will be determined not only by absolute differences in competitive ability ("resource holding potential") but by relative differences in the value each places on that piece of territory. If benefits do level off as territories increase in size, as shown in Figure 8.6, there should come a point where the value (in fitness) of an additional piece of territory is worth less to the resident than to an intruder who has a smaller territory, or no territory at all. At that point (other things equal), it no longer pays the resident to fight for it. Asymmetries of this sort may be an important determinant of territory size, and would be consistent with the empirical relationship between abundance and territory size noted earlier.

8.4.3. Why Be Territorial?
Economic Defendability

Brown (1964) put the study of territoriality on its modern footing by arguing that, where competition exists for resources, territoriality should be found only where resources are economically defendable. Resources are economically—as opposed to physically—defendable when the benefits exceed the costs of defense. One important factor in determining defendability, discussed at length above, is range size; smaller ranges should be less costly to defend, other things equal. Mitani and Rodman (1979) computed an index of defendability based on range size relative to normal day range, to provide a measure of the frequency with which individuals should encounter the perimeter of their territory. This index was a strong predictor of territoriality in their primate sample.

It does not pay to defend a territory unless one can be reasonably confident that the resources will be there when needed; the predictability of the resource, therefore, should also be considered. Brown argued that mobile or transient resources cannot be economically defended, and there is empirical support for his argument (see, for example, Brown and Orians 1970:252). Individuals may also respond flexibly to changes in resource predictability. Davies (1976) has shown that pied wagtails change foraging strategies as the distribution of resources changes, defending individual territories when food is dense and predictable and foraging in flocks when food supplies are patchy and transient (see also Kruuk 1972).

Dyson-Hudson and Smith (1978) were the first to evaluate these economic defendability arguments with the human literature. They argued that territories would be most defendable when resources were abundant and predictable, and they supported their argument with ethnographic material from a variety of sources. Among the Basin–Plateau Indians, for example, one finds both a diversity of habitats and of land tenure arrangements. The Western Shoshone of the U.S. Great Basin inhabit a very arid area, where most resources are both sparse and unpredictable. As we would expect, "the Shoshoni lacked any form of ownership of land or resources on it" (Steward 1938:254). The ranges exploited by families and villages overlapped, and were different from year to year. The Owens Valley Paiute, at the edge of the Great Basin, present a sharp contrast to the Western Shoshone. Their land, which lay between the Sierra Nevada and the White Mountains, was a comparatively fertile zone fed by mountain streams. Resources were abundant and varied, enabling them to obtain all necessary food resources within 20 miles of their villages. The natural abundance and predictability was increased still further by the irrigation of wild seed patches. Because of the local abundance, the Owens Valley Paiute lived in permanent villages and had clearly demarcated and defended territories. The territories were owned by bands (villages or groups of villages), and plots of pine nut trees within band territories were owned by individual families (Steward 1938; Dyson Hudson and Smith 1978).

We can use similar cost–benefit arguments to understand patterns of land tenure among cultivators. Boserup (1965; see also Netting 1969 and Brown and Podolefsky 1976) argued that there is a regular shift from communal to individual forms of land tenure as cultivators intensify their use of the land in response to increases in population density. With communal tenure, individuals have use rights over land but relinquish claims to it when all traces of cultivation are gone. This form of land tenure makes sense when there is abundant land, since there is no payoff for territorial defense when there is no competition for land. As competition increases, however, individuals make efforts to keep the land in continuous cultivation, thereby effectively "defending" the land against competitors. The improvements often made to intensively cultivated land (terracing, irrigation, etc.) should further enhance its value and the benefits of defending it.

The economic defendability arguments linking territoriality to abundant and predictable resources explain much, but not all, of the variation in the ethnographic record. Among the San (Kalahari foragers), ethnographic accounts suggest that the most territorial groups are located where resources are sparsest and most variable (Barnard 1979; Cashdan 1983), precisely the opposite of what we might expect. In order to understand why this should be so, one must understand something about San patterns of land tenure. While San foragers claim rights to particular territories, usually ones that they inherit from their parents, territorial boundaries are not marked or defended. The lack of boundary marking and defense is reasonable, given the large size of Kalahari territories (300–600 km^2 for the !Kung [Lee 1979:334] and 457–1036 km^2 for the G/wi [Silberbauer 1981:198]). Yet people are reluctant, even fearful, to enter territories other than their own unless they have relatives there and feel sure that they will be welcome (Heinz 1972; Marshall 1976). In some respects, the Kalahari situation is similar to the spatiotemporal territories found among lions (Schaller 1972), whose large territories preclude boundary defense but who nonetheless repel intruders when they see them. The fearfulness of the San to enter strange territories, their reluctance to enter even known areas unless they are visiting the residents, suggests that the likelihood of being caught, even without systematic boundary maintenance, is not small. Although I have no systematic data about this, I was repeatedly struck by how much people seemed to know concerning the whereabouts of everyone in the region. There are two reasons why this might be so. The first is that human cognitive and communicative abilities ensure that if one person spots an intruder, everyone else will soon know about it. The second is that the scarcest and most critical resource in the Kalahari is water (and water-bearing plants), and to exploit such a resource one must remain in the territory, thereby increasing one's chances of being noticed. It might be possible to bag some game and leave with it without attracting notice, but this would not be possible with water, which would require an extended stay. If we add to these factors the difficulty of exploiting a strange territory, we can see why outsiders might prefer to limit their interterritorial moves to places where they know people and can use them as a source of information and help.

Why should reluctance to enter strange areas, and animosity to outsiders, be greatest among these groups where resources are sparsest and most variable? Probably because competition for resources in such areas is more intense, increasing the benefits of exclusion, whereas the costs of territoriality without boundary maintenance are minimal (Cashdan 1983). If Kalahari foragers were distributed in an ideal free manner, competition for resources should be similar in all areas. But, as was explained earlier (see section 8.4.2), this seems not to be the case.

8.4.4. Territorial Contests: Who Wins and Why

Whether one should attempt to defend a territory and the territory size one can defend depend not only on the physical characteristics of the resources but also on the characteristics and strategies of one's competitors. We will conclude this section, therefore, with a brief illustration of how the study of territorial contests can illuminate issues of territoriality.

A consistent empirical finding in the animal literature is that residents typically win territorial contests. There are two likely ways in which such contests could be decided, each of which might give rise to such a result. First, the winner could be bigger, stronger, or in some other way have greater resource holding potential (RHP). If the original residents won their position as a result of their greater RHP, then most territorial contests would be decided in favor of residents. This seems to be the case for a number of species (see Petrie 1984 and references therein). A second possibility is that the value of the territory might be worth more to residents than to intruders. If this were the case, it would pay residents to fight harder, even if the RHP of combatants were equal. Why might territories be more valuable to residents? Krebs (1982) suggests two possibilities: The first is that the greater familiarity of residents with the territory and its resources might enhance its value to them. The second is that as neighbors learn to recognize and evaluate each other, the frequency and intensity of their disputes lessens. A resident who had already gone through this process, therefore, would pay fewer defense costs, and the territory would be correspondingly more valuable to him. Krebs (1982) explored this in an ingenious experiment with great tits, where he first removed the original residents, waited for replacements to occupy the territory, and then freed the original residents. He was able to show that the probability of a replacement bird evicting a former resident increased with the length of time the original resident was away, eventually reaching a probability of 90%. Clearly, then, residents of this species do not win territorial contests because of differences in RHP. The asymmetry is more likely to result from differences in the fitness value of the territory to residents, probably because the original residents would have to renegotiate boundaries after a long absence.

How are territorial contests decided among humans? Differences in RHP are obviously important, particularly in interclass and interethnic group struggles. In this case, greater RHP typically consists of greater economic and military strength, and sometimes a more centralized political organization that can mobilize larger groups. However, asymmetries of the sort explored by Krebs may also be important. If food has diminishing fitness returns, the last morsel of a food package would add less fitness to its possessor than to someone without food. Blurton Jones (1984) has argued that, under these circumstances, one can expect "tolerated theft" of the item, since the possessor will be less willing to fight for it. Hawkes (this volume) argues that much of what looks like "sharing" is actually better explained as tolerated theft. A similar situation may prevail with territorial intrusions; the literature of anthropology is full of discussions of reciprocal interterritorial visiting, but it is possible that this is, in part, a result of asymmetries in the degree to which residents and intruders value access to the territory. If its value is higher to intruders than to residents, we might expect to see residents tolerating access, just as they might tolerate theft. While both Krebs and Blurton Jones emphasize that possession of a resource may affect its value, it is worth noting that their arguments make opposite predictions about the outcome of territorial contests. An evaluation of these arguments in humans awaits empirical study.

8.5. CONCLUSION

Anthropologists have been explaining spatial organization in ecological terms at least since the time of Julian Steward. Human patterns of settlement, mobility, and territorial organization have all been explained as adaptations to the environment. In view of this, it is reasonable to ask: Does evolutionary ecology contribute anything new to our understanding of these topics?

In addition to the rigor of the theoretical arguments and the power of using arguments that apply to a wide variety of species, evolutionary ecology has sharpened our thinking about adaptation by forcing us to (a) consider explicitly the costs and benefits of alternative strategies, and (b) address explicitly the question: Adaptive for whom? Since natural selection acts on the individual, we are led to consider how a particular strategy is adaptive for one individual at the expense, perhaps, of others in the group. When considering optimal group size, for example, we see that the optimal strategy for a newcomer may be suboptimal for existing members of the group. When considering when an individual should defend a territory, we see that the optimal strategy depends not only on material resources but on the characteristics and strategies of competitors.

Conflicts of interest have not been handled well in classical cultural ecology. Cultural ecological explanations of spatial organization within anthropology have tended to ignore the possibility of winners and losers, even when considering behaviors such as warfare. Anthropologists and sociologists concerned with conflicts of interest, on the other hand, have tended to focus on conflicts between classes or other social units, assuming a homogeneity of interests within these units. The perspective of evolutionary ecology offers a powerful way to bridge this gap.

REPRODUCTION AND SOCIAL RELATIONS

IV

Sharing and Collective Action

Kristen Hawkes

9

9.1. INTRODUCTION

9.1.1. Purpose

Frequent sharing and exchange of goods and services are striking features of human social life. People under the widest array of circumstances seem more interdependent than other primates because so much of what anyone consumes is acquired, modified, and transported by others. Students of hominid evolution have speculated on both the causes and effects of this difference between humans and other apes and monkeys (e.g., Isaac 1978; Tiger and Fox 1971). At the same time ethnologists have long noted a wide and patterned range of variation in the character of cooperation and exchange across types of human social organizations (Service 1962; Fried 1967; Sahlins 1968b).

Recently these generalizations have been complicated by increasing appreciation of the sharing and cooperation that occur among nonhumans (e.g., Boesch and Boesch 1989; de Waal 1989b; Emlen 1991) and of the variation in sharing within and between human societies of similar social scale and subsistence type (e.g., Kaplan and Hill 1985b). Evolutionary ecologists are interested in measuring and explaining this variability, not only between species, and between communities of the same species, but also variation associated with resource types and contexts, as well as the sex, age, and relationships of the individuals involved. The topic is a broad one. I focus especially on food sharing among ethnographically known hunter–gatherers and subsistence cultivators to illustrate some of the patterns, the explanatory problems they present, and some of the competing hypotheses that evolutionary ecologists pose to account for them.

9.1.2. Overview

The chapter begins with a brief discussion of the contrast between the phenomenon labeled "reciprocity" by ethnologists and "reciprocal altruism" by behavioral ecologists (section 9.2). The usages overlap to some degree but the differences are important. The discussion reviews some ethnographic patterns for later reference. When goods are collectively consumed, those who provide the goods contribute benefits to others. This engages the problem of collective action: If those who provide more do not consume more, those who provide less obtain greater net benefits. As a consequence, individuals often serve their own interests by providing less of a collective good than would best serve the group. Some influential treatments of this problem are reviewed (9.3), and the economic logic and the kinds of explanations that are favored by evolutionary ecologists investigating these topics described (9.4). Three models used to explore problems of sharing and collective action are introduced (9.5). The models illustrate three kinds of explanation—delayed reciprocity, mutualism, and manipulation—and underline the overlap of the latter two. The following section (9.6) reviews the effects of time lags, ancillary benefits, and resource "lumpiness" on collective action. Some applications to "the sexual division of labor" are briefly discussed. Finally (9.7), ethnographic examples in which variations in patterns of food sharing have been described are summarized and examined in light of issues raised in preceding sections.

9.2. TWO MEANINGS OF RECIPROCITY

The field-defining contribution to the ethnology of "reciprocity" is Mauss's 1925 *Essay on the Gift* (Mauss 1967). In it he argued that giving and receiving gifts was the mechanism for making social contracts with strangers in the absence of state institutions. Levi-Strauss subsequently labeled giving and receiving the principle of reciprocity (1949, English translation 1969) and called it the fundamental rule of human society. These influential ideas about the social effects of transfers of goods were complemented by White (1959) and Polanyi (1957), who saw that social relationships could profoundly affect transfers. In some contexts, they argued, the flow of goods between individuals and groups is governed by the social relationships, not by the value of the goods themselves. Polanyi labeled exchanges ruled by the social relationship between equivalent parties "reciprocity." Sahlins (1965) constructed an influential synthesis incorporating these generalizations and added an important empirical observation: Much that ethnologists call reciprocity is not literally reciprocal. He cited numerous ethnographic reports in which goods moved mostly in one way. Sahlins noted that the disposition to give or share without concern for balancing accounts is characteristic of relationships between good friends and close kin. He labeled this "generalized reciprocity." Where social ties are more distant and fragile, exchanges must be more literally reciprocal to maintain the relationships.

Reciprocity in evolutionary ecology refers to Trivers's "reciprocal altruism" (1971) in which individuals take short-term costs for their sharing or assistance, in exchange for delayed but larger return benefits. This usage emphasizes that the repayment to reciprocators results in an overall net benefit, so that they are acting in their own self-interest. Reciprocal altruists discriminate against those who do not return favors. Otherwise they would be vulnerable to exploitation by "free riders" who took the benefits dispensed but did not reciprocate themselves. Unchecked by sanctions, free riders net higher benefits than those who repay assistance, and so evolutionary ecologists expect free riding to increase in frequency against unconditional sharing. In contrast, commensurate-return gifts govern the reciprocity of ethnology only at the edges of sociability where the relationships are fragile. Otherwise it is the *lack* of attention to balancing accounts, the "sustained one way flow" that is diagnostic (Sahlins 1965, 1972). If this ethnological characterization is an accurate description of empirical patterns, the reciprocal altruism model does not explain them. These different uses of the same word are recognized here by restricting the term *reciprocity* to reciprocal altruism unless otherwise indicated.

9.3. THE PROBLEM OF COLLECTIVE ACTION

The perspective of evolutionary ecology directs attention to likely differences between individual and group interests. It focuses on the fitness costs and benefits to the individuals involved in any behavior pattern. The tendency for "individual selection" to swamp "group selection," so influentially exposed by Williams (1966a; see 2.2.2), is also the problem of collective action described by Olson (1965) for human social groups. Olson showed that individuals acting in their own self-interest will often fail to provide goods that are used in common by members of their social groups, even though all members agree on the value of these common goods and even on the means to achieve them. G. Hardin (1968), taking his title from instances in which individuals increase their own net benefits by overgrazing a common pasture, called this the "tragedy of the commons." The problem has drawn attention from a long line of commentators in Western political philosophy. R. Hardin (1982), cites Plato as well as Hobbes, Hume, J. S. Mill, and Adam Smith. All note what Hardin (1982) calls "the back of the invisible hand."

Paradoxically, both sides of the invisible hand can have welfare-enhancing as well as welfare-inhibiting effects, depending on whose welfare is at issue (Hirshleifer 1982). The conflict between individual and group interests unravels powerful cartels and monopolies as well as participation in community enhancement projects. The interests of individuals are rarely either perfectly coincident or mutually exclusive, so that characterizing "a group" as even having "an interest" may obscure differences in the costs and benefits that affect the behavior of each member.

Olson relied on the distinction made by Samuelson (1954) between private goods, which can be divided up for consumption, and public goods, which are consumed concurrently (see also 10.4). If someone pays for lighthouses, public radio, or community defense, all can consume them, including those who did not pay. One person's consumption of a public good does not preclude others from consuming the same unit. Since goods can fall along a spectrum from perfectly public to perfectly private, complex technical problems have emerged around the distinction. But as Hardin points out, "the good need not be a public good in the narrow, technical sense" (1982:5) to engage "the logic of collective action." The classic example of a private good is a loaf of bread. It is perfectly divisible and you are excluded from consuming any slice I consume. Yet if I make a loaf of bread and cannot refuse you a share without paying a cost, the loaf is our collective good. For the present discussion the important point is that where individuals can consume a good whether or not they pay for it, those not paying have the advantage—unless there are separate incentives for those who pay.

Sharing gives benefits to those who did not pay for them, a prime opportunity for free riding. Taylor, in an investigation into alternative solutions to the problem of collective action, observes that general sharing promotes free riders. It is the fundamental difficulty in "intentional communities," explicitly constructed on cooperative charters, where free access to goods and services is not denied to those who do not work:

> In all these intentional communities a central problem was inequality of work effort. Every adult member of a community was expected to put in a certain number of hours of work, or to contribute as much labor as he was able; but since an individual's rewards were not dependent on the amount or quality of his work, there was always the temptation to be a free rider on the efforts of others—to find excuses for not working some days, to put little effort into the work to contribute the minimum amount of work acceptable. There are few studies of any of these communities which do not furnish examples of such free riders, and it is my impression that it is the chief source of discontent in contemporary communes. (1982:123)

What then of the sharing among hunter–gatherers? Sahlins's influential analysis of the "original affluence" of hunter–gatherer societies (1968a, 1972) led him to suggest that sharing was the source of their "nonacquisitiveness." Sahlins began with three generalizations documented from an impressively wide array of sources. First, he showed that ethnographically known hunter–gatherers do not spend more time in food acquisition than do cultivators. In fact, work efforts are often surprisingly modest (1972:14–28). Sahlins used only two quantitative data sets, but Hames (1989) has since found the same pattern in a larger sample (see also Chapter 7). Second, foragers are commonly reported to be quite prodigal with occasional plenty. They feast now rather than storing for later (Sahlins 1972:29). Third, there is the "sloppiness" of hunter–gatherers, who are not careful of their possessions (1972:12). These three patterns suggested to Sahlins the "zen road to affluence": Foragers must want little, since they do not work as hard as they might, do not save, and place little value on their material goods. So "wanting little, they have all they want."

To account for the modest wants at the root of zen affluence, Sahlins nominated a central contradiction faced by foragers: that between mobility and accumulation (1972:33). If local resources can be exhausted or if distant resources come into season, those who move more easily may have fuller stomachs. Having less means less to move. But he argued further that limited wants are not a direct practical response to transport costs but instead a response to the family organization of band societies. People do not treasure stocks of goods because accumulation depends on refusal to give or share. A stingy person is the opposite of a "good kinsman," and forfeits the esteem of kin–neighbors. If it is "bad" not to share and so all share, then "an attempt to stock up food may only reduce the overall output of a hunting band, for the have-nots will content themselves with staying in camp and living off the wherewithal amassed by the more prudent" (1972:32).

By this reading, Sahlins is arguing that the "limited needs" of foragers are set by sharing, which makes food and other objects collective goods. This makes food procurement—and even artifact manufacture and maintenance —a collective action problem. The examples he adduced and the characteristics he noted are all quite consistent with the view that a free rider problem sets "standards of living" low among many ethnographically known foragers. Several ethnographic reports as well as synthetic accounts that have subsequently appeared are also consistent with this view. Wiessner's rich description of !Kung San sharing is a particularly clear example. She reports that

> in deciding whether or not to work on a certain day, a !Kung may assess debts and debtors, decide how much wild-food harvest will go to family, close relatives and others to whom he or she really wants to reciprocate, versus how much will be claimed by freeloaders. A person may consider whether the extra effort is worthwhile, or if time would be better spent gathering more information about the status of partners and trying to collect from one of them. . . . Limiting work effort over the long run can result in bringing lower than possible mean income. (1982:79)

So ethnologists have recognized that sharing can make "work" a collective action problem. But if these are effects of sharing, why the sharing? Ought it not to be self-limiting? If more sharing leads to less work, there must be less and less to share. Yet the empirical generalizations suggest variation in sharing (as well as work). Moreover, this construction implies three mutually exclusive extremes: One is to acquire no more than one can immediately consume, another is to acquire more and share it, and a third is to acquire more and store it for future consumption. Each of these possibilities occurs empirically, sometimes even in the same household. This variability provides the opportunity to test alternative explanations.

9.4. THE ECONOMIC LOGIC OF EVOLUTIONARY ECOLOGY

9.4.1. Trade-Offs and Conflicts of Interest

Evolutionary ecologists seek to explain how any pattern they study is maintained. Economic logic is central to the inquiry. That makes two notions especially important. First, in a world of limited time and other resources, individuals regularly face trade-offs. If more is invested in one thing, less can go to something else. This, in turn, poses questions about the costs and benefits of the behavior under study. Why not more or less work, more or less sharing in any particular case? What adjustments are possible? What would be the costs and benefits of these alternatives?

The second important notion is that while there are often overlapping fitness interests among individuals, perfect coincidence is rare. For example, we may both eat better if one of us kills an antelope, or if we clear the drainage ditch between our gardens (the antelope and the cleared ditch are collective goods); but only one of us need track the animal, and my garden may suffer more than yours if the ditch remains clogged. Where social interactions are involved, behavior that would maximize the fitness of one party is unlikely to maximize the fitness of the other. This is so even among the closest of kin. Moreover, the costs and benefits for alternative actions often depend directly on what others are doing. If the costs and benefits for each depend on the choices others make, what outcomes can be predicted?

9.4.2. Four Kinds of Explanation

Kin Selection. Explanations that seek to predict how (and under what limits) patterns of sharing will be maintained fall into four categories. First, there is kin-selected altruism, in which individuals assist others whose consequent gains in reproductive success are gains to the benefactor's inclusive fitness (Hamilton 1964; see section 2.2.2). Assistance given by parents to offspring, as well as some assistance given to other kin, will be consistent with kin-selected altruism as long as the cost to the benefactor is less than her probable gains in inclusive fitness.

Note that although individuals have more overlapping inclusive fitness interests with closer kin, only identical twins have identical genetic interests. The inclusive fitness of even mothers and their infants is only partly coincident (Trivers 1974). This means that the remaining explanatory categories that do not depend on shared inclusive fitness are relevant not only to interactions among nonkin but kin as well, with appropriate adjustments in expectation for the inclusive fitness each gains and loses in the fitness costs and benefits to the other.

Reciprocal Altruism: Delayed Reciprocity. The second kind of explanation developed in evolutionary ecology to account for persistent transfers of benefits from one individual to another is reciprocal altruism, perhaps usefully termed "delayed reciprocity," where a short-term cost to the "altruist" is exceeded by benefits returned to him later (Trivers 1971). Here the current shares given up are the "advance payment" for the future shares to be returned. Theorists have noted that if individuals live long enough and interact repeatedly with the same others, and especially if individuals can provide highly beneficial services to others at low cost, those who participate in delayed reciprocity will have higher fitness than those who do not (Trivers 1985).

Immediate Mutual Benefits. The third category might be called mutualism, where individuals all do better, *in terms of immediate accounting*, by mutual assistance. If, for example, there are economies of scale in some resource procurement activity, then individuals who join in mutual procurement and then mutual consumption might do better than those who do not. But self-interested actors will often fail to produce collective goods even though they would gain substantial benefits. The benefits alone are an insufficient explanation for cooperation. A complete analysis will consider the controls on "cheating." This requires an evaluation of the costs and benefits to hypothetical free riders who try to join in consumption without participating in the procurement.

Manipulation. Fourth, there are cases of manipulation, coercion, or social parasitism in which individuals contribute to the fitness of others because it would cost them more not to. In the preceding example individuals who pay the cost of procurement may do so because, in spite of the free riders, they net a gain. Even if they would do better without free riders, the cost of excluding them may be higher than the benefit. Intuitively mutualism and manipulation seem distinct, but actually there is considerable overlap between them. Since individuals rarely have an identity of interests, and since individuals differ in myriad ways, costs and benefits are unlikely to fall evenly on cooperators. Thus mutualism grades into manipulation where benefits are unequal and individuals help or share because the cost of not doing so would be higher. Paradoxically, as Olson noted (1965:35), there is thus "*a surprising tendency for the 'exploitation' of the great by the small*" (original emphasis). Any who stand to gain more from a collective good will find it in their own interest to "bear a disproportionate share of the burden." Inequalities of wealth and power can thus serve the interests of those low in the hierarchy by increasing the provision of collective goods (see section 10.2.4). Of these four categories of explanation, this chapter will focus on the latter three. For further discussion of kin selection see section 2.2.2.

9.5. INTERDEPENDENT COSTS AND BENEFITS: THREE MODELS

9.5.1. Frequency Dependence and Game Theory

Whether or not sharing yields net benefits to those who give depends on what recipients do. The infinite regress created by such interdependencies is initially daunting. But these are precisely the problems familiar to economists (Schelling 1978). Game theory was originally developed by von Neumann and Morgenstern (1944) to deal with such frequency-dependent choices (See Luce and Raiffa 1957). Applications by economists and political scientists to problems of sharing and collective action are usually *not* (sometimes quite explicitly not) motivated by evolutionary theory. But some of their modeling provides results of direct interest to evolutionary ecology. The technique allows the exploration of trade-offs and calculation of outcomes where individuals have conflicting interests and where the costs and benefits of the various options depend on what others do. Evolutionary ecologists have thus found game theory to be a particularly useful analytical tool (Maynard Smith 1982a; see section 2.2.3).

The simplest games involve two players and two strategies that can be represented by a matrix in which one player's options define the rows and the other's define the columns. The four cells contain the payoffs for each of the possible combinations of strategies. Of the large variety of possible games, one, the Prisoner's Dilemma, has stimulated an enormous literature (see Chapter 2, Box 2.2). That game and a second, Chicken, which has received a fair amount of attention as well, are especially useful ways to represent problems of sharing and collective action.

The example of group size will serve to illustrate the games. It is itself a problem of some anthropological interest (see Chapter 10) and can, as in this illustration, involve a collective-action problem. How large will groups be under different circumstances? The case of special-purpose hunting groups may be one of the simplest (Smith 1981; Hill and Hawkes 1983; see section 10.2.1). Similar problems may confront gardeners cooperating on a swidden. If the harvest per gardener varies with the number of cooperators, then some number(s) of cooperators will maximize individual harvest rates. For illustration, assume that the number of cooperators that maximizes this rate is two. Two solitary gardeners both do better if they join together. Imagine now a third gardener choosing whether to garden separately or join the group of two. If groups of three have higher rates/person than solitary gardeners (though lower rates/person than do groups of two) the gain to the third gardener, if she joins, is the difference between her rate alone and her rate as a member of a group of three. If each of the gardeners is trying to maximize her own rate, there is a conflict of interest between the current cooperators and this potential joiner. If she joins, their rate goes down, hers goes up.

9.5.2. The Prisoner's Dilemma and Reciprocity

There is another potential conflict of interest here, *between* the two current cooperators. Since they stand to lose if the newcomer joins, they may either allow her to join and take the cost of reduced rates or try to exclude her. Since it is in her interest to join, assume that it will cost the excluder(s) to keep her out. If one of the current cooperators could exclude her, which of them will provide this collective good? Perhaps this cost of excluding the potential joiner could be shared. The current cooperators face a collective action problem that can be represented as a 2 × 2 symmetrical game. One possible game is represented in the following matrix, where the letters are used to define the cells and the numbers in each cell indicate the value of the payoffs to row if she plays the indicated strategy against the intersecting strategy of column:

Payoff matrix 1

	Exclude	Don't exclude
Exclude	$c = 3$	$a = 1$
Don't exclude	$d = 4$	$b = 2$

The payoff to row depends on what column does. In this game, if column excludes, row will do better to let column take the whole cost and not to exclude, that is, $d > c$. If column does *not* exclude, row will also do better not to exclude, since otherwise row will pay the whole cost herself, that is, $b > a$. Whatever column does, row will do better not to exclude. Since this is a symmetrical game, either player's payoffs appear in the cell defined by her strategy as row and her opponent's strategy as column. If Alice excludes and Ann doesn't, the payoff to Alice is indicated in cell a, the payoff to Ann in cell d. The strategy that dominates this game is to allow the joiner into the group. Maynard Smith called strategies that dominate a game evolutionarily stable strategies (ESS; section 2.2.3). Since not providing the common good dominates in matrix 1, this is an example of a Prisoner's Dilemma (Chapter 2). If each player acts in her own interest the joiner will not be excluded. The potential joiner's exclusion is a collective good for the current cooperators. They have a collective action problem because it is not in their individual interests to provide this good, even though they would both have done better if only they had cooperated.

Where games are repeated and players can make their responses contingent on previous rounds with the same opponents, patterns emerge in Prisoner's Dilemmas that are impossible with "one-shot" games. Trivers relied on this in his model of reciprocity (1971). He and others have seen this opportunity for contingent strategies to be the key to the evolution of cooperation. To model some possibilities, Axelrod (Axelrod and Hamilton 1981; Axelrod 1984) invited contestants to enter strategies in computer tournaments in which each played a series of two-person Prisoner's Dilemma games against all the others, with a total score for each strategy determined by the average of its scores over each series. In every game, each player could either cooperate or defect. Submitted strategies specified the basis for choosing between these moves. The winning strategy (submitted by the game theorist A. Rapoport) was tit-for-tat (TFT), in which a player cooperates on the first play and then responds in each subsequent round with whatever the opponent played last time. This is the strategy of reciprocal altruism, in which individuals forgo the temptation to defect in the company of other reciprocators, and so, as long as their opponents cooperate, they accumulate delayed rewards for cooperation.

In his analysis of the tournament results, Axelrod noted that strategies that were "nice, retaliatory, and forgiving" generally did better than their opposites. Nice strategies began by cooperating; thus they took immediate advantage of any tendency in their opponents to cooperate. Quick retaliation for a defection prevented exploitative strategies from abusing their niceness. But quick forgiveness was as important as quick revenge. Those that forgave after a single retaliatory defection avoided long costly periods of mutual recrimination. Axelrod pointed out that TFT never did better than any opponent in a series. It won because it took advantage of mutual cooperation when the opportunity arose, but, unlike a strategy of pure cooperation, it did not allow itself to be exploited. Its short memory was a clear asset since holding a grudge slowed return to mutually advantageous cooperation. TFT did well itself by allowing others to do well too, but not at *its own* expense.

Axelrod (1984) deduced very general implications about delayed reciprocity and the evolution of cooperation from these results. However, the special characteristics of the tournaments have since been emphasized by the construction of alternative models showing TFT to be less robust. Boyd and Lorberbaum (1987) show that TFT may be collectively stable, that is, no other strategy doing better against it than it does against itself, but not evolutionarily stable. Other nice strategies can do *as well* against it as it does against itself, and so TFT cannot prevent them from increasing in frequency. Hirshleifer and Martinez-Coll (1988) show that (for the same reason) in triadic playoffs, TFT players support the persistence of unconditional cooperators. Since TFT stops cooperating with defectors, it limits their success, which limits the damage defectors can do to unconditional cooperators. Cooperators "free ride" on TFT's punishment of defectors. The presence of these cooperators is an opportunity for defectors, in turn, to free ride on them. Hirshleifer and Martinez-Coll also show that introducing a probability of error can reduce the ability of unconditional cooperators to free ride and made TFT a more likely ESS. But as Rasmusen (1989:120ff.) points out, accidents can readily catch two TFT players in a "miserable alternation" of irrational punishments.

Sugden (1986) suggested a variant that Boyd (1989) calls "contrite tit-for-tat," which avoids this problem. With it, individuals "apologize" for their mistakes by taking their punishment but then cooperating rather than replying with further defection. Boyd (1989) showed that contrite TFT can be evolutionarily stable. In addition to the problems that these contributions reveal about the interplay of strategies even with small groups of players, the larger the group of players the more difficult it is for delayed reciprocity to persist (Taylor 1987; Boyd and Richerson 1988a).

Another source off vulnerability for delayed reciprocity is the time between a cost incurred and the compensating benefit returned. Iterated games differ from single contests because the possibility that players might meet again allows their current choices to influence subsequent decisions. "The future can therefore cast a shadow back upon the present and thereby affect the current strategic situation" (Axelrod 1984:12). Axelrod noted that the shadow of the future will be larger if replies are more frequent, smaller if they are not (more on this in 9.6.1.).

Recall that delays of notable length are *diagnostic* of the pattern that Sahlins labeled "generalized reciprocity." This prompts a search for benefits (or costs) other than future repayment as possible determinants of sharing. The focus on the payoff structure of the Prisoner's Dilemma and on delayed reciprocity as the solution to the riddle of cooperation may have defined the problem too narrowly. Models that posit different payoff structures and are less dependent on delayed returns provide some insights.

9.5.3. Chicken and "Cooperation"
(with a Bit of Manipulation)

There is another form that the group size problem introduced in (9.5.1) might take. Assume that one of the current cooperators can successfully exclude the potential joiner, and that the cost to one member of keeping him out is less than the cost to that member of letting him in. This reverses the order of payoffs for cells a and b in payoff matrix 1. The game is then not a Prisoner's Dilemma. Allowing the joiner into the group is no longer an ESS. The game is now Chicken (Rapoport et al. 1976), familiar to evolutionary ecologists as one form of the Hawk–Dove game (Maynard Smith and Price 1973; Maynard Smith 1982a; Chapter 2, Box 2.1). In Chicken, row would do better not to pay any of the cost of excluding the joiner if column excludes, but if column fails to exclude, row would do better to pay the cost of exclusion herself than accept the greater loss of allowing the joiner into the group. Taylor (1987; Taylor and Ward 1982) has argued that many collective-action problems are better represented by games other than the Prisoner's Dilemma. Chicken is one of them.

Maynard Smith first used game theory (Maynard Smith and Price 1973) and first elaborated the concept of an ESS (Maynard Smith 1974a) to address a question of direct relevance to the topic of sharing. He asked what strategy natural selection would favor among potential consumers meeting over a resource. Imagine two individuals arriving at a food item. Consider first two alternative courses of action. One strategy is Hawk: fight for exclusive use of the valuable, escalating the fight as necessary to win or until injured and defeated. The other is Dove: never fight, share the resource, or retreat if a competitor threatens a fight. To construct a payoff matrix for individuals playing these two strategies against each other, Maynard Smith defined the following payoff variables (ignoring here the cost of display): V, the value of the resource (i.e., the gain in fitness it provides), and C, the cost of injury in a fight over the resource. Entries in the matrix show the payoff to row against column, assuming that any Hawk is likely to win about half its contests with another Hawk:

Payoff matrix 2

	Hawk	Dove
Hawk	$(V - C)/2$	V
Dove	0	$V/2$

If the value of the resource is greater than the cost of defending it ($V > C$), then Hawk is the ESS. A Hawk does better both against other Hawks and against Doves than a Dove does. Under these circumstances the payoff structure is a Prisoner's Dilemma. When both play Hawk, they earn lower payoffs than if they both played Dove, yet neither player acting in its own interest will choose Dove because it can be exploited by a Hawk free riding on Dove's defenselessness.

If $C > V$, however, the payoff structure is no longer a Prisoner's Dilemma. It is Chicken. Neither pure Hawk nor pure Dove is an ESS, since Hawk does better than Dove in a population of Doves, and Dove does better than Hawk in a population of Hawks. For these payoffs the ESS is a mixed strategy. At the ESS there can be no relative increase in either Hawk or Dove, that is, neither can do better than the other. So the ESS can be calculated from the payoff matrix by solving for the relative frequency of encounters with Hawks at which the average payoffs to Hawk and Dove are equal. In this case the ESS is to play Hawk with a probability of V/C in any encounter. Any individual playing either Hawk or Dove with probabilities different from V/C for Hawk and $1 - (V/C)$ for Dove does worse overall than those adopting the ESS. Thus some cooperation or sharing is in the immediate self-interest of the players.

Taylor and Ward (1982) and Taylor (1987) argue that such payoff structures may be quite common. Jousting knights and jalopy-driving teenagers would prefer that the other guy swerve, but would prefer to chicken out rather than suffer the dire consequences if no one backs down. Chickens abound: from fetching the daily load of firewood to claims on a resource and fending off predators. With Chicken neither pure unconditional cooperation (Dove) *nor* pure unconditional defection (Hawk) is an ESS. The mixed strategy that *is* the ESS depends on the relative value of the goods being produced or contested and the costs associated with providing or fighting over them.

The payoff structure for a contest over an existing good, the Hawk–Dove game, differs from the payoffs for procuring or producing a good that all can use. The second of these can be represented as follows. Imagine here a public good, like a campfire or community defense, which is not divisible and is consumed concurrently by both players. If only one contributes and that contribution ensures that there is some fraction s (where $0 < s < 1$) of the good, then that much benefit is available to both. The payoff structure looks like this:

Payoff matrix 3

	Cooperate	Defect
Cooperate	$V - C$	$sV - C$
Defect	sV	0

If $C > V(1 - s)$ and $C > sV$, then this is a Prisoner's Dilemma. Row will do better to defect whatever column does. But if $sV > C > V(1 - s)$ (which requires that $s > \frac{1}{2}$) this is a Chicken. Row will do better to defect if column cooperates but if column defects row will do better to cooperate. Any public good that can be provided in increments with incremental benefits might pose this payoff structure. If, on the other hand, $C < V(1 - s)$ and $C < sV$, then *cooperation* is the best strategy for row whatever column does. Unconditional cooperation would then be the only ESS.

Compare this payoff structure to the Hawk–Dove game (inverted from above to make that easier):

Payoff matrix 4

	Dove	Hawk
Dove	$V/2$	0
Hawk	V	$(V - C)/2$

In this game there are no production costs, the good is divisible, and exclusion is possible. The goods in question are different, the costs are different, but both games can be Prisoner's Dilemmas or Chickens. If $V > C$, then row will do better to play Hawk whatever column does: a Prisoner's Dilemma. If $C > V$, then this is a game of Chicken.

Maynard Smith (1974a) defined a third strategy in the Hawk–Dove game that uses an arbitrary asymmetry between the contestants to decide who gets the resource. His conditional strategy, "Bourgeois," uses the following convention. Play Hawk if you arrive first at a resource ("the owner"), and play Dove if you arrive later ("the intruder"). The payoff matrix that includes this strategy, and assumes that either player is equally likely to be the first to arrive at a resource, looks like this (again ignoring the cost of display):

Payoff matrix 5

	Hawk	Dove	Bourgeois
Hawk	$(V - C)/2$	V	$(3V - C)/4$
Dove	0	$V/2$	$V/4$
Bourgeois	$(V - C)/4$	$3V/4$	$V/2$

In general, a strategy is an ESS if its diagonal entry is greater than any entry in that column, that is, it does better against itself than any other strategy does against it. Consider first the Hawk column of the matrix, which shows how all others do against Hawk. If the cost of injury (C) is greater than the value of the resource (V), Hawk as a pure strategy can never be an ESS because $(V - C)/2 < 0$ and Dove, never paying the cost of a fight, will always be able to invade a population of Hawks. Inspection of the Dove column shows that Dove can never be an ESS since both Hawk and Bourgeois can invade a population of Doves (because $V > V/2$, and $3V/4 > V/2$, respectively). The Bourgeois column shows that if $V < C$, then this arbitrary asymmetry, which settles each contest with other Bourgeois unambiguously without a fight, can invade a population of Hawks. Since the Bourgeois strategy is to play Hawk only as the first arriver, it will play Dove when arriving second and so give up to Hawk half the time. In the other half of its encounters with Hawk, Bourgeois will be first to arrive and so it will fight (winning the resource in half of those fights and paying the cost of injury in the other half). Bourgeois also outcompetes Dove, because $V/2 > V/4$, regardless of C. Hence Bourgeois is an ESS, in fact the only ESS in this game. Players using this strategy play Hawk half of the time and Dove half of the time in their contests with both Hawks and Doves. Bourgeois players do better than either Hawks or Doves against other Bourgeois because they never pay the cost of injury when they meet each other, but, unlike Dove, they do not always yield the resource to Hawk.

9.5.4. Tolerated Theft and Manipulation

Blurton Jones (1984, 1987b) has discussed a third payoff structure for problems of sharing and collective action. He pointed out the potential importance of payoff differences likely to arise in contests over resources that (1) are divisible, (2) come in package or clump sizes large enough that the value of successive bits diminishes to consumers, and (3) are unpredictably acquired. A resource with the first two features can be characterized by a gain curve of diminishing marginal value with each successive bit consumed (Figure 9.1). If resources are unpredictably acquired, individuals will have unsynchronized successes. Those who have consumed more will value the remaining bits of the resource less than will others. If all individu-

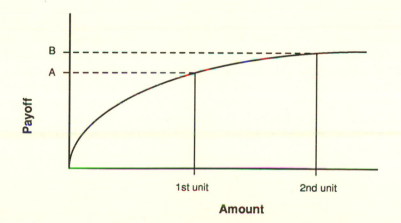

Figure 9.1. A gain curve of diminishing returns showing that initial units of a resource are worth less than subsequent units. The fitness payoff for consumption is on the y-axis. The amount of the resource consumed is on the x-axis.

als will pay a cost to get or keep the next unit commensurate with the value it has for them, and if individuals have similar competitive abilities, those who have more will relinquish additional amounts to those who have less. They will "tolerate the theft" because the cost of defending the extra is more than its worth to them. (See 10.3.2 for further discussion of tolerated theft.)

The group size problem would contain this kind of asymmetry if the joiner would gain more than the current members would lose were he to join them. Under those circumstances it would be in the interest of the joiner to take a higher cost to enter the group than a current member could afford to pay to exclude him.

The tolerated-theft model focuses attention on the importance of differences in the value that the same amount of the same resource may have to different consumers, as well as the consequences of different types of gain curves. Under some circumstances, the relationship between the payoff and the amount of the resource could be convex up, gains accelerated rather than decelerating, or it could be linear—constant increases in value for each additional unit—or even sigmoid (see Figure 10.5). But a diminishing-returns curve is likely to represent a wide array of empirical circumstances. The familiar notion of superabundances is nicely accommodated by this model. It allows discrimination of "relative" superabundance, the extreme being resources available in sufficient richness that the gain curve of all consumers in a group reaches the asymptote at which they get no additional benefits for additional consumption.

With tolerated theft, goods that are divisible, that display a payoff curve of diminishing returns, and that are asynchronously acquired will come to be distributed so that each individual keeps no more than she can economically defend. Since the costs of defense will depend on what others have, economically defendable amounts cannot be calculated directly from one individual's gain curve and her current holdings. It is a relative matter. Whenever anyone has more than others, the extra portion will be worth more to those who do not have it. They will thus be ready to pay more to get it than holders of equal competitive ability can afford to pay to keep it. As Blurton Jones noted, the movement of goods in many ethnographic contexts seems very much this sort of distribution by threat. On the other hand, marked differences in coercive power, or resources with accelerating gain curves, can result in very unequal resource distributions, as discussed in section 10.3.2.

The Cost of Sharing.   A slight modification of Maynard Smith's Hawk–Dove game allows us to consider the effect of resources that vary in size or richness relative to the appetite or consumption capacity of users. Define another variable: L, the change in value imposed by sharing with another consumer. Whereas matrices 2, 4, and 5 assumed that a user lost ½ the value of a resource if it was shared, substituting $V - L$ for $V/2$ will show what happens as the "cost of sharing" varies. Incorporating this variable alters the payoff matrix as follows.

Payoff matrix 6

	Hawk	Dove	Bourgeois
Hawk	$(V - C)/2$	V	$(3V - C)/4$
Dove	0	$V - L$	$(V - L)/2$
Bourgeois	$(V - C)/4$	$V - L/2$	$V/2$

The Hawk column is unchanged. If $C > V$, Hawk cannot be an ESS. If $C <$ V, it is an ESS, but it may not be the only one. Consider the Dove column. The variable L allows Dove to be an ESS, but only if L has a negative value, that is, if sharing the resource with another individual *increases* the payoff to Dove. This may be the case if the resource is very large relative to Dove's appetite, so that Dove's consumption is not reduced, *and* there is some additional benefit from the presence of another feeder. For example, if predators (or raiders) are a serious danger, the presence of others as alternative targets and as additional eyes and ears may allow Dove to spend less time in vigilance and so more in consumption. Or it could be that other sharers actually increase Dove's productive efficiency. Any cooperative task in which additional hands increase the per capita returns (e.g., building a barrier for fish, harvesting a very perishable crop, driving game), could have these payoffs (Hames 1990; Smith and Boyd 1990; and Kaplan et al. 1990). As long as L is negative, Dove will be an ESS.

The Bourgeois column shows that Bourgeois can be an ESS only if $C > V$ and $L > 0$. If $C < V$ and $L > 0$, then Hawk is the only ESS. If $C > V$ and $L < 0$, then Dove is the only ESS. If $C < V$ and $L < 0$, then both Hawk and Dove are ESSs. When both are ESSs then one *or* the other will be reached—the ESS is a pure strategy, not a mixed one (Hawk *and* Dove) as in matrix 2. Which ESS prevails depends on the relative frequencies of the strategies when the game begins. If Dove is at high frequency, neither Hawk nor Bourgeois can increase in frequency against it, but if instead Hawk is at high frequency, then neither Dove nor Bourgeois can invade it.

9.6. DISCOUNTING, DIFFERENT KINDS OF BENEFITS, LUMPINESS, AND ASYMMETRIES WITH SPECIAL REFERENCE TO SEX

9.6.1. Time and Discounting

The observation that the patterns labeled reciprocity in the ethnographic record are rarely literally reciprocal prompts analysts to ask why one-way flows persist in these cases. A simple answer could be that benefits are usually reversed in the long run. While long delays make literal reciprocation hard to observe and measure, short-term "imbalances" could add up to longer-term balances. But there are reasons to suspect that long delays in themselves make future favors less likely to compensate current costs.

The relative value of future benefits depends on the discount rate and the length of the delay between a good given and a good returned. The discount rate is the proportional decline in the present value of a good when its expected consumption is a unit of time into the future. For example, the interest rate is a measure of how much the value of money is discounted over time. Money loans cost more as the value of a dollar returned declines with higher interest rates and longer delays to repayment. So also the future compensating benefit must increase with larger discount rates and longer time delays if the present value of that future benefit is to exceed the temptation to defect.

Those who study the rates at which rewards lose their value as delays lengthen report extremely high discount rates for both human and nonhuman subjects (Logue 1988; Kagel et al. 1986; Rogers n.d.). If discounting is steep and if, moreover, there are long delays as ethnographic reports suggest, then the value of any expected repayment may be insufficient to account for the persistence of sharing.

The longer the delay, the lower the value of the expected repayment for two reasons. First, the future is always uncertain. Givers may themselves not be around to receive the future returns. Current recipients may not be around to reciprocate. The longer the distance into the future, the greater the likelihood that something might interrupt the repayment (Taylor 1987; Stephens 1990; Clark 1973). Second, the longer the delay, the higher the likely opportunity costs (alternative dispositions of the favor, which could draw quicker net benefits). Delay means losing chances to "earn interest" on the investment in the meantime (Stephens 1990). In sum, as Axelrod (1984) noted, the longer the time between goods or assistance given and anticipated return, the smaller the shadow of the future, and so the larger anticipated future benefits must be to offset current costs.

The discounting problem is not restricted to reciprocal altruism. Other costs and benefits that might play a role in the persistence of sharing often imply some delay. Consider, for example, tolerated theft. What costs of not sharing might others impose? Physical threats would not be very credible from smaller and weaker contestants (Kaplan and Hill 1985b; Kaplan et al. 1990). But crying complaints, even (perhaps especially) from a very small child, might pose not only the cost of irritation, but more general disapproval with important fitness consequences. These consequences of social disapproval, like refusal of subsequent sexual access or of support in later disputes, are delayed and so should be discounted accordingly.

There is another issue that involves time in a different way. Reciprocity is expected where the same individuals interact regularly and can swap benefits often. Axelrod noted that one way to enlarge the shadow of the future is to make the relationship more "durable." Paradoxically, if Axelrod's tournaments are a relevant model, this is not because of "long track records" to establish trust. As Axelrod's analysis of his results indicated, tit-for-tat was successful in part because of its *short* memory. Instead of "holding a grudge" this strategy won partly because it responded only in terms of the very last play. In his tournaments, strategies that did have longer memories got caught up in mutual recriminations. As noted above (9.5.2), contrite reciprocity is an ESS when there is some probability of mistakes because it so quickly recovers from an exchange of defections with "apologetic" cooperation and "forgets" the past. These models contradict the view that long-term relationships are ripe for reciprocity because time allows an accumulation of confidence. What counts is the future. From this perspective, it is not a past of mutual trust that makes friends and neighbors better candidates for reciprocity than strangers but the greater likelihood that they will be around tomorrow.

9.6.2. *Different Kinds of Benefits*

Olson (1965) talked about the role of "selective incentives" in extracting collective goods, and emphasized that these must themselves be private goods, that is, "they must distinguish between those individuals who support action in the common interest and those who do not" (1965:61, fn. 17). Kaplan and Hill (1985b) suggested that exchanges of different kinds of benefits, which they called trade, were important among the Aché. They showed that men who were more successful hunters were more often named as sexual partners and had more surviving children (1985a). Winterhalder (1986) called exchanges "involving goods or services in addition to food," "differentiated exchange," and suggested that this would be likely to occur where some individuals were consistently more successful than others at acquiring food. It seems likely that, other things the same, people would prefer companions who were more generous over those who were less. They might, as a consequence, treat those they prefer favorably so as to increase the likelihood of their continued proximity.

The fitness value of "favorable treatment" among nonhuman primates has been emphasized by Smuts (1985), who describes friendships between adult male and female anubis baboons and points out the important consequences these may have for the fitness of both. Although anthropologists have tended to see "divisions of labor" in food acquisition as the basis for cooperation in other aspects of social life (e.g., Isaac 1978; White 1959), a view that encompasses other primates suggests the converse argument:

Exchanges of nonfood goods come first. Contributions of food may then be an additional way to elicit other fitness-enhancing goods. Ethnologists have long noted associations between generous food distributions and higher social status. Sahlins summarizes this:

> Insofar as the society is socially committed to kin relationships, morally it is committed to generosity; whoever, therefore is liberal, automatically merits the general esteem. . . . The economic relation of giver-receiver is the political relation of leader follower. (1972:133)

If esteem and deference are associated with sexual favors, support in disputes, or favors to children of the esteemed, then "generosity" has fitness benefits that may be greater than its fitness costs.

These hypotheses about "selective incentives" do not, however, escape some of the problems noted for more literal delayed reciprocity. First there are the problems of delay (9.6.1), and second the familiar problem of free riding. While the selective incentives themselves may be private goods to the recipient, they elicit collective goods. This makes the *contribution* of the selective incentives a payment for the collective good. So such contributions themselves pose collective-action problems. Some might do better to free ride on the favor giving of others, with favor giving consequently underprovided. Prisoner's Dilemmas and Chickens could occur throughout. Favors to elicit favors for food providers could add more nests of Chickens. Both prospects of future benefits (i.e., some version of delayed reciprocity) and also short-term costs (i.e., tolerated theft, Chicken) may be operating at the same time. To be more concrete, Wiessner's description (1982) of the choice of *hxaro* partners and the fostering of partnerships among the !Kung shows attention to both probable future and more immediate benefits and costs.

9.6.3. Lumpiness and Thresholds

The character of the goods themselves has important effects on the kind of collective-action problems arising. If goods cannot be provided in continuous increments but only in large "lumps," this affects both sharing and work. Food resources that are acquired unpredictably in large packages tend to be more widely shared (see 9.7). Hunters cannot bring down part of a giraffe. If each forager, knowing that most of his prey will be consumed by others, can still expect to get more food for himself (and his family) by hunting big game, then in making the best choice to feed his family he also provides a collective good. Whether his direct consumption payoff is sufficient to account for his work will depend on his costs, including the opportunity cost of things he might have done instead. Among the Hadza of Northern Tanzania men specialize in hunting and scavenging large animals.

Recent observational and experimental data show that in this case (Hawkes et. al. 1991), hunters would provide a more regular income for themselves and their families with alternative foraging strategies, for example, hunting small prey in addition to large game. Since Hadza men continue to be big-game specialists, other incentives for providing these collective goods are implicated.

Tasks in which several must cooperate to gain any payoff at all may be prone to critical-mass effects, which limit free riding because moderate participation is unstable (Schelling 1978:91ff.). Hirshleifer's (1983) modeling and Harrison and Hirshleifer's (1989) experiments show that individuals tend to contribute to a public good that depends on the "weakest link," that is, when the failure of one member to contribute is fatal to the whole. Expensive and lumpy goods may stimulate both more work and more sharing than cheaper, smaller lumps (Taylor and Ward 1982). If there are more potential participants than the minimum required, however, games of Chicken arise over who shall complete the working group.

The size of the lumps, the relative value of lumpy goods, and the steepness of thresholds differ from one time and place to another. Ecological variation in local resources along these dimensions, as well as in other features of local circumstances such as the density of enemies and competitors, will lead to different kinds of collective-action problems, with implications for both work and sharing.

9.6.4. The Sexual Division of Labor

The sexual "division of labor" is the standard term for typical task differentiation between women and men. The implication of the label—that *family* (or larger group) agendas somehow set the optimal allocation of work, dividing jobs so as to best serve "family interests"—is so widely taken for granted as to seem simply a factual description. But a collective interest, even for a family, can pose collective-action problems.

Sugden (1986:33ff.), building on Schelling (1960), showed how readily consistent distinctions among players that do not initially affect costs and benefits can come to do so, developing into conventions that turn symmetrical into asymmetrical games. In asymmetrical games the same strategy has different payoffs for different players. Only a few players need initially respond to the distinctions to alter payoffs so that others follow. The success of contingent strategies, like Bourgeois, illustrates the importance even arbitrary distinctions may have in altering games.

As Schelling pointed out (1960:Chapter 3), prominent features are especially likely to trigger conventions. Gender is not only prominent, it can also be associated with initial differences in the fitness costs and benefits of a wide array of production and consumption activities, so that gender-based conventions are especially likely to evolve. Some kinds of work, for example, may exact higher fitness opportunity costs from women than from men (Brown 1970a; Murdock and Provost 1973; Hurtado 1985; Hurtado et al. 1985). And some kinds of work may give greater benefits to men than to women. If people prefer the company of those who share with them, and if they adjust social favors like sexual access and support in disputes accordingly, then men may gain more fitness from sharing and the work that supports it than do women (Hawkes 1990, 1991).

Consider the cooperative group problem posed earlier (9.5.2). Instead of a gardening group, however, make it a local residential group whose members will suffer lowered foraging returns or reduced arable land (per capita) with the arrival of additional residents. Exclusion of newcomers would be a collective good for current members (see 10.2.30). If the current group is composed of a man and a woman, and if size and strength differences require the woman to mount a more expensive defense to give her equal chances of success, then the game over who will do the defending might look like payoff matrix 7 (with the woman as row, the man as column). This is an asymmetrical game in which the payoffs to row, the first number in each cell, are a Prisoner's Dilemma, while column, whose payoffs are the second number, faces a Chicken.

Payoff matrix 7
(Male strategy)

		Defend	Don't defend
(Female strategy)	Defend	3,3	1,4
	Don't defend	4,2	2,1

Taylor, considering such a payoff structure (1987:39), notes that the outcome of this game is not at all problematic. Since row's best strategy, no matter what column does, is not to defend, column's best strategy, limited by row's obvious choice, is to defend. The payoff structure commits row not to defend. Schelling (1960) showed that, paradoxically, clear restrictions on one player's choice can provide the committed player a powerful bargaining advantage. If the group includes more adults, however, other collective-action problems are posed. If these payoffs hold for a man and a woman, the simplest additional assumption is that a game of Chicken would arise among the men (see section 10.4.1 for additional discussion). A man would do better to free ride on the defensive actions of others but would prefer to defend than leave the job undone. This would make defending men preferred companions (for both women and men) and lead to hypotheses about selective incentives for the provision of this collective good.

9.7. SOME APPLICATIONS OF EVOLUTIONARY ECOLOGY TO PATTERNS OF FOOD SHARING

Of the models reviewed here, delayed reciprocity has been more often applied than any other to food sharing among hunter–gatherers. Foraging is a chancy business. Many ethnologists and archaeologists have suggested that foragers share food and foraging areas to reduce risks of failure, that is, they give up shares when they can, to claim repayment when in need. By this hypothesis, variation in sharing may be associated with variation in the magnitude of such risks (Draper 1978; Hames 1990; Harpending 1981; Hayden 1981: Jochim 1981; Kaplan and Hill 1985b; Kaplan et al. 1990; Lee 1968, 1979; O'Shea 1981; Smith 1988; Washburn and Lancaster 1968; Whitelaw 1989; Wiessner 1977; 1982; Winterhalder 1986, 1990; Yellen and Harpending 1972). The distribution of sharing and storing as alternative means to increased security has been of particular interest to anthropologists (Sahlins 1972; Binford 1980; Gould 1981, 1982; Whitelaw 1989) including those employing evolutionary ecology (Cashdan 1980, 1985; Smith 1988; Smith and Boyd 1990; Winterhalder 1986, 1990).

Behavioral ecologists studying non humans have also been increasingly interested in risk. Although the classic optimal forager was assumed to make foraging decisions that would maximize mean values for model variables, subsequent modeling has taken variance into account (see Chapter 6, Stephens 1990; and Stephens and Krebs 1986). Both modeling and observation point to situations in which foragers do better to minimize variance, but also situations in which they do better to choose *higher* variance alternatives. Because of the several ways "risk" is defined, individuals sometimes *minimize* their risk of complete failure, by *increasing* their risks of getting less. If nothing but $2000 will stop foreclosure on the mortgage, risking the only $200 on long-shot gambles that give a *possible* payoff of $2000 makes loss of the farm *less* likely than investing the $200 for a sure gain of 20%.

The widespread argument that sharing would be an especially effective means to reduce variance in daily income for foragers under many circumstances has been borne out by formal modeling. Winterhalder (1986) showed that sharing could have large effects on the daily income variance of foragers. Moreover, it took only a few sharers to eliminate most of the variation in the income of participants. Winterhalder considered the alternatives of sharing and storing and showed that two variables—(1) the extent to which successes among foragers are synchronized, and (2) the extent of variation in the success of any individual forager over time—predicted whether sharing or storing would reduce risks of failure more effectively. If foraging success is variable and unsynchronized, then sharing will buffer risk best. If foragers have synchronized successes and failures then sharing will not reduce risk but storing will. Low variation in foraging success will mean that neither sharing nor storing will repay their costs.

Kaplan (1983), Kaplan and Hill (1985b), and Kaplan et al. (1990) noted the wide variation in the extent to which different kinds of food resources are shared. They tested several hypotheses about this variation on observations of the foraging Aché of Eastern Paraguay. The data show the Aché to be notable sharers: On average three quarters of what anyone eats was acquired by someone outside the consumer's nuclear family. Some resources are more likely to go to close kin, but other kinds of resources show no such kin-biased sharing. The extent of this sharing is positively correlated with the average package size of resources and the unpredictability of securing them (Figure 9.2a, b). As Kaplan and associates noted, wide sharing of large and unpredictable resources reduces the variance in daily consumption, lessening the risk of a hungry day. They modeled the "nutritional consequences" of sharing and not sharing various categories of resources, using the Aché data on patterns of daily acquisition and assuming a ceiling on daily consumption. This exercise showed that the benefits for sharing some categories of resources were greater than benefits for sharing others, those in larger and more unpredictably acquired packages giving the greatest increase in "mean nutritional status" when shared. Moreover, almost all individuals and families, including those who produced significantly more than others, consumed more with sharing than they would have done without.

Cashdan (1985) also focused on the variance reduction effect of sharing, and explored the circumstances that would favor sharing rather than storage as a means of reducing risks of failure. Drawing on insurance theory, she noted that for sharing to reduce risks of loss effectively, the possible losses of sharing units must be independent accidents. Thus (as Winterhalder's subsequent formal model showed), where potential sharing units are subject to correlated fortunes, sharing will be an ineffective means of variance reduction. She nominated two variables as especially important in determining the relative costs and benefits of sharing or storing to buffer risk: distance and mobility. The shorter the distance over which losses are uncorrelated and the more mobile the participating units, the more readily sharing can reduce variance and the less it costs relative to storage.

Cashdan compared Basarwa and Bantu-speaking people along the Nata River in Northeastern Botswana, showing that the Basarwa had smaller harvests, often insufficient to last the year. The Basarwa engaged in more interhousehold food sharing, while the Bantu speakers stored more food. The source of smaller Basarwa harvests was their much smaller fields. This was, in turn, the result of more frequent household moves, dictated by opportunities to care for cattle. For these Basarwa, the mobility attendant on acquiring cattle products would make sharing more "cost-effective" than storing.

The authors cited above have pointed to circumstances in which individu-

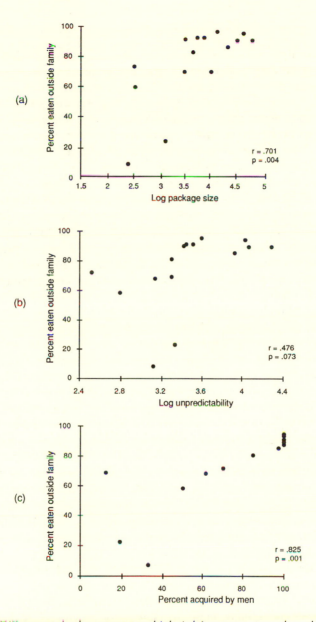

Figure 9.2. Differences in the extent to which Aché resources are shared (Hawkes 1991: figures 1–3). Each point represents 1 of 15 resource types acquired by Aché hunter–gatherers on 9 foraging trips in 1981–1982. On all graphs, the y-axis shows the percentage of times subjects were observed consuming a resource type acquired by someone outside their own nuclear family (Kaplan and Hill 1985b). (a) The x-axis indicates the log of package size, defined as the mean number of calories in a single acquisition of the resource (Kaplan and Hill 1985b). (b) The log of unpredictability, defined as the mean of the standard deviations of the family totals in calories of the resource acquired each day (Kaplan and Hill 1985b). (c) The percentage of total acquisitions of the resource by men.

als reduce their risks of failure if they share because they receive shares when they have little or nothing. If one receives because one has given, then this is delayed reciprocity. But if individuals receive shares whether or not they give them, they can free ride. The shared items are then collective goods, and providing them poses a collective action problem. The expectation of future shares is not the reason for the giving.

The circumstances in which delayed reciprocity would have sizable variance reduction effects are also the circumstances that promote tolerated theft. If successes are synchronized, there is no inequality of holdings to promote theft. Under these circumstances, storing poses no prohibitive defense costs, and so Blurton Jones (1987b) suggested that seasonal gluts might promote storage. On the other hand, marked and unsynchronized variations in acquisition produce large differences between those who have and those who do not. If some are much hungrier than others, the strategy of *not* sharing could be costly. One obvious kind of cost would be the time, energy, and potential injury of a fight, but there may be penalties for refusals to share even in the absence of a physical struggle. Others may see sharers as more attractive companions than nonsharers. They may be readier to join and support sharers in other contests.

Storing can thus occur where the variance in successes is low because there the pressure of "theft" is low. But where the variance in successes is high, so is the pressure for shares. Tolerated theft has the same *effect* of reducing variance in consumption as does reciprocity. But there is a key difference. With delayed reciprocity, individuals who share or cooperate less will get less sharing and cooperation in return. Reciprocity depends on discriminations against those who do not share. Conversely, strategies like tolerated theft, for which net benefits depend on immediate accounting, are not contingent on past (and predicted future) sharing. Assuming equal competitive ability, individuals who acquire more tolerate more theft. Individuals who acquire less take more from others. If some individuals consistently acquire more, then the differential that emerges is a one-way flow to the less successful.

Consider the data on Aché food sharing. The wider sharing of resources that come more unpredictably and in larger packages is consistent with delayed reciprocity to reduce risks of failure, because the cost to a successful hunter of giving up extra bits of a large resource is less than the benefit to him of getting bits from another when he has failed to score himself. As Kaplan and associates point out, this follows from a diminishing-returns shape for the gain curve of nutritional payoff for increasing consumption (as in Figure 9.1).

But risk of failure is reduced by giving shares only if the giving obligates recipients to return them, which implies giving to those more likely to return in future, and not giving to those who have failed to return them in the past.

A striking feature of the Aché data is the *lack* of such a differential. Hunters who "give" more do not get more. Their work provides a collective good.

Tolerated theft offers an alternative framework in which to explain the wider sharing among Aché foragers of large resources that are unpredictably acquired. If the gain curve for consuming these foods is one of diminishing returns, and consumers have similar competitive abilities (cf. Kaplan and Hill 1985b; Kaplan et al. 1990), then the economics of defense will lead to even sharing. From this perspective the question is not why these resources are widely shared, but why they are acquired in the first place. If foragers know these items will be widely shared, if they expect no consumption advantage for themselves (or their wives and children), why do they do the work? How could it be in their interest to pay the acquisition costs? Why not free ride and, as Blurton Jones (1987) asked, be scroungers instead? If there were only two foragers, the problem could be modeled as the game reviewed earlier (section 9.5.3, matrix 3), except that here the resource is divisible. V is the amount of resource acquired if both forage, C is the cost of foraging, s is some fraction of V that one forager could acquire:

Payoff matrix 8

	Forage	Scrounge
Forage	$(V/2) - C$	$(sV/2) - C$
Scrounge	$sV/2$	0

As with matrix 3, this would produce several different payoff structures depending on the values of the variables. The values will determine whether there is a pure ESS. If $(1 - s)V > 2C$ *and* $sV > 2C$, row should forage whatever column does. Here the fraction of the resource a forager can expect to keep is worth the costs paid to acquire it. If the inequalities are both reversed, row should scrounge whatever column does, since the cost is not worth paying, making it a Prisoner's Dilemma. If $(1 - s)V < 2C$ but $sV > 2C$, the game is Chicken with no pure ESS. Note that whatever row does, he will do better if column foragers. Blurton Jones suggested that "prestige" awarded to energetic foragers might, for these reasons, be a form of "self-serving deceit." But why should energetic foragers allow themselves to be duped?

Some resources are more widely shared than others. Why not target resources that could be kept within the family? The question is given special force by the surprising finding that Aché men could more than double their energetic rate of gain by taking palm starch at every opportunity (Hill et al. 1987; Kaplan et al 1990; see section 6.5.1). Instead they choose to hunt and take honey, part of a preference for widely shared foods, which distinguishes men's from women's resource choice (Figure 9.2c). Hawkes (1990, 1991) associates this gender bias in foraging strategies with the hypothesis that mating advantages (Kaplan and Hill 1985a) serve as selective incentives for men to provide collective goods instead of provisioning their families.

Cashdan's data on Basarwa sharing also conflict in some ways with a hypothesis that this is delayed reciprocity to buffer risk. Here, as in the Aché case, a diagnostic feature of reciprocity must be differential sharing, with those most likely to give in the future receiving the most. Otherwise reciprocators are exploited by free riders. If benefits can be enjoyed without paying prior costs, those who do not pay do better. Her data show a clear but *negative* correlation between the number of food items received per household and the number of bags of grain harvested. Those who harvest least receive most. This could only be consistent with reciprocity if those who harvested least this year are likely to harvest most next year. But a year-long time lag and high mobility suggest that uncertainty about repayment would be high. Discounting could be a barrier to reciprocity. Moreover, if Basarwa who have just begun to plough a field are no *less* likely to move than those who have been ploughing longer, those who have been ploughing longer are likely to harvest more next year than those with newer fields. Those who have larger harvests and receive less this year are likely to have even larger harvests and receive even less next year. Those who receive more this year are likely to receive more next year as well. This is a pattern inconsistent with delayed reciprocity.

Tolerated theft on the other hand would level differences. Data are not available to see whether those who harvest little or nothing consume as much as those who harvest more. Again the collective action problem arises. If all have similar consumption levels, then why plow and harvest at all? If "scroungers" can eat as well without paying the cost of farming, self-interested individuals should choose to scrounge.

If we assume similar consumption for all (due to tolerated theft) then some of the elements of the problem of whether to plant in this situation could be represented by payoff matrix 8, with plowing rather than foraging the alternative to scrounging. As above, the value of the variables would determine the game. As with the foraging version, whatever row does he would do better if column ploughed. As with the case of Aché hunters, some other benefits dispensed to those who plow might encourage their industry. But the striking pattern in this case is how truncated that industry is. While harvest depends on field size, which depends on years plowed, the Basarwa move much more readily and so plow the same fields for much shorter periods than their Bantu-speaking neighbors. Changing opportunities to care for the cattle of Bantu speakers is the suggested reason. But, as Cashdan notes, this pattern is unlike arrangements for cattle tending elsewhere in Botswana, where the cattle come to the tenders rather than vice versa. Perhaps the reason Basarwa households move so often is precisely to avoid exploitation by scrounging kin and neighbors. If more productive fields only mean more insistent begging, more tolerated theft, households may find little benefit in expanding their fields and less cost in moving, which reduces their productivity and the pressure on them to give. As Blurton Jones suggested, the dynamics of tolerated theft may be implicated in the otherwise paradoxical observation that often small-scale cultivators do not plant quite enough to meet annual family needs.

Comparison of these analyses of Aché hunting and Basarwa farming highlights the following question: Under what circumstances do those who provide collective goods net benefits for themselves even though some free ride on their work? Why would Aché hunters gain by hunting long hours, with better hunters hunting even longer than other men (Hill and Hawkes 1983, Hawkes et al. 1985), while (the hypothesis is) Basarwa farmers do not gain from and so do not sustain high levels of productivity? If better hunters earn favors for their hunting among the Aché, why would not better farmers earn favors among the Basarwa?

This returns attention to the collective-action problem that Sahlins found pointing to "the zen road to affluence." In spite of free riders, there is empirical variation in the amount people work as well as the amount they share. Again, consider three mutually exclusive extremes: One is to acquire no more than one can immediately consume, another is to acquire more and share it, and a third is to acquire more and store it for future consumption.

Features of local ecology such as the lumpiness of resources, the way they are encountered in both space and time, the effects these have on the costs and benefits of sharing versus not sharing, the costs and benefits for alternative subsistence strategies, the opportunity costs of foraging or farming, and the extent to which these differ according to sex differences, may all affect the payoffs for work.

Details of local circumstances set the constraints and the trade-offs: the costs and benefits for possible alternatives. Aché hunters apparently earn quite unambiguous fitness benefits for their industry. Each man faces trade-offs—more hunting means less of something else—and optimizing these trade-offs depends on what the alternatives are and the costs and benefits of each. Special features of the Aché foraging pattern, in which the entire party moves through the forest rather than returning each night to the same central place, surely affect the suite of possible alternative activities available to men. Further exploration of the constraints and costs and benefits would attend to such details of local circumstance, including not only the character and distribution of resources in the forest, but the way these affect the behavior of other people who are potential mates, competitors, and allies.

Wiessner's discussion of !Kung San sharing cited above underlines the point. Much of the sharing follows special rules and operates between carefully chosen partners. Wiessner describes !Kung sharing as reciprocity to reduce risks. But she reports the prevalence and importance of tolerated theft, and also the effect it has on reducing "mean" levels of productivity. This pattern among the !Kung sharply contrasts with the Aché. Foraging Aché men spend almost 50 hours a week in food acquisition (Hill et al. 1985). Lee reports that !Kung men at Dobe spent less than half that (Lee 1979:278). As Wiessner's descriptions indicate (and see Shostak 1983) people prefer companions and neighbors who are energetic foragers with more to share to companions who share less or have less to share. Why do the !Kung not dispense favorable treatment to those inclined to active foraging so that compensating benefits make more work the best strategy, at least for some? From the perspective employed here, answers would be sought in two directions. First, what are the patterns of income foragers can earn given the character of local resources? What daily rates are likely and how large and predictable are the resources foragers can acquire? Some prey species may be very large and so very widely shared. But, if successful captures are sufficiently rare, the value of hunting neighbors may not be high. So favors given to encourage them may be few (Hawkes 1990: 165–166). Second, what are the opportunities forgone when foraging? Wiessner's comments cited above suggest more high-benefit/low-cost alternatives to foraging among the !Kung than the mobility pattern of the Aché allows.

Returning to the Basarwa, there is a second difference between the Aché and the Basarwa patterns, especially pertinent to the issues of this chapter. Among the Aché, *men* hunt; among the Basarwa, *households* farm. While individual men are expected to have numerous and important conflicts of interest with other men as well as with women and children, members of households not only have conflicts of interest with members of other households, but with each other as well. Thus what any "household does" will be, from this perspective, the outcome of its individual members each acting from self-interest. Even if it were the case that men who are industrious farmers are preferred neighbors by members of other households, benefits dispensed to them to encourage their continued industry might not be benefits to the fitness of their wives. Women who are industrious farmers might be preferred neighbors but fitness costs to them of energetic farming might be higher than for men. And while both men and women might benefit from neighborly dispensations of food or solicitude toward offspring, some favors neighbors could return to men might have less value to women (e.g., sexual favors and support in disputes over sexual access). Moreover, household members might see different costs and benefits for sharing with different claimants. Collective-action problems posed by defending household goods against persistent demands could result in Prisoner's Dilemmas or games of Chicken in which "household fortunes" suffer. Only further research can show how much of the difference between Basarwa, !Kung, Aché, and others can be explained from this perspective.

9.8. SUMMARY

Among hunter-gatherers and small-scale horticulturalists, many goods are collectively consumed. The common pattern labeled reciprocity by ethnologists is paradoxically distinguished by the lack of definite commitment to reciprocate. With widespread sharing, some can take a "free ride" on what others give. This may point the way to Sahlins's "zen road to affluence," where people work less than they might because any extra will be consumed by others.

If collective-action problems dampen work effort, sharing patterns still persist. Moreover, both work and sharing vary from one ethnographic setting to another, and among seasons, resources, and the age and gender of workers. More systematic investigation of the costs and benefits and the sources of their variability is indicated.

The costs and benefits to individuals who share varies with the effects this sharing has on what others do. This reverberating interdependence makes game theory a suitable framework for building models to suggest the circumstances in which those who share do better than those who do not. Three of the kinds of explanations that evolutionary ecologists employ to account for sharing patterns are discussed. The first is reciprocal altruism, which, unlike the reciprocity of ethnology, entails definite, though delayed repayment for short-term costs. The game known as the Prisoner's Dilemma has been widely used to illustrate the problem of collective action, and to explore the possibility of cooperation among self-interested actors using the strategy of delayed reciprocity. Mutualism is the second kind of explanation. Individuals may sometimes do better in terms of immediate personal costs and benefits if they share than they would if they did not. The game of Chicken, best known to evolutionary ecologists as a version of the Hawk–Dove game, shows how easily mutualism can turn into manipulation, which is the third kind of explanation. Individuals may be manipulated or coerced into sharing because it costs too much not to. The payoff structure of tolerated theft shows how the costs of *not* sharing can be too high to be worth paying.

Four issues arising from discussion of these models deserve emphasis. First, because the future is uncertain, individuals are expected to discount the value of benefits that are delayed. Observation and experiment are consistent with this expectation and encourage skepticism toward the view that ethnographers miss compensating returns for sharing because their observation periods are short. Steep discounting makes the value of future benefits and thus the probability that they might compensate current costs, diminish rapidly with hypothesized longer delays.

Second, where those who give do not thereby gain greater shares of the collective good, other benefits, selectively awarded, could provide incentives for continued giving. The character and value of such selective incentives also depends on specific features of local circumstances. Such incentives, however, can pose other collective-action problems. If favors are given to sharers to promote their continued sharing, others could free ride on the favor givers.

Third, the suite of goods that people acquire or produce may be more or less "lumpy." If lumps are large, individuals may be unable to acquire "just enough" for their own consumption. If expected consumption makes the cost worth paying, at least for some, collective goods may be provided as a consequence. Thus, the character of the goods themselves and the local alternatives to providing them determine whether collective-action problems arise.

The fourth issue is the strong effect that differences among individuals can have on the payoffs for strategic interaction among them. This can happen even if initially the differences are quite arbitrary. Prominent differences may be especially likely to stimulate conventional responses. A few individuals responding in consistent but different ways can alter the payoffs for all and generate a convention that is then self-reinforcing. Gender as a prominent asymmetry would be a likely basis for frequency-dependent conventions. Moreover, it is associated with fairly consistent differences in fitness costs and benefits for various activities. This makes it an even more likely basis for the development of conventions, as individuals adjust their behavior to take advantage of frequency-dependent payoffs.

Some particular applications of models and concepts from evolutionary ecology to ethnographic patterns of food sharing are summarized and problems are revisited as they apply. The hypothesis that sharing is a means to reduce risks of failure has appealed to a wide array of scholars, including those employing the perspective of evolutionary ecology. Aspects of the empirical variation in sharing seem consistent with this hypothesis; that is, items that are large and unpredictably acquired, like game animals, are often shared. But if these items are consumed collectively, a producer's contribution now has no effect on the shares he can claim in the future. Tolerated theft suggests a simpler explanation for the wider sharing of large unpredictably acquired goods. But it does not explain why they are acquired in the first place. Modeling and measuring the payoffs for this work will include appraisals of the local alternatives and of possible selective incentives, with continuing attention to why and how these might vary among and within communities.

ACKNOWLEDGMENTS

I thank N. Blurton Jones, M. Borgerhoff Mulder, E. Cashdan, R. Cooter, K. Hill, J. Hirshleifer, J. O'Connell, A. Rogers, and E. Smith for good advice.

Competition, Conflict, and The Development of Social Hierarchies

James L. Boone

10

10.1. INTRODUCTION

This chapter outlines some evolutionary ecological approaches to analyzing and explaining the formation of hierarchical social groups among humans. Following the approach of methodological individualism (section 2.3.1), this chapter is built around the idea that the size and structure of social groups can be explained in terms of the aggregate consequences of individual behavioral strategies aimed at maximizing access to or control over limiting resources through competitive and cooperative interaction with other individuals. Such strategies involve costs in the form of investment of time, energy, resources, and—under some conditions—bodily risk. At the same time, individuals organizing and cooperating in groups rather than acting solitarily accrue benefits related to acquiring, producing, processing, and defending access to resources.

Thus the process of group formation may be seen from a cost-benefit point of view, wherein individuals weigh the costs of group affiliation (increased competition for resources, increased exposure to disease) against the benefits (enhanced access to resources or mates) versus the costs and benefits of leaving the group for a less competitive environment or affiliating with another group under more favorable terms. Where benefits outweigh costs, groups should form and continue to grow as long as all the members benefit relative to dispersal or alternative affiliation. Sections 10.2.1 and 10.2.2 present some simple optimization models that define more rigorously the conditions under which group formation occurs.

The question then arises: If groups form out of mutual self-interest, how can we explain the development of inequality and exploitation within groups? The answer to this question revolves around the issue of resource competition within and between groups and the "stay or leave" option that exists, at least in theory, for every group member. Under conditions of intense competition or where unoccupied territory no longer exists, the lack of alternative strategies for individuals may promote group affiliation even in the face of extreme disadvantage to some, perhaps most, of its members. And it is under these conditions that particular individuals, kingroups, or coalitions can exploit the lack of alternative strategies as leverage to gain control of resources at the expense of others. The result is hierarchical social organization based on unequal access to resources. Hence, from an analytical point of view, groups characterized by exploitation and inequality can be said to develop out of mutual self-interest, even if many members of the group are seriously disadvantaged. Some optimization models that clarify the dynamics of resource competition and hierarchy formation are presented in section 10.3

While small-group foraging activities and central-place sharing of resources in high-risk environments are discussed in some detail as factors in the formation of small groups (10.2.2), group formation based on reciprocity has serious size limitations (10.2.3). What then explains the formation of large, areally extensive corporate groups? To answer this, we turn to the problem of the maintenance of public goods, specifically defense and the maintenance of complex production systems, as a basis for corporate group formation (10.4).

10.2. MODELING GROUP FORMATION

10.2.1. Optimal and Equilibrium Group Size

Smith (1981, 1983, 1985, 1987a) has developed some simple models of optimal group size among Inuit hunting parties. With a few modifications, these models can be extended to cover group formation in more permanent kinds of groups. Smith's model is based on the hypothesis that foragers seek to form groups that maximize per capita net rate of energy capture, which he defined as:

$$R = \frac{\Sigma(E_a - E_e)}{tn}$$

where n is the foraging group size, t is the duration of the foraging period (in this case, the duration of a single hunt), E_a and E_e are the food energy acquired and metabolic energy expended, respectively, by each member of the foraging group during time t. In analyzing the dynamics of group formation on this view, Smith assumes there are two options available to an individual: (1) to join a group of $n - 1$ foragers and become the nth member, or (2) to forage solitarily. Further assuming that the harvest is divided equally at the end of the foraging period, an optimal forager should seek to join a group as long as

$$R_n > R_1$$

where R_n is the per capita return rate for a forager group of size n. At the point where this inequality reverses, the optimal forager should forage alone. This Smith terms the "joiner's rule."

Once a member of a foraging group, an individual should favor the addition of yet more members only as long as

$$R_n > R_{n-1}$$

This is the "member's rule." It follows that a conflict between the joiner's rule and the member's rule will develop when

$$R_{n-1} > R_n > R_1$$

In other words, under some conditions, it may be in the joiner's interests to join a group even when it is not in the interests of the members of the group to include the joiner (as illustrated graphically in Figure 10.1). In the context of this kind of conflict of interest between members and joiners, whether a group grows to optimal size and stops (due to the member's rule) or continues to grow past optimal size (due to the joiner's rule), depends on the costs to individual members of excluding additional members relative to the costs of including them.

Conflicts of Interest in the Formation of Groups. Predicting whether group members will exclude or include new members beyond the optimal group size takes us into the realm of game theory, issues that are dealt with in detail by Hawkes in Chapter 9. Briefly, it may be that the addition of a new member beyond the optimal group size will decrease the benefits of the existing members, but excluding the would-be joiner might also entail costs. For example, if the benefits of joining such a group are high enough, would-be joiners might adopt various tactics, such as refusing to acquiesce peacefully, in order to make it more costly for existing members to exclude them. Equilibrium group size is determined as much by the costs and benefits to joiners as to members.

If the costs of excluding a joiner are *more* than the costs of admitting him or her, it will be cheaper to let the joiner into the group even though the benefits of all the existing members are reduced. Hence, group size may continue to grow beyond the optimal group size to the point where the fitness of group members is equal to what it would be if they foraged solitarily. This point is called a Nash equilibrium, which is the best group size that can exist given that everyone is maximizing their own self-interests (i.e., in this case by not paying the costs of excluding new members past the optimal group size).

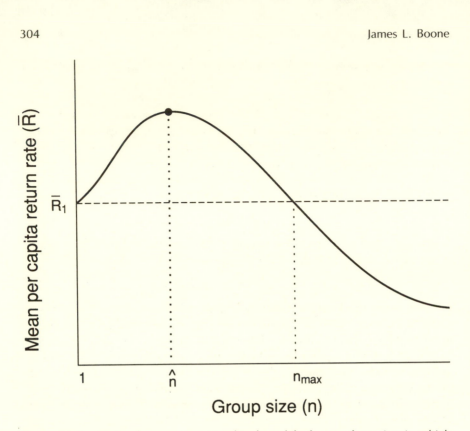

Figure 10.1. Optimal group size. Graphical model of group formation in which mean per capita return rate first increases, then decreases with group size. Optimal group size is at n, maximum group size is at n_{max}. Group size may grow beyond optimal size because of conflict between members and joiners (after Smith 1987a:212).

Alternatively, it may be that the costs of admitting the joiner are *greater* than the costs of excluding him or her. Here, it will eventually be to someone's best interests to pay the costs of excluding the new member, but it is still best for any individual member to have someone else pay those costs. Hence, the game of who among the members will pay the costs takes the form of a game of Chicken (see 9.5.3).

Central-Place Sharing. The joiner–member model addresses itself to the situation where per capita harvest rate is enhanced by grouping during the foraging activity itself. What happens if foragers range out from a central place, singly or in groups, and return to camp at the end of the hunt to pool their catch and divide it equally? The central-place sharing scenario results in a different optimization rule wherein the sharing group will increase in size as long as

$$nR_n - (n - 1)R_{n-1} > R_1$$

The optimization rule for central-place sharing has several new and different implications that stand in contrast to the previous model (Smith 1987a). First, the equation defines the decision rule for all individuals in the sharing network, regardless of whether they are currently members or joiners. Second, the sharing foragers will benefit by maximizing the per capita share of the entire network, rather than just their own harvest rates. Hence, unlike the previous case, there is no conflict of interest between members and joiners over how large the group should be. In fact, the "optimal (equilibrium) group size will always be greater than or equal to that which maximizes per capita returns for a foraging group . . . , but less than or equal to the maximum size determined by the joiner's rule" (Smith 1987a:213). Thus,

> as long as the sharing rule is strictly adhered to, and foragers attempt to maximize their own share (and hence total harvest for the sharing network), the equilibrium group size will approach Pareto-optimality (maximizing total benefits to the community) rather than the pessimistic Nash equilibrium (selfish maximizing) that might otherwise prevail . . . because the communal-sharing rule results in a payoff structure where the marginal contribution of a foraging group member is equal to the marginal cost of not joining the group (i.e., the expected solitary return rate)". (pp. 213–214; emphasis added)

Several issues are raised by the communal-sharing model. First, it could easily be extended to include horticulturalists and agriculturalists who produce food, pool it, and divide it equally among themselves, or to any cooperative production activity in which there are *economies of scale* (see discussion in section 10.2.3). Second, it would seem that in the absence of intervening conditions not explicitly specified in this simple model, groups forming around central-place sharing networks could become very large indeed, and ought to be rather common. But large, truly egalitarian pooling and sharing groups are not common and have a seemingly inevitable tendency to move toward conditions of inequality. Hence, we might ask: (1) Under what conditions should a central-place communal-sharing network arise and persist? (2) Are there hidden limitations to or problems with grouping on basis of reciprocal sharing? These questions will be addressed in 10.2.

10.2.2. Conditions Under Which Group Formations Occurs

Group Formation Through Resource Sharing. Smith (1987a; see also Kaplan and Hill 1985b; Schaffer 1978) has specified the conditions under which resource sharing should occur. He uses an optimization model based on the idea that individuals living in a risky, variable environment attempt to minimize variance in resource income through sharing. The assumptions of the model, which essentially constitute the conditions under which sharing should occur, are:

1.   Each actor is subject to random variation in harvest rates.
2.   Actors in each locale experience the same expected harvest rate over the long run.
3.   Stochastic variation in harvest rates is asynchronic between actors.
4.   The resource being exploited exhibits diminishing returns (that is, the more of a resource one has the less the value of each additional unit).
5.   The actors seek to maximize the total expected value gained from the resource in the long run (resource value is distinct from the actual harvest or consumption rate of the resources).
6.   The actors are self-sufficient and have no better resources available (other than the ones they are pooling and sharing).

This risk reduction model of resource sharing is presented in graphic form in Figure 10.2. Harvest or consumption rate of resources used by a population is plotted along the x-axis, with a mean of x and a range from a to b (in this case, harvest rates are assumed to follow a normal distribution). A diminishing-returns utility function (symbolized by the curve) transforms the harvest rate into resource *value, V,* along the y-axis of the graph. If an individual forages (or cultivates) alone, he or she can expect to harvest resources at a stochastic rate with an average of x and a range of α to β (i.e., the same distribution as the average harvest rate for members of the group). The expected return in *value, V,* as a function of harvest rate would then be given by the midpoint on the y-axis between $V(\alpha)$ and $V(\beta)$, that is, $V(\alpha + \beta)/2$. If the same group pooled their resources and divided them equally among each other, each individual's expected return would be $V(\bar{x})$, which in this graph is a greater value. In other words, they would get better value for their efforts by pooling and sharing than by harvesting and consuming solitarily.

This situation would obtain only if the resource being harvested were characterized by a *diminishing-returns utility function* (see further discussion in section 10.3.2). If the resource exhibited either a linear or an accelerating function, such that increasing quantities of the resource do *not* become less and less valuable, $V(\bar{x})$ would be less than $V(\alpha + \beta)/2$, and individuals in the population would do better to harvest and consume alone.

Unequal Exchange and Development of Inequality.   Two key assumptions in Smith's model of resource sharing were that each actor is subject to random variation in harvest rates, and that actors in each locale experience the same expected harvest rate over the long run. What might happen if these conditions do not obtain?

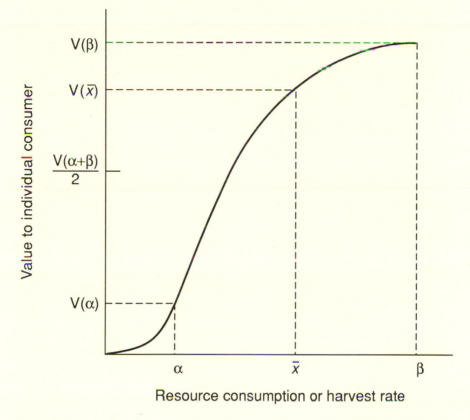

Figure 10.2.   *Risk reduction model of resource sharing (after Smith 1987a:215).*

If local patches are about equal in quality and in the likelihood of falling short in a given year, and all patches do not usually fall short in the same year, systems of exchange of foodstuffs and valuables would be expected to remain on a more or less reciprocal basis indefinitely. If, however, some patches are of consistently better quality, particularly in the sense that they are subject to shortfall less frequently, the flow of valuables and foodstuffs becomes asymmetrical (i.e., they flow in one direction more often than the other). Under these conditions a series of asymmetric relations between less risk-prone and more risk-prone patches could occur, resulting in the development of patron–client relationships (O'Shea 1981). Hence, local variation in patch quality, particularly in terms of levels of susceptibility to harvest failure in areas that are already characterized by a relatively high degree of risk, should be a major factor in the formation of relations of inequality, resulting in some degree of social stratification. The importance of agricultural risk and local variation in resource patch quality in the formation of asymmetric exchanges in the form of patron–client relations and resulting social stratification have been emphasized in several recent case studies (Halstead 1981; Halstead and O'Shea 1982; Sanders and Webster 1978; G. Webster 1990).

Limitations on Size of Groups Based on Sharing. There are some serious limitations to sharing based on reciprocity when groups begin to increase in size. The problem of whether individuals should cooperate in sharing or hoard their resources takes the form of the Prisoner's Dilemma game, which was outlined in 2.2.3 and 9.5. Briefly, the paradox in this game is that in order for cooperation to arise among selfish individuals, and for the players to realize the benefits of sharing, they have to accept lower short-term payoffs in return for the long-term benefits of reciprocity. If groups are small, reciprocal sharing can develop on a tit-for-tat basis if all the individuals involved are likely to have repeated interactions (Axelrod 1980). But in larger groups, the problems of cheating and free riding become insurmountable.

Herein lies the crux of a really fundamental problem in evolutionary ecological theory regarding the formation of complex societies. Boyd and Richerson (1988b) have recently presented a theoretical analysis of an extended *n*-person Prisoner's Dilemma, in which they show that reciprocity tends to break down in groups larger than about 6 to 10 individuals, due principally to the free rider problem. The implication of their analysis is that cooperative groups consisting of selfish individuals cannot form without some evolutionary mechanism to "short-circuit" individual selfishness. Campbell (1983) also presents a narrative account of the same position, arguing for a kind of group selection at the cultural level that overcomes the problem of the selfishness of the individual, and allows for the development of what he terms human "ultrasociality." The only other ultrasocial species are the social insects, which have evolved ultrasociality through the mechanism of kin selection; this has an important but much more limited role in human sociality.

However, Boyd and Richerson (1988b) point out that their analysis of the effects of group size on reciprocity does not take into account several possibilities that might allow cooperation to arise in larger groups. These include:

1. Individuals in the group could directly punish defectors, using various sanctions.

2. Hierarchical structure in a group could function to enforce cooperation in larger groups (using sanctions).

3. The Prisoner's Dilemma may not be the only relevant game with which to model reciprocity in sizable groups.

4.   More complex payoffs schedules may alter the outcome of the Prisoner's Dilemma and other games.

Each of these possibilities is discussed in more detail below.

Sanctions involve some form of punishment of noncooperators to provide incentives for cooperation. But punishing noncooperators involves costs as well: Who will pay these costs? This is called a *second-order collective-action problem* and takes the same form as the dilemma of who should pay the costs of excluding excess members in a simple public goods problem, as outlined above (10.2.1). Boyd and Richerson (in press b) show, however, that if sanctions are adopted that will punish nonpunishers, that is, those who fail to punish noncooperators, the second-order problem is solved and any behavior can become a stable strategy, even if it is maladaptive. Of course, the costs of invoking such sanctions to punish the nonpunishers must be paid by someone as well (otherwise there would be a third-order collective-action problem!).

One way out of the dilemma of who will pay the costs of enforcing cooperation would be if a special-interest group has more to gain from group cooperation and the resulting increased production than others in the group, and hence is willing to pay the extra costs to maintain the affiliation and cooperation of others in the group. A group is termed *privileged* if it "pays at least one of its members to provide some public good unilaterally, that is to bear the cost of providing it alone" (Taylor 1987:8–9; following Olson 1965).

Political entrepreneurs are one kind of individual or interest group that might pay the costs of maintaining some public good unilaterally (see discussion in Taylor 1987:24–26). Imagine a situation in which a dominant gains benefits from maintaining subordinates within his or her group. Benefits might include food production, materiel, personnel, and other logistic support in, for example, defending his or her position against other competing groups (more specifically, in competition with other group leaders, as discussed in sections 10.2.3, 10.2.4, and 10.4.3). Even if the productivity or well-being of the subordinates is either dependent upon or at least enhanced by cooperative effort in production, they may not have as much to gain from enhanced production as the dominants (as discussed in section 10.2.3), and hence they may not be able to surmount the Prisoner's Dilemma.

This view of group formation and persistence constitutes a departure from the view presented thus far, in which group formation arises within the context of cooperation between individuals with more or less equal interests. Here, a special-interest group or individual is financing group formation in its own interests. In doing so, the special-interest group may offer prospective affiliates a "better deal" than they would get operating alone, particularly if production risks or armed conflict are involved.

In this sense, the introduction of hierarchy probably facilitates the enforcement of sanctions. But while it seems clear that sanctions aimed at enhancing civil order are a common feature of hierarchical social systems, it is another thing to say social hierarchies initially develop *in order* to enforce such sanctions. This kind of argument is a common feature of group benefit, systems-level models of social evolution (for example, Johnson 1982). Again, the problem here is that cooperation in enforcement of cooperation involves a second-order collective-action problem that entails costs as well. The only way out of this dilemma is if some special-interest group has something more to gain from paying these costs unilaterally.

Another possibility is that reciprocity could be enforced by small subgroups of peers embedded in a much larger group constituted of similarly partitioned peer groups (Robert Boyd, personal communication; see also Olson 1965:63). For example, it is often argued that while armies are organized into large, hierarchical corporate groups, much of the cooperative, altruistic behavior seen in combat is conditioned by peer group pressure within patrols. This is a potentially interesting solution to the large-group problem, but the models needed to determine whether and under what conditions such partitioned cooperation would actually develop have yet to be developed.

Most Prisoner's Dilemma games have been modeled assuming that there is a linear relationship between time or resources put into a strategy and the fitness payoff. Other payoff schedules are possible, and will alter the outcome of the game. The effects of changing the payoff schedule on the outcome of games designed to model collective-action problems are beyond the scope of this chapter, though some progress has been made in this area by Smith and Boyd (1990). It can be pointed out, however, that changing the shape of utility function curves in other kinds of models (as in the sharing model in sections 10.2.2 and 10.3.3) has a strong effect on the resulting predictions of these models.

The fourth possibility Boyd and Richerson cite is that the Prisoner' Dilemma payoff structure may not be the only appropriate framework for understanding cooperation. For example, it is Taylor and Ward's (1982) contention that the game of Chicken is often a more appropriate model for understanding cooperation among individuals in a "public goods" situation (see also Reichert and Hammerstein 1983; and Chapters 2 and 9). The issue can be briefly summarized as follows, using the example developed in section 10.2.1 of the conflict among members over who should pay the costs of excluding would-be joiners beyond optimal group size.

The maintenance of optimal group size is the public good—it is to every existing member's benefit that the group not grow too large. In the Prisoner's Dilemma case, the costs to any particular individual of excluding a member is *greater* than the costs of letting him or her in. The members might cooperate in sharing the costs of exclusion, but this kind of cooperation is difficult to get started because the members would have to pay higher costs to cooperate in excluding than they would if they simply did nothing. But other payoffs schedules are possible.

In the Chicken example, the costs of letting a new member in are *greater* than the costs of excluding him or her. Here, exclusion will eventually occur; it is simply a matter of deciding who in the group will pay the exclusion costs (since it is still better to let someone else pay them), or whether these costs will be shared. On the basis of a "one-shot" game, there is no pure solution to this problem; that is, it is unpredictable whether or not someone will pay the costs, and the public good be upheld.

However, if the analysis is extended to an *n*-person game through a number of iterations, eventually a balance should be struck between "good citizens" who share the costs and "free riders" who enjoy the benefits of the public good without paying for it. This balance is referred to as a mixed ESS, in contrast to a pure strategy of either all cooperation or all noncooperation. The balance between cooperators and defectors is determined by the value of the public good being maintained relative to the costs of maintaining it. We will return to the issue of public goods in section 10.4; at this stage, the critical point is that the Prisioner's Dilemma framework may be an unduly restrictive way to look at the possibilities for cooperation.

Other Conditions Fostering Group Formation. Pooling and sharing of resources or information in a risky environment is not the only, and perhaps not even the most important, context in which group formation can occur. I discussed the pooling and sharing example in some detail as a vehicle to introduce the various aspects of collective-action problems. Group cooperation can also develop in production systems characterized by *economies of scale,* wherein increases in the scale of production result in increasing returns in output per unit of time or effort that is put into production.

The most familiar example of this kind of production (at least in industrial societies) is assembly line production, where goods are more efficiently produced through the division of production into specialized tasks that are then performed in series by an organized work group. But increasing the scale of production can also be critical when there is some kind of time limit on production, for example, in the harvesting of ripe crops. Ten people can probably harvest only 10 times faster than one person (hence, there is no efficiency gained in grouping per se), but if there is a threat of the crop spoiling or being ruined by rain, then cooperating as a group in harvesting will result in a gain for everyone involved. A similar benefit is gained in tasks such as sowing, weeding, drying and smoking meat or fish, or other tasks where there is a time limit. Production systems involving economies of scale are important to the issue of social hierarchy formation in several respects, and I will return them again in sections 10.3 and 10.4.

Group formation can also occur as a defensive or offensive strategy in the protection or acquisition of certain kinds of resources. Some theorists (e.g., Alexander 1974) have argued that defense, first against predators and later against other human competitors, has been the principal formative factor in the development of increasingly larger and more complex human groups. This may be to a certain extent an overstatement in view of the many other circumstances under which groups may form and where group defense of resources would not necessarily be predicted to occur (see section 10.3.2). I will return to the issue of defense as a special topic in the discussion of public goods in section 10.4. First, I want to set the stage for that discussion with a consideration of *group structure* as a consequence of competition within and between groups.

10.2.3. Optimal and Equilibrium Group Structure

The group formation model outlined in 10.2.1 assumes that the actors have the option of either joining and staying with a group or leaving it to live solitarily or with another group on more favorable terms. But suppose there is no empty habitat for a dispersing individual to move into, or the habitat is filled with groups that have reached their equilibrium size, so that the option of leaving the group is not available. Under such conditions, we should expect the level of within-group competition to increase, encouraging the development of group structure based on unequal access to resources or benefits of group membership. Let us now consider some optimization of models of the dynamics of group size and structure in this context.

Vehrencamp has developed a model of optimal and equilibrium group structure based on the idea that "the opposing forces of competition and cooperation within most groups reach a stable equilibrium that determines both the optimal group size and the degree of bias" (1983:667; see also Brown 1982; and Pulliam and Caraco 1984). *Bias* refers to the degree to which the benefits of grouping "accrue disproportionately to a few individuals in the group *at the expense of others*" (Vehrencamp 1983:667; emphasis added). According to this view, social groups can be ranked along a continuum in terms of the degree to which benefits within the groups are biased.

Vehrencamp has used this position as a point of departure for a model designed to define rigorously some of the conditions under which individuals living in groups interact in "despotic" versus "egalitarian" social groups. Her analysis begins with the assumption that group living entails both competition and cooperation. Cooperation leading to group formation occurs when individuals benefit more in terms of foraging, brood care, or predator defense than they would if they engaged in these activities solitarily. Competition is reflected in unequal division of resources or group benefits among members of such groups. Egalitarian groups are thus defined as groups in which "benefits derived from group living are divided roughly equally or in proportion to the risk or effort taken" (1983:667).

According to the model Vehrencamp develops, group size and structure (i.e., the degree of bias in resources, benefits, or fitness within the group) are determined by a balance between the ability of dominants to aggrandize resources at the expense of subordinates, and the ability of subordinates to do better either solitarily or as members of another group. As implied above, group benefits could include a variety of factors, but for generality and simplicity Vehrencamp models benefits with a single measure of fitness, W.

A model incorporating the effects of dominance interaction, resource allocation, group size and composition, and kinship interactions would be too complex to present in the form of an easily understandable optimization model. Hence, Vehrencamp employs the following simplifying assumptions:

1.   In any particular group there is a single manipulator, or dominant (whose fitness is defined as W_α, who can appropriate resources from subordinate members of the group, each of whom has fitness W_ω.

2.   Average (per capita) fitness is a function of group size k, and is denoted as W_k: There are no behaviors available to either the dominants or subordinates to change the functional relationship between W and k.

3.   The dominant's only strategy is to redistribute benefits within the group to his or her own benefit (the costs of dominating are not incorporated into this model).

4.   The subordinate's only options are either to accept the biased distribution of benefits or to *disperse* (leave the group) and operate solitarily.

Under these conditions subordinates would not stay in a group if fitness $W_\omega(k)$ in a group of size k were biased such that it fell below the mean fitness they would obtain solitarily, $W(1)$. The coefficient of variation of individual fitnesses within the group is used as an index of the degree of within-group bias. Vehrencamp also introduces inclusive fitness effects into the model, in order to analyze the effects of kinship on the degree of bias possible under given ecological conditions.

Since the options available to subordinates are to remain with the group or to disperse and operate solitarily or with another group, it was necessary to incorporate the costs of dispersal among subordinates into the model. This is accomplished by defining the probability of dispersing successfully, d, which for the purposes of Vehrencamp's model is defined as the number of unoccupied slots in the environment relative to the number of dispersing individuals competing for them.

The resulting analysis centers around determining "the allocation of resources or fitness to the dominants and subordinates that maximizes the fitness of the dominant . . . [that is,] the maximum degree of biasing that a

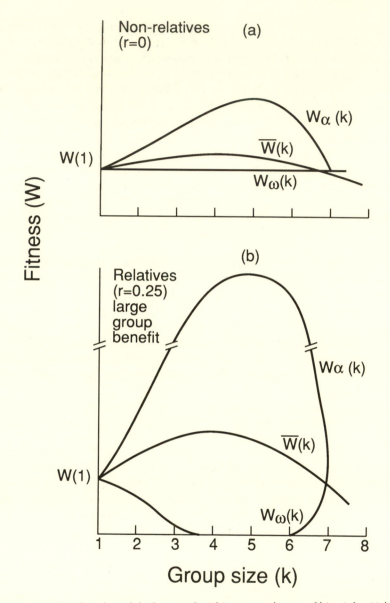

Figure 10.3.   Graphical model of optimal within-group degree of bias (after Vehren-camp 1983).

dominant should favor, given the ecologically determined $W(k)$ function and d'' (p. 669). Figure 10.3 shows the degree of bias possible under two conditions: one in which group members are nonrelatives, the other in which the degree of relatedness (r) among individuals in the group is 0.25. These graphs are analogous to the group size graph in Figure 10.1, except that the fitness as a function of group size is graphed separately for the dominant [$W_\alpha(k)$], the subordinates [$W_\omega(k)$], and the group mean [$W(k)$]. In these examples, d, the probability of subordinates dispersing successfully, is 1.0. Hence, subordinates must do better than they would solitarily in order to remain in the group, except in the cases where they are related to the dominant, wherein their fitness can actually fall below $W(1)$, as a result of inclusive fitness effects. Among nonrelatives, the degree to which $W_\omega(k)$ could fall below $W(1)$ would be a function of d. Note that the optimal group size for the dominant is always higher than it is for the group as a whole; this means that dominants might be expected to employ strategies to make subordinates remain in the group even when it is against subordinates' interests.

10.3. RESOURCE STRUCTURE AND COMPETITION WITHIN AND BETWEEN GROUPS

How the dynamics of group structure play out in any particular situation depends not only on political factors, but also on the structure of resources over which competition occurs. Below, I discuss the relation between resource structure, forms of competition, and resulting group structure.

10.3.1. Resource Structure and Forms of Competition

Scrambles and Contests. Competition over resources can be divided into two main categories: scrambles and contests (Parker 1984; Łomnicki 1988). Łomnicki's treatment of this subject seems most useful in terms of characterizing within-group competition and resulting group structure, and I will follow it here (see also section 12.4.1).

Scrambles can be likened to what happens when a group of children run in to collect candies that have fallen from a piñata. Ideally, in a scramble competition, each addition of another individual into the competition for a limited resource results in the lowering of the fitness of every other individual in the group (for example, through the lowering of per capita resource intake—i.e., the more children that scramble for the piñata candies, the fewer candies there will be for each child). Hence, average individual fitness is a function of group size (i.e., the number of consumers in relation to some more or less fixed resource base). Foragers consuming and competing over resources that are distributed such that they are not economically defendable (see discussion below on resource quality and distribution) would be a good example of scramble competition.

Contests consist of pairwise competitions between individuals over particular resource patches. In the simplest case, competitors are either successful or unsuccessful in winning or holding a patch in any particular contest. Hence, the addition of competitors into group competition in a pure contest situation does not necessarily lower the fitness of individuals who already hold resource patches, and individual fitness is independent of group size. (However, once the costs of resource *defense* to resource holders are factored in, it becomes clear that increases in group size, by raising per capita defense costs, will lower individual fitness.) Intensive agriculturalists competing over arable land would be a good example of contest competition.

The relationship between scrambles and contests on one hand, and *ideal free* and *despotic distributions* of individuals on the other, becomes important at this point (Pulliam and Caraco 1984:138–146; Lomnicki 1988:170–173). In an ideal free distribution, every individual is assumed to be able to choose the best available resource patch or strategy. Hence, given equal power and information, the fitnesses of individuals are equal (Lomnicki 1988:170; Fretwell 1972:86; see section 8.3). In this way, scramble competition is closely tied to the concept of the ideal free distribution.

In a despotic distribution, the fact that some proportion of the higher-quality patches are already occupied (and are economically defendable) means that free choice of patches is precluded. Accordingly, individual fitness vary and are correlated with patch quality. Hence, despotic distributions are likely to result from contest competition. Table 10.1 summarizes the relationship between form of competition, resource distribution, and individual fitnesses.

In scramble competition within a growing population, the growth rate can be slowed (i.e., regulated) through the lowering of fitness of all the individuals in the population. Adjustment of group size occurs when the average fitness of group members falls below the fitness of individuals if they operated solitarily. Adjustment of group size in despotic distributions results from dispersal of subordinates when their fitness within the group falls below what they could achieve alone or in another group.

Resource Quality and Distribution.   Generally speaking, what kinds of resource characteristics determine whether competition will resemble more a scramble or a contest, and hence whether distributions will be ideal or despotic? Resource quality and distribution are the most obvious factors (Davies and Houston 1984:149–151), and to the extent that social hierarchies are the social analog of territoriality (Wilson, 1975), optimization models of resource defense and territoriality appear to be the shortest path to an understanding to the relationships between resource structure and group structure.

Table 10.1.   The Relationship between Form of Competition, Resource
         Distribution, and Individual Fitnesses

Form of competition	Resource distribution	Individual fitnesses
Scramble	Ideal-free	Equal
Contest	Despotic	Unequal

Dyson-Hudson and Smith (1978) argued that territoriality is favored among populations that exploit densely distributed, spatiotemporally predictable resources. This is because such resources are the most economically defendable: The benefits of maintaining exclusive access to certain resources within an area outweigh the costs in time and effort of defending them (further discussion in 8.4.3).

Densely distributed, temporally and spatially predictable resources also constitute the most attractive object of competitive aggression, since they present the highest potential net gain to the successful aggressor (Parker 1974). It is for this reason that among individuals or groups competing for densely distributed, spatially and temporally stable resources, an "arms race" involving continually escalating offensive and defensive strategies may develop (Boone 1983). For humans, organizing and cooperating in groups is an important strategy in acquiring, maintaining, and defending access to resources. Hence, under conditions of increased competition within and between groups, group size may tend to increase all around, as long as all the members (as individuals, kin groups, larger subgroups) benefit relative to emigration or alternative affiliation.

The above discussion makes it clear that social hierarchy formation is a density-dependent phenomenon and develops around resources that are in some way defendable and divisible. As more individuals are added to the population, the competition leads to "latecomers" accepting lower-quality resource patches within the group, if resource structure is such that limiting resources exploited by the group is economically defendable by dominants within the group. The other side of the coin of population density is the resource-containing space exploited by a population. As long as there is unoccupied territory available and emigration/dispersal remains an economically viable strategy relative to staying in a group under reduced circumstances, no hierarchy should form.

If an area is circumscribed environmentally (by geographical barriers) or socially (by the presence of other groups), emigration becomes much less attractive, and hierarchical social organization should begin to develop under conditions of increasing population density. This is the essential point of Carneiro's (1970) classic formulation of the "environmental circumscription" theory of state formation.

10.3.2. Resource Holding Potential and Resource Value in Contest Competition

In the following two subsections, I will discuss in more detail the internal dynamics of group formation and structuring in the context of resource structure.

Contest Competition and Resource Holding Potential. Contests over resources are strategic games in which the best strategy for any particular individual depends upon what others are doing. Natural selection should favor evolution of psychological mechanisms that lead individuals to fight only for fitness gain. A contest may gain a fitness-enhancing resource, but it may also incur costs in terms of time, energy, or injury. The greater the fitness value of a resource to an individual, the greater the costs it can incur in a fight while still coming out with a net gain in fitness value in the end.

The classic game that captures contest competition over resources is Hawk–Dove (Maynard Smith 1982a). Hawk–Dove games are described in detail in 2.3 and 9.5.3. Briefly, assuming a symmetrical game (that is, fighting ability or resource holding potential—RHP—is equal; see Parker 1974), if the value of a contested resource is greater than the cost of defending it, the Hawk strategy (fight for the resource) is an ESS. If the cost of defending the resource is greater than the value, there will be no pure ESS, but rather a mixed strategy: to play Hawk with a probability defined by the ratio of value to cost; otherwise play Dove.

Dunbar (1991) has recently suggested that the "war-band" and "peace-band" organization among the Cheyenne (which was widely distributed among North American Indians) is a case of a mixed ESS between Hawk and Dove strategies that may have arisen under the conditions described here. The conditions for a mixed ESS are that the "net payoffs for its constituents be in equilibrium in terms of their frequencies in the population . . . [which] means that the numbers of individuals opting for the two strategies should be inversely proportional to their relative payoffs" (Dunbar 1991:171). In an ingenious reanalysis of data presented by Moore (1990), Dunbar shows that the ratio of males in peace bands to war bands approximates the inverse of the ratio between the respective payoff of joining one or the other band (Dunbar used the mean fertility of each kind of chief as a measure of payoff). Dunbar's suggestion may apply to a number of Hawk–Dove moiety or alternative-strategy organizational phenomena found in middle-range and complex societies, including the knights and monks of Medieval Europe, and the Pakhtun–Saint dichotomy that exists among the Swat Pathans (discussed in section 10.3.3).

Contests are asymmetrical if RHP is not equal. It is often assumed that individuals who already hold a resource have a defensive advantage over the interloper, all other things being equal. In this case, the Bourgeois strategy (play Hawk if you are an owner, Dove if you are a latecomer) may be favored. The Bourgeois strategy becomes an ESS if we assume that players have a .5 probability of being an owner in any given contest (see further discussion in 9.5.3).

Asymmetries in RHP can be an important factor in maintaining social hierarchies. For example, Pettengill, in a microeconomic approach quite similar to the one adopted here, has argued that the sharp drop in peasant income in Europe between 1500 and 1650 A.D. was ultimately due to the "development of the firearm into an effective weapon, which enabled the upper classes to exploit the peasants more harshly (1979:201). The development of firearms brought the cost of force or threat against the peasants so low that the ruling class was able to extract the maximum amount of rents and taxes without fear of resistance and without the exorbitant costs of maintaining large private armies or police forces on retainer.

RHP affects how social groups are structured within and among themselves in a number of other ways. Military and transport technology influence polity building in that they determine how large an area a polity can effectively control, exploit, and defend. More effective weaponry can be a supplement to group size as an aggressive or defensive strategy. Anthony (1986) provides an illustrative account of how the Plains Indian adoption of the horse as a food source, mount, and transport animal on the North American grasslands affected group and territory size and structure. This model (see Figure 10.4) in turn illustrates the general relationship between group size and structure, resource structure, and military and transport technology. The horse allowed an increase in the amount of territory that could be exploited, both directly through warfare and raiding, and indirectly through increases in the distance and amount of goods that could be transported in trade. Horses themselves became a concentrated, divisible, excludable form of wealth, and competition over them resulted in increased social differentiation. Anthony applied this model to the late Neolithic development of nomadic pastoralist groups on the Eastern European steppes.

Contest Competition and Resource Value.   RHP is not the only thing that determines the outcome of contest competition. Blurton Jones (1987b) has presented an analysis of competition and within-group partitioning of resources in which RHP is equal, but *value* of the resource to each of the competitors differs. Like the resource-sharing model outlined in 10.2.2, the model assumes that resource harvests are asynchronized, so that at any given time, there are likely to be differences among individuals in the amount of resource currently held. Under such conditions, if RHP is about equal, then the *value* of the resource to each of the competitors (which may differ, depending upon how much of the resource each one already con-

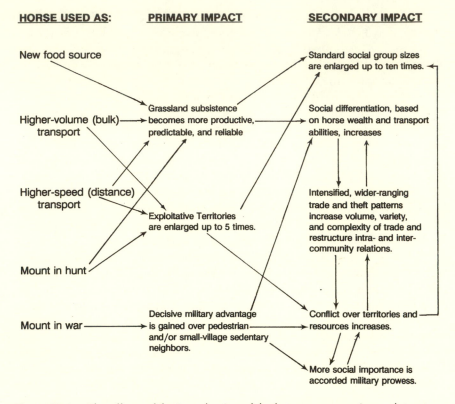

HORSE USED AS: **PRIMARY IMPACT**   **SECONDARY IMPACT**

New food source

Higher-volume (bulk) transport

Higher-speed (distance) transport

Mount in hunt

Mount in war

Grassland subsistence becomes more productive, predictable, and reliable

Exploitative Territories are enlarged up to 5 times.

Decisive military advantage is gained over pedestrian and/or small-village sedentary neighbors.

Standard social group sizes are enlarged up to ten times.

Social differentiation, based on horse wealth and transport abilities, increases

Intensified, wider-ranging trade and theft patterns increase volume, variety, and complexity of trade and restructure intra- and inter-community relations.

Conflict over territories and resources increases.

More social importance is accorded military prowess.

Figure 10.4. The effects of the introduction of the horse on group size and structure and resource structure among the Plains Indians (Anthony 1982).

trols) should determine the outcome of the contest. The one who has the most to gain from either keeping or appropriating the resource should hold out longest and bear greatest costs in the dispute. In such cases, transfer of resources that results is not, properly speaking, exchange or reciprocity, but is more like "scrounging," or what Blurton Jones termed "tolerated theft" (see also section 9.5.4).

Blurton Jones considers a series of fitness functions that specify how valuable a given incremental resource gain will be to an individual in given contest (Figure 10.5). Graph A depicts a linear fitness function in which each incremental gain x of a resource results in an equal gain in fitness y, no matter how much of the resource an individual already possesses. A series of contests over a resource with this kind of utility curve would produce a classic rank order or dominance hierarchy, one based entirely on differences in fighting ability or RHP.

Graph B represents a classic diminishing-returns curve. For an individual

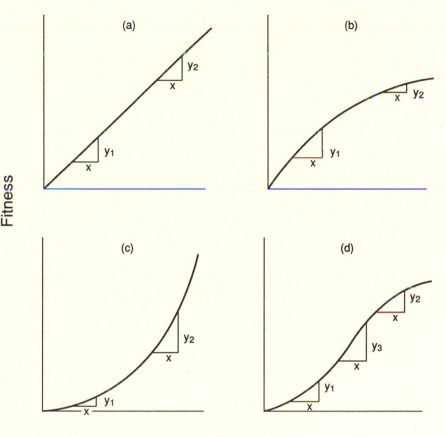

Figure 10.5.   Fitness functions that transform the amount of resource held by an individual into fitness payoffs (after Blurton Jones 1987b).

who already possesses a large quantity of a resource, each incremental resource results in a smaller gain in fitness than it would for an individual currently holding relatively less. This asymmetry in resource *value* means that contests between individuals at different points on the curve would result in everyone ending up with roughly equal amounts of the contested resource. A series of such contests would result in a situation that looks very much like sharing, particularly among a population of foragers, where individuals may return to camp on some days with a big catch (and hence be high up on the curve), and empty-handed (lower on the curve) on others.

   Graph C depicts an *increasing* returns curve: The more of a resource one already controls, the higher the gain in value that results from each incremental gain of the resource. A series of contests among haves and have-nots over resources characterized by this kind of curve would be resolved in favor of the haves. Blurton-Jones suggests that such curves may obtain in productive systems in which there are *economies of scale* (recall section 10.2.3). In fact, it would appear that the increasing-returns curve would primarily be applicable in situations where a controlling individual is reaping the benefits of the efforts of more than one (perhaps many) subordinate individual engaged in production. But it may apply also for some individually utilized resources, for example, a minimal agricultural plot, which if further subdivided, would be insufficient to support two farmers.

Taken to its logical limit, the increasing-returns variant of the tolerated-theft model predicts that a series of contests over such a resource would ultimately result in all of the resource being concentrated in the hands of the individual highest on the curve (that is, highest in terms of resource currently held). In reality, this would probably never happen except among small groups on a relatively temporary basis, because the costs of resource defense, independent of resource value, would eventually increase faster than the gains from resource control. And in the case of despotically organized social groups, a despot who claimed *all* resources would have all the subordinates desert or die.

Nevertheless, cases of societies where an overwhelming proportion of the wealth is concentrated in a small proportion of the populace are familiar, and might profitably be viewed in the light of this model. For example, Garfinkel (1981:120–122), who adopts a view of the development of inequality much like the one outlined here, reports that according to 1969 figures, among 300,000 U.S. corporations, the 500 largest had 60% of sales and 70% of profits, the result of capitalist competition in an economy favoring mass marketing.

Finally, graph D is based on a combination of curves B and C. It seems likely that few, if any, resources realistically continue indefinitely in an upward acceleration in the relationship between harvest rate and value. Hence, there may be an area on the curve where value increases rapidly and then levels off. With regard to the economy-of-scale argument outlined above, returns may level off when further increases in the scale of productivity no longer result in lower production costs per unit; the inflection point at which this leveling off occurs is referred to as the *minimal optimal scale* of a production organization. This may be an interesting way to look at limits to the size of groups engaged in production of some *public good* that is more efficiently produced by a group than by an individual (see further discussion in section 10.4). This curve may prove useful in characterizing the dynamics of resource competition in stratified social groups, particularly in the sense that inflection points in the utility curves may mark boundaries between social strata.

10.3.3. Modeling Equilibrium Group Size
and Structure: A Summary and Case Study

Simple optimization models such as those outlined in section 10.2 offer many insights into conditions determining group size and structure, but it is clear that what constitutes the best strategy for an actor in these contexts depends largely upon what others are doing. It is also evident that group dynamics are closely tied to resource structure and the forms of competition that develop over resources. To capture these aspects of group dynamics, it will ultimately be necessary to shift to game-theoretical orientations.

Hierarchical relations in human social systems result from a series of asymmetric compromises, which ultimately amount to transactions involving the two-way transfer of resources, rights, services, or other benefits. Hence, the addition of individuals to a group *can* result in the lowering of the amount of resources available to a dominant (or dominants). These compromises clearly entail variation in the functional relationship between group size and individual fitness (which, for example, was highly simplified in Vehrencamp's model, reviewed above). The addition of subordinate individuals entails costs to the controllers, and benefits in terms of increasing their competitive ability, through services in defense and production within and between polities. In this sense, subordinates constitute a "resource" for dominants.

One-option or alternative-option *n*-person scrambles may be the most relevant category of game to capture the processes inherent in the formation of human social hierarchies. In a pure scramble, the ESS would be reached when individuals have distributed themselves in relation to resources such that their resource intake or fitness is equal—an ideal free distribution. If resource structure is such that resource distribution is unequal, a despotic distribution results, and ESS is reached under two conditions that could be said to function as homeostatic constraints for each other. First, the number of subordinates tolerated by dominants will reach a maximum, such that if their number increased, the dominants would not further share their resources. Second, the amount of exploitation or bias in access to resources tolerated by subordinates will similarly reach a maximum, such that if it increased, they could do better solitarily or affiliated with alternative groups. The amount of toleration possible would depend ultimately on the fitness value of resources, services, or other benefits that passed between dominants and subordinates.

A clearer view of the range of interactions that are possible is suggested by the matrix in Table 10.2. (I thank E.A. Smith for suggesting this.) This matrix categorizes the possible interactions between individuals involved in asymmetric relations. In hierarchical systems, dominants have a disproportionate share of power and resources, and hence probably gain fitness relative to

Table 10.2. *The Potential Interactions between Dominants and Subordinates in Within-Group Competition*[a]

| | | Dominant | |
		Exploit	Patronize
Subordinate	Steal	Antagonism (−, −)	Benevolent despotism (+, −)
	Serve	Exploitation (−, +)	Mutualism (+, +)

[a]The plus sign indicates that an individual gains from the interaction; a minus sign indicates that he or she loses; the left sign corresponds to the subordinate's gain or loss; the right sign to the dominant's.

subordinates. Some of this fitness gain is exploitative (that is, it reduces subordinate fitness over what it would be if dominants did not exist) and some is mutualistic (both gain through their interaction). Any or all of these interactions may be present side by side in a given social situation. The form interactions eventually take is the result of negotiations between dominants and subordinates, each of whom has his/her own interests, which sometimes conflict and sometimes overlap with the interests of others in the group.

Structurally, this kind of situation has some similarities to Parker's (1984:49–54) parent–offspring conflict game, which he modeled as a one-option *n*-person scramble with two continuous strategies. In Parker's model, the two strategies were parent's investment in offspring and offspring's solicitation of investment from the parent. There are really two scrambles going on here: The parents scramble against other parents to produce the best number of offspring, and the offspring in each family scramble against one another to receive the most investment. Likewise, there are two scrambles going on in the competition model outlined above: The dominants scramble against each other to optimize the number of subordinates, and subordinates scramble to get the most resources controlled by the dominants.

This strategic perspective on competition and group structure introduces two aspects of within-group competition that are relevant at this point. First, competition is *divisive* in the sense that under the right conditions of resource structure (i.e., economic defendability; see section 8.4.3), it will create differentiation on the basis of access to wealth among individuals by "factionalizing a group into rivals vying for support" (Earle 1978:172). Second, resource competition requires *additional energy expenditure* (for example, in the form of costs of defense) beyond that needed strictly for reproduction.

There are at least four ways in which individuals can garner the extra resources required in competition: (1) intensification of individual effort; (2) reciprocal pooling and sharing of resources or effort; (3) enlistment of aid from subordinates either in a mutualistic or exploitative interaction; (4) formation of subgroups, or *coalitions,* of individuals of more or less equal standing within a group, who are set apart from other individuals in the group in the sense that they cooperate in the formation of mutualistic or exploitative relationships with other subgroups in the population (Roberts and Holdren 1972:107–110).

The Swat Pathans: A Case Study of Scramble Competition among Patrons and Clients.   Fredrik Barth's (1965) analysis of political leadership among the Swat Pathans presents a picture of scramble competition within and between groups of patrons and clients very similar to the one outlined above. Barth (see especially his 1967 article) advocated a methodological individualist, cost–benefit approach to social organization based on the allocation of time and resources; his approach even anticipated interactions in strategic contexts between individuals. The main difference between his approach and the one presented here is that Barth's never incorporated an evolutionary dynamic or causal force such as natural selection. Hence, his approach does not explain why humans should engage in optimizing behavior.

The Swat Valley is an area of relatively high agricultural potential sealed in by high mountain ranges on both sides. In the valley bottom, two crops a year (of wheat, barley, rice, maize, and mustard) are grown, watered by irrigation systems that require a high level of capital investment. These lands are highly productive and densely populated. The portion of the valley populated by Pathans is approximately 1250 square miles and populated by 400,000 people (area measurement taken from Barth's map; estimated population is by Barth in 1956), equalling approximately 320 inhabitants per square mile. Further up the slopes from the river channel, crops are dry farmed, produce only one crop a year, and are subject to failure due to drought.

The Swat Valley is divided into 13 territorial subdivisions of 20,000 to 40,000 inhabitants, within which land rights are shared by members of a patrilineal descent group. Within each territory are a number of villages of 500 to 10,000 inhabitants, and each village is divided into two or more wards. The wards are the primary political and administrative units, headed by ward chiefs, who are Yusufzai landholders (Yusufzai are the tribal descendants of the original conquering elite, who arrived in the valley around 1600 A.D.). Wards consist of between 30 and 40 houses occupied by tenant nuclear families who are tied to the landholding chief.

The Pathans are divided into approximately 23 occupational castes, of which only the Pakhtuns and Saints are landholders. Pakhtuns are the descendants of the conquering Yusufzai tribesmen and are known for their competitive, warlike values. The Saints are a hereditary caste of religious leaders who take an essentially nonviolent, or Dove role in land competition and often act as as mediators in land disputes among Pakhtuns. Saints tend to take up landholdings in more marginal areas of the Swat Valley. They apparently undertake conquest only against non-Pathans. The other castes consist of tenant farmers, agricultural laborers, and various craft specialists and service personnel such as barbers, all of whom are tied to Pakhtun or Saint in patron–client relationships. Tenants are tied to their patron chiefs by land tenancy and agricultural labor contracts in which the landholder grants use-rights to agricultural land in return for 60–80% of the crops they produce. Members of the craft castes pay their rent in kind in the form of goods or services. Ideally then, each landholder is the head of an organized production unit including himself, tenants and laborers, a carpenter, a blacksmith, a rope and thong maker, and a muleteer. These individuals are tied together in a complex series of contracts involving patron–client relations between the landholder and all others, land-sharing contracts, contracts between crafts specialists and agriculturalists, and so on.

The basis for political and economic power of the chief is the security of his tenure on his landholdings, which is dependent on his ability to defend his land rights against other competing landholding lineage equals by rallying and maintaining a loyal following, who in the last resort will support him militarily. The size of a chief's following will weigh heavily in a competing chief's decision to push a land claim or some other grievance to a military level.

Maintaining the loyalty of his following depends on the chief's ability to dispense gifts and hospitality, primarily through the institution of the men's house maintained by each chief. Loyalty to a chief is signaled by a male tenant's attendance in the men's house. There the chief provides various forms of hospitality, including meals and tea. A tenant may have a land contract with a chief, but not necessarily be his political supporter. A man may break his tie of loyalty to a landowner by having his servant announce the break at the door of the men's house. Sometimes a chief's following can collapse rather precipitously if his followers get the sense that their chief is losing power, or if another chief in the area is rapidly gaining power.

The source of all wealth (and hence political influence) in Swat is land, and competition over land among chiefs is intense. Land can be gained peacefully through sale, but land is also gained through coercive means, and as reward for political support in a dispute. Powerful landowners will try to encroach on a weaker neighbor by plowing an additional furrow around their holdings during planting, gradually increasing the size of their own plots. There is constant vigilance against this practice. Additionally, since there is no survey or registration of land in Swat, there are many real and fabricated disputing claims over entire plots. In order to make a claim to a tribal assembly or mediator, a land owner needs witnesses and the political support of other powerful landowners. Often, powerful landowners will back the claims of small landowners in return for as much as half the share of the property concerned. In this way, they can increase their own holding and that of their weaker clients. Land is also gained by frightening a weaker landowner into selling his land or by murdering the landowner and occupying his land outright. When a landowner loses his land, so do his loyal tenants. Hence, a conflict over land has the power to rally everyone with interests in a plot of land.

Barth makes the argument that a kind of equilibrium is maintained through competition among political blocs led by the landholding chiefs. Followers are constantly shifting their loyalties to the landholders who offer them the most hospitality and protection, and the chiefs protect themselves and their holdings by maintaining the largest following they possibly can through redistributing the surplus they extract from their tenants. Hence, the competition between landowners (patrons) on one hand, and between followers (clients) for the best deal under a patron, closely parallels the *n*-person scramble with two continuous strategies outlined above in this section. There are two scrambles going on: one between patrons for the best number of followers needed to support their position in conflicts over land, and another among followers to get the best deal in terms of plots of land to sharecrop, provisioning in the form of meals at the men's house, and protection in times of conflict.

This case further illustrates the role of competition over limited and economically defendable resources in fostering the development of despotic group structure, as outlined in section 10.2.3 and earlier in this section. Productive agricultural lands are extremely limited along the Swat River. Competition over these lands among the hereditary landowners is intense and apparently fostered the development of patronage of groups of followers who are needed not only for defense, but in producing the surplus necessary to maintain a following in the first place. Barth's view of an equilibrium between and among blocs is virtually the same one set forth in Vehrencamp's model of equilibrium group structure, discussed above.

10.4. COOPERATION, CONFLICT, AND PUBLIC GOODS

The resource competition model outlined in section 10.3. implicitly assumed competition over what are called *private goods*, that is, goods that are more or less perfectly divisible and excludable. A good is *excludable* if its use can be appropriated by a single individual or subgroup such that it cannot then be used by others. (Excludability is closely related to the idea of defendability, introduced above, but does not necessarily imply that benefits of having access to the good exceed the costs.) *Divisibility* refers to whether a good can be divided among individual consumers without a reduction in total utility. For example, a store of grain can be divided into a series of individual meals; a road or irrigation system cannot be divided into parcels amenable to exclusive access—to a certain extent they must be intact to have any value to their users (although, of course, branches of each can be divided off and still have utility).

Private goods, then, are excludable and divisible among individuals such that "once any part of it has been appropriated by one individual, the same part cannot be simultaneously made available to others" (Taylor and Ward 1982:351). But not all goods that are pertinent to group and individual survival and reproduction are private. Goods that are in some sense either imperfectly excludable or divisible, or both, are termed *public goods,* and any good that is not purely private has some degree of "publicness." In section 10.2.3, I developed the idea of guarding the group against unneeded extra members as a public good, and outlined some game-theoretical approaches to the problem. As it turns out, there are a number of resources, services, and benefits that fall into the public goods category, and they relate to the problem of group formation and structure in a number of interesting ways.

Table 10.3 illustrates the interaction between excludability and divisibility. Goods that are perfectly divisible and perfectly excludable (food and various forms of wealth are good examples) can be considered perfectly private goods. The other three general categories of goods can be all considered public to some degree, although goods that are perfectly indivisible and nonexcludable are probably quite rare. However, defense, particularly in the form of deterrence against outside attacks, is a good example of this form of public good, and is considered in detail in section 10.4.2.

Goods that are divisible but nonexcludable would appear to be associated with scramble competitions and resulting ideal free distributions. Taylor cites bees exploiting a field of flowers as an example (Taylor 1987:6). The flowers and the pollen they hold are divisible, but it is practically impossible to exclude individual bees or bees from a specific hive from a field of flowers. Most kinds of resources that are economically undefendable, either because they are too thinly distributed in space or are unpredictable in time or space, would fall into this category.

Goods that are indivisible but excludable are potentially the most interesting category of public goods with regard to the problems of cooperation and conflict that develop around systems of production. Such goods would include, for example, road systems: A road cannot be completely divided up into short units for exclusive private use, but individuals can be excluded from using it, and hence be made to pay to use it. Large, interconnected irrigation systems and some other kinds of prepared cultivation and har-

Table 10.3. The Possible Combinations of Excludability and Divisibility of Goods

	Excludable	Nonexcludable
Divisible	Private goods, contest competition (food, wealth)	Partially public, scramble competition (dispersed, undefendable resources)
Nondivisible	Partially public (public works, production with economies of scale)	Purely public goods (defense/deterrence)

vesting systems can also fall under this category, as would many kinds of productive systems in which there are economies of scale. As I will argue, these kinds of public goods are particularly susceptible to exploitation by special-interest groups (indeed they may be financed by such interest groups, characterized as political entrepreneurs in section 10.2.3), and hence are important in the analysis of the development of social inequality.

10.4.1. Defense as Public Good

Organized defense against outside attackers is a good example of a public good that is relatively indivisible and nonexcludable: It benefits everyone who is a part of the group, cannot normally be apportioned or hoarded, and once in place it is not excludable. This is especially true of the deterrence aspect of group defense: If the group is safe from attack because of organized defense, *everyone* in the group is safe.

Cooperation in the production and maintenance of a public good such as defense raises some distinct issues in the problem of group formation and maintenance. First, as implied above, a group member can benefit from the good regardless of whether he or she contributes anything to its maintenance (i.e., the problem of free riding). Further, the costs of not maintaining the public good can be very high indeed. In the joiner-exclusion model developed in section 10.2.3., the worse that could happen if members failed to uphold the public good and exclude joiners beyond optimal group size was that everyone would experience a reduced harvest rate. If the group got too large, it would simply begin to dissolve. In the defense case, failure to maintain the public good could very well result in the entire group being routed, enslaved, or massacred. At the same time, the costs of contributing to the "war effort" are high; there is the risk of death or injury in fighting, and at the very least, there is a high expenditure of time, resources, and lost opportunities (although some individuals may benefit greatly from participation in warfare). It is a game with very high stakes.

Maring Ritual and Defense Alliance Formation. One important case study illustrating defense as a public goods problem is James Peoples's (1982) reinterpretation of Rappaport's (1968) analysis of Maring ritual. Peoples argues that the ritual regulating the onset of Maring warfare arose and persisted as means by which a local group compensates its allies for their assistance in warfare. These compensations allow a local group to retain its allies and perhaps attract new ones, thus increasing its chances of military success (Peoples 1982:295).

In order to succeed in the hostilities with its enemies, a local group must establish and maintain alliances with members of other local groups lest it be defeated by the enemy, aided by its own allies. However, it is difficult to maintain support of allies during prolonged fighting because the allies are less enthusiastic about defending other groups' lands than their own. Victory often goes to the local group that can keep its allies in the struggle longest.

Ideally, military assistance of allies is reciprocated in kind and no additional compensation should be required. This would indeed be the case if (1) mutual aid were reciprocated on a group-to-group basis, and (2) every individual gave about the same amount of assistance. However, groups are not of equal size, and in any case requests for help are from one individual to another. Hence there is individual variation within allied groups in the amount of assistance rendered and in relation to its costs.

Perfect group-to-group reciprocity works only if any behavior advantageous to the group is also equally advantageous to each individual member. Clearly all members have a common interest in the defense of their land. But since the accumulation of pigs and valuables is costly and since (unless groups are very small) any particular individual's contribution will have little effect on the outcome—that is, even if an individual does not share equally the costs of recruiting allies, he or she will still receive the benefits of military assistance—it seems likely that individual selection or rational choice will favor individuals who will free ride (minimize personal payment while enjoying the benefit of security). If everyone calculated his or her costs similarly, a group would be unable to maintain allies and would go extinct even though all its members could be said to be acting rationally and in their own interests. Under this scenario, the amount of military assistance a local group receives is likely to be less than optimal for its survival.

Peoples argues for at least three mechanisms that counter the tendency of individuals to avoid the costs of reciprocation: (1) due to the network of intermarriage, individuals from various groups are likely to be closely related, and egoism may be counteracted by kin selection effects; (2) individuals may gain private rewards (even though defense is a public good) for compensating their allies in the form of prestige gained through open generosity and access to exchange networks in resources and valuables not locally available; and (3) there are sanctions against individuals who shirk their duty, in the form of accusations of witchcraft. Individuals who are wealthy in pigs and valuables but who are not generous seem to end up as suspected sorcerers, and suffer higher mortality in warfare and homicide. The last two mechanisms, Peoples argues, violate self-interest—they raise the same "second-order" collective action problems discussed earlier (10.2.2)—but could arise through group selection at the cultural level.

In truth, the defense problem posed by Peoples implies a different payoff structure than the Prisoner's Dilemma he seems to assume. In section 10.2.4, I outlined the distinction between Prisoner's Dilemma and the game of Chicken. Chicken implies a payoff structure in which the per capita benefits of the public good are greater than the per capita costs of doing whatever is necessary to maintain it. If the public good in question can be maintained by one person alone, the collective-action problem could be modeled using a simple game of Chicken: After several iterations of the game, someone would eventually pay the costs of maintaining the public good.

In the Maring defense problem, however, it is clear that the efforts of just one person would not be sufficient to ensure the defense of the group: The efforts of many (but not necessarily all) individuals are necessary in keeping up the war effort. Taylor and Ward (1982) have outlined a game called the Assurance game to model this kind of collective-action problem. The game has two variants. In its simple dyadic (2-person) form, if neither individual through his or her efforts alone can maintain any of the public good, the game is called the First Variant of the Assurance game. If one individual can through his or her efforts alone maintain at least some of the public good, it is called the Second Variant.

A n-person version of the First Variant would seem most applicable to the Maring defense problem. Some proportion of the group can provide sufficient contributions to the group defense, but as group size increases, eventually enough people are contributing to the defense effort to allow some individuals to contribute nothing, or free ride. But at the same time, too much free riding would result in the failure of the defense system. Hence, the Assurance game can revert to a Prisoner's Dilemma–like game when group size is large.

10.4.2. Complex Agrarian Production Systems as Public Goods

Taylor and Ward (1982) use irrigation works as an example of a public goods problem. Two cultivators have the option of cooperating in building and maintaining dykes and ditches for an irrigation system. If one or both of them do not contribute the necessary work, both their crops will fail, and they will starve. If either one of them can do all the work necessary alone, one of them will eventually do it, because if neither of them does it, the payoffs to each are lower than if one of them does it. This interaction, then, resembles a game of Chicken. If neither of them can do any of the work alone, it becomes a First Variant of the Assurance game. If each can do *some* of the work alone (as in the example of weeding a cultivated plot), it becomes a Second Variant game.

Large complex irrigation systems can be built and maintained on a more or less egalitarian basis by a cooperative of self-interested cultivators if the payoff to individual cultivators is high, the whole system cannot be maintained by one person, and the alternatives to irrigation are insufficiently productive (Earle 1978:39–41 has made a similar point and cites examples of such systems). But there are free-rider problems to be solved in such cases.

In any such production system, the required per capita input of effort decreases with the size of the work force. Eventually, for an indivisible or "lumpy" good, the required labor input for any particular individual will dwindle to insignificance, and problems of free riding will appear. Hence, even cooperative situations with Chicken- or Assurance-like payoff structures may eventually revert to Prisoner's Dilemma. At the same time, too much free riding will result in the failure of cooperation altogether, and/or the failure of the production system. The mechanisms by which cooperation continues in the face these problems would appear to be a fundamental issue in understanding the development and persistence of complex societies.

It is also worth pointing out that while the maintenance of a complex production system, such as irrigation, is a public good, the crops produced by it, once they are harvested and stored, are by definition private (they are divisible and excludable). Depending upon the structure of the system, this may be true of the water that flows through it as well. Hence, the potential for political conflict and the opportunities for political entrepreneurship in irrigation systems (as well as other kinds of productive systems requiring cooperative effort) are great.

Earle (1978) and Hunt and Hunt (1978) in particular have cited (1) defense of the system against raiding from outside groups; (2) settlement of disputes over water; and (3) the allocation of water in systems where water is scarce. In some of the cases cited by Earle, the chief or sheik was responsible for organizing defense of cultivated lands against outside raiders, but had little or nothing to do with managing the irrigation system itself. In Hunt and Hunt's analysis of traditional irrigation systems in Mexico, individuals involved in water allocation and the settlement of disputes over water were almost always members of the elite and were deeply embedded in politics dealing with other areas of society as well. In these cases, conflict and the benefits of some kind of organized and predictable response present political opportunities for leaders (who could be termed political entrepreneurs) to step in and ultimately control and exploit the system.

It remains to be said that because complex production systems involving cooperative effort are often more efficient in the production of resources, they allow population to grow above the level that would be possible in an organizationally simpler, less labor-intensive system. Once the population has grown to the higher level made possible by a complex production system, the individuals maintaining it may not be able to revert to a simpler system without experiencing political conflict over the resulting lower production levels and/or mortality due to starvation. This situation is similar in its effects to environmental or social circumscription, in that it limits the options available to individuals participating in the production system. It is this kind of circumscription that contributes to the often remarked upon ratchetlike nature of sociopolitical development.

10.4.3. Elite Competition, Intensification of Production, and Public Works: Complex Chiefdoms in the Hawaiian Islands

The colonization and political development of Polynesia, particularly of the Hawaiian Islands, constitutes one of the clearest examples of pristine development of statelike political structures from groups of relatively egalitarian beginnings that exists in the literature. There is a rich body of ethnographic, ethnohistorical, and archaeological evidence to illustrate this development, summarized in such recent works as Earle (1978), Hommon (1986), and Kirch (1984). Below, I present a brief summary of the main arguments regarding sociopolitical development in the Hawaiian Islands to illustrate some of the key ideas developed in this chapter. Of particular interest is the relationship between increasing population density and packing of habitable land, the development of competition between paramount chiefs, and their role in instigating public works to finance the maintenance and expansion of their role as corporate territorial group leaders.

The Hawaiian Islands were first colonized sometime between 1 and 400 A.D., apparently by populations from the Marquesas Islands some 3900 km distant (Kirch 1984). Hommon (1986) divides the colonization and sociopolitical development of the Hawaiian Islands into three stages, or phases. In phase 1 (500–1400 A.D.), following the initial colonization of the islands by small groups of colonists, the population grew at a rate in which it doubled about every 107 years, reaching a population of about 14,000 by 1350, or approximately 1/16 the size it would attain by the time of western contact in 1788. During this initial period, the population was distributed sparsely and discontinuously in small settlements along the coasts of all the major islands (p. 60), subsisting on marine resources and agricultural production that could be undertaken in the coastal zones. Separating areas of settlement were "buffer zones" comprising arid zones, mountain chains, lava flows and other areas of low productivity. According to radiocarbon data from excavated sites, the inland regions of the islands were virtually devoid of permanent settlement during this period.

Social organization of settlements during this period was characterized by lineage-based corporate groups in the form of conical clans, which Hommon terms "archaic maka'ainana." In later periods, maka'ainana referred only to the commoner class. Conical clans are largely endogamous, bilateral, or ambilateral lineage groups ranked by the principle of seniority and genealogical distance from the senior, or primary line. The highest rank at any particular node in the political structure was inherited by the eldest son. Through the growth, segmentation, and fissioning of secondary, or cadet, lineages, lineage groups proliferate, disperse, and colonize new lands until an island or island group is fully colonized.

Settlement patterns and population growth rates appear to have changed radically around AD 1400 (the beginning of Phase II, 1400–1600), when the habitable coastal areas were apparently filled up and the inland regions of the islands began to be colonized. It is during this period that the first clear evidence of a separate chiefly class (the ali'i) appears. Settlement of these inland areas required the implantation of intensive agricultural techniques such as the construction of irrigation systems and pond fields. These intensification projects appear to have been instigated and financed by chiefs, and overseen by their field managers, called konohiki.

While internal colonization may have been stimulated by increasing population density on the coastal margins, intensification and expansion of productive zones in turn allowed even more rapid population expansion of Hawaiian populations, and between approximately 1350 and the time of Western contact in 1788, the population of the archipelago grew from an estimated 14,000 to about 225,000. By 1600 (the beginning of Phase III, 1600 to contact), even the arid regions of the islands were being colonized and dry-farmed. Settlement expansion into the arid areas, which were characterized by much greater interannual fluctuations in rainfall, meant that agricultural production in these areas was much more subject to failure. Hommon (1986) argues localized failures in these newly developed arid zones fueled conflicts between territorial groups.

Social organization apparently changed in several ways during the period of colonization of the interior zones. First, local groups were no longer organized entirely on the basis of kinship. Instead, stratification began to develop in which local groups were divided into an elite class (ali'i) still organized on the basis of kinship in the form of conical clans, and a commoner class (*maka'ainana*), in which extended kin groups had broken down to the point where they were now more accurately characterized as bilateral kindreds. Second, territorial organization of the islands changed from scattered coastal settlement zones separated by "buffer zones" to a series of pie-slice–like land divisions called *ahuapa'a*, which stretched from forested mountainous interior zones, across lower valleys where intensive agricultural systems were maintained, to coastal zones where marine resources were exploited. Hence, ideally, each *ahuapa'a* encompassed a full range of Hawaiian ecozones from which different kinds of resources could be exploited.

Under this new social–territorial organization, the commoner class, which comprised the primary producers, was subject to the *ali'i*, which was composed of the paramount chiefs. Inheritance of high offices among the *ali'i* retained the pattern inherent in the earlier conical clan system, but because leadership could pass either through the male or female line, there was always potential for conflict among would-be leaders (Earle 1978). In the final stages of Hawaiian political development, succession to paramountcy came to depend much less on inheritance and more on a particular individual's ability to rally armed support, eliminate his rivals through armed conflict, and conquer new lands (Earle 1978:172). Such competition was financed by *capital investment*, which required the use of the surplus labor of the commoners to effect intensification of local production. Surplus produce was then used to reward and feed retainers (including corvee labor groups and warriors), make shows of generosity to lesser nobles and commoners, and finance warfare.

The Hawaiian case has many similarities with the Swat example discussed in section 10.3.3. Proliferation of lineage-based corporate groups eventually led to the filling up of the most productive coastal areas, and the colonization of less-productive interior zones. As competition intensified, group structure became increasingly characterized by a series of patron–client– like relationships between the *ali'i* class and the commoners. But in Swat, centralized and territorially extensive political organization did not develop until the twentieth century, as a result of more global political factors, whereas by the time of European contact in 1788, Hawaii was approaching a statelike political system.

Two main factors seem to have prevented the Hawaiian social system from maintaining the kind of fluid, shifting competitive equilibrium that existed between and among the Pakhtun chiefs and their followers. First, agricultural production in the interior zones of the Hawaiian Islands necessitated considerable cooperative effort to initiate and maintain. These public works were instigated and financed through capital investment by the chiefs largely for the purpose of financing warfare with competing chiefs and their constituents. The "public" nature of these production systems fostered the cohesion of much larger groups of commoner-producers. Second, the character of the resources produced in these systems, as well as the high risk of failure in the more marginal zones, apparently necessitated the control of extensive areas that encompassed a variety of ecological zones (hence the development of the pie-shaped *ahuapa'a* territories). Thus competition between chiefs in the Hawaiian case ultimately resulted in much more politically centralized, demographically larger, and territorially more extensive polities.

10.5. CONCLUSION

Western social scientific thought about the origins of complex political systems has, generally speaking, fallen into two traditions distinguished principally by their fundamental unit of analysis, and by the kinds of questions they ask about origins. The oldest tradition, with its origins in the Renaissance and the Enlightenment, begins with the individual and asks how government can arise from individual self-interest. What is the nature of government as collective action? What is the nature of the individuals that comprise it? What are the terms under which governmental institutions arise? Are they voluntary, coercive, mutually beneficial, exploitative? These were the issues raised by Hobbes, Rousseau, Locke, Hume, and many other political theorists during the Enlightenment. Over the past two or three decades, there has been something of a renaissance in this tradition brought about by political theorists employing methodological individualism, rational-choice theory, and game theory (Hampton 1986; Sugden 1986; Taylor 1987 are some recent examples). Within this tradition, the question of why complex political systems developed where they did, when they did (and just as importantly, where they did not and why), has never been a very important one.

Working out of a somewhat different and more recent tradition, anthropologists, especially cultural evolutionists, have been very much concerned with explaining variability in the timing, location, and ecological circumstances surrounding the formation of "the state," "civilizations," and other complex sociopolitical systems (good summaries of this work are found in Flannery (1972), Wright (1978), and Brumfiel (1983). A vast amount of comparative data has been amassed, and a number of (often) competing "macro" theories attempting to explain variability in political development have been offered, many of which approximate some, even a large, measure of truth. But while the social philosophers of the Enlightenment and the political scientists of today are less concerned about variability in the timing, the form, and the location of early state formation, anthropologists have been somewhat cavalier in their assumptions about the character of individual behaviors that would be capable of producing higher-level social structure.

In sections 10.2 through 10.4, I have been concerned with outlining and making explicit the assumptions involved in explaining how and why social groups form out of individual choices and how and why they are structured the way they are. I have proceeded from the basic position that groups form out of individual self-interest, and that group dynamics arise from the option each individual has to remain in a group, operate alone, or affiliate with another group (section 10.2). But there are many circumstances, particularly those related to intense competition within and between groups, under which alternative options are severely limited, and under those conditions individuals will remain in a particular group even under severe disadvantage. Here lie the conditions for the development of inequality (section 10.3). How group structure develops under conditions of competition is highly dependent upon the structure of resources exploited by the group, including the structure of systems of production. I have summarized what appear to be the most important aspects of resource production structure under two categories: (1) resource defendability and the related issue of marginal utility (section 10.3), and (2) the public or private nature of goods produced through collective action (10.4). In this chapter, I have only been able to scratch the surface of the complex and subtle relationships between the various aspects of resource structure and the dynamics of competition within and between groups; but I hope to have shown that a closer investigation of these relationships using ideas from evolutionary ecology and rational-choice theory promises to bring us closer to the goal of explaining and predicting the size and structure of human social groups.

ACKNOWLEDGMENTS

I thank Eric Smith for his close readings and extensive comments on several earlier drafts of this chapter. Thanks also to Hillard Kaplan, Jane Lancaster, Robert Santley, Michael Taylor, and Bruce Winterhalder for reading and commenting on earlier drafts.

Reproductive Decisions

Monique Borgerhoff Mulder

11

In 1838 at the age of 29, Charles Darwin was contemplating marriage. His thoughts survive on a scrap of paper (Macfarlane 1986), an unusually candid statement of a common dilemma.

This Is The Question

Marry
Children—constant companion, who will feel interested in one (a friend in old age)—object to be beloved and played with— better than a dog anyhow— someone to take care of house— unthinkable to think of spending one's whole life, like a neuter bee, working—nice soft wife on a sofa with good fire.

Not Marry
Conversation of clever men at clubs—Not forced to visit relatives—the expense and anxiety of children—perhaps quarrelling—terrible loss of time—cannot read in the Evenings—fatness and idleness— less money for books—if many children forced to gain one's bread.

11.1. INTRODUCTION

11.1.1. The Problem

When to mate and to start breeding? How many children to produce? How much care and solicitude to be given to each, and over how long a period? With whom to mate, and whether to remain faithful to that partner? When to terminate reproduction entirely? Not only Darwin, but men and women all over the world face these decisions, and their solutions generate the fascinating diversity in patterns of marriage and kinship that lie at the heart of anthropological research. This chapter examines some of the principles that guide reproductive decision-making.

11.1.2. The Role of Natural and Sexual
Selection in Shaping Life History

Fisher (1958) first called attention to how natural selection might adjust the allocation of an organism's limited resources between growth and maintenance (collectively somatic effort) and reproduction (reproductive effort). Resources allocated to reproduction can be subdivided (Alexander and Borgia 1979) into parental effort (the provisioning and rearing of off-spring) and mating effort (the pursuit of mating opportunities). These patterns of allocation differ among individuals, both within and between species, and are called an individual's life history. Characteristics that shape these patterns of allocation, such as longevity and number of reproductive bouts during a lifetime, are termed life history traits.

Since Fisher's time, and particularly since the 1960s, there has been a massive growth in studies that examine how different patterns of allocation are adapted to the socioecological conditions an individual can expect to experience in its lifespan. There are two areas that are of particular relevance to human reproductive decision-making: the offspring quantity/quality dilemma (11.2) that grew, in part, from the literature on clutch size, and the mate/invest dilemma (11.3—11.5) that developed within sexual selection theory. By focusing on these and other concepts derived from animal studies, this chapter explores how evolutionary ecology can frame analyses of some of the diverse reproductive decisions referred to in this chapter's epigram.

11.1.3. Outline

Reproductive decisions are shaped by both natural and sexual selection, and are therefore influenced by the specific demography, ecology, and social organization of a population. In humans, the study of reproductive decisions inevitably leads us into a web of complexities traditionally tackled by such different disciplines as ecology, evolution, demography, economics, and sociology or anthropology. In order to introduce useful analytical principles for future studies we focus initially on simple models. In the following section (11.2) we consider the offspring quality/quantity dilemma, specifically with respect to an optimal birth interval model. This provides a good example of how far simple models can take us. It also raises broader issues of interest to demographers and reproductive ecologists, the solution to which will require different models.

The evolutionary ecology of mating systems is an even more complex topic, again entailing an articulation of life history theory with sexual selection theory. We consider how models developed in the study of nonhu-

mans (11.3) can be used to determine the effects of resource monopolization (11.4) and parental care (11.5) on patterns of marriage and mating.

11.2. DECISIONS ABOUT REPRODUCTION AND PARENTAL CARE

11.2.1. Optimal Life Histories and Concept of Trade-Offs

Trade-offs have to be made when two traits are limited by a resource,
such as time or energy, that can only be spent once (the "principle of
allocation"; Levins 1968). In considering life history decisions a multitude
of potential life history trade-offs can be subsumed under two major categories (Lessels 1991): (a) current versus future reproduction; (b) offspring
quantity versus quality.

The Cost of Reproduction. Reproduction can be both costly in terms of
energy and dangerous in terms of survival, since both future fecundity
(Williams 1966b) and subsequent survivorship (Bell and Koufopanou 1986)
may be negatively affected by the allocation of resources to reproduction.
These are the costs of reproduction.

Fisher (1958) defined reproductive value (RV) as the number of offspring
an individual of a given age can expect to produce in the remaining years of
its life multipled by the probability of surviving each of those years. RV (or
expected fitness) at age x (Williams 1966b) is given by

$$RV_x = \sum_{y=x}^{\infty} (l_y/l_x)\, m_y e^{-r(y-x+1)} \tag{11.1}$$

where x is age; l_y and l_x are the probabilities of survival to ages y and x,
respectively; m_y is the number of daughters produced by a female at age y
(Fisher's Malthusian parameter measuring the rate of increase of a genotype); e is the base of the natural logarithms; and r is the instantaneous
rate of increase per individual. The equation is a summation of three
components: the probability of a female surviving between ages x and y, her
fecundity at age y, and $e^{-r(y-x+1)}$; this latter term incorporates the effects of
expanding or shrinking populations on various reproductive schedules by
weighting the value of offspring according to how far in the future they are
produced.

By partitioning reproductive value at any given moment into current (m_x)
and future components (*residual* reproductive value RRV; Williams 1966b)

$$RV_x = m_x e^{-r} + \sum_{y=x}^{\infty} (l_y/l_x)\, m_y e^{-r(y-x+1)} \tag{11.2}$$

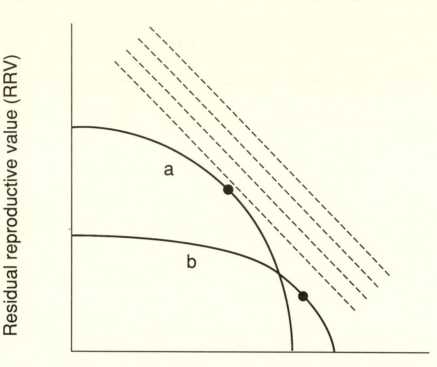

Fecundity at age x (m_x)

Figure 11.1. Trade-offs between current reproductive expenditure and parent's expectation of future offspring. Two hypothetical curves represent the trade-off between current reproductive effort (measured as fecundity at age x, m_x) and residual reproductive value (RRV), as defined in text. Dashed lines represent a family of straight lines corresponding to the equal lifetime production of offspring through both current and future reproduction; the slopes are negative because of the negative association between current and future reproduction, and are at 45° because in a stable population immediate progeny and offspring in the more distant future are of equivalent value in perpetuating an organism's genes. The point of intersection with the line of equal lifetime production of offspring (dots) marks the optimal expenditure of reproductive effort that maximizes reproductive value and lifetime production of offspring. After Pianka and Parker (1975).

it becomes possible to assess the effects on overall fitness of various schedules of reproductive effort. Models of parental care (see Figure 11.1) assume that parental expenditure in current offspring increases the reproductive value of the current offspring at the expense of the parent's subsequent reproductive success (RRV) measured *after* investment in the current brood is complete; retention of resources for future reproduction, by contrast, lowers the reproductive value of the current offspring but increases the parent's RRV. For example, a gazelle that has opted for current reproduction loses valuable time—that could have been spent feeding—scanning the environment for predators on her newborn fawn; any resulting reduction in her nutritional status might diminish her future reproductive success, while a decision to spend more time feeding might reduce her fawn's survival and hence reproductive value.

Pianka and Parker's (1975) model can be used to determine optimal levels of expenditure in reproduction, which are likely to vary between individuals, according to age and environmental conditions. For example, as an individual ages, the depicted trade-off between current reproductive effort and future reproductive success might change from curve (a) to curve (b) (see Figure 11.1). Curve (a) represents a high cost of reproduction at an early age; an example of this in humans is the impaired growth of poorly nourished teens who become pregnant (Fleming et al. 1985).

In this section we have seen how different options (e.g., "produce a child now" versus "continue to work and save") must be evaluated in terms of their consequences on overall lifetime reproductive success. Darwin faced just such a trade-off when he deliberated the fact that if he started a family he would have less time and money to pursue his passion for natural history; but with declining health and encroaching age would anyone want to marry him, even if he became an eminent professional?

The Quantity/Quality Trade-Off. If an individual does opt for current reproduction, how many offspring should he or she produce? As more offspring are produced the amount of investment that can be given to each necessarily declines such that offspring survival will be negatively affected by the number produced (Figure 11.2a). Only in circumstances where offspring survivorship decreases exponentially with respect to the number of offspring produced (e.g., 100% from a clutch of 10, 50% from a clutch of 20, 33% from one of 30) will parental fitness be independent of numbers of offspring produced.

Clearly whether the relationship is exponential or less steep (the latter situation is depicted in Figure 11.2a) will depend on the nature of parental care and the potential for sibling cooperation. For example, if the main component of parental care is providing food, we would expect a strong negative decrease in offspring survivorship with increasing numbers of offspring produced; this is because there will be less food available for each offspring. However, if the main component of parental care is protection (say from predators), there are less likely to be survivorship costs to offspring born into large families; this is particularly likely if siblings cooperate in scanning the environment for predators (for discussion of depreciability in parental care, see section 11.5.1).

Considering variable clutch sizes in birds, Lack (1947) proposed that where offspring mortality does not increase exponentially with clutch size,

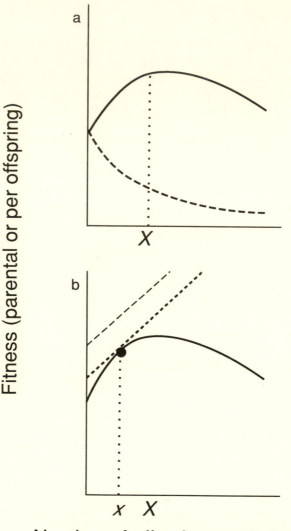

Figure 11.2. *Models predicting the optimal numbers of offspring to produce. (a) Offspring fitness and parental fitness plotted as a function of the number of offspring produced (or clutch size), assuming a fixed total reproductive effort. Offspring fitness (dashed line) is shown to decrease with clutch size, whereas parental fitness (solid line) peaks at an intermediate optimal clutch size (X). In this example, offspring fitness does not increase exponentially with clutch size; were this so, parental fitness would be independent of clutch size (after Pianka and Parker 1975). (b) Parental fitness (solid line) is shown as in (a). If parental mortality (long dashes) increases with the number of offspring produced because of the costs of reproduction, the optimal number of offspring produced (dot) maximizes the difference between gains through reproduction and losses through adult mortality. The optimal number of offspring produced is found where a line (short dashes) parallel to the parental mortality line is a tangent to the parental fitness curve. It is lower (X − x) than the optimal clutch size shown in (a) (after Charnov and Krebs 1974).*

production of an intermediate number of offspring yields the greatest number of survivors; he also proposed that as a result of natural selection on clutch size variability the *commonest* clutch size would be the one that was most productive (Figure 11.2a), a somewhat problematic assertion (11.2.3).

The Allocation of Reproductive Effort. While these two trade-offs are conceptually separate, in practice both must be considered in the analysis of reproductive allocation (Williams 1966b). For example, experimental manipulations in birds show that the mean clutch size is often lower than the most productive brood size. However, if the costs of reproduction increase as the number of offspring produced increases, clutches smaller than the most productive brood size maximize lifetime fitness (Figure 11.2b). The links between these two trade-offs are likely to be important in humans, despite the fact that generally single young are produced; this is because the allocation of reproductive effort is not limited to a single season (as it is in most birds), and parents may have to care simultaneously for a number of dependent young.

Optimality models can be used to identify the selection pressures (or critical constraints) operating on decisions over how many offspring a female should produce and at what interval. Because of its detail and heuristic value, we focus here on Blurton Jones and Sibly's (1978) optimal birth spacing model (11.2.2). Then we examine some issues raised that are important for the study of human life history trade-offs, relating to phenotypic correlations, exclusion of the costs of reproduction, comparative questions, and future directions (11.2.3).

11.2.2. Birth Spacing as a Life History Trait

The Optimal Birth Interval Model. In testing life history models we need to assess what factors affect the shape of the curves in Figure 11.2a. Length of the interval between the birth of one child and a subsequent birth seems like a good candidate, insofar as it is an indicator of the amount of care invested in the first, in particular, of the amount of time this child is breastfed. Furthermore, extensive evidence from human populations that offspring survivorship is poor when births are closely spaced (Knodel 1978; Hobcraft et al.1983) indicates that parental care in these first years of life enhances offspring survival. Consequently mothers face a trade-off between producing a large number of closely spaced offspring with low survival chances (low RV) and a smaller number of widely spaced offspring with higher survival probabilities (high RV).

Blurton Jones and Sibly (1978) investigated such trade-offs among the Central Kalahari !Kung, where the mean birth interval of 4 years had previously been attributed to the strain on mothers who must carry their young children on daylong foraging trips, camp moves, and visiting trips, often in the heat of the day (Lee 1979). First they determined the mortality consequences of birth interval variations, describing a curvilinear relationship between length of interval and the probability of an offspring surviving. Then, by calculating the weight of plant food needed to fulfill the mother's contribution to her children's daily caloric requirements, and adding to this the average weight of the children to be carried, simulations were used to describe the association between different interbirth intervals and the backloads that result from such spacing; these simulations were based on the observed frequency with which children of different ages are carried by !Kung women on foraging trips. The results showed that backloads increase sharply for birth intervals shorter than 4 years, and then level off.

But are mothers spacing their offspring in such a way as to maximize their lifetime reproductive output? To test this Blurton Jones (1986) used the optimality logic implicit in Lack's proposition (11.2.1): The best number of offspring to produce is that which yields the highest number of surviving offspring. Using the curvilinear function of offspring mortality on interbirth interval (described above), he could determine which interval (if repeated throughout a reproductive career of a constant length) leaves the greatest number of surviving offspring. This *expected* distribution is then matched to the *observed* distribution of birth intervals in the population. The results (Figure 11.3) show a striking parallel between predicted and observed interbirth intervals. They suggest that !Kung women, by spacing their offspring at 4-year intervals, maximize the number of offspring surviving to 10 years (the age beyond which mortality is very low in this population).

Subsequent analyses offer additional support for the model (Blurton Jones 1987a). First, the survival of children of first birth intervals is less strongly influenced by the length of the interval than that of children of later intervals; this is presumably because mothers do not have to carry food for elder children and are in a better position to carry and care for two toddlers. Second, there is no significant relationship between birth interval and mortality among !Kung settled at cattle posts, women who are under very different constraints with respect to foraging and travel (Lee 1979).

There are three strengths to Blurton Jones's model. First, it is deductive, predicting an optimal value that can be tested against empirical data. Second, because of its deductive structure, it can be used to test the importance of different factors in contributing to a "failed" birth interval, that is, one in which one or both of the children die. Thus total backload (with food and toddler) is a better predictor of failure than toddler weight alone, both of which are better than simply the length of the birth interval. Third, the model can be applied in different human populations in order to determine the importance of such parameters as foraging practices, the contributions of others to subsistence, and the availability of alternative caretakers, in shaping different birth interval optima. For example, when

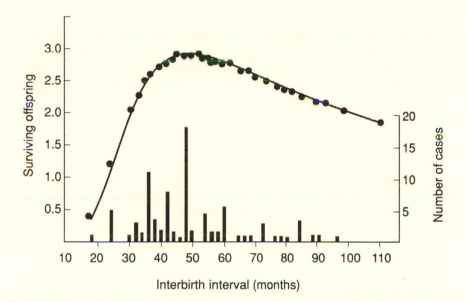

Figure 11.3. Modeling and testing optimal interbirth intervals in the !Kung. The number of surviving offspring to mothers spacing their births at any specific interval can be calculated as [(reproductive lifespan/interbirth interval) × probability of survival if born at that interval], and is shown by dots connected by a hand-drawn curve. The optimal birth interval, calculated in this way, is 50 months. The observed frequency distribution of interbirth intervals, shown by the vertical bars, has a mean value of 55 months and a modal and median value of 48 months (based on 96 intervals for 65 women (after Blurton Jones 1986).

compared to the !Kung, the high total fertility (and presumably shorter birth intervals) of the savanna-living Hadza of Tanzania may reflect the shorter foraging trips of Hadza women and the greater self-sufficiency of their children, both of which probably result from ecological differences (Blurton Jones et al. 1989).

11.2.3. Issues Raised by the Model

Phenotypic Correlations.   Most studies of the evolution of life history traits use phenotypic correlations to determine the shape of trade-offs between different patterns of expenditure; for example, the values of each of two traits are plotted against one another for a sample of individuals. These curves are then used to determine optima. This is also the approach used by Blurton Jones, although he focuses on two traits associated with birth intervals (length and offspring survivorship) rather than individuals.

Such trade-offs should be measured for individuals who do not differ in terms of their resources, their environments, or any other traits (subsequently termed their "condition"). If individuals differ in condition, we may find unexpected patterns. For example, returning to the birth interval study, women who space their births most closely might also be those who are able to raise the *highest* number of surviving offspring; perhaps they live near good sources of food and water, have a relative who helps carry the children, or are so strong and healthy that the quality of care they provide their children is not compromised by carrying heavy backloads in the hot sun. Such positive correlations tell us nothing about life history trade-offs. They may even obscure the fact that the optimal solution to the quantity/ quality dilemma can differ for women according to their condition. Indeed, some women might maximize the number of their surviving offspring by spacing widely whereas others, in better condition, could attain a different optimum by spacing more closely (for alternative strategies, see section 11.5.4).

Blurton Jones (1986) is aware of this problem; it plagues all field and even many experimental studies (Lessels 1991). Consequently he limited his analysis to !Kung women whose reproductive years were spent predominantly in the bush; other extrinsic sources of variation among women actually render Blurton Jones's particular test conservative (reduce the likelihood of empirical data matching the optimum). Nevertheless the abundance of intervals shorter than the median value of 48 months (Figure 11.3) suggests there may be some heterogeneity among women: In other words, some women can "get away with" shorter intervals, due perhaps to environmental, phenotypic, or genetic differences. Future investigations could examine whether there is anything particular about the women who contribute to the unusually short (and long) intervals. Furthermore, a more systematic analysis of how birth intervals vary over the lifespan could be explored in relation to age-specific changes in reproductive value.

Reproductive Costs.   The optimal birth interval model focuses only on the offspring quantity/quality trade-off. It does not incorporate the longer-term effects of short interbirth intervals on either the survivorship, subsequent fertility, or age of last reproduction of a mother. Indeed, women who space their births closely may suffer a precipitated decline in maternal condition ("maternal depletion"; Jelliffe and Maddocks 1964), assuming all else is equal (as discussed above).

Because of this exclusion of reproductive costs, Blurton Jones's model predicts *only* the optimal birth interval; it makes no prediction about optimal completed fertility, nor the optimal mix of fertility and mortality. Hence Pennington and Harpending's (1988) failure to find a trade-off (negative correlation) between completed fertility (total number of live births) and offspring mortality in a slightly different sample of !Kung women does not

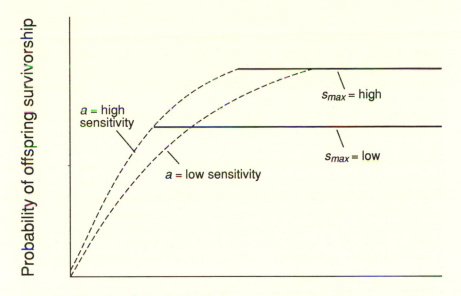

Parental care interval

Figure 11.4.   Environmental effects on offspring mortality. The probability of off-spring survival increases as the period of parental care is extended. The function a denotes the sensitivity of offspring survival to parental care. At s_{max}, the maximum probability of survival in a given environment, parental care no longer enhances this probability. The different curves depict high and low values for s_{max} and a (dotted line) (after Pennington and Harpending 1988).

necessarily contradict Blurton Jones's conclusions. The reason for this is as follows: If there are phenotypic differences (see above) that enable some women to have shorter birth intervals *and* reproduce for longer than others, we would not expect to find a negative relationship between offspring mortality and completed fertility; a positive association between these two life history parameters is particularly likely if women in good health can space children closely without prejudicing the survival of these children, or without precipitating rapid maternal depletion.

Comparative Issues.   The potential value of optimality models in deter-mining the critical factors influencing reproductive schedules has already been reviewed (11.2.1, 11.2.2). With respect to the study of birth intervals, new directions can be taken.

A central idea within life history theory is that the *strength of the effects* of parental care on offspring survival is an important factor influencing repro-ductive schedules (e.g., Schaffer 1974; Hirshfield and Tinkle 1975). Pennington and Harpending (1988) pursue this in the context of human demography. They propose that to explain variability in parental strategies we need to consider two parameters (Figure 11.4). The function a is the sensitivity of offspring survival to parental care. We can think of this as describing how much an increase in the time or energy invested in feeding, defending, or minding a child improves the child's probability of survival. In Figure 11.4 this investment is measured in terms of the interval following the birth of a child (a useful measure that, as discussed above, probably approximates the number of months a child is breastfed). The positive effects of breastfeeding on child survival decrease as the child ages, and this leveling-off in the function probably occurs earlier in populations where high-quality weaning foods are available than in those without such foods.

The second parameter is the impact of care-independent sources of mortality. s_{max} denotes the maximum probability of survival in any given environment and can be thought of as the risk of mortality to which a child is exposed *irrespective* of the amount of care it receives from its parents. s_{max} will vary between populations (see again Figure 11.4) according to, for example, the prevalence of diseases against the fatal effects of which parents can do nothing to protect their children. Pennington and Harpending (1988) note that parental care "saturates" where a reaches the value of s_{max}; at this point a parent cannot increase its fitness by investing further or prolonging the birth interval.

If we think of parental care primarily in terms of the duration of the birth interval, some interesting predictions arise from the model, which might well affect variability in life history parameters across populations. First, if s_{max} (care-independent mortality) is held constant, increased sensitivity of offspring survival to parental care should *shorten* the interbirth interval, that is, s_{max} is reached earlier (Figure 11.4). Second, if a is held constant, in populations where care-independent mortality is low (s_{max} is high) birth intervals should be *longer* than where s_{max} is low. The nonintuitive message from this second prediction is that in many Third World environments where we think of parental care as critical to offspring survival, care may be curtailed and interbirth intervals short, simply because s_{max} is so low (see also Daly and Wilson 1978).

How far can birth interval models explain differences in fertility between populations? There are still many problems and inadequacies with the models discussed above insofar as neither fully explores the costs of reproduction. Pennington and Harpending examine parental care solely in terms of strategies that maximize offspring survival. Blurton Jones extends this focus by determining the trade-off between offspring survivorship and the time remaining for subsequent births. Neither offers a full examination of how RRV (as defined in Section 11.2.1) is affected by current reproduction.

Second, there are clearly reproductive costs that extend beyond the ensuing birth interval. Indeed it is most unlikely that high s_{max} and high a in industrial nations can by themselves account for our comparatively low levels of fertility. And what about variable levels of fertility in horticultural, pastoral, and other more complex agrarian societies? For these questions we need to consider not only the association between offspring survivorship and the interbirth interval, but the broader costs (and possible benefits) of children. This is a growing topic in demography (e.g., Caldwell 1982), and can be tackled from varying perspectives. Particularly interesting areas include: (a) the nature of the costs of parental care (for example, Is it depreciable? Is it compatible with other activities? and Can it be shared with a partner? Section 11.5); (b) the length of the dependency period, and the extent to which these might overlap with one another, as investigated for the London Quakers (Landers 1990); (c) the potential for children to "repay" some of their costs, particularly if this occurs during the reproductive years (Turke 1988); (d) the trade-off between conserving wealth for future offspring and providing large gifts for current offspring (Rogers 1990a; see also section 12.5.1).

Mechanisms and New Directions. What mechanisms might be responsible for the apparently adaptive variations in interbirth intervals among the !Kung? Suckling frequency seems unlikely, as there is no indication that maternal nutrition or work load reduces either the quantity or quality of her milk (Prentice 1980), such that infants of stressed mothers might increase their suckling attempts, frequency, or duration. More generally, an evolutionary perspective that incorporates parent/offspring conflict (Trivers 1974) would require birth spacing mechanisms that respond to cues other than the baby's behavior: Because long interbirth intervals benefit the baby more than the parent, babies would be selected to exaggerate suckling demands. For mothers to break out of this evolutionary arms race, return to ovulation should be stimulated by their *own* condition as well as that of their infant (Blurton Jones 1987a). Independent effects of nutrition, stress, energy balance, and exercise would therefore be expected on purely theoretical grounds. An evolutionary approach to such questions is opening up a new field of reproductive ecology (Ellison 1991), which attempts to determine what environmental, developmental, and intrinsic factors might affect a woman's probability of conceiving and successfully bringing a fetus to parturition, within the context of her overall life history.

11.3. VARIABILITY IN MATING SYSTEMS

Animal studies make it clear that variability in mating systems is the outcome of adaptive adjustments of males and females to the specifics of their social and ecological environments, as well as to variations in individual capabilities. To this end reproductive decisions concerning mating and parental behavior have been examined in socioecological context, focusing on both parametric and strategic (cf. Chapter 2) aspects of the environment, through the use of optimality and game-theoretic analyses. Despite an extensive literature on human reproductive strategies (reviewed in Betzig 1988a), there is as yet no comprehensive understanding of the evolutionary ecology of human mating systems. After a summary review of major factors affecting nonhuman breeding systems (11.3.2) we consider the importance of resource monopolization (11.4) and parental, particularly paternal, care (11.5) in human systems of marriage and mating.

11.3.1. Mating System Classification:
Criteria and Caveats

Mating systems can be classified on many criteria, perhaps the most salient of which are the number of mates an individual takes (either sequentially or concurrently), the duration and exclusivity of the pair bond, and the relative impact of inter- and intrasexual selection in contributing to mating arrangements.

Nonhuman mating systems have been categorized as monogamous, polygynous, polyandrous (or polygynandrous), or promiscuous, according to the different configurations of the criteria noted above (mate number, pair bond duration and exclusivity, and the relative impact of inter- and intrasexual selection). As with most classificatory labels for behavioral patterns, each type contains many variants: Polygyny, for example, may be serial or concurrent; it may or may not be associated with high within-bond fidelity, as revealed by DNA fingerprinting; furthermore it may result from male–male competition or from female choice, or some combination of the two. Such diversity often renders functional explanations for a particular mating system type contrived, as demonstrated by Searcy and Yasukawa's (1989) analysis of all the different factors that can contribute to avian polygyny.

Anthropologists classify human mating systems using similar categories, usually relying not on observed or presumed patterns of mating but on marriage rules and practices. Increasingly they too appreciate how a term such as polygyny may obscure a variety of marriage systems driven by very different dynamics (White 1988). Indeed the term *marriage* itself proves to be almost undefinable for rigorous cross-cultural analysis (Needham 1975); partners who are "married" may be linked by any combination of sexual, economic, political, or ritual obligations to one another, and with widely diverse expectations as concerns the stability and exclusivity of the relationship. These intriguing aspects of the diversity of marital arrangements in the cross-cultural record have not yet been seriously investigated in an evolutionary ecological framework.

11.3.2. Nonhuman Models for Polygyny

Variability in mating systems is generally explained in terms of sex differences in the provision of parental care. Trivers's (1972) proposal that the sex investing less care will compete over mating opportunities provides a convincing explanation for why polygyny is so common in mammals (where due to gestation and lactation females are high obligate investors). Indeed in about 95% of all mammalian species some males monopolize more than one breeding female. This is usually achieved through intense levels of mating competition, which may take the form of scrambles or contests (see Chapters 10 and 12); here males control females and defend them against other males ("females-defense polygyny"; Emlen and Oring 1977), or monopolize resource-rich sites that attract aggregations of females ("resource-defense polygyny"; Emlen and Oring 1977). The former strategy is favored when females aggregate independently, the latter when there are patchily distributed and defendable resources. The exceptions (monogamy) occur where the male can play a significant role in increasing the rate at which his partner produces surviving offspring (Kleiman 1977, evidence reviewed in Clutton-Brock 1989), where paternity certainty is high, and where the opportunities for additional matings are low (section 11.5).

In birds polygyny is much rarer, presumably because males can brood eggs and feed nestlings just as effectively as can females. It usually arises through resource defense: Males monopolize females indirectly through the control of scarce resources that are critical to female breeding success, such as food or nest sites (Wittenberger 1976). Where males contribute little or nothing to direct parental care (such as feeding of nestlings), polygyny results simply from female preferences to settle on territories where resources are most plentiful (resource-defense polygyny). Females may even benefit from polygyny if aggregation or cooperation enhances their access to resources or protection from predators (Altmann et al. 1977).

In so far as males *do* contribute to parental care (either directly or indirectly), polygyny becomes potentially costly to females because they must share parental resources with others; the relationship between these costs and harem size will depend on the extent to which the invested resources are "depreciable," that is, that the total benefits of any invested resource cannot be gained by more than one offspring (11.5.1). For this situation, a more precise trade-off model was developed based on female interests and assuming free choice—the so-called polygyny threshold model (Verner and Willson 1966; Orians 1969). These authors proposed that female choice for males with high-quality resources may contribute to the evolution of polygyny, if the differences in quality between resources held by males are great enough that females raise as many or more offspring by mating with already-paired males on superior territories than with bachelors on inferior territories (Figure 11.5). This trade-off could take several forms. Either a female simply maximizes resource accesses by choosing the male who has most resources on offer, taking into consideration the number of females with whom she will have to share these resources; or she trades a reduction in direct paternal care (such as feeding rate) for access to the better territory. Functionally either form of this trade-off leads to an ideal free distribution (Fretwell 1972; see also section 8.3.2) if females are entirely unconstrained in their choices of mates.

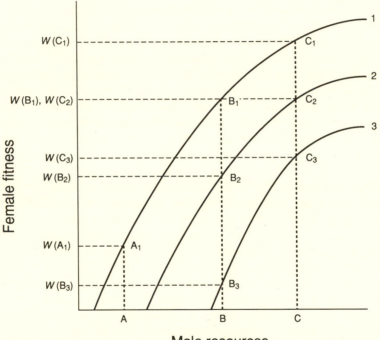

Figure 11.5. The polygyny threshold model. Curves 1, 2, and 3 represent hypothetical fitness values of females (mated monogamously or with 1 or 2 cowives, respectively), as a function of the amount of resources controlled by males. Male resources vary from low (A) to high (C). $W(X_n)$ is the expected fitness of a female with $n - 1$ cowives mated to male X, where X denotes a male controlling a particular amount of resources. The horizontal distance between two fitness functions (e.g., $C_2 - B_1$) is termed the polygyny threshold, i.e., the minimum difference in male-controlled resources sufficient to favor female choice of polygynous mating (after Orians 1969). The interests of males and females will conflict. Consider male B's preference versus that of the fourth arriving female: B prefers a second mate, because $2W(B_2) > W(B_1)$, whereas the female prefers to become the third mate of C, since $W(C_3) > W(B_2)$. B would not want a third mate, however, since $3W(B_3) < 2W(B_2)$. In general, males will prefer to add the nth mate as long as $nW(X_n) > (n - 1)W(X_{n-1})$, while the nth female will prefer to mate with X only if $nW(X_n)$ exceeds the fitness she can get from mating any available male.

An important aspect of the relationship between polygyny and male parental care is seen in many species of fish, where males commonly guard a territory and protect eggs or fry from predation. As noted by Gross and Sargent (1985), because male fishes defend sites that females visit to mate and lay their eggs, the *mating* costs to providing parental care are very small; indeed, the presence of eggs makes a male *more* attractive to additional females, perhaps because it indicates successful protection from predation.

In sum, nonhuman studies reveal certain conditions under which polygyny may evolve as a breeding system (see also Chapter 5 re nonhuman primates). The relative importance of different explanations varies between orders. In birds the ability of males to monopolize resources, irrespective of their actual role in providing parental care, appears to be important. This resource-defense model has received much attention in the human literature and is examined in section 11.4. In mammals, focus has fallen primarily on the importance of paternal care to juvenile survival in inhibiting polygyny. In fish, emphasis has been on the absence of a mating cost to paternal care; this has been little examined in the human literature. These latter issues are explored in section 11.5.

11.4. RESOURCE MONOPOLIZATION AND MATE NUMBER

Both within- and between-population comparisons have been used to assess the relationship between male monopolization of resources and polygyny. We turn first to the evidence from within-population comparisons, then to broader social and ecological explanations for variability in mate number between societies.

11.4.1. Within-Population Comparisons

Extensive qualitative and some quantitative (e.g., Grossbard 1976) evidence of a correlation between differential resource control by men and the number of wives that they marry suggests that nonhuman models for polygyny may be of relevance to human mating systems (Irons 1979a, 1983). Such correlations between male resource holding power (RHP) and mate number (see also section 12.5) have been replicated in many historical and contemporary populations (reviewed in Betzig 1988a), using a variety of measures of RHP such as land, livestock, capital, and status. These studies suggest that resource-defense polygyny does occur in humans. A number of alternative interpretations for these correlations, for example, that high resource ownership among polygynous men is a *consequence* of their wives' and children's economic productivity, can to some extent be excluded; this can be done through restricting analyses to young men with children too young to work (Borgerhoff Mulder 1987, 1989b; Cronk 1991); in addition, longitudinal data can be used to determine whether, over time, wealth is a better predictor of polygyny or vice versa (Irons 1980).

Correlations between levels of polygyny and hunting success (Aché; Kaplan and Hill 1985a), chiefly rank (Ifaluk, Turke and Betzig 1985), headmanship, and personal violence (Yanomamö; Chagnon 1979, 1988) can also be assessed in relation to nonhuman models for polygyny (Flinn and Low 1987). In some cases, the reproductive advantage of high status may operate through resource access; for example, on the Micronesian atoll of Ifaluk, men of chiefly rank can appropriate the fish caught by commoners (Betzig 1988b). In other cases it is argued that material wealth differences among men are not responsible for polygyny; thus Chagnon (1979) proposes that in the rich and homogeneous Yanomamo environment (where game and cultivable land are plentiful) men differ not in their access to wealth, but rather in their *utilization* of it, insofar as some men can use their broad kinship networks to exploit the productive labor of others. This kind of differentiation among men with respect to their control of others' labor is probably a very common form of RHP in human populations (cf. "wealth in people"; Bledsoe 1980). The Yanomamo case also demonstrates how men differ in their ability to accumulate wives through violence (Chagnon 1988), and presumably in protection of wives against harassment.

Few of the studies of the relationship between resource monopolization and mating system consider the role of female choice in contributing to polygyny. However among the Kipsigis, agropastoralists of Kenya, there are some indications that women distribute themselves according to the ideal free distribution depicted in the polygyny threshold model (11.3.2). In the traditional communities studied, only men have the right to own farms. A longitudinal analysis of a group of pioneers' accumulation of wives during a period of territorial expansion in midcentury shows that men offering greater breeding opportunities were preferred over men offering lesser breeding opportunities, with breeding opportunity measured as the land available for an incoming wife to settle on (Table 11.1). Thus of the 3 and 5 pioneers with farms in Abosi in 1932 and 1933, respectively, the men (A and B) offering the largest breeding opportunity got married. In 1934 the man (C) offering the second largest breeding opportunity was married, and so forth. Results of a Cox stepwise regression show independent effects of 2 covariates on a man's probability of marrying in any particular year: Men offering larger breeding opportunities were preferred over those offering smaller opportunities, and men were more likely to be chosen if married to fewer wives (Borgerhoff Mulder 1990). The fact that women chose men on the basis of the resources available to an incoming wife rather than according to the total size of a man's farm (a covariate that did not reach statistical significance in the multivariate model) suggests the potential importance of female choice *versus* male competition in this population.

Table 11.1. Marriages (N = 29) in a Community of Kipsigis Pioneers

Year of marriage	Pioneer	Breeding opportunity (in acres)[a]	Size of plot pioneer settled	Pioneers currently settled to choose from	Rank of breeding or opportunity selected	Above below median rank[b]
1932	A	40	160	3	1	+
1933	B	300	300	5	1	+
1934	C	100	100	5	2	+
1935	B	150	300	6	1	+
1936	D	33	100	7	4	
—	E	30	30	7	6	−
—	F	16.7	50	7	7	−
1938	C	50	100	9	2	+
1939	G	120	120	11	1	+
1939	H	30	60	11	6	
1941	G	60	120	12	2	+
—	I	23.3	70	12	8	−
1943	B	100	300	15	2	+
—	J	180	180	15	1	+
1944	B	75	300	17	2	+
1945	G	40	120	18	3	+
—	K	10.7	32	18	16	−
—	L	20	40	18	10.5	−
1946	B	60	300	20	2	+
—	D	25	100	20	8	+
—	M	20	40	20	10	+
—	N	18	36	20	12	−
1947	J	90	180	22	1	+
1948	O	37.5	150	22	3	+
—	P	30	60	22	5.5	+
—	E	15	30	22	12	−
1949	B	50	300	25	2	+
—	Q	29	29	25	8	+
—	R	10	20	25	17	−

[a] [Total farm size/number of wives (+1)], reflecting the number of acres available to an incoming wife, given the approximately equal distribution of land among cowives.
[b] Sign text X = 2.16, n = 27 (2 tied observations), P = .05; for report of multivariate statistics, see text.

In short, nonhuman models for polygyny have directed us to some important correlates of mating systems. Monopolization of the material resources on which women depend for reproduction may drive polygyny in some societies at some points in their history, but many other routes to polygyny are possible, such as the monopolization of labor or the use of force. Ideal free models may be appropriate in circumstances where the resources critical to female reproduction are defensible and limited, where there are no alternative means to economic support for women, and where female choice is possible. But many problems remain. First, no studies have looked at how the proportion of investment in reproduction varies by wealth. We know wealthier men have higher reproductive success, but do they allocate higher or lower percentages of their resources to fitness, and what alternative investments do they make? In short, how does wealth affect life history decisions? Second, what features of the natural and social environment permit resource monopolization, and how can they be measured? Hypotheses proposed for the between-population variability in mating systems provide some clues.

11.4.2. Between-Population Comparisons

Broader social, ecological, and institutional explanations for variations in mate number between populations are listed in Table 11.2.

Social and Economic Hierarchies. Hypothesis 1 follows directly from the observation that differences in RHP, status, and skill are associated with mate number within societies. It predicts that polygyny will be most prevalent in populations in which the differences in wealth and power among men are most extreme.

Betzig (1986) finds a strong correlation between degree of social hierarchy and maximum harem size, indicating the importance of wealth and status on the outcome of mate competition. However, there are two problems with this hypothesis. First it fails to account for other samples that show a curvilinear relationship between social complexity and polygyny (see hypothesis 5 below), in which monogamy characterizes both egalitarian *and* the most hierarchical of societies. Second, recent and more finely controlled analysis shows that social stratification has no effects on polygyny (White and Burton 1988). Both these difficulties suggest that we need to look in more detail at the nature of the resource base, the type of competition that occurs between males, and aspects of the ecology and political economy that might affect both; some hypotheses below explore these issues further. Finally, it is important to note that factors like RHP that are important in determining mate number differentials within some populations may hold less explanatory power across a diverse array of societies.

Environmental and Political Fluctuations. Environmental and political fluctuations contribute to high levels of polygyny, because such conditions generate the differences among men in wealth or status that permit some men to monopolize wives. While Dickemann (1979, hypothesis 2) is primarily concerned with instability contingent on political and economic processes, Low (1990, hypothesis 3) aims at determining an ecological basis to differences in mate number.

Table 11.2. Ecological and Social Factors Generating Variability
   in Mate Number

Hypothesis	Supported[a]	Source
1. Monopolization of power and wealth: Where resources can be monopolized, men successful in acquiring resources (culturally successful men) can also monopolize mates	Yes	Irons 1979a; Betzig 1986
2. Environmental/political fluctuation: Unpredictable fluctuations such as famine, war, and revolution generate sharp social hierarchies, leading to hypergyny and polygyny	U	Dickemann 1979
3. Environmental extremeness and uncertainty: Polygyny will occur in environments with rainfall levels that are seasonal and unpredictable, because of increased variability in male competitive ability	Yes	Low 1990
4. Geopolitical conscription: Where the costs to an individual of leaving a socially defined unit are greater than those of staying intense differentials in mate number will be tolerated	U	Betzig 1986
5. Socially imposed monogamy: Because of the risks of armed insurrection in stratified modern societies, high-ranking men forgo multiple marriages in order to maintain group solidarity and enhance intergroup competitive ability	U	Alexander et al. 1979
6. Low carrying capacity environments: Restricted resource base limits the marriage chances of sons, leading to polyandry	Yes	Crook and Crook 1988

[a]U, untested.

Low uses Colwell's indices (see also section 8.1.1) to measure the predictability of rainfall. She finds that polygyny (as measured by the proportions of men and women married polygynously) decreases with the constancy of rainfall over the year and increases with seasonality (contingency). This intriguing result is difficult to interpret insofar as it is probably confounded by subsistence type, with which polygyny is correlated (White and Burton 1988). The impact of environmental variability on human behavior will necessarily depend on the sophistication of technology (technology buffers us from the environment), such that analyses of environmental uncertainty *within* subsistence types will have much greater explanatory power than environmental uncertainty across all societies. Thus, among African farmers and pastoralists, extremes of rainfall affect the dynamics of polygynous households, with cowives being less autonomous in areas with low rainfall (Hakansson 1989); in addition, bridewealth payments are lower (Turton 1980).

Using grosser ecological categories than Low, White and Burton (1988) find that societies where more than 20% of men are married polygynously are commonest in high-quality and spatially homogenous habitats; this they attribute to the need for both plentiful resources to support a large family and new land on which to settle additional wives; polygyny is therefore seen as part of an expansionist strategy in rich environments.

To reconcile these findings with those of Low it becomes important to distinguish different kinds of polygyny. White and Burton differentiate between different types of polygyny previously lumped by other authors. They show that "class-based polygyny" and "polygyny for leaders" are most commonly found in spatially heterogeneous habitats. It is conceivable that male variance in reproductive success is actually greater in these latter types of polygynous societies than in "general polygyny" societies, where number of wives is highly age dependent and most men get two wives by the time they are elders. If so, heterogeneous environmental conditions would contribute to marked variance in male reproductive success, consistent with Emlen and Oring's original formulaton (11.3.2). These speculative conclusions suggest future directions for ecologically oriented research on mating systems.

Other Hypotheses and Review.   Hypothesis 4 is an expansion of Carneiro's theory for the origin of the state. Betzig (1986) utilizes Vehrencamp's (1983) notion of bias (see also section 10.2.3) to suggest that lower-ranking or powerless individuals might be willing to concede to lifelong bachelorhood if the costs of leaving the group are greater than the costs of remaining a subordinate. Given the predominant asymmetries in practically all polygynous societies, this explanation seems plausible. Unfortunately White and Burton's data show that residence on small islands has a strong negative effect on the frequency of polygyny; if island residence inhibits emigration, these findings counter Betzig's hypothesis. Clearly carefully controlled multivariate empirical work is needed.

More generally as regards each of the foregoing hypotheses, the problem arises of how to determine the monopolizability of resources. In principle we could use measures of the extent to which resources are clumped in space and predictable over time, using the three-dimensional spectral analyses models discussed by Cashdan (Chapter 8). In practice it is hard to know a priori what aspects of the environment should be so categorized, and at what scale. Clearly the significance of different resource distributions will depend on technology. Even more importantly, it is probably not generally valid to assume that the distribution of most human populations with respect to resources is "ideal free" (see also section 8.3.2) insofar as individuals are usually not of equal competitive ability. Rogers's discussion of how resource distributions might ideally be described (see section 12.4.1) highlights the dearth of empirical documentation of these dynamics in the anthropological literature. For societies in which there is differential ownership and control of material wealth or political office, a more tractable approach in the future might be to focus on three dimensions: variability in resource holding among individuals in the population, stability in resource ownership over the lifetime, and stability between generations. The heuristic value of this approach is that it obviates the need to measure the distributions of natural resources that have often already been aggregated for use and defense by humans.

Hypothesis 5 has not as yet been tested but raises interesting questions with respect to the provision of collective goods. It argues that high-ranking individuals forgo reproductive advantages in return for retaining the loyalty and labor of the less powerful members of society, services that enable high-ranking individuals to remain dominant in an autonomous group. However, it is not clear whether this restraint is advantageous to the individual dominants, the dominant class, or to the whole population, and hence whether a potential for cheating might destabilize such "socially imposed" monogamous systems (see also section 10.2.3).

Polyandry (hypothesis 6) has been little studied. Crook and Crook (1988) provide a qualitative test of their hypothesis that cooperative fraternal polyandry in the Himalayas is an adaptation to resource shortage by comparing rates of polyandry before and after alternative economic opportunities become available for younger sons. They find that where off-farm sources of income and subsistence are more accessible, polyandrous marriage is rare. One problem with this hypothesis is that many populations depend on highly restricted resources, and yet polyandry is not common.

The conditions contributing to other forms of polyandry, such as wife sharing in many African societies and sequential monogamy by means of which women obtain the support of a number of different males over their lifetime, have yet to be investigated on a systematic basis. As in the nonhuman literature, it seems unlikely that a unitary explanation for polyandrous systems will emerge (Clutton-Brock 1991).

11.5. PARENTAL CARE AND MATING SYSTEMS

The costs and benefits to the two sexes of providing parental care are important determinants of mating systems. The theory here is well formulated. Maynard Smith (1977) recognized that when one parent cares for the young the benefits of providing care are likely to be *reduced* for the second parent. Biparental care is likely to evolve only when the benefits of additional care are extremely high, or the costs extremely low. Insofar as the optimal investment pattern of males will depend on how females respond to desertion (and vice versa), game theory models become appropriate analytical tools.

In the simplest formulation of Maynard Smith's model, equilibrium parental expenditure depends both on the function of offspring survivorship in relation to number of parents providing care and on the mating opportunities (and associated fitness consequences thereof) for the deserting sex. In this sense it is a trade-off model parallel to those used in life history studies (11.2.1). The model can be rendered more complex (and realistic) by considering differences in the effects of maternal and paternal care, by exploring how the strategy of an individual is affected by its partner (Lazarus 1989), and by examining how mates respond to *variation* in each other's parental behavior (Chase 1980; 11.5.5).

Maynard Smith's model is clearly relevant to analyses of the wide variability in mate number, pair bond stability, and parental roles across human societies (e.g., Irons 1979b). Given the basic sexual asymmetries in mammalian reproduction (11.3.2) we can most usefully focus on the male dilemma of whether to invest time and energy in obtaining copulations (mating effort) or increasing the survivorship of their offspring (parental effort). Resources invested in growth and survivorship (somatic effort) can be viewed as contributing to both mating and parental effort, and therefore excluded from the model. In the simplest terms, we need only specify the relative fitness function of investing a given amount of time or energy in mating or parental care: When an additional unit of paternal care yields a lower fitness return than would an equal investment in obtaining copulations, males would be expected to seek matings rather than continue to invest in their offspring; conversely, expenditure should be in parental care where the payoff exceeds that of an identical expenditure in mating.

In order to identify the important demographic, sociological, and ecological factors that might affect these functions, we address three important questions: What are the costs (11.5.1), benefits (11.5.2), and opportunity costs (11.5.3) of parental care to either sex? In reality, answers to these questions will vary on a case-by-case basis within populations (depending on a man's age, reproductive value, the viability of his children, and other things, such that it may be useful to look at alternative strategies; 11.5.4).

Similarly, we expect individuals to vary their expenditure on parental care in response to increases or decreases in the care offered by their mates, leading to stable or unstable equilibria (11.5.5). We discuss these issues primarily from the male perspective, referring to studies of trade-offs for females where these are relevant.

11.5.1. The Costs of Parental Care

Parental care will be favored in either sex where its fitness costs are low, but how do we determine these costs? While parental expenditure can easily be measured (e.g., feeding rates in birds, duration of egg fanning periods in fish, and measures of proximity to infants in mammals), the cost of such variability in time/energy expenditure to subsequent survival and reproduction is rarely known (Clutton-Brock 1991). Conclusions concerning how sex differences in the fitness costs of parental expenditure might influence mating patterns are therefore speculative.

It is nevertheless possible to make some qualitative observations on how the costs of care might be affected by social and ecological factors. On the gross assumption that many productive activities undertaken by adult males and females within the household constitute parental investment (which may well be problematic) we can use data on the sexual division of labor to give some indication of the different parental roles of men and women and how they might vary between populations. Women are necessarily responsible for childbearing, usually for nursing, and commonly for child carrying, child care, cooking, grain grinding, fuel collection, water carrying, gathering, and cultivation. Men usually take primary responsibility for defense, trade, herding, fishing, household maintenance, politics, and ritual duties (Murdock 1965).

How do these activities differ in their fitness costs? Hunting and defense are likely to impose high survivorship costs; for example, Irwin (1989) interprets the positive association between male mortality and latitude among different Arctic foragers as reflecting the danger of hunting. Similarly childbearing, lactation, child care, and secondary food processing are likely to impose metabolic costs that depress subsequent survivorship and fertility, as suggested in comparative studies of birth intervals in desert and savanna habitats (see section 11.2.2). We as yet have no good measures of how parental expenditure affects rates of subsequent fertility and mortality for each sex in any population. There are nevertheless some interesting dimensions along which sex differences in parental care between different populations might be compared, to which we now turn.

Alternative Sources of Parental Care.   How might the decision of whether or not to care for a child be affected by the availability of alternative caretakers? We need first to address the extent to which men's and women's parental roles are unique and nonsubstitutable by the nondeserting sex. We need then to assess whether other individuals in the population might contribute parental effort toward the raising of nondescendants.

As regards the first question, there has been no empirical investigation of how different marriage patterns are influenced by overlap between the sexes in the provision of parental care. One evolutionary ecological prediction would be that high levels of divorce and promiscuity are more common where the economic roles of women and men are similar, hence more easily substitutable. The theoretical issue of the conflict of interests between care-givers in such circumstances is discussed in section 11.5.5.

On the second question, studies of women's time allocation suggest that the fitness costs of reproduction may be reduced when women can rely on alternative caretakers and/or subsistence providers for support during the late stages of pregnancy and during lactation. An extreme case of this is the employment of wet nurses (Hrdy 1992); by delegating lactation women can resume cycling within a few months of parturition. However, there are other mechanisms whereby women can reduce the fitness costs of reproduction. Hames (1988a), for example, attributes the reduced work of nursing women among the horticultural Venezuelan Ye'kwana to the help they receive from female kin with garden labor. Aché women of Paraguay also reduce the amount of time they spend foraging during lactation (Hurtado et al. 1985), and lactating Tanzanian Hadza women appear to lower their foraging efficiency compared to nonlactating women (Hawkes et al. 1989). Conversely, among Nepalese Tamang cultivators, lactating women do not reduce their work load in the season of heaviest work (Panter-Brick 1989); in the extremely seasonal Nepalese environment there may be times of year when no women have any time to help others.

The extent to which men's parental roles are substitutable by others, and the conditions under which others might be cajoled into providing investment, are unknown. In patrilineal patrilocal societies where agnates assist one another with defense and subsistence and where even postreproductive widows and their offspring are inherited by the deceased's brothers, there are high levels of polygyny (White and Burton 1988); this may suggest that the costs of paternal care are low where men can elicit the support of their kin. In populations with neolocal residence rules and where nuclear families constitute independent economic units, paternal investment may be less easily substitutable.

Both these dimensions of the substitutability of parental care could be explored with cross-cultural data. We might, for example, predict that where women receive help in provisioning their offspring during lactation, men can withhold investment and thereby avoid its associated fitness costs. Such dynamics are most likely where male and female provisioning roles overlap significantly, as in some horticultural societies.

Depreciability. Another important dimension of parental care is its depreciability. With "nondepreciable" care (Altmann et al. 1977) such as nest defense, the benefits to offspring of a given amount of care do not decline with increasing brood size; with "depreciable" care, such as food provisioning, the benefits of a given amount of care *do* decline as brood size increases. While most types of care will fall between these two ideal types, the parent who provides nondepreciable care suffers fewer costs as the number of dependent offspring increases than does the parent providing care that is more depreciable.

Can we say that females specialize in care that is more depreciable than that provided by males? Clearly this is true for pregnancy, lactation, and (to some extent) child care in the younger years; effort devoted to the gestation and carrying of a child does not benefit other children. As regards secondary food processing, cultivation, hunting, herding, and household maintenance, the question is more complicated, requiring data on economies of scale that are not available on a comparative basis. Effort expended in politics, ritual, and other activities securing allies and status for the family as a whole is largely nondepreciable. In populations where this constitutes an important component of male parental care we might speculate that parental care is less costly for males than females (see also Low 1988). Clearly empirical research could be directed to such questions.

11.5.2. Benefits of Parental Care

Mortality Patterns. Building on one component of Maynard Smith's model, Harpending and Draper (1986) propose that stable pair bonds in human societies will be most common in circumstances where fathers have a strong effect on the survival of their offspring. Conversely, high divorce rates will be favored where the presence of fathers in households has negligible effects on offspring survivorship.

The sex-specific benefits of parental care can to some extent be investigated by looking at a child's chances of survival if its mother or father dies or deserts. For single fathers the chances of raising offspring are often (e.g., Aché; Hill and Kaplan 1988) but not necessarily (e.g., !Kung; Pennington and Harpending 1988) low. For single mothers the chances of raising offspring are in some populations considerably lower than those of women with coresident husbands (e.g., !Kung, Pennington and Harpending 1988; and seventeenth- to early nineteenth-century European data; Voland 1988); in other populations there is no effect (e.g., Hiwi; Hurtado and Hill 1992). The links between these patterns and environmental factors that influence risks of starvation and disease in different populations have not yet been examined on a broad comparative basis, nor have the socioecological factors favoring biparental care.

Correlations between offspring mortality and parental absence may over-estimate the true benefits of parental care if desertion is precipitated by a spouse who is a poor provider of care or by an offspring who is inviable, or if desertion and/or parental mortality are exacerbated in poor conditions. Furthermore, they fail to take into consideration how the remaining parent *alters* its investment; this might increase in compensation, or decline in response to the decline in the offspring's reproductive value, with variable effects on offspring survival. Nevertheless, such data can give a very rough estimate of qualitative differences between populations or subpopulations in the benefits of parental care provided by each sex.

Paternity Certainty.   For males paternity certainty directly impinges on the benefits of parental care: Why provide parental care to offspring that may not be yours? Between-society comparisons reveal that where men are unsure of their paternity, as measured by the reported societywide incidence of adultery, they tend not to invest in their spouses' children but in their sisters' children (Hartung 1985, and references therein). Furthermore, anec-dotal accounts of within-society variability indicate that men who are cer-tain of their paternity are more likely to provide for their offspring than are men who are less certain (Flinn 1981).

However, low paternity certainty, matrilineality, and matrilocality are all highly intercorrelated; it is therefore difficult to tease out the extent to which paternal investment is withheld as a result of low paternity certainty rather than as a result of the low fitness returns associated with investing in the children of a woman who is living with (and perhaps can depend on) her kin (see discussion of alternative sources of parental care, section 11.5.1). Furthermore, it is unclear whether men in these societies direct effort from parental care toward seeking extra mates, although the high rates of adultery that distinguish these matrilineal societies suggest that they might (Flinn 1981). In short, sociobiological models have focused on the association between low paternity certainty and the tendency of men to invest in their sisters' children, to whom they are on average more closely related than their wives' children. The relative fitness payoffs to mating *versus* parental effort in the context of low paternity certainty have not yet been investigated.

What socioecological factors might contribute to infidelity among mates, thus lowering the benefits of parental care? One important factor might be the absence of heritable property: Through monopolizing the resources that women need to raise their children, men can accumulate wives (11.4.1, 11.4.2), and then coerce or reward their fidelity with the threat of withdraw-ing these resources (Kitcher 1985:299ff.; Flinn 1981). Another important factor might be male absence. The case of the colonial era matrilineal Iroquois provides a good example of how marital tensions arise in situations where men spend long periods absent as a result of long-distance trade,

hunting and fishing expeditions, and warfare (Brown 1970b). The correlation between matrilocal residence and external warfare (Ember and Ember
1971) provides some support for the generality of this phenomenon.

11.5.3. Opportunity Costs

Finally we need to consider how men might increase their fitness if they
chose to do other things with their time, energy, or resources than invest in
offspring. This entails an assessment of the so-called opportunity costs of
parental care. Opportunity costs are generally measured in terms of lost
mating opportunities and the potential fitness gains associated with them.
Such opportunities can be affected by both demographic (e.g., sex ratio, age
structure) and sociological factors (e.g., the autonomy of men and women
with respect to their sexual relations). We now explore some of these
factors.

Sex Ratio.   Hurtado and Hill (1992) examine the impact of the operational sex ratio on the marriage practices of two lowland South American
foraging groups, the Aché and the Hiwi. The Aché are promiscuous and the
Hiwi largely monogamous. These authors decided to look at the sex ratio
because, contrary to Harpending and Draper's (1986) prediction discussed
above (11.5.2), paternal effects of offspring survival are much stronger in the
Ache, the promiscuous group, than in the Hiwi. If Aché men are so important to the survival of their children, why are their marriages so unstable?
Conversely, if Hiwi men have so little effect on their children's survival, why
are they so faithful? Hurtado and Hill use the ratio of reproductive-aged
females to males, devalued by differences in the total fertility rates of both
groups, as an approximation of the fitness payoffs to mating effort, and find
that this index is more than twice as high for the Aché than for the Hiwi.
Thus Aché marriages are unstable because the opportunities for extramarital
fertilizations are so high.

The strength of this analysis is that the measure of male mating opportunity is independent of the level of marital instability that the authors are
trying to explain. The weakness is that in many societies sex ratios of
breeding-aged females to males will tell us little about the opportunities for
mating *precisely because* of the culturally sanctioned conventions limiting
extramarital sexual activity and marital breakup. Hurtado and Hill's explanation is of heuristic value in the Hiwi/Aché comparison, but there are many
instances where social conventions backed by formal and informal sanctions (that may be exogenously imposed) must be incorporated into evolutionary ecological models of ethnographic diversity (see section 11.6).

Differences in Male Competitive Ability or Attractiveness.   The opportunity costs of parental behavior to males will also be affected by their

probable success in attaining extra mates, thus contributing to within- and between-population variability in paternal behavior.

We might expect males of high resource potential (see section 11.4.1) to play a minor role in at least some forms of paternal care; this has not been investigated. More indirectly, we might examine whether fathers play a small paternal role in environments where there are easily monopolizable resources over which males can compete to gain multiple matings and/or polygynous marriage (11.4.2); in such circumstances competitive behavior brings greater fitness returns than paternal behavior, thus favoring nonpaternal fathers. This is indirectly supported by the finding that husband/wife intimacy is greatest in societies without capital resource ownership (Whiting and Whiting 1975).

Cumulable resources are not, however, the only avenue to male mating success. Among the Aka Pygmies, Hewlett (1988) suggests that it is not a man's material resources *per se* but the size of his fraternal sib group that affects his future mating prospects, and consequently his willingness to provide paternal care. This idea is backed with evidence that men with several brothers offer less direct paternal care than those with fewer brothers (cf. also Ye'kwana; Hames 1988).

Clearly there are many factors that affect male mating success, merely hinted at in the studies referred to earlier (section 11.4.1). While it is generally thought that with intense male–male competition (e.g., some forms of polygyny) paternal behavior will not yield high fitness returns, noncompetitive males would be expected to specialize in paternal care because for them the opportunity costs are small. Such a divergence of condition-dependent strategies seems to characterize the Aka. It also suggests the need for investigating alternative mating and parental strategies *within* populations (see section 11.5.4).

Compatibility.   As in all life history treatments, models for the allocation of parental care assume that effort devoted to mating yields no parental benefits, and *vice versa* (i.e., that the two activities are exclusive), but this is not necessarily the case (see section 11.3.2). We can consider this problem using the Aché as an example. As noted above, Aché fathers are critical to the survival of their offspring. More specifically, they appear to play a key role in protecting their offspring from conspecific infanticide, a significant risk to children in this population. Yet they are also highly promiscuous, devoting much effort to extramarital copulations. One explanation for this unexpected pattern is the strongly female-biased operational sex ratio (discussed above).

Another important factor might be the compatibility of paternal care with mating effort. Although the precise mechanisms whereby men protect their children from infanticide are unclear, it appears that coresidence is important. Does this particular form of paternal investment, coresidence with children, seriously damage a man's chance of seeking extra matings? Real opportunity costs associated with paternal investment among the Aché are only likely if the age and sex structure of the band offers poor fitness prospects through extramarital matings.

Such observations on the compatibility of paternal care with other activities suggest that to explain differences between mating systems and pair bond stability we need to determine not simply the effects of father absence on offspring survival, but the social and ecological *mechanisms* responsible for this effect. We also need to be cautious in our interpretations of studies that use indices of association to measure investment. For example, fathers and offspring may associate for common purposes (to eat or work) without any parental care being offered. Furthermore, even if parental care is entailed in, for example, a behavioral observation in which a man is demonstrating a particular construction technique to his son, the cost to the father (in terms of forgone opportunities) will be minimal if the structure had to be built anyhow.

11.5.4. Alternative Strategies

The existence of alternative reproductive strategies within populations has been largely ignored. Here we briefly consider what forms these might take. One possibility is that some males specialize in mating competition and others in parental investment—the "faithful" and "philandering" strategies (Dawkins 1976), or "dad" and "cad" (Harpending and Draper 1986). Hewlett (1988) identified such tendencies among Aka men in Central African Republic, insofar as the amount of direct child care exhibited by males varies significantly: Direct paternal care is lower among men who have many brothers and are more likely to acquire multiple mates than among men with fewer brothers (and reduced mating opportunities). Hawkes (1990) suggested that a similar suite of alternative strategies might characterize Aché men—"providers" who supply reliable food to their wives and children, and "showoffs" who distribute large bonanzas of high-variance food items (primarily meat) for everyone in camp, in return for sexual favors from fecund women. The success of each strategy is dependent on its frequency in the population (see section 2.2.3).

Empirical investigations of such patterns within populations can prove problematic. For example, positive correlations between the size of mating and parental effort may reflect phenotypic differences among males, such that those males who are most successful in exerting mating effort are also those best able to contribute high parental care (see also section 11.2.3). Hence, even though individuals may face trade-offs between specializing in mating or parenting, such pure strategies may not be apparent in the population unless wealth and other differences are controlled. Thus in the Kipsigis men who pay the largest amount of cattle as bridewealth (mating expenditure) are generally those who also provide most land on which maize can be grown to feed their offspring (parental expenditure; Borgerhoff Mulder n.d.).

Finally, there is no a priori reason why potentially reproductively successful members of the population, for example, those with resources or, as in the Aka, fraternal support, should necessarily specialize in mating rather than parental care. Where parents attempt to maximize offspring quality, as is hypothesized in postdemographic transition societies (11.2.3), high paternal investment (in the form of bequeathed wealth) may be the best route to fitness maximization, ensuring the entrance of competitive offspring into the breeding pool.

It seems important to keep potential alternative reproductive tactics in mind when we assess demographic studies. For example, the much discussed disappearance of a positive relationship between status and female fertility in postdemographic transition societies (Vining 1986) may obscure variable tactics among women with respect to trading their careers against their family lives. Thus measures of completed fertility may conceal marked differences in the timing of reproduction that have important fitness effects: By delaying reproduction women can attain higher income than those who reproduce earlier, thus improving the quality of care they can offer their children. In a stationary or declining population, delayed reproduction could maximize fitness.

11.5.5. Conflicts of Interests between Caregivers

Optimal levels of parental effort for each sex reflect not simply the costs and benefits of providing care, but the amount of care provided by its partner (Chase 1980; Houston and Davies 1985; Lazarus 1989). The mate desert model (11.5) that has structured most discussion of the evolution of parental care is useful for tackling questions like Which parent cares? or Why is biparental care so rare? But subtle variations in the level of care may be of particular interest to anthropologists studying variable family systems.

Game theory models can be used to examine the kinds of bargaining processes that might arise between partners with conflicting interests. Chase's (1980) model has two steps. First, he starts from the simple assumption that an individual will allocate her effort between noncooperative behavior (somatic or mating effort) and cooperative behavior (parental care) according to the variety of constraints discussed above. Care devoted to offspring is most likely to have diminishing returns after a certain threshold is reached (this function was discussed for Figure 11.4). Chase then examines what happens if her partner *increases* the resources expended on offspring

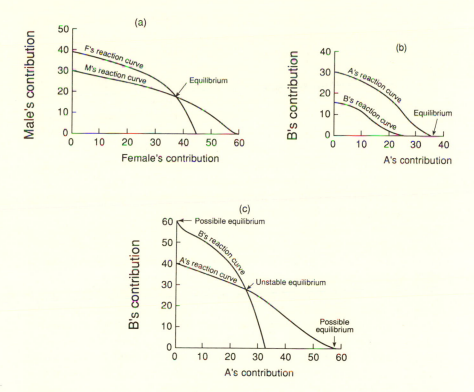

Figure 11.6.   *Optimal parental expenditure for males and females plotted on the level of expenditure by the other sex. (a) Reaction curves for an equilibrium in which both individuals supply the parental behavior. This equilibrium is always reached no matter which individual makes the first contribution and no matter how large the contribution is, if the reaction curves intersect and each has a slope < −1 at the intersection (see note, below). (b) Reaction curves for an equilibrium in which one particular individual (sexes randomly assigned as A or B in parts b and c) supplies all the parental behavior. This equilibrium is always reached no matter which individual makes the first contribution and no matter how large the contribution is, if the reaction curves do not intersect. (c) Reaction curves for equilibria in which one individual or the other, depending on initial conditions, supplies all the parental behavior. At one of the possible equilibria, A provides all the parental behavior and B contributes nothing. At the other possible equilibrium, B provides all the parental behavior and A contributes none. These unstable equilibria arise if the slopes are > −1 at their intersection (after Chase 1980). Note: Specifications for the steepness of the slopes at the intersection must characterize both A's reaction to variations in B's contribution, and B's reaction to variations in A's contribution, with the axes similarly aligned. Only if the slopes are < −1 does an increase in the contribution of one partner entail a proportionately smaller decrease in its partner's contribution, and hence arrival at a stable equilibrium. If the slopes are > −1, an increase in one individual's contribution provokes a proportionately larger decrease in its partner's contribution, precipitating instability.*

such that, given the diminishing returns, the payoff to her investment in parental care declines. Under these circumstances it may pay her to invest any additional resources in somatic or mating effort rather than in parental effort.

The second step of the model uses this logic to predict a female's reaction to any contribution by a mate, and vice versa. To do this, Chase utilizes reaction curves (Figure 11.6). In this model each reaction curve describes one partner's decrease or increase in the provision of parental care in response to an increase or decrease in the care provided by its partner. In Figure 11.6a the female's contribution to parental care is plotted as a function of the male's contribution, and is termed the female's reaction curve (F). Similarly the male's contribution (M) is plotted as a function of the female's contribution. Two such curves are shown in the three parts of Figure 11.6.

An equilibrium (Figure 11.6a) can be reached as a result of mutual adjustments by each partner to the other's expenditure; it represents the male's optimal expenditure given the female's contribution, and the female's optimal expenditure given the male's contribution. If the reaction curves intersect and each has a slope < -1 at the intersection point, the intersection is stable. Other outcomes are possible. If one partner's reaction curve is completely above that of the latter (Figure 11.6b) then the other former should desert and the latter should take care of the offspring, and vice versa. If the slopes are > -1 at the intersection, the intersection point is unstable (Figure 11.6c); reductions in expenditure by one parent lead to reductions by its partner, such that either one parent or the other ends up doing all the work; which parent it will be depends on initial conditions.

Although reaction curves cannot be determined empirically from observational and demographic studies, broad differences in their shape can be inferred on the basis of the survival chances of orphaned offspring (11.5.2). The potential for detailed behavioral and longitudinal studies could most usefully be explored using within-population variability. If, as is probable, optimal allocations of parental effort reflect such factors as the age and earning power of both partners, different couples are likely to reach different equilibria. The scope for application of such "bargaining process" models seems great in the study of marital relations.

11.6. CONCLUSIONS

Reproduction, marriage, parental roles, and relationships among kin have been core issues of anthropological interest since the founding of the discipline. What can evolutionary ecology contribute to our understanding of ethnographic variability in these areas?

We have seen that models for the study of life history effort, mating systems, and parental care in nonhumans point to social and ecological constraints that are important in shaping diverse family patterns in the ethnographic record. Applications of simple models have been quite successful, as in the case of birth intervals, polygyny, and the distribution of paternal care. However, there are problems with using these models in the study of human populations, as indeed there always are when *general* models are applied to *specific* cases. These have been mentioned in passing, and include how to describe the distribution of resources in a species with sophisticated technology and how to measure the costs of reproduction or parental care without recourse to experimental manipulations.

Finally, care is needed in identifying what exactly we are trying to explain: behavior or constraints. In a classic statement of the goals of human sociobiology, Alexander (1979:68) proposed that human culture represents "the cumulative effects of . . . inclusive-fitness-maximizing behavior (i.e., reproductive maximization via all socially available descendant and non-descendant relatives) by all humans who have lived." The goal is to tackle both behavior *and* its constraints, providing an explanation for both the fine-tuning of parental investment (Voland et al. 1991) *and* the particular marriage and inheritance system characterizing any population at that time in history.

The goal of evolutionary ecologists is at least *initially* somewhat less ambitious than that of Alexander, insofar as constraints are taken as given. Abiotic constraints cannot be changed by individual behavior, or at least only very indirectly. Changes in biotic constraints, such as institutional and social factors, may in some exciting cases be reducible to individual strategies (e.g., Boone 1986; Cronk 1989), but are often most usefully seen as resulting from historical processes that are often exogenous to the behavior of individuals in the target population, and are hence not wholly attributable to these individuals' fitness-maximizing strategies. Thus polygyny is not simply the outcome of domestic calculations given certain resource and investment constraints, but can be affected by the proximity of a neighboring population from whom to raid wives, which may in itself be attributable to a particular historical migration. Similarly, religiously sanctioned monogamous marriage may exist as a result of a history of conquest. The extent to which such constraints are themselves products of fitness-maximizing strategies is a fascinating second-order question on which we have as yet made little progress. Sociocultural diversity, with its full complement of rules, conventions, and sanctions, is nevertheless what evolutionary ecologists, like sociobiologists, ultimately strive to explain (see Chapter 1). Advances toward this goal will depend on rigorous hypothesis testing with new empirical data, and clearer statements of what exactly is being explained.

ACKNOWLEDGMENTS

Many thanks to Nick Blurton Jones, Tim Caro, Claudia Engel, Sarah Hrdy, Daniel Sellen, and Daniela Sieff, who read and commented on various versions of this manuscript, to the editors for their persistent suggestions and encouragement, and to the participants in the Behavioral Ecological Anthropology Seminar (Spring 1991) at Davis for their bright ideas.

Resources and Population Dynamics

Alan R. Rogers

12

12.1. INTRODUCTION

Population ecology is concerned with the growth (and decline) of populations of plants and animals, including humans. This interest, of course, is also shared by demography, economics, and several other disciplines. Population ecology differs in its emphasis on ecology and evolution—the ecological interactions among individuals and among species, and the evolutionary forces that shape these interactions.

Earlier chapters in this volume discuss how natural selection shapes the characteristics of individuals: their use of resources, their distribution across the landscape, their life histories, and so forth. This chapter is concerned with the effects that these characteristics have on the dynamics and stability of populations. It will show that these effects are profound, and have important practical consequences.

This chapter begins by introducing the fundamental principles of population growth: the exponential increase of unregulated populations, various mechanisms that regulate population growth, and a method called "cobwebbing" that is useful for understanding the consequences of population regulation. As we shall see, these consequences may include not only the stability that the term *regulation* seems to imply, but also various forms of instability. Next, we shall take a closer look at the effects of dwindling resources, using the models of "scramble" and "contest" competition. Finally, we turn to the effect of resources on the reproduction of individuals, with particular attention to the case in which wealth can be inherited by offspring.

12.2. DEPENDENCE OF POPULATION GROWTH ON POPULATION DENSITY

In 1990, there were roughly 5.292 billion people in the world, and this number was expected to increase to 6.251 billion by the year 2000 (Brown 1990). At this rate, the population would double every 42 years. Should this rate of growth continue for 420 years, the world population would double ten times and there would be over a thousand humans for each human alive today—over 5 trillion in all. It seems unlikely that this can happen. As a population increases in size, its rate of growth must eventually slow.

In the literature of population ecology, anything that limits the growth of a population is called a "mechanism of population regulation." These mechanisms fall into two important categories. *Density-independent* mechanisms are those whose frequency and severity are unaffected by population density. This category would include, for example, natural disasters such as blizzards and earthquakes, but would not include hunger or infectious diseases that are transmitted more easily in dense than in sparse populations. Mechanisms that are affected by population density are called *density dependent*.

Nearly 200 years ago, Thomas Malthus (1914 [1798]) argued that density-dependent mechanisms have a profound effect on human affairs. It seemed inconceivable to him that food production could increase rapidly enough to match the growth of an unconstrained population, and he concluded that population growth must ultimately be limited by starvation and disease. This view has been extremely influential, and tempts us to view the history of human population growth as a series of responses to technological innovations. For example, archaeological evidence (Klein 1989) shows that new kinds of stone tools appeared and spread out from an African origin some 40,000 years ago, and genetic evidence (Rogers and Harpending 1991) suggests that a dramatic burst of population growth occurred at roughly the same time. Archaeological data suggest that another burst of population growth followed the origin of agriculture some 6000 years ago. More recently, the industrial revolution in Europe allowed another spurt of population growth that still continues.

One influential point of view holds that the human population is usually regulated at a level, called the *carrying capacity*, that is determined by the availability of resources. The carrying capacity is determined not only by the environment, but also by our ability to extract resources from it. The major episodes of population growth may have resulted when technological innovations increased the carrying capacity.

This point of view has been criticized by authors who point out that the rate at which innovations are adopted or invented is itself density dependent. Population growth leads to gradually increasing scarcity, which encourages efforts to invent or adopt new technologies. This effect has been documented both in rural (Boserup 1965, 1981) and industrial economics (Simon 1977). Even in foraging societies, technological complexity increases with the number of people per unit of environmental productivity (Keeley 1988). Thus, it may be more useful to view innovation as an effect, rather than a cause, of population growth. If so, perhaps humankind has not

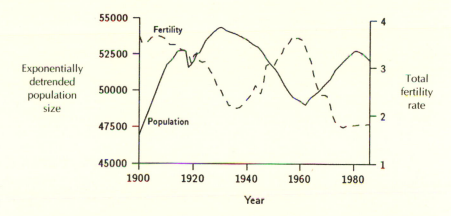

Figure 12.1. Fertility and population size. Data refer to the US during the 20th century. Population size has been "exponentially detrended." In other words, an exponential curve was fit to the original data, and the graph shows the deviations from this curve. After Lee (1987).

been faced with the chronic shortages that Malthus envisioned; perhaps density-dependent population regulation has played no important role.

This last point of view is also influential, but is probably incorrect. That rates of innovation respond to density seems clear, but it does not follow that the rate of population growth is unaffected by density. Consider Figure 12.1, which displays Lee's (1987) data on fertility and population size in the twentieth-century United States. Fertility is high when population size is relatively low (i.e., below the long-term trend), and vice versa. These data suggest that some mechanism of density-dependent population regulation is at work, even during a period of uninterrupted population growth. Analogous density-dependent effects on mortality are reported by Wood and Smouse (1982) in a study of a very different population: the Gainj, a horticultural people in Papua New Guinea. Density-dependent effects are weak, and may be masked by larger density-independent effects. Over the long run, however, a weak effect with a persistent direction may overwhelm stronger effects with no persistent direction (Lee 1987). Thus, even weak density dependence may be important. Let us consider, therefore, how it affects the dynamics of population growth.

This is a subject to which unaided intuition is a poor guide. It is tempting to assume that density-dependent regulation will produce a time path like the logistic growth curve in Figure 12.2. The population in that figure grows steadily until it reaches a limit determined by available resources, and then remains constant in size. Unfortunately, this is not necessarily so. Other, less pleasant effects are also possible, and it behooves us all to be aware of them. The best way to develop intuition about population dynamics is to

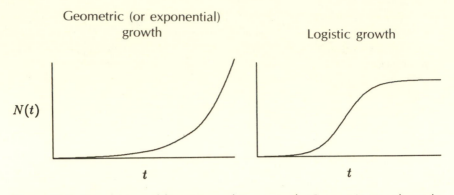

Figure 12.2. Geometric and logistic population growth. Geometric growth results when age-specific rates of birth and death are constant. Logistic growth is one of many patterns that may arise when these rates are density dependent.

study simple mathematical models. Let us consider, then, the dynamics of simple models of population growth.

12.3. THE DYNAMICS OF SIMPLE POPULATIONS

A population can change in size in only four ways: by birth, by death, by immigration, and by emigration. In this chapter, I deal only with the first two of these in order to keep things simple. This still leaves plenty of complexity, since rates of birth and death can vary in complex ways. Before plunging into these complexities, it will be useful to consider first the case in which these so called *vital rates* do not change.

12.3.1. Geometric (or Exponential) Growth

Even when vital rates do not change, the situation is far from simple. Since death rates are higher for the elderly, more deaths per capita will occur in a population with many elderly people than in a young population. By the same token, since fertility is highest for young adults, the number of births per capita will be high if there are lots of young adults. Thus, age-specific birth and death rates alone cannot tell us how fast a population will grow. We also need to know the *age structure* of the population, that is, the number of individuals in each age category. And as if this were not bad enough, there is also the matter of sex. A population with no females cannot grow, regardless of its age structure. Furthermore, vital rates often vary among social classes. When vital rates vary according to categories of any type—age, sex, social class, geographic region, or whatever—the population is said to be *structured*. In such a population we cannot predict how a population will grow until we know how many people are in each category.

Confronted by these complications, we can proceed either by building a complicated model to deal with them or by sweeping them under the rug and pretending that they do not exist. This latter approach sounds irresponsible, but it is the best way to start. A realistic model will not help much if it is too complex for its workings to be understood. We proceed by looking first at models so simple that they are easy to understand. Then, one at a time, we add complications.

The simplest case is that of an organism without sex that lives a single season, reproduces, and then dies. Suppose that each individual produces R offspring. If there is one individual to begin with, there will be R after 1 generation, R^2 after 2 generations, R^3 after 3 generations, and R^t after t generations. If there are N_t individuals in generation t, there will be

$$N_{t+1} = RN_t \qquad (12.1)$$

in generation $t + 1$. This pattern of growth, in which the population size increases by a constant multiple each generation, is called *geometric* or *exponential* growth, and the time path of a population growing in this way is shown in Figure 12.2.

In this simple case it is easy to see why growth is geometric. The remarkable thing about this result is that it usually holds even when you add the complications of age and sex structure back in, still assuming vital rates to be constant in time. Thus, the simple unrealistic model tells most of the story. This suggests that it will still be worthwhile to ignore age structure and sex as we explore the effect of relaxing our other assumption: that vital rates do not vary.

12.3.2. Population Regulation

It is not hard to see that the pattern of geometric growth shown in Figure 12.2 cannot continue forever. Mechanisms of population regulation alter this pattern by adjusting rates of birth or death. Therefore, let us drop the assumption that the vital rates do not change, and assume instead that they vary as a function of N, the population size. To indicate this, I write the number of offspring per parent as $R(N)$, thus emphasizing its dependence on N. Now the equation for population change becomes

$$N_{t+1} = R(N_t)N_t \qquad (12.2)$$

In Eq. (12.2) the rate of growth depends on the size, or density, of the population: It is *density dependent*. The supposition is that when N_t is large enough, R will be less than 1, so the population will decrease in size. When the population is small, R will be greater than 1 and the population will

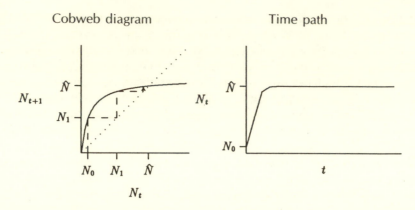

Figure 12.3. Monotonic convergence toward an equilibrium. This figure illustrates a trick called "cobwebbing" for studying population dynamics. The solid line on the left plots the size of a population in generation t + 1 against its size in generation t. The dotted line shows the points at which $N_{t+1} = N_t$. The time path of the population, beginning at point N_0, is derived by reflecting the dashed line back and forth as shown. This time path is graphed against t on the right.

grow. At some intermediate *equilibrium* value $\hat{N}$, population size will tend to remain the same because $R = 1$.

Graphs such as the "cobweb diagram" in Figure 12.3 are useful for thinking about density-dependent population growth. The solid line is a plot of N_{t+1} against N_t for some hypothetical population. The dotted line connects the points at which $N_{t+1} = N_t$. To the left of $\hat{N}$, the solid line lies above the dotted line, which means that $N_{t+1} > N_t$, that $R(N) > 1$, and that the population is growing. The reverse is true to the right of $\hat{N}$, which means that large populations will shrink. The curve in Figure 12.3 does not (so far as I know) describe any real population; it is purely hypothetical. Analysis of hypothetical models cannot tell us what nature is really like, but can illustrate the range of behaviors that are possible. Let us consider, therefore, what Figure 12.3 implies about the dynamics of growth in this hypothetical population.

12.3.3. Cobwebbing and Dynamic Stability

Given a graph like the left side of Figure 12.3, it is natural to wonder what the time path of the population will be like. This is easy to figure out using a trick called "cobwebbing." Suppose that N_0, the population size in generation 0, is known. The size in the next generation, N_1, can be read off the vertical axis of the graph. In order to get N_2 we need to transfer the value of N_1 from the vertical axis to the horizontal axis. You could do this with a ruler and a pencil, but there is an easier way. Notice that the horizontal dashed line level with N_1 on the vertical axis strikes the diagonal line directly above N_1 on the horizontal axis. Thus, we can work out the time path of population size as shown by the dashed line in Figure 12.3. Going straight up from N_0 to the solid line gives us N_1. Then "reflecting" a horizontal line from this point off the diagonal gives us N_2, and so forth.

Let us now use cobwebbing to investigate several kinds of dynamical behavior, which are illustrated in Figures 12.3–12.5. The time paths generated are shown on the right in each figure. Try starting the population at different values on both sides of $\hat{N}$ in Figures 12.3–12.5. Equilibria such as those in Figures 12.3 and 12.4 (or the logistic curve in Figure 12.2) are said to be *stable*, since populations away from the equilibrium tend to move closer to it. Equilibria such as that in Figure 12.5 are called *unstable* since populations near them tend to move farther and farther away. Among stable equilibria there are two possibilities. The first of these, illustrated by Figure 12.3, is called *monotone convergence* and is the sort of thing that comes immediately to mind when we talk about population size being regulated. A small population will increase gradually toward its equilibrium value, while a large population will decrease gradually. The other possibility is that a stable equilibrium may exhibit *damped oscillations*, as illustrated in Figure 12.4. There the population always overshoots the equilibrium so that its time path oscillates back and forth about the equilibrium. Each overshoot, however, is smaller than the last so the oscillations get smaller and smaller. Finally, the unstable equilibrium in Figure 12.5 exhibits what is called *diverging oscillations*. These oscillations get larger and larger rather than dwindling away. Actually, the oscillations in Figure 12.5 do not continue to

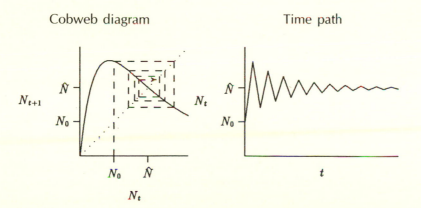

Cobweb diagram   Time path

Figure 12.4. Damped oscillations. The solid line in the cobweb diagram crosses the dotted line with a steeper slope in this figure than in figure 12.3, producing damped oscillations.

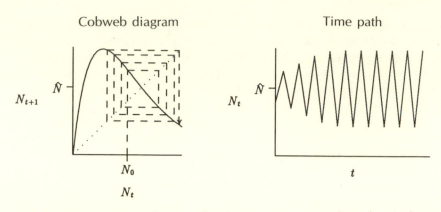

Figure 12.5. Diverging oscillations. The slope is even steeper here than in figure 12.4, and produces diverging oscillations in the neighborhood of the unstable equilibrium, Ň. The oscillations increase in magnitude until a stable limit cycle is reached.

diverge indefinitely. They increase only until they reach a certain amplitude, which is then maintained. This is called a *stable limit cycle*.

These cases illustrated in Figures 12.3–12.5 are by no means an exhaustive list of the kinds of dynamical behavior that can arise. Some models, for example, give rise to a phenomenon called "chaos," in which population size fluctuates but does not follow any cyclical pattern (May 1981). None of these models is complex enough to be an accurate description of any real population. The same sorts of instability, however, often arise in more complex and realistic models (Winterhalder et al. 1988). The lesson here is that population regulation need not lead to a stable, equilibrium population size. It can do so, but it can also lead to oscillations. Natural populations often fluctuate in size, and the principles that generate instability in the simple models may contribute to this instability.

The next section will consider a variety of mechanisms that tend to "regulate" populations in that they tend to increase the size of small populations, and to decrease the size of large ones. The hypothetical graphs we have just considered show that even populations that are regulated may differ greatly in the stability of their equilibria. Unstable dynamics such as those in Figure 12.5 might well drive a population to extinction. The equilibrium in Figure 12.4 is somewhat more stable, but the violent swings in population size exhibited there would probably also increase the likelihood of extinction. The most stable equilibrium is that in Figure 12.3, and it is only equilibria such as these that are likely to have the favorable results that are suggested by the phrase "population regulation." Thus, as we consider mechanisms of density-dependent population regulation, it will be important to ask how they affect the stability of equilibria.

12.4. COMPETITION FOR LIMITED RESOURCES

All organisms need food, and some need special dens or nesting sites in order to reproduce or to survive the winter. Populations that grow large enough to deplete the supply of such resources are said to be *resource limited.* In such populations, an individual's ability to survive or reproduce may depend on its success in competition with others for scarce resources. The larger a population grows, the more likely it is to deplete its resources. The human population has recently enjoyed several generations of uninterrupted growth, but there are indications that this trend is about to end. While the world population has continued to grow, the growth in agricultural production has slowed because of "environmental degradation, a worldwide scarcity of cropland and irrigation water, and a diminishing response to the use of additional chemical fertilizer" (Brown and Young 1990). The result, shown in Figure 12.6, is that per capita food production has begun to drop, and is projected to drop further. The world population may be approaching its carrying capacity. As food becomes increasingly scarce, competition for it will surely intensify.

Competition for limited resources is clearly a mechanism of density-dependent population regulation since it tends to decrease the size of large populations, but allows small populations to grow. Yet as we have already seen, this is no guarantee that the dynamics of population growth will be stable. Will the world human population converge gradually toward its carrying capacity like the hypothetical population in Figure 12.3, or is it

Figure 12.6. World per capita grain production (After Brown and Young 1990:76).

about to enter into a series of oscillations like those illustrated in Figure 12.4 or 12.5? We cannot know, but some insight can be gained by considering how competition affects stability in simple models.

In order to predict how a change in the supply of resources would affect the growth of some population, we would need to know (1) how it would affect the way resources are distributed among individuals, and (2) how resources affect individual survival and reproductive success. The second of these factors can be described by the *fitness function*, $w(x)$, whose value is the expected number of offspring born to individuals with x units of re-source. For the sake of brevity, I will hereafter refer to x as "wealth," with the understanding that this term will apply to a squirrel's supply of acorns as well as to money that one of us might have in the bank.

At the outset, let us make a simplistic assumption about the second of these factors in order to concentrate on the first: Let us assume that $w(x)$ is a step function, as shown in Figure 12.7. The vertical axis, $w(x)$, is the average number of offspring per individual of wealth x, and the horizontal axis is wealth. The graph illustrates the assumption that individuals whose wealth is below a threshold value x_0 have zero fitness, whereas the wealthier have fitness m. In real populations, fitness may often increase with wealth (more on this later), but it would be surprising to find a threshold as abrupt as the one in Figure 12.7. Thus, our assumption is only a caricature of reality. Nonetheless, it will illuminate effects that are only dimly perceived in more realistic models.

12.4.1. The Distribution of Resources among Individuals

The distribution of resources among individuals is affected both by the nature and spatial distribution of foods that are eaten, and by social and foraging behaviors. Some behavior patterns tend to concentrate resources in the hands of a few successful individuals, while others tend to distribute resources more evenly. For example, where rich, dependable patches of resource can be found, a system of behavior called *territoriality* (discussed further in Chapter 8 of this volume) is common. Powerful individuals gain exclusive access to rich patches, or "territories," by defending them against all comers. Those who acquire rich territories are well provided for; the others may starve, freeze, or be eaten by predators. Social dominance has a similar effect, if subordinate individuals are unable to feed until the domi-nant individuals are satisfied.

At the other end of the spectrum are populations in which resources are relatively evenly distributed among individuals. This may occur, for exam-ple, if resource patches are not rich enough or lasting enough to be worth defending, and foraging is done by individuals rather than groups. These

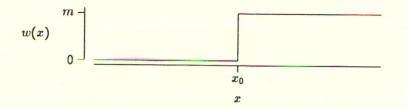

Figure 12.7. A step function. The simplest assumption about the fitness function, w(x), is that fitness is nil if wealth (x) is less than a threshold value, x_0, and is equal to a constant value, m, if x exceeds this threshold.

differing patterns of behavior have profoundly different consequences for population dynamics. This can be seen most easily in two extreme cases: *scramble competition*, in which resources are divided evenly, and *contest competition*, in which they are monopolized by a few individuals.

Scramble Competition. Scramble competition will here refer to the hypothetical extreme case in which resources are divided perfectly evenly. [This usage of the term *scramble competition* follows that of Begon and Mortimer (1986), and differs from that of Nicholson (1954) and Łomnicki (1988).] The idea of an even distribution of resources sounds nice, but its effect on population dynamics can be decidedly unpleasant. To demonstrate this we make use of the cobweb method described above.

The cobweb method requires a graph relating N_{t+1} to N_t, and this requirement impels us to ask how scramble competition affects the reproductive success of individuals. Suppose that each generation is allotted c units of resource. Since wealth is divided evenly, each individual in generation t will have wealth c/N_t. We can read the consequences of this from Figure 12.7. If individual wealth (c/N_t) exceeds x_0, then each individual will produce m offspring, so $N_{t+1} = mN_t$. This occurs when $N_t < c/x_0$. When the population is larger than this, no offspring are produced at all, and $N_{t+1} = 0$.

The critical population size, $K = c/x_0$, is the carrying capacity of the environment. In Figure 12.8, the cobweb method is used to demonstrate the catastrophic consequences of pure scramble competition. The population grows until it exhausts the supply of resources (i.e., until $N_t > K$), and then "crashes" and goes extinct. If some small fraction of the population is able to survive the crash, the population will grow again until it reaches carrying capacity, and will then crash again.

The term *carrying capacity* is used in the literature in two different ways (Dewar 1984). One usage takes carrying capacity to be the maximum number of individuals that can survive if resources are divided evenly. The other takes it to be the equilibrium population size. In either case, we may

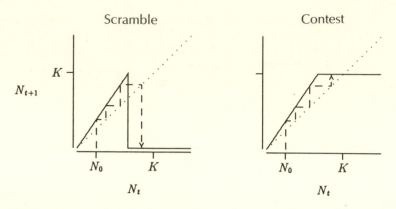

Figure 12.8. Scramble and contest. Under scramble competition, $N_{t+1} = mN_t$ if $mN_t \leq c/x_0$, and otherwise $N_{t+1} = 0$. Under contest competition, $N_{t+1} = mN_t$ if $N_t \leq K$, and otherwise $N_{t+1} = mK$. In both plots, $m = 1.5$.

expect the carrying capacity to vary, and these variations generate interesting kinds of instability (May 1974; Harpending and Bertram 1975). This chapter, however, deals only with the simple case in which carrying capacity (in either sense) is constant.

The model of scramble competition shows that the two definitions of carrying capacity are not equivalent. In our model, K is the carrying capacity since all the individuals in a population that size (but no larger) would be able to survive and reproduce. On the other hand, K is not an equilibrium because the mK children of such a population would all perish. Thus, the carrying capacity is not necessarily an equilibrium. A catastrophic fate may await any population that—like the human population of planet earth—is approaching carrying capacity. The extreme case of scramble competition gives us the worst case imaginable. What of the other extreme?

Contest Competition. The other extreme is contest competition. In this case everyone gets an equal share if $N_t < K$, but not if $N_t > K$, for the available resources are then divided evenly among only K individuals, and the rest get nothing. The consequences of this form of social inequality can be derived using the cobweb method, as before.

For concreteness, let us consider a system of territoriality in which there are K territories, each rich enough to enable one individual to breed. This implies that each territory contains at least x_0 units of resource, and that each territory holder will produce m offspring. If there are no more than K adults, each will acquire a territory and produce m children. If fewer than K children are thus produced, each child will acquire a territory and survive. Thus, $N_{t+1} = mN_t$ provided that $mN_t \leq K$. If there are more adults than this, more children will be produced, but only K of them will find territories, and the rest will perish. Thus, $N_{t+1} = K$ if $mN_t > K$. The cobweb diagram representing this case is shown in Figure 12.8, and demonstrates that contest competition produces stable population dynamics. The population will increase monotonically to its equilibrium value, K, and then stay there. In contrast to the case of scramble competition, the carrying capacity *is* an equilibrium under contest competition.

This is good news, because the human population approximates the case of contest competition a good deal more closely than that of scramble competition. Not only do individual humans own property of various sorts, and defend it against one another, they maintain police forces that aid them in these efforts. In addition, vast resources are also controlled and defended collectively, by corporations and by nations. Even when resources are shared, larger shares often go to individuals of high status (Betzig 1988b). Consequently, resources are not divided evenly among nations, or among individuals within them. As resources become scarce, poor nations (and individuals) will suffer more than rich nations (and individuals). This inequality causes a great deal of suffering that, in my opinion, justifies the prevailing view that inequality is a social evil. All the same, its beneficial effects on population dynamics should not be overlooked.

The Distribution of Individuals Across the Landscape.   Ordinarily, individuals that are far apart do not compete. The intensity of competition depends less on the number of other individuals in the species as a whole than on the number of near neighbors. If individuals are distributed evenly in space, the number of neighbors will be smaller than if individuals are clumped together. For example, Lewontin and Levins (1989) point out that although there are about 60 humans per square mile in the United States as a whole, the average U.S. citizen shares his or her square mile with 3105 neighbors. This is because the U.S. population is "clumped" into cities and towns whose population density is quite high.

These observations suggest that any behavior that, like those discussed by Cashdan (Chapter 8), affects the way in which individuals are distributed in space, will also affect the stability of population dynamics. In simple mathematical models, clumping reduces stability (Hassell and May 1985). However, this effect is most pronounced in populations that are capable of extremely rapid growth. The effect of clumping on human population dynamics may be small because of the limitation on growth rate that is imposed by our comparatively low reproductive capacity.

12.4.2. Relaxing Assumptions

The analysis above of scramble and contest competition produced rather unpleasant results, which should not be accepted uncritically. Perhaps they are due to some unrealistic feature of the models. To find out, we must add realism to the models.

We have relied on simplistic assumptions both about the shape of the fitness function and also about the way in which resources are divided among individuals. To add realism, let us drop the restrictive assumption that w is a step function, and assume only that it is a nondecreasing function of wealth—that wealthier people produce at least as many children, on average, as those who are less wealthy. This seems plausible, and is not a controversial assumption in animal ecology. It is not at all clear, however, that this pattern holds among humans. This controversy is discussed below, but let us ignore it for the moment.

I have also made extremely simple assumptions about the distribution of wealth among individuals. I now assume instead that wealth is distributed among individuals in some arbitrary fashion. I shall not specify whether wealth is distributed evenly or unevenly, or whether poor individuals are common or rare. I shall say only that there is some arbitrary function, $f_N(x)$, that measures the relative frequency of individuals of wealth x in a population of size N. To be precise, if dx is some very small value, then $f_N(x)\ dx$ is the number of individuals whose wealth lies between x and $x + dx$. (In the language of probability theory, I am saying that $f_N(x)$ is the *probability density* of individuals with wealth x.) In this notation, the function R can be written as

$$R(N) = \int_0^\infty w(x)f_N(x)\ dx \qquad (12.3)$$

which is merely a formal way of saying that R is the average reproductive success of the individuals in the population.

In this more general context, the method of cobwebbing breaks down, for in order to construct the necessary graph, we would first need to specify the functions w and f_N, thereby losing the generality we seek to introduce. To evaluate the stability of Eq. (12.2) *in general*, we must abandon graphical analysis in favor of mathematics. The price that is paid for this generality (apart from the need for mathematics) is an enormous loss of detail. The mathematical analysis will tell us only about the behavior of populations that are already very near the equilibrium. An equilibrium is said to be *locally stable* if a population very near to it tends to get closer, and locally unstable if such populations tend to move away. The mathematics will not tell us what happens to populations that are far from the equilibrium, nor will it allow us to reconstruct the time path of population growth.

Mathematical analysis of local stability rests on a well-known relationship (Maynard Smith 1968:22) between the local stability of an equilibrium at $\hat{N}$, and the derivative $dR/d \log N|_{N=\hat{N}}$. As explained in the legend of Figure 12.9, this derivative tells how the rate of reproduction (R) changes when the

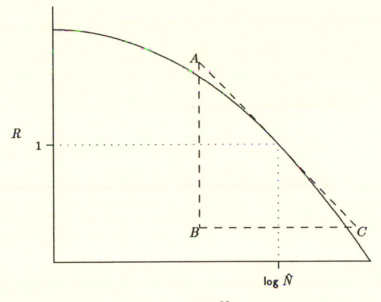

Figure 12.9. The meaning of dR/d log N$|_{N=\hat{N}}$. The solid line graphs R as a function of log N for some hypothetical population. The equilibrium, N = $\hat{N}$, occurs at the point where R = 1, as shown by the dotted lines. Line AC is drawn tangent to R at this point, so that the slope of AC is equal to that of R at the equilibrium point. This slope is equal in magnitude to the ratio of lengths of line segments AB and BC, and is negative because R decreases as log N increases. Thus, dR/d log N$|_{N=\hat{N}}$ = $-\overline{AB}/\overline{BC}$.

Table 12.1.   Criteria for Local Stability of an Equilibrium at $\hat{N}^a$

dR/d log N$|_{N = \hat{N}}$	Behavior near $\hat{N}$
>0	Monotone divergence (unstable)
−1 to 0	Monotone convergence (stable)
−2 to −1	Damped oscillations (less stable)
<−2	Diverging oscillations (unstable)

[a]The quantity dR/d log N$|_{N = \hat{N}}$ is the derivative (or slope) of R as a function of log N, evaluated at the equilibrium point, where N = $\hat{N}$ (see Figure 12.9).

population is perturbed a little ways away from its equilibrium. Table 12.1 says that an equilibrium is stable provided that a small increase in population size reduces the rate of reproduction, but not by too much.

   To use these results, we must evaluate the derivative, dR/d log N, which depends both on the fitness function w and on the way in which the frequency distribution of wealth changes as the population grows. Let us reexamine the two forms of competition discussed above in this more general context.

Generalized Scramble Competition. In the earlier model of scramble competition, a reduction in overall wealth would have produced an equal proportional reduction in the wealth of each individual. For example, if each individual in a population of size 100 had wealth 10, then there must have been 10 × 100 = 1000 units of wealth in all. If the population had doubled, each individual would have had 1000/200 = 5 units. Thus, doubling the population size would halve the wealth of each individual. We now dispense with the assumption that wealth is evenly divided, but let us continue to assume that an increase in population size produces an equal proportional reduction in the wealth of each individual. This provides a generalized model of scramble competition, in which the ratios of the wealths of individuals are unaffected by changes in overall wealth. The generalized model includes the earlier one as a special case in which all individuals have the same wealth, so that the ratios of individual wealths are all 1 : 1. The generalized model is more realistic, and may be a fair description of *exploitation competition* (Park 1954), the case in which individuals compete by exploiting a resource to which all have access. Under exploitation competition, differences in wealth arise solely from differences in ability to exploit the resource. If Joe can harvest twice as much resource per hour as Jack can, then he will be twice as wealthy. We are assuming that the magnitude of Joe's advantage does not depend on the richness of the habitat.

The question is, Under what circumstances is this new, generalized model stable? This will depend on the slope ($dR/d \log N$) that is referred to in Table 12.1. In an earlier paper (Rogers 1986), I showed that, under the assumptions just stated, this slope is equal to -1 times the slope of the graph of mean fitness ($\overline{w}$) against the mean of log wealth. If this latter slope is small—if mean fitness increases only slowly with the mean of log wealth— then Table 12.1 ensures that equilibria will be stable under generalized scramble competition. Before trying to decide whether this condition is likely to be satisfied, consider carefully what it means.

Three hypothetical graphs relating mean fitness ($\overline{w}$) against mean log wealth are shown in Figure 12.10. Log wealth is assumed to follow a normal distribution (the familiar bell-shaped curve), and curves are shown for three different values of the standard deviation, σ. When $\sigma = 0$, all individuals have identical wealth, so mean fitness ($\overline{w}$) is the same as individual fitness ($\overline{w}$). In that case, the curve shown is strongly sigmoid, or S-shaped. Why? Because in most species, reproduction is probably impossible unless wealth exceeds some minimum value, so below that value the slope of w will be near zero. The slope will also be near zero where x is large, since there will be some physiological limit to the number of young that can be produced even if unlimited resources are available. Thus, the graph of w should be flat at the left edge of the graph (where x is small) and also at the right edge (where x is large). The slope should be steepest for intermediate values of x,

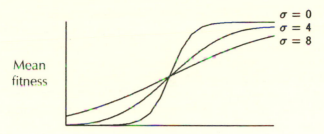

Figure 12.10. Mean fitness, $\overline{w}$, as a function of mean log wealth. Here σ^2 is the variance of log x. It is assumed that $f_k(x)$ is log-normally distributed and that $w \propto 1/(1 + 1/x)$.

and may even approximate a step function there. Thus, when there is no variation among individuals ($\sigma = 0$), the slope of the graph may be very steep in the central portion. Since this slope is -1 times $dR/d \log N$, Table 12.1 shows that equilibria may easily be unstable. In general, the steeper the graph of $\overline{w}$ against log wealth, the more likely dynamics will be unstable.

Now study the curves for $\sigma = 4$ and $\sigma = 8$, which refer to populations with greater variation in wealth. Increasing variation tends to flatten out the curves, and thus makes equilibria more stable. Conclusion: An even partitioning of resources reduces the stability of population dynamics even in this generalized model of scramble competition. (For further discussion of this topic, see Łomnicki 1978, 1980, 1982; Łomnicki and Ombach 1984; Łomnicki and Sedziwy 1988, 1989; Rogers 1989b.)

So far, the news about the effects of scramble competition is mostly bad: The unpleasant results of the earlier model still hold. On the other hand, there is also good news. If the slope of the fitness function is everywhere less than 2, then the slope of mean fitness ($\overline{w}$) must also be less than 2, and equilibria will be stable regardless of the distribution of resources among individuals. Thus, the earlier unrealistic assumption that w is a step function served to exaggerate the adverse effect of social equality. Real populations may be able to survive these adverse effects, provided that their fitness functions are not too steep. It will be important, therefore, to consider how evolution affects the slope of the fitness function. But first let us generalize the earlier model of contest competition to see whether w plays an equally important role there.

Generalized Contest Competition. The task now before us is that of constructing a model of contest competition that allows an arbitrary distribution of wealth, and an arbitrary fitness function. To make it a sensible model of contest competition, we shall require that additional individuals do not affect the wealth of the individuals already there. Consider, therefore, a hypothetical territorial population that inhabits an environment in which the number of territories whose wealth lies between x and $x + dx$ is $h(x)\, dx$, where dx is some very small number. Assume that individuals always inhabit the best available territory, and let $x_0(N)$ denote the wealth of the poorest territory inhabited in a population of size N.

Appendix 1 shows that, in this model, $dR/d \log N|_{N=\hat{N}} = w(x_0) - 1$. Consequently, Table 12.1 implies that population dynamics will be stable provided that $0 < w(x_0) < 1$. In other words, stability requires that the fitness of the poorest individual in the equilibrium population be between zero and unity. Now a fitness cannot be negative, so the first of these inequalities is always satisfied. The second will be satisfied provided only that w is an increasing function of wealth. With a bizarre fitness function in which fitness *decreases* with wealth over at least a part of its range, $w(x_0)$ might exceed unity, making equilibria unstable even under contest competition. But if, as intuition suggests (see below), fitness always increases with wealth, then contest competition will always lead to stable population dynamics, at least in deterministic models such as we have studied.

Real populations, however, are subjected to random perturbations of various kinds, and these tend to make dynamics less stable than Table 12.1 would suggest. For example, if $w(x_0) = 0$, the analysis above indicates that the population will fall on the boundary between monotone convergence and damped oscillations. In reality, random effects would cause such a population to oscillate toward its equilibrium. On the other hand, if the fitness function is fairly flat so that $w(x_0)$ is close to unity, population dynamics will be more resistant to random perturbations, and therefore more stable. Thus, even in the case of contest competition, a steep fitness function tends to destabilize population dynamics.

12.5. EVOLUTION OF THE FITNESS FUNCTION

Evolution affects population dynamics in various ways. Since the behavior of individuals affects both the distribution of resources among individuals and the distribution of individuals across the landscape, the evolution of behavior affects population dynamics. In addition, evolution also affects population dynamics via its effect on life history strategies, for these strategies determine the fitness function w. In simple evolutionary models, selection favors those who produce the largest number of surviving offspring. If, in addition, one assumes that the ability to rear offspring is constrained by wealth, then it follows that the rich should reproduce faster than the poor. Thus, it seems reasonable to expect that natural selection will favor a fitness function that increases with wealth.

The evolution of the fitness function is probably also affected by mechanisms of population regulation. MacArthur and Wilson (1967; MacArthur

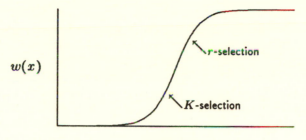

Wealth, x

Figure 12.11. How r- *and* K-*selection would affect the fitness function. In a* K-*selected species, resources are usually scarce, and selection will push up the left side of the graph. In an* r-*selected species, resources are usually abundant, and selection will push the right side up.*

1972) distinguished between "r-selected" populations, which are usually kept well below their equilibrium size by density-independent mechanisms, and "K-selected" populations, which are usually near equilibrium. The terms refer to the suggestion that r-selection will increase r (the instantaneous growth rate), whereas K-selection will increase K (the equilibrium size, usually called the carrying capacity; Armstrong and Gilpin 1977). This classification has been of enormous heuristic value in ecology, although it is of only limited value in describing nature (Begon and Mortimer 1986). More realistic classifications are available (Caswell 1982; Sibly and Calow 1985; Begon 1985), but require more detail than is present in the models developed here.

These selection regimes should have quite different effects on the fitness function, as illustrated in Figure 12.11. Under r-selection, resources are usually abundant, so selection would tend to push the right side of the fitness function up, increasing its slope. On the other hand, resources are usually scarce under K-selection, so selection will tend to push up the left side of the fitness function, decreasing its slope. Consequently, r-selection should reduce the stability of population dynamics.

Humans are generally regarded as a K-selected species, so these arguments would lead us to expect fitness to increase gently with human wealth. There is a good deal of evidence, however, that this is not so. Figure 12.12 shows that the fertility of Brazilian males *decreases* with wealth, a blatant contradiction of our expectations. Similar data from a variety of sources are summarized by Vining (1986), who argues that they indicate that evolutionary arguments are of little relevance in the study of human behavior. If these data truly represent the human fitness function, then the arguments presented above suggest that

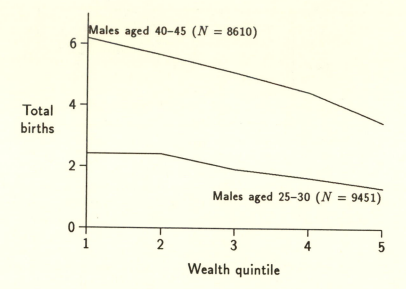

Figure 12.12. Mean fertility of Brazilian males by wealth quintile (Lam 1986).

1.   Under scramble competition, $d\overline{w}/d\overline{z} < 0$ and therefore $dR/d \log N > 0$, which means (as Table 12.1 shows) that population dynamics will be unstable.

2.   Under contest competition, it is possible that $w(x_0) > 1$, since the fitness function apparently has a negative slope. This would make population dynamics unstable even under contest competition!

Thus, a fitness function such as that in Figure 12.12 would have bizarre consequences for population dynamics. It might produce instability even in a population such as our own, which resembles the ideal of contest competition more than that of scramble competition.

There are, however, reasons to be skeptical of such conclusions. Even if the poor do enjoy an advantage during good times, it is hard to imagine that this advantage could survive under conditions of extreme scarcity. In addition, other evidence suggests a positive relationship between wealth and reproduction (Simon 1977; Mealey 1985; Irons 1979a; Turke and Betzig 1985; Essock-Vitale 1984; Borgerhoff Mulder 1989a). Furthermore, the number of one's offspring may not be a good indicator of reproductive success in the long run. This is particularly true of species, such as our own, in which wealth can be passed on from generation to generation. To show why, the next section will discuss a model (Rogers 1990a; Harpending and Rogers 1990) of natural selection with heritable wealth.

12.5.1. Optimal Reproduction When Wealth Is Heritable

Humans are unusual in that they can inherit wealth, as well as genes, from their parents, and can pass these bequests on to their own children if they choose. Thus, a bequest left by a parent may affect the reproductive success of his or her descendants for several generations. Wealthy parents must choose between producing many offspring who will each inherit relatively little, or a few who will each inherit much more. Which choices would be favored by natural selection?

To answer this question, we need an evolutionary model that allows reproductive opportunities to vary with wealth, that allows wealth to be inherited, and that uses an unusual measure of fitness. In this context, the appropriate measure of fitness is not the number of one's offspring, but the number of one's descendants in some generation in the distant future. In a recent paper (Rogers 1990a), I developed such a model, and showed that reproductive strategies that maximize the number of one's offspring do not necessarily maximize the number of one's descendants in the long run. Similar effects arise even when wealth is not heritable. For example, David Lack (1948) showed that birds must limit the number of offspring hatched in order to maximize the number that survive to breed. R.A. Fisher's (1958) model of sex ratio evolution looked beyond the number of offspring produced, and showed that selection maximizes the number of one's grandchildren. The novelty introduced by heritable wealth is that one must also look beyond the number of grandchildren. It no longer suffices to count either the surviving children or the grandchildren produced. One must count the number of descendants produced in some generation in the distant future.

My model allowed each parent to allocate some portion of her wealth (the "fertility allocation") toward the production of offspring, and divided the rest as bequests among the offspring that she produced. A reproductive strategy was taken to be a rule specifying the fertility allocation as a function of wealth, and optimal reproductive strategies were those which maximized the long-term rate of increase in the numbers of one's descendants. Increasing fertility allocations yielded increasing fertility, as specified by the fitness function, which was assumed to follow a law of diminishing returns. One of the fitness functions that was used is illustrated by the open circles in the upper panel of Figure 12.13. In addition to inheriting wealth, offspring also earn some on their own, as specified in the figure legend.

The optimal reproductive strategy is the one that maximizes the ultimate rate of increase in the number of one's descendants, and is found by a method that is discussed in the next section. For now, it is important only to notice that, as the upper panel in Figure 12.13 shows, optimal fertility is *not*

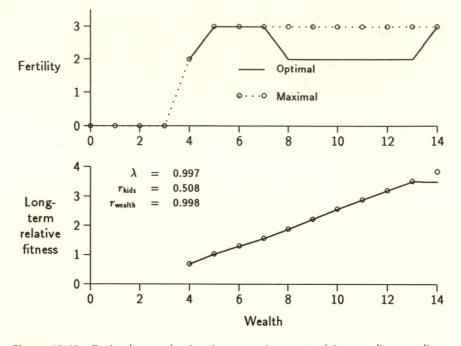

Figure 12.13. Optimal reproduction in an environment of intermediate quality. Upper panel: The dotted line panel shows the relationship between fertility and the allocation of wealth to fertility. The solid line shows optimal fertility as a function of total wealth, assuming that, in addition to her inheritance, each offspring may "earn" some wealth on her own. Earnings are a Poisson random variable with mean 3. Lower panel: The solid line graphs, as a function of total wealth, the long-term fitness of individuals adopting the optimal reproductive strategy. The open circles show long-term fitness in a model with the same parameters except that maximal wealth is 40 instead of 15. λ is the long term growth rate, r_{kids} is the correlation between long-term fitness and fertility, and r_{wealth} the correlation between long-term fitness and wealth.

an increasing function of wealth under these assumptions. It increases, then decreases, then increases again. The lower panel in this figure graphs what is called long-term fitness as a function of wealth. Long-term fitness is discussed further below, and measures one's genetic contribution to generations in the distant future. Note that long-term fitness increases with wealth even though fertility does not.

The assumptions of this model are too unrealistic for it to be of much use in data analysis. Its value lies in what it shows us about the possibilities that may arise under evolution in structured populations. When individuals may belong to one of several classes, and when these classes offer differing reproductive opportunities, we cannot measure fitness in terms of offspring produced. As we have just seen, there need be no simple relationship between the number of one's offspring, and one's expected genetic contribution to future generations. Thus, in structured populations, we should seek ways to measure long-term fitness. The next section shows how this can be done using, as an example, the fertility and mobility among four social classes in the population of England and Wales.

12.6. LONG-TERM FITNESS AND SOCIAL CLASS

Berent (1952:247) described the fertility and mobility among four British social classes. For convenience, I number these from 1 to 4, with 1 representing the lowest class and 4 the highest (Berent, incidentally, used the opposite system). The pattern of fertility and mobility among the classes in Berent's data can be described by a matrix,

$$
\mathbf{G} = \begin{array}{cc}
 & \begin{array}{cccc} 1 & 2 & 3 & 4 \end{array} \\
\begin{array}{c} 1 \\ 2 \\ 3 \\ 4 \end{array} &
\begin{pmatrix}
1.81 & 0.77 & 0.33 & 0.15 \\
1.34 & 1.36 & 0.72 & 0.30 \\
0.37 & 0.49 & 0.94 & 0.57 \\
0.04 & 0.12 & 0.18 & 0.86
\end{pmatrix}
\end{array}
$$

whose *ij*th entry (the entry in row *i* and column *j*) is the mean number of offspring of social class *i* produced per parent of class *j*, after one generation. Clearly, we could construct such a matrix for categories of wealth, religion, or anything else. The approach described here is a simplified version of the methods described by Bartholomew (1982), Lam (1986), Chu (1987), Rogers (1990a), and Harpending and Rogers (1990).

12.6.1. Projecting Fitness Forward in Time

We are interested in the genetic contribution made by members of each class to the distant future, but let us begin by summing the rows of **G** to calculate the number of offspring born to members of each class. This gives 3.56 for class 1, 2.73 for class 2, 2.17 for class 3, and 1.88 for class 4. Now we can calculate the numbers of grandchildren for each class as follows.

$$
\begin{aligned}
10.98 &= 1.81 \times 3.56 + 1.34 \times 2.73 + 0.37 \times 2.17 + 0.04 \times 1.88 \\
7.72 &= 0.77 \times 3.56 + 1.36 \times 2.73 + 0.49 \times 2.17 + 0.12 \times 1.88 \\
5.51 &= 0.33 \times 3.56 + 0.72 \times 2.73 + 0.94 \times 2.17 + 0.18 \times 1.88 \\
4.20 &= 0.15 \times 3.56 + 0.30 \times 2.73 + 0.57 \times 2.17 + 0.86 \times 1.88
\end{aligned}
$$

Note that each row above uses the values from one column of **G** along with the fertility values that we just calculated. The first row says that each parent in class 1 produces 1.81 class 1 offspring that each produce 3.56 grandchildren, 1.34 class 2 offspring that each produce 2.73 grandchildren, 0.37 class 3 offspring that each produce 2.17 grandchildren, and 0.04 class 4 offspring that each produce 1.88 grandchildren. Adding these up gives 10.98, the total grandchildren per parent in class 1.

To summarize these calculations, it is helpful to have an algebraic formula. Let us write $w_i(1)$ for the expected number of offspring of individuals of class i, $w_i(2)$ for the expected number of their grandchildren, $w_i(3)$ for their expected great-grandchildren, and so forth. In general $w_i(t)$ will be called the t-generation fitness of individuals in class i. The arithmetic of the preceding paragraph is summarized by the formula

$$w_i(t + 1) = \sum_j g_{ji} w_j(t) \qquad (12.5)$$

By applying this recipe again and again, we can find the number of descendants in any future generation produced by individuals in each social class. The results of this procedure are shown in Figure 12.14. Notice that the curves for the four social classes form straight, parallel lines after the first few generations. Since the y-axis is on log scale, these lines can be straight only if the t-generation fitnesses are increasing exponentially. The fact that the four lines are parallel means that all four classes have the same rate of exponential increase. It also means that the ratios, $w_i(t)/w_j(t)$, between pairs

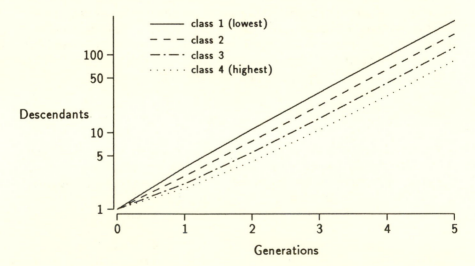

Figure 12.14. Projection of fitnesses using British social mobility matrix. Numerical projection of fitnesses using Berent's data (matrix G) on fertility and social mobility.

Table 12.2.   Stable Wealth Distribution and Long-Term Fitness[a]

Social class	Fertility	Long-term fitness	Stable distribution
1	3.56	1.37	0.36
2	2.73	0.92	0.41
3	2.17	0.61	0.18
4	1.88	0.41	0.05

[a]Fertility is the number of offspring born per family within a 10-year period, and long-term fitness of each class measures the eventual reproductive success per family in that class relative to that of an average family (see text for details). As the population grows, the relative frequencies of the four social classes converge to the stable distribution.

of social classes have stopped changing. Thus, after two or three generations the t-generation fitnesses have converged to the long-term fitness values. These can be written in standard form by dividing $w_i(t)$ by the mean t-generation fitness. The result (Table 12.2) shows that long-term fitness declines steadily with wealth, and that the poorest class has over three times the long-term fitness of the wealthiest class. This means that, eventually, individuals of the lowest class will achieve more than three times the genetic representation of individuals in the highest class. Incidentally, long-term fitness is equivalent to a quantity that is called the *reproductive value* in demography (Fisher 1958; see section 11.2.1). I have used a different term here since reproductive vale conventionally refers to categories of age rather than social class.

We are now in a position to reevaluate my criticism of Vining's (1986) argument that since fertility declines with social class, humans must not be striving to maximize reproductive success. In response to Vining's article (Rogers 1990a), I objected that his conclusion was not justified because the number of one's offspring may be a poor indicator of long-term fitness. Poor parents might have lower long-term fitness in spite of their higher fertility. However, the long-term fitnesses in Table 12.2 suggest that Vining was right after all, at least for this British population. The poor have greater reproductive success even in the long run. If these data are to be believed, and if the pattern of reproduction that they describe continues, then the British population will eventually be dominated by the genes of those now in the lower classes, as Fisher (1958) first suggested in 1930.

There are, however, reasons to be skeptical of this conclusion. Berent's data on reproductive success tell us only the number of births during the 10 years before the sample was taken. We do not know what fraction of the infants born survived to maturity, nor do we know what fraction of these survivors were able to form families of their own. It is possible that lower-class individuals are less likely to survive, or to marry, than their upper-class counterparts. Furthermore, I have taken no account of nonpaternity—the possibility that some of the offspring in Berent's data have been attributed to men not their biological fathers. Estimated rates of nonpaternity vary from population to population, ranging from 2.3 to 30% (Potthoff and Whittinghill 1965; Peritz and Rust 1972; Philipp 1973; Neel and Weiss 1975; Ashton 1980; Lathrop et al. 1983). If the biological father tends to come from a different social class than the putative father, then my calculation of the long-term fitnesses from Berent's data may be badly in error.

On the other hand, it is also possible that human adaptation is out of date, as Vining suggested. Perhaps we behave in ways that increased the reproductive success of our ancestors, but no longer do so today. If so, evolutionary theory will still be useful in discovering why the human mind has evolved into its present form, but we should not expect humans to maximize reproductive success in modern environments (Symons 1989; Blurton Jones 1990).

12.7. CONCLUSIONS

The human population has grown at an unprecedented rate for longer than anyone now alive can remember, but this epoch of rapid growth appears to be drawing to a close. Mechanisms of density-dependent population regulation will have increasingly severe effects in the decades to come. Yet this need not imply that our population is converging toward some equilibrium size. Density-dependent population regulation can also generate various kinds of unstable dynamics, in which population numbers rise and fall cyclically. The response of our population to increasing scarcity will depend on a variety of factors. Behaviors such as territoriality and behavioral dominance tend to stabilize population dynamics while the clumping of populations into towns and cities may have the reverse effect.

All of these effects are mediated by the fitness function, which relates reproductive success to wealth. Plausible assumptions about the fitness function imply that population dynamics will be somewhat more stable than simple models predict. However, there is evidence of a bizarre relationship between wealth and human reproduction. In many human societies, the poor consistently have more children than the rich. This need not imply that they have more descendants in the long run, for wealthy offspring may enjoy improved reproductive opportunities. Thus, the small, wealthy progeny of a rich woman may generate more great-great-grandchildren than the large, poor progeny of her impoverished sister. However, data from the post–World War II population of England and Wales suggest that exactly the opposite is true. Individuals of the poorest class produce roughly twice the offspring of the richest class, and their advantage in long-term fitness is even greater. Members of the poorest class will ultimately produce more than three times as many descendants as do members of the richest class.

This finding does not settle the issue, for it is based on data that are inadequate in several ways. What it will do, I hope, is to show clearly what is at issue, and how that issue might be settled with better data.

Appendix 1. Stability under Generalized Contest Competition

Let $H(x)$ denote the number of territories whose quality is less than x. Now x can take only integer values, but if the total number of territories is large, we can approximate $H(x)$ by a smooth curve, and write its derivative as $h(x) = dH(x)/dx$. The number of individuals in a small interval, $[x, x+dx]$, is $H(x+dx) - H(x)$, which approaches $h(x)\,dx$ as $dx \to 0$. The total number of territories is therefore $\int_0^\infty h(x)\,dx$.

To model contest competition, let us assume that each territory can contain at most one individual, and that the best territories are always occupied first. Let $x_0\,(N)$ denote the quality of the worst territory occupied in a population of size N. Then

$$N = \int_{x_0(N)}^{\infty} h(x)\,dx \tag{12.4}$$

and the population size in generation $t + 1$ is related to that in generation t by

$$N_{t+1} = \int_{x_0(N_t)}^{\infty} h(x)w(x)\,dx = N_t R(N_t)$$

where $w(x)$ is the fitness (reproductive success) of an individual in a territory of quality x, and

$$R(N) = N^{-1} \int_{x_0(N)}^{\infty} h(x)w(x)\,dx$$

The stability of population dynamics depends on the derivative,

$$dR/dN = (-N^{-2}) \int_{x_0(N)}^{\infty} h(x)w(x)\,dx + N^{-1}[w(x_0(n))h(x_0'(N)]$$

where $x_0'(N) = dx_0(N)/dN$. To find $x_0'(N)$, differentiate both sides of Eq. (12.4) to get $dN/dN = 1 = -h(x_0(N))x_0'(N)$, whence

$$x_0'(N) = -1/h(x_0(N))$$

$$\frac{dR}{dN} = N^{-1}[w(x_0(N)) - R(N)]$$

$$\frac{d \log R}{dN} = N \frac{dR}{dN} = w(x_0(N)) - R(N)$$

Since we are evaluating this derivative at the equilibrium, where $R(N) = 1$, we have

$$\frac{d \log R(\hat{N})}{dN} = w(x_0(\hat{N})) - 1.$$

This result, together with Table 12.1. shows that the stabilities of equilibria under generalized contest competition are determined by $w(x_0(\hat{N}))$, the fitness of the individual in the poorest inhabited territory in the equilibrium population.

References

Aiello, L. C. (1981) Locomotion in the Miocene Hominoidea. In *Aspects of Human Evolution*, C. B. Stringer, ed., pp. 63–98. London: Taylor & Francis.

Aiello, L. C. and M. C. Dean. (1990) *An Introduction to Human Evolutionary Anatomy*. London: Academic Press.

Alexander, R. D. (1974) The evolution of social behavior. *Annual Review of Ecology and Systematics* 5:325–383.

Alexander, R. D. (1979) *Darwinism and Human Affairs*. Seattle: University of Washington Press.

Alexander, R. D. (1987) *The Biology of Moral Systems*. New York: Aldine de Gruyter.

Alexander, R. D. (1990) Epigenetic rules and Darwinian algorithms: The adaptive study of learning and development. *Ethology and Sociobiology* 11:241–303.

Alexander, R. D. and G. Borgia. (1979) On the origin and basis of the male-female phenomenon. In *Sexual Selection and Reproductive Competition in Insects*, M. F. Blum and N. Blum, eds., pp. 413–440. New York: Academic Press.

Alland, A., Jr. (1985) *Human Nature: Darwin's View*. New York: Columbia University Press.

Altmann, J. (1974) The observational study of behavior. *Behaviour* 48:1–41.

Altmann, J. (1980) *Baboon Mothers and Infants*. Cambridge: Harvard University Press.

Altmann, S. A. (1974) Baboons, space, time and energy. *American Zoologist* 14:221–248.

Altmann, S. A. (1979) Altruistic behaviour: The fallacy of kin deployment. *Animal Behaviour* 27:958–959.

Altmann, S. A. and J. Altmann, (1970) *Baboon Ecology*. Chicago: University of Chicago Press.

Altmann, S. A., S. Wagner, and S. Lenington. (1977) Two models for the evolution of polygyny. *Behavioural Ecology and Sociobiology* 2:397–410.

Amoss, P. and S. Harrell. (1981) Introduction: An anthropological perspective on aging. In *Other Ways of Growing Old: Anthropological Perspectives*, P. Amoss and S. Harrell, eds., pp. 1–24. Stanford: Stanford University Press.

Andelman, S. J. (1986) Ecological and social determinants of cercopithecine mating systems. In *Ecological Aspects of Social Evolution. Birds and mammals*, D. I. Rubenstein and R. W. Wrangham, eds., pp. 201–216. Princeton NJ: Princeton University Press.

Andrews, P. J. and L. C. Aiello. (1984) An evolutionary model for feeding and positional behaviour. In *Food Acquisition and Processing in Primates*, D. J. Chivers, B. A. Wood, and A. Bilsborough, eds., pp. 429–466. New York: Plenum Press.

Anthony, D. W. (1986) The "Kurgan Culture," Indo-European origins, and the domestication of the horse: A reconsideration. *Current Anthropology* 27(4):291–313.

Armstrong, R. and M. Gilpin. (1977) Evolution in a time-varying environment. *Science* 195:591–592.

Ashton, G. C. (1980) Mismatches in genetic markers in a large family study. *American Journal of Human Genetics* 32:601–613.

Axelrod, R. (1984) *The Evolution of Cooperation.* New York: Basic Books.

Axelrod, R. and D. Dion. (1989) The further evolution of cooperation. *Science* 242:1385–1390.

Axelrod, R. and W. D. Hamilton. (1981) The evolution of cooperation. *Science* 211:1390–1396.

Babchuck, W., R. Hames, and R. Thompson. (1985) Sex differences in the recognition of infant facial expressions of emotion: The primary caretaker hypothesis. *Ethology and Sociobiology* 6:89–101.

Bailey, H. P. (1960) A method of determining the warmth and temperateness of climate. *Geografiska Annaler* 43:1–13.

Barash, D. (1974) An advantage of winter flocking in the black-capped chickadee, *Parus atricapillus*. *Ecology* 55:674–76.

Barkow, J. (1989) *Darwin, Sex, and Status: Biological Approaches to Mind and Culture.* Toronto: University of Toronto Press.

Barnard, A. (1979) Kalahari bushman settlement patterns. In *Social and Ecological Systems*, P. Burnham and R. Ellen, eds., pp. 131–144. New York: Academic Press.

Barth, F. (1956) Ecological relationships of ethnic groups in Swat, North Pakistan. *American Anthropologist* 58: 1079–1089.

Barth, F. (1965) *Political Leadership Among Swat Pathans.* London: Athlone.

Barth, F. (1967) The study of social change. *American Anthropologist* 69:661–669.

Bartholomew, D. J. (1982) *Stochastic Models for Social Processes*, 3rd ed. New York: Wiley.

Bates, D. G. and S. H. Lees. (1979) The myth of population regulation. In *Evolutionary Biology and Human Social Behavior*, N. Chagnon and W. Irons, eds., pp. 273–289. North Scituate, MA: Duxbury Press.

Beckerman, S. (1983) Carpe diem: an optimal foraging approach to Bari fishing and hunting. In *Adaptive Responses of Native Amazonians*, R. Hames and W. Vickers, eds., pp. 269–299. New York: Academic Press.

Beckerman, S. (1989) Hunting and fishing in Amazonia. Paper presented at Wenner-Gren Symposium 109, Nova Friburgo, Brazil.

Begon, M. (1985) A general theory of life-history variation. In *Behavioural Ecology: Ecological Consequences of Adaptive Behaviour*, R. M. Sibly and R. H. Smith, eds., pp. 91–97. Boston: Blackwell.

Begon, M. and M. Mortimer. (1986) *Population Ecology: A Unified Study of Animals and Plants*, 2nd ed. Boston: Blackwell.

Behrensmeyer, A. K. and A. P. Hill. (1981) *Fossils in the Making.* Chicago: University of Chicago Press.

Bell, G. and V. Koufopanou. (1986) The cost of reproduction. *Oxford Surveys in Evolutionary Biology* 3:83–131.

Belovsky, G. (1987) Hunter-gatherer foraging: A linear programming approach. *Journal of Anthropological Archaeology* 3:29–76.

Belovsky, G. (1988) An optimal foraging-based model of hunter-gatherer population dynamics. *Journal of Anthropological Archaeology* 7:329–372.

Belovsky, G., M. Ritchie, and J. Moorehead. (1989) Foraging in complex environments: when prey availability varies over time and space. *Theoretical Population Biology* 36(2):144–160.

Bentley, G. R. (1985) Hunter-gatherer energetics and fertility: A reassessment of the !Kung San. *Human Ecology* 13:79–109.

Berent, J. (1952) Fertility and social mobility. *Population Studies* 5:244–260.

Bernstein, I. S. (1981) Dominance: The baby and the bathwater. *Behavioral and Brain Sciences* 4:419–458.

Bertram, B. C. R. (1978) Living in groups: Predators and prey. In *Behavioural Ecology, an Evolutionary Approach*, J. R. Krebs and N. B. Davies, eds., pp. 64–96. Sunderland, MA: Sinauer Association.

Bertram, B. C. R. (1980) Vigilance and group size in ostriches. *Animal Behaviour* 28:278–286.

Bettinger, R. L. (1987) Archaeological approaches to hunter-gatherers. *Annual Review of Anthropology* 16:121–42.

Bettinger, R. L. and M. A. Baumhoff. (1982) The Numic spread: Great Basin cultures in competition. *American Antiquity* 47:485–503.

Betzig, L. L. (1986) *Despotism and Differential Reproduction: A Darwinian View of History*. New York: Aldine.

Betzig, L. L. (1988a) Mating and parenting in Darwinian perspective. In *Human Reproductive Behaviour: A Darwinian Perspective*, L. Betzig, M. Borgerhoff Mulder, and P. Turke, eds., pp. 3–20. Cambridge: Cambridge University Press.

Betzig, L. L. (1988b) Redistribution: Equity or exploitation? In *Human Reproductive Behaviour: A Darwinian Perspective*, L. Betzig, M. Borgerhoff Mulder, and P. Turke, eds., pp. 49–63. Cambridge: Cambridge University Press.

Betzig, L. L. and P. Turke. (1986) Measuring time allocation: Observation and intention. *Current Anthropology* 26:647–650.

Beynon, A. D. and M. C. Dean. (1988) Distinct dental development patterns in early fossil hominids. *Nature* 335:509–514.

Beynon, A. D. and B. A. Wood. (1987) Patterns and rates of molar crown formation times in East African hominids. *Nature* 326:493–496.

Binford, L. R. (1978) *Nunamuit Ethnoarcheology*. New York: Academic Press.

Binford, L. R. (1980) Willow smoke and dogs' tails: Hunter-gatherer settlement systems and archaeological site formation. *American Antiquity* 45:4–20.

Binford, L. R. (1984) *Faunal Remains from Klasies River Mouth*. New York: Academic Press.

Binford, L. R. (1989) Isolating the transition to cultural adaptations: An organizational approach. In *The Emergence of Modern Humans*, E. Trinkaus, ed., pp. 18–41. Cambridge: Cambridge University Press.

Binford, L. R. (1990) Mobility, housing and environment: A comparative study. *Journal of Anthropological Research* 46.119–152.

Binford, L. R. (1991) Is Australian site structure explained by the absence of predators? *Journal of Anthropological Archaeology* 10:255–82.

Birdsell, J. (1953) Some environmental and cultural factors influencing the structuring of Australian aboriginal populations. *American Naturalist* 87:169–207.

Blackfan, K. D. (1933) Growth and development of the child: Part II, anatomy and physiology. In *White House Conference on Child Health and Protection*, pp. 176–190. New York: Appleton Century Crofts.

Bledsoe, C. (1980) *Women and Marriage in Kpelle Society*. Stanford: Stanford University Press.

Blurton Jones, N. G. (1984) A selfish origin for human food sharing: Tolerated theft. *Ethology and Sociobiology* 5:1–3.

Blurton Jones, N. G. (1986) Bushman birth spacing: A test for optimal interbirth intervals. *Ethology and Sociobiology* 7:91–105.

Blurton Jones, N. G. (1987a) Bushman birth spacing: Direct tests of some simple predictions. *Ethology and Sociobiology* 8:183–203.

Blurton Jones, N. G. (1987b) Tolerated theft, suggestions about the ecology and evolution of sharing, hoarding and scrounging. *Social Science Information* 26:31–54.

Blurton Jones, N. G. (1990) Three sensible paradigms for research on evolution and human behavior. *Ethology and Sociobiology* 11:353–359.

Blurton Jones, N. G. and R. Sibly. (1978) Testing adaptiveness of culturally determined behaviour: Do Bushman women maximize their reproductive success by spacing births widely and foraging seldom? In *Human Behavior and Adaptation*, Society for the Study of Human Biology, Symposia 18, N. Blurton Jones and V. Reynolds, eds., pp. 135–158. London: Taylor and Francis.

Blurton Jones, N. G., K. Hawkes, and J. F. O'Connell. (1989) Modelling and measuring costs of children in two foraging societies. In *Comparative Socioecology: The Behavioral Ecology of Humans and Other Mammals*, V. Standen and R. A. Foley, eds., pp. 367–390. Oxford: Blackwell Scientific Publications.

Bock, K. (1980) *Human Nature and History: A Response to Sociobiology*. New York: Columbia University Press.

Boesch, C. and H. Boesch. (1983) Optimization of nut-cracking with natural hammers by wild chimpanzees. *Behaviour* 83:265–86.

Boesch, C. and H. Boesch. (1989) Hunting behavior of wild chimpanzees in the Tai National Park. *American Journal of Physical Anthropology* 78:547–573.

Boinski, S. (1987) Birth synchrony in Squirrel monkeys (*Saimiri oerstedi*): A strategy to reduce neonatal predation. *Behavioral Ecology and Sociobiology* 21:393–400.

Boone, J. L. (1986) Parental investment and elite family structure in preindustrial states: A case study of late medieval-early modern Portuguese genealogies. *American Anthropologist* 88:859–878.

Boone, J. L. (1987) Parental investment, social subordination, and population processes among the 15th and 16th century Portuguese nobility. In *Human Reproductive Behavior: A Darwinian Perspective*, L. L. Betzig, M. Borgerhoff Mulder, and P. W. Turke, eds. Cambridge: Cambridge University Press.

Borgerhoff Mulder, M. (1987) On cultural and biological success: Kipsigis evidence. *American Anthropologist* 89:619–634.

Borgerhoff Mulder, M. (1989a) Early maturing Kipsigis women have higher reproductive success than late maturing women and cost more to marry. *Behavioral Ecology and Sociobiology* 24:145–153.

Borgerhoff Mulder, M. (1989b) Polygyny and the extent of women's contribution to subsistence. *American Anthropologist* 91:178–180.

Borgerhoff Mulder, M. (1990) Kipsigis women's preferences for wealthy men: Evidence for female choice in mammals. *Behavioral Ecology and Sociobiology* 27: 255–264.

Borgerhoff Mulder, M. (n.d.) Tradeoffs between mating and parental effort in the Kipsigis. Manuscript in author's files, Dept. of Anthropology, UC Davis.

Borgerhoff Mulder, M. and T. Caro. (1985) The use of quantitative observation techniques in anthropology. *Current Anthropology* 26:232–262.

Borgerhoff Mulder, M. and M. Milton. (1985) Factors affecting infant care among the Kipsigis. *Journal of Anthropological Research* 4:231–262.

Boserup, E. (1965) *The Conditions of Agricultural Growth: The Economics of Agrarian Change under Population Pressure*. Chicago: Aldine.

Boserup, E. (1970) *Women's Role in Economic Development*. New York: St. Martin's.

Boserup, E. (1981) *Population and Technological Change: A Study of Long-Term Trends*. Chicago: University of Chicago Press.

Boyd, R. (1988) Is the repeated prisoner's dilemma game a good model of reciprocal altruism? *Ethology and Sociobiology* 9:211–221.

Boyd, R. (1989) Mistakes allow evolutionary stability in the repeated prisoner's dilemma game. *Journal of Theoretical Biology* 136:47–56.

Boyd, R. (n.d.) The evolution of cooperation when conditions vary. Manuscript (Sept. 1990).

Boyd, R. and J. Lorberbaum. (1987) No pure strategy is evolutionarily stable in the repeated prisoner's dilemma game. *Nature* 327:58–59.

Boyd, R. and P. J. Richerson. (1982) Cultural transmission and the evolution of cooperative behavior. *Human Ecology* 10:325–351.

Boyd, R. and P. J. Richerson (1985) *Culture and the Evolutionary Process*. Chicago: University of Chicago Press.

Boyd, R. and P. J. Richerson. (1987) The evolution of ethnic markers. *Cultural Anthropology* 2:65–79.

Boyd, R. and P. Richerson. (1988a) The evolution of reciprocity in sizeable groups. *Journal of Theoretical Biology* 132:337–356.

Boyd, R. and P. J. Richerson. (1988b) The evolution of social learning: The effects of spatial and temporal variation. In *Social Learning: Psychological and Biological Perspectives*, T. R. Zentall and B. G. Galef, Jr., eds., pp. 119–139. Hillsdale, NJ: Lawrence Erlbaum.

Boyd, R. and P. J. Richerson. (1989a) Social learning as an adaptation. *Lectures on Mathematics in the Life Sciences* 20:1–26.

Boyd, R. and P. J. Richerson. (1989b) The evolution of indirect reciprocity. *Social Networks* 11:213–236.

Boyd, R. and P. J. Richerson. (1990a) The evolution of ethnic markers. *Ideas in Anthropology*, pp. 27–39. Santa Fe, NM: School of American Research.

Boyd, R. and P. J. Richerson. (1990b) Group selection among alternative evolutionarily stable strategies. *Journal of Theoretical Biology* 145:331–342.

Boyd, R. and P. J. Richerson. (in press a) How microevolutionary processes give rise to history. In *Evolution and History*, M. Nitecki, ed. Chicago: University of Chicago Press.

Boyd, R. and P. J. Richerson. (in press b) Punishment allows the evolution of cooperation (or anything else) in sizable groups. *Ethology and Sociobiology.*

Brandon, R. N. (1990) *Adaptation and Environment.* Princeton, NJ: Princeton University Press.

Brandon, Robert N. and R. M. Burian. (1984) *Genes, Organisms, Populations: Controversies over the Units of Selection.* Cambridge: MIT Press.

Bromage, T. G. and M. C. Dean. (1985) Re-evaluation of the age at death of Plio-Pleistocene fossil hominids. *Nature* 317:525–528.

Brown, J. (1970a) A note on the sexual division of labor. *American Anthropologist* 72:1073–1078.

Brown, J. (1970b) Economic organization and the position of women among the Iroquois. *Ethnohistory* 17:151–167.

Brown, J. L. (1964) The evolution of diversity in avian territorial systems. *Wilson Bulletin* 76:160–169.

Brown, J. L. (1982) Optimal group size in territorial animals. *Journal of Theoretical Biology* 95:793–810.

Brown, J. L. and G. H. Orians. (1970) Spacing behavior in mobile animals. *Annual Review of Ecology and Systematics* 1:239–62.

Brown, L. R. (1990) The illusion of progress. In *State of the World, 1990,* L. R. Brown et al., eds., pp. 3–16. New York: Norton.

Brown, L. R. and J. E. Young. (1990) Feeding the world in the nineties. In *State of the World, 1990,* L. R. Brown et al., eds., pp. 59–78. New York: Norton.

Brown, P. and A. Podolefsky. (1976) Population density, agricultural intensity, land tenure, and group size in the New Guinea highlands. *Ethnology* 15:211–238.

Brumfiel, E. (1983) Aztec state-making: Ecology, structure, and the origin of the state. *American Anthropologist* 85:261–284.

Brush, S. (1976) Introduction to cultural adaptations to mountain ecosystems (a symposium). *Human Ecology* 4:125–133.

Bunn, H. T. and E. Kroll. (1986) Systematic butchery by Plio-Pleistocene hominids at Olduvai Gorge, Tanzania. *Current Anthropology* 27:431–452.

Byrne, R. and A. Whiten, eds. (1986) *Machiavellian Intelligence.* Oxford: Claredon.

Calder, W. A. (1984) *Size, Function, and Life History.* Cambridge: Harvard University Press.

Caldwell, J. C. (1982) *Theory of Fertility Decline.* New York: Academic Press.

Campbell, D. T. (1965) Variation and selective retention in socio-cultural evolution. In *Social Change in Developing Areas,* H. R. Barringer et al., eds., pp. 19–49. Cambridge, MA: Schenkman.

Campbell, D. T. (1975) On the conflicts between biological and social evolution and between psychology and moral tradition. *American Psychologist* 30:1103–1126.

Campbell, D. T. (1983) The two distinct routes beyond kin selection to ultrasociality: Implications for the social sciences and humanities. In *The Nature of Prosocial Development: Theories and Strategies,* D. Bridgeman, ed., pp. 11–39. New York: Academic Press.

Cann, R. L., M. Stoneking, and A. C. Wilson. (1987). Mitochondrial DNA and human evolution. *Nature* 325:31–36.

Caraco, T. (1979) Time budgeting and group size: A theory. *Ecology* 60:611–617.

Carneiro, R. (1970) A theory of the origin of the state. *Science* 169:733–738.

Carneiro, R. (1979) Tree felling with the stone axe: An experiment carried out among the Yanomamö Indians of southern Venezuela. In *Ethnoarchaeology: Implications of Ethnography for Archaeology*, C. Kramer, ed., pp. 21–58. New York: Columbia University Press.

Carrier, D. R. (1984) The energetic paradox of human running and hominid evolution. *Current Anthropology* 25:483–495.

Cashdan, E. (1980) Egalitarianism among hunters and gatherers. *American Anthropologist* 82:116–120.

Cashdan, E. (1983) Territoriality among human foragers: Ecological models and an application to four Bushman groups. *Current Anthropology* 24:47–66.

Cashdan, E. (1984a) G//ana territorial organization. *Human Ecology* 12:443–463.

Cashdan, E. (1984b) The effects of food production on mobility in the Central Kalahari. In *From Hunters to Farmers*, J. D. Clark and S. A. Brandt, eds., pp. 311–327. Berkeley: University of California Press.

Cashdan, E. (1985) Coping with risk: Reciprocity among the Basarwa of Northern Botswana. *Man* 20:454–474.

Cashdan, E. (1987) Trade and its origins on the Botletle River, Botswana. *Journal of Anthropological Research* 43:121–138.

Caswell, H. (1982) Life history theory and the equilibrium status of populations. *American Naturalist* 120:317–339.

Cavalli-Sforza, L. L. and M. W. Feldman. (1981) *Cultural Transmission and Evolution: A Quantitative Approach*. Princeton, NJ: Princeton University Press.

Chagnon, N. A. (1968) *Yanomamö: The Fierce People*. New York: Holt, Rinehart, Winston.

Chagnon, N. A. (1979) Is reproductive success equal in egalitarian societies? In *Evolutionary Biology and Human Social Behavior: An Anthropological Perspective*, N. A. Chagnon and W. Irons, eds., pp. 374–401. North Scituate, MA: Duxbury Press.

Chagnon, N. A. (1988) Life histories, blood revenge, and warfare in a tribal population. *Science* 239:985–992.

Chagnon, N. A. and W. G. Irons, eds. (1979) *Evolutionary Biology and Human Social Behavior: An Anthropological Perspective*. North Scituate, MA: Duxbury Press.

Chagnon, N. A., J. V. Neel, L. Weitkamp, H. Gershowitz, and M. Ayres. (1970) The influence of cultural factors on the demography and pattern of gene flow from the Makiritare to the Yanomama Indians. *American Journal of Physical Anthropology* 32:339–350.

Chapais, B. and S. Schulman. (1980) An evolutionary model of female dominance relations in primates. *Journal of Theoretical Biology* 82:48–89.

Chapman, C. (1988) Patch use and patch depletion by the spider and howling monkeys of Santa Rosa National Park, Costa Rica. *Behaviour* 105:99–116.

Charles-Dominique, P. (1977) *Ecology and Behaviour of Nocturnal Prosimians*. London: Duckworth.

Charlesworth, B., et al. (1982) A neo-Darwinian commentary on macroevolution. *Evolution* 36:474–498.

Charnov, E. L. (1976) Optimal foraging: the marginal value theorem. *Theoretical Population Biology* 9:129–136.

Charnov, E. L. and J. R. Krebs. (1974) On clutch size and fitness. *Ibis* 116:217–219.

Charnov, E. L. and G. Orians. (1973) *Optimal Foraging: Some Theoretical Explorations.* Mimeo. Department of Biology. University of Utah, Salt Lake City.

Chase, I. D. (1980) Cooperative and noncooperative behavior in animals. *American Naturalist* 115:827–857.

Chayanov, A. (1966) *The Theory of Peasant Economy.* D. Thorner, D. Kerblay, and R. Smith, eds. (Engl. translation). New York: American Economic Association.

Cheney, D. L. (1981) Inter-group encounters among free-ranging vervet monkeys. *Folia Primatologica* 35:124–146.

Cheney, D. L. and R. R. Seyfarth. (1985) Social and non-social knowledge in vervet monkeys. *Philosophical Transactions of the Royal Society of London, Series B* 308:187–201.

Cheney, D. L. and R. R. Seyfarth. (1987) The influence of inter-group competition on the survival and reproduction of female vervet monkeys. *Behavioral Ecology and Sociobiology* 21:375–386.

Cheney, D. L. and R. W. Wrangham. (1987) Predation. In *Primate Societies,* B. B. Smuts, D. L. Cheney, R. M. Seyfarth, R. W. Wrangham, and T. T. Struhsaker, eds., pp. 227–239. Chicago: University of Chicago Press.

Cheverud, J. M., M. M. Dow, and W. Leutenegger. (1985) The quantitative assessment of phylogenetic constraints in comparative analyses: Sexual dimorphism in body weight among primates. *Evolution* 39:1335–1351.

Chu, C. Y. C. (1987) The dynamics of population growth, differential fertility, and inequality: Note. *American Economic Review* 77:1054–1056.

Clark, A. (1978) Sex ratio and local resource competition in a prosimian primate. *Science* 201:163–165.

Clark, C. W. (1973) The economics of overexploitation. *Science* 181:630–634.

Clark, C. W. and M. Mangel. (1984) Foraging and flocking strategies: Information in an uncertain environment. *American Naturalist* 123:626–641.

Clark, C. W. and M. Mangel. (1986) The evolutionary advantages of group foraging. *Theoretical Population Biology* 30:45–74.

Clark, P. J. and F. C. Evans. (1954) Distance to nearest neighbour as a measure of spatial relationships in populations. *Ecology* 35:445–453.

Cliff, A. D. and J. K. Ord. (1973) *Spatial Autocorrelation.* London: Pion.

Cliff, A. D., P. Haggett, J. K. Ord, K. Bassett, and R. Davies. (1975) *Elements of Spatial Structure: A Quantitative Approach.* Cambridge: Cambridge University Press.

Clutton-Brock, T. H. (1974) Primate social organization and ecology. *Nature* 250:539–542.

Clutton-Brock, T. H. (1983) Sons and daughters. *Nature* 298:11–13.

Clutton-Brock, T. H. (1989) Mammalian mating systems. *Proceedings of the Royal Society of London, Series B* 236:339–372.

Clutton-Brock, T. H. (1991) *The Evolution of Parental Care.* Princeton, NJ: Princeton University Press.

Clutton-Brock, T. H. and P. H. Harvey. (1977a) Primate ecology and social organization. *Journal of Zoology, London* 183:1–39.

Clutton-Brock, T. H. and P. H. Harvey. (1977b) Species differences in feeding and ranging behaviour in primates. In *Primate Ecology, Feeding and Ranging Behaviour in Lemurs, Monkeys and Apes,* T. H. Clutton-Brock, ed., pp. 539–556. New York: Academic Press.

Clutton-Brock, T. H. and P. H. Harvey. (1980) Primates, brains and ecology. *Journal of Zoology* 190:309–323.

Coale, A. J. (1986) The decline of fertility in Europe since the Eighteenth Century as a chapter in human demographic history. In *The Decline in Fertility in Europe*, A. J. Coale and S. C. Watkins, eds., pp. 1–30. Princeton, NJ: Princeton University Press.

Cody, M. L. (1974) Optimization in ecology. *Science* 183:1156–1164.

Cody, M. L. and C. B. J. Cody. (1972) Territory size, clutch size, and food in populations of wrens. *Condor* 74:473–477.

Cody, M. L. and J. M. Diamond, eds. (1975) *Ecology and the Evolution of Communities*. Cambridge, MA: Harvard University Press.

Cohen, G. A. (1978) *Karl Marx's Theory of History: A Defence*. Princeton, NJ: Princeton University Press.

Collins, D. A. and W. C. McGrew. (1988) Habitats of three groups of chimpanzee (*Pan troglodytes*) in Western Tanzania compared. *Journal of Human Evolution* 17:553–574.

Colwell, R. K. (1974) Predictability, constancy, and contingency of periodic phenomena. *Ecology* 55:1148–1153.

Cords, M., B. Mitchell, N. M. Tsingalia, and T. E. Rowell. (1986) Promiscuous mating among blue monkeys in the Kakamega forest, Kenya. *Ethology* 72:214–226.

Cosmides, L. and J. Tooby. (1989) Evolutionary psychology and the generation of culture, II. Case study: A computational theory of social exchange. *Ethology and Sociobiology* 10:51–97.

Crockett, C. M. and J. F. Eisenberg. (1987) Howlers: Variations in group size and demography. In *Primate Societies*, B. B. Smuts, D. L. Cheney, R. M. Seyfarth, R. W. Wrangham, and T. T. Struhsaker, eds., pp. 54–68. Chicago: University of Chicago Press.

Cronk, L. (1989) Low socioeconomic status and female-biased parental investment: The Mukogodo example. *American Anthropologist* 91:414–429.

Cronk, L. (1991) Wealth, status and reproductive success among the Mukogodo of Kenya. *American Anthropologist* 93:345–360.

Crook, J.H. (1965) The adaptive significance of avian social organization. In *Social Organization of Animal Communities*, P. E. Ellis, ed., pp. 181–218. London: Zoological Society of London.

Crook, J.H. (1970) The socio-ecology of primates. In *Social Behavior in Birds and Mammals*, J. H. Crook, ed., pp. 103–166. London: Academic Press.

Crook, J.H., and S. J. Crook. (1988) Tibetan polyandry: Problems of adaptation and fitness. In *Human Reproductive Behavior: A Darwinian Perspective*, L. Betzig, M. Borgerhoff Mulder, and P. Turke, eds., pp. 97–114. Cambridge: Cambridge University Press.

Crook, J.H. and J. S. Gartlan. (1966) On the evolution of primate societies. *Nature* 210:1200–1203.

Daly, M. and M. Wilson. (1978) *Sex, Evolution, and Behavior*. North Scituate, MA: Duxbury Press.

Darwin, C. (1859) *The Origin of Species*, 1st ed. London: John Murray.

Darwin, C. (1871) *The Descent of Man and Selection in Relation to Sex*. London: John Murray.

Datta, S. (1988) The acquisition of rank among free-ranging rhesus monkey siblings. *Animal Behavior* 36:754–772.

Datta, S. (1989) Demographic influences on dominance structure among female primates. In *Comparative Socioecology: The Behavioural Ecology of Humans and Other Mammals*, V. Standen and R. A. Foley, eds., pp. 265–284. Oxford: Blackwell.

Davies, N. B. (1976) Food, flocking, and territorial behaviour of the pied wagtail (*Motacilla alba yarrellii Gould*) in winter. *Journal of Animal Ecology* 45: 235–54.

Davies, N. B. and A. I. Houston. (1984) Territory economics. In *Behavioural Ecology: An Evolutionary Approach*, J. R. Krebs and N. B. Davies, eds., pp. 122–147. Oxford: Blackwell Scientific Publications.

Dawkins, R. (1976) *The Selfish Gene*. Oxford: Oxford University Press.

Dawkins, R. (1979) Twelve misunderstandings of kin selection. *Zeitschrift für Tierpsychologie* 51:184–200.

Dawkins, R. (1980) Good strategy or evolutionarily stable strategy? In *Sociobiology: Beyond Nature/Nurture?* G. W. Barlow and J. Silverberg, eds., pp. 331–367. Boulder, CO: Westview Press.

Dawkins, R. (1982) *The Extended Phenotype*. San Francisco: W. H. Freeman.

de Ruiter, J. R. (1986) The influence of group size on predator scanning and foraging behaviour of wedge-capped capuchin monkeys (*Cebus olivaceus*). *Behaviour* 98: 240–258.

de Waal, F. (1989a) *Peacemaking Among Primates*. Cambridge: Harvard University Press.

de Waal, F. (1989b) Food sharing and reciprocal obligations among chimpanzees. *Journal of Human Evolution* 18:433–459.

Denham, W. W. (1974) Infant transport among the Alyawara tribe, central Australia. *Oceania* 44:253–257.

Denham, W. W. (1978) *Alyawara Ethnographic Data Base*. New Haven: HRAF Press.

DeVore, I. and S. L. Washburn. (1963) Baboon ecology and human evolution. In *African Ecology and Human Evolution*, F. C. Howell and F. Bourliere, eds., pp. 335–367. Chicago: Aldine.

Dewar, R. E. (1984). Environmental productivity, population regulation and carrying capacity. *American Anthropologist* 86:601–614.

Dickemann, M. (1979) The ecology of mating systems in hypergynous dowry systems. *Social Science Information* 18:163–195.

Dittus, W. P. J. (1977) The social regulation of population density and age-sex distribution in the toque monkey. *Behaviour* 63:281–322.

Dittus, W. P. J. (1986) Sex differences in fitness following a group take-over among toque macaques: Testing models of social evolution. *Behavioral Ecology and Sociobiology* 19:257–266.

Draper, P. (1978) The learning environment for aggression and anti-social behavior among the !Kung. In *Learning Non-Aggression*, Ashley Montagu, ed., pp. 31–53. New York: Oxford University Press.

Duby, G. (1977) *The Chivalrous Society*. C. Postan, trans. London: Edward Arnold.

Dunbar, R. I. M. (1979) Population demography, social organization, and mating strategies. In *Primate Ecology and Human Origins*, I. S. Bernstein and E. A. Smith, eds., pp. 65–88. New York: Garland Press.

Dunbar, R. I. M. (1984) *Reproductive Decisions: An Ecological Analysis of Gelada Baboon Social Strategies*. Princeton NJ: Princeton University Press.

Dunbar, R. I. M. (1988) *Primate Social Systems*. London: Crook Helm.

Dunbar, R. I. M. (1990) Ecological modelling in an evolutionary context. *Folia primatologica* 53:235–247.

Dunbar, R. I. M. (1991) On sociobiological theory and the Cheyenne case. *Current Anthropology* 32:169–173.

Dunnell, R. C. (1980) Evolutiuonary theory and archaeology. In *Advances in Archaeological Method and Theory*, vol. 3, M. Schiffer, ed., pp. 35–99. New York: Academic Press.

Dupré, J., ed. (1987) The *Latest on the Best: Essays on Evolution and Optimality*. Cambridge, MA: Bradford Books/MIT Press.

Durham, W. H. (1976) The adaptive significance of cultural behavior. *Human Ecology* 4:89–121.

Durham, W. H. (1990) Advances in evolutionary culture theory. *Annual Review of Anthropology* 19:187–210.

Durnin, J. and G. Passmore. (1967) *Energy, Work, and Leisure*. London: Heinemann.

Durrenberger, E. P. (1984a) Operationalizing Chayanov. In *Chayanov, Peasants, and Economic Anthropology*, E. P. Durrenberger, ed., pp. 39–50. New York: Academic Press.

Durrenberger, E. P. (1984b) *Chayanov, Peasants, and Economic Anthropology*. New York: Academic Press.

Dwyer, P. (1974) The price of protein: Five hundred hours of hunting in the New Guinea highlands. *Oceania* 44:278–293.

Dwyer, P. and M. Minnegal. (1985) Andaman islanders, Pygmies, and an extension of Horn's model. *Human Ecology* 13:111–119.

Dyson-Hudson, R. (1983) An interactive model of human biological and behavioral adaptation. In *Rethinking Human Adaptation: Biological and Cultural Models*, R. Dyson-Hudson and M. A. Little, eds., pp. 79–96. Denver, CO: Westview Press.

Dyson-Hudson, R. and E. A. Smith. (1978) Human territoriality: An ecological reassessment. *American Anthropologist* 80:21–41.

Earle, T. (1978) *Economic and Social Organization of a Complex Chiefdom: The Halelea District, Kaua'i, Hawaii*. Anthropological Papers, No. 63. Ann Arbor: Museum of Anthropology, University of Michigan.

Earle, T. and A. L. Christensen. (1980) *Modeling Change in Prehistoric Subsistence Economies*. New York: Academic Press.

Eberhard, W. G. (1985) *Sexual Selection and Animal Genitalia*. Cambridge, MA: Harvard University Press.

Ebersole, J. P. (1980) Food density and territory size: An alternative model and a test on the reef fish *Eupomacentrus leucostictus*. *American Naturalist* 115:492–509.

Eisenberg, J. F. (1981) *The Mammalian Radiations: An Analysis of Trends in Evolution, Adaptation, and Behavior*. Chicago: University of Chicago Press.

Eisenberg, J. F., H. A. Muckenhirn, and R. Rudran. (1972) The relation between ecology and social structure in primates. *Science* 1976:863–874.

Eldredge, N. (1985) *Unfinished Synthesis: Biological Hierarchies and Modern Evolutionary Thought*. New York: Oxford University Press.

Elgar, M. A. and C. P. Catterall. (1981) Flocking and predator surveillance in house sparrows: Test of an hypothesis. *Animal Behaviour* 29:868–876.

Ellen, R. (1981) *Environment, Subsistence and System: The Ecology of Small-Scale Social Formations*. Cambridge: Cambridge University Press.

Ellison, P. T. (1991) Human ovarian function and reproductive ecology: New hypotheses. *American Anthropologist* 92:933–952.

Elster, J. (1982) Marxism, functionalism, and game theory: The case for methodological individualism. *Theory and Society* 11:453–482.

Elster, J. (1983) *Explaining Technical Change: A Case Study in the Philosophy of Science*. Cambridge: Cambridge University Press.

Elster, J. (1985) *Making Sense of Marx*. Cambridge: Cambridge University Press.

Elster, J. (1986) Introduction. In *Rational Choice*, J. Elster, ed., pp. 1–33. New York: New York University Press.

Ember, C. (1983) The relative decline in women's contribution to agriculture with intensification. *American Anthropologist* 85:285–304.

Ember, M. and C. R. Ember. (1971) The conditions favoring matrilocal versus patrilocal residence. *American Anthropologist* 73:571–594.

Emlen, J. M. (1966) The role of time and energy in food preferences. *American Naturalist* 100:611–617.

Emlen, J. M. (1973) *Ecology: An Evolutionary Approach*. Reading, MA: Addison-Wesley.

Emlen, S. T. (1984) Cooperative breeding in birds and mammals. In *Behavioural Ecology: An Evolutionary Approach*, J. R. Krebs and N. B. Davies, eds., pp. 305–339. Oxford: Blackwell Scientific.

Emlen, S. T. (1991) Evolution of cooperative breeding in birds and mammals. In *Behavioral Ecology: An Evolutionary Approach*, 3rd ed., J. Krebs and N. Davies, eds., pp. 301–337. Oxford: Blackwell Scientific Publications.

Emlen, S. T. and L. W. Oring. (1977) Ecology, sexual selection, and the evolution of mating systems. *Science,* 197:215–223.

Endler, J. A. (1984) *Natural Selection in the Wild*. Princeton, NJ: Princeton University Press.

Engle, P. (1988) How accurate are time use reports? Paper presented at the Annual Meeting of the American Ethnological Society, Santa Fe, NM, April 14.

Epple, G. and Y. Katz. (1980) Social influences on first reproductive success and related behaviors in the saddle back tamarin (*Saguinus fuscicollis*, Callitrichidae). *International Journal of Primatology* 1:171–183.

Erasmus, C. (1956) Culture, structure, and process: The appearance and disappearance of reciprocal farm labor. *Southwestern Journal of Anthropology* 12:444–469.

Erasmus, C. (1980) Comment on: Does labor time decrease with industrialization? *Current Anthropology* 21:289–291.

Essock-Vitale, S. (1984) The reproductive success of wealthy Americans. *Ethology and Sociobiology* 5:45–49.

Ewald, P. W., G. L. Hunt, and M. Warner. (1980) Territory size in western gulls: Importance of intrusion pressure, defense investments, and vegetation structure. *Ecology* 61:80–87.

Fagen, R. (1987) A generalized habitat matching rule. *Evolutionary Ecology* 1:5–10.

Felsenstein, J. (1985) Phylogenies and the comparative method. *American Naturalist* 125:1–15.

Fisher, R. A. (1930) *The Genetical Theory of Natural Selection.* Oxford: Oxford University Press.

Fisher, R. A. (1958) *The Genetical Theory of Natural Selection,* 2nd ed. New York: Dover.

Flannery, K. V. (1972) The cultural evolution of civilizations. *Annual Review of Ecology and Systematics* 3:395–425.

Fleming, A. F., N. D. Briggs, and C. E. Rossiter. (1985) Growth during pregnancy in Nigerian teenage primigravidae. *British Journal of Obstetrics and Gynaecology,* Supplement 5:32–39.

Flinn, M. V. (1981) Uterine versus agnatic kinship variability and associated cousin marriage preferences: An evolutionary biological analysis. In *Natural Selection and Social Behavior: Recent Research and New Theory,* R. D. Alexander and D. W. Tinkle, eds., pp. 439–475. New York: Chiron Press.

Flinn, M. (1988a) Mate guarding in a Caribbean village. *Ethology and Sociobiology* 9:1–29.

Flinn, M. (1988b) Parent-offspring interactions in a Caribbean village: Daughter guarding. In *Human Reproductive Behaviour,* L. Betzig, M. Borgerhoff Mulder, and P. Turke, eds., pp. 189–200. Cambridge: Cambridge University Press.

Flinn, M. V. and B. S. Low. (1987) Resource distribution, social competition, and mating patterns in human societies. In *Ecological Aspects of Social Evolution: Birds and Mammals,* D. I. Rubenstein and R. W. Wrangham, eds., pp. 217–243. Princeton, NJ: Princeton University Press.

Foley, R. A. (1985) Optimality theory in anthropology. *Man* 20:222–242.

Foley, R. A. (1987a) *Another Unique Species: Patterns in Human Evolutionary Ecology.* Harlow: Longman.

Foley, R. A. (1987b) Hominid species and stone tool assemblages: How are they related? *Antiquity* 61:380–392.

Foley, R. A. (1988) Hominids, humans and hunter-gatherers: an evolutionary perspective. In *Hunters and Gatherers 1: History, Evolution and Social Change,* T. Ingold, D. Riches, and J. Woodburn, eds., pp. 207–221. London: Berg.

Foley, R. A. (1989a) The evolution of hominid social behaviour. In *Comparative Socioecology: The Behavioural Ecology of Mammals and Man,* V. Standen and R. A. Foley, eds., pp. 473–494. Oxford: Blackwell Scientific Publications.

Foley, R. A. (1989b) The ecology of speciation: Comparative perspectives on the origins of modern humans. In *The Human Revolution: Behavioural and Biological Perspectives on the Origins of Modern Humans,* P. A. Mellars and C. B. Stringer, eds., pp. 298–320. Edinburgh: Edinburgh University Press.

Foley, R. A. (1990) The causes of brain enlargement in human evolution. *Behavioural and Brain Science* 13:354–356.

Foley, R. A. (in press) African terrestrial primates: The comparative evolutionary biology of *Theropithecus* and the Hominidae. In *Theropithecus as a Case Study in Primate Evolutionary Biology*, N. Jablonski, ed. Cambridge: Cambridge University Press.

Foley, R. A. and R. I. M. Dunbar. (1989) Bones of contention. *New Scientist*, 14 October, pp. 37–41.

Foley, R. A. and P. C. Lee. (1989) Finite social space, evolutionary pathways and reconstructing hominid behavior. *Science* 243:901–906.

Frank, R. H. (1988) *Passions Within Reason*. New York: Norton.

Fratkin, E. (1989) Household variation and gender inequality in Ariaal pastoral production: Results of a time allocation survey. *American Anthropologist* 91:430–440.

Frayer, D. (1984) Biological and cultural change in the European late Pleistocene and early Holocene. In *The Origins of Modern Humans: A World Survey of Fossil Evidence*, F. Smith and F. Spencer, eds., pp. 211–250. New York: Alan Liss.

Freeland, W. J. (1976) Pathogens and the evolution of primate sociality. *Biotropica* 8:12–24.

Fretwell, S. D. (1972) *Populations in a Seasonal Environment*. Princeton, NJ: Princeton University Press.

Fretwell, S. D. (1975) The impact of Robert MacArthur on ecology. *Annual Review of Ecology and Systematics* 6:1–13.

Fretwell, S. D. and H.L. Lucas. (1970) On territorial behaviour and other factors influencing habitat distribution in birds. *Acta Biotheoretica* 19:16–36.

Fried, M. (1967) *The Evolution of Political Society: An Essay in Political Anthropology*. New York: Random House.

Frisch, R. (1984) Body fat, puberty, and fertility. *Science* 199:22–30.

Froemming, S. (1986) *Public Goods, Limited Good, and Peasant Rationality: Cargos and Cost Sharing in Mesoamerican Indian Communities*. Research Competency Paper for Master's Degree in Anthropology, University of Washington, Seattle.

Galef, B. G., Jr. (1988) Communication of information concerning distant diets in a social, central-place foraging species: *Rattus norvegicus*. In *Social Learning: Psychological and Biological Perspectives*, T. R. Zentall and B. G. Galef, Jr., eds., pp. 119–139. Hillsdale, NJ: Lawrence Erlbaum.

Galt, A. H. (1979) Exploring the cultural ecology of field fragmentation and scattering on the island of Pantelleria, Italy. *Journal of Anthropological Research* 35:93–108.

Garber, P. A. (1988a) Foraging decisions during nectar feeding by tamarin monkeys (*Saguinus mystax* and *Saguinus fuscicollis*, Callitrichidae, Primates) in Amazonian Peru. *Biotropica* 20:100–106.

Garber, P. A. (1988b) Diet, foraging patterns, and resource defense in a mixed species troop of *Saguinus mystax* and *Saguinus fuscicollis* in Amazonian Peru. *Behaviour* 105:18–34.

Garber, P. A., L. Moya, and C. Malaga. (1984) A preliminary field study of the moustached tamarin (*Saguinus mystax*) in northeastern Peru: Questions concerned with the evolution of a communal breeding system. *Folia Primatologica* 42:17–32.

Garfinkel, A. (1981) *Forms of Explanation: Rethinking the Questions of Social Theory.* New Haven, CT: Yale University Press.

Gaulin, S. and R. W. FitzGerald. (1986) Sex differences in spatial ability: An evolutionary hypothesis and test. *American Naturalist* 127:74–88.

Gaulin, S. and H. Hoffman. (1988) Evolution and development of sex differences in spatial ability. In *Human Reproductive Behavior: A Darwinian Perspective*, L. L. Betzig, M. Borgerhoff Mulder, and P. Turke, eds., pp. 129–152. Cambridge: Cambridge University Press.

Gaulin, S. and L. Sailer. (1985) Are females the ecological sex? *American Anthropologist* 87:111–189.

Gautier-Hion, A. and J.-P. Gautier. (1978) Le singe de Brazsa: Une strategie originale. *Zeitschrift für Tierpsychologie* 46:84–104.

Geertz, C. (1973) Thick description: Toward an interpretive theory of culture. In *The Interpretation of Cultures*, pp. 3–30. New York: Basic Books.

Ghiglieri, M. P. (1984) *The Chimpanzees of Kibale Forest.* New York: Columbia University Press.

Ghiglieri, M. P. (1987) Sociobiology of the great apes and the hominid ancestor. *Journal of Human Evolution* 16:319–357.

Gill, F. B. and L. L. Wolf. (1975) Economics of feeding territoriality in the golden-winged sunbird. *Ecology* 56:333–345.

Godin, J. and M. Keenleyside. (1984) Foraging on patchily distributed prey by a cichlid fish (Teleostei, Cichlidae): A test of the ideal free distribution theory. *Animal Behaviour* 32:120–131.

Goldizen, A. W. and J. W. Terborgh. (1986) Cooperative polyandry and helping behavior in saddle-backed tamarins (*Saguinus fuscicollis*). In *Primate Ecology and Conservation*, J. G. Else and P. C. Lee, eds., pp. 191–198. Cambridge: Cambridge University Press.

Goodall, J. (1986) *The Chimpanzees of Gombe: Patterns of Behavior.* Cambridge, MA: Harvard University Press.

Goodman, M., P. Griffin, A. Estioko-Griffin, and J. Grove. (1985) The compatibility of hunting and mothering among the Agta hunter-gatherers of the Philippines. *Sex Roles* 4:132–141.

Gould, R. (1981) Comparative ecology of food-sharing in Australia and Northwest California. In *Omnivorous Primates: Gathering and Hunting in Human Evolution*, R. Harding and G. Teleki, eds., pp. 422–454. New York: Columbia University Press.

Gould, R. (1982) Sharing among hunter-gatherers. In *Resource Managers: North American and Australian Hunter-Gatherers*, N. Williams and E. Hunn eds., pp. 69–91. Boulder, CO: Westview Press.

Gould, R. and J. E. Yellen. (1987) Man the hunted: Determinants of household spacing in desert and tropical foraging societies. *Journal of Anthropological Archaeology* 6:77–103.

Gould, S. J. (1980) Is a new and general theory of evolution emerging? *Paleobiology* 6:119–130.

Gould, S. J. (1981) *The Mismeasure of Man.* New York: Norton.

Gould, S. J. (1982) Darwinism and the expansion of evolutionary theory. *Science* 216:380–387.

Gould, S. J. and R. C. Lewontin. (1979) The spandrels of San Marco and the Panglossian paradigm: A critique of the adaptationist programme. *Proceedings of the Royal Society of London, Series B* 205:581–598.

Grafen, A. (1984) Natural selection, kin selection and group selection. In *Behavioural Ecology: An Evolutionary Approach*, 2nd ed., J. R. Krebs and N. B. Davies, eds., pp. 62–84. Sunderland, MA: Sinauer Associates.

Greene, P. J. (1978) Promiscuity, paternity, and culture. *American Ethnologist* 5:151–159.

Grieg-Smith, P. (1983) *Quantitative Plant Ecology*, 3rd ed. Berkeley: University of California Press.

Griffin, D. (1981) *The Question of Animal Awareness*. New York: Rockefeller University Press.

Griffin, D. (1982) *Animal Mind–Human Mind*. Berlin: Springer-Verlag.

Grine, F. E. (1981) Trophic differences between "gracile" and "robust" australopithecines: A scanning electron microscope analysis of occlusal events. *South African Journal of Science* 77:203–230.

Grine, F. E., ed. (1989) *The Evolutionary History of the "Robust" Australopithecines*. Hawthorne, NY: Aldine de Gruyter.

Gross, D. (1985) Time allocation: a tool for the study of cultural behavior. *Annual Review of Anthropology* 14:214–255.

Gross, M. R. and R. C. Sargent. (1985) The evolution of male and female parental care in fishes. *American Zoologist* 25:807–822.

Grossbard, A. S. (1976) An economic analysis of polygyny: The case of Maiduguri. *Current Anthropology* 17:701–707.

Gruber, H. E. (1974) *Darwin on Man: A Psychological Study of Scientific Creativity*. New York: Dutton.

Hakansson, T. (1989) Family structure, bridewealth, and environment in Eastern Africa. *Ethnology* 28:117–134.

Hallpike, C. R. (1986) *Principles of Social Evolution*. Oxford: Clarendon.

Halstead, P. (1981) From determinism to uncertainty: Social storage and the rise of the Minoan palace. In *Economic Archaeology: Towards an Integration of Ecological and Social Approaches*, A. Sheridan and G. Bailey, eds., pp. 187–214. BAR International Series 96.

Halstead, P. and J. O'Shea (1982) A friend in need is a friend indeed: Social storage and the origins of social ranking. In *Ranking, Resource and Exchange*, C. Renfrew and S. Shennan, eds., Cambridge: Cambridge University Press.

Hames, R. (1978) *A Behavioral Account of the Division of Labor among the Ye'kwana*. Ph.D thesis, Dept. of Anthropology, University of California, Santa Barbara.

Hames, R. (1979a) Interaction and relatedness among the Ye'kwana: A preliminary analysis. In *Evolutionary Biology and Human Social Behavior*, N. Chagnon and W. Irons, eds., pp. 201–209. North Scituate, MA: Duxbury Press.

Hames, R. (1979b) A comparison of the efficiencies of the shotgun and bow in neotropical forest hunting. *Human Ecology* 7:219–252.

Hames, R. (1980) Games depletion and hunting zone rotation among the Ye'kwana and Yanomamö of Amazonas, Venezuela. In *Working Papers on South American Indians*, R. Hames ed., pp. 24–62. Bennington, VT: Bennington College.

Hames, R. (1983) The settlement pattern of a Yanomamö population bloc: A behavioral ecological interpretation. In *Adaptive Responses of Native Amazonians*, R. B. Hames and W. T. Vickers, eds., pp. 393–427. New York: Academic Press.

Hames, R. (1987a) Relatedness and garden labor exchange among the Ye'kwana. *Ethology and Sociobiology* 8:354–392.

Hames, R. (1987b) Game conservation or efficient hunting? In *The Question of the Commons*, B. McCay and J. Acheson, eds., pp. 92–107. Tucson: University of Arizona Press.

Hames, R. (1988) The allocation of parental care among the Ye'kwana. In *Human Reproductive Behaviour*, L. Betzig, M. Borgerhoff Mulder, and P. Turke, eds., pp. 237–254. Cambridge: Cambridge University Press.

Hames, R. (1989) Time, efficiency, and fitness in the Amazonian protein quest. *Research in Economic Anthropology* 11:43–85.

Hames, R. (1990) Sharing among the Yanomamö, the effects of risk. In *Risk and Uncertainty in Tribal and Peasant Economies*, E. Cashdan, ed., pp. 89–105. Boulder, CO: Westview.

Hames, R. (1992) Variation in paternal investment among the Yanomamö. In *Father–Child Relations: Cultural and Biosocial Contexts*, B. Hewlett, ed. Chicago: Aldine de Gruyter.

Hames, R. and W. Vickers. (1982) Optimal foraging theory as a model to explain variability in Amazonian hunting. *American Ethnologist* 9:358–378.

Hamilton, W. D. (1964) The genetical evolution of social behaviour, I, II. *Journal of Theoretical Biology* 7:1–52.

Hamilton, W. D. (1971) Geometry for the selfish herd. *Journal of Theoretical Biology* 31:295–311.

Hamilton, W. D. (1975) Innate social aptitudes of man: An approach from evolutionary genetics. In *Biosocial Anthropology*, R. Fox, ed., pp. 133–155. London: Malaby.

Hampton, J. (1986) *Hobbes and the Social Contract Tradition*. Cambridge: Cambridge University Press.

Hanna, J. and P. Baker (1983) Human heat tolerance. *Annual Review of Anthropology* 12:259–284.

Harcourt, A. H. (1989) Environment, competition and reproductive performance of female monkeys. *Trends in Ecology and Evolution* 4:101–105.

Hardin, G. (1968) The tragedy of the commons. *Science* 162:1243–1248.

Hardin, R. (1982) *Collective Action*. Baltimore: Johns Hopkins University Press.

Harestad, A. S. and F. L. Bunnell. (1979) Home range and body weight—A reevaluation. *Ecology* 60:389–402.

Harpending, H. C. (1981) Perspectives on the theory of social evolution. In *Current Developments in Anthropological Genetics*, Vol. 1: Theory and Methods, J. H. Mielke and M. H. Crawford, eds., pp. 45–64. New York: Plenum Press.

Harpending, H. C. and J. Bertram. (1975) Human population dynamics in archaeological time. *American Antiquity* 40:82–91.

Harpending, H. C. and H. Davis. (1977) Some implications for hunter-gatherer ecology derived from the spatial structure of resources. *World Archaeology* 8:275–286.

Harpending, H. C. and P. Draper. (1986) Selection against human family organization. In *On Evolutionary Anthropology: Essays in Honor of Harry Hoijer 1983*, B. J. Williams, ed., pp. 37–75. Malibu, CA: Undena Publications.

Harpending, H. C. and A. R. Rogers. (1987) On Wright's mechanism for intergroup selection. *Journal of Theoretical Biology* 127:51–61.

Harpending, H. C. and A. R. Rogers. (1990) Fitness in stratified societies. *Ethology and Sociobiology* 11:497–509.

Harpending, H., A. Rogers, and P. Draper. (1987) Human sociobiology. *Yearbook of Physical Anthropology* 30:127–150.

Harper, D. G. C. (1982) Competitive foraging in mallards: "Ideal free" ducks. *Animal Behaviour* 30:575–584.

Harris, M. (1979a) *People, Culture, and Nature*. New York: Harper and Row.

Harris, M. (1979b) *Cultural Materialism: The Struggle for a Science of Culture*. New York: Random House.

Harrison, G. and J. Hirshleifer. (1989) An experimental evaluation of weakest link/best shot models of public goods. *Journal of Political Economy* 97:201–225.

Hart, J. (1978) From subsistence to market: A case study in Mbuti net hunters. *Human Ecology* 6:325–353.

Hartung, J. (1985) Matrilineal inheritance: new theory and analysis. *Behavioral and Brain Sciences* 8:661–688.

Harvey, P. H., M. Kavanagh, and T. H. Clutton-Brock. (1978) Sexual dimorphism in primate teeth. *Journal of the Zoological Society of London* 186:475–485.

Harvey, P. H., R. D. Martin, and T. H. Clutton-Brock. (1987) Life histories in comparative perspective. In *Primate Societies*, B. B. Smuts, D. L. Cheney, R. M. Seyfarth, R. W. Wrangham, and T. T. Struhsaker, eds., pp. 181–196. Chicago: University of Chicago Press.

Hassell, M. P. and R. M. May. (1985) From individual behaviour to population dynamics. In *Behavioural Ecology: Ecological Consequences of Adaptive Behaviour*, R. M. Sibly and R. H. Smith, eds., pp. 3–32. Boston: Blackwell.

Hausfater, G. (1984) Infanticide in langurs: Strategies, counterstrategies, and parameter values. In *Infanticide: Comparative and Evolutionary Perspectives*, G. Hausfater and S. B. Hrdy, eds., pp. 257–281. Hawthorne, NY: Aldine.

Hausfater, G. and B. J. Meade. (1982) Alternation of sleeping groves by yellow baboons (*Papio cynocephalus*) as a strategy for parasite avoidance. *Primates* 23:287–297.

Hawkes, K. (1987) Limited needs and hunter-gatherer time allocation. *Ethology and Sociobiology* 8:87–91.

Hawkes, K. (1990) Why do men hunt? Some benefits for risky choices. In *Risk and Uncertainty in Tribal and Peasant Economies*, E. Cashdan, ed., pp. 145–166. Boulder, CO: Westview Press.

Hawkes, K. (1991) Showing off: Tests of another hypothesis about men's foraging goals. *Ethology and Sociobiology* 11:29–54.

Hawkes, K., K. Hill, H. Kaplan, and A. M. Hurtado (1987) Some problems with instantaneous scan sampling. *Journal of Anthropological Research* 43:239–247.

Hawkes, K., K. Hill, and J. O'Connell. (1982) Why hunters gather: Optimal foraging and the Aché of Eastern Paraguay. *American Ethnologist* 9:379–398.

Hawkes, K., K. Hill, J. O'Connell, and E. Charnov. (1985) How much is enough? Hunters and limited needs. *Ethology and Sociobiology* 6:3–15.

Hawkes, K. and J. O'Connell. (1983) Affluent hunters? Some comments in light of the Alyawara case. *American Anthropologist* 83:622–626.

Hawkes, K., J. O'Connell, and N. Blurton Jones. (1989) Hardworking Hadza grand-mothers. In *Comparative Socioecology: The Behavioural Ecology of Mammals and Man*, V. Standen and R. Foley, eds., pp. 341–366. London: Blackwell Scientific Publications.

Hawkes, K., J. O'Connell, and N. Blurton Jones. (1991) Hunting income patterns among the Hadza: Big game, common goods, foraging goals, and the evolution of the human diet. In *Philosophical Transactions of the Royal Society*, in press.

Hayden, B. (1981) Subsistence and ecological adaptations of modern hunter-gatherers. In *Omnivorous Primates*, R. S. O. Harding and G. Teleki, eds., pp. 344–421. New York: Columbia University Press.

Heffley, S. (1981) The relationship between northern Athapaskan settlement patterns and resource distribution. In *Hunter-Gatherer Foraging Strategies*, B. Winterhalder and E. A. Smith, eds., pp. 126–147. Chicago: University of Chicago Press.

Heinz, H. J. (1972) Territoriality among the Bushmen in general and the !Ko in particular. *Anthropos* 67:405–416.

Hewlett, B. S. (1986) Intimate fathers: paternal patterns of holding among Aka Pygmies. In *The Father's Role in Cross-Cultural Perspective*, M. Lamb, ed., pp. 34–61. New York: Erlbaum.

Hewlett, B. S. (1988) Sexual selection and paternal investment among Aka Pygmies. In *Human Reproductive Behavior: A Darwinian Perspective*. L. Betzig, M. Borgerhoff Mulder, and P. Turke, eds., pp. 263–276. Cambridge: Cambridge University Press.

Hewlett, B. S. ed. (1992) *Father–Child Relations: Cultural and Biosocial Contexts*. Hawthorne, NY: Aldine.

Hill, A. (1985) Early hominids from Baringo, Kenya. *Nature* 315:222–224.

Hill, A. (1987) Causes of perceived faunal change in the later Neogene of East Africa. *Journal of Human Evolution* 16:583–596.

Hill, K. (1982) Hunting and human evolution. *Journal of Human Evolution* 11:521–544.

Hill, K. (1988) Macronutrient modifications of optimal foraging theory: An approach using indifference curves applied to some modern foragers. *Human Ecology* 16:157–197.

Hill, K. and K. Hawkes. (1983) Neotropical hunting among the Aché of Eastern Paraguay. In *Adaptive Responses of Native Amazonians*, R. Hames and W. Vickers, eds., pp. 223–267. New York: Academic Press.

Hill, K. and H. Kaplan. (1988) Tradeoffs in male and female reproductive strategies among Aché foragers. In *Human Reproductive Effort*, L. Betzig, M. Borgerhoff Mulder, and P. Turke, eds., pp. 277–306. Cambridge: Cambridge University Press.

Hill, K. and H. Kaplan. (1989) Population description and dry season subsistence among the newly contacted Yora (Yaminahua) of Manu National Park, Peru. *National Geographic Research* 5(3):317–334.

Hill, K., H. Kaplan, K. Hawkes, and A. Hurtado. (1984) Seasonal variance in the diet of Aché hunter-gatherers in Eastern Paraguay. *Human Ecology* 12:145–180.

Hill, K., H. Kaplan, K. Hawkes, and A. Hurtado. (1985) Men's time allocation to subsistence work among the Aché of Eastern Paraguay. *Human Ecology* 13:29–47.

Hill, K., H. Kaplan, K. Hawkes, and A. Hurtado. (1987) Foraging decisions among Aché hunter-gatherers: New data and implications for optimal foraging models. *Ethology and Sociobiology* 8:1–36.

Hirshfield, M. F., and D. W. Tinkle. (1975) Natural selection and the evolution of reproductive effort. *Proceedings of the National Academy of Sciences* 72:2227–2231.

Hirshleifer, J. (1977) Economics from a biological viewpoint. *Journal of Law and Economics* 20:1–52.

Hirshleifer, J. (1980) *Price Theory and Applications,* 2nd ed. Englewood Cliffs, NJ: Prentice-Hall.

Hirshleifer, J. (1982) Evolutionary models in economics and law: Cooperation versus conflict strategies. *Research in Law and Economics* 4:1–60.

Hirshleifer, J. (1983) From weakest-link to best-shot: The voluntary provision of public goods. *Public Choice* 41:371–386.

Hirshleifer, J. (1987) On the emotions as guarantors of threats and promises. In *The Latest on the Best: Essays on Evolution and Optimality,* John Dupré, ed., pp. 307–326. Cambridge, MA: MIT Press.

Hirshleifer, J. and J. C. Martinez Coll. (1988) What strategies can support the evolutionary emergence of cooperation? *Journal of Conflict Resolution* 32:367–398.

Hladik, C. M. (1975) Ecology, diet, and social patterns in Old and New World primates. In *Socioecology and Psychology of Primates,* R. H. Tuttle, ed., pp. 3–35. The Hague: Mouton.

Hladik, C. M. (1977) Chimpanzees of Gabon and chimpanzees of Gombe: Some comparative data on diet. In *Primate Ecology,* T. H. Clutton-Brock, ed., pp. 481–501. London: Academic Press.

Hobcraft, J. N., J. W. McDonald, and S. O. Rutstein. (1983) Child-spacing effects on infant and early child mortality. *Population Index* 49:585–618.

Hoffman, J. (1984) *The Gramscian Challenge: Coercion and Consent in Marxist Political Theory.* Oxford: Basil Blackwell.

Hofstadter, R. (1944) *Social Darwinism in American Thought, 1860–1915.* Philadelphia: University of Pennsylvania Press.

Homans, G. C. (1967) *The Nature of Social Science.* New York: Harcourt, Brace.

Hommon, R. J. (1986) Social evolution in ancient Hawaii. In *Island Societies: Archaeological Approaches to Evolution and Transformation,* P. V. Kirch, ed., pp. 55–68. Cambridge: Cambridge University Press.

Horn, H. (1968) The adaptive significance of colonial nesting in the brewer's blackbird *Euphagus cyanocephalus. Ecology* 49:682–694.

Houston, A. I. and N. B. Davies. (1985) The evolution of cooperation and life history in the dunnock *Prunella modularis.* In *Behavioural Ecology,* R. M. Sibley and R. H. Smith, eds., pp. 471–487. Oxford: Blackwell Scientific Publications.

Howe, H. F. (1980) Monkey dispersal and waste of a neotropical fruit. *Ecology* 61:944–959.

Howell, F. C. (1978) The hominidae. In *Evolution of African Mammals*, V. J. Maglio and H. B. S. Cooke, eds., pp. 154–248. Cambridge: MA: Harvard University Press.

Hrdy, S. B. (1974) Male-male competition and infanticide among the langurs (*Presbytis entellus*) of Abu, Rajasthan. *Folia Primatologica* 22:19–58.

Hrdy, S. B. (1981) *The Woman That Never Evolved*. Cambridge, MA: Harvard University Press.

Hrdy, S. B. (1992) Fitness tradeoffs in the history and evolution of delegated mothering with special reference to wet-nursing, abandonment and infanticide. In *Protection and Abuse of Infants*, S. Parmigiania, B. Svare, and F. vom Saal, eds. London: Harwood.

Humphrey, N. K. (1976) The social function of intellect. In *Growing Points in Ethology*, P. P. G. Bateson and R. A. Hinde, eds., pp. 303–317. Cambridge: Cambridge University Press.

Hunt, E. and R. C. Hunt. (1978) Irrigation, conflict and politics: a Mexican case. In *Origins of the State: The Anthropology of Political Evolution*, R. Cohen and E. R. Service, eds., pp. 69–124. Philadelphia: ISHI Press.

Hurtado, A. M. (1985) *Women's Subsistence Strategies Among Aché Hunter-Gatherers of Eastern Paraguay*. Ph.D. dissertation. Department of Anthropology, University of Utah.

Hurtado, A. M. and K. Hill. (1989) Seasonality in a foraging society: variation in diet, work effort, fertility, and the sexual division of labor among the Hiwi of Venezuela. *Journal of Anthropological Research* 34:293–346.

Hurtado, A. M. and K. Hill. (1990) Experimental studies of tool efficiency among Machiguenga women and implications for root-digging foragers. *Journal of Anthropological Research* 35:207–217.

Hurtado, A. M. and K. Hill (1992) Tradeoffs between female food acquisition and childcare among Hiwi and Aché foragers. *Human Nature* 3:185–216.

Hurtado, A. M. and K. Hill. (1992) Paternal effect on offspring survivorship among Aché and Hiwi hunter-gatherers: implications for modelling pair-bond stability In *Father–Child Relations: Cultural and Biosocial Contents*, B. Hewlett, ed., Hawthorne, NY: Aldine de Gruyter.

Hurtado, A.M., K. Hawkes, K. Hill, and H. Kaplan. (1985) Female subsistence strategies among the Aché of Eastern Paraguay. *Human Ecology* 13:1–28.

Hutchinson, G. E. (1965) *The Ecological Theater and the Evolutionary Play*. New Haven, CT: Yale University Press.

Hutchinson, G. E. (1978) *An Introduction to Population Ecology*. New Haven, CT: Yale University Press.

Huxley, L. (1920) *Thomas Henry Huxley: A Character Sketch*. Freeport, NY: Books for Libraries Press.

Ingold, T. (1986) *Evolution and Social Life*. Cambridge: Cambridge University Press.

Irons, W. (1979a) Cultural and biological success. In *Evolutionary Biology and Human Social Behavior: An Anthropological Perspective*, N. A. Chagnon and W. Irons, eds., pp. 257–272. North Scituate, MA: Duxbury.

Irons, W. (1979b) Investment and primary social dyads. In *Evolutionary Biology and Human Social Behavior*, N. A. Chagnon and W. Irons, eds., pp. 181–212. North Scituate, MA: Duxbury Press.

Irons, W. (1980) Is Yomut social behavior adaptive? In *Sociobiology: Beyond Nature/Nurture?* G. Barlow and J. Silverberg, eds., pp. 417–463. Boulder, CO: Westview Press.

Irons, W. (1983) Human female reproductive strategies. In *Social Behavior of Female Vertebrates*, S. K. Wasser, ed., pp. 169–213. New York: Academic Press.

Irons, W. (1990) Let's make our perspective broader rather than narrower: A comment on Turke's "Which humans behave adaptively, and why does it matter?" and on the so-called DA-DP debate. *Ethology and Sociobiology* 11:361–374.

Irwin, C. (1989) The sociocultural biology of Netsilingmiut female infanticide. In *The Sociobiology of Sexual and Reproductive Strategies*, A. E. Rasa, C. Vogel, and E. Voland, eds., pp. 234–264. London: Chapman and Hall.

Isaac, G. (1978) The food sharing behavior of protohuman hominids. *Scientific American* 238(4):90–108.

Isaac, G. (1984) The archaeology of human origins: Studies in the Lower Pleistocene of East Africa. *Advances in World Archaeology* 3:1–79.

Janson, C. N. (1984) Female choice and mating system of the brown capuchin monkey *Cebus apella* (Primates: Cebidae). *Zeitschrift für Tierpsychologie* 65:177–200.

Janson, C. N. (1985) Aggressive competition and individual food intake in wild brown capuchin monkeys. *Behavioral Ecology and Sociobiology* 18:125–138.

Janson, C. N. (1986) The mating system as a determinant of social evolution in capuchin monkeys (Cebus). In *Primate Ecology and Conservation*, J. G. Else and P. C. Lee, eds., pp. 169–179. Cambridge: Cambridge University Press.

Janson, C. N. (1988a) Intra-specific food competition and primate social structure: A synthesis. *Behaviour* 105:1–17.

Janson, C. N. (1988b) Food competition in brown capuchin monkeys (*Cebus apella*): Quantitative effects of group size and tree productivity. *Behaviour* 105:53–76.

Janson, C. N. (1990) Ecological consequences of individual spatial choice in foraging brown capuchin monkeys (*Cebus apella*). *Animal Behaviour* 38:922–934.

Janson, C. N. and C. P. van Schaik. (1988) Recognizing the many faces of primate food competition: Methods. *Behaviour* 105:165–186.

Jelliffe, D. B. and I. Maddocks (1964) Notes on ecologic malnutrition in the New Guinea Highlands. *Clinical Pediatrics* 3:432–438.

Jerison, H. J. (1973) *Evolution of the Brain and Intelligence*. New York: Academic Press.

Jochim, M. A. (1981) *Strategies for Survival*. New York: Academic Press.

Jochim, M. A. (1983) Optimization models in context. In *Archaeological Hammers and Theories*, A. S. Keene and J. A. Moore, eds., pp. 157–172. New York: Academic Press.

Johanson, D. C., C. O. Lovejoy, W. H., Kimbel, T. D. White, S. C. Ward, M. E. Bush, B. M. Latimer, and Y. Coppens. (1982) Morphology of the Plio-Pleistocene partial skeleton AL288-1 from the Hadar Formation, Ethiopia. *American Journal of Physical Anthropology* 57:403–452.

Johnson, A. (1975) Time allocation in a Machiguenga community. *Ethnology* 14:301–310.

Johnson, A. (1977) The energy costs of technology in a changing environment: A Machiguenga Case. In *Material Culture*, H. Latchman and R. Merrill, eds., pp. 155–168. St. Paul, MN: West Publishing.

Johnson, A. and C. Behrens. (1982) Nutritional criteria in Machiguenga food production decisions: A linear-programming analysis. *Human Ecology* 10:167–190.

Johnson, A. and O. Johnson. (1989) *Machiguenga Time Allocation Data Base*. Cross-Cultural Studies in Time Allocation. New Haven: HRAF Press.

Johnson, G. A. (1982) Organizational structure and scalar stress. In *Theory and Explanation in Archaeology*, C. Renfrew et al., eds. New York: Academic Press.

Jones, K. J. and D. B. Madsen. (1989) Calculating the cost of resource transportation: A Great Basin example. *Current Anthropology* 30:529–534.

Jorde, L. B. (1977) Precipitation cycles and cultural buffering in the prehistoric Southwest. In *For Theory Building in Archaeology: Essays on Faunal Remains, Aquatic Resources, Spatial Analysis, and Systemic Modeling*, L. R. Binford, ed., pp. 385–396. New York: Academic Press.

Jorde, L. B. and H. C. Harpending. (1976) Cross-spectral analysis of rainfall and human birth rate: An empirical test of a linear model. *Journal of Human Evolution* 5:129–138.

Jungers, W. L. (1982) Lucy's limbs: Skeletal allometry and locomotion in *A. afarensis*. *Nature* 297:676–678.

Kagel, J., L. Green, and T. Caraco. (1986) When foragers discount the future: Constraint or adaptation? *Animal Behaviour* 34:271–283.

Kaplan, H. (1983) *Food Sharing Among Adult Conspecifics: Research with the Aché Hunter-Gatherers of Eastern Paraguay*. Ph.D. dissertation. Department of Anthropology, University of Utah.

Kaplan, H., and K. Hill (1985a) Hunting ability and reproductive success among male Aché foragers: Preliminary results. *Current Anthropology* 26:131–133.

Kaplan, H., and K. Hill. (1985b) Food sharing among Aché foragers: Tests of explanatory hypotheses. *Current Anthropology* 26:223–245.

Kaplan, H., K. Hill, K. Hawkes, and A. M. Hurtado. (1984) Food sharing among Aché foragers. *Current Anthropology* 25:223–245.

Kaplan, H., K. Hill, and A. Hurtado. (1988) Risk, foraging and food sharing among the Aché. In *Risk and Uncertainty in Tribal and Peasant Economies: Ecological and Economic Perspectives*, E. Cashdan, ed., pp. 104–177. Boulder, CO: Westview Press.

Kaplan, H., K. Hill, and A. Hurtado. (1990) Risk, foraging, and food sharing among the Aché. In *Risk and Uncertainty in Tribal and Peasant Economies*, E. Cashdan, ed., pp. 107–144. Boulder, CO: Westview Press.

Katz, M. and M. Konner. (1981) The role of the father: An anthropological perspective. In *The Role of the Father in Child Development*, M. Lamb, ed., pp. 189–222. New York: Wiley.

Kay, R. F. (1985) Dental evidence for the diet of *Australopithecus*. *Annual Review of Anthropology* 14:315–342.

Keegan, W. F. (1986) The optimal foraging analysis of horticultural production. *American Anthropologist* 88:92–107.

Keeley, L. H. (1988) Hunter-gatherer economic complexity and "population pressure": A cross-cultural analysis. *Journal of Anthropological Archaeology* 7: 373–411.

Keene, A. S. (1981) Optimal foraging in a nonmarginal environment: A model of prehistoric subsistence strategies in Michigan. In *Hunter-Gatherer Foraging Strategies*, E. Smith and B. Winterhalder, eds., pp. 171–193. Chicago: University of Chicago Press.

Keene, A. S. (1982) *Prehistoric Foraging in a Temperate Forest: A Linear Programming Model*. New York: Academic Press.

Kelly, R. C. (1985) *The Nuer Conquest*. Ann Arbor: University of Michigan Press.

Kelley, R. L. (1983) Hunter-gatherer mobility strategies. *Journal of Anthropological Research* 39:277–306.

Kershaw, K. A. (1973) *Quantitative and Dynamic Plant Ecology*. London: William Clowes and Sons.

Kingsland, S. E. (1985) *Modeling Nature*. Chicago: University of Chicago Press.

Kirch, P. V. (1984) *The Evolution of the Polynesian Chiefdoms*. Cambridge: Cambridge University Press.

Kirkpatrick, M. and R. Lande. (1989) The evolution of maternal characters. *Evolution* 43:485–503.

Kitcher, P. (1985) *Vaulting Ambition: Sociobiology and the Quest for Human Nature*. Cambridge, MA: MIT Press.

Kleiman, D. G. (1977) Monogamy in mammals. *Quarterly Review of Biology* 52:39–69.

Klein, L. L. and D. J. Klein. (1975) Social and ecological contrasts between four taxa of neotropical primates. In *Socioecology and Psychology of Primates*, R. Tuttle, ed., pp. 59–86. The Hague: Mouton.

Klein, R. G. (1989) *The Human Career: Human Biological and Cultural Origins*. Chicago: University of Chicago Press.

Knauft, B. M. (1987) Divergence between cultural success and reproductive fitness in preindustrial cities. *Cultural Anthropology* 2:94–114.

Knodel, J. (1978) Natural fertility in preindustrial Germany. *Population Studies* 32:481–510.

Kodric-Brown, A. and J. H. Brown. (1978) Influence of economies, interspecific competition, and sexual dimorphism on territoriality of migrant rufous hummingbirds. *Ecology* 59:285–296.

Konner, M. (1982) *The Tangled Wing*. New York: Holt, Reinhart, and Winston.

Konner, M. and C. Worthman (1980) Nursing frequency, gonadal function, and birth spacing among !Kung hunter-gatherers. *Science* 207:788–791.

Kortlandt, A. (1984) Habitat richness, foraging range and diet in chimpanzees and some other primates. In *Food Acquisition and Processing in Primates*. D. J. Chivers, B. A. Wood, and A. Bilsborough, eds., pp. 119–160. New York: Plenum Press.

Krebs, J. R. (1982) Territorial defence in the great tit (*Parus major*): Do residents always win? *Behavioral Ecology and Sociobiology* 11:185–194.

Krebs, J. R. and N. B. Davies, eds. (1978) *Behavioural Ecology: An Evolutionary Approach.* Oxford: Blackwell.

Krebs, J. R. and N. B. Davies, eds. (1991) *Behavioral Ecology: an Evolutionary Approach,* 3rd ed. Oxford: Blackwell.

Krebs, J. R. and R. H. McCleery. (1984) Optimization in behavioural ecology. In *Behavioural Ecology: An Evolutionary Approach,* J. R. Krebs and N. B. Davies, eds., pp. 91–121. Sunderland, MA: Sinauer Associates.

Krebs, J. R., M. H. MacRoberts, and J. M. Cullen. (1972) Flocking and feeding in the great tit *Parus major* —An experimental study. *Ibis* 114:507–530.

Kroeber, A. (1917) The superorganic. *American Anthropologist* 19:163–213.

Kruuk, H. (1972) *The Spotted Hyena.* Chicago: University of Chicago Press.

Kruuk, H. and D. MacDonald (1985) Group territories of carnivores: Empires and enclaves. In *Behavioural Ecology: Ecological Consequences of Adaptive Behaviour,* R. M. Sibly and R. H. Smith, eds., pp. 521–536. Oxford: Blackwell Scientific Publications.

Kuchikura, Y. (1988) Efficiency and focus of blowpipe hunting among Semaq Beri hunter-gatherers of Peninsular Malaysia. *Human Ecology* 16(3):271–305.

Kurland, J. A. (1979) Paternity, mother's brother, and human sexuality. In *Evolutionary Biology and Human Social Behavior,* N. Chagnon and W. Irons, eds., pp. 86–132. North Scituate, MA: Duxbury Press.

Kurland, J. A. and S. Beckerman. (1985) Optimal foraging and hominid evolution: Labor and reciprocity. *American Anthropologist.* 87:73–93.

Lack, D. (1947) The significance of clutch size. *Ibis* 89:302–352.

Lack, D. (1948) Selection and family size in starlings. *Evolution* 2:95–110.

Lack, D. (1954) The evolution of reproductive rates. In *Evolution as a Process,* J. S. Huxley, A. C. Hardy, and E. B. Ford, eds., pp. 143–156. London: Allen and Unwin.

Lack, D. (1968) *Ecological Adaptations for Breeding in Birds.* London: Methuen.

Lam, D. (1986) The dynamics of population growth, differential fertility, and inequality. *The American Economic Review* 76:1103–1116.

Lancaster, J. and C. Lancaster. (1983) Parental investment: The hominid adaptation. In *How Humans Adapt,* D. Ortner, ed., pp. 33–69. Washington, DC: Smithsonian Institute Press.

Lande, R. (1979) Quantitative genetic analysis of multivariate evolution, applied to brain-body size allometry. *Evolution* 33:402–416.

Lande, R. (1981) Models of speciation by sexual selection on polygenic traits. *Proceedings of the National Academy of Sciences USA* 78:3721–3725.

Landell, W. (1964) Terrestrial animals in humid heat: Man. In *Handbook of Physiology: Adaptation to the Environment,* D. Dill, ed., pp. 76–99. New York: Wiley Interscience.

Landers, J. (1990) Fertility decline and birth spacing among London Quakers. In *Fertility and Resources,* J. Landers and V. Reynolds, eds., pp. 92–117. Cambridge: Cambridge University Press.

Lathrop et al. (1983) Evaluating pedigree data. I. The estimation of pedigree error in the presence of marker mistyping. *American Journal of Human Genetics* 35:241–262.

Lazarus, J. (1989) The logic of mate desertion. *Animal Behaviour* 39:657–671.

Leakey, M. D. and R. L. Hay. (1979) Pliocene footprints in the Laetolil Beds at Laetoli, north Tanzania. *Nature* 278:317–323.

Lee, P. C. (1989) Comparative ethological approaches in modelling hominid behaviour. *Ossa* 14:113–126.

Lee, P. C. (1991) Adaptations to environmental change: An evolutionary perspective. In *Primate Responses to Environmental Change*, H. O. Box, ed., pp. 39–56. London: Chapman and Hall.

Lee, R. B. (1968) What hunters do for a living, or, how to make out on scarce resources. In *Man the Hunter*, R. Lee and I. DeVore, eds., pp. 30–48. Chicago: Aldine.

Lee, R. B. (1969) !Kung Bushman subsistence: an input-output analysis. In *Ecological Essays*, D. Damas, ed., pp. 18–33. Ottawa: National Museum of Canada.

Lee, R. B. (1979) *The !Kung San: Men, Women, and Work in a Foraging Society.* Cambridge: Cambridge University Press.

Lee, R. D. (1977) Methods and models for analyzing historical series of births, deaths, and marriages. In *Population Patterns in the Past*, R. D. Lee, ed., pp. 337–370. New York: Academic Press.

Lee, R. D. (1987) Population dynamics of humans and other animals. *Demography* 24:443–465.

Lefebvre, L. and B. Palameta. (1988) Mechanisms, ecology, and population diffusion of socially learned, food-finding behavior in feral pigeons. In *Social Learning: Psychological and Biological Perspectives*, T. R. Zentall and B. G. Galef, Jr., eds., pp. 141–164. Hillsdale, NJ: Lawrence Erlbaum.

Lehrman, D. S. (1970) Semantic and conceptual issues in the nature-nurture problem. In *Development and Evolution of Behavior*, L. R. Aronson, E. Tobach, D. S. Lehrman, and J. S. Rosenblatt, eds., pp. 17–52. San Francisco: W. H. Freeman.

Leighton, M. and D. R. Leighton. (1982) The relationship of size of feeding aggregate to size of food patch: Howler monkeys (*Alouatta palliata*) feeding in *Trichilia cipo* fruit trees on Barro Colorado Island. *Biotropica* 14:81–90.

Lessels, C. M. (1991) The evolution of life histories. In *Behavioural Ecology*, 3rd ed., J. R. Krebs and N. B. Davies, eds., pp. 32–68. Oxford: Blackwell Scientific Publications.

Levi-Strauss, C. (1969) *The Elementary Structures of Kinship.* Boston: Beacon Press (first published in 1949).

Levins, R. (1966) The strategy of model building in population biology. *American Scientist* 54:421–431.

Levins, R. (1968) *Evolution in Changing Environments.* Princeton, NJ: Princeton University Press.

Lewontin, R. C. (1970) The units of selection. *Annual Review of Ecology and Systematics* 1:1–18.

Lewontin, R. C. (1974). The analysis of variance and the analysis of causes. *American Journal of Human Genetics* 26:400–411.

Lewontin, R. C. (1979) Fitness, survival, and optimality. In *Analysis of Ecological Systems*, D. J. Horn, R. Mitchell, and G. R. Stairs, eds., pp. 3–21. Columbus: Ohio State University Press.

Lewontin, R. C. (1987) The shape of optimality. In *The Latest on the Best: Essays on Evolution and Optimality*, J. Dupré, ed., pp. 151–159. Cambridge: MIT Press.

Lewontin, R. C. and R. Levins. (1989) On the characterization of density and resource availability. *American Naturalist* 134:513–524.

Little, M. and M. Morren. (1976) *Ecology, Energetics, and Human Variability.* Dubuque, IL: W. C. Brown.

Logue, A. (1988) Research on self control: An integrating framework. *Behavioral and Brain Sciences* 11:665–709.

Łomnicki, A. (1978) Individual differences between animals and natural regulation of their numbers. *Journal of Animal Ecology* 47:461–475.

Łomnicki, A. (1980) Regulation of population density due to individual differences and patchy environment. *Oikos* 35:185–193.

Łomnicki, A. (1982) Individual heterogeneity and population regulation. In *Current Problems in Sociobiology*, King's College Sociobiology Group, eds., pp. 153–167. New York: Cambridge University Press.

Łomnicki, A. (1988) *Population Ecology of Individuals.* Princeton: Princeton University Press.

Łomnicki, A. and J. Ombach. (1984) Resource partitioning within a single species population and population stability: A theoretical model. *Theoretical Population Biology* 25:21–28.

Łomnicki, A. and S. Sedziwy. (1988) Resource partitioning and population stability under exploitation competition. *Journal of Theoretical Biology* 132:119–120.

Łomnicki, A. and S. Sedziwy. (1989) Do individual differences in resource intakes without monopolization cause population stability and persistence? *Journal of Theoretical Biology* 136:317–326.

Lovejoy, C. O. (1988) The evolution of human walking. *Scientific American* 259:82–29.

Low, B. S. (1988) Pathogen stress and polygyny in humans. In *Human Reproductive Behaviour: A Darwinian Perspective*, L. Betzig, M. Borgerhoff Mulder, and P. Turke, eds., pp. 115–127. Cambridge: Cambridge University Press.

Low, B. S. (1990) Human responses to environmental extremeness and uncertainty: A cross-cultural perspective. In *Risk and Uncertainty in Tribal and Peasant Economies*, E. Cashdan, ed., pp. 229–255. Boulder, CO: Westview Press.

Luce, R. D. and H. Raiffa. (1957) *Games and Decisions.* New York: Wiley.

Lumsden, C. J. and E. O. Wilson. (1981) *Genes, Mind, and Culture: The Coevolutionary Process.* Cambridge, MA: Harvard University Press.

MacArthur, R. H. (1958) Population ecology of some warblers of northeastern coniferous forests. *Ecology* 39:599–619.

MacArthur, R. H. (1960) On the relation between reproductive value and optimal predation. *Proceedings of the National Academy of Sciences* 46:143–145.

MacArthur, R. H. (1961) Population effects of natural selection. *American Naturalist* 95:195–199.

MacArthur, R. H. (1972) *Geographical Ecology.* New York: Harper and Row.

MacArthur, R. H. and E. R. Pianka. (1966) On optimal use of a patchy environment. *American Naturalist* 100:603–609.

MacArthur, R. H. and E. O. Wilson. (1967) *The Theory of Island Biogeography.* Princeton, NJ: Princeton University Press.

Macdonald, D. W. (1981) Resource dispersion and the social organization of the red fox, *Vulpes vulpes*. In *Proceedings of the Worldwide Furbearer Conference,* Vol. 2, J. A. Chapman and D. Pursley, eds., pp. 918–949. Baltimore: University of Maryland Press.

Macdonald, D. W. and G. M. Carr. (1989) Food security and the rewards of tolerance. In *Comparative Socioecology,* V. Standen and R. A. Foley, eds., pp. 75–99. Oxford: Blackwell Scientific Publications.

Macfarlane, A. (1986) *Marriage and Love in England: Modes of Reproduction 1300–1840.* Oxford: Basil Blackwell.

Malthus, T. R. (1914 [1798]) *An Essay on Population,* vol. 1. London: John M. Dent.

Marshall, L. (1976) *The !Kung of Nyae Nyae.* Cambridge: Harvard University Press.

Martin, P. and G. Bateson. (1986) *Measuring Behaviour: An Introductory Guide.* Cambridge: Cambridge University Press.

Martin, R. D. (1983) *Human Brain Evolution in an Ecological Context.* 52nd James Arthur Lecture on the Evolution of the Brain. American Museum of Natural History.

Martin, R. D. (1985) Primates: A definition. In *Major Topics in Primate and Human Evolution,* B. A. Wood, L. Martin, and P. J. Andrews, eds., pp. 1–31. Cambridge: Cambridge University Press.

Martin, R. D. (1989) *Primate Origins and Evolution: A Phylogenetic Reconstruction.* London: Chapman and Hall.

Mauss, M. (1967 [1925]) *The Gift: Forms and Functions of Exchange in Archaic Societies.* New York: Norton.

May, R. M. (1974) *Stability and Complexity in Model Ecosystems,* 2nd ed. Princeton, NJ: Princeton University Press.

May, R. M., ed. (1976) *Theoretical Ecology: Principles and Applications,* 1st ed. Philadelphia: W. B. Saunders.

May, R. M. (1981) Models for single populations. In *Theoretical Ecology: Principles and Applications,* R. M. May, ed., pp 5–29. Sunderland, MA: Sinauer.

Maynard Smith, J. (1964) Group selection and kin selection. *Nature* 201:1145–1147.

Maynard Smith, J. (1968) *Mathematical Problems in Biology.* New York: Cambridge University Press.

Maynard Smith, J. (1974a) The theory of games and the evolution of animal conflicts. *Journal of Theoretical Biology* 47:209–221.

Maynard Smith, J. (1974b) *Models in Ecology.* Cambridge: Cambridge University Press.

Maynard Smith, J. (1976) Commentary: Group selection. *Quarterly Review of Biology* 51:277–283.

Maynard Smith, J. (1977) Parental investment—a prospective analysis. *Animal Behaviour* 25:1–9.

Maynard Smith, J. (1978) Optimization theory in evolution. *Annual Review of Ecology and Systematics* 9:31–56.

Maynard Smith, J. (1982a) *Evolution and the Theory of Games.* Cambridge: Cambridge University Press.

Maynard Smith, J. (1982b) The evolution of social behaviour—A classification of models. In *Current Problems in Sociobiology*. King College Sociobiology Group, eds., pp. 29–44. Cambridge: Cambridge University Press.

Maynard Smith, J. (1987) How to model evolution. In *The Latest on the Best: Essays on Evolution and Optimality*, John Dupré, ed., pp. 119–132. Cambridge: MIT Press.

Maynard Smith, J. and G. A. Parker. (1976) The logic of asymmetric contests. *Animal Behaviour* 24:159–175.

Maynard Smith, J. and G. R. Price. (1973) The logic of animal conflict. *Nature* 246:15–18.

Mayr, E. (1974) Behavior programs and evolutionary strategies. *American Scientist* 62:650–659.

Mayr, E. (1976 [1961]) Cause and effect in biology. In *Evolution and the Diversity of Life*, E. Mayr, ed., pp. 359–371. Cambridge, MA: Harvard University Press.

Mayr, E. (1977) Darwin and natural selection. *American Scientist* 65:321–327.

Mayr, E. (1988) Is biology an autonomous science? In *Toward a New Philosophy of Biology*, E. Mayr, ed., pp. 8–23. Cambridge, MA: Harvard University press.

McCloskey, D. M. (1975a) The persistence of English common fields. In *European Peasants and Their Markets*, W. N. Parker and E. L. Jones, eds., pp. 73–119. Princeton: Princeton University Press.

McCloskey, D. M. (1975b) The economics of enclosure: A market analysis. In *European Peasants and Their Markets*, W. N. Parker and E. L. Jones, eds., pp. 123–160. Princeton, NJ: Princeton University Press.

McCloskey, D. M. (1976) English open fields and behavior toward risk. *Research in Economic History* 1:144–170.

McGrew, W. C. (1978) Evolutionary implications of sex differences in chimpanzee predation and tool use. In *The Great Apes*, D. Hamburg and E. McCown, eds. Palo Alto, CA: Benjamin Staples.

McGrew, W. C. (1989) Why is ape tool-use so confusing? In *Comparative Socioecology: The Behavioral Ecology of Humans and Other Mammals*, V. Standen and R. A. Foley, eds., pp. 457–494. Oxford: Blackwell.

McGrew, W. C. (in press) *Chimpanzee Material Culture*. Cambridge: Cambridge University Press.

McHenry, H. M. (1988) New estimates of body weight in early hominids and their significance to encephalization and megadontia in "robust" australopithecines. In *Evolutionary History of the "Robust" Australopithecines*, F. E. Grine, ed., pp. 133–148. Hawthorne, NY: Aldine de Gruyter.

McNab, B. (1963) Bioenergetics and the determination of home range size. *American Naturalist* 97:133–140.

McNamara, J. M. and A. I. Houston. (1986) The common currency for behavioral decisions. *American Naturalist* 127:358–378.

McNeill, W. H. (1963) *The Rise of the West: A History of the Human Community*. Chicago: University of Chicago Press.

McNutt, C. (1981) Nearest neighbors, boundary effect, and the old flag trick: A general solution. *American Antiquity* 46:471–591.

Mealey, L. (1985) The relationship between social status and biological success: A case study of the Mormon religious hierarchy. *Ethology and Sociobiology* 6:249–257.

Medawar, P. (1982) *Pluto's Republic*. Oxford: Oxford University Press.

Mellars, P. A. and C. B. Stringer, eds. (1989) *The Human Revolution: Behavioural and Biological Perspectives on the Origins of Modern Humans*. Edinburgh: Edinburgh University Press.

Metcalfe, D. and K. R. Barlow. (1992) A model for exploring the optimal tradeoff between field processing and transport. *American Anthropologist*, in press.

Michod, R. E. (1982) The theory of kin selection. *Annual Review of Ecology and Systematics* 13:23–55.

Milinski, M. (1984) Competitive resource sharing: an experimental test of a learning rule for ESSs. *Animal Behaviour* 32:233–242.

Mills, S. and J. Beatty. (1984) The propensity interpretation of fitness. In *Conceptual Issues in Biology*, E. Sober, ed., pp. 34–57. Cambridge, MA: The MIT Press. (Originally published in *Philosophy of Science* 46: 263–286, 1979.)

Milton, K. (1981) Distribution patterns of tropical plant foods as an evolutionary stimulus to primate mental development. *American Anthropologist* 83:534–548.

Minge-Kalman, W. (1980) Does labor time decrease with industrialization? A survey of time allocation studies. *Current Anthropology* 21:279–298.

Mitani, J. and P. Rodman. (1979) Territoriality: The relation of ranging pattern and home range size to defendability, with an analysis of territoriality among primate species. *Behavioral Ecology and Sociobiology* 5:241–251.

Mitchell, C. L., B. Boinski, and C. P. van Schaik. (1991) Competitive regimes and female bonding in two species of squirrel monkeys (*Saimiri oerstedi* and *Saimiri sciureus*). *Behavioral Ecology and Sociobiology* 25:55–60.

Moore, B. Jr., (1966) *Social Origins of Dictatorship and Democracy: Lord and Peasant in the Making of the Modern World*. Boston: Beacon Press.

Moore, J. H. (1990) The reproductive success of Cheyenne war chiefs: A case contrary to Chagnon's Yanomami. *Current Anthropology* 31:322–330.

Mori, A. (1979) Analysis of population changes by measurement of body weight in the Koshima troop of Japanese monkeys. *Primates* 20:371–397.

Munroe, R. H., R. L. Munroe, A. Koel, R. Bolton, C. Michelson, and C. Bolton (1983) Time allocation in four societies. *Ethnology* 22:355–370.

Munroe, R. H., R. L. Munroe, and H. Shumin (1984) Children's work in four cultures: Determinants and consequences. *American Anthropologist* 83:369–379.

Murdock, G. (1965) *Culture and Society*. Pittsburgh: University of Pittsburgh Press.

Murdock, G. and C. Provost. (1973) Factors in the division of labor by sex: A cross-cultural analysis. *Ethnology* 12:203–225.

Myers, J. P., P. G. Connors and F. A. Pitelka. (1979) Territory size in wintering sanderlings: the effects of prey abundance and intruder density. *Auk* 96:551–561.

Nag, M., B. White, and R. Peet. (1978) An anthropological approach to the study of the economic value of children in Java and Nepal. *Current Anthropology* 19:293–306.

National Research Council (1981) *Techniques for the Study of Primate Population Ecology*. Washington DC: National Academy Press.

Needham, R. (1975) Polythetic classification: Convergence and consequences. *Man* 10:349–369.

Neel, J. V. and K. M. Weiss. (1975) The genetic structure of a tribal population, the

Yanomama Indians. XII. Biodemographic studies. *American Journal of Physical Anthropology* 42:25–52.

Nelson, R. R. and S. G. Winter. (1982) *An Evolutionary Theory of Economic Change.* Cambridge, MA: Harvard University Press.

Netting, R. (1969) Ecosystems in process: A comparative study of change in two West African societies. In *Contributions to Anthropology: Ecological Essays,* D. Damas, ed., pp. 102–112. Ottawa: Queen's Printer.

Nicholson, A. J. (1954) An outline of the dynamics of animal populations. *Australian Journal of Zoology* 2:9–65.

Nisbett, R. and L. Ross. (1980) *Human Inference: Strategies and Shortcomings of Social Judgment.* Englewood Cliffs, NJ: Prentice-Hall.

Nishida, T. (1987) Local traditions and cultural transmission. In *Primate Societies,* B. B. Smuts, D. L. Cheney, R. M. Seyfarth, R. W. Wrangham, and T. T. Struhsaker, eds., pp. 462–474. Chicago: University of Chicago Press.

North, Douglass (1981) *Structure and Change in Economic History.* New York: Norton.

Nudds, T. (1978) Convergence of group size strategies by mammalian social carnivores. *American Naturalist* 112:957–960.

Nunney, L. (1985) Group selection, altruism, and structured deme models. *American Naturalist* 126:212–230.

O'Connell, J. F. (1987) Alyawara site structure and its archaeological implications. *American Antiquity* 52:74–108.

O'Connell, J. and K. Hawkes. (1981) Alyawara plant use and optimal foraging theory. In *Hunter-Gatherer Foraging Strategies,* E. Smith and B. Winterhalder, eds., pp. 99–125. Chicago: Chicago University Press.

O'Connell, J. and K. Hawkes. (1984) Food choice and foraging sites among the Alyawara. *Journal of Anthropological Research* 40:504–535.

Olson, M. (1965) *The Logic of Collective Action: Public Goods and the Theory of Groups.* Cambridge MA: Harvard University Press.

Orians, G. H. (1969) On the evolution of mating systems in birds and mammals. *American Naturalist* 103:589–603.

Orians, G. H. (1973) A diversity of textbooks: ecology comes of age. *Science* 181:1238–1239.

Orians, G. H. and N. E. Pearson (1979) On the theory of central place foraging. In *Analysis of Ecological Systems,* D. J. Horn, B. R. Stairs, and R. D. Mitchell, eds., pp. 155–177. Columbus: Ohio State University Press.

Orlove, B. S. (1976) Integration through production: The use of zonation in Espinar. *American Ethnologist* 4:84–101.

O'Shea, J. (1981) Coping with scarcity: exchange and social storage. In *Economic Archaeology: Towards an Integration of Ecological and Social Approaches,* A. Sheridan and G. Bailey, eds., pp. 167–186. BAR International Series 96.

Oster, G. and E. O. Wilson. (1984) A critique of optimization theory in evolutionary biology. In *Conceptual Issues in Evolutionary Biology,* Elliott Sober, ed., pp. 271–288. Cambridge, MA: MIT Press. (Originally published as Chapter 8 in *Caste and Ecology in the Social Insects,* G. F. Oster and E. O. Wilson, Princeton University Press Monographs in Population Biology, No. 12, 1978.)

Packer, C. (1977) Reciprocal altruism in olive baboons. *Nature* 265:441–443.

Pagel, M. D. and P. H. Harvey. (1989) Taxonomic differences in the scaling of brain on body weight among mammals. *Science* 244:1589–1593.

Panter-Brick, C. (1989) Motherhood and subsistence work: The Tamang of rural Nepal. *Human Ecology* 17:205–228.

Park, T. (1954) Experimental studies of interspecific competition. II. Temperature, humidity and competition in two species of tribolium. *Physiological Zoology* 27:177–238.

Parker, G. A. (1974) Assessment strategy and the evolution of fighting behaviour. *Journal of Theoretical Biology* 47:223–243.

Parker, G. A. (1984) Evolutionarily stable strategies. In *Behavioural Ecology: An Evolutionary Approach*, 2nd ed., J. R. Krebs and N. B. Davies, eds., pp. 30–61. Sunderland, MA: Sinauer Associates.

Parker, G. A. and P. Hammerstein. (1985) Game theory and animal behaviour. In *Evolution: Essays in Honour of John Maynard Smith*, P. J. Greenwood, P. H. Harvey, and M. Slatkin, eds., pp. 73–94. Cambridge: Cambridge University Press.

Parker, G. A. and N. Knowlton (1980) The evolution of territory size—some ESS models. *Journal of Theoretical Biology* 84:445–476.

Parker, S. T. and K. R. Gibson. (1979) A model of the evolution of intelligence and language in early hominids. *Behavioural and Brain Sciences* 2:367–407.

Passingham, R. (1982) *The Human Primate*. San Francisco: Freeman.

Passmore, R. and J. B. G. Durnin. (1955) Human energy expenditure. *Physiological Review* 35:801–835.

Pennington, R. and H. Harpending. (1988) Fitness and fertility among Kalahari !Kung. *American Journal of Physical Anthropology* 77:202–319.

Peoples, J. G. (1982) Individual or group advantage? A reinterpretation of the Maring ritual cycle. *Current Anthropology* 23:291–310.

Peritz, E. and P. F. Rust (1972) On the estimation of the nonpaternity rate using more than one blood-group system. *American Journal of Human Genetics* 24:46–53.

Peterson, N. (1972) Totemism yesterday: Sentiment and local organization among the Australian aborigines. *Man* 7:12–32.

Petrie, M. (1984) Territory size in the moorhen (*Gallinula chloropus*): An outcome of RHP aysmmetry between neighbours. *Animal Behaviour* 32:861–870.

Pettengill, J. S. (1979) The impact of military technology on European income distribution. *Journal of Interdisciplinary History* 10(2):201–225.

Philipp, E. E. (1973) Discussion remark in "Law and ethics of A. I. D. and embryo transfer." *Cibe Foundation Symposium* 17:66.

Pianka, E. R. (1974) *Evolutionary Ecology*. New York: Harper and Row.

Pianka, E. R. (1978) *Evolutionary Ecology*, 2nd ed. New York: Harper and Row.

Pianka, E. R. and W. S. Parker. (1975) Age-specific reproductive tactics. *American Naturalist* 109:453–464.

Pielou, E. C. (1977) *Mathematical Ecology*. New York: Wiley.

Pinder, D., I. Shimada, and D. Gregory. (1979) The nearest-neighbor statistic: archaeological applications and new developments. *American Antiquity* 44:430–445.

Pitcher, T. J., A. E. Magurran, and I. J. Winfield. (1982) Fish in larger shoals find food faster. *Behavioral Ecology and Sociobiology* 10:149–151.

Platt, T. and K. L. Denman. (1975) Spectral analysis in ecology. *Annual Review of Ecology and Systematics* 6:189–210.

Polanyi, Karl (1957) The economy as instituted process. In *Trade and Market in the Early Empires: Economies in History and Theory*, K. Polanyi, C. Arensberg, and H. Pearson, eds., pp. 243–270. Chicago: Henry Regnery Company.

Pomianowski, A. (1988) Evolution of female mate preference for male genetic quality. *Oxford Surveys in Evolutionary Biology* 5:136–184.

Pope, G. G. (1988) Current issues in Far Eastern palaeoanthropology. *Proceedings of the Second Conference on the Palaeoenvironment of East Asia from the Mid-Tertiary*, Vol. 2, pp. 1097–1123.

Post, D., G. Hausfater, and S. A. McCuskey. (1980) Feeding behaviour of yellow baboons (*Papio cynocephalus*): Relationship to age, gender and dominance rank. *Folia Primatologica* 34:170–195.

Potthoff, R. F. and M. Whittinghill. (1965) Maximum-likelihood estimation of the proportion of nonpaternity. *American Journal of Human Genetics* 17:480–494.

Potts, R. (1989) *Early Hominid Activities at Olduvai*. Chicago: Aldine de Gruyter.

Powell, R. A. (1989) Effects of resource productivity, patchiness and predictability on mating and dispersal strategies. In *Comparative Socioecology: The Behavioral Ecology of Humans and Other Mammals*, V. Standen and R. A. Foley, eds., pp. 101–124. Oxford: Blackwell.

Prentice, A. M. (1980) Variations in maternal dietary intake, birthweight, and breast milk output in the Gambia. In *Maternal Nutrition During Pregnancy and Lactation*, H. Aebi and R. G. Whitehead, eds., pp. 167–183. Bern: Hans Huber.

Provine, W. B. (1971) *The Origins of Theoretical Population Genetics*. Chicago: University of Chicago Press.

Pulliam, H. R. (1973) On the advantages of flocking. *Journal of Theoretical Biology* 38:419–422.

Pulliam, H. R. (1974) On the theory of optimal diets. *American Naturalist* 108:59–75.

Pulliam, H. R. (1976) The principle of optimal behavior and the theory of communities. In *Perspectives in Ethology*, P. P. G. Bateson and P. H. Klopfer, eds., vol. 2, pp. 311–332. New York: Plenum.

Pulliam, H. R. and T. Caraco (1984) Living in groups: is there an optimal group size? In *Behavioral Ecology*, 2nd ed., J. R. Krebs and N. B. Davies, eds., pp. 122–147. Oxford: Blackwell.

Pulliam, H. R. and C. Dunford. (1980) *Programmed to Learn: An Essay on the Evolution of Culture*. New York: Columbia University Press.

Pulliam, H. R., G. H. Pyke, and T. Caraco. (1982) The scanning behavior of juncos: A game-theoretical approach. *Journal of Theoretical Biology* 95:89–103.

Radcliffe-Brown, A. R. (1952) *Structure and Function in Primitive Society*. Oxford: Oxford University Press.

Rambo, A. (1978) Bows, blowpipes, and blunderbusses: Ecological implications of weapons change among the Malaysian Negritos. *Malayan Nature Journal* 32(2):209–216.

Rapoport, A. (1974) Prisoner's dilemma—Recollections and observations. In *Game Theory as a Theory of Conflict Resolution*, A. Rapoport, ed., pp. 17–34. Dordrecht: D. Reidel.

Rapoport, A., M. J. Guyer, and D. G. Gordon. (1976) *The 2 × 2 Game*. Ann Arbor: University of Michigan Press.

Rappaport, R. A. (1968) *Pigs for the Ancestors*. New Haven: Yale University Press.

Rappaport, R. A. (1987) *Pigs for the Ancestors: Ritual in the Ecology of New Guinea People*, enlarged edition. New Haven, CT: Yale University Press.

Rapport, D. (1981) Foraging behavior of *Stentor coeruleus*: a microeconomic approach. In *Foraging Behavior*, A. Kamil and T. Sargent, eds., pp. 77–93. New York: Garland STPM.

Rapport, D. and J. Turner. (1977) Economic models in ecology. *Science*. 195: 367–373.

Rasmusen, E. (1989) *Games and Information*. Oxford: Basil Blackwell.

Reichert, S. E. and P. Hammerstein. (1983) Game theory in the ecological context. *Annual Review of Ecology and Systematics* 14:377–411.

Renfrew, C. (1984) *Approaches to Social Archaeology*. Cambridge, MA: Harvard University Press.

Reynolds, V. (1976) *The Biology of Human Action*. San Francisco: Freeman.

Rhine, R. J. (1975) The order of movement of yellow baboons *(Papio cynocephalus)*. *Folia Primatologica* 23:72–104.

Rhoades, R. E. and S. I. Thompson. (1975) Adaptive strategies in alpine environments: beyond ecological particularism. *American Ethnologist* 2:535–551.

Richards, T. (1983) Weather, nutrition, and the economy: short-run fluctuations in births, deaths, and marriages, France 1740–1909. *Demography* 20: 197–212.

Richerson, P. J. and R. Boyd. (1984) Natural selection and culture. *BioScience*. 34:430–434.

Richerson, P. J., and R. Boyd. (1987) Simple models of complex phenomena: The case of cultural evolution. In *The Latest on the Best*, J. Dupré, ed., pp. 27–52. Cambridge, MA: MIT Press.

Richerson, P. J. and R. Boyd. (1989) A Darwinian theory for the evolution of symbolic cultural traits. In *The Relevance of Culture*, M. Freilich, ed., pp. 121–142. Boston: Bergin and Garvey.

Ricklefs, R. E. (1973) *Ecology*. Newton, MA: Chiron Press.

Rindos, D. (1985) Darwinian selection, symbolic variation, and the evolution of culture. *Current Anthropology* 26:65–88.

Rindos, D. (1989) Undirected variation and the Darwinian explanation of cultural change. *Archaeological Method and Theory*, vol. 1. M. Schiffer, ed., pp. 1–45. Tucson: University of Arizona Press.

Roberts, B. and B. Holdren. (1972) *Theory of Social Process: An Economic Analysis*. Ames: Iowa State University Press.

Robinson, J. G. (1981) Spatial structure in foraging groups of wedge-capped capuchin monkeys (*Cebus nigrivittatus*). *Animal Behavior* 29:1036–1056.

Robinson, J. G. (1982) Intrasexual competition and mate choice in primates. *American Journal of Primatology Supplement* 1:131–144.

Robinson, J. G. (1988) Group size in wedge-capped capuchin monkeys *Cebus olivaceus* and the reproductive success of males and females. *Behavioral Ecology and Sociobiology* 23:187–197.

Rodman, P. S. (1984) Foraging and social systems of orangutans and chimpanzees.

In *Adaptations for Foraging in Non-Human Primates,* P. S. Rodman and J. G. H. Cant, eds., pp. 134–160. New York: Columbia University Press.

Rodman, P. S. and H. M. McHenry. (1980) Bioenergetics and origins of bipedalism. *American Journal of Physical Anthropology* 52:103–106.

Roemer, J. E. (1982a) Methodological individualism and deductive Marxism. *Theory and Society* 11:513–20.

Roemer, J. E. (1982b) *A General Theory of Exploitation and Class.* Cambridge, MA: Harvard University Press.

Roemer, J. E., ed. (1986) *Analytical Marxism.* Cambridge: Cambridge University Press.

Rogers, A. R. (1986) Population dynamics under exploitation competition. *Journal of Theoretical Biology* 119:363–368.

Rogers, A. R. (1989a) Does biology constrain culture? *American Anthropologist* 90:819–831.

Rogers, A. R. (1989b) Resource partitioning and the stability of population dynamics: A reply to Łomnicki and Sedziwy. *Journal of Theoretical Biology* 138: 545–549.

Rogers, A. R. (1990a) The evolutionary economics of human reproduction. *Ethology and Sociobiology* 11:479–495.

Rogers, A. R. (1990b) Group selection by selective emigration: The effects of migration and kin structure. *American Naturalist* 135:398–413.

Rogers, A. (n.d.) Evolution of time preference. Unpublished manuscript.

Rogers, A. and W. J. Chasko. (1979) The spatial distribution of archaeological sites: A clue to subsistence behavior. In *Archaeological Investigations in Cochiti Reservoir, New Mexico, Vol. 4: Adaptive Change in the Northern Rio Grande Valley,* J. V. Biella and R. C. Chapman, eds., pp. 283–294. Albuquerque: Office of Contract Archaeology, University of New Mexico.

Rogers, A. R. and H. C. Harpending. (1991) Population growth makes waves in the distribution of pairwise genetic differences. Manuscript.

Rogers, E. M. (1983) *Diffusion of Innovations.* New York: Free Press.

Rogers, E. S. (1969) Band organization among the Indians of Eastern Subarctic Canada. In *Contributions to Anthropology: Band Societies,* D. Damas, ed., pp. 21–50. Ottawa: Queen's Printer.

Rosenberg, A. (1980) *Sociobiology and the Preemption of Social Science.* Baltimore, MD: Johns Hopkins University Press.

Rosenblum, L. A. and I. C. Kaufman. (1967) Laboratory observations of early mother–infant relations in pigtail and bonnet macaques. In *Social Communication Among Primates,* S. A. Altmann, ed., pp. 33–41. Chicago: University of Chicago Press.

Roughgarden, J. (1979) *Theory of Population Genetics and Evolutionary Ecology: An Introduction.* New York: Macmillan.

Roughgarden, J., R. M. May, and S. A. Levin, eds. (1989) *Perspectives in Ecological Theory.* Princeton, NJ: Princeton University Press.

Rowell, T. E. (1988) Beyond the one-male group. *Behaviour* 104:189–201.

Rubenstein, D. I. (1982) Risk, uncertainty, and evolutionary strategies. In *Current Problems in Sociobiology,* King's College Sociobiology Group, eds., pp. 91–111. Cambridge: Cambridge University Press.

Ruse, M. (1986) *Taking Darwin Seriously*. Oxford: Blackwell.

Rutberg, A. T. (1983) The evolution of monogamy in primates. *Journal of Theoretical Biology* 104:93–112.

Sackett, R. (1988) Cross-cultural variation in time allocation. Paper presented at the Annual Meeting of the American Ethnological Society, Santa Fe, NM, April 14.

Sahlins, M. (1963) Poor man, rich man, big man, chief: Political types in Melanesia and Polynesia. *Comparative Studies in Society and History* 5:285–303.

Sahlins, M. (1965) On the sociology of primitive exchange. In *The Relevance of Models for Social Anthropology*, M. Banton, ed., pp. 139–236. ASA Monographs 1. London: Tavistock.

Sahlins, M. (1968a) Notes on the original affluent society. In *Man the Hunter*, R. Lee and I. DeVore, eds., pp. 85–89. Chicago: Aldine.

Sahlins, M. (1968b) *Tribesmen*. Englewood Cliffs, NJ: Prentice-Hall.

Sahlins, M. (1972) *Stone Age Economics*. Chicago: Aldine.

Sahlins, Marshall (1976) *The Use and Abuse of Biology: An Anthropological Critique of Sociobiology*. Ann Arbor: University of Michigan Press.

Salisbury, R. (1962) *From Stone to Steel*. Cambridge: Cambridge University Press.

Samuelson, P. A. (1954) The pure theory of public expenditure. *Review of Economics and Statistics* 36:387–389.

Sanders, W. T. and D. Webster (1978) Unilinealism, multilinealism, and the evolution of complex societies. In *Social Archaeology: Beyond Subsistence and Dating*, C. L. Redman, M. J. Berman, E. V. Curten, W. T. Langhorne, Jr., N. M. Versaggi, and J. C. Wanser, eds., pp. 249–302. NY: Academic Press.

Sarich, V. (1983) Appendix: retrospective on hominoid macromolecular systematics. In *New Interpretations of Ape and Human Ancestry*, R. Ciochon and R. S. Corruccini, eds., pp. 137–150. New York: Plenum Press.

Schaffer, W. M. (1974) Optimal reproductive effort in fluctuating environments. *American Naturalist* 108:783–790.

Schaffer, W. (1978) A note on the theory of reciprocal altruism. *American Naturalist* 112:250–253.

Schaller, G. B. (1972) *The Serengeti Lion*. Chicago: University of Chicago Press.

Schelling, T. (1960) *The Strategy of Conflict*. Cambridge: Harvard University Press.

Schelling, T. (1978) *Micromotives and Macrobehavior*. New York: Norton.

Schoener, T. (1971) Theory of feeding strategies. *Annual Review of Ecology and Systematics* 2:369–404.

Schoener, T. (1979) Generality of the size-distance relation in models of optimal feeding. *American Naturalist* 114:902–914.

Schultz, A. H. (1940) Growth and development of the chimpanzee. *Contributions to Embryology* 170:1–63.

Searcy, W. A. and K. Yasukawa. (1989) Alternative models of territorial polygyny in birds. *American Naturalist* 134:323–343.

Service, E. (1962) *Primitive Social Organization*. New York: Random House.

Shackleton, N. J. and N. D. Opdyke. (1976) Oxygen isotope and paleomagnetic stratigraphy of Pacific core V28-239, late Pliocene to latest Pleistocene. *Geological Society of America Memoir* 145:449–464.

Shostak, M. (1983) *Nisa: the Life and Words of a !Kung Woman*. New York: Vintage.

Sibley, C. and J. Ahlquist (1984) The phylogeny of hominoid primates as indicated by DNA-DNA hybridization. *Journal of Molecular Evolution* 20:2–15.

Sibly, R. M. and P. Calow. (1985) Classification of habitats by selection pressures: A synthesis of life-cycle and r/K theory. In *Behavioural Ecology: Ecological Consequences of Adaptive Behaviour*, R. M. Sibly and R. H. Smith, eds., pp. 75–90. Boston: Blackwell.

Sih, A. and K. Milton (1985) Optimal diet theory: Should the !Kung eat mongongos? *American Anthropologist* 87:395–401.

Silberbauer, G. B. (1981) *Hunter and Habitat in the Central Kalahari Desert.* Cambridge: Cambridge University Press.

Silk, J. B. (1983) Local resource competition and facultative adjustment of sex ratio in relation to competitive abilities. *American Naturalist* 121:56–64.

Simms, S. (1984) *Aboriginal Great Basin Foraging Strategies: An Evolutionary Approach.* Unpublished Ph.D. dissertation, University of Utah, Salt Lake City.

Simon, C. A. (1975) The influence of food abundance on territory size in the iguanid lizard *Sceloporus jarrovi. Ecology* 56:993–98.

Simon, H. A. (1955) A behavioral model of rational choice. *Quarterly Journal of Economics* 69:7–19.

Simon, H. A. (1969) *The Sciences of the Artificial.* Cambridge, MA: MIT Press.

Simon, J. L. (1977) *The Economics of Population Growth.* Princeton, NJ: Princeton University Press.

Skinner, B. F. (1972) *Cumulative Record.* New York: Appleton-Century-Crofts.

Slobodchikoff, C. N. (1984) Resources and the evolution of social behavior. In *A New Ecology: Novel Approaches to Interactive Systems*, P. Price, C. N. Slobodchikoff, and W. S. Gaud, eds., pp. 228–251. New York: Wiley.

Slobodkin, L. B. (1978) Is history a consequence of evolution? In *Perspectives in Ethology*, P. P. G. Bateson and P. H. Klopfer, eds., Vol. 3, pp. 233–255. New York: Plenum.

Smith, A. (1979) Chayanov, Sahlins, and the labor-consumer balance. *American Ethnologist* 35:477–480.

Smith, B. H. (1989) Dental development as a measure of life history in primates. *Evolution* 43:683–688.

Smith, E. A. (1979a) Human adaptation and energetic efficiency. *Human Ecology* 7:53–74.

Smith, E. A. (1979b) Data and theory in sociobiological explanation: Critique of van den Berghe and Barash. *American Anthropologist* 81:360–363.

Smith, E. A. (1980) *Evolutionary Ecology and the Analysis of Human Behavior.* Unpublished Ph.D. dissertation. Cornell University.

Smith, E. A. (1981) The application of optimal foraging theory to the analysis of hunter-gatherer group size. In *Hunter-Gatherer Foraging Strategies*, B. Winterhalder and E. A. Smith, eds., pp. 36–65. Chicago: University of Chicago Press.

Smith, E. A. (1983) Anthropological applications of optimal foraging theory: A critical review. *Current Anthropology* 24:625–651.

Smith, E. A. (1985) Inuit foraging groups: Some simple models incorporating conflicts of interest, relatedness, and central-place sharing. *Ethology and Sociobiology* 6:27–47.

Smith, E. A. (1987a) Optimization theory in anthropology: applications and critiques. In *The Latest on the Best: Essays on Evolution and Optimality*, J. Dupré,
ed., pp. 201–249. Cambridge, MA: Bradford Books/MIT Press.

Smith, E. A. (1987b) On fitness maximization, limited needs, and hunter-gatherer
time allocation. *Ethology and Sociobiology* 8:73–85.

Smith, E. A. (1987c) Folk psychology versus pop sociobiology. *Behavioral and Brain
Sciences* 10:85–86.

Smith, E. A. (1988) Risk and uncertainty in the "original affluent society": Evolutionary ecology of resource sharing and land tenure. In *Hunters and Gatherers 1:
History, Evolution, and Social Change*, T. Ingold, D. Riches, and J. Woodburn,
eds., pp. 222–252. Oxford: Berg.

Smith, E. A. (1991) *Inujjuamiut Foraging Strategies: Evolutionary Ecology of an
Arctic Hunting Economy*. Hawthorne, NY: Aldine de Gruyter.

Smith, E. A. and R. Boyd. (1990) Risk and reciprocity: hunter-gatherer socioecology
and the problem of collective action. In *Risk and Uncertainty in Tribal and
Peasant Economies*, E. Cashdan, ed., pp. 167–192. Boulder, CO: Westview
Press.

Smuts, B. (1985) *Sex And Friendship in Baboons*. Hawthorne, NY: Aldine.

Sober, E. (1984) *The Nature of Selection*. Cambridge, MA: MIT Press.

Southwood, T. R. E. (1977) Habitat, the templet for ecological strategies? *Journal of
Animal Ecology* 46:337–365.

Speth, J., and K. Spielmann (1983) Energy source, protein metabolism, and hunter-
gatherer subsistence strategies. *Journal of Anthropological Archaeology* 2:1–31.

Stacey, P. B. (1986) Group size and foraging efficiency in yellow baboons. *Behavioral Ecology and Sociobiology* 18:175–187.

Stanley, S. M. (1975) A theory of evolution above the species level. *Proceedings of
the National Academy of Sciences* 72:646–650.

Stanley, S. M. (1979) *Macroevolution: Pattern and Process*. San Francisco: W. H.
Freeman.

Starfield, A. M. and A. L. Bleloch. (1986) *Building Models for Conservation and
Wildlife Management*. New York: Macmillan.

Stearns, S. C. (1976) Life-history tactics: a review of the ideas. *Quarterly Review of
Biology* 51:3–47.

Stephens, D. W. (1985) How important are partial preferences? *Animal Behavior:*
33:667–669.

Stephens, D. W. (1990) Risk and incomplete information in behavioral ecology. In
Risk and Uncertainty in Tribal and Peasant Economies, E. Cashdan, ed., pp.
19–46. Boulder, CO: Westview Press.

Stephens, D. W. and J. R. Krebs. (1986) *Foraging Theory*. Princeton, NJ: Princeton
University Press.

Steward, J. (1938) *Basin Plateau Aboriginal Sociopolitical Groups*. Bureau of American Ethnology, Bulletin 120. Washington, D. C.: Smithsonian Institution.

Steward, J. (1955) *Theory of Culture Change*. Urbana, IL: University of Illinois Press.

Stringer, C. B. and P. Andrews. (1988) Genetic and fossil evidence for the origin of
modern humans. *Science* 239:1263–1268.

Struhsaker, T. T. (1969) Correlates of ecology and social organization among African
cercopithecines. *Folia Primatologica* 11:80–118.

Sugden, R. (1986) *The Economics of Rights, Co-operation and Welfare*. Oxford: Basil Blackwell.

Susman, R. L., J. T. Stern, and W. I. Jungers. (1984) Arboreality and bipedality in the Hadar hominids. *Folia primatologica* 43:113–156.

Sutherland, W. J. and G. A. Parker. (1985) Distribution of unequal competitors. In *Behavioural Ecology: Ecological Consequences of Adaptive Behaviour*, R. M. Sibly and R. H. Smith, eds., pp. 255–274. Oxford: Blackwell Scientific Publications.

Symington, M. McFarland (1987) Sex ratio and maternal rank in wild spider monkeys: when daughters disperse. *Behavioral Ecology and Sociobiology* 20:421–425.

Symington, M. McFarland (1988) Food competition and foraging party size in the black spider monkey *(Ateles paniscus chamek)*. *Behaviour* 105:117–134.

Symons, D. (1978) *Play and Aggression: A Study of Rhesus Monkeys*. New York: Columbia University Press.

Symons, D. (1989) A critique of Darwinian anthropology. *Ethology and Sociobiology* 10:131–144.

Symons, D. (1990) Adaptiveness and adaptation. *Ethology and Sociobiology* 11:427–444.

Tanaka, J. (1980) *The San Hunter-Gatherers of the Kalahari: A Study in Ecological Anthropology*. Translated by D. Hughes. Tokyo: University of Tokyo Press.

Taylor, C. R. and V. J. Rowntree. (1973) Running on two legs or four: Which consumes more energy? *Science* 179:186–187.

Taylor, M. (1982) *Community, Anarchy and Liberty*. Cambridge: Cambridge University Press.

Taylor, M. (1987) *The Possibility of Cooperation*. Cambridge: Cambridge University Press.

Taylor, M. and H. Ward (1982) Chickens, whales and lumpy goods: Alternative models of public goods provision. *Political Studies* 30:350–370.

Taylor, R. J. (1976) Value of clumping to prey and the evolutionary response of ambush predators. *American Naturalist* 110:13–29.

Taylor, R. J. (1979) The value of clumping to prey when detectability increases with group size. *American Naturalist* 113:299–301.

Terborgh, J. W. (1983) *Five New World Primates*. Princeton, NJ: Princeton University Press.

Terborgh, J. W. (1990) Mixed flocks and polyspecific associations: Costs and benefits of mixed groups of birds and monkeys. *American Journal of Primatology* (in press).

Terborgh, J. W. and A. W. Goldizen. (1985) On the mating system of the cooperatively breeding saddle-backed tamarin *(Saguinus fuscicollis)*. *Behavioral Ecology and Sociobiology* 16:293–299.

Terborgh, J. W. and C. H. Janson. (1986) The socioecology of primate groups. *Annual Review of Ecology and Systematics* 17:111–135.

Terhune, K. W. (1974) A review of the actual and expected consequences of family size. *Calspan Report N. DP-5333-G-1, Center for Population Research*. National Institute of Child Health and Human Development, U. S. Dept. of Health Education and Welfare Publ. (NIH) 75–779.

Thomas, R. B. (1973) *Human Adaptation to a High Andean Energy Flow System*. Occasional Papers in Anthropology (No. 7), Department of Anthropology, Pennsylvania State University.

Tiger, L. and R. Fox. (1971) *The Imperial Animal*. New York: Dell.

Tilly, C. (1983) War making and state making as organized crime. In *Bringing the State Back In*, P. Evans, D. Rueschemeyer, and T. Skocpol, eds., pp. 3–37. Cambridge: Cambridge University Press.

Tinbergen, N. (1963) On aims and methods of ethology. *Zeitschrift für Tierpsychologie* 20:404–433.

Tinbergen, N. (1968) On war and peace in animals and man. *Science* 160:1411–1418.

Tooby, J. and L. Cosmides. (1989) Evolutionary psychology and the generation of culture, part I: Theoretical considerations. *Ethology and Sociobiology* 10: 29–49.

Tooby, J. and L. Cosmides. (1990) The past explains the present: Emotional adaptations and the structure of ancestral environments. *Ethology and Sociobiology* 11:375–424.

Trinkaus, E. (1983) Neanderthal post-crania and the adaptive shifts to modern humans. In *The Mousterian Legacy*, E. Trinkaus, ed., pp. 165–200. Oxford: British Archaeological Reports S164.

Trinkaus, E. (1989a) The Upper Pleistocene transition. In *The Emergence of Modern Humans*, E. Trinkaus, ed., pp. 42–66. Cambridge: Cambridge University Press.

Trinkaus, E., ed. (1989b) *The Emergence of Modern Humans*. Cambridge: Cambridge University Press.

Trivers, R. L. (1971) *The evolution of reciprocal altruism. Quarterly Review of Biology* 46:35–57.

Trivers, R. L. (1972) Parental investment and sexual selection. In *Sexual Selection and the Descent of Man, 1871–1971*, B. Campbell, ed., pp. 136–179. Chicago: Aldine.

Trivers, R. L. (1974) Parent-offspring conflict. *American Zoologist* 14:249–262.

Trivers, R. L. (1985) *Social Evolution*. Menlo Park: Benjamin Cummings.

Trivers, R. L. and D. E. Willard. (1973) Natural selection of parental ability to vary the sex ratio of offspring. *Science* 179:90–92.

Tsingalia, H. M. and T. E. Rowell. (1984) The behaviour of adult male blue monkeys. *Zeitschrift für Tierpsychologie* 64:253–268.

Turke, P. W. (1984) On what's not wrong with a Darwinian theory of culture. *American Anthropologist* 86:663–668.

Turke, P. W. (1988) Helpers at the nest: childcare networks on Ifaluk. In *Human Reproductive Behaviour: A Darwinian Perspective*, L. Betzig, M. Borgerhoff Mulder, and P. W. Turke, eds., pp. 173–188. Cambridge: Cambridge University Press.

Turke, P. W. (1990) Which humans behave adaptively, and why does it matter? *Ethology and Sociobiology* 11:305–339.

Turke, P. W. and L. L. Betzig. (1985) Those who can do: Wealth, status, and reproductive success on Ifaluk. *Ethology and Sociobiology* 6:79–87.

Turton, D. (1980) The economics of Mursi Bridewealth. In *The Meaning of Marriage Payments*, J. L. Comaroff, ed., pp. 67–92. London: Academic Press.

Ulijaszek, S. J. and S. Strickland. (in press) *Nutritional Anthropology*. Cambridge: Cambridge University Press.

Uyenoyama, M. and M. W. Feldman. (1980) Theories of kin and group selection: A population genetics perspective. *Theoretical Population Biology* 17:380–414.

Valentine, J. W. (1973) *Evolutionary Paleoecology of the Marine Biosphere*. Englewood Cliffs, NJ: Prentice Hall.

van den Berghe, P. L. (1981) *The Ethnic Phenomenon*. New York: Elsevier.

van Schaik, C. P. (1983) Why are diurnal primates living in groups? *Behaviour* 87:120–144.

van Schaik, C. P. (1989) The ecology of social relationships amongst female primates. In *Comparative Socioecology: The Behavioural Ecology of Humans and Other Mammals*, V. Standen and R. A. Foley, eds., Oxford: Blackwell.

van Schaik, C. P. and R. I. M. Dunbar (1990) The evolution of monogamy in large primates: a new hypothesis and some crucial tests. *Behaviour* 115:30–62.

van Schaik, C. P. and S. B. Hrdy. (n. d.) The intensity of local resource competition determines the relationship between maternal rank and sex ratio at birth in cercopithecine primates. (submitted to *American Naturalist*).

van Schaik, C. P. and J. van Hooff. (1983) On the ultimate causes of primate social systems. *Behaviour* 85:91–117.

van Schaik, C. P. and M. A. van Noordwijk. (1985) Evolutionary effect of the absence of felids on the social organization of the macaques on the island of Simeulue (*Macaca fascicularis fusca*, Miller 1903). *Folia Primatologica* 44:138–147.

van Schaik, C. P. and M. A. van Noordwijk. (1988) Scramble and contest in feeding competition among female long-tailed macaques (*Macaca fascicularis*). *Behaviour* 105:77–98.

van Schaik, C. P. and M. A. van Noordwijk. (1989) The special role of male Cebus monkeys in predation avoidance and its effect on group composition. *Behavioral Ecology and Sociobiology* 24:265–276.

van Schaik, C. P., M. A. van Nordwijk, B. Warsono, and E. Sutriono. (1983) Party size and early detection of predators in Sumatran forest primates. *Primates* 24:211–221.

Vayda, A. P. (1986) Holism and individualism in ecological anthropology. *Reviews in Anthropology* 13:295–313.

Vayda, A. P. and R. A. Rappaport. (1968) Ecology, cultural and non-cultural. In *Introduction to Cultural Anthropology*, J. Clifton, ed., pp. 477–497. Boston: Houghton-Mifflin.

Vehrencamp, S. L. (1983) A model for the evolution of despotic versus egalitarian societies. *Animal Behavior* 31:667–682.

Vehrencamp, S. C. and J. W. Bradbury. (1984) Mating systems and ecology. In *Behavioural Ecology, an Evolutionary Approach*, J. R. Krebs and N. B. Davies, eds., pp. 251–278. Sunderland, MA: Sinauer Association.

Verner, J. and M. F. Willson. (1966) The influence of habitats on mating systems of North American passerine birds. *Ecology* 47:143–147.

Vickers, W. (1988) Game depletion hypothesis of Amazonian adaptation: Data from a native community. *Science* 239:1521–1522.

Vine, I. (1971) Risk of visual detection and pursuit by a predator and the selective advantage of flocking behaviour. *Journal of Theoretical Biology* 30:406–422.

Vine, I. (1973) Detection of prey flocks by predators. *Journal of Theoretical Biology* 40:207–210.

Vining, D. R. (1986) Social versus reproductive success—the central theoretical problem of human sociobiology. *Behavioral and Brain Sciences* 9:167–260.

Voland, E. (1988) Differential infant and child mortality in evolutionary perspective: Data from late 17th to 19th century Ostfriesland (Germany). In *Human Reproductive Behaviour: A Darwinian Perspective*, L. Betzig, M. Borgerhoff Mulder, and P. Turke, eds., pp. 253–261. Cambridge: Cambridge University Press.

Voland, E., Siegelkow, E., and C. Engel. (1991) Cost/benefit orientated parental investment by high status families: The Krummhorn case. *Ethology and Sociobiology* 12:105–118.

von Neumann, J. and O. Morgenstern. (1944) *Theory of Games and Economic Behavior*. Princeton, NJ: Princeton University Press.

Voorips, A. and J. O'Shea. (1987) Conditional spatial patterning: Beyond the nearest neighbor. *American Antiquity* 52:500–521.

Vrba, E. S. (1985). Ecological and adaptive changes associated with early hominid evolution. In *Ancestors: The Hard Evidence*, E. Delson, ed., pp. 63–71. New York: Alan R. Liss.

Wade, M. J. (1978) A critical review of models of group selection. *Quarterly Review of Biology* 53:101–114.

Wade, M. J. (1985) Soft selection, hard selection, kin selection, and group selection. *American Naturalist* 125:61–73.

Walker, A. C. (1981) Dietary hypotheses in human evolution. *Philosophical Transactions of the Royal Society, London Series B* 292:47–64.

Walker, A. C. and R. E. F. Leakey. (1986) *Homo erectus* skeleton from West Lake Turkana, Kenya. *American Journal of Physical Anthropology* 69:275.

Wallace, A. R. (1913) *Social Environment and Moral Progress*. New York: Cassell and Company.

Ward, P. and A. Zahavi. (1973) The importance of certain assemblages of birds as "information centres" for food finding. *Ibis* 115:517–534.

Waser, P. M. (1977) Feeding, ranging, and group size in the mangabey *Cercocebus albigena*. In *Primate Ecology: Feeding and Ranging Behaviour in Lemurs, Monkeys, and Apes*, T. H. Clutton-Brock, ed., pp. 183–222. London: Academic Press.

Waser, P. M. and T. J. Case. (1981) Monkeys and matrices: On the coexistence of "omnivorous" forest primates. *Oecologia* 49:102–108.

Washburn, S. and C. Lancaster (1968) The evolution of hunting. In *Man the Hunter*, R. Lee and I. DeVore, eds., pp. 293–303. Chicago: Aldine.

Watanabe, K. (1981) Variations in group composition and population densities of two sympatric Mentawan leaf-monkeys. *Primates* 22:145–160.

Webster, G. (1990) Labor control and emergent stratification in prehistoric Europe. *Current Anthropology* 31:337–366.

Webster, S. (1973) Native pastoralism in the South Andes. *Ethnology* 12:115–133.

Whallon, R. (1974) Spatial analysis of occupation floors I: Application of dimensional analysis of variance. *American Antiquity* 38:266–278.

Wheeler, P. (1985) The evolution of bipedalism and the loss of functional body hair in hominids. *Journal of Human Evolution* 14:23–28.

White, D. R. (1988) Rethinking polygyny: Co-wives, codes, and cultural systems. *Current Anthropology* 29:529–572.

White, D. R. and M. L. Burton. (1988) Causes of polygyny: Ecology, economy, kinship, and warfare. *American Anthropologist* 90:871–887.

White, F. J. and R. W. Wrangham. (1988) Feeding competition and patch size in the chimpanzee species *Pan paniscus* and *Pan troglodytes. Behaviour* 105:148–163.

White, L. (1949) *The Science of Culture.* New York: Farrar, Straus, and Giroux.

White, L. (1959) *The Evolution of Culture: The Development of Civilization to the Fall of Rome.* New York: McGraw-Hill.

White, T. D. (1984) Pliocene hominids from the Middle Awash, Ethiopia. *Courier Forschunginstitut Senckenberg* 69:57–68.

Whitelaw, T. (1989) *People and Space in Hunter-Gatherer Communities: Some Implications for Social Inference in Archaeology.* Ph.D. dissertation, Faculty of Archaeology and Anthropology, University of Cambridge.

Whiting, B. B. and K. W. M. Whiting. (1975) *Children of Six Cultures: A Psychocultural Analysis.* Cambridge, MA: Harvard University Press.

Whitten, P. L. (1983) Diet and dominance among female vervet monkeys (*Cercopithecus aethiops*). *American Journal of Primatology* 5:139–159.

Wiens, J. A. (1966) On group selection and Wynne-Edwards' hypothesis. *American Scientist* 54:273–287.

Wiens, J. A. (1977) On competition and variable environments. *American Scientist* 65:590–597.

Wiens, J. A. (1984) Resource systems, populations, and communities. In *A New Ecology: Novel Approaches to Interactive Systems,* P. W. Price, C. N. Slobodchikoff, and W. S. Gaud, eds., pp. 397–436. New York: Wiley.

Wiessner, P. (1977) *Hxaro: A Regional System of Reciprocity for Reducing Risk among the !Kung San.* Ph.D. dissertation, Department of Anthropology, University of Michigan.

Wiessner, P. (1982) Risk, reciprocity and social influences on !Kung San economics. In *Politics and History in Band Societies,* E. Leacock and R. B. Lee, eds., pp. 61–84. Cambridge: Cambridge University Press.

Williams, G. C. (1966a) *Adaptation and Natural Selection: A Critique of Some Current Evolutionary Thought.* Princeton, NJ: Princeton University Press.

Williams, G. C. (1966b) Natural selection, the costs of reproduction and a refinement of Lack's Principle. *American Naturalist* 100:687–690.

Williams, G. C. (1979) The question of adaptive sex ratio in outcrossed vertebrates. *Proceedings of the Royal Society of London Series B* 205:567–580.

Williams, G. C. (1985) A defense of reductionism in evolutionary biology. *Oxford Surveys in Evolutionary Biology* 2:1–27.

Williamson I. and M. Sabath. (1982) Island population, land area, and climate: A case study of the Marshall Islands. *Human Ecology* 10:71–84.

Wilmsen, E. (1973) Interaction, spacing behavior, and the organization of hunting bands. *Journal of Anthropological Research* 29:1–31.

Wilson, E. O. (1971) Competitive and aggressive behavior. In *Man and Beast: Comparative Social Behavior,* J. F. Eisenberg and W. S. Dillon, eds., pp. 183–217. Washington, D. C.: Smithsonian Institution Press.

Wilson, E. O. (1975) *Sociobiology: The New Synthesis.* Cambridge, MA: Harvard University Press.

Wilson, D. S. (1977) Structured demes and the evolution of group-advantageous traits. *American Naturalist* 111:157–185.

Wilson, D. S. (1980) *The Natural Selection of Populations and Communities.* Series in Evolutionary Biology, Institute of Ecology, University of California at Davis. Menlo Park: Benjamin/Cummings.

Wilson, D. S. (1983) The group selection controversy: History and current status. *Annual Review of Ecology and Systematics* 14:159–187.

Winter, S. G. (1964) Economic natural selection and the theory of the firm. *Yale Economic Essays* 4:225–272.

Winterhalder, B. (1977) *Foraging Strategies and Adaptations of the Boreal Forest Cree: An Evaluation of Theory and Models from Evolutionary Ecology.* Unpublished Ph.D. dissertation, Cornell University.

Winterhalder, B. (1980) Environmental analysis in human evolution and adaptation research. *Human Ecology* 8:135–170.

Winterhalder, B. (1981) Foraging strategies in the boreal environment: an analysis of Cree hunting and gathering. In *Hunter-Gatherer Foraging Strategies,* B. Winterhalder and E. Smith, eds., pp. 66–98. Chicago: University of Chicago Press.

Winterhalder, B. (1983) Opportunity-cost foraging models for stationary and mobile predators. *American Naturalist* 122:73–84.

Winterhalder, B. (1986) Diet choice, risk, and food sharing in a stochastic environment. *Journal of Anthropological Archaeology.* 5:369–392.

Winterhalder, B. (1987) The analysis of hunter-gatherer diets: Stalking an optimal foraging model. In *Food and Evolution: Toward a Theory of Human Food Habits,* M. Harris and E. Ross, eds., pp. 311–339. Philadelphia: Temple University Press.

Winterhalder, B. (1990) Open field, common pot: Harvest variability and risk avoidance in agricultural and foraging societies. In *Risk and Uncertainty in Tribal and Peasant Economies,* E. Cashdan, ed., pp. 67–88. Boulder, CO: Westview Press.

Winterhalder, B., W. Baillargeon, F. Cappelletto, J. I. Randolph Daniel, and C. Prescott. (1988) The population ecology of hunter-gatherers and their prey. *Journal of Anthropological Archaeology* 7:289–328.

Wittenberger, J. F. (1976) The ecological factors selecting for polygyny in altricial birds. *American Naturalist* 110:779–799.

Wood, J. W. and P. E. Smouse. (1982) A method of analyzing density-dependent vital rates with an application to the Gainj of Papua New Guinea. *American Journal of Physical Anthropology* 58:403–411.

Wrangham, R. W. (1977) Feeding behaviour of chimpanzees of Gombe National Park, Tanzania. In *Primate Ecology,* T. H. Clutton-Brock, ed., pp. 504–537. London: Academic Press.

Wrangham, R. W. (1980) An ecological model of female-bonded primate groups. *Behaviour* 75:262–300.

Wrangham, R. W. (1986) Ecology and social relationships of two species of chimpanzee. In *Ecological Aspects of Social Evolution: Birds and Mammals,* D. I. Rubenstein and R. W. Wrangham, eds., pp. 352–378. Princeton, NJ: Princeton University Press.

Wrangham, R. W. (1987) The significance of African apes for reconstructing human evolution. In *The Evolution of Human Behavior: Primate Models,* W. G. Kinzey, ed., pp. 28–47. Albany: SUNY Press.

Wrangham, R. W. and D. I. Rubenstein. (1986) Social evolution in birds and mammals. In *Ecological Aspects of Social Evolution: Birds and Mammals,* D. I. Rubenstein and R. W. Wrangham, eds., pp. 452–470. Princeton, NJ: Princeton University Press.

Wrangham, R. W. and B. B. Smuts. (1980) Sex differences in the behavioural ecology of chimpanzees in the Gombe National Park, Tanzania. *Journal of Reproduction and Fertility Supplement* 28:13–31.

Wright, H. T. (1978) Toward an explanation of the origin of the state. In *Origins of the State: The Anthropology of Political Evolution,* R. Cohen and E. R. Service, eds., pp. 49–68. Philadelphia: ISHI Press.

Wright, P. C. (1984) Biparental care in *Aotus trivirgatus* and *Callicebus moloch.* In *Female Primates: Studies by Female Primatologists,* M. Small, ed., pp. 59–75. New York: Alan Liss.

Wright, S. (1945) Tempo and mode in evolution: A critical review. *Ecology* 26:415–419.

Wynne-Edwards, V. C. (1962) *Animal Dispersion in Relation to Social Behavior.* Edinburgh: Oliver and Boyd.

Yellen, J. and H. C. Harpending. (1972) Hunter gatherer populations and archeological inference. *World Archaeology* 4:244–253.

Yost, J. and P. Kelley. (1983) Shotguns, blowguns, and spears: An analysis of technological efficiency. In *Adaptive Responses of Native Amazonians,* R. Hames and W. Vickers, eds., pp. 189–224. New York: Academic Press.

Young, R. M. (1974) The human limits of nature. In *The Limits of Human Nature,* J. Benthall, ed., pp. 233–274. New York: E. P. Dutton.

Zentall, T. R. and B. G. Galef, Jr. (1988) *Social Learning: Psychological and Biological Perspectives.* Hillsdale, NJ: Lawrence Erlbaum.

Biographical Sketches of the Contributors

James L. Boone is Associate Professor at the University of New Mexico, where he teaches in the archaeology and biosocial programs of the Anthropology Department. His research has ranged from analysis of political and reproductive strategies among medieval Portugese nobility to historical archaeology in North Africa. At present, he is conducting research on the historical biogeography of the Christian-Muslim interface in the Mediterranean region.

Monique Borgerhoff Mulder is Assistant Professor of Anthropology at the University of California at Davis, and co-editor of *Human Reproductive Behaviour* (Cambridge University Press). She has conducted research with pastoral populations in East Africa and has published papers on various aspects of life history strategy, including marriage, reproduction and inheritance. She is currently analysing data on work effort and cooperation among Kenyan agropastoralists, and editing a collection of stories about fieldwork.

Robert Boyd is Professor of Anthropology at the University of California, Los Angeles. He coauthored *Culture and the Evolutionary Process* (University of Chicago Press) and a variety of papers on cultural evolution, population genetics, and evolution of cooperation. His current research focuses on the evolution of cooperation and ethnicity.

Elizabeth Cashdan is Associate Professor of Anthropology at the University of Utah. She has conducted ecological and economic research among G//ana people in Botswana, and edited *Risk and Uncertainty in Tribal and Peasant Economies* (Westview Press). Her current research concerns how expectations about paternal investment shape reproductive strategies of both women and men, and evolutionary aspects of food learning in children.

Robert Foley is a University Lecturer in Biological Anthropology and a Fellow of King's College, Cambridge University. He has authored *Another Unique Species: Patterns in Human Evolutionary Ecology* (Wiley) and many papers on hominid evolution. He is currently investigating interactions between climatic change and patterns of human evolution, as well as the ecological basis of life history changes in hominid evolution.

Raymond Hames is Associate Professor of Anthropology at the University of Nebraska. He has edited *Adaptive Responses of Native Amazonians* (with W. T. Vickers, Academic Press), and published papers on time allocation, social relations, the organization of production, and settlement patterns of Amazonian peoples. He is currently preparing a set of papers on Yanomamö food exchange, collaborative labor, and the economic costs and benefits of polygyny for men and women, based on field research conducted from 1985-87.

Kristen Hawkes is Professor of Anthropology at the University of Utah. Topics of her publications include foraging and reproductive strategies. She has conducted field research in Papua New Guinea, Paraguay, and Tanzania, and is currently engaged in a long-term research project on Hadza behavioral ecology.

Kim Hill is Associate Professor of Anthropology at the University of New Mexico. He has conducted extensive field research with several lowland South America foraging peoples, and has published papers on foraging strategies, nutrition, food sharing, time allocation, and life history characteristics. He is currently completing a book on Aché demography and life history.

Charles Janson is Associate Professor in the Department of Ecology and Evolution, SUNY at Stony Brook. His research includes field studies of capuchin monkeys in South America. He is currently studying how a lack of predators affects capuchin social structure in Iguazu, Argentina.

Hillard Kaplan is Associate Professor in the Department of Anthropology, University of New Mexico. He has published papers on reciprocity, communication, and foraging and reproductive strategies based on his research with Aché, Yanimanjua, Machiguenga and Piro in Lowland South America. He is currently collaborating on a study of male reproductive strategies in the Albuquerque area.

Peter J. Richerson is Professor in the Division of Environmental Studies and member of the Center for Population Biology, University of California at Davis. Besides his publications on human adaptation and cultural evolution (including *Culture and the Evolutionary Process*, coauthored with Robert Boyd), he conducts research on the ecology of lakes, including Tahoe and Clear Lake in California, and Lake Titicaca in Peru.

Alan Rogers is Associate Professor of Anthropology at the University of Utah. He has authored papers on population ecology, population genetics, and cultural and behavioral evolution. His current research concerns evolutionary economics, the evolution of time preference, and human molecular evolution.

Eric Alden Smith is Associate Professor of Anthropology, University of Washington. He has conducted fieldwork on subsistence ecology and economics among Hudson Bay Inuit, and is currently analyzing demographic data collected in the same area. His publications include *Inujjuamiut Foraging Strategies* (Aldine de Gruyter) and *Hunter-Gatherer Foraging Strategies* (coedited with Bruce Winterhalder, University of Chicago Press)

Bruce Winterhalder is Associate Professor and Chairman, Department of Anthropology, and a member of the Ecology Curriculum, University of North Carolina at Chapel Hill. He has conducted fieldwork on foraging strategies of boreal forest Cree in Ontario, and agropastoral tactics and ecology among Quechua peasants in highland Peru. He is currently investigating prey exploitation, population dynamics, and work effort of foragers using simulation models, and analyzing data on time allocation of Peruvian peasants.

Author Index

Subject Index